"Written with characteristic erudition, wit and exquisitely crafted prose, this is a glorious collection of almost four decades of scholarship from a leading Markan scholar. With sophistication and candor, C. Clifton Black provides a masterly guide to the wild and mysterious terrain of Mark's Gospel, bursting with both sophisticated scholarship and personal reflections. A must-read for scholars, students and ministers of religion."

—**Helen K. Bond**
University of Edinburgh

Mark's Gospel

History, Theology, Interpretation

❧

C. Clifton Black

William B. Eerdmans Publishing Company

Grand Rapids, Michigan

Wm. B. Eerdmans Publishing Co.
4035 Park East Court SE, Grand Rapids, Michigan 49546
www.eerdmans.com

29 28 27 26 25 24 23   1 2 3 4 5 6 7

ISBN 978-0-8028-7918-9

Library of Congress Cataloging-in-Publication Data

A catalog record for this book is available from the Library of Congress.

Scripture quotations marked NEB are from the New English Bible. Scripture quotations marked NIV are from the New International Version. Scripture quotations marked NJPS are from the New Jewish Publication Society version. Scripture quotations marked NRSV are from the New Revised Standard Version. Scripture quotations marked REB are from the Revised English Bible. Scripture quotations marked RSV are from the Revised Standard Version.

The Acknowledgments on pp. 427–29 constitute an extension of the register of permissions from copyright holders.

All author's royalties from the sale of this book are donated to The NAACP Legal Defense and Educational Fund, Inc., Washington, DC. www.naacpldf.org

In memory of
William B. Eerdmans Jr.
(1923–2020)

Contents

Tables

Preface

WHILE I HAVE ROAMED MANY AREAS OF THE Bible and its interpretation, ancient and modern, the Gospel according to Mark is the home to which I have always returned. It has been focal in three of my books for scholars or clergy and one book for laity. The earliest of this volume's chapters was originally drafted in the spring of 1983. The first to be published was in 1988. Second only to introducing students to the NT, the course I have most often offered in classrooms of three schools has been on Mark. All save one of the eight PhD dissertations I have directed have concentrated on the Second Gospel. After completing my own dissertation in 1986, its director, D. Moody Smith (1931–2016), quipped, "You are a Marked man." How right he was.

These collected essays span almost four decades. Because many plumb the depths of Markan scholarly interpretation as much as the gospel itself, the reader will find here one explorer's soundings of the history of Markan exegesis in the latter decades of the twentieth century and the early decades of the twenty-first. That is also the principal subject of chapter 6, written for this book and heretofore unpublished. Perhaps their assemblage here may serve a useful purpose. The remainder concentrates on those aspects of the gospel that have most attracted me: its tenebrous history, intricate construction, and unfathomable theology. These topics continue to fascinate other scholars. I hope that this compilation may spur them to further study.

No book is easily written, not even one that draws heavily on previous publications. Here I must settle my debts. At the top of the list are James D. Ernest, vice-president and editor in chief, and Trevor W. Thompson, senior acquisitions editor, of William B. Eerdmans Publishing. Both were quickly receptive to my modest proposal in the Plague Year of COVID (2020) and wise counselors at every stage of a complicated process. With the endorsement of President M. Craig Barnes, the Trustees of Princeton Theological Seminary granted me a research leave in 2019–2020, during which I was able to gain initial traction on this volume. The copyright holders of the various books and journals in which the book's contents originally appeared were uniformly gracious in granting permissions for reprinting. Kate Finn, an editor of SAGE Publishing in London, unearthed and dispatched to me electronic offprints for articles of yore. Under the direction of Joan Petrowski, senior administrative assistant at Princeton Seminary, Joy Crosley laboriously processed the words of essays whose typescripts and floppy-disk files had vanished long ago. After I had finished a first round of revisions, Devlin R. McGuire, candidate for the PhD in New Testament at Princeton, edited them with exceptional care, often under extraordinary circumstances. Laurel Draper and Justin Howell then subjected the entire manuscript to meticulous copyediting. I am profoundly grateful to Ray Wiersma for proofreading and to Holly Knowles for preparation of this book's indexes. The production staff at Eerdmans, including Amy Kent, editorial administrator, and Tom DeVries, subsidiary rights manager, rendered me valuable service. To all these friends and colleagues, I am sincerely grateful. In no way are any of these professionals to be held responsible for those errors of style, fact, or judgment that remain.

By an ugly but unforgettable coincidence, preliminary negotiations for this book coincided with the murder of George Perry Floyd Jr., on 25 May 2020. Soon thereafter I received a cri de coeur from a colleague who lamented that so much biblical scholarship did nothing to alter the vicious bigotry that blights our country and world. It is a reasonable assumption that Mark's Gospel was written for a community persecuted for no reason other than that they were Christian. It is a fact that Mr. Floyd and millions like him have died for no cause other than the color of their skin. Assumption and fact became fused in my mind. Stirred by my colleague's anguish, and in consultation with my family, I decided to donate all royalties I may accrue from sales of this book, in perpetuity, to the NAACP Legal Defense and Educational Fund, Inc. In the words of Albert Camus, who founded the series *Espoir* ("Hope") for Éditions Gallimard, "All I can say is that on this earth there are pestilences and there are victims—and as far as possible one must refuse to be on the side of the pestilence." In Mark's Gospel, Jesus does all in his power to destroy pestilence. That is where I want to stand.

This book is dedicated to the memory of William B. Eerdmans Jr., who in 1966 took from his father the reins of a Dutch Calvinist enterprise and steered the company into one of the world's premiere publishers of religious scholarship. For reasons inexplicable beyond pure grace, Bill Eerdmans bestowed on me extraordinary gifts of laughter, hospitality, and support. I savor memories when, out of the blue, the phone would ring and a mischievous voice in Grand Rapids would ask to speak to "Boston Blackie." For those too young to remember, Blackie was a jewel thief-*tunc*-safecracker-*tunc*-detective in movies (1918–1949), radio (1944–1945), and television (1951–1953). I lack firsthand experience in crime and popular media, but for Bill that made no difference. I was Blackie, "enemy to those who make him an enemy, friend to those who have no friend." If Bill had enemies, I imagine it was from envy alone. His friends were legion. I was privileged to be one. I miss him.

C. C. B.
June 2022
Princeton, New Jersey

Abbreviations

b. Yoma	Yoma (Babylonian Talmud)
Cal.	Suetonius, *Gaius Caligula*
Cels.	Origen, *Contra Celsum*
Claud.	Suetonius, *Divus Claudius*
Comm. Matt.	Jerome, *Commentariorum in Matthaeum libri IV*
Comp.	Dionysius of Halicarnassus, *De compositione verborum*
Comp. vit.	Plutarch, *Comparatio vitas*
Conf.	Philo, *De confusione linguarum*
Congr.	Philo, *De congressu eruditionis gratia*
Cons.	Augustine, *De consensu evangelistarum*
Cupid. divit.	Plutarch, *De cupiditate divitiarum*
De an.	Aristotle, *De anima*
De or.	Cicero, *De oratore*
Dial.	Justin Martyr, *Dialogus cum Tryphone*; alternatively, Seneca, *Dialogi*
Diatr.	Epictetus, *Diatribai*
Doctr. chr.	Augustine, *De doctrina christiana*
Dom.	Suetonius, *Domitianus*
Eloc.	Demetrius, *De elocutione* (*Peri hermēneias*)
Ep. Tra.	Pliny the Younger, *Epistulae ad Trajanum*
Euthyphr.	Plato, *Euthyphro*
Flac.	Cicero, *Pro Flacco*
Fug.	Philo, *De fuga et inventione*
Galb.	Suetonius, *Galba*
Gorg.	Plato, *Gorgias*
Haer.	Irenaeus, *Adversus haereses*; alternatively, Hippolytus, *Refutatio omnium haeresium* (*Philosophoumena*)
Herm. Mand.	Shepherd of Hermas, Mandatum
Herm. Sim.	Shepherd of Hermas, Similitudo
Herm. Vis.	Shepherd of Hermas, Visio
Hier.	Xenophon, *Hiero*
Hist.	Tacitus, *Historiae*; alternatively, Thucydides, *De bello peloponnesiaco*; Herodotus, *Historiae*
Hist. eccl.	Eusebius, *Historia ecclesiastica*
Hist. rom.	Cassius Dio, *Historia romana*
Hom. Matt.	John Chrysostom, *Homiliae in Matthaeum*
Ign. *Eph.*	Ignatius, *To the Ephesians*
Ign. *Rom.*	Ignatius, *To the Romans*
Inst.	Quintilian, *Institutio oratoria*

Inv.	Cicero, *De inventione rhetorica*
Jub.	Jubilees
Jul.	Suetonius, *Divus Julius*
LAE	Life of Adam and Eve
Legat.	Philo, *Legatio ad Gaium*
Marc.	Tertullian, *Adversus Marcionem*
m. Ber.	Berakot (Mishnah)
Mem.	Xenophon, *Memorabilia*
m. Giṭ.	Giṭṭin (Mishnah)
Mor.	Plutarch, *Moralia*
Mos.	Philo, *De vita Mosis*
m. Šabb.	Šabbat (Mishnah)
m. Sanh.	Sanhedrin (Mishnah)
Nat.	Pliny the Elder, *Naturalis historia*
Nat. d.	Cicero, *De natura deorum*
Nero	Suetonius, *Nero*
Nigr.	Lucian, *Nigrinus*
Od.	Homer, *Odysseia*
Oed. col.	Sophocles, *Oedipus coloneus*
Opif.	Philo, *De opificio mundi*
Or.	Cicero, *Orator*
Orat.	Dio Chrysostom, *Orationes*
Pan.	Epiphanius, *Panarion* (*Adversus haereses*)
Paralyt.	John Chrysostom, *In paralyticum demissum per tectum*
Pelag.	Jerome, *Adversus Pelagianos dialogi III*
Per. id.	Hermogenes of Tarsus, *Peri ideōn* (Περὶ ἰδεῶν)
Phaedr.	Plato, *Phaedrus*
Praescr.	Tertullian, *De praescriptione haereticorum*
Prov.	Seneca, *De Providentia*
Rab. Perd.	Cicero, *Pro Rabirio Perduellionis Reo*
Resp.	Plato, *Respublica*
Rhet.	Aristotle, *Ars rhetorica*
Rhet. ad Alex.	Anaximenes of Lampascus (?), *Rhetorica ad Alexandrum* (*Ars rhetorica*)
Rhet. ad Her.	*Rhetorica ad Herennium*
Sat.	Juvenal, *Satirae*
Saturn.	Macrobius, *Saturnalia*
Sib. Or.	Sibylline Oracles
Spec.	Philo, *De specialibus legibus*

Subl.	Longinus, *De sublimitate*
T. Benj.	Testament of Benjamin
Tib.	Suetonius, *Tiberius*
T. Iss.	Testament of Issachar
Tit.	Suetonius, *Divus Titus*
T. Job	Testament of Job
T. Jos.	Testament of Joseph
T. Levi	Testament of Levi
T. Mos.	Testament of Moses
T. Naph.	Testament of Naphtali
Tract. Ev. Jo.	Augustine of Hippo, *In Evangelium Johannis tractatus*
Verr.	Cicero, *In Verrem*
Vesp.	Suetonius, *Vespasianus*
Vir. ill.	Jerome, *De viris illustribus*
Vit.	Suetonius, *Vitellius*
Vit. Apoll.	Philostratus, *Vita Apollonii*

SECONDARY SOURCES

AB	Anchor Bible
ABD	*Anchor Bible Dictionary*. Edited by David Noel Freedman. 6 vols. New York: Doubleday, 1992
ABRL	Anchor Bible Reference Library
AcBib	Academia Biblica
ACCSNT	Ancient Critical Commentary on Scripture: New Testament
ACNT	Augsburg Commentary on the New Testament
AJP	*American Journal of Philology*
Alter	*The Book of Psalms: A Translation with Commentary*. Translated by Robert Alter. New York: Norton, 2007
AmJT	*American Journal of Theology*
AnBib	Analecta biblica
ANTC	Abingdon New Testament commentaries
ARCA	ARCA Classical and Medieval Texts, Papers and Monographs
ASE	*Annali di Storia dell'Esegesi*
ASNU	Acta Seminarii Neotestamentici Upsaliensis
ATANT	Abhandlungen zur Theologie des Alten und Neuen Testaments
ATLAMS	American Theological Library Association Monograph Series
AUSS	American University Studies Series

AYBRL	Anchor Yale Bible Reference Library
BBB	Bonner biblische Beiträge
BEH	Bibliothêque de l'Evolution de l'Humanité
BETL	Bibliotheca ephemeridum theologicarum Lovaniensium
BHT	Beiträge zur historischen Theologie
Bib	*Biblica*
BibInt	*Biblical Interpretation*
BIS	Biblical Interpretation Series
BJRL	*Bulletin of the John Rylands University Library of Manchester*
BNTC	Black's New Testament Commentaries
BPC	Biblical Performance Criticism
BR	*Biblical Research*
BSac	*Bibliotheca Sacra*
BSR	Biblioteca di scienze religiose
BTB	*Biblical Theology Bulletin*
BTS	Biblisch-theologische Studien
BZ	*Biblische Zeitschrift*
BZNW	Beihefte zur Zeitschrift für die neutestamentliche Wissenschaft
CBET	Contributions to Biblical Exegesis & Theology
CBNT	Commentaire Biblique Nouveau Testament
CBQ	*Catholic Biblical Quarterly*
CBR	*Currents in Biblical Research*
CBRA	Collectanea Biblica et Religiosa Antiqua
CEC	Collection d'études classiques
ConBNT	Coniectanea Biblica: New Testament Series (= Coniectanea Neotestamentica)
CRBR	*Critical Review of Books in Religion*
DBI	*Dictionary of Biblical Interpretation*. Edited by John Hayes. 2 vols. Nashville: Abingdon, 1999
Di	*Dialog*
EBib	Etudes bibliques
EC	*Early Christianity*
ECCA	Early Christianity in the Context of Antiquity
ÉHPR	Études d'histoire et de philosophie religieuses
EKKNT	Evangelisch-katholischer Kommentar zum Neuen Testament
EpRev	*Epworth Review*
ETL	Ephemerides Theologicae Lovanienses
ETR	Etudes théologiques et religieuses
EvT	*Evangelische Theologie*

ExAud	*Ex Auditu*
ExpTim	*Expository Times*
FBBS	Facet Book Biblical Series
FF	Foundations and Facets
FMFS	Faith Meets Faith Series
FRLANT	Forschungen zur Religion und Literatur des Alten und Neuen Testaments
GBS	Guides to Biblical Scholarship
GNS	Good News Studies
HBT	*Horizons in Biblical Theology*
HNT	Handbuch zum Neuen Testament
HTKNT	Herders theologischer Kommentar zum Neuen Testament
HTR	*Harvard Theological Review*
HUCA	*Hebrew Union College Annual*
HUT	Hermeneutische Untersuchungen zur Theologie
HZ	*Historische Zeitschrift*
IBT	Interpreting Biblical Texts
ICS	*Illinois Classical Studies*
IDBSup	*Interpreter's Dictionary of the Bible: Supplementary Volume.* Edited by Keith Crim. Nashville: Abingdon, 1976
Int	*Interpretation*
IPS	Institute of Preaching Series
IRT	Issues in Religion and Theology
IRUSC	Interpretation: Resources for the Use of Scripture in the Church
JAAR	*Journal of the American Academy of Religion*
JBL	*Journal of Biblical Literature*
JBR	*Journal of Bible and Religion*
JJS	*Journal of Jewish Studies*
JMS	Johannine Monograph Series
JSHJ	*Journal for the Study of the Historical Jesus*
JSJSup	Supplements to Journal for the Study of Judaism
JSNT	*Journal for the Study of the New Testament*
JSNTSup	Journal for the Study of the New Testament Supplements
JSOT	*Journal for the Study of the Old Testament*
JSP	*Journal for the Study of the Pseudepigrapha*
JTI	*Journal of Theological Interpretation*
JTS	*Journal of Theological Studies*
KBANT	Kommentare und Beiträge zum Alten und Neuen Testament
KEKNT	Kritisch-exegetischer Kommentar über das Neue Testament

KJV	King James Version
LCL	Loeb Classical Library
LEC	Library of Early Christianity
LJS	Lives of Jesus Series
LNTS	Library of New Testament Studies
LTT	Library of Theological Translations
MnemSup	Mnemosyne Supplements
NAC	New American Commentary
NBf	*New Blackfriars*
NCB	New Century Bible
NEB	New English Bible
NedTT	*Nederlands theologisch tijdschrift*
Neot	*Neotestamentica*
NGS	New Gospel Studies
NIGTC	New International Greek Testament Commentary
NIV	New International Version
NJPS	*Tanakh: The Holy Scriptures; The New JPS Translation according to the Traditional Hebrew Text.* 2nd ed. 1999
NovT	*Novum Testamentum*
NovTSup	Supplements to *Novum Testamentum*
NPNF[1]	*The Nicene and Post-Nicene Fathers*, Series 1. Edited by Philip Schaff. 1886–1889. 14 vols. Repr., Peabody, MA: Hendrickson, 1994
NRSV	New Revised Standard Version
NTL	New Testament Library
NTS	*New Testament Studies*
NTT	New Testament Theology
NTTS	New Testament Tools and Studies
NYRB	New York Review of Books
OBT	Overtures to Biblical Theology
OEBI	*The Oxford Encyclopedia of Biblical Interpretation.* Edited by Steven McKenzie. 2 vols. New York: Oxford University Press, 2013
OTKNT	Ökumenischer Taschenbuch-Kommentar zum Neuen Testament
OTL	Old Testament Library
OTP	*Old Testament Pseudepigrapha.* Edited by James H. Charlesworth. 2 vols. New York: Doubleday, 1983, 1985
Per	*Perspective*
PGC	Pelican Gospel Commentaries
PNTC	Pillar New Testament Commentary

PR	*Philosophy and Rhetoric*
PRSt	*Perspectives in Religious Studies*
PSB	*Princeton Seminary Bulletin*
PSTJ	*Perkins School of Theology Journal*
RB	*Revue biblique*
RBL	*Review of Biblical Literature*
RBS	Resources for Biblical Study
REB	Revised English Bible
RelS	*Religious Studies*
RelSRev	*Religious Studies Review*
RelStTh	*Religious Studies and Theology*
ResQ	*Restoration Quarterly*
RevExp	*Review & Expositor*
RIPS	Royal Institute of Philosophy Supplements
RNTS	Reading the New Testament Series
RP	Religious Perspectives
RSV	Revised Standard Version
SBLDS	Society of Biblical Literature Dissertation Series
SBLMS	Society of Biblical Literature Monograph Series
SBT	Studies in Biblical Theology
SEÅ	*Svensk exegetisk årsbok*
SemeiaSt	Semeia Studies
SHBC	Smyth & Helwys Biblical Commentary
SJT	*Scottish Journal of Theology*
SM	*Speech Monographs*
Smith-Goodspeed	*The Holy Bible: An American Translation.* The Old Testament, translated by J. M. Powis Smith et al.; The New Testament, translated by Edgar J. Goodspeed. Chicago: University of Chicago Press, 1939
SNTI	Studies in New Testament Interpretation
SNTSMS	Society for New Testament Studies Monograph Series
SNTW	Studies of the New Testament and Its World
SP	Sacra Pagina
SPNT	Studies on Personalities of the New Testament
SR	*Sewanee Review*
SRR	Studies in Religion and Rhetoric
StPatr	*Studia Patristica*
StPB	Studia Post-biblica
SwJT	*Southwestern Journal of Theology*

TC	Trends in Classics
TDNT	*Theological Dictionary of the New Testament*. Edited by Gerhard Kittel and Gerhard Friedrich. Translated by Geoffrey W. Bromiley. 10 vols. Grand Rapids: Eerdmans, 1964–1976
TeolT	*Teologisk tidsskrift*
Them	*Themelios*
ThTo	*Theology Today*
TJT	*Toronto Journal of Theology*
TLS	*The Times Literary Supplement*
TLZ	*Theologische Literaturzeitung*
TRu	*Theologische Rundschau*
TS	*Theological Studies*
TSAJ	Texte und Studien zum antiken Judentum
TTKi	*Tidsskrift for Teologi og Kirke*
TZ	*Theologische Zeitschrift*
UJT	Understanding Jesus Today
Vid	*Vidyajyoti Journal of Theological Reflection*
VPT	Voices in Performance and Text
VTSup	Supplements to *Vetus Testamentum*
WBC	Word Biblical Commentary
WGRW	Writings from the Greco-Roman World
WMANT	Wissenschaftliche Monographien zum Alten und Neuen Testament
WUNT	Wissenschaftliche Untersuchungen zum Neuen Testament
WW	*Word and World*
WWSup	Word and World Supplement Series
YPR	Yale Publications in Religion
ZNW	*Zeitschrift für die neutestamentliche Wissenschaft und die Kunde der älteren Kirche*
ZWKL	*Zeitschrift für Wissenschaft und kirchliches Leben*

Sigla

Alt.	Alternative reading
AT	Author's translation
BCE	Before Common Era (= BC)
bis	(Appearing) Twice
CE	Common Era (= AD)

ET	English translation
Exp.	Expanded
Gk.	"in Greek"
Heb.	"in Hebrew"
LXX	Septuagint
MT	Masoretic Text
N.B.	*nota bene*, note carefully
n.s.	new series
NT	New Testament
o.s.	old series
OT	Old Testament
Par(r).	and parallel(s)
Repr.	Reprinted
sc.	*scilicet*, to wit, namely
s.v.	*sub verbo*, under the word or titular entry
Trans.	Translation, translated by

A Brief Commentary
on the Gospel According to Mark

> In every fat book there is a thin book trying to get out.
>
> —Unknown

MARK'S GOSPEL MAY HAVE BEEN the first sustained, literary interpretation of the traditions about Jesus in primitive Christianity. Although testimonies from as early as the second century CE ascribe the Second Gospel to "Mark," Peter's companion in Rome (1 Pet 5:13), nowhere in the gospel is its author identified or correlated with other NT figures. Mark's presumption that its readers are unfamiliar with Jewish customs, Aramaic terms, and Palestinian geography (7:2–4, 31, 34) suggests an origin beyond Palestine. The pervasiveness of Latin customs and vocabulary (5:9; 10:12; 12:42) points to a provenance in Syria, Italy, or elsewhere in the Roman Empire. If the tumult forecast in 13:5–23 mirrors that of Mark's readers, then the gospel may have arisen during the era of Nero's persecution of Christians (64 CE) and the Jewish revolt against imperial Rome (66–73 CE). Such a setting is consistent with Mark's emphasis on the tribulations of Jesus and his followers (4:17; 10:30, 33–34) (see chapter 1). Such dating squares with the judgment, accepted by most scholars, that Mark was a source for Matthew and Luke, both of which may have been written toward the end of the first century CE. Mark's own sources appear to have included miracle stories (4:35–5:43), sayings (9:42–50), and an account of Jesus's final days in Jerusalem (14:1–15:47).

Mark bears the stamp of many literary genres in antiquity: OT prophetic and apocalyptic narratives (1 Kgs 17–2 Kgs 9; Dan 1–6), legends of the rabbis, and lives of Hellenistic philosophers (see chapter 15). Like the other gospels, Mark is essentially a religious proclamation based on historical event. Though vivid, its Greek is cruder than that of Matthew or Luke. Closely examined, however, Mark exhibits care in composition, creatively juxtaposing disparate traditions.

Preeminent among Mark's emphases is an interpretation of Jesus that recognizes his authority (1:21–27; 2:1–3:6) yet stresses his suffering and death (8:31; 9:31; 10:33–34, 45). Authentic discipleship is depicted as self-sacrificial service to God for the sake of the gospel (8:34–9:1; 9:33–50; 10:35–45). Ironically, Jesus's disciples (10:35–41; 14:66–72) display such discipleship less often than do a cast of minor characters (5:21–43; 12:41–44) and Jesus himself (14:32–42). Jesus's followers are summoned to faithful vigilance during an arduous, ambiguous time between the inauguration and consummation of God's kingdom (1:14–15; 4:1–34; 10:1–31; 13:28–37).

Compared with Matthew and Luke, Mark contains much less of Jesus's teaching (cf. Matt 5:1–7:27) and none of the infancy narratives (Luke 1:1–2:52). Only later endings appended to Mark describe appearances of the risen Christ. Unlike John, whose Jesus unveils himself at length (6:35–51; 10:1–18), Jesus in Mark is a cryptic figure who conceals as much as he reveals (4:1–34; 9:2–13) (see chapter 9). Despite its mysterious character, Mark's place in the NT has been secure, perhaps because no gospel probes more intensely the implications of "proclaim[ing] Christ crucified" (1 Cor 1:23) (see chapter 12).

Outline of the Gospel

1:1–15	Prologue: Introducing Jesus
1:16–3:12	The Early Days: Jesus's Galilean Ministry and Its Opposition
3:13–6:6a	"Who, Then, Is This?"
6:6b–8:21	Revelation over Bread
8:22–10:52	Christology and Discipleship
11:1–13:37	The Final Days: Jerusalem and the Temple
14:1–15:47	The Passion Narrative
16:1–8	Epilogue: The Empty Tomb
	[The Shorter Ending of Mark]
	[16:9–20: The Longer Ending of Mark]

Analysis

1:1–15. Prologue: Introducing Jesus

Mark's prologue consists of five seamless segments: the *title and epigram* (1:1–3), a *description of John the Baptist* (1:4–8), the *stories of Jesus's baptism* (1:9–11) *and temptation* (1:12–13), and *a transitional passage that opens Jesus's Galilean ministry* (1:14–15). This introduction orients the reader to several interrelated themes.

A christological concentration: Jesus Christ ("messiah" or "anointed one": 8:29; 9:41; 12:35; 13:21; 14:61; 15:32) stands at the beginning of this evangelist's "good news" or "glad tidings of salvation" (vv. 1, 14; cf. Isa 52:7; 61:1; Matt 11:5; Rom 1:1; 1 Cor 15:1; 1 Thess 2:2, 8–9). Although missing from some ancient witnesses, "Son of God" is another significant title for Jesus in Mark (1:11; 3:11; 9:7; 15:39). In the OT, it connotes an obedient servant within God's salvation history (2 Sam 7:13–14; Hos 11:1; Wis 2:18).

An Old Testament backdrop: The epigram in verses 2–3 conflates material from Isa 40:3 with Exod 23:20 and Mal 3:1, suggesting that John's ministry fulfills Scripture and prepares the way of one mightier than he (v. 4). In the wilderness (vv. 3, 12, 13), Israel rebelled against God (Pss 78:17–18; 106:13–33) yet was delivered (Exod 19–24). The baptizer shares the prophets' concern for repentance and forgiveness (Isa 1:10–20; Jer 31:34; Joel 2:12–13; Zech 1:4) in association with baptism (Mark 1:4; Ezek 36:25–28); his attire recalls that of Elijah (Mark 1:6; 2 Kgs 1:8). The heavenly acclamation of Jesus at his baptism (v. 11) combines elements of Ps 2:7 and Isa 42:1, with possible allusions to Gen 22:2–16 and Exod 4:22–23. A sojourn of forty days is reminiscent of Exod 34:28 and 1 Kgs 19:8. Though the significance of Jesus's being with the wild beasts (v. 13) is obscure, it may suggest the restoration of a paradisiacal condition before the fall (see Gen 2:19–20; Isa 11:6–9; 65:25) or, in conjunction with angels, providential protection (Ps 91:11–13).

An apocalyptic aura: Elijah's return was sometimes regarded as a sign of the age's end (Mal 4:5). In John, he has indeed returned (Mark 9:13); the whole countryside around Judea's capital, Jerusalem, is responding to his message (v. 5). Israel's reinfusion with the Holy Spirit was expected in the last days (vv. 8, 10; Isa 11:1–2; Joel 2:28–32; Acts 2:17–22); the Spirit hovers over Jesus at his baptism (vv. 9–10; Gen 1:2) before driving him into the desert (v. 12). The rending of the heavens is an apocalyptic image of divine disclosure (v. 10; 15:38; Isa 64:1 Ezek 1:1; John 1:51; Acts 7:56; Rev 4:1; 11:19; 19:11). By the NT era, Satan, Jesus's tempter (v. 13), is considered God's eschatological adversary (Mark 4:15; John 13:27; Acts 5:3; 26:18; 2 Cor 11:14; 1 Tim 5:15; Rev 20:1–10). The pith of Jesus's proclamation, repentance and trust on the threshold of God's sovereign reign (v. 15b; 4:11; 9:1; 15:43), is apocalyptically tinged: "The time"—God's appointed moment—"is fulfilled" (v. 15a; 11:13; 12:2; Ezek 7:12; Dan 7:22; Gal 4:4). Such a time is painful (13:1–23): Jesus's own ministry in Galilee, a region of northern Palestine, begins only after John's arrest (v. 14), which presages Jesus's own (14:46).

1:16–3:12. The Early Days: Jesus's Galilean Ministry and Its Opposition

Mark's first major section comprises a series of *five anecdotes that characterize Jesus's earliest ministry* (1:16–45) and *their stimulation of five controversies* (2:1–3:6).

At the beginning of each of Mark's major sections (3:12–19a; 6:6b–13; 8:27–9:1; 11:1–11; 14:1–11) Jesus's disciples are prominent. In 1:16–20, *the first disciples are summoned* along the Sea of Galilee, an inland freshwater lake. Fishermen enjoyed a lucrative business, as suggested by Zebedee's hired men (1:20). Brief though it is, this passage highlights features that will recur: the extraordinary authority of Jesus's actions (1:27; 4:41); his initiative in making disciples (2:14; 3:13–19a); and the rupture such discipleship creates within families (3:19b–21; 10:28–30).

Jesus's casting out of an unclean spirit in Capernaum (1:21–28), on the northwestern shore of the Sea of Galilee, is the first of four such stories in Mark's four major sections (see 5:1–20; 7:24–30; 9:14–29). Jesus triumphs over the demon's attempt to wrest power through assertion of his antagonist's identity (v. 24b; cf. Gen 32:27–29). Subtle details cast long narrative shadows: Jesus wields authority over Satan's dominion (vv. 24a, 27c; 1:32; 3:11–12), which astounds (vv. 22a, 27a; 2:12; 5:20, 42b; 7:37; 11:18) and causes his fame to spread (v. 28; 3:7–10; 5:20; 6:14, 53–56). Jesus's teaching is fresh (v. 27b; 2:21–22), unlike that of the scribes (v. 22): quasi-professional interpreters of the law who will return as Jesus's nemeses (2:6, 16; 3:22; 11:27). This healing takes place on the Sabbath in a synagogue (v. 21; also 3:1–2), a place of teaching and prayer, even as Jesus will resist later attacks in Jerusalem's temple (11:27–12:27).

Describing *Jesus's cure of all of Capernaum's sick*, including Peter's mother-in-law (1:29–34), Mark generalizes the exorcism's effect. Three other nuances are introduced: the ministry of women to Jesus (v. 31b; 14:3–9; 16:1); his silencing of demons, who know his true identity (v. 34b; 3:11–12); and the impossibility of keeping Jesus's power a secret (vv. 32–33; 1:43–45; 7:36).

Jesus's ministry has begun with preaching (1:14–15); Mark broadens that aspect by narrating the buildup to *a preaching tour throughout Galilee* (1:35–39). More details are introduced for later development: Jesus as a person of prayer (v. 35b; 6:46; 14:32–42); his distance from the multitudes and their incursions upon him (vv. 35, 37; 1:45; 2:1–2; 3:7, 19b–20; 6:31–34; 9:2–15); and those searching for Jesus, often with hostile intent (vv. 36–37; 3:32; 11:18; 12:12; 14:1b).

Jesus's healing of a leper (1:40–45) declares many of Mark's remaining preoccupations. This tale demonstrates Jesus's compassion for those in distress (v. 41; 5:21–24a; 6:34–36, 48a; 8:2–3) and his divine power for its alleviation (v. 42; 4:39; 6:41–44, 48b–51b; 8:7–9; cf. 2 Kgs 5:7). Because leprosy (Hansen's disease) was regarded as contagious impurity (Lev 13:1–14:47), its sufferers were subject to banishment (2 Kgs 7:3–10; 2 Chr 26:19–21). Accordingly, Jesus insists that this leper's cleansing be ratified by a priest and honored with an offering (v. 44; cf. Lev 14:48–57). Social reintegration of outcasts and appreciation of genuine piety recur throughout Mark (3:4; 5:19, 23–34; 7:18b–23; 12:29–31).

Mark 1:16–45 highlights Jesus's power while resistance stirs in the shadows. In 2:1–3:6, opposition to Jesus moves onto center stage. Controversy stitches together five anecdotes arranged as a chiasm, or inverted ladder:

> A. Dispute over blasphemy: a paralytic (2:1–5, 10b–12) and some scribes (2:6–10a)
>> B. The scribes' challenge to the disciples about Jesus's eating (2:13–17)
>>> C. The disciples' feasting and the bridegroom's removal (2:18–22)
>> B.' The Pharisees' challenge to Jesus about his disciples' eating on the Sabbath (2:23–28)
> A.' Dispute over the Sabbath: Pharisees (3:1–2, 6) and a man with a withered hand (3:3–5)

Two healings (2:1–12; 3:1–6) encompass three debates, all of which involve eating (2:13–17, 18–22, 23–28). The two bookends, tainted by spiritual heart disease (2:6, 8; 3:5), conflate common elements in a mirror image: the first healing (2:1–4, 10b–12) frames an accusation (2:5–10a); murderous suspicion (3:1–2, 6) frames the second healing (3:3–5).

The scribes' repudiation of Jesus's healing of a paralytic (2:1–12) is the first instance of Mark's characteristic technique of intercalating or "sandwiching" two traditional pieces in such a way that each provides commentary on the other (see also 3:1–6; 3:19–35; 5:21–43; 6:6b–30; 11:12–25; 14:1–11; 14:53–72). The primary concern of 2:1–12 is Jesus's authority, manifested in his extraordinary ability to heal (vv. 10–11); the passage's theological springboard is the OT's correlation of healing with forgiveness (2 Chr 7:14; Pss 41:4; 103:3; Isa 57:17–19). Other issues rise to the fore. The scribes' rejection of Jesus's pronouncement of forgiveness is framed as blasphemy (v. 7a), a capital offense (Lev 24:15–16) with which Jesus will ultimately be charged by Jerusalem's high priest (Mark 14:64). Its relevance here presumes that forgiveness was God's exclusive prerogative (v. 7b; Exod 34:6–7; Isa 43:25). As elsewhere (3:4; 11:30), Jesus counters with an ambiguous question that puts his accusers on the spot (v. 9); the paralytic's healing suggests Jesus's authority to forgive sins without proving it. By contrast, faith (v. 5) manifests itself as aggressive confidence in Jesus's healing power (see also 5:34, 36; 10:52). Though he exhibits preternatural discernment (v. 8), the only authority Jesus claims for himself is that of "the Son of Man" (v. 10), his customary yet obscure expression of self-reference throughout Mark (2:28; 8:31, 38; 9:9, 12, 31; 10:33, 45; 13:26; 14:21, 41, 62).

The summoning of Levi from a roadside tollhouse (2:13–14) dissolves into a larger tableau: *disgruntlement among Pharisaic scribes over Jesus's eating with social outcasts* (2:15–17). Jewish tax collectors were despised for their presumed dishonesty, interaction with gentiles, and collaboration with Roman authorities. "Sinners" were the notoriously wicked who flouted Jewish law. In Mark, the Pharisees are ranged among Jesus's typical adversaries (v. 18; 2:24; 3:6; 7:1, 5; 8:11; 10:2; 12:13), even though they were a popular reform movement within Judaism that piously applied the law to all aspects of life (Josephus, *B.J.* 2.162–66). Here the dispute turns on the proper expression of righteousness: distancing one's self from sinners or fraternizing with them, as a physician consorts with the infirm (Mark 2:16–17).

A criticism of eating shifts into one of *fasting* (2:18–22): a Jewish rite observed annually (Lev 16:29; Zech 7:5) and occasionally (Ezra 8:21–23; Jonah 3:7–9) as a sign of contrition. Early Christians eventually adopted the practice (Acts 13:2–3; 14:23), as Mark 2:20b suggests. Jesus's rejoinder challenges not the act but its timing: the time to mourn is not at a wedding (cf. Isa 54:5–6; 62:4–5; Ezek 16:1–63; Hos 2:19; Eph 5:32; Rev 19:7) but rather when the bridegroom is taken away (vv. 19–20a; 14:21). Jesus's ministry represents something new (cf. 1:27) that the old cannot contain (vv. 21–22).

Another dispute erupts over *plucking grain on the Sabbath* (2:23–28). During and after the biblical era, Jews debated the legality of particular activities on the Sabbath, the day set apart from all work (Exod 20:8–11; Deut 5:12–15; m. Šabb. 1:1–24:5). Plucking heads of grain (v. 23) may have been reckoned a violation of the proscription of reaping on the Sabbath (Exod 34:21). In rabbinic style, Jesus defends his disciples' actions by countering with scriptural precedent (Lev 24:5–9; 1 Sam 21:1–6) whose effect is more liberal (Mark 7:1–23). The underlying question—Who decides?—is resolved in favor of Jesus, "the Son of Man [who] is lord even of the Sabbath" (v. 28; cf. 2:10).

The healing of the man with a withered hand (3:1–6) is the last in this series of initial disputes. The narrative pattern inverts that of 2:1–12: a mighty work (vv. 3–5) is sandwiched inside a controversy (vv. 1–2, 6). The issue is the same as in 2:23–28: Jesus's contemporaries would have accepted a violation of the Sabbath to save life but would have questioned that exception's relevance in this case. Jesus attributes pitiless legality to "hardness of heart," stubborn obtuseness (see also 6:52; 8:17; 10:5; Exod 9:34–35; 1 Sam 6:6; 2 Chr 36:13; Ps 95:8). The climax of this passage, indeed of 2:1–3:6, lies in 3:6. The Herodians may have been partisans of the Herodian dynasty or officials appointed by Herod Antipas, tetrarch of Galilee and Perea (4 BCE–39 CE). Either way, Mark foreshadows a conspiracy of Jewish and Roman authorities to destroy Jesus (see also 6:14–29; 12:13; 15:1).

Mark 3:7–12 is a transitional summary that underscores Jesus's growing popularity (1:28, 35–37, 45) while foreshadowing his ministry beyond Palestine (7:24–31). Judea and Jerusalem (v. 8) lay south of Galilee; Idumea ("Edom," Gen 32:3) was a region southeast of Judea. Beyond the Jordan was Perea, northeast of Judea and southeast of Galilee; Tyre and Sidon were cities northwest of Galilee. Mark gathers several threads in this digest: the enormous, life-threatening crowds (3:8–10; 3:20; 6:31) that want to touch Jesus (1:41; 5:27–28; 6:56); the unclean spirits' submission to him (v. 11; 1:23–26; 5:1–13; 9:25–26); and their recognition of Jesus as the Son of God (see also 1:24; 5:7) and his silencing of that acclamation (v. 12; 1:34).

3:13–6:6a. "Who, Then, Is This?"

Mark's previous section crystallized Jesus's ministry and its ensuing controversy; this one focuses on Jesus's mysterious identity and its challenge to faith. Opening and closing with disputes in which Jesus's family is implicated (3:21, 31–35; 6:1–6a), two episodes highlight Jesus's contest with unclean spirits (3:22–30; 5:1–20), and a trio explores the dynamics of faith amid hopeless circumstances (4:35–41; 5:21–43). At this section's heart is Jesus's teaching in parables (4:1–34), addressing God's kingdom while characterizing its principal herald.

Mark's first major section opened with Jesus's calling of his first disciples (1:16–20); this section begins with *the filling out of the Twelve* (3:13–19a). The setting is a mountain or "the hill country" (v. 13), a typical place for supernatural disclosures in the OT (e.g., Exod 19:3–25) and elsewhere in Mark (9:2–13; 13:3–37). Jesus "makes" (3:14, 16) twelve whom he wants: a number that may symbolize Israel's twelve tribes (Num 1:4–16; 13:1–16; cf. Matt 19:28; Luke 22:30). The term "apostles" is rare in Mark (elsewhere only at 6:30). Its basic meaning, emissaries who discharge a specific commission, is its likely connotation (see 6:7–13). Besides affording him company, the Twelve are authorized to do precisely what Jesus has done in 1:21–3:12: to preach and wield authority over demons (3:14–15; 6:12–13). The names and ordering of the Twelve (3:16–19a) vary across the NT (see Matt 10:2–4; Luke 6:14–16; John 1:40–49; 21:2; Acts 1:13). Jesus gives Simon the name *Petros* (Gk., "stone" or "rock"; 1:16; cf. Matt 16:18–19 and its Aramaic equivalent *Kēphas* in John 1:42; 1 Cor 1:12; Gal 1:18). Despite Mark's translation (3:17), the derivation and meaning of *Boanērges*, nicknames for James and John (1:19), remain obscure. The "Cananaean," applied to another Simon (v. 18), may derive from an Aramaic term denoting religious zeal (*qananan*; see Luke 6:15; Acts 1:13). The meaning of "Iscariot" (3:19a) is cloudy; it could be rooted in different Semitic terms for "one from Kerioth" (see Josh 15:25; Jer 48:24) or "a fraud" (*sakar*), perhaps even in a Latin loanword for an "assassin" (*sicarius*). Mark immediately identifies Judas as the one who will hand Jesus over: the same verb used to describe John the Baptist's arrest (1:14).

The embedding of *a harsh controversy over Jesus's authority* (3:22–30) inside a framing narrative that *redefines his family* (3:19b–21, 31–35) exemplifies a classic Markan technique first witnessed in 2:1–12. Indeed, that traditional sandwich and this one evince interesting parallels. In both cases, the setting is "at home" (2:1; 3:19b), where an overflow crowd has gathered, impeding access (2:2; 3:20). Accusatory scribes are present in both cases (2:6; 3:22); here they have come "from Jerusalem," where Jesus's death awaits (10:32–34). Coloring both scenes are spirits, whether discerning (2:8) or unclean (3:30), and a charge of blasphemy (2:7; 3:28–29) associated with Jesus's healing power (2:9; 3:22) and his forgiveness of sins (2:7; 3:28–29). Both tableaux turn on the scope or source of Jesus's authority: either to forgive sins (2:7) or to cast out demons (3:22). The cords braiding 3:22–30 with its surrounding material in 3:19b–21 and 3:31–35 are (1) a serious misapprehension of Jesus as "out of his mind" (v. 21) or demon possessed (v. 22; cf. John 8:48–52; 10:20) and (2) the division of households revealed by that charge. While Jesus counters his attackers with the claim that a house internally divided cannot stand (3:25–27), his own family show themselves as divided against Jesus (3:21, 31–32). Jesus suggests that his ministry spells the toppling of Satan (vv. 26–27) or "Beelzebul" ("lord of the flies" [2 Kgs 1:2] or "lord of the dwelling" [Matt 10:25]); strangely, the lord of an ancient household—the father—is absent from among Jesus's mother and brothers (Mark 3:31–32). Both components of this Markan sandwich of traditions end on a jarring note. In 3:28–30, Jesus solemnly affirms that confusing the Holy Spirit (see 1:8, 10, 12) or the Spirit's agent (3:30) with unclean spirits is tantamount to commission of an unforgiveable sin—perhaps because a patient so gravely ill will never solicit the physician's healing (2:17). In 3:33–35, Jesus radically redefines members of the family, antiquity's most basic social organization. No longer are they his relatives by blood; now they are all who do God's will. The broadening of that family to include "sister[s]" (v. 35) probably bespeaks female disciples in the earliest churches.

Mark characterizes Jesus's speech "in parables" (3:23), which in the OT are riddles or enigmatic stories that provoke without necessarily illuminating

(Ps 78:2; Prov 1:6; Ezek 17:2; Hab 2:6). The stage is set for 4:1–34, *Mark's largest cluster of parables*, which, like 2:1–3:6, is chiastically arranged:

A. Introduction (vv. 1–2)
   B. The sower (vv. 3–9)
      C. The parables' purpose: mystery given or withheld (vv. 10–12)
         D. The sower explained (vv. 13–20)
      C.' The parables' purpose: disclosure and secrecy (vv. 21–25)
   B.' The growing seed (vv. 26–29) and the mustard seed (vv. 30–32)
A.' Conclusion (vv. 33–34)

The setting (vv. 1–2, 10, 33–34) swings between poles of publicity and privacy, between distance and proximity, between parables and explanation. Three parabolic stories (vv. 3–9, 26–29, 30–32) liken God's kingdom (v. 11) to seeds whose inauspicious origins—random or inattentive sowing, minute size—eventuate in astonishing outcomes: a hundredfold yield (v. 8), automatic growth (v. 28), "the greatest of all shrubs" (v. 32). Fertility and fruitlessness are common metaphors in Jewish and early Christian apocalypticism (2 Esd 4:26–32; 1 Cor 3:6–8), even as sickle and harvest (v. 29) refer to final judgment (Joel 3:13a; Rev 14:14–20), and nesting in large branches (v. 32) suggests protection of God's elect (Ezek 17:23; 31:6; Dan 4:12, 21).

Punctuated by prophetic exhortations to listen and to look (vv. 3, 9, 23–24a; cf. Isa 28:23; Rev 2:7, 11), apocalypticism is even more pronounced in Jesus's baffling reasons for the parables (vv. 10–12, 21–25). In Daniel (2:18–19, 27–30), intertestamental Judaism (1 En. 63.3), the Pauline tradition (Rom 11:25; 1 Cor 4:1; Eph 3:3–9), and Revelation (10:7), the "secret" or "mystery" (Mark 4:11) refers to God's cosmic purposes, graciously unveiled to a select few. Things temporarily hidden are intended for disclosure (vv. 21–22). Attending that revelation, however, is a paradoxical concealment, a deafening and blinding, which the parables themselves are meant to inflict (v. 12). Like other NT authors (John 12:40; Acts 28:26–27), Mark adapts Isa 6:9–10 to interpret rejection of the gospel: preaching the word both gives and deprives to those mysteriously disposed to receive or to refuse (vv. 24–25; cf. 2 Esd 7:25). Even more puzzling is the reality that "those outside" (v. 11) can be those seemingly closest to Jesus (3:31–32). Mark sustains this enigma. Parables told as his listeners "were able to hear it" (v. 33) is highly ambiguous; disciples to whom everything is explained (v. 34) persistently do not understand (v. 13; 6:52; 7:18a; 8:17, 21; 14:68).

The heart of this section (4:13–20) is an allegorical interpretation of the sower (vv. 3–9), which may have originated among early Christians in reflection on their missionary hardships and the difficulty of discipleship (cf. 2 Cor 4:7–12; 2 Thess 1:4). The seed of Jesus's original parable is inconsistently interpreted as "the word" (i.e., the gospel: 4:14, 15b) and various responses to it (vv. 15a, 16–20; cf. 2 Esd 8:41–44; 9:31). Mark 4:13–20 is a précis of his entire narrative, which recounts the vicissitudes of Jesus's ministry in the face of satanic temptation (v. 15; 1:13; 8:33), his disciples' temporary acceptance but apostasy under fire (vv. 16–17; 9:42–47; 14:27), and this world's lures of wealth and prestige (vv. 18–19; cf. 9:33–37; 10:17–27). At the end, in spite of everything, good soil bears astonishing fruit (v. 20)—perhaps an allusion to Jesus's own vindication by resurrection (14:28; 16:6–7; cf. John 12:23–24).

If Mark 3:19b–4:34 bespeaks tacit Christology, then 4:35–6:6a pointedly raises the question, "Who is Jesus?" This segment exhibits balanced architecture:

> A. "Who then is this?" Jesus stills a storm (4:35–41)
> B. Three healings: the Gerasene demoniac (5:1–20), Jairus's daughter (5:21–24, 35–43), the woman suffering from hemorrhages (5:25–34)
> A.' "Where did this man get all this?" Jesus provokes controversy (6:1–6a)

Mark's christological question generates human reactions of faith, fear, or disbelief: the other thread tying these passages together (4:40; 5:15, 33, 34, 36; 6:3, 6a).

Jesus's stilling of a storm (4:35–41) is a mighty work that reverberates with both the OT and Mark's exorcism narratives. The windstorm, waves, and boat's being swamped (v. 37) recall Ps 107:23–25 and Jonah 1:4. Jesus's sleep in the stern (v. 38) suggests the repose of trust in God (Job 11:18–19; Pss 3:5; 4:8). In its desperation (Pss 44:23–24; 59:4b), the disciples' plea for deliverance (v. 38) recalls the Psalms (69:1–2, 14–15; 107:26–28a). Like unclean spirits in Mark 1:25 and 9:25, the wind is "rebuked" and the roiling seas are "muzzled" (v. 39a; cf. Ps 104:6–7). The quelling of chaotic waters (vv. 39a, 41b) implies divine power (Gen 1:2, 6–9; Pss 65:5–8; 74:12–14; 93:3–4; Isa 51:10); great awe (v. 41a) characterizes human response to divine manifestations (Isa 6:1–5; Jonah 1:10, 16). The most obviously Markan stamp on this tale is the sharp contrast between Jesus's serenity and his disciples' terror: "Why are you afraid? Have you still no faith?" (4:40).

After the storm's stilling, likened to an exorcism, Mark recounts an actual *exorcism* on the Galilee's east bank, *in Gerasa* (modern Jerash: 5:1–20; cf. 1:21–28; 7:24–30; 9:14–29). The story comprises Jesus's contest with a demon (vv. 1–13) and its social consequences (vv. 14–20). As before (3:11), the unclean spirit bows before a superior force (v. 6) even while attempting to repel the exorcist with divine adjuration (v. 7b). The battle ensues with retaliatory commands (vv. 8,

12–13) and incantation of names (vv. 7a, 9; cf. 1:24). Defilement pervades the scene. The victim, possessed by an unclean spirit (v. 2), lives among tombs, the abode of the dead and of social outcasts (v. 3; cf. Isa 65:1–7). Gentiles applied the title "the Most High God" (v. 7a) to Israel's God (Gen 14:18–20; Num 24:16; Dan 3:26). A Roman "Legion" (v. 9), a regiment of about six thousand soldiers, is a massive gentile occupation; equally defiling is a herd of two thousand swine (vv. 11–13; cf. Lev 11:7–8; Isa 65:4). The duel's outcome is simultaneously satisfying and terrifying: thousands of demons take possession of thousands of swine; all are drowned in chaotic waters (v. 13; cf. 4:41). The aftermath (5:14–20) abounds with conflicting emotions—fear (v. 15), gratitude (v. 18), amazement (v. 20b)—and social tensions. After the swineherds publicize the occurrence in city and countryside, the populace comes out, broadcasts its own witness, and entreats Jesus to depart (vv. 14, 16–17). Now clothed and calm, the erstwhile demoniac begs for Jesus's fellowship (vv. 15, 18). That Jesus refuses (v. 19), instead commissioning him to tell his friends of the Lord's mercy: presumably that of God (see 12:11, 29–30, 36; 13:20), though this new missionary proclaims Jesus (v. 20; cf. 2:28; 11:3; 12:37). The news spreads throughout the Decapolis (v. 20a), ten cities lying within a predominantly gentile region west and east of the Jordan River (see also 7:31).

While *the raising of Jairus's daughter* (Mark 5:21–24a, 35–43) is reminiscent of healings by Elijah (1 Kgs 17:17–24) and Elisha (2 Kgs 4:18–37), the deepest reverberations are those with the interlaminated story of *the healing of a woman with hemorrhages* (Mark 5:24b–34). Each tale mirrors the other, down to the smallest details. Both center on women—"daughters" (vv. 23, 34)—whose lives are running out after twelve years (vv. 25, 42). The sufferers' medical conditions—chronic menstruation (v. 25) or death (v. 35)—restrict or exclude them from normal social intercourse (see Lev 12:1–8; 15:19–30). Circumstances are hopeless and growing worse (vv. 23a, 26b, 35). In both tales, someone pitifully falls at Jesus's feet (vv. 22, 33); in both, he displays uncommon insight that appears laughably absurd (vv. 30–33, 39–40). Jesus's power trumps that of professionals: physicians (v. 26) and mourners (v. 38). By touch (vv. 23b, 27–28, 41a), both women are healed (σῴζω: vv. 23b, 28, 34a) and restored to wholeness (vv. 34b, 43b). Most important, both stories pivot on faith that penetrates fear (vv. 33–34, 36; cf. 4:40; 9:23–24). Mark stipulates that the little girl is "at the point of death" (v. 23b; cf. Matt 9:18) before recounting at excruciating length the tale of the older woman, capped by a false ending (v. 35). This is performative theology: the narration itself raises the stakes for *the reader's* trust in God.

With *Jesus's return home* (6:1–6a), Mark's second major segment ends as it began: with the disciples in tow (cf. 3:13–19a), Jesus is repudiated by association with his family (3:31–32). This passage recalls much that has occurred to this point: Jesus's teaching in synagogue (1:21, 39; 3:1–4), astonishment over his powerful deeds (1:22, 27, 2:12), and rejection by those nearest him (3:19b–21). Here they "stumble" (v. 3b; the same Greek verb, σκανδαλίζομαι, translated as "fall away" in 4:17) because they think they know him, his everyday occupation (carpentry, or any material craftsmanship), and his kinfolk (v. 3a; as in 3:19b–35, Jesus's father remains curiously missing). Insiders again stand on the outside (4:11–13); honorable prophets divide their households (v. 4; 3:25). The conclusion is sadly predictable and doubly ironic: hometown folk receive from their native son the very nothing they expect (v. 5a; 4:24–25)—though he does cure a few (v. 5b). Now it is *Jesus* who is amazed (v. 6a; cf. 1:27; 2:12; 5:42)—by their lack of faith (cf. 4:40).

6:6b–8:21. Revelation over Bread

Pulsing throughout Mark's third major section is the capacity of Jesus's ministry to reveal the kingdom's "insiders" and "outsiders" in surprising ways. Curiously, most of these episodes have something to do with food: a royal banquet (6:14–29), two wilderness feedings (6:30–44; 8:1–10), and a debate over kosher practice (7:1–23). A woman pleads for crumbs from Israel's loaf (7:24–30); the disciples bumble over bread (8:14–21).

Food is conspicuous by its absence in *the commissioning of the Twelve* (6:6b–13). In 3:13–15, Jesus assembles the Twelve to extend his ministry; after a transitional summary of his work (6:6b), that is precisely what happens. Their assignment consists of exorcism, healing, and preaching repentance (vv. 7, 12), all of which they accomplish (v. 13). Sending in pairs (v. 7) reflects biblical custom, in the interest of safety and corroboration (Deut 17:6; 19:15; 1 Tim 5:19). For room and board, they are utterly dependent on others' hospitality (v. 10). Their traveling gear—a mere staff and sandals (vv. 8–9)—is extraordinarily sparse; other itinerant preachers in antiquity carried with them bread in a beggar's bag. Shaking dust off the feet against those who refuse them (v. 11) is an obscure gesture, reminiscent of the practice of Jews who, upon returning home, guarded against contaminating Israel with pagan dust (cf. Acts 10:28).

The tale of *John the Baptist's death* (6:14–29) is Mark's only anecdote in which not Jesus but a contemporaneous political figure predominates. True, Jesus's fame occasions its placement here (v. 14); debate over his true identity (vv. 14b–16) recalls earlier encounters (3:22; 4:41; 6:2–3) and anticipates later ones (8:28–30; 9:11–13; 12:35–38; 14:61; 15:2). The protagonist is Herod Antipas, son of Herod the Great and tetrarch of Galilee and Perea (4 BCE–39 CE), popularly acknowledged as "king." His conclusion that Jesus is John raised from the dead (vv. 14b, 16) is the first intimation of the latter's death (cf. 1:14). As retold by Mark, the miserable tale in 6:14–29 recalls personages and events in Israel's history. John is a righteous man like Eleazar (2 Macc 6:18–31; 4 Macc 5:1–7:23), martyred for his fidelity to the law (vv. 18, 20, 27–28; cf. Lev 18:16; 20:21). Herodias is a schemer like Jezebel (1 Kgs 19:1–3; 21:5–15), bent on destroying a prophet who challenges her (vv. 19, 24). Like Ahab (1 Kgs 21:1–4, 27), Herod is a weak ruler, manipulated by his shrewd wife (vv. 16–17, 20, 26–27a). Herod presages Pilate: both seemingly in control, both easily outmaneuvered (vv. 21–25; 15:1–15). John's disciples give their teacher's body a decent burial (v. 29). How will Jesus's disciples dispose of his remains?

The apostles' (or envoys') report of all they have done and taught (v. 30) harks back to verses 13–14, suggesting that 6:14–29 has been another Markan intercalation, casting a shadow on the Twelve's success stories. *The feeding of five thousand* (6:31–44) offers sharp contrast between two very different meals: a private state banquet, twisted into an innocent man's execution (6:21–28), and a public feast in the wilderness, refreshing the lives of all. This tale also chimes with remembrance of things past and hope for things to come: Israel's miraculous sustenance by God in the wilderness (Exod 16:13–35; Num 11:1–35) and Jewish expectations of an end-time feast for God's elect (Isa 25:6–8). Although retreat to the desert is intended for restful solitude (Mark 6:31–32; 1:35), Jesus's compassion for the multitude, "like sheep without a shepherd" (vv. 33–34), is a poignant reminder of a faithful king's proper response to needy Israel (Num 27:15–17; Ezek 34:1–31). The disciples' suggestion that the throng be disbanded elicits Jesus's command that they be fed (Mark 6:35–37a): a manifestly impossible assignment, whose cost would require two-thirds of a day laborer's annual income (v. 37b). Equally ridiculous are Jesus's query of how much food is available and the puny reckoning (v. 38). No matter: The crowd is divided into "groups" (literally, συμπόσια, suggesting a banquet's conviviality: v. 39), companies "of hundreds and of fifties" (v. 40) like Israel's jurisdictions in the wilderness (Exod 18:21, 25). Jesus's look to heaven (v. 41a) indicates the source of his power (also 7:34; Ps 121:1); his taking, blessing, breaking, and giving (v. 41b) are a host's customary actions at a Jewish meal, prefiguring Jesus's last supper (14:22). The symbolic significance, if any, of twelve baskets and five thousand men (*sic*) is obscure (v. 44; so also 8:8–9). Clearer is the miracle's confirmation by the multitude's satisfaction and the plentiful leftovers (vv. 42–43; cf. 2 Kgs 4:42–44).

Reminiscent of appearances of the risen Christ in Luke (24:36–37) and John (21:1–14), Mark 6:45–52 presents this gospel's second *epiphany of Jesus on the sea* (see 4:35–41). Again Jesus removes himself for prayer (6:46; 1:35; 3:13) as evening falls (6:35, 47). Events unfold "early in the morning" (v. 48b: "around the fourth watch of the night," between three and six a.m.). This tale's imagery reaches deep into the OT: Jesus's bestriding the waves (v. 48b) recalls the LORD God's own power (Ps 93:3–4); "It is I" (ἐγώ εἰμι: v. 50), a classic expression of divine self-identification (Exod 3:13–15; Isa 43:10–11); the numinous evokes human terror (Exod 3:6b; Jonah 1:9–10). Jesus's intent to bypass them (v. 48c) is baffling. Perhaps it alludes to God's veiled self-disclosure to Moses (Exod 33:18–23) and Elijah (1 Kgs 19:11–12), though Jesus in Mark is typically ahead of his disciples (10:32; 16:7). The climax in 6:51 is much like 4:39b–41. Here, however, Mark emphasizes the Twelve's incomprehension (cf. 4:13), attributed to their hardness of heart (v. 52; 3:5; Ps 95:8) and focused on "the loaves": a veiled reference to their earlier incredulity (6:37).

Their misperception of Jesus (vv. 49–52) is immediately juxtaposed with another throng's recognition of him as one with power to heal (6:53–56). This *transitional summary* (see 3:7–12) is located at Gennesaret (v. 53), on the lake's northwest shore, instead of Bethsaida on the northeast, where the boat was headed (v. 45). Mark emphasizes Jesus's openness to Galilee's widespread need of healing (1:28–45), communicated through a simple touch of his tassel (v. 56; 5:27–28; Num 15:37–41).

From destruction (6:14–29) to nourishment (6:30–44); from obtuseness (6:45–52) to recognition (6:53–54): between such poles, Mark's narrative swings. From beseeching (6:55–56) to criticism—*Jesus's and the Pharisees' mutual rejection* (7:1–23)—the pendulum swings again, with a discernible arc.

1. *The Pharisees' critique of eating with unwashed hands* (vv. 1–2, 5) seems decades ahead of its time: the earliest mishnaic prescription for scrupulous washing among priests is about 100 CE (cf. m. Ber. 8:2–4). By Mark's day, some laity may have adopted this pious practice. The parenthetical explanation (vv. 3–4) appears for the benefit of gentile readers unfamiliar with Jewish customs. Some Pharisees (2:16) from Jerusalem (the place of danger: 3:22; 10:32) challenge the disciples' ritually unclean "eating [of] the loaves" (7:2): a Semitic expression that recalls 6:38b, 41, 44, 52.

2. Disregarding the point at issue, *Jesus sets the written law—"the word of God"—over "the [oral] tradition of the elders"* (vv. 6–8, 13). Quoting Isa 29:13, he likens eating with unwashed hands to vacuous worship, castigated by Israel's prophets (Isa 1:10–20; 58:1–14; Amos 5:21–24). Jesus extends his critique (Mark 7:9–13) to Corban, a ritual offering (Lev 1:2) withdrawn from secular uses like parental support, as violating the fifth commandment (Exod 20:12; Deut 5:16).

3. After a withering repudiation of Pharisaic piety (Mark 7:13), Jesus answers their critique with *a blatant repudiation of laws for keeping a kosher table* (vv. 15, 18–19; cf. Lev 11:1–47). All hear this "parable"; privately the disciples, who "still fail to understand" (v. 18; 6:52), receive extended interpretation (vv. 14, 17; 4:34). Adopting a list of vices common in ancient exhortations (vv. 21–22; see Rom 1:29–31; Gal 5:19–21; 2 Tim 3:2–5), Jesus reasons that the organ in need of purification is not the stomach but rather the heart, the seat of moral sensibility and religious conduct (Ps 24:4; Jer 32:39–40). Defilement comes not from without but from within (vv. 18–20, 23). Mark draws the obvious if scandalous conclusion: "Thus he declared all foods clean" (v. 19b).

Immediately following this controversy are two healings in disreputable gentile territory (Tyre, Sidon, the Decapolis: vv. 24, 31; cf. 3:8; Ezek 26:1–28:19). The healings themselves—*the daughter of a Syro-Phoenician woman* (7:24–30) and *a deaf-mute* (7:31–37)—do not receive as much attention as the tensions attending them. Seclusion and disclosure pull against each other (vv. 24b, 33a; cf. 1:44–45; 6:31–33). The infirmities (possession by an unclean spirit, v. 25; deafness and speech impediment, v. 32) place the sufferers at odds with their own bodies. Suspense is further created by Jesus's responses—at first, refusal (v. 27); later, a "gag-order" (v. 36a)—which others immediately overturn (vv. 28–29, 36b). The focus of 7:31–37 is on the healer's technique (vv. 33–35) and the vaguely scriptural astonishment his work evokes (v. 37; Isa 35:5). In Mark 7:24–30, the dynamics are reversed: the healing occurs at long distance (vv. 29b–30) while the foreign woman's acceptance of Jesus's harsh rebuff ("dog": cf. 1 Sam 17:43), her insistence on receiving even the crumbs of Israel's "bread" (vv. 26–28), stand at the center.

The feeding of four thousand (8:1–10) twins the tale in 6:30–44, reprising the same narrative components: desert ambience (6:31; 8:4), a famished horde (6:34–36; 8:2), Jesus's compassion (6:34; 8:2), the disciples' dubiety (6:37; 8:4), meager provisions of bread and fish (6:38; 8:5, 7), their offering to God (6:41; 8:6b–7) and orderly distribution (6:39–40; 8:6a), and satisfaction of everyone's hunger (6:42; 8:8a) with abundant leftovers (6:43; 8:8b). Although Dalmanutha's location is unknown (8:10), the overarching setting is gentile (7:31).

The earlier feeding miracle triggered misunderstanding (6:51b–52); so it is here, twofold. First, certain *Pharisees return* (8:11–13; cf. 7:1), demanding of Jesus knockdown verification of his divine authority (as though heavenly feedings of thousands were an inadequate "sign"; cf. Num 14:11). Jesus refuses to comply with this generation's faithlessness (v. 12; 8:38; 9:19; cf. Deut 32:5, 20; Ps 95:10). Second, Jesus's own *disciples have forgotten the bread* (8:14–21). Their hardened hearts (v. 17; see 4:13) align them with the Pharisees (3:5) and

Herod (6:14–29) when by now they should beware their antagonists' insidious corruption (the "yeast" that ferments within bread: 8:15; cf. 1 Cor 5:6) and recognize in Jesus the power of God (8:19–20). This section of Mark, which opened with the Twelve's ability to follow Jesus (6:7–13, 30), ends with an off-key demonstration of their resistance and incomprehension (8:17–18, 21; cf. Jer 5:21; Ezek 12:2)—pointing the way into Mark's fourth major section.

8:22–10:52. *Christology and Discipleship*

This section is the pivot around which this gospel turns. To this point, Jesus's identity and activity have been correlated with that of his disciples (1:9–20; 3:7–19a; 6:1–13). In this section, lying near the gospel's center, the character of Jesus's messiahship and the responsibilities of his disciples forcefully converge in the dawning light of Mark's passion narrative, which immediately follows (11:1–15:47). This section adopts a tripartite structure that is framed by the gospel's only two stories about the healing of blind men:

A Two-Stage Healing: Mark 8:22–26

Prediction of the Son of Man's Destiny	*The Disciples' Misunderstanding*	*Teaching about Discipleship*
Mark 8:31	8:32–33	8:34–9:1
Mark 9:31	9:32–34, 38	9:35–37, 39–50
Mark 10:33–34	10:35–41	10:42–45

The Calling of Bartimaeus: Mark 10:46–52

The intercalated correspondences between blindness and incomprehension (4:12; 8:18), between healing and teaching (1:27), are unmistakable.

The first healing story (8:22–26) returns the reader to Bethsaida (6:45), as well as to the motifs of healing by touch (5:23), with saliva (7:33), and in seclusion (5:37, 43; 7:24, 36). This story's anomalous feature is its sufferer's progressive relief, requiring more than one touch by the healer (vv. 23–25). Likewise, the Twelve's perception of Jesus is fuzzy, requiring of their teacher multiple corrections.

The first of Jesus's pointed exchanges with his disciples (8:27–9:1) occurs at Caesarea Philippi (v. 27), a city on Mount Hermon's southwestern slope. As in 6:14–15, those with whom Jesus is identified (v. 28) were popularly regarded as harbingers of "the Day of the Lord." While correct (1:1), Peter's identification of Jesus as "the Messiah" (v. 29) is susceptible of misunderstanding and, therefore, is sternly silenced (literally, "rebuked": v. 30; see 3:12).

Cryptically referring to himself as "the Son of Man" (2:10, 28), Jesus fore-tells his suffering, death, and vindication in twenty-five words (v. 31) that synopsize Mark's last seventy-five verses. The elders were senior Jewish lay leaders (Luke 7:3) who with the chief priests and the scribes constitute the Sanhedrin, or supreme Jewish council, in Mark (14:43, 53–55). That the Son of Man "must undergo" all these things is a way of expressing its conformity to God's will. This is no parable; it is said as plainly as Peter rebukes it (v. 32). Regarding all his disciples (vv. 33, 34), Jesus rebukes his rebuker as offering a satanic deviation from God's intentions (v. 33; cf. 1:13). Jesus then draws Mark's clearest connection between his own destiny (the cross) and his followers' responsibility to deny themselves, even to the point of death, for the sake of the good news (vv. 34–37; 1:1, 14). Honor and shame preoccupied ancient so-ciety (Xenophon, *Hier.* 7.3); here Jesus associates shame with alignment to the values of "this adulterous and sinful generation," honor with fidelity to God (v. 38). Jesus's first reference in Mark to an apocalyptic Son of Man (8:38; also 13:26–27; 14:62; cf. Dan 7:13–14) is ambiguous. In this figure, is he pointing to another or to himself? Perhaps the latter (v. 31), as early Christians deduced (Matt 19:28; Acts 7:55–56). Equally mysterious is Jesus's promise in 9:1, so easily disconfirmed in Mark's own day—unless the kingdom's coming with power points to the very next episode.

Jesus's transfiguration (9:2–8) and *its ensuing deliberation* (9:9–13) are sat-urated with apocalyptic imagery. A high mountain (v. 2) is a place of divine disclosure in the OT (Exod 19:3–25; 1 Kgs 19:8). Here the revelation is privately witnessed by an inner circle (cf. 5:37; 13:3), ordered to withhold report of their experience until after the resurrection (v. 9). Transfiguration, or supernatural metamorphosis (v. 3), is rooted in Jewish apocalypticism (Rom 12:2; 2 Cor 3:18; Phil 3:21); dazzling whiteness often connotes glorification (Dan 12:3; 2 Esd 7:97; Rev 4:4). In Mal 4:4–5, Moses and Elijah (Mark 9:4) are linked as heralds of the Lord's Day. A cloud (v. 7) often accompanies OT theophanies (Exod 24:12–18; Isa 4:5; Ezek 1:4), which characteristically evoke terror (Mark 9:6; Exod 3:1–6; Isa 6:1–5). What sets this theophany apart is the heavenly voice's identification of Jesus as God's beloved or unique Son, comporting with Jesus's singular trans-figuration. This divine announcement recalls that of Jesus's baptism (1:9–11); this time, however, an audience beyond Jesus is addressed and instructed to pay attention to him (v. 7). Rather than housing God's self-revelation on a moun-tain top (v. 5; cf. Exod 25:1–9), the disciples are redirected to the world below (v. 9). Their questioning (vv. 10–11) elicits from Jesus another pronouncement of the divine necessity of his many sufferings (v. 12), with the assurance that his precursory Elijah, John the Baptist, has come and was similarly received (v. 13; see 1:6; 6:15).

The last of four exorcisms in Mark (1:21–28; 5:1–20; 7:24–30), *the healing of an epileptic child* (9:14–29), counterpoises desperate anguish (vv. 18, 20–22, 26) against the requisite of faith (vv. 19, 23). Whereas the scribes, like the disciples, are divided (vv. 10, 14), and the boy's father sways from trust to unbelief (v. 24), Jesus exerts mastery over the demonic (v. 25) so that its victim may arise (v. 27; cf. 5:41–42). Nothing is possible apart from faith and prayer (vv, 19, 23, 29), a lesson reiterated in Mark 11:22–26.

With another change of scene (Galilee, v. 30), Mark unfolds *the second of Jesus's predictions and corrections of his disciples* (9:31–50). The major differences between the wording of 9:31 and 8:31 are the former's simplicity and emphasis on the Son of Man's betrayal (cf. 1:14; 3:19). The disciples are typically uncomprehending and fearful (4:13, 40), as evidenced by their private argument in Capernaum over who among them is greatest (vv. 33–34): a point of debate within antiquity's social groups (Luke 22:24–25). Jesus upends the conventional premise by demanding of his disciples servanthood (Mark 9:35), exemplified by accepting a little child—an exemplar of powerlessness—as one would accept Jesus himself (vv. 36–37). Nor are there rigid boundaries between disciples and other sympathizers, like the exorcist casting out demons in Jesus's name (vv. 38–39). If the bar for those receiving Jesus's disciples is low and easily reached (vv. 40–41), that for faithful discipleship is high indeed. On that note, this segment concludes, with a chain of what may originally have been detached sayings about radical self-sacrifice, now linked by catchwords ("causes to stumble," vv. 42, 43, 45, 47; "fire," vv. 48, 49; "salted," vv. 49, 50a, 50b). The primary exhortations are for protection of Jesus's "little ones" (disciples: v. 42), elimination of any impediment that might prevent entry into eternal life, or God's kingdom (vv. 43–48), and the importance of vital peace among disciples (vv. 49–50).

Focused on life within the family, Mark 10:1–31 explores *the ethics of discipleship*. Appropriately, the subject opens with marriage (vv. 2–12). Proper grounds for divorce were debated among later rabbis (m. Giṭ. 9:10); their Pharisaic antecedents raise the question here (vv. 2–4). Jesus argues (vv. 5–12) that their cited precedent (Deut 24:1) arose from human stubbornness (cf. 3:5) and is trumped by Genesis (1:27; 2:24; 5:2). God wills union, not division (see 9:50b). As elsewhere in the NT (Matt 5:32; 19:9; 1 Cor 7:10–16), Mark 10:11–12 seems to relax absolute prohibition of divorce. By OT definition (see Exod 20:14; Deut 5:18; 22:22), adultery violates only the husband's prerogative. By contrast, Jesus asserts also the wife's protection against adultery (v. 11) and assumes her right to initiate divorce (without remarriage, v. 12). Effectively placed on a level plane, wives and husbands owe each other mutual rights and responsibilities.

The subject turns to children brought to Jesus for blessing but rebuked by his disciples (vv. 13, 16). Jesus defends these little ones as candidates for God's kingdom (v. 14) and urges upon his disciples a child's vulnerable receptivity (v. 15; 9:36–37). Before the kingdom's demands, Jesus himself renounces any claim of goodness (v. 18; cf. 2 Cor 5:21). Such a disposition differs sharply from the man wanting to do something to inherit eternal life (v. 17), God's new creation in the age to come (9:43–47; Dan 12:2; 2 Macc 7:9). Though religiously observant (Mark 10:19–20; Exod 20:12–17; Deut 5:16–20; 24:14), he cannot satisfy the outstanding requirement: to relinquish his riches for heavenly treasure—to receive God's kingdom like a child (v. 15)—and to follow Jesus (vv. 21–22). Read in context, the problem with wealth (vv. 23–25) lies in its inhibition of self-denial (8:35–37) and unreserved dependence on God, for whom nothing is impossible (vv. 26–27). Jesus accepts Peter's affirmation that he and others have indeed abandoned all for the gospel (v. 28), promising them that they shall inherit a new family in this life and eternal life in the coming age (vv. 29–30). That promise is, however, laced with surprises: no paterfamilias (the supreme head of antiquity's households) replaces an earthly father (v. 29); the rewards to come are comparatively modest (cf. 1 Esd 7:88–89); persecutions remain on the horizon (v. 30); and God retains sovereignty for reversing expectations (v. 31).

Mark 10:32–45 presents this section's *third contrast between suffering Christology and recalcitrant discipleship*, set amid the disciples' fearful amazement as they approach the Judean capital from which hostility to Jesus has radiated (v. 32; 3:22). Verses 33–34 offer the most detailed forecast of the Son of Man's destiny; verses 35–41, the most blatant display of his followers' failure to get the point. The wording of James and John's request (vv. 35–37) echoes Herod's impetuous offer to Herodias's daughter (6:22); moreover, they mistake the cup they must drink as that of bliss (Pss 23:5; 116:13), not woe (Isa 51:17, 22). The rest of the Twelve are predictably indignant (v. 41); Jesus implies that all of them still construe authority in the gentiles' self-aggrandizing terms (v. 42), not as the radical inversion of social norms that obtains in God's kingdom (vv. 43–44; 9:35). Discipleship derives from Christology: the Son of Man who gives life as ransom or compensatory redemption for many (v. 45; 14:24; cf. Isa 43:1–7; 1 Tim 2:5–6).

The healing of blind Bartimaeus (10:46–52) in Jericho (v. 46), twenty miles northeast of Jerusalem, bookends the healing of Bethsaida's blind man

(8:22–26). Many themes are reprised in this brief encounter: partial apprehension of Jesus ("Son of David," vv. 47–48; cf. 12:35–37); refusal to be diverted (v. 48a, 51b; 8:33; 9:43–47); and faith that heals (v. 52a; 9:23; 10:27). Timaeus's son not only receives his sight; he also acts toward Jesus, who calls him (v. 49; 1:17, 20), as a disciple should (vv. 50, 52b; 9:23b; 10:14).

11:1–13:37. The Final Days: Jerusalem and the Temple

Mark's fifth major section narrates Jesus's arrival, activities, and discourses in Jerusalem during his life's last days. The focal point is the Herodian temple, Israel's religious and political center. There, after his arrival in the city (11:1–11), Jesus performs and interprets a prophetic act (11:12–26). Later, facing the temple, he speaks of its annihilation within the context of God's final judgment (13:1–37). The heart of this section (11:27–12:44) is a series of controversies arising from Jesus's teaching in the temple court about God's will.

In Jerusalem, Mark slows down the narrative by clocking days (11:11, 12; 14:1, 12), then hours (14:17, 72; 15:1, 25, 33, 34, 42; 16:1–2). The first day is marked by *Jesus's arrival* (11:1–11), whose description in Mark is less lofty than in other gospels (cf. Matt 21:1–11; Luke 19:28–40; John 12:12–19). Bethpage's location is uncertain; Bethany was about two miles southeast of the Judean capital (John 11:18). The Mount of Olives, a high hill east of Jerusalem (Ezek 11:23), was associated with both the city's defeat (2 Sam 15:15–30) and hope for God's end-time triumph (Zech 14:4). Speculation about prearrangements for the colt (Mark 11:2–4) is pointless; the point is acknowledgment of Jesus's authority (vv. 5–6; cf. 1 Sam 10:1–8). Apart from the textually suspect Mark 16:19, "the Lord" appears only in verse 3 with clear reference to Jesus. The animal (v. 7) may allude to a humble king's conveyance (Zech 9:9); its having never been ridden (v. 2) is reminiscent of unyoked, consecrated animals (Num 19:2; Deut 21:3; 1 Sam 6:7). Spreading of cloaks and branches on the road (v. 8) is a motif in Israel's royal and festal processions (2 Kgs 9:13; 1 Macc 13:51; 2 Macc 10:7), accented here (vv. 9–10) by acclamations approximating Ps 118:25–26 (a thanksgiving for military deliverance). "Hosanna" (literally, "Save now!") was a liturgical formula for God's praise. "The kingdom of our ancestor David" recalls Bartimaeus's blind recognition in 10:47–48, which Jesus himself will challenge in 12:35–37. Jesus's visit to the temple, rebuilt by Herod the Great (37–4 BCE), is anticlimactic and suspenseful (v. 11). Jesus's arrival does not neatly match customary expectations of Israel's king.

Mark 11:12–25 comprises one of the evangelist's characteristic narrative intercalations (see 2:1–12). In the center is *the cleansing of the temple* (vv. 15–19):

a debatable characterization, as its defilement is not evident. Purchasing cultic paraphernalia in the Court of the Gentiles, the outermost plaza of the temple complex, was legitimate, even necessary. Jesus's bewildering conduct—affronting both buyers and sellers (vv. 15–16)—suggests the temple's destruction (see also 13:1–2). Those seeking refuge there, as bandits regard a secure lair (Jer 7:1–11), must look elsewhere for "a house of prayer for all the nations" (v. 17; Isa 56:7). The understandable animosity of chief priests and scribes (Mark 11:18) harks back to 3:22 and 8:31, and will be amplified in 11:27–33.

Surrounding Jesus's prophetic action is *the withering of a fig tree and its interpretation* (vv. 12–14, 20–25). Old Testament prophets likened Israel to a fruitless fig tree (Jer 8:13; Joel 1:7; Mic 7:1; cf. Luke 13:6–9). That it was not the season for figs (v. 13) holds an important clue: a season—καιρός, the climactic time appointed by God (see 1:15)—of fruitlessness (on a tree, in the temple) invites judgment, which Jesus twice invokes (vv. 14–17; also 13:28–29). From a chain of exhortations with catchwords ("faith," "believe," vv. 22, 23, 24; "prayer," "praying," vv. 24, 25; cf. 9:42–50), Mark constructs Jesus's consolatory instruction about prayer, emphasizing forgiveness among disciples (vv. 14b, 20–21, 25). Because the temple was situated on a rise, faith's moving of a mountain is apropos (v. 23). Trusting in God is itself promised rescue from calamity (v. 24; see also 2:5; 5:34, 36; 9:23–29; 10:26–27).

Mark 2:1–3:6 clusters five controversies between Jesus and his antagonists in Capernaum; Mark 11:27–12:44 comprises another *five controversies in Jerusalem* (11:27–12:34), to which are appended *three provocative barbs* about Christology (12:35–37), destructive piety (vv. 38–40), and authentic discipleship (vv. 41–44).

The first of *five controversies* in the temple is *a frontal assault on Jesus's authority* to challenge its cultic practice (11:15–19) by those most heavily invested in it: chief priests, scribes, and elders (vv. 27–28). From Mark's beginning, Jesus's authority has occasioned amazement (1:22, 27) and contention (2:7–8). As elsewhere (2:25–26; 10:3), in rabbinic fashion, Jesus counters one question with another: the origin of John the Baptist's authority (vv. 29–30). This was a delicate matter. Ancient Jews (Josephus, *A.J.* 18.117–118) and Christians (Matt 21:32; Luke 7:28–30; Acts 19:1–7) esteemed John and his baptism of repentance for their alignment with God's righteousness. Mark 11:31–32 captures the Hobson's choice Jesus offers his antagonists. Typically (2:6; 3:4; 9:10), his interlocutors are divided (v. 31), finally copping a plea of ignorance (v. 33a) that justifies Jesus's reply: If his accusers are in no position to adjudicate John's credibility, then neither can they judge Jesus's (v. 33b).

Jesus elaborates his parabolic answer with *a controversial parable* (12:1–12), Mark's longest and most allegorical (cf. 3:23–27; 4:1–34). The planter's procedure (vv. 1–2), customary for its era, is also reminiscent of Isa 5:1–7, which identifies God's vineyard with wayward Israel (Jer 2:21; Ezek 19:10–14). The coming of the season (v. 2, καιρός) strikes an eschatological note (see Mark 1:15; 11:13). Old Testament prophets, styled as God's slaves (Jer 7:25; 25:4; Amos 3:7; Zech 1:6), suffered comparable brutality at the hands of their countrymen (Mark 12:2–5; 1 Kgs 18:12–13; 2 Chr 24:20–22; Neh 9:26). "A beloved son" (Mark 12:6), murdered for being the true heir (vv. 7–8), is a veiled yet direct pointer to Jesus (1:11; 9:7); likewise, the religious leadership (11:27) recognize themselves as the parable's killers (v. 12; 3:6). As elsewhere in the NT (Acts 4:11; Eph 2:20; 1 Pet 2:7), Ps 118:22–23 is cited to interpret Jesus's rejection by his coreligionists and to assert the church's vindication.

Returning to the spotlight in this section's *third controversy* (Mark 12:13–17) are Pharisees (first appearing in 2:16) and Herodians (3:6). Their identification is pertinent to the trap they lay (vv. 13–15a): Poll (per capita) taxes were a detested aspect of the Jews' subjugation to imperial Rome. If Jesus can be maneuvered into sanctioning their payment, his piety is compromised; if he advocates nonpayment, sedition is whispered. Jesus recognizes their hypocrisy (v. 15b); Mark's reader perceives the truth in their obsequiousness (v. 14). The head (literally, "image") on the requested denarius (a laborer's daily wage; v. 15) is the emperor's (v. 16); its title (literally, "inscription"), "Tiberius, Emperor, Son of the Divine Augustus." Jesus evades the trap with a neat double entendre: Caesar is entitled to his own (see also Matt 17:24–27; Rom 13:1–7; 1 Pet 2:13–17), as is God (to whom belongs everything).

Next come *the Sadducees* (Mark 12:18–27), ancient Judaism's priestly aristocracy (Acts 23:6–8), whose denial of resurrection was likely based on its absence from the Pentateuch (cf. Isa 26:19; Dan 12:2–3; 2 Macc 7:14, 23; Josephus, *A.J.* 13.197; 18.17). Presupposing Deuteronomy's law of levirate marriage (25:5–6), their question issues from an absurd exaggeration: Whose wife will a seven-time widow be after she herself dies (Mark 12:19–23)? Jesus's initial answer rejects the question's premise: in postmortem life, there is no marriage (v. 25). More to the point (vv. 26–27a), the wording of God's self-identification to Moses (Exod 3:6, 15–16) implies that Abraham, Isaac, and Jacob still live under divine dominion. Formally, Jesus's argument resembles rabbinic exegesis and reasoning. Its point is emphatic: his social superiors are altogether wrong about "the scriptures [and] the power of God" (Mark 12:24, 27b). The end of this gospel will verify that soon enough.

The final controversy in the temple (vv. 28–34) proves unexpectedly noncontroversial. Since scribes have opposed Jesus since Mark's beginning (1:22), the reader anticipates the same here (v. 28). Surprise: This scribe simply inquires about first principles, a question of scriptural precedent debated among the rabbis (m. Ber. 2:2, 5; b. Mak. 23b–24a; Sifra Lev 19:18). Jesus's reply to a sincere question is an impeccably orthodox answer (vv. 29–31): love of God and neighbor, the Shema (Deut 6:4–5), wedded to the Holiness Code (Lev 19:18). Jesus's questioner not only commends but also amplifies his assessment (Mark 12:32–33; Deut 4:35; 1 Sam 15:22; Isa 45:5, 21; Hos 6:6). Jesus has the last, enigmatic word (12:34a): If the scribe were any closer to God's kingdom than this, would he then be Jesus's disciple?

Having silenced all further debate (v. 34b), Jesus takes the initiative with *three brief rejoinders*, linked by catchwords ("scribes," vv. 28, 32, 38; "widow[s]," vv. 40, 42; cf. 9:42–50; 11:22–25). His first riposte (vv. 35–37a) mysteriously *questions the Messiah's Davidic sonship* (2 Sam 7:4–17; Ps 89:3–4; cf. Matt 1:1; Rom 1:3; 2 Tim 2:8) by assuming the traditional attribution of Ps 110 to "David himself." Since his audience hears this with delight (v. 37b), the force of Jesus's remark is worth teasing out. First, utterance "by the Holy Spirit" is with presumed prophetic authority (Acts 1:16; 28:25; Heb 3:7; 10:15). Second, Mark may concur with other NT authors in regarding Ps 110:1 as descriptive of Jesus's ultimate exaltation (Acts 2:34–35; 1 Cor 15:25; Heb 1:13). Most important, David's concession of a Lord greater than himself (12:37a) may be Mark's way of qualifying the suffering Son of Man's superior messiahship (8:29–31).

Denunciation of pretentious scribes follows in verses 38–40. The OT castigates oppression of economically vulnerable widows (Ps 94:1–7; Isa 10:1–2; Zech 7:10; Mal 3:5). Speaking of widows, Jesus concludes his teaching in the temple with a surprising comment made opposite the treasury (v. 41), a temple chamber that abutted the Women's Court as well as a receptacle for offerings located in that precinct (John 8:20). By contrast with the wealthy, making large donations, *a poor widow* offers two small copper coins (the smallest in circulation at that time), equal in value to a penny (a Roman *quadrans*, about one-sixty-fourth of a laborer's daily wage; v. 42). The surpassing value of her gift is a lesson for disciples, underlined by Jesus's solemn assurance (v. 43; see 3:28; 9:1, 41). Like another nameless woman memorable for her extravagance (14:3–9), this widow gives "all she had to live on": literally, "her whole life" (v. 44)—as Jesus himself will do (10:45). The irony that she gives everything for a seemingly lost cause (13:1–2) is no greater than Jesus's own sacrifice soon to come.

Mark 13:1–37 is Jesus's last extended discourse to members of the Twelve, some of whom comment on the temple's massive stones and wondrous structures (v. 1). The Jewish historian Josephus corroborates just how magnificent the temple was: Soaring fifty meters into heaven and covered on all sides with massive golden plates, "the outside of the building lacked nothing to astonish the mind or eye" (*B.J.* 5.222). Examining the temple's remains, today's visitors to Jerusalem observe building blocks whose weight ranges from two to nearly four hundred tons. Regardless of whether Mark knew of the Romans' destruction of the temple in 70 CE, as Luke seems to (19:41–44), Jesus's forecast of its future is prescient (Mark 13:2), much as OT prophets accurately predicted devastation of its predecessor, Solomon's Temple (Jer 26:18; Mic 3:12).

The temple was more than an architectural marvel. As the locus of the nation's priestly ritual, it represented Israel's sacrifice of itself to the God who had called it into covenant existence. Its decorative tapestry "typified the universe" (Josephus, *B.J.* 5.212–214), suggesting to worshipers that the world itself was held together by the divine-human interaction occurring within these sacred precincts. No little anxiety percolates in the questions of the disciples in private colloquy with their teacher while seated east of the temple on the Mount of Olives (Mark 13:3).

The discourse that follows (vv. 5–37), the longest uninterrupted speech in Mark, is a familiar genre in antiquity: a farewell address of leaders to their followers (see Gen 49:1–33; Deut 33:1–29; Josh 23:1–24:30; Tob 14:3–11; John 14:1–17:26; Acts 20:18–35). Like them, Jesus's address at Olivet is braided with common forms of expression: exhortations to vigilance, predictions of things to come, commissions or prohibitions, and authoritative pronouncements. Moreover, Jesus's address is clearly structured. About three-quarters is devoted to the *second* of his disciples' queries, "the sign when these things will be accomplished." Jesus offers not one sign but many, each more obvious than the last.

1. *Earthly calamities that will befall everyone* (vv. 6–8): While images of sociopolitical turbulence are common in prophetic portents (Isa 19:2; Jer 22:23; Rev 6:8; 11:13), first-century Jews and Christians were aware of specific tumults (Acts 5:36–37). Jesus warns that such lie within divine providence and are not in themselves proof of the end (cf. 2 Thess 2:1–12).

2. *Particular forms of stress that believers will undergo* (vv. 9–13): As Jesus himself must suffer (14:17–21), his disciples will be targeted for arrest before sanhedrins (local Jewish courts: Matt 10:17–18) and suffer abuse (cf. Deut 25:1–3; 2 Cor 11:24). All is for the sake of the good news (Mark 1:1, 14) proclaimed to all nations (11:17): an OT theme (Isa 49:6; 52:10) adapted in the NT (Mark 16:20; Rom 11:11–32; Eph 3:1–10). Anxiety is answered by reassurance that in the hour of trial, God's Holy Spirit will support those suffering for the gospel (also Matt 10:19–20; Luke 12:11–12; John 14:26). Interfamilial betrayal is a stock apocalyptic motif (Mic 7:6), yet such divisions occurred among first-century Christians (John 9:18–23; 16:2), even as the

Roman historian Tacitus attests to widespread hatred of early Christians (*Ann.* 15.44). This is not yet the end; there's more to endure.

3. *Particular human reactions to the great tribulation* (vv. 14–23)—especially flight—are triggered by "the desolating sacrilege," pagan desecration of the temple (see Dan 9:27; 11:31; 12:11). This is an era of unparalleled tribulation, sometimes expected to precede the end (Dan 12:1; Rev 7:14); if occurring in winter, heavy rains would impede travel. Again believers are assured of their election by God (cf. Ps 105:6; Rom 8:33; Eph 1:4–5) and are warned against losing their heads over signs performed by false prophets (v. 6; Matt 7:15–23; 2 Thess 2:9–10).

4. *Particular supernatural responses* (vv. 24–27): Celestial convulsions are commonplace in OT prophecy (Isa 13:10; 34:4; Ezek 32:7–8; Joel 2:10, 31). Expecting the advent of an end-time Son of Man may have its origins in Daniel (7:13–14); Christian apocalypticism associates that figure with Jesus (Rev 1:7, 13). The ingathering of God's dispersed elect is a pervasive biblical hope (Isa 11:11; Ezek 39:25–29; 2 Bar. 5.5–9; 1 Thess 4:15–17).

   The disciples *began* by asking when these things will happen. Jesus defers this query until last, reworking the question into a matter of discipleship.

5. *Predictable imminence and assurance of the time* (vv. 28–31) are parabolically represented by a maturing fig tree (cf. 11:12–14, 20–21). The language here is vague yet urgent: exactly who "is near, at the very gates" is unclear; "this generation" is regarded pejoratively in Mark (8:12). Still, all these things are soon to happen (see 9:1). All else may fade, but Jesus's promise is dependable.

6. There remains, nevertheless, *unpredictable suddenness and ignorance of the precise time* (vv. 32–37). "That day" likely refers to "the Day of the Lord" (Isa 2:12; Jer 46:10; Ezek 30:2–3; Amos 5:18–20; Zeph 1:14–18); "that hour," God's appointed time for the consummation of the age (cf. 1:15; 14:35; Dan 8:17–19). Instead of futile attempts to clock that hour—unknown even to "the Son" (cf. Luke 10:22)—faithful disciples remain vigilant and accountable (see also Matt 25:1–30; Luke 12:35–40; Rom 13:11–14). The stages of night in Mark 13:35—evening, midnight, cockcrow, and dawn—may refer to the Romans' four nocturnal watches (6:48).

In presentation and substance, the Olivet discourse is apocalyptic pastoral care: dialing down anxiety, reminding disciples that God remains mysteriously and faithfully in control.[1]

---

1. For more detailed analysis of Mark 13:3–37, see chapter 14.

14:1–15:47. The Passion Narrative

Mark's last major section recounts events culminating in Jesus's betrayal and arrest (14:1–52), his arraignment (14:52–15:15), his execution (15:16–41), and burial (15:42–47). Appreciation of Mark's irony-saturated treatment is critical.

The anointing of Jesus (14:3–9) is illuminated against *a conspiracy for his arrest* (14:1–2, 10–11). Entwining two sharply contrasting anecdotes that complement each other, Mark frames a theologically significant gift for Jesus from an unnamed woman (vv. 3–9) with the consummation of long-standing machinations against him by religious authorities (3:6; 8:31; 11:18; 12:12) assisted by a named member of the Twelve (vv. 1–2, 10–11; 3:19a). The effect is one of ironic simultaneity: the woman is publicly, albeit unwittingly, preparing Jesus's body for burial (14:8) while others aggressively seek (vv. 1, 11; 1:37) his secret betrayal (9:31). Her gift is incredibly lavish: fragrant perfume (Song 1:12; 4:13, 14), worth over three hundred denarii (almost a full year's wages for a day laborer; cf. 6:37), seems wasted from the viewpoint of conventional religiosity (v. 5; see also 12:38–44; Deut 15:11). Colluding with the religious establishment, Judas is promised an unspecified reward (Mark 14:10–11). Pouring the ointment on his head (v. 3) suggests Jesus's royal anointment (1 Sam 10:1; 2 Kgs 9:6); this is a messianic coronation (Mark 1:1). Later Jesus will be crucified as "King of the Jews" (15:26). Here (14:9) as elsewhere in Mark (1:14; 8:35; 13:9–10), "gospel" is embedded in suffering that God's will be done. Mark's timing for these events (v. 1) is apparently Wednesday, 13 Nisan (March–April), two days before Passover: the annual celebration of God's liberation of Israel from captivity (Exod 12:1–13:16), later conjoined with the seven-day harvest festival of Unleavened Bread (2 Chr 35:17; Ezek 45:21–24). In spite of concern that it not happen during the festival (v. 2), Jesus's arrest occurs on Passover evening (14:12–50).

Jesus's last observance of Passover (14:12–31) comprises four vignettes: preparation for the feast (vv. 12–16); his betrayal's prediction at table (vv. 17–21); the institution of the Lord's Supper (vv. 22–26); and a foretelling of all the Twelve's desertion (vv. 27–31).

The preparation (vv. 12–16) is introduced by one of Mark's calendrical anomalies: the first day of Unleavened Bread (v. 12; usually 15 Nisan) seems inconsistent with 14 Nisan, when the Passover lamb is sacrificed (Exod 12:1–20; cf. John 18:28; 19:14, 31, which clocks Jesus's last day twenty-four hours later than in the Synoptics). Jesus's prescience about the dining room in verses 13–16 is reminiscent of his disciples' dispatch for a colt (Mark 11:1–6).

Prediction of betrayal (vv. 17–21) occurs after all had taken their places ("were reclining," the customary posture at banquets: Luke 5:29). Jesus's poignant language (v. 18) echoes earlier phrases in Mark: "Truly I tell you" (also vv. 25, 30; 3:28), "will betray" (9:31). The betrayer at table—in Eastern culture the last place a bosom friend should knife his host in the back—chimes with Ps 41:9. Elsewhere in Mark (2:10; 10:33), "the Son of Man" speaks of himself with authority about the suffering he must endure. That he goes "as it is written" means in accordance with the divine purpose (also 8:31; 1 Cor 15:3–4).

Passover slides into *institution of the Lord's Supper* (vv. 22–26), variously expressed elsewhere in the NT (cf. Luke 22:14–23; John 6:48–58; 1 Cor 11:24–25). At previous banquets in Mark (6:41; 8:6), Jesus "took, bless[ed], broke, and gave" (v. 22); likewise he earlier spoke of his sacrifice for many (v. 24; 10:45). In Greek, as in English, one's "body" is a flexible metaphor: "My selfhood" or "personality" may capture some nuances here (cf. 1 Cor 10:16–17). "Blood of the covenant" (v. 24) is a classic OT image for ratification (Exod 24:6–8; Jer 31:31; Zech 9:11), christologically developed in Hebrews (9:11–10:18). "That day . . . in the kingdom of God" suggests the new eschatological age, sometimes envisioned as a magnificent banquet (1 Chr 12:38–40; Isa 25:6–8; Matt 22:1–4).

Jesus's prediction of the Twelve's desertion (vv. 27–31) occurs en route to the Mount of Olives (see 11:1; 13:3). The sheep's scattering after their shepherd's smiting accords with Scripture (Zech 13:7; cf. Mark 6:34; 14:21). To "become deserters" (vv. 27, 29) is tantamount to "falling away," much as rocky, rootless hearers of the word fold under pressure (4:16–17). One such "rock"—Peter (Πέτρος [3:16])—twice repudiates his threefold defection (vv. 29–31a); his peers join in for a third denial (v. 31b). Jesus promises his own postmortem fidelity in Galilee (v. 28; 16:7). The mind reels at ironies past and to come: Jesus's injunction that his followers must deny themselves (8:34), their precipitate denial of their denials, and Jesus's denial of himself out of loyalty to the traitorous.

At *Gethsemane* (14:32–52), Jesus is arrested as all of the Twelve forsake him. Verses 32–42 present Jesus's most extended crisis of faith in Mark. In many ways, it is a flashback to Jairus, his daughter, and the woman with chronic bleeding in 5:21–43. All these stories are drenched in apocalyptic imagery: Jesus's declaration that the woman depart in peace (5:34), his raising of the little girl (5:41–42), his references to "the cup" (14:36; see also 10:38–39; Isa 51:17, 22) and "the time of trial" (14:38; cf. Jas 1:2; 1 Pet 1:6; Rev 2:10), and his repeated rousings (14:34, 37–38, 41a–b) of disciples who cannot stay awake (vv. 37, 40, 41; cf. 13:33–37). All culminates in his announcement that "the hour" has come (vv. 35, 37, 41c; cf. 13:11, 32). Present in all three stories are Peter, James, and John (5:37; 14:32–33), who characteristically flout their teacher (5:31; 14:34, 37–38, 40). Suffusing these tableaux is utter hopelessness: Jairus's little girl is at death's door (5:23a); the woman's bleeding has only worsened (5:25–26); here Jesus is tormented, even to death (14:34a). All the protagonists' initial responses to crisis is fear (5:33, 36; 14:33): distress that throws its victims to the ground (5:22, 33; 14:35), a grief whose source is human frailty, "weakness of the flesh" (14:38; cf. Isa 31:3; 40:6; Rom 8:1–17). "Daughters" (5:23a, 34) and a "beloved Son" (1:11; 9:7) addressing "Abba" (Rom 8:15; Gal 4:6) beg for relief (5:23b, 27–28; 14:36, 39, 41). Like the woman (5:28), Jesus temporarily resists discovery yet ultimately steps forward to face the truth (5:32–33; 14:36): the Son of Man's ordained betrayal into sinful hands (14:41–42, 49b).

Immediately *Jesus's arrest* (14:43–52) compounds the irony. The betrayer is Judas, one of the Twelve (v. 43; 3:19; 14:10), using as his signal the kiss to which a rabbi was entitled from his disciples (Prov 27:6; Luke 7:38). Just as he predicted (Mark 8:31), those to whom Jesus is delivered are the religious elite who first challenged him in the temple (11:27): chief priests, scribes, and elders, whose associates Jesus implicated for the very banditry for which he is now apprehended (11:17–18; 14:48–49a). Various interpretations have been proposed for the mysterious incident in 14:51–52. Is it an anticipation of the linen shroud in 15:46, soon to be discarded? Is this the same young man in 16:5? Should we recall naked flight in Gen 39:12 or Amos 2:16? None is compelling. Perhaps Mark intends a contrast between Jesus's calm courage and his followers' panicked flight (14:50).

"On the night he was betrayed" (1 Cor 11:23) not one but *two interrogations* took place at the high priest's house. Mark heightens the irony by folding one (that of Jesus: 14:55–65) inside the other (that of Peter: 14:53–54, 66–72). Inside Mark portrays a kangaroo court, with Jesus the silent center (v. 61; cf. Ps 38:12–14) amid a rash of judicial irregularities. A formal trial by the entire council, or Sanhedrin (Mark 14:55; cf. 13:9), should not be convened at night, especially on a festal evening; nor should a verdict to convict be reached in a single day (m. Sanh. 4:1). The charge that Jesus threatened to destroy the temple is bogus (Mark 14:57–58) and contradicted (vv. 56, 59; cf. Deut 19:15; Ps 109:2–3). The temple's replacement with one not made with hands braids a strand of the OT (2 Sam 7:4–17) with later Christian reflection (Acts 7:48; 1 Cor 3:16; 1 Pet 2:4–6). Finally (v. 61b) the high priest, presumably Caiaphas (18–37 CE; Matt 26:3; John 18:13, 24), oddly charges Jesus as the Messiah, the Son of the Blessed One: all terms central to Christian preaching (Mark 1:1; John 20:31), none culpable of capital punishment. Jesus accepts that claim (Mark 14:62), again predicting the advent of an apocalyptic Son of Man (8:38; 12:36; 13:26) along the lines of Ps 110:1 and Dan 7:13–14. Rending his garment (Mark 14:63; Gen 37:29), the high priest charges blasphemy (v. 64), which here seems unfounded (see Lev 24:16; cf. Mark 2:7). The court's conduct in verse 65 is reminiscent of Isa 50:6; 53:3–5; at the precise moment they taunt him to "prophesy," Jesus's prophecies are fulfilled in the courtyard outside (vv. 66–72). There a motley group, chiefly the high priest's maid, accurately spot Peter as having been "with Jesus" (v. 67; 3:14). Not only does Peter lie thrice about his discipleship (v. 71); he does so in a manner revealing unintended truth about all of the Twelve: "I do not know or understand" (v. 68; see 4:13; 6:52; 8:17, 21; 9:32). The cock crows (whether a bird or a Roman signal: 13:35), Peter remembers (14:30–31) and collapses (v. 72): one who lost himself by trying to save himself (8:35).

Jesus's arraignment continues by his transfer to Roman jurisdiction (15:1–15). Mark's specification of morning (v. 1) is the first of five carefully measured, temporal indicators in this chapter (vv. 25, 33a, 33b, 42). The Pharisees, Jesus's antagonists earlier in Mark, have faded from the picture; henceforth the chief priests, representing the entire Sanhedrin, are his principal accusers (vv. 3, 10, 11, 31). Recalling the second passion prediction in 9:31, Mark emphasizes Jesus's being handed over (15:1, 10, 15) to Pontius Pilate, fifth Roman prefect of Judea (26–36 CE). Philo (*Legat.* 301–302) and Josephus (*A.J.* 18.55–57; *B.J.* 2.169–177) characterize Pilate as stubbornly vicious; the evangelists, as a reluctant pawn (Matt 27:18–25; Luke 23:1–24; John 18:28–19:16). Appearing for the first time in Mark 15:2, the title "the King of the Jews" is the first of five ironic acclamations of Jesus by Roman agents (vv. 9, 12, 18, 26; cf. v. 32). Their unbelieving affirmation chimes with the high priest's in 14:61, as does Jesus's silence in 15:5. The trial before Pilate concludes with the so-called Passover amnesty (vv. 6, 8), evidence for which is uncorroborated outside the gospels. Benefitting from this custom is one Barabbas (literally, "Son of the Father"). In which insurrection he may have committed murder (v. 7) is uncertain; Luke (13:1; Acts 5:36–37) and Josephus (*A.J.* 18.55–62, 65–87; *J.W.* 2.167–177) report numerous Jewish revolts against their Roman overlords. Pilate's offer to release Jesus and the crowd's decision for Barabbas underscore two further ironies: yet another authority in Mark proves feckless (see 6:14–29); a known malefactor goes free while a righteous innocent (cf. 6:20; 15:15) pays the ultimate penalty.

The execution of Pilate's sentence (15:16–47) begins with Jesus's humiliation by the Roman guard (15:16–20). Torture often preceded crucifixion (Plato, *Gorg.* 473b–c). A whole cohort numbered between two hundred and six hundred soldiers; if this be exaggeration, its effect is to dramatize the enormous odds against Jesus. Like the crown, purple suggests royal raiment (15:17; see 1 Macc 10:20). Bowing in worship (v. 19) while uttering, "Hail, King of the Jews!" (v. 18) is altogether ironic, possibly a cruel parody of the legionary salute, "Hail, Caesar, conqueror, emperor" (Suetonius, *Claud.* 21.6). Mockery by physical abuse (vv. 19–20) recalls Jesus's prediction in 10:34, which in turn brings to mind Isa 50:6 and Mic 5:1.

A condemned prisoner like Jesus carried only the crossbar (v. 21); the gibbet awaited at the place of execution. By reporting that a passerby named Simon (cf. 14:37) was pressed to carry his cross (cf. 8:34), Mark may cut the irony deeply indeed. Cyrene (Acts 11:20) was a city in what is now Libya. Evidently Mark's audience would have recognized Rufus and Alexander; identification of the former with Paul's associate (Rom 16:13) is impossible to confirm. Though it can no longer be certainly located, Golgotha (v. 22) was apparently outside Jerusalem's city walls (John 19:20; Heb 13:12). Myrrh-spiked wine (v. 23) was likely offered as an analgesic (cf. Prov 31:6); because he has chosen to drink from another cup (10:38; 14:36), Jesus refuses this one.

Cicero describes crucifixion—impaling a victim onto a stake and crossbar—as the supreme penalty over burning, decapitation, and a simple noose (*Verr.* 2.5). It was commonly used in cases of imperial sedition, which matches several of Mark's details: the placard of the charge, "the King of the Jews" (15:26); the identification of fellow victims as revolutionary bandits (v. 27; cf. 14:48). The intent of crucifixion was sadistic: cruel, shameful, protracted torture of society's most heinous offenders of lower class. In that context, Mark's portrait of Jesus's crucifixion is in four respects noteworthy. First, the evangelist does not milk the event for pity: he simply states the matter (v. 24). Second, the details of Jesus's final hours, effectively tolled (vv. 25, 33), remind a biblically knowledgeable reader of Pss 22 and 109, two classic laments: casting lots for a victim's clothes (Mark 15:24 // Ps 22:18), taunting by head-shaking (Mark 15:29 // Ps 22:7; 109:25), the cry of dereliction (Mark 15:34 // Ps 22:1). For those able to perceive, "the scriptures [are being] fulfilled" (14:49b; made explicit in 15:28, which is absent from the oldest manuscripts). Third, reminiscent of Jesus's prediction at Olivet (13:24), midday darkness over the whole land (v. 33) is an apocalyptic portrayal of divine judgment (Amos 8:9).

The fourth characteristic of Mark's narration is by now predictable: its hellish irony. Malefactors are crucified on Jesus's right and left (15:27): the places of honor that James and John had requested (10:37). Even Jesus's fellow victims join with bystanders in ridiculing him (v. 32b; cf. Luke 23:39–43). The mockery, rendered in the NRSV as "derision" (v. 29), is described in Greek as "blaspheming" (see 14:64); singled out among the blasphemers are the chief priests and scribes (v. 31). The substance of their jeer in verse 29, like the testimony of impeached witnesses in 14:58, demonstrates that to the very end most of Jesus's auditors have misunderstood him altogether. The taunt that he save himself (v. 30) directly contradicts the Son of Man's mission in 8:35; that he is the Messiah, Israel's king (v. 32a) who cannot save himself as he saved others (v. 31), is not for a moment believed but exactly right (1:1; 10:45; 14:24; 15:2). In effect, Golgotha's audience is enacting the attitude of the unrighteous in the Wisdom of Solomon (2:12–24); their insistence on signs as a basis of faith (v. 32a) Jesus has already repudiated (8:11–12). In Mark, the relationship between faith and mighty works is precisely opposite: nothing can happen unless first one trusts God (2:5; 5:34; 9:23; 11:22–24).

Irony persists in Mark's depiction of Jesus's death and its immediate aftermath. His lament in Aramaic (v. 34; see also 5:41; 7:34) occasions still more misunderstanding by his audience (see also 4:12; 8:14–21): they mistake "Eloi" (God) as a cry to Elijah (v. 35). Perhaps evolving from 2 Kgs 2:9–12, later Jewish tradition envisioned Elijah as protector of the righteous in distress. In John the Baptist, however, Elijah has already returned and been disposed of (1:6; 6:27–28; 9:11–13). While an allusion to Ps 69:21 may be intended, sour wine, a common drink of the time, is offered in a final, unavailing attempt to pump a miracle from heaven (Mark 15:36). After a final shriek lacking either confidence (Luke 23:46) or triumph (John 19:30), Jesus dies (Mark 15:37). Immediately (v. 38) Mark redirects the reader's attention to the curtain of the temple, perhaps that which veiled the holy of holies (Exod 26:31–37), ripped from top to bottom. As a bookend to the heavens' rending at Jesus's baptism (1:10), this is surely a revelatory sign. Just what it reveals is debatable. It may symbolize the temple's eventual eradication (see also 11:15–19; 13:1–2). Another possibility, effectively developed in Hebrews (9:1–28; 10:19–20) is unmediated access to God created by Jesus's death. Equally ironic and no less ambiguous is the centurion's reaction (v. 39). For the first and only time in Mark, a human being besides Jesus identifies him as God's Son (cf. 1:1; 3:11; 9:7; 13:32). This person is a gentile, and gentiles have been receptive to Jesus (3:8; 5:20; 7:24–31; 11:17; 13:10). Ironically this gentile is one of Jesus's executioners, facing Jesus who has thus expired (cf. Matt 27:54). Whether his assertion betokens sincerity or sarcasm (15:9, 32) is impossible to determine. Only the reader who faithfully accepts the Son of Man's self-assessment (8:31; 10:45) is in position to judge the accuracy of the centurion's verdict and the basis on which it is reached (cf. 1 Cor 1:18–2:5).

Women observing from a distance (v. 40; cf. Ps 38:11) perform three important functions. First, they remind the reader of those *absent* from the scene: the Twelve, who have long since abandoned Jesus (14:50). Second, their presence clarifies that Jesus's ministering entourage has included from the beginning many women, disciples beyond the Twelve (v. 41; see also 1:31; 14:6). Third, Mary Magdalene, Mary the mother of Joses, and Salome know where Jesus was buried (v. 47), anticipating any objection that they later visited the wrong tomb (16:1). Whether Mary the mother of James and of Joses is the same woman as Jesus's mother (6:3) is impossible to determine. The negotiations for disposition (vv. 42–45) of Jesus's body ring true, and archaeological remains confirm the burial customs implied (v. 46; see also Deut 21:22–23; Isa 22:16). It is unclear on which council served Joseph of Arimathea (in northwest Judea), but respected membership could have allowed him such access to Pilate as Mark describes (vv. 43, 45). If not a disciple as such, Joseph was "himself awaiting expectantly" the kingdom that Jesus preached (1:15); with courage, Joseph performs for the body those services John's disciples rendered for their dead teacher (6:29). Since death after crucifixion often occurred after "long drawn-out agony" (Seneca, *Dial.* 3), Pilate's surprise that Jesus was gone after only six hours is as understandable as his determination to verify it (vv. 44–45)—confirmation that may have served as additional defense against later charges of Christian fraud (cf. Matt 27:62–66). Evening on the Day of Preparation (v. 42) suggests the three hours before sundown on Friday; even a hurried burial before the Sabbath suggests Jewish piety and provides reason for the women's return to anoint the body after the Sabbath was past (16:1).

16:1–8. Epilogue: The Empty Tomb

[The Shorter Ending of Mark]

[16:9–20: The Longer Ending of Mark]

The earliest and finest manuscripts of Mark end at 16:8. This gospel's textual tradition includes three other endings, two of which the NRSV places in brackets. The latter two are obvious attempts by scribes to close this gospel in conformity with the other gospels' conclusions. (The fourth ending, an expansion of "the longer ending," is not rendered in the NRSV and will not be discussed further.)

The shorter ending of Mark, thirty-four Greek words in length, was added not earlier than the fourth century CE. This conclusion offers the women's report to the eleven and others (see Matt 28:8; Luke 24:9) and a variant of Matthew's Great Commission (28:19–20). Through "Peter and those with him," the risen Jesus disseminates "the sacred and imperishable proclamation of eternal salvation" (cf. 1 Tim 1:11; 2 Tim 1:10; 1 Pet 1:23–25). This announcement's sweep "from east to west" presumes, or at least aspires for, subsequent expansion of the Christian proclamation (cf. Mark 13:10; Acts 1:8; Rom 15:22–29).

Dating to the late second century and present in a majority of witnesses is *the longer ending of Mark* (16:9–20), well known to readers of the KJV. Mixing a variety of NT motifs, many foreign to Mark, this ending reads as a pastiche of the other gospels. The risen Jesus's first appearance to Mary Magdalene (16:9) recalls different traditions in Matt 28:9–10 and John 20:11–18. From Luke 8:2 is probably derived the detail that he had cast out seven demons from Magdalene. The disbelief confronting Mary's testimony (16:10–11) is reminiscent of Luke 24:9–11. Mark 16:12–13 seems an abbreviated version of the Emmaus road episode in Luke 24:13–35. The clearest intersection of this ending's theology with that expressed elsewhere in Mark lies at 16:14: Jesus appears and upbraids the eleven for their "lack of faith" (see 4:40b; 6:6a; 9:24) and their "stubbornness" (literally, "hardness of heart"; see 3:5; 6:52; 8:17; 10:5). Recalling Mark's opening reference to the good news (1:1), 16:15 and 16:20 paraphrase Matt 28:19, with additional cautions and encouragements. "The one who does not believe will be condemned" (16:16b) is without precedent in Mark but akin to John (3:18; 16:17). "The one who believes and is baptized will be saved" (16:16a) approximates assertions made elsewhere in the NT (Matt 28:19; Acts 2:38; Tit 3:5; 1 Pet 3:21). Though Mark is suspicious of signs as warrants for belief (8:11; 13:22), the longer ending accords credibility to many signs done in Jesus's name (vv. 17, 20; cf. 9:39; John 2:23; 4:48; 6:30). Casting out demons is not beyond the purview of Jesus's disciples in Mark (3:15; 6:7; cf. 9:38). Other convincing signs (16:17–18) are characteristically Lukan: speaking in tongues (Acts 2:4–11; 10:46; 19:6), safely picking up snakes (Luke 10:19; Acts 28:3–6), healing the sick by the laying of hands (Acts 3:1–10; 5:12–16; 9:12, 17–18; also Jas 5:14–15). Divine cooperation with and confirmation of Christian believers (Mark 16:20) are assured throughout the NT (Matt 28:20; Acts 4:30; 6:8; 14:3; 15:12; Rom 15:19; Heb 2:3–4). Even more prevalent is the image, developed from Ps 110:1, of the Lord Jesus as gloriously seated at God's right hand (Acts 2:33–34; 5:31; 7:55–56; Rom 8:34; Eph 1:20; Col 3:1; Heb 1:3; 8:1; 10:12; 12:2; 1 Pet 3:22). His being "taken up into heaven" (Mark 16:19) recalls Jesus's ascension in Luke (24:51; see also Acts 1:2, 11; 1 Tim 3:16) as well as Elijah's departure in a chariot of fire (2 Kgs 2:11).[2]

What, then, of *Mark's original epilogue* (16:1–8), on which all other endings are based? As elsewhere in the passion narrative (14:1, 12, 17; 15:1, 25, 33, 42), Mark sets the stage with temporal precision: "when the Sabbath was over [after six o'clock on Saturday evening] . . . very early on the first day of the week

2. For a discerning analysis of Mark 16:9–20, see Kara J. Lyons-Pardue, *Gospel Women and the Long Ending of Mark*, LNTS 614 (London: T&T Clark, 2020).

[Sunday]" (vv. 1, 2). Those visiting the tomb are the same women named as witnesses of Jesus's death (15:40). They have come to anoint the hastily buried body (15:42, 46). Their mission is doubly futile: another woman has already performed that task (14:8); repeatedly Jesus has promised that his body would be raised three days after his death (8:31; 9:31; 10:34). While superficially an expression of poor planning, their concern for moving from the tomb's mouth a stone so large (vv. 3–4) tacitly rebuts any accusation that the body was stolen (thus, Matt 28:11–15). Again their concern proves needless: the stone has already been rolled back (v. 4). Entering the tomb, they are astonished to see a young man dressed in white (v. 5), which suggests apocalyptic glorification (9:3; Dan 7:9; 12:3; Matt 13:43; Rev 7:9, 13). In verse 6, he assures them (1) there's no cause for alarm: (2) Jesus, the crucified Nazarene they are seeking, (3) is not there because (4) he has been raised from death (implicitly, by God). This is one of the NT's fundamental claims (John 5:21; Acts 4:10; 13:30; Rom 4:24; 1 Cor 15:3–4; 2 Tim 2:8). Verse 7 is an assignment: (1) Go and tell his disciples, especially Peter (see 14:30–31, 66–72), (2) that Jesus is going ahead of them back to Galilee (the starting point: 1:9, 14), (3) where they will see him (cf. Acts 2:32; 3:15; 10:40–41; 1 Cor 9:1; 15:5–8), (4) just as he said (Mark 14:28). Verse 8 describes the women's response: (1) they flee the tomb, (2) tremulous and bewildered, (3) and say nothing to anyone (4) because they are afraid. The final irony: even these women, who followed Jesus longer than anyone else, fall short from fear—as his disciples have done as far back as Mark 4:40–41. When all else and all others fail, God remains faithful to the promise relayed by Jesus himself (8:31; 9:31; 10:33–34). Mark's Gospel is but the beginning of the good news (1:1), now sandwiched into its readers' lives, where it may continue to unfold as a parable most surprising (4:1–34).

Part One

HISTORICAL STUDIES

CHAPTER 1

Was Mark a Roman Gospel?

> Checked for the moment, this pernicious superstition[, Christi-
> anity,] again broke out, not only in Judea, the home of the disease,
> but in the capital itself [Rome]—that receptacle for everything
> hideous and degraded from every quarter of the globe, which
> there finds a vogue.
>
> —Publius Cornelius Tacitus, *Annales* 15.44 (AT)

OF ALL THINGS ATTRIBUTED by the early fathers to Mark's Gospel, its origination from Rome may be the item accorded greatest plausibility at the bar of
critical scholarship. To the minds of modern investigators, however, the most
persuasive reasons for that assignment of provenance are not those suggested
by patristic sources, which for their part tend toward an explanation that is
roundly rejected by most moderns.

To come straight to the point: in Christian tradition, the connection of
Mark, both evangelist and gospel, with Rome appears to have been made on
the basis of Mark's prior association with Peter. In their comments on Mark,
most of the fathers yoke Peter and Rome (Irenaeus, Clement, Origen, Eusebius, Epiphanius, and Jerome) or Peter and Italy (the "anti-Marcionite" and
Monarchian gospel prologues).[1] For these details, several testimonies appear
to be dependent on one another. All of these witnesses, moreover, had access to 1 Pet 5:13 and its affiliation of Peter, Mark, and Rome (= "Babylon"; cf.
Rev 14:8; 16:19; 17:5; 18:1–24). Some of the fathers link Mark with Peter but not
with Rome (Papias, Tertullian, John Chrysostom); others associate Mark with

---

1. Patristic testimonies on Mark and the other evangelists are conveniently gathered in
Kurt Aland, ed., *Synopsis Quattuor Evangeliorum*, 10th ed. (Stuttgart: Deutsche Bibelstiftung,
1978), 531–48.

neither Peter nor Rome (Hippolytus, Adamantius, the Apostolic Constitutions, Augustine). *Nowhere in patristic testimony, however, is a link between Mark and Rome ever wrought in the absence of a coincident coupling of Mark and Peter.* That is to say, Rome seems to have entered the traditions about Mark only by way of Peter's association with that city, as a function of the assumption of Mark's Petrine authority. And there's the rub: while the gospel's affinity with Petrine tradition is not implausible,[2] its actual derivation from the apostle Peter is seriously contested within critical scholarship. Consequently, more recent appraisals of a Roman origin for Mark's Gospel tend to be made not on the face but in the teeth of the early fathers' conclusions.

Still, it is worth asking whether the patristic location of Mark's Gospel in Rome makes sense in the light of what we have come to learn of (1) the social and religious setting of first-century Roman Christianity and (2) the content of the Second Gospel. Is the situation of Mark's Gospel in Rome a claim that is, if not historically demonstrable, at least coherent with what can be reasonably inferred about the *Sitz im Leben* of early Roman Christianity?

CHRISTIANS IN FIRST-CENTURY ROME

With allowance for expected differences in critical assessment of finer details, a fairly sharp and rather textured reconstruction of first-century Roman Christianity seems to emerge from current research.

Ethnicity and Social Background

From the second century BCE onward, a substantial portion of Rome's population consisted of non-Romans who, as enslaved war captives, had been imported from their homelands in the Hellenized east (Greece, Asia Minor, Syria, Judea, Egypt, and elsewhere). One of the largest segments of that foreign population consisted of Jews, who by the first century CE numbered around forty to fifty thousand.[3] Paul's epistle to the Romans (ca. 57) presumes a sim-

---

2. See John H. Elliott, *A Home for the Homeless: A Sociological Exegesis of 1 Peter, Its Situation and Strategy* (Philadelphia: Fortress, 1981), 267–95; C. Clifton Black, *Mark: Images of an Apostolic Interpreter*, SPNT (Minneapolis: Fortress; Edinburgh: T&T Clark, 2001), 60–66.

3. The foundational studies in this area are by George La Piana, "The Roman Church at the End of the Second Century," *HTR* 18 (1925): 201–77, and "Foreign Groups in Rome during the First Centuries of the Empire," *HTR* 20 (1927): 183–403.

ilar ethnic mix among Christians in the imperial capital (see Rom 2:1, 9–12, 17; 11:13). If chapter 16 was originally part of Romans, the names mentioned in its concluding salutations imply a concentration of Christians in Rome whom Paul had met during his missionary travels (Rom 16:3, 4, 5, 7, 9, 13), among whom were a significant number of Jews (Prisca and Aquila: Rom 16:3; cf. Acts 18:2; Paul's "kinsfolk" in Rom 16:7, 11). Eleven of the twenty-six persons in Rom 16 bear names that are held by slaves in literary references or inscriptions associated with Rome (Mary, Junia, Ampliatus, Tryphaena, Tryphosa, Asyncritus, Phlegon, Hermes, Philologus, Julia, Nereus: Rom 16:6, 7, 8, 12, 14, 15).

Economic and Social Standing

In an exhaustive analysis of the archaeological, epigraphic, and literary evidence, Peter Lampe has made a convincing case for the relatively low economic status of Rome's first Christians. That religion appears to have been centered in two swampy, urban districts: the harbor of Trastevere (west of the River Tiber), one of the city's most densely populated, heavily Jewish, and rundown areas; and beyond the Porta Capena around the heavily traveled Appian Way (to the southeast). The population in these areas consisted of laborers, artisans, traders, transport workers, and in general some of the poorest from among Rome's citizenry. On the other hand, traces of a Christian presence linger from the city's more affluent Aventine between Trastevere and Porta Capena. Christians there may have enjoyed better prospects for limited upward mobility, whether as freedmen or as the slaves of Roman aristocrats.[4] James Jeffers has argued that very different social levels among Roman Christians are implied by two documents, both issuing from Rome near the turn of the first century: 1 Clement (ca. 95), which assumes the values of an educated elite (1 Clem. 37.4; 62.3), and the Shepherd of Hermas (ca. 135), whose perspective tends toward advocacy for destitute Christians (Herm. Mand. 2.4; 8.3, 4, 10; Sim. 5.3.7; 9.27.2; Vis. 3.9.5, 6).[5] Even earlier, in Rom 16, Paul greets several persons who were able either to own or to rent houses in which Christians might gather for worship (vv. 5, 14, 15).

---

4. Peter Lampe, *Die städtromischen Christen in den ersten beiden Jahrhunderten: Untersuchungen zur Sozialgeschichte*, 2nd ed., WUNT 2/18 (Tübingen: Mohr Siebeck, 1987), 36–52.

5. James S. Jeffers, *Conflict at Rome: Social Order and Hierarchy in Early Christianity* (Minneapolis: Fortress, 1991), 90–120.

Religious Organization

From Rom 16 and other sources, Lampe reckons that Roman Christians congregated in a half-dozen circles, located in houses and separated from each other geographically, socially, and intellectually. Early Christian worship in Rome appears to have been a heterogeneous, even fragmented, affair. Probably not by happenstance, Paul encourages Christian solidarity among various house-congregations (Rom 16:16), an ideal that by the second century had begun to founder on the shoals of ethnic and ideological diversity. By that time, a countervailing pull was exerted toward a more centralized, even hierarchical, administration among Roman congregations: thus, 1 Clement presumes as its provenance "*the* church of God that sojourns in Rome" (preface, emphasis added) and points up an apostolic succession of authority (42.4; 44.1–2). Eventually, though probably not earlier than the mid-second century, a single bishop pattern of leadership prevailed.

Political Turbulence

Long before then, conflicts for Roman Christians were appearing, the earliest of which are traceable to the religion's roots in Judaism. Relations between the empire and Roman Jews had tended at best toward uneasiness: though the Jews had been conceded various religious privileges (Josephus, *A.J.* 14.10.1–8), their religious insularity made them objects of suspicion and ridicule (Cicero, *Flac.* 28, 69; Juvenal, *Sat.* 3.14; 6.542–548; 14.105–106). By 49 or 50, there was enough tension in Rome to provoke the emperor Claudius (41–54) to expel from the capital a large number of Jews (Suetonius, *Claud.* 25.4; cf. Acts 18:2), who were not allowed to return until five years later. The effect of this imperial ban for the future of Roman Christianity was profound: it pushed to the outer edges its indigenous Jewish quality, which already had been marginalized by the large number of gentiles among Christian converts.

By the mid-sixties, a distinction between Christians and Jews in the imperial capital was recognizable even to pagan historians like Tacitus, who chronicled the next major chapter in Roman Christianity's stormy political history: Nero's arrest, torture, and execution of Christians on the trumped-up charge of culpability for the great Roman fire (*Ann.* 15.44). Trastevere, the harbor in which many poor Christians were concentrated, suffered no damage from the fire, which may partially explain how Nero was able to make his scapegoating stick. Moreover, the grotesque punishments suffered by Roman Christians at the emperor's hand—dismemberment by dogs, crucifixion, immolation—tally with our inferences of their social standing: Roman law forbade such means of execution for citizens of the state.

If, by the end of the sixties, Christians in Rome were no longer the bull's-eye for imperial harassment, they surely were caught up in the general upheavals that shook the empire. Following military and senatorial revolts against him, Nero killed himself in 68; within the following year, four emperors were installed in rapid succession, only to die by murder or suicide. By the time Vespasian (69–79) had restored a degree of stability, the state's economy and spirit had been depleted by civil war, including a disastrous Jewish insurrection against Rome (66–74). The climax of this revolt came in 70, when Jerusalem was first starved, then slaughtered, and its temple burned by order of Vespasian's son, Titus. Such events were of more than regional significance: Titus's quelling of the Judean uprising was commemorated in late first-century Roman coinage and in the Arch of Titus, which still stands at the Roman Forum.

For reasons disputed among historians, evidence for contemporaneous Christian reactions to its ambient turmoil is hard to come by. Contrary to the once popular notion that Christianity was the seedbed for a social unrest that ultimately toppled the empire, Christians of this and subsequent periods adopted a rather low political profile. For instance, Jewish Christians in Jerusalem did not join in the revolt against Rome but fled to gentile territory (Eusebius, *Hist. eccl.* 3.5.2–3). This, in a sense, was symptomatic of Christianity's destiny: as evidenced by Paul's letters and corroborated by the book of Acts, the fledgling religion had already flown beyond Israel, to nest in numerous gentile regions throughout the Mediterranean basin. During the second half of the first century, Christians were busily sculpting a new religious identity from the materials of their religious heritage. To that end, though in different ways, both Paul and Clement probe some common themes: the question of Christianity's relationship with Judaism (Rom 9:1–11:36; 1 Clem. 40.1–5; 41.2), the distinctive structure of Christian belief (Rom 3:21–31; 5:1–8:39) and practice (1 Clem. 42.4; 44.1–4), and a stance of reflective compliance with the Roman government (Rom 13:1–7; 1 Clem. 60.4–61.2).[6]

Hints within the Second Gospel

Does the message of Mark comport with first-century Roman Christianity, thus reconstructed? I think that an affirmative verdict may be rendered.

---

6. Consult Raymond E. Brown and John P. Meier, *Antioch and Rome: New Testament Cradles of Catholic Christianity* (New York: Paulist, 1983), 105–83.

Ethnic and Religious Assumptions

The Second Gospel presents Christian traditions that originated in Palestinian Judaism, interpreted for an audience that would no longer find some of its Jewish references intelligible or sufficient. On the one hand, the Markan narrative is laced with biblical quotations (thus, 1:2–3; 7:6–7; 12:10–11, 36) and riddled with biblical imagery (e.g., 6:30–44; 8:1–10; cf. Exod 16:13–35; Mark 9:2–8, 9–13; cf. Mal 3:1–2; 4:5–6). Significantly, Jesus and a sincere scribe concur on the first principles of a life lived in accordance with God's will (Mark 12:28–34, working out of Deut 6:4–5; Lev 19:18; 1 Sam 15:22; Isa 45:21). On the other hand, the Second Gospel betokens a certain distance from Judaism. Accordingly, the evangelist explains Jewish customs (Mark 7:3–4, 11, 19b) and translates Semitic expressions (5:41; 7:34; 14:36; 15:22, 34, 42). Indeed, the author's own grasp of Jewish Scripture (1:2; cf. Exod 23:20; Mal 3:1; Mark 2:25–26; cf. 1 Sam 21:1–6) and practice (7:3; cf. Lev 22:1–16), of Palestinian idiom (3:17) and geography (5:1; 6:53; 7:31; 10:1), seems rather unsure.

Even as new wine inevitably bursts from old wineskins (Mark 2:22), the movement inaugurated by Jesus in Mark's Gospel has spilled out of Judaism into the gentile world, whose communities (3:8; 5:1, 20; 7:31; 8:27) and customs (10:2–12; cf. Deut 24:1–4) figure prominently in the narrative. Remarkably, Jesus dismisses Levitical discriminations between things clean and unclean (Mark 7:14–23; cf. Lev 11:1–47), which signals a clear break from Pharisaic tradition (Mark 7:1–9) and an effective justification for "the proclamation of the good news to all nations" (13:10; 14:9; cf. 15:39). Nevertheless, the shift in Mark from a Jewish past to a gentile future is effected with considerable resistance, both among Jews (2:1–3:6; 12:1–9) and toward gentiles (7:24–30). The same transition, as we have seen, was no smoother for first-century Christians in Rome.

Economic and Social Standing

Positive interactions with Jesus are typically displayed in the Second Gospel by characters whose social identity or standing is analogous to that of early Roman Christians. While largely rural in orientation, in Mark Jesus's mission attracts adherents from both urban and rural settings (1:45; 6:32–33, 56). The condition for entrance into God's reign is described by Jesus as being childlike in receptivity (10:15; cf. 9:36–37), which may allude to the powerlessness of children in antiquity. Sparks of discipleship in the Second Gospel are struck by a band of minor characters living on society's margins (1:40–45; 2:1–12; 8:22–

26; 10:46–52), many of whom are women (5:25–34; 7:24–30; 12:41–44; 14:3–9; 15:40–41; 16:1). The stability created by possessions is actually or potentially manifest among some of Jesus's disciples and would-be followers (1:16–20; 10:17–22), such that they must be cautioned concerning "the lure of wealth and the desire for other things" (4:18–19; 10:23–31). Jesus's models of discipleship consistently subvert conventional assumptions about social status: many who are first will be last, and the last—notably, those who are others' servants and slaves—will be first (9:35; 10:31, 43–44).

Religious Organization

Another cluster of images in Mark would not have gone unnoticed by Christians, at Rome and elsewhere, who gathered for worship in houses as real and surrogate families. Repeatedly Jesus interacts with his followers in "a house" (1:29, 32–33; 2:1, 15; 3:19b; 7:24b); pointedly he satisfies a hungry horde, far from home (8:1–10, N.B. v. 3). Pervading the Second Gospel is a related theme, the constitution of Jesus's disciples into a new family: "houses, brothers and sisters, mothers and children" who do God's will in this age (3:33–35; 10:29–30). The absence in Mark 10:29 of the paterfamilias, the clan's customary patriarch, is conspicuous yet coherent with this gospel's aforementioned egalitarian tendencies. Accordingly, disciples who bicker among themselves over greatness, or clamber over each other for exalted positions, are immediately reproved by Jesus (9:33–37; 10:35–45). Although consideration for one's natural parents fulfills God's commandment and is thus no negligible matter (7:9–13), divisions within families over the pursuit of Jesus's way are painfully real (3:21, 31–32; 6:1–6a; 10:28–30). Indeed, Mark is keenly aware of divisions that can occur even among those surrogate families who follow Jesus (see 6:7–13; 9:38–48). Rectified communion among Christians entails judgment, repentance, and prayerful forgiveness (6:11–12; 11:25): "Have salt in yourselves, and be at peace with one another" (9:50b).

Unrest and Harassment

Probably no feature of the gospel enjoys a greater degree of exegetical consensus than Mark's acknowledgment of the turmoil, even persecution, to which Jesus and his followers are inevitably subject. Such hostility assumes manifold social shapes in Mark, all of which resonate with the experience of first-century Roman Christians. First, Jesus and the Twelve are perpetually at loggerheads with their fellow Jews, a conflict dramatized most obviously through

43

Jesus's repeated conflicts with Israel's leaders (e.g., 2:6–10; 7:1–13; 11:27–12:27; 14:53–65), more subtly through such matters as the presence of demonism in the synagogue (1:23–24) and the absence of "fruit" in the temple (11:12–21; cf. 13:1–2; 15:38). Second, because of their implied challenge to the claims of the imperial cult (cf. 1:1, 15; 11:9–10), Jesus and his followers fall afoul of the Roman authorities (10:33–34; 13:9).

Here one detects in Mark some ambivalence. Whereas no illusions are harbored about "those whom [the gentiles] recognize as their rulers" (10:42), the evangelist draws on traditions that effectively endeavor to repair Christians' relationship with the empire: thus, the delicacy of Jesus's position on paying Caesar's taxes (12:13–17) and the presentation of Pilate as feckless though not malicious (15:1–15). Although its theological reasons are complex and irreducible to solely political motivations, the mystery in which the Second Gospel enshrouds Jesus's identity as Christ and Son of God (1:34; 3:11–12; 8:27–30) has the practical effect of defusing, among Mark's contemporaries, any charge that Jesus and his successors were downright seditious.[7]

Other forms of jeopardy, implied by Mark, are poignant but ill-defined, much as the experience of first-century Roman Christians appears to have been. Though clothed in the stock motifs of prophecy and apocalypticism (cf. 2 Chr 15:6; Isa 19:2; Rev 16:18), some of Jesus's warnings at Olivet may not be merely imaginative. Since, as both Jewish and Roman historians attest, "nation [did] rise against nation" during the sixties (cf. Mark 13:8), the gospel's readers might well have been shaken by turmoil and in need of settling down (thus, 13:6–7, 14–23). To "be hated by all because of [Jesus's] name" (13:13) need be interpreted neither as mere rhetoric nor as religious paranoia: Tacitus and Pliny (*Ep. Tra.* 10.96) remind us of the indiscriminate contempt heaped upon Christians by many pagans. Although fraternal betrayal doubtless occurred in various historical contexts, Tacitus's record of the persecution of Roman Christians confirms the fact that occasionally "brother [did] betray brother to

---

7. In *Mark 15:39 as a Markan Theology of Revelation: The Centurion's Confession as Apocalyptic Unveiling*, LNTS 458 (London: Bloomsbury T&T Clark, 2017), 3–4 and passim, Brian K. Gamel argues that the centurion's confession of the dead Jesus as υἱὸς θεοῦ (Mark 15:39) is, in effect, the gospel's punch line. While that reading ties up some of the gospel's loose ends, I remain uncertain whether the evangelist intends for the legionnaire's betrayal of imperial fealty to be taken at face value or as the capper in a series of other sarcastically ironic affirmations by Jewish and Roman authorities in the passion narrative (14:61; 15:9, 32). Without direction from the evangelist of the kind that Matthew (27:51–54) and Luke (23:47–48) provide, it is impossible to judge with certainty. See C. Clifton Black, *Mark*, ANTC (Nashville: Abingdon, 2011), 332–33, and chapter 9 of the present volume.

death" (Mark 13:12). If its substance is more than biblically allusive (cf. Mic 7:6; 2 Esd 6:24), such a comment might help us in understanding why Jesus's disciples in Mark are characterized as such craven, faithless incompetents (4:35–41; 8:14–21; 14:17–31, 66–72). For some early Christians, at Rome and elsewhere, it was indeed the case that "when trouble or persecution [arose] on account of the word, immediately they [fell] away" (4:17).

To summarize, if the book's accents permit such inferences as these, we might reasonably suppose that Mark was written for Christians of low to middling social status, who could have gathered for worship in independent house-churches. By the time of the gospel's composition, Markan Christianity evidently had begun to break away, ethnically and religiously, from its roots in Palestinian Judaism. The tension experienced between Markan Christians and erstwhile Jewish coreligionists was but one aspect of a larger panorama of tumult, in which the Roman state and even other Christians were implicated. Between the social, political, and religious conditions implied by Mark's Gospel and the circumstances attending first-century Roman Christians, there are, in short, some fascinating parallels.

A CAUTIOUS CONCLUSION

One might ask, If the correspondence seems so marked, why not cut the Gordian knot, vindicate the majority patristic opinion, and flatly assert that Mark's Gospel was written in Rome?[8] At least three factors, I think, retard our progress toward a conclusion so confident.

First, we are deprived of the hard, corroborative evidence that is a historian's bread and butter.[9] If other Christian documents issuing from Rome during the

---

8. In recent study, Adam Winn has made a strong argument for this: *The Purpose of Mark's Gospel: An Early Christian Response to Roman Imperial Propaganda*, WUNT 2/245 (Tübingen: Mohr Siebeck, 2008). The propaganda to which Winn refers is "Vespasian['s] claim] to be the fulfillment of Jewish messianic prophecy" (160; also 178, 180, 183, 199). While Josephus (*B.J.* 6.312), Tacitus (*Hist.* 5.13.1–2), and Suetonius (*Vesp.* 4.5) connect Vespasian with a Jewish prophecy, none of them states that Vespasian himself made such a claim or that it figured heavily in imperial propaganda of the mid to late first century. For further consideration of this subject, see chapter 6 of the present volume.

9. Pursuing a different cluster of assumptions, Brian J. Incigneri argues for a broad range of veiled historical allusions to the Flavians' persecution of Roman Christians in Mark in the late 60s and early 70s (*The Gospel to the Romans: The Setting and Rhetoric of Mark's Gospel*, BIS 65 [Leiden: Brill, 2003]). Reviewing this monograph in *JTS* 58 (2007): 206–14, William R. Telford offers an extensive analysis and rebuttal of many of its claims, which tend

same period demonstrated the use of Mark, that fact would substantially support the gospel's Roman provenance. Such documents we have (1 Peter; 1 Clement; Shepherd of Hermas); indisputable references to Mark within them we lack.

Second, the social, religious, and political aspects that we have inferred are patient of alternative interpretations, which do not require Mark's origination from Rome. While many believe that the Second Gospel would have been read most meaningfully within the context of actual persecution, there is nothing in it that demands such a reading. The book could have arisen from a community (say, in Syria or Galilee) where troubles loomed on the horizon, or for that matter from any church that pondered the meaning of suffering within the Christian confession.[10] Some consider the gospel's evidence too ambiguous, our knowledge of circumstances in the first century too spotty, to permit determination of Mark's origins.

Third, even more basic questions can be raised about the method by which any assessment of Mark's provenance is ventured. The historical analysis of ancient documents is anything but an exact science. Furthermore, the manifest content of Mark's Gospel is far less *descriptive* of its original readership, far more *prescriptive* of that community's theological stance.

Weighing the probabilities, I consider the relevant evidence strong enough to support the assumption of Mark's Roman provenance, yet too weak to nail down that hypothesis. Given our present state of knowledge, we can nevertheless acknowledge an appreciable social, religious, and theological congruence between the Second Gospel and first-century Roman Christianity. If they were as much in the dark about the book's origins as we, the church fathers could have reasoned their way to an intelligible conclusion (Mark's consonance with Roman Christianity) from an uncertain premise (the association of Peter and the Second Evangelist). It is worth remembering, however, that the sheer con-

---

to underplay the gospel's Jewish apocalypticism and to overstate what historians have yet been able to verify. "In discussing 8:33 ('Get behind me, Satan!') Incigneri claims that Satan is 'a term that elsewhere always points to Roman society' ([*Gospel to the Romans*], 337), but what is the evidence for this, or for any deep, underlying hostility on the part of Mark for Rome? Indeed, from a strictly historical point of view, what evidence do we have, for the immediate post-70 CE period, that Roman Christians were actually thrown to the lions, crucified, or otherwise executed by the Roman means of punishment that Incigneri sees adumbrated in the Gospel?" (212–13).

10. Contrast the alternative conclusions drawn in the perceptive analyses by Joel Marcus, "The Jewish War and the *Sitz im Leben* of Mark," *JBL* 111 (1992): 441–62; Hendrika Nicoline Roskam, *The Purpose of the Gospel of Mark in Its Social and Religious Context*, NovTSup 114 (Leiden: Brill, 2004); Bas M. F. van Iersel, "The Gospel according to St Mark—Written for a Persecuted Community?," *NedTT* 34 (1980): 15–36.

nection of Mark with that apostle did not necessitate a secondary derivation of the gospel *from Rome*. The figure of Peter played a significant role in Syrian Christianity, but none of the early fathers—even those from Syria themselves—located the composition of the Second Gospel there.[11]

What appears to have prompted, or at least bolstered, the triangulation of Peter-Mark-Rome was the forceful testimony, not to Peter's mere presence in Rome (much less the later tradition of his Roman pontificate), but to his Roman martyrdom (cf. 1 Clem. 5.4–7; 6.1; Ignatius, *Rom.* 4.2–3; Irenaeus, *Haer.* 3.3.2; Eusebius, *Hist. eccl.* 2.25.7). The fathers seem to have been impressed not only with the Second Gospel's Petrine derivation but also with its strong overtones of sacrifice for the Christian cause, an impression shared by a host of current commentators. In any case, the association of Mark's Gospel with Rome, formulated by most patristic scholars and perpetuated by some of their modern counterparts, is, if not proven, then at least not improbable.

11. See Glanville Downey, *A History of Antioch in Syria from Seleucus to the Arab Conquest* (Princeton: Princeton University Press, 1961), 272–316, 583–86.

CHAPTER 2

The Second Evangelist:
Authorship and Apostolicity

> John Mark, the cousin of St. Barnabas (Col. 4.10), a Jew, set out
> with St. Barnabas and St. Paul on their first missionary jour-
> ney, but for reasons which failed to satisfy St. Paul turned back
> (Acts 12.25, 13.5, 13, 15.37f.). Afterwards he accompanied Barnabas
> on a mission to Cyprus (Acts 15.39), and he was in Rome with St.
> Paul (Col. 4.10, Philem. 24, 2 Tim. 4.11) and St. Peter (1 Pet. 5.13),
> whose 'interpreter' (ἑρμηνευτής), acc[ording] to Papias, he was;
> and it was no doubt in Italy, if not at Rome itself, that he wrote
> his Gospel. Acc[ording] to Eusebius (H.E. II.xvi.1 and xxiv.1), he
> afterwards went to Alexandria and was its first bishop, while in
> later tradition he is also associated with Venice. The tradition that
> Mark was κολοβοδάκτυλος (prob[ably] "stump-fingered," i.e., of
> Mark himself, and not an allusion to the brevity of his Gospel),
> is found in the Anti-Marcionite Prologue and in St. Hippolytus,
> Haer., vii.3D.

> —*The Oxford Dictionary of the Christian Church*[1]

FROM AMONG SEVERAL GOSSAMER STRANDS embedded in small patches
of the NT, patristic authors plucked one, sometimes two, for weaving into a
traditional miniature that characterized the composition of the anonymous
Second Gospel.[2] The effect of their portrayal has been, paradoxically, both

---

1. F. L. Cross and E. A. Livingstone, eds., 2nd ed. (New York: Oxford University Press,
1974), 1038, s.v. "Mark, St., Evangelist."

2. Patristic testimonies on Mark and the other evangelists are conveniently gathered in
Kurt Aland, ed., *Synopsis Quattuor Evangeliorum*, 10th ed. (Stuttgart: Deutsche Bibelstiftung,
1978), 531–48.

ephemeral and enduring: for while the "personality" of Mark has never pre-occupied biblical interpreters, whether patristic or contemporary, that gospel has ever since been personalized, by custom ancient and modern, as the one "according to Mark."

However deep or shallow its historical grounding, the attribution of the Second Gospel to Mark and the sustenance of that ascription across the centuries need never have happened. Just why patristic observers settled on Mark, among other possibilities, as an appropriate identification of that gospel's author is a riddle that invites more rumination than it has received. Beyond that puzzle, one might wonder why the early church took the trouble to remember and to embellish a Markan personality, basted into stories about that gospel's creation. Indeed, an even more fundamental question could be raised: why bother with an ascription of human authorship at all? If the crucial factor were ultimately the legitimation of a religious text, why not simply impute to Mark's Gospel a divine origin, much as the Vedas are regarded in traditional Hinduism?

Considered as a dimension of the broader study of Christian religious phe-nomena, such questions are neither trivial nor easily answerable, whether one assumes of patristic traditions some basis in fact or dismisses their historical foundation altogether. More vexing still, the early fathers offer us little explicit guidance in addressing such questions, since they were understandably more occupied with practicing Christianity than with self-referentially abstracting its practical peculiarities.

Personification and Apostolicity

I think it likely that the formation of a rudimentary personality for Mark the Evangelist was one component of a larger process, by which the early church came to recognize Mark's Gospel as an apostolic document. The fathers' reason-ing probably traversed a circle. On the one hand, patristic figurations of the Sec-ond Evangelist helped the church to understand, and to appropriate as apostolic, the gospel they associated with Mark. On the other hand, the general shape and to some degree the motivations of that gospel molded the fathers' personifica-tion of its putative evangelist as an apostolic associate and interpreter. While this circular maneuver may have been informed by some extrinsic assumptions about apostolicity, the fathers probably arrived at their understanding of both gospel and evangelist as apostolic by virtue of that reflective process itself.

Within the framework of Christian theology, discourse about apostolicity is not necessarily tantamount to the claim that an apostle actually authored a given religious text (like a gospel or creed) or authorized a given religious practice (like a ritual or form of ministry). Nor is apostolicity interchangeable with the concept of "catholicity," which usually refers to some general, if not universal, consensus on authentic Christian belief and practice. Apostolicity, rather, is essentially an expression of the church's hope for its own integrity across time. It refers to the actual or potential continuity of a normative Christian witness, extending from the earliest testimonies to Jesus through each successive Christian generation:[3] a constancy that persists among inevitably variable formulations, throughout history, of the meaning of Christian faith. Even as an individual Christian changes across the experience of a lifetime, yet remains a recognizably unified self, apostolicity embraces the church's quest for "'a visible, historical community,' possessing an identity and yet developing in response to new demands and opportunities."[4] The formation of a Christian canon and the emergence of an episcopate were institutional embodiments of the church's commitment to maintain and to perpetuate its practical and theological heritage, styled as "the faith of the apostles."

With respect to Mark, an early but significant step was taken when the patristic church not only aligned the Second Gospel conceptually with the apostle Peter but also distanced the book's creation from the ministry of the earthly Jesus.[5] Although the rise of modern historical consciousness has enabled us to appreciate some of its implications with a clarity and force impossible for them to have realized, Papias (Eusebius, *Hist. eccl.* 3.39.4), Irenaeus (*Haer.* 3.1.1; cf. *Hist. eccl.* 5.20.5–7), and their successors presumed, indeed theologically esteemed, an important insight: namely, that the Second Gospel (like other gospels) does not so much offer "the life of Jesus" as a remembrance of that life, a commemoration born of Christian faith.[6] Within that context it is surely no accident that a chain of reminiscence looms large in some of our earliest testimonies to Mark's proclamation of Jesus: hence Justin Martyr's character-

---

3. Indeed, the early fathers tended to trace that line of continuity back to God, the source of all revelation, by way of Jesus Christ (see 1 Clem. 42.2; Irenaeus, *Haer.* 5.1.1; Tertullian, *Praescr.* 32.6). See also Maurice Wiles, *The Making of Christian Doctrine* (Cambridge: Cambridge University Press, 1967), 45–46.

4. John Macquarrie, *Principles of Christian Theology* (New York: Scribner's Sons, 1977), 411.

5. This bifocal characterization of apostolicity, embracing both proximity to and mediated distance from Jesus Christ, might be compared with John Knox's treatment of the topic in *Criticism and Faith* (New York: Abingdon-Cokesbury, 1952). Knox emphasizes, rather one-sidedly in my view, "nearness to the normative event" (100; see also 68–70).

6. On which, consult Nils A. Dahl, *Jesus in the Memory of the Early Church* (Minneapolis: Augsburg, 1976), 11–29.

ization of the gospels as apostolic memoirs (e.g., *1 Apol.* 1.66.3; *Dial.* 105.1, 5, 6); thus, the unbroken sequence of memory that is recalled, backward, from Eusebius to Papias to John the Elder, from John to Mark to Peter (Eusebius, *Hist. eccl.* 3.39.14–15).

As decades, then centuries, passed after the Second Gospel's creation, the traditions about its author eventually melded into an image exhibiting a considerable degree of coherence. Naturally, the Second Evangelist was presumed to have been related to an acknowledged apostle; for the early church, however, it was not merely that predication that rendered the Second Gospel apostolic. The figure of Mark itself acquired a discernible measure of definition and stability. Once a relationship was established between the evangelist and Peter, it persisted to the usual, though not complete, exclusion of other traditional options, even alternatives suggested elsewhere in the NT (Acts 12:12, 25; 13:5b, 13b; 15:36–40; Col 4:10; 2 Tim 4:11; Phlm 24).[7] Moreover, the figure of Mark came to acquire other, relatively consistent embellishments: thus, for example, the evangelist's somewhat chastened apostolicity and his activity in Rome (thus Irenaeus, Clement of Alexandria, Origen, and Eusebius, among others [*Hist. eccl.* 2.15.1–2; 5.8.2–3; 6.14.5–7, 25.3–6]). Though neither historically implausible nor readily amenable to historical confirmation, these recurrent features (like Mark's association with Peter) arguably manifest an external coherence with the concerns of the Second Gospel and its general regard by the early church.[8] As such, the figure of Mark—his patristic personality, if you will—appears to have contributed a dimension to the broader interpretive framework within which the early church read the Second Gospel and heard its witness as continuous with Christ: that is, as apostolic.[9]

7. Within patristic Christianity, only "Adamantius" (*The Dialogue on the Orthodox Faith*), the Apostolic Constitutions, and Jerome (*Commentary on Philemon*) associate Mark the Evangelist with the apostle Paul. Among characterizations of the Second Evangelist within the first four centuries, only the late Monarchian gospel prologue implies use of the Lukan portrayal of John Mark (in Acts). The least developed of NT traditions about someone named Mark, which couples that figure with Peter (only at 1 Pet 5:13), is, ironically, the firmest and most highly elaborated among the early church fathers.

8. See John H. Elliott, *A Home for the Homeless: A Sociological Exegesis of 1 Peter, Its Situation and Strategy* (Philadelphia: Fortress, 1981), 267–95; Martin Hengel, *Studies in the Gospel of Mark*, trans. John Bowden (Philadelphia: Fortress, 1985), 1–58; and part 3 of my study, *Mark: Images of an Apostolic Interpreter*, SPNT (Minneapolis: Fortress; Edinburgh: T&T Clark, 2001), 193–250.

9. While the notion of apostolicity, as presented here, may strike some moderns as an artificial imposition upon ancient texts, we might bear in mind that scholars since the nineteenth century have typically viewed the NT through a similar lens, polished during the

The Evangelists on Jesus and the Fathers on Mark

The personification of Mark not only shaped the early church's acceptance of the Markan Gospel; that document appears to have influenced the manner in which the church personified the evangelist. In support of this thesis, one might recall some general features, characteristic of the early fathers' *modus operandi* in their presentations of Mark. There is, to begin with, the notable *sketchiness* of that figure's patristic profile. On the teeming stage of Christian antiquity, Mark emerges as little more than a bit player. Second, one may discern, I believe, a characteristic *treatment*, among the fathers, *of traditions about Mark*. At least through the fourth century, patristic interpreters tended, in general, toward conservation of their inheritance of lore regarding the evangelist, rather than ad hoc, much less capricious, fabrication of legendary novelties. Without doubt, some of their presentations lean toward the improbable (Bishop Mark of Alexandria) or the fantastic (Mark the Levite, who tried to disqualify himself from the priesthood by amputating his thumb). Yet, with a fair degree of confidence, one can usually infer the bases for these portraits by Jerome (*Comm. Matt.* Pref.) and the Monarchian prologue to the gospel, precisely because they preserve (with elaborations) recognizably stable aspects of "the patristic Mark." The variations on this common theme may bring to mind a third recurring aspect: be they conventional (as with Hippolytus, *Haer.* 7.30.1) or venturesome (as in Clement's *Letter to Theodore*), inevitably *the traditionists' own interests and biases* tend to color their presentations of the evangelist Mark.

Little wonder that the Markan traditions of the early church flowed along these lines: for, in compatible ways, traditions about Jesus were reconstituted in the gospels themselves. First, although a minority demurs, most scholars regard Mark's Gospel as a conservation, to some degree, of antecedent traditions about Jesus.[10] That the bulk of the book was outrightly or largely concocted

---

Enlightenment. Thus, when the Second Gospel was judged to be the earliest of the four, and was for that reason often (albeit fallaciously) considered the most historically reliable, then Mark finally emerged from the canon's penumbra to a position of equality, if not centrality, among the gospels.

10. Thus, for instance, Ernest Best, "Mark's Preservation of the Tradition," in *L'Évangile selon Marc: Tradition et rédaction*, ed. M. Sabbe, BETL 34 (Leuven: Leuven University Press, 1988), 21–34. See also Larry W. Hurtado, "The Gospel of Mark: Evolutionary or Revolutionary Document?," *JSNT* 13 (1990): 15–32, which challenges proposals for Mark's "revolutionary" creativity suggested by Werner H. Kelber (*The Oral and the Written Gospel:*

by the Second Evangelist is a highly remote possibility. The same observation manifestly holds for the other Synoptic Gospels: on the prevailing assumption that they adopted Mark as a source, we can actually track the degree to which Matthew and Luke have been patterned after Mark. With its distinctive character, the Fourth Gospel presents special problems of assessment in this regard; still, few scholars would deny that John, too, is the product of some conservation of earlier sources, however indeterminate their exact nature and use by the Fourth Evangelist may be.

Second, on the other hand, as patristic interpreters like Augustine observed (*Cons.* 2.12.27), the evangelists more than merely replicated earlier sources. They purposefully, even ingeniously, adapted those traditions in the light of various historical and religious circumstances attending their gospels' composition. The later, canonical consequence of the evangelists' creative enterprise was a common gospel, focused on Jesus, expressed in four different editions, each with a distinguishable theological slant (as Irenaeus recognized: *Haer.* 3.11.8). Likewise, patristic interpreters filtered their renderings of the evangelist Mark through the mesh of their own religious concerns: thus, Mark is variously portrayed as an eminent ecclesiarch (Jerome, *Vir. ill.* 8) or as Peter's shadow (Tertullian, *Marc.* 5.3–4), as an advocate of either catholic orthodoxy (Hippolytus, *Haer.* 7.30.1; Epiphanius, *Pan.* 51.6.10–13), catholic Gnosticism (Clement, *To Theodore*), or dynamic Monarchianism (the Monarchian prologue). Canonically and traditionally, the results are comparable: virtually as many different perspectives on Jesus as there are evangelists; almost as many different perspectives on Mark as there are patristic testimonies.

Third, nevertheless, for the early church, the figure of Mark or of any evangelist was nowhere nearly as significant as that of the Christ whom they proclaimed. In a sense, the fragmented sketches of Mark in patristic witnesses conform with the Second Gospel's complete lack of reference to its author. In another sense, of course, even a marginal curiosity about the evangelists' personalities veers from the gospels' own unwavering concentration on Jesus. Yet this slight shift of focus may be intelligible when regarded in the context of an even more profound influence that probably was exerted by the Second Gospel upon patristic musings on its evangelist.

The Hermeneutics of Speaking and Writing in the Synoptic Tradition, Mark, Paul, and Q [Philadelphia: Fortress, 1983]) and Burton L. Mack (*A Myth of Innocence: Mark and Christian Origins* [Philadelphia: Fortress, 1988]).

Jesus and Mark as Biographical Subjects

The similarities between the gospels' presentation of Jesus and the fathers' presentation of the evangelists are more than merely formal. When viewed in a particular light, the motivations underlying those presentations appear to have been kindred. What I wish to suggest, finally, is that patristic figurations of the evangelist Mark may have been religious byproducts of the need, manifested by early Christians, to recall and to recast Jesus's activities.

Of course, neither I nor anyone would argue that the figure of Mark was accorded, by the early church, an esteem equal to that of Jesus. To the contrary, the significance of any evangelist was measured against, and thus relativized by, the alleged author's representation of Jesus and, specifically, that representation's fidelity to the church's emergent understanding of Jesus's lordship. Nevertheless, from the middle of the first century onward, the Second Gospel's sheer existence proved to be no more sufficient for Christians than their sheer acceptance of Jesus as Lord: in both cases, there seems to have been a religious pressure to construe apostolic testimony to Jesus, and to construe Jesus himself, within the landscape of time and space. Although historical questions as such appear to have held for them little or no interest, early Christians were profoundly concerned about the situation of their faith within history, both Jesus's history and their own.[11] The principal literary precipitate of that concern was the creation of gospels like Mark's, which eulogized and proclaimed in faith what God had done through Jesus of Nazareth. A collateral literary offshoot of the same historical concern appears to have been the preservation of anecdotes about the authors of those gospels and the circumstances under which those works came to be produced. This two-pronged interest in positioning both Jesus's and Mark's activities within a historical framework is clearly signaled by Papias, quoting the elder John in the oldest of our patristic witnesses to the Second Evangelist: "Mark became Peter's interpreter and wrote accurately whatever he remembered, but not in order, of the things said or done by the Lord" (Eusebius, *Hist. eccl.* 3.39.15).

A further analogy can be drawn when comparing early Christian portrayals of Jesus the Christ and Mark the Evangelist. In both cases, the genre adopted in the resulting literature was that of "classical popular biography": a sketch

---

11. For acute soundings of this subject, consult Paul W. Meyer, "Faith and History Revisited," *PSB* 10 (n.s. 1989): 75–83; repr. Meyer, *The Word in This World: Essays in New Testament Exegesis and Theology*, ed. John T. Carroll, NTL (Louisville: Westminster John Knox, 2004), 19–26.

of a figure, perceived as historical, rendered for an edifying purpose. Between these depictions of Jesus and of Mark, there is, of course, a decided difference in degree: whereas the Markan Gospel is a coherent narrative, most of the patristic traditions about the evangelist Mark are mere narrative scraps. Yet the anecdotal quality of the fathers' rendition of Mark is not entirely unlike what form critics imagine to have been the mode of early Christian presentations of Jesus, prior to their congealment into any of the gospels. Indeed, with patristic testimonies like the Monarchian gospel prologue and Jerome's *De viris illustribus*, we can observe how many of those anecdotal snippets were being reformulated into biographical cameos of Mark. Viewed from this perspective, popular and even scholarly reconstructions of a *vita Marci* such as that which introduced this essay—the slightly picaresque tale of the Jewish-Christian backslider who ultimately turned apostolic companion, evangelist, and missionary bishop—amount to an innocent, occasionally fanciful culmination of a religious impulse that is intelligible, scarcely reprehensible, and as old as Christianity itself.

Again, make no mistake: early Christians did *not* venerate the Second Evangelist as they revered Jesus. The point, rather, is the church's inclination to personify Mark and to position that personality on the horizon of ecclesiastical events—a tendency reflective of, and perhaps indirectly stimulated by, the gospel's own location of Jesus Christ within human history.[12]

CONCLUSION

The fashioning of the figure of Mark as apostolic associate and interpreter was neither arbitrary, scattershot, nor purposeless. Historically unverifiable and therefore debatable: yes, in many if not most respects. Yet to allow our historical preoccupations to dominate the early fathers is every bit as anachronistic as their own procedure is sometimes branded by modern critics. Moreover, such reservations distract us from what their personifications of the evangelist were arguably attempting to achieve, religiously and theologically. Carefully crafted, the figure of Mark the Evangelist was one aspect of the larger hermeneutical context within which the Second Gospel was preserved, read, and interpreted by

---

12. Such an assessment harmonizes with a more general judgment, rendered by many church historians: that, in the patristic era, Scripture and tradition were thought to be reciprocally interpretive, not polarized. See Ellen Flesseman-van Leer, *Tradition and Scripture in the Early Church* (Assen: Van Gorcum, 1954), N.B. 186–97.

the early church as a faithful testimony to the significance of Jesus.[13] The "character" of the evangelist helped to lend apostolicity to the gospel; yet the gospel's own character helped to lend apostolicity to its putative author's personification. Verification of this judgment lies ultimately in the church's own tradition: the evangelist Mark was canonized as Alexandria's bishop, and the Gospel according to Mark was canonized as Scripture.

13. On the larger framework within which the early church interpreted its Scripture, with special stress on Irenaeus's formulation of a "rule of faith," consult James L. Kugel and Rowan A. Greer, *Early Biblical Interpretation*, LEC 3 (Philadelphia: Westminster, 1986), 155–99.

CHAPTER 3

The Quest of Mark the Redactor: Why Has It Been Pursued, and What Has It Taught Us?

It is better to ask some of the questions than to know all the answers.

—James Thurber[1]

"NEW WINDS ARE BLOWING in Marcan research," claimed Jack Dean Kingsbury four decades ago.[2] As always, the heartiest gusts had been methodological in character, as fresh literary, rhetorical, sociological, and tradition-critical strategies were adopted in the interpretation of the Second Gospel.[3] Yet the steady breeze of redaction criticism has wafted for over sixty years. In some

---

1. "The Scotty Who Knew Too Much," from *Fables for Our Time and Famous Poems Illustrated* (1940), repr., James Thurber, *The Thurber Carnival* (New York: The Modern Library, 1957), 249.

2. Jack Dean Kingsbury, "The Gospel of Mark in Current Research," *RelSRev* 5 (1979): 106.

3. Among the major contributions in literary strategies of that era, see David Rhoads, Joanna Dewey, and Donald Michie, *Mark as Story: An Introduction to the Narrative of a Gospel* (Minneapolis: Fortress, 2012); Jack Dean Kingsbury, *The Christology of Mark's Gospel* (Philadelphia: Fortress, 1983); Dan O. Via Jr., *The Ethics of Mark's Gospel—In the Middle of Time* (Philadelphia: Fortress, 1985); Elizabeth Struthers Malbon, *Narrative Space and Mythic Meaning in Mark* (San Francisco: Harper & Row, 1986). For rhetorical approaches, see B. H. M. G. M. Standaert, *L'Évangile selon Marc: Composition et genre littéraire* (Brugge: Sint Andreisabdij, 1978); Joanna Dewey, *Markan Public Debate: Literary Technique, Concentric Structure, and Theology in Mark 2.1–3.6*, SBLDS 48 (Chico, CA: Scholars, 1980). See the sociological approach of Vernon K. Robbins, *Jesus the Teacher: A Socio-rhetorical Interpretation of Mark* (Philadelphia: Fortress, 1984). As its subtitle suggests, Robbins's monograph blends social analysis with classical rhetoric. And for tradition-critical strategies, note especially Rainer Riesner, *Jesus als Lehrer: Eine Untersuchung zum Ursprung der Evangelien-Überlieferung*, WUNT 2/7 (Tübingen: Mohr Siebeck, 1981); Werner H. Kelber, *The Oral and the Written Gospel: The Hermeneutics of Speaking and Writing in the Synoptic Tradition, Mark, Paul, and Q* (Philadelphia: Fortress, 1983); J. Duncan M. Derrett, *The Making of Mark: The Scriptural Bases of the Earliest Gospel*, 2 vols. (Shipston-on-Stour: Drinkwater, 1985).

quarters, it continues to propel Markan scholarship,[4] despite manifold uncertainties surrounding its execution that have long been recognized by cautious investigators.[5] Given the considerable theoretical and practical problems entailed by the practice of Markan redaction criticism, especially when predicated on the assumption of Markan priority, one wonders why this exegetical approach has for so long held so many interpreters in thrall. This chapter addresses that question: first, by reviewing salient features in the conceptualization of Markan *Redaktionsgeschichte*; second, by revisiting the scholarly *Sitz im Leben* in which the method was germinated and nurtured; third, by identifying both the contributions and the liabilities of redaction-critical analysis, as an aid in one's ongoing reappraisal of appropriate methods of Markan study.

A Profile of the Redaction-Critical Method

To understand the past half-century of Markan exegesis, which has exerted influence on all who currently labor in the field, we might begin by recalling the

4. Noteworthy specimens include William R. Telford, *The Barren Temple and the Withered Tree: A Redaction-Critical Analysis of the Cursing of the Fig-Tree Pericope in Mark's Gospel and Its Relation to the Cleansing of the Temple Tradition*, JSNTSup 1 (Sheffield: JSOT Press, 1980); Ernest Best, *Following Jesus: Discipleship in the Gospel of Mark*, JSNTSup 4 (Sheffield: JSOT Press, 1981); Rolf Busemann, *Die Jüngergemeinde nach Markus 10: Eine redaktionsgeschichtliche Untersuchung des 10. Kapitels im Markusevangelium*, BBB 57 (Bonn: Hanstein, 1983). Though divergent in their presuppositions and practice of the method, most of the major commentaries on Mark of the past forty years have been avowedly redaction-critical in orientation: Rudolf Pesch, *Das Markusevangelium*, 2 vols., HTKNT 2 (Freiburg: Herder, 1976, 1977); Joachim Gnilka, *Das Evangelium nach Markus*, 2 vols., EKKNT 2/1-2 (Neukirchen-Vluyn: Neukirchener Verlag, 1978, 1979); Walter Schmithals, *Das Evangelium nach Markus*, OTKNT 2/1-2 (Gütersloh: Gerd Mohn; Würzburg: Echter, 1979); C. S. Mann, *Mark: A New Translation with Introduction and Commentary*, AB 27 (Garden City, NY: Doubleday, 1986); Joel Marcus, *Mark 1-8: A New Translation with Introduction and Commentary*, AB 27 (New York: Doubleday, 2000); Marcus, *Mark 8-16: A New Translation with Introduction and Commentary*, AB 27A (New Haven: Yale University Press, 2009); Adela Yarbro Collins, *Mark: A Commentary*, Hermeneia (Minneapolis: Fortress, 2007).

5. Acknowledgments of the difficulty in differentiating tradition from redaction in the Second Gospel are *de rigueur* among Markan redaction critics and are usually invoked by them in qualifying the certitude of their analyses. Two recent studies have responded to this hesitation in contrasting ways: in *Mark as Composer*, NGS 1 (Macon, GA: Mercer University, 1987), David B. Peabody has sought to refine the procedure by which putative redactional features in Mark might be identified; in my own study, *The Disciples according to Mark: Markan Redaction in Current Debate*, 2nd ed. (Grand Rapids: Eerdmans, 2012), 254-87, the methodological quandaries involved in the enterprise have been underscored and judged impossible to resolve.

fundamental concerns voiced by the first self-reflective redaction critics of the Second Gospel. Early on, and in contrast to the form-critical emphasis on the gospel traditions as products of early Christian communities, redaction critics of Mark emphasized its production by *an individual author*.[6] It is almost impossible to find a *redaktionsgeschichtlich* treatment of Mark and the other gospels, of either older or more recent vintage, that does not stress this understanding of their literary origins. Thus Willi Marxsen urged that Markan interpreters take into account "an author personality who pursues a definite goal with his work, . . . an 'individualistic' trait oriented to the particular interest and point of view of the evangelist concerned."[7] Repeatedly in the secondary literature, the claim was made that, with *Redaktionsgeschichte*, "We are dealing with individual authors, not with the 'community,'" "evangelists [who] are genuine authors," "authors in their own right," whose existence "must at all costs be stressed, even if the extent and delimitation of [each author's] sources, his share in shaping them, his name, his home, his fortunes could never be established with complete certainty."[8]

Why were redaction critics so insistent on locating the evangelist-author at the center of exegetical attention? In part, it reflected their common-sense judgment that only from the redactor's hands have we directly received the biblical literature; thus, Franz Rosenzweig once suggested that "R" (referring to the lowly esteemed redactor of the Hexateuch) should be interpreted as *rabbenu*, "our master."[9] In part, this accent on the author attempted to correct the exaggerated importance conferred by form critics on the *urchristliche Gemeinde* in the production of the gospels, a perspective that virtually excluded any contribution by the individual evangelists.[10] However, the principal reason

6. Most of the observations on redaction criticism presented in this section would apply not only to Mark but to the other gospels as well.

7. Willi Marxsen, *Mark the Evangelist: Studies on the Redaction History of the Gospel*, trans. James Boyce, Donald Juel, and William Poehlmann, with Roy A. Harrisville (Nashville: Abingdon, 1969), 18, 24. The first German edition of Marxsen's seminal volume appeared in 1956 (Göttingen: Vandenhoeck & Ruprecht).

8. Respectively, Robert H. Stein, "What Is *Redaktionsgeschichte*?," *JBL* 88 (1969): 49; Norman Perrin, "The Evangelist as Author: Reflections on Method in the Study and Interpretation of the Synoptic Gospels and Acts," *BR* 17 (1972): 9 (notice the very title of Perrin's article); Joachim Rohde, *Rediscovering the Teaching of the Evangelists*, trans. Dorothea M. Barton, NTL (Philadelphia: Westminster, 1968), 9 (cf. Norman Perrin, *What Is Redaction Criticism?* GBS [Philadelphia: Fortress, 1976], 33); Rohde, *Rediscovering the Teaching of the Evangelists*, 18.

9. Cited by Gerhard von Rad, *Genesis: A Commentary*, rev. ed., trans. John H. Marks, OTL (Philadelphia: Westminster, 1972), 42–43.

10. Thus, Marxsen, *pace* Martin Dibelius (*Mark the Evangelist*, 20): "Tradition is indeed

for this emphasis on the evangelist as author seems to have been its association with the idea of the evangelist as *religious thinker* and his gospel as the vehicle for *predominantly theological perspectives.* This connection between authorial and theological intention in the evangelist's work is expressly wrought by Ernest Best in an early redaction-critical volume: "All this means that we must treat Mark seriously as an author. He has his place in the canon, not because he gives certain historical facts about the life of Jesus, but because, in the same sense as Paul, he preaches Christ."[11]

Alongside regard for the evangelists as genuine authors, this perception of Mark and the other gospel writers as theologians might be considered the most significant redaction-critical concern. Certainly it was one of the most often voiced: "the evangelists were not merely *Sammler* but individual theologians,"[12] "their redactional work . . . undertaken to serve a theological conception and particular theological themes"[13] and reflecting "a distinctive, definable theological outlook as it seeks to relate the story of Jesus in its own manner."[14] The sort of religious coloration, applied to the narrative of Jesus, that had long been recognized in the Fourth Gospel was now acknowledged as pervasive in the Synoptics as well: "Each Evangelist was a theologian in his own right and possessed a theological purpose for writing his gospel."[15] From this point of view, redaction-critical exegesis was often depicted as a process of textual threshing, separating the wheat of an evangelist's theology from the chaff of his sources:

---

the primary factor which we encounter, but it is the tradition of the evangelists, that is, the tradition laid down in the Gospels. When we reconstruct their world (and that means the world of the evangelists) we approach the individual tradition. Can it then be our first task to proceed to an investigation of the material of the synoptic tradition, ignoring the evangelists? Is not our primary task twofold—that of arriving at redaction *and* tradition?"

11. Ernest Best, *The Temptation and the Passion: The Markan Soteriology*, SNTSMS 2 (Cambridge: Cambridge University Press, 1965), xi. Note also the subtitle of Ernst Haenchen's introductory section in *Der Weg Jesu: Eine Erklärung des Markus-Evangeliums und der kanonischen Parallelen* (Berlin: Alfred Töpelmann, 1966), 32–37: "Die Evangelisten als Schriftsteller und Theologen."

12. Stein, "What Is *Redaktionsgeschichte?*," 47.

13. Rohde, *Rediscovering the Teaching of the Evangelists,* 17. Cf. Eduard Schweizer, "Die theologische Leistung des Markus," *EvT* 4 (1964): 337–55; Schweizer, *The Good News according to Mark,* trans. Donald H. Madvig (Atlanta: John Knox, 1970), 380–86.

14. John H. Hayes and Carl R. Holladay, *Biblical Exegesis: A Beginner's Handbook* (Atlanta: John Knox, 1982), 99; cf. Haenchen, *Der Weg Jesu,* 24.

15. Robert H. Stein, "The Proper Methodology for Ascertaining a Markan Redaction History," *NovT* 13 (1971): 181; cf. Morna D. Hooker, *The Message of Mark* (London: Epworth, 1983), 20.

having ascertained the evangelist's redaction we seek to find: (1) What unique *theological views* does the evangelist present which are foreign to his sources? . . . (2) What unusual *theological emphasis or emphases* does the evangelist place upon the sources he received? . . . (3) What *theological purpose or purposes* does the evangelist have in writing his gospel?[16]

No less than the consideration of the gospels as individual rather than communal products, this focus on the theology of the evangelists was regarded as a departure from the form-critical approach.[17] If, according to *Formgeschichte*, the evangelist's role was understood as dusting off, refinishing, and rearranging the furniture of the Synoptic tradition, "from the redaction critical viewpoint, . . . each evangelist functioned as the architect of his conceptual house of gospel, for which he chose, refurbished, and in part constructed the fitting furniture."[18]

Beyond this slant on the synoptists as authors and theologians, redaction criticism ostensibly emphasized two other aspects of the gospels: one literary, the other sociological. The literary insight was expressed by different scholars in different ways. Some spoke of the significance of the gospel's narrative framework, overriding its constituent traditions;[19] others expressed a critical concern for larger units of tradition up to and including the entire gospel.[20] However they put it, redaction critics saw themselves as treating *the gospels as unitary textual artifacts, to be interpreted holistically*: "By contrast [to tradition and form criticism], redaction criticism emphasizes the wholeness of the Gospels, their literary integrity, and seeks to see not simply the individual parts, but what they were saying when arranged together as a single whole."[21]

Moreover, redaction critics claimed to contribute an important sociological insight: namely, an understanding of the gospels in light of *the evangelist's historical context and of the social setting of the communities for which they were writing*. Most scholars concurred with Marxsen's characterization of this

16. Stein, "*What Is Redaktionsgeschichte?*," 54; in the original, each of the numbered questions is italicized. Stein further indicates a fourth concern of the method, the *Sitz im Leben* out of which the gospel emerged. This we shall consider momentarily.

17. Thus, Rohde, *Rediscovering the Teaching of the Evangelists*, 16.

18. Werner H. Kelber, "Redaction Criticism: On the Nature and Exposition of the Gospels," *PRS* 6 (1979): 12.

19. Thus, Marxsen, *Mark the Evangelist*, 23; Rohde, *Rediscovering the Teaching of the Evangelists*, 14, 19.

20. So Perrin, *What Is Redaction Criticism?*, 34.

21. Hayes and Holladay, *Biblical Exegesis*, 99. Similarly, Haenchen, *Der Weg Jesu*, 23; Stephen S. Smalley, "Redaction Criticism," in *New Testament Interpretation: Essays on Principles and Methods*, ed. I. Howard Marshall (Exeter: Paternoster, 1977), 191–92.

component of *Redaktionsgeschichte* as *der dritte Sitz im Leben*: "If Joachim Jeremias [in his work on the parables] differentiates the 'first situation-in-life' located in the unique situation of Jesus' activity, from the 'second situation-in-life' mediated by the situation of the primitive church (which form criticism seeks to ascertain), we are dealing here with the '*third* situation-in-life.'"[22]

With allowance for minor modifications and varying shades of emphasis, these three ideas—the evangelist as author and theologian, his gospel as the immediate product of his and his community's "setting in life," and that gospel as a literary entity to be interpreted holistically—have been basic in the formulation of redaction criticism from its inception up to the present day. As such, redaction criticism was conceived to be not merely another instrument to be added to the toolbox of gospel exegesis but a comprehensive interpretive approach, equipped to address the theological, sociological, and literary issues raised by a text. Although comprehensive, the method did not intend, however, to award each of these concerns equal weight; for the center of gravity in redaction criticism, no less than in source and form criticism, remained with the author-theologian.[23] To be sure, practitioners of *Redaktionsgeschichte* believed that the method permitted them to intuit the particulars of the redactor's historical and sociological matrix and to interpret a gospel as a literary product; *but the point of entry, as well as the confirmation, for both of these investigations resided with the identification of the redactor's theology*. On this point, John Barton's comments regarding OT redaction criticism are no less accurate as a characterization of gospel *Redaktionsgeschichte*: "the original author in some sense is the place where the method comes to rest. Once we have found the meaning or intention of whoever first wrote the text, we have achieved our goal."[24]

REDACTION CRITICISM IN THE CONTEXT
OF TWENTIETH-CENTURY THEOLOGY AND SCHOLARSHIP

Inasmuch as redaction critics of the gospels have been absorbed in the delineation of the evangelists' social and historical setting, it seems not inappropriate

22. Marxsen, *Mark the Evangelist*, 23.

23. Thus D. Moody Smith: "The *basic* insight of redaction criticism was that *the evangelists were authors and theologians* painting their own portraits of Jesus and addressing themselves to important theological issues, albeit in the church of the first century" (*Interpreting the Gospels for Preaching* [Philadelphia: Fortress, 1980], 32, emphasis mine).

24. John Barton, *Reading the Old Testament: Method in Biblical Study* (Philadelphia: Westminster, 1984), 202. In context (201), Barton's comments apply to source and form criticism as well.

to inquire why redaction criticism itself has been pursued with such vigor, and what historical and cultural forces in this century have encouraged that pursuit. The following factors do not constitute a complete explanation; however, no explanation would be complete without mention of these.

First, initially at least, Markan redaction criticism was a somewhat late-blooming offshoot of the method's application to the other Synoptics. The impressive exegetical results of *Redaktionsgeschichte*, when applied by Günther Bornkamm and his students to Matthew,[25] and by Hans Conzelmann to Luke,[26] were noted by Markan investigators, and the conclusion was drawn by them, either openly or tacitly, that the method would yield equally impressive results when applied to the Second Gospel.[27] The popularity of redaction criticism was accelerated further by the freedom and rapidity with which Anglo-Saxon and Continental scholarship could be exchanged and translated in the period following World War II.

Second, to say that redaction criticism characterized the *Zeitgeist* of postwar Markan research as did no other interpretive tool is, while true, insufficient to explain why the method so thoroughly captured the imaginations of Synoptic scholars to start with. Surely one reason for the ascendance of *Redaktionsgeschichte* was its perceived continuity with previous exegetical methods. In the last section of his form-critical *magnum opus*, Bultmann himself had set the stage for this perception by suggesting that the composition of the gospels "involves nothing in principle new, but only completes what was begun in the oral tradition."[28] Redaction critics ever since have debated among themselves the degree of continuity between their discipline and form criticism;[29]

---

25. Günther Bornkamm, Gerhard Barth, and Heinz Joachim Held, *Tradition and Interpretation in Matthew*, trans. Percy Scott, NTL (Philadelphia: Westminster, 1963). The German original of the essays collected in this volume span the period from 1948 to 1957.

26. Hans Conzelmann, *The Theology of St. Luke*, trans. Geoffrey Buswell (New York: Harper & Row, 1961). The first German edition of this work, under the title *Die Mitte der Zeit*, was published in 1953 (Tübingen: Mohr).

27. For example, see Marxsen, *Mark the Evangelist*, 16 n. 3, 28 n. 38; Perrin, "Evangelist as Author," 9. Like most Markan redaction critics, Marxsen and Perrin assumed the priority of the Second Gospel; thus it was natural for the origination and preliminary development of Synoptic *Redaktionsgeschichte* to occur with gospels other than Mark.

28. Rudolf Bultmann, *The History of the Synoptic Tradition*, trans. John Marsh, rev. ed. (New York: Harper & Row, 1963), 321.

29. Contrast Ernest Best's postulation of the Second Evangelist's positive respect for, and conservative adaptation of, traditional material ("Mark's Preservation of the Tradition," in *L'Évangile selon Marc: Tradition et Rédaction*, ed. M. Sabbe, BETL 34 [Leuven: Leuven University Press, 1974], 21–34) with Kelber's argument for a radical disjunction between oral and literary transmission (*Oral and the Written Gospel*, passim).

nevertheless, that there was *some* conceptual consonance between them, that *Redaktionsgeschichte* at least grew out of and presupposed the existence of the preliterary, typical traditions analyzed by the form critics, has never been a serious subject of debate. Similarly, redaction-critical discussion of the evangelists' distinguishing literary traits and theological ideas was congenial with, and an extension of, the procedure adopted by such older source critics as Julius Wellhausen and Burnett Hillman Streeter.[30]

However fruitful or abortive the attempt may be judged, however valuable or valueless its pursuit be regarded, redaction criticism of Mark and the other gospels promised to throw more light on the oral and literary history of those texts by means of a method based on accepted principles of critical analysis.

Third, perhaps an even more significant reason for redaction criticism's hold upon Synoptic scholarship is this: the method has ostensibly offered biblical theologians and preachers constructive theological insights at a time when two important theological movements were disintegrating, much to the chagrin of many adherents of historical criticism. These were the old quest of the historical Jesus and the mid-twentieth century's "biblical theology movement."

The first of these trends was in its death throes in the early decades of the twentieth century. In a real sense, a proleptic exercise in *Redaktionsgeschichte* was directly responsible for its demise. In the last half of the nineteenth century, the "old quest" had been predicated largely on acceptance of "the Markan hypothesis": the theory that Mark not only was the earliest gospel and a source employed by Matthew and Luke but also was the closest chronologically to the original eyewitnesses of Jesus and could therefore be regarded as historically trustworthy for information about the life and ministry of Jesus.[31] Although this position still claims some proponents, its logic was sawn off at the root in the course of William Wrede's explosive and *redaktionsgeschichtlich*-clairvoyant presentation of the secrecy motif in the gospels: "It therefore remains true to say that as a whole the Gospel no longer offers a historical *view* of the real life of Jesus. Only pale residues of such a view have passed over into what is a suprahistorical view for faith. In this sense the Gospel of Mark belongs to the history of dogma."[32]

---

30. Julius Wellhausen, *Einleitung in die drei ersten Evangelien* (Berlin: Georg Reimer, 1905); B. H. Streeter, *The Four Gospels: A Study of Origins* (New York: Macmillan, 1925).

31. Though with varying modifications, this theory was most closely associated with C. G. Wilke (*Der Urevangelist: Oder, Exegetische kritische Untersuchung über das Verwandtschafts-verhältnis der drei ersten Evangelien* [Dresden: G. Fleischer, 1838]) and C. H. Weisse (*Die Evangelienfrage in ihrem gegenwärtigen Stadium* [Leipzig: Breitkopf & Härtel, 1856]).

32. William Wrede, *The Messianic Secret*, trans. J. C. G. Greig (Cambridge: James Clarke,

When, some fifty years later, Ernst Käsemann reopened "the problem of the historical Jesus" with the skeptical (and hyperbolic) observation that "the Gospels offer us primarily the primitive Christian kerygma, and . . . [historical] criticism can only help us to arrive at corrections and modifications in the kerygma but never at a word or action of the earthly Jesus himself,"[33] he was adding in substance nothing new to Wrede's depiction of a historical-critical blind alley, which, if anything, looked by now even blinder after form criticism.[34]

In the face of such increasing skepticism about history in the gospels and the possibility of conventional *Leben-Jesu-Forschung*, Markan redaction critics could and did assume one of two positions. On the one hand, many joined Marxsen in simply bracketing out the bothersome historical questions and devoting themselves exclusively to the discernment of the evangelist's theology: "With this [redaction-critical] approach, the question as to what really happened is excluded from the outset. . . . [That question] is of interest only to the degree it relates the situation of the primitive community in which the Gospels arose."[35] Marxsen was prepared to grant only minimal credence to the historicity of Mark's Gospel;[36] however, a secret of redaction criticism's success

---

1971), 131, also 115–45. Cf. the similar conclusions of R. H. Lightfoot, *History and Interpretation in the Gospels* (London: Hodder & Stoughton, 1935), 23–24.

33. Ernst Käsemann, *Essays on New Testament Themes*, trans. W. J. Montague, SBT 41 (London: SCM, 1964), 34–35; see also Ernst Käsemann, "Blind Alleys in the 'Jesus of History' Controversy," in *New Testament Questions of Today*, trans. W. J. Montague (Philadelphia: Fortress, 1969), 23–65.

34. Thus, e.g., Martin Dibelius: "The first understanding afforded by the standpoint of *Formgeschichte* is that there never was a 'purely' historical witness to Jesus" (*From Tradition to Gospel*, trans. Bertram Lee Woolf [New York: Scribner's Sons, 1965], 295). Of course, other form critics maintained a guardedly positive estimation of the historicity of the gospels' framework and contents: C. H. Dodd, "The Framework of the Gospel Narrative," *ExpTim* 43 (1932): 396–400; Joachim Jeremias, *The Parables of Jesus*, 2nd rev. ed., trans. S. H. Hooke (New York: Scribner's Sons, 1972). Taking an expressly American evangelical stand, the commentary by James A. Brooks (*Mark*, NAC 23 [Nashville: Broadman, 1991]) is ambivalent. In many cases, he speaks of Mark's phraseology and point of view as distinguishable from that of the protagonists in the narrative (thus, 53, 60, 115, 120, 128, 143, 179, 248, 252); with equal frequency, Brooks suggests that the gospel is transparent or at least translucent to the intentions of Jesus and the Twelve (39, 51, 55, 143–45, 159, 169, 178) and their *ipsissima verba* (63, 116, 142, 158). Occasionally Brooks infers from the gospel that the speech or purposes of Jesus and Mark converge without demonstrating how, on redaction-critical premises, such inferences could be verified (151, 158, 185, 200).

35. Marxsen, *Mark the Evangelist*, 23–24. Conzelmann, *Theology of St. Luke*, 9, expresses a similar statement of purpose.

36. See Marxsen's *Introduction to the New Testament: An Approach to Its Problems*, trans. Geoffrey Buswell (Philadelphia: Fortress, 1968), 120–45.

lay in the fact that one had not to agree with Marxsen's judgment in this matter in order to adopt the method and be repaid with positive exegetical results.

On the other hand, as *Redaktionsgeschichte* increasingly came to carry a certain scholarly cachet, it so fundamentally redefined what the gospels were that no longer was the riddance of historical questions merely possible or permissible; it was now considered virtually mandatory. As a growing number of scholars came to accept the dictum that "the gospels must be understood as *kerygma*, and not as biographies of Jesus of Nazareth,"[37] the appropriation of the gospels in a reprise of the old quest of the historical Jesus came to be regarded not so much as problematic but as illegitimate: "The fact is that the very project of redaction criticism methodologically precludes the quest for the historical Jesus. . . . The historical Jesus forms the basis and presupposition of theology. Interestingly, what the gospels give us is not the presupposition, but the theologies."[38]

Although more conservative exegetes found cold comfort in the notion that neither Mark nor any of the evangelists proclaimed the *historical* Jesus,[39] more liberal interpreters tended to regard this as a positive contribution of redaction criticism. It seemed to bridge the enormous temporal and hermeneutical gap between Mark as interpreter of the Jesus traditions and the twentieth-century theologian as interpreter of the Second Gospel by functionally locating both in the same position: that of elucidator not of Jesus of Nazareth but of the early Christian kerygma about Jesus. As Eduard Schweizer expressed it, "[Jesus] can only be proclaimed and witnessed to by a believer like Mark. . . . [Although] the historical Jesus is, in the highest possible degree, essential for the faith of the church[,] . . . this does not mean that we could see anything which would really help us in the historical Jesus, without the miracle of God's Spirit who, in the word of the witness [i.e., Mark], opens our blind eyes to the 'dimension' in which all these events took place."[40]

In short, redaction criticism responded to the problem of the historical Jesus either by ignoring it entirely or by regarding it as of only tangential exegetical or

37. Rohde, *Rediscovering the Teaching of the Evangelists*, 11. Of course, this view had been anticipated by Wrede and, in 1915, by Clyde Weber Votaw, *The Gospels and Contemporary Biographies in the Greco-Roman World*, FBBS (Philadelphia: Fortress, 1970), esp. 1–5.

38. Kelber, "Redaction Criticism," 13–14. See also David Blatherwick, "The Markan Silhouette?," *NTS* 17 (1970–1971): 184–92, esp. 192.

39. Naturally, some rejected such a formulation: thus T. W. Manson, *Studies in the Gospels and Epistles*, ed. Matthew Black (Philadelphia: Westminster, 1962), 40–83.

40. Eduard Schweizer, "Mark's Contribution to the Quest of the Historical Jesus," *NTS* 10 (1963–1964): 423, 431.

theological consequence, since, on particular *redaktionsgeschichtlich* premises, the evangelists themselves had responded to the matter in precisely the same way.

The waxing of redaction criticism during the middle of the twentieth century should be viewed also in the context of the waning of a second scholarly enterprise during the same period: the so-called "biblical theology movement."[41] In some respects, the *redaktionsgeschichtlich* approach was antagonistic to some of that movement's traits:[42] thus, given the nonchalance of the method toward matters historical, few proponents of "revelation in history" found a home among Markan redaction critics, even though some of the earliest *redaktionsgeschichtlich* efforts reckoned with the Second Evangelist's understanding of history.[43] And redaction criticism did nothing if not stimulate a heightened sensitivity to theological diversity among the gospels, contrary to the emphasis of biblical theology on the unity of the Bible.

On the other hand, so clearly in sympathy with other aspects of the biblical theology movement was *Redaktionsgeschichte* that it proved to be the movement's successor, in perspective if not in method. To those weary of the sort of biblical exegesis associated with liberal Protestant theology—dry historical analysis, complacent or indifferent to theological concerns—redaction criticism promised, and often delivered, robust interpretations of the evangelists' theologies,[44] based on established exegetical principles of source and form criticism yet readily appropriable by both theologians and pastors. Indeed, for the church and its ministry of preaching, a concern of vital importance for the biblical theology movement, redaction criticism was regarded as having immediate and positive implications: not only did it provide new exegetical content for preachers; it also offered them new paradigms for understanding the homiletical task. From Willi Marxsen's early, heuristic analogy between the evangelist, his gospel, and their *Sitz* with a modern preacher, sermon,

41. The growth and decline of this movement was chronicled by Brevard S. Childs, *Biblical Theology in Crisis* (Philadelphia: Westminster, 1967), 13–87.

42. For a concise summary and assessment of the characteristics of postwar biblical theology, consult James Barr, "Biblical Theology," *IDBSup*, 104–11.

43. James M. Robinson, *The Problem of History in Mark*, SBT 21 (London: SCM, 1957); T. Alec Burkill, *Mysterious Revelation: An Examination of the Philosophy of St. Mark's Gospel* (Ithaca, NY: Cornell University Press, 1963).

44. The very notion that the synoptists displayed such developed and distinctive theological understandings was revolutionary: by contrast, Rudolf Bultmann had used the Synoptics as the source only for "the message of Jesus" and "the kerygma of the earliest church" (*Theology of the New Testament*, vol. 1, trans. Kendrick Grobel [New York: Scribner's Sons, 1951], 3–62).

and congregation,[45] it was but a short step to Leander Keck's characterization of biblical preaching as that which not only "imparts [the Bible's] message-content, but . . . does so in a manner that repeats the Bible's own way of using normative tradition"—namely, "in response to particular occasions (usually crisis situations) in the life of communities of faith."[46]

To summarize, in the mid-twentieth century a number of forces conspired to promote the pursuit of Markan *Redaktionsgeschichte*. Especially significant were the apparent fruitfulness of the method when applied to the other Synoptics, its ostensible continuity with previous exegetical procedures, and its perceived theological fecundity during the decline of the biblical theology movement and the old quest of the historical Jesus.

The Contributions and Liabilities of Redaction Criticism

Contributions

In retrospect, the *redaktionsgeschichtlich* perspective on Mark and the other gospels has offered, and continues to offer, some genuinely positive contributions. First, as we have seen, redaction criticism was intended to be a comprehensive method, melding concerns for the author, his historical and sociological background, and the literary features displayed by his text. Whether the method was in fact successful in holding together these various interests, particularly by situating the author as its fulcrum, is a moot point, and one to be considered presently. For now, let this much be underscored: by incorporating the historical, traditional, literary, and theological concerns of its methodological predecessors, especially source and form criticism, *Redaktionsgeschichte virtually set the agenda for the full range of critical inquiry into the gospels* during the second half of the twentieth century. That amounts to no small contribution.

In the second place, *Redaktionsgeschichte* has drawn the attention of biblical scholars to *the evangelists as authors of literary products*. At first blush, such an observation may seem self-evident if not trivial. In fact, however, it is of

45. Marxsen, *Mark the Evangelist*, 24 n. 30.
46. Leander E. Keck, *The Bible in the Pulpit: The Renewal of Biblical Preaching* (Nashville: Abingdon, 1978), 115. Keck considers this to be a characteristically *redaktionsgeschichtlich* insight: "It is precisely at this point that especially redaction criticism becomes fruitful for preaching" (115).

utmost significance in light of redaction criticism's methodological precursors and successors. Prior to *Redaktionsgeschichte*, the primary critical tasks in the gospels' interpretation were the delineation of their literary sources (if any) and the discernment of their preliterary traditions: that is, source and form criticism. While these approaches were not repudiated with the onset of redaction criticism, the critical perspectives were realigned toward the evangelists as authors and their gospels as literary wholes. Of course, a shift in interpretive perspective does not necessarily entail a substantive shift in exegetical procedure or results: many advocates of "new criticism" in the twentieth century's middle decades and other literary-critical strategies retorted, with some justification, that redaction criticism remained every bit as "disintegrating" of the gospels, oblivious to their narrative wholeness, as were source and form criticism.[47] Nevertheless, without the countervailing stress of *Redaktionsgeschichte* on the synthesis of the gospels by evangelists who functioned as creative authors, the force of those literary critics' response might have been lost on us. Without the redaction-critical emphasis on authors and literary products, the movement toward current literary-critical approaches might not have been as expeditious.

Third, *Redaktionsgeschichte* has made a persuasive case for *the fundamentally theological character of Mark and of the other gospels*. To say that various themes are interwoven by the author of Mark in his gospel is, for the redaction critic, accurate but insufficient: these themes carry theological freight and communicate the evangelist's peculiar *Tendenzen*.

To speak of the evangelists' authorial intentions, and of the gospels as vehicles of their creators' religious beliefs, has come to be regarded in some quarters as reflective of engagement in exegetical pursuits that are passé at best and spurious at worst. (1) Some scholars, for instance, have adopted a position of critical agnosticism: in their view, the notion that the evangelists molded their source materials in accordance with kerygmatic convictions has been merely assumed, not demonstrated. As John Meagher has put it, "We simply do not know how [the gospels] were meant to be read."[48] Doubtless it is possible for redaction critics to exaggerate the extent to which an evangelist like Mark orchestrated his received tradition to the tune of his special

47. Among others, see Roland Mushat Frye, "Literary Criticism and Gospel Criticism," *ThTo* 36 (1979): 207–19; Augustine Stock, *Call to Discipleship: A Literary Study of Mark's Gospel*, GNS 1 (Wilmington, DE: Glazier, 1982), 12–15. Also see below, note 61.

48. John C. Meagher, *Clumsy Construction in Mark's Gospel: A Critique of Form- and Redaktionsgeschichte* (New York: Mellen, 1979), 20.

concerns; on the other hand, the communication of a distinctive, theological point of view is by no means an improbable assessment of a significant aspect of Mark's intentions (see 1:1; 15:39).[49] Moreover, to discredit from the start the possibility of the evangelists' theological interests is in itself a critical over-statement. (2) Among interpreters influenced by "new criticism," the recovery of authorial intent, even if possible, is irrelevant if not critically fallacious. For them, the meaning of a text resides in the sense or senses that the words bear or might come to bear, altogether apart from the intention of the author in penning those words. However, it is one thing to suggest, as did William Wimsatt and Monroe Beardsley, "that the design or intention of the author is neither available nor desirable as a standard for judging the *success* of a work of literary art";[50] it is quite another thing, and rather doctrinaire, to argue that the meaning intended by an author like Mark evaporated once the ink was dry, or that such meaning is unworthy of critical pursuit, or that a text is only some free-floating sequence of words whose meaning has nothing what-ever to do with the author who wrote them.[51] (3) Other scholars insist that Mark's Gospel, like any work of literary art, cannot and should not be mined for the historical data to which it purportedly refers or for such theological insights as are stressed by redaction critics; the meaning of Mark is utterly nonreferential and resides entirely in its own narrative shape.[52] Admittedly, the narrative form of Mark should be respected, not manipulated facilely as a convenient repository for historical or theological data. Still, when Luke prefaces his narrative with the express intention that Theophilus "may know the truth concerning the things of which [he has] been informed" (1:4), and when John concludes his narrative with the hope "that you may believe that Jesus is the Christ, the Son of God, and that believing you may have life in his name" (20:31), is not the reader of these works justified in moving beyond the

---

49. If Meagher is correct (*Clumsy Construction*, 22) that Mark's readers were just curi-ous about Jesus, such inquisitiveness likely betokened a theological judgment among that readership that Jesus was an especially apt object of curiosity.

50. William K. Wimsatt Jr. and Monroe C. Beardsley, "The Intentional Fallacy," *SR* 54 (1946): 468.

51. For a now classic defense of authorial intention in texts, see E. D. Hirsch Jr., *Validity in Interpretation* (New Haven: Yale University Press, 1967).

52. Thus Frank Kermode, *The Genesis of Secrecy: On the Interpretation of Narrative* (Cambridge: Harvard University Press, 1979), 116–23. Similar arguments are presented by M. Weiss, "Die Methode der 'Total-Interpretation,'" in *Congress Volume Uppsala 1971*, ed. P. A. H. de Boer, VTSup 22 (Leiden: Brill, 1972), 88–112, and Hans W. Frei, *The Eclipse of Biblical Narrative: A Study in Eighteenth and Nineteenth Century Hermeneutics* (New Haven: Yale University Press, 1974), 267–324.

acknowledged character of the gospels as works of narrative art,[53] following their authors' lead in pursuing legitimately ostensive theological issues?[54]

Notwithstanding such criticisms of their validity, three contributions of *Redaktionsgeschichte* as applied to Mark and to the other gospels seem secure: its emphasis on the evangelists as creative authors in their own right; its recognition of the fundamentally theological character of their intentions; its multiple concerns for the gospels' history, tradition, theology, and literary character. To affirm these assets of *Redaktionsgeschichte* is not to deny the many procedural quandaries that have plagued Markan redaction criticism (or, for that matter, *Redaktionsgeschichte* when applied to the other gospels). At this point, I am not speaking strictly of method or procedure as such. Redaction criticism has always been more than merely a step-by-step recipe for interpreting texts; often its practitioners have not even bothered to articulate such "steps."[55] At heart, the term "redaction criticism" has described a particular way of viewing biblical texts, the salient aspects of which were outlined in this chapter's first part. An interpretive approach to the Bible, or to any literature, can present a valid or at least defensible *point of view* on textual interpretation, apart from the success or validity of a specific *method* of interpretation that it may propose. For all of its problems, to which we now must turn, Markan redaction criticism has brought to bear on the text some salient perspectives: the importance of the author and his intention, the gospel as expressive of theological interests, and the need for an exegetical approach incorporating concerns historical, religious, and literary. These hermeneutical *Tendenzen* may prove to be the enduring contribution of redaction criticism of Mark and the other gospels.

Liabilities

On the other hand, the *redaktionsgeschichtlich* approach is not without its drawbacks. In most cases, they are the obverse, more accurately the overextension, of the very assets we have just observed.

---

53. The same should apply, mutatis mutandis, to Matthew and Mark.

54. Historically, Christian readers have believed that they were so justified: thus Papias (ca. 130) asserts, "I did not rejoice in the loquacious, but in those who teach the truth, nor in them who recount others' dicta, but in those who repeated commandments given to the faith by the Lord and derived from truth itself" (Eusebius, *Hist. eccl.* 3.39.3 AT). Note also Irenaeus's well-known comments on Mark's preservation of the preaching of Peter (Eusebius, *Hist. eccl.* 5.8.3). Throughout the history of biblical exegesis, it was assumed that the gospels are intended to call attention to what they are *about*.

55. Stein's "Proper Methodology for Ascertaining a Markan Redaction History" (see above, n. 15) is a conspicuous exception to this general neglect of *redaktionsgeschichtlich* procedure.

For starters, it is one thing to accent the evangelists' authorial intention; it is something else to situate this concern at the center of one's interpretive procedure. As I have suggested, Markan redaction critics were justified in doing the former. The latter, however, has created nothing but headaches for the method's practitioners.

First, by placing the author and his intention(s) at the methodological center, redaction criticism of Mark, predicated on Mark's chronological priority among the Synoptics, has sought answers to exegetical questions that are, by definition, unverifiable.[56] Select, at random, any redaction-critical study of Mark, or any critical exercise in the refinement of that method's application to the Second Gospel, and notice the pattern that emerges: in order to discern the earliest evangelist's redactional (= authorial) activity, every investigator is compelled to engage in often highly speculative conjectures about the history of traditions *behind* the evangelist, assumptions unamenable to empirical analysis yet invariably determinative of that researcher's exegetical or methodological results. Typically, those conclusions scatter in all directions and are impossible to validate, for they are primarily a function of their proponents' divergent perspectival starting points, and only minimally the result of a controlled method of interpretation.[57] In short, by locating the author at the center of critical attention, Markan redaction criticism has raised fundamental questions that it cannot answer, at least with any reasonable degree of confidence.

Second, another problem flows directly from the preceding: by concentrating on the author, Markan redaction criticism (again presupposing Markan priority) has been forced to appeal to interpretive clues lying beyond the boundaries of the gospel itself.[58] The paradox of Markan redaction criticism is that it must traffic in evidence that is not redactional: the key to the enterprise lies in the fragile reconstruction of the shape, development, and utilization of pre-Markan (nontextual) tradition. Since the method demands speculation about hypothetical sources, the *Geschichte* of whose *Redaktion* can be plotted, its practitioners are compelled to devise traditio-historical scenarios of greater or lesser plausibility, extrinsic to the actual content of the gospel. Periodically, Markan scholars balk at such a dubious procedure and decide to treat the gos-

56. The same could be said of the redaction criticism of Matthew, presupposing the Griesbach hypothesis, and of John, on the assumption of its independence from the Synoptics.

57. See Black, *Disciples according to Mark*, 178–203, and my comments on the quest for a pre-Markan passion narrative in chapter 15 of the present volume.

58. More narrowly in connection with Markan Christology, this point was made by Jack Dean Kingsbury, "The 'Divine Man' as the Key to Mark's Christology—The End of an Era?," *Int* 35 (1981): 243–57.

pel as a whole, taking it for what it says and refusing to quarry for pre-Markan strata; then, however, they are no longer practicing redaction criticism as it has been customarily defined—nor do they need to do so.

Third, at least intuitively, many Markan redaction critics seem aware that their interpretations cannot ultimately be made to turn upon the author and his editorial activity. It is for this reason, I believe, that the focus of so many *redaktionsgeschichtlich* studies of the Second Gospel is not so much on precise redactional discriminations as on particular *themes* that are evident in the text: the mystery of the kingdom of God, the disciples' incomprehension, the suffering Son of Man, and so forth. Of course, many exegetes have regarded the specification of such themes as an inherently redaction-critical operation;[59] that, however, is a point of methodological confusion. Although the identification of the gospel's themes could be incorporated into a larger redaction-critical paradigm, *such a determination is not an intrinsically redaction-critical criterion but a literary-critical assessment.*

It is equally misleading, I suspect, to follow the redaction-critical path of identifying Mark's thematic concerns as strictly theological in character. Doubtless many motifs in Mark *do* connote special theological interests of the author; yet such themes may also, or in some cases primarily, reflect the historical or social circumstances in Mark's environment or community, or may resonate at a deeper psychological level with the readers of that gospel.[60] Furthermore, any one or a combination of these referents (the historical, social, religious, or psychological) may be addressed not only by themes but also by other literary devices (such as plot, settings, and characters, if one proceeds as a formalist literary critic). In any case, themes and other such literary characteristics rightly belong in the center of an interpretation of Mark in a way that "theology" or "theological themes" do not, if for no reason other than that the form of the Second Gospel is not that of a self-consciously theological treatise. Mark is, first of all, a *narrative*. At least on initial approach, it should be treated as such. Even so, the temptation to smuggle one's own biases into complex narratives is not easily resisted.

59. To select one example among many, Eduard Schweizer argued that the methodological starting point for distinguishing tradition and redaction in Mark should be the delineation of such themes as *Wundercharakter*, teaching, and the suffering Son of Man ("Anmerkungen zur Theologie des Markus," *Neotestamentica et Patristica: Freundesgabe O. Cullmann*, NovTSup 6 [Leiden: Brill, 1962], 35–46).

60. For an insightful discussion of the subtle interconnections that may exist between an author and his readers in the realm of emotions, values, and beliefs, consult Wayne C. Booth, *The Rhetoric of Fiction*, 2nd ed. (Chicago: University of Chicago Press, 1983), 89–147.

A fourth major liability of the redaction-critical approach has been its tendency toward "methodological imperialism": by attempting to answer questions not only of theology and *Traditionsgeschichte* but of literary composition and sociohistorical setting as well, redaction criticism has taken on more issues than its critical apparatus was designed to handle. Even more pointedly, one may argue that the very procedure of *Redaktionsgeschichte* operates at cross-purposes with that method's intention to treat the gospels as literary wholes. "Literary criticism seeks to apprehend a text as a whole or as a totality. From Marxsen up to the most recent times, however, redaction critics . . . have split Mark into tradition (sources) and redaction and have sought to establish chronological-genetic-causal relations between these two strata. As provocative and interesting as these studies often are for historical purposes, the text as a whole, as a narrative, in the form in which it confronts the reader and needs explication, is lost sight of."[61]

Nor has redaction criticism adequately fulfilled its promise to illuminate the historical and sociological *Sitz im Leben* of Mark's Gospel. Thus, while reaping the fruits of *Redaktionsgeschichte* in his own study of the Second Gospel, Howard Clark Kee urges the adoption of more sophisticated tools of social analysis, since "much of what passes for historical writing about the New Testament is docetic. It fails to take account of the full range of social and cultural factors that shaped the Christian communities and their ideas, their understanding of themselves, and their place in the universe."[62] Overall, redaction criticism has set forth many of the different kinds of critical questions that can reasonably be posed of the gospels. It is doubtful, however, that *Redaktionsgeschichte*, or any methodological approach, is conceptually or practically equipped to answer all of those questions. Other modes of analysis come into play; other questions are worth asking.

---

61. Dan O. Via Jr., *Kerygma and Comedy in the New Testament: A Structuralist Approach to Hermeneutic* (Philadelphia: Fortress, 1975), 72–73. Note the similar criticisms of Thomas E. Boomershine, "Mark the Storyteller: A Rhetorical-Critical Investigation of Mark's Passion and Resurrection Narrative" (PhD diss., Union Theological Seminary [New York City], 1974), 23, 25, 31, 334–38, and Norman Perrin, "The Interpretation of the Gospel of Mark," *Int* 30 (1976): 120.

62. Howard Clark Kee, *Community of the New Age: Studies in Mark's Gospel* (Philadelphia: Westminster, 1977), ix. Likewise, Leander E. Keck, "On the Ethos of Early Christians," *JAAR* 42 (1974): 435–42, upholds the corrective value of an etiological approach to the study of Christian origins.

CONCLUSION

Markan redaction criticism is neither a sacred cow nor a white elephant.[63] Born of the marriage of the twentieth century's scholarly occupations and religious preoccupations, the *redaktionsgeschichtlich* point of view has schooled us in the appreciation of the Second Evangelist's literary creativity, the theological cast of his gospel, and the need for critical breadth in the interpretation of Mark and the other gospels. Corresponding to these contributions have been certain liabilities of the redaction-critical perspective: its misplacement of the author at the center of textual interpretation, occasioning tendentious and unverifiable exegeses; its overemphasis on the strictly theological quality of the Markan narrative; and its incompetence to answer all of the critical questions that it has raised. The way forward in Markan research lies in the exploration and interrelation of the historical, social, theological, and literary contexts to which *Redaktionsgeschichte* has directed us, and in the clarification and refinement of the critical disciplines germane to those interpretive contexts. In pondering appropriate strategies in the study of Mark, we need not only to move beyond redaction criticism but also to move forward in a manner respectful of the lessons it has taught us.[64]

63. The double metaphor is borrowed from Victor Paul Furnish, *The Moral Teaching of Paul: Selected Issues*, rev. 2nd ed. (Nashville: Abingdon, 1985), 11–28.

64. For a general assessment of the method's application to the canonical gospels overall, see C. Clifton Black, "Redaction Criticism," in *Encyclopedia of the Historical Jesus*, ed. Craig A. Evans (New York: Routledge; London: Taylor & Francis, 2008), 491–95; Black, "Redaction Criticism, New Testament," *OEBI* 2:240–51.

CHAPTER 4

Thirty Years On:
Mark's Disciples and Markan Redaction

> A person who publishes a book willfully appears before the populace with his pants down. . . . If it is a good book nothing can hurt him. If it is a bad book nothing can help him.
>
> —Edna St. Vincent Millay[1]

THE IRREPRESSIBLE MISS MILLAY was on the money. So, too, was the author of 2 Pet 2:22, whose motto I resist out of gratitude to William B. Eerdmans for publishing a second edition of *The Disciples according to Mark*.[2] This was my first scholarly monograph: originally published in 1989, its *Vorleben* was a doctoral dissertation approved in 1986.[3] Though nothing created at age thirty-one qualifies as juvenilia, neither is it a mature work. It is a novice's offering on the guild's altar, whose aroma drifted south of heaven.

My aim in this chapter is fourfold. First, I wish to explain this book's motivation and its academic lineage, insofar as I am conscious of it. Second, full disclosure necessitates a report of how competent critics received the book upon its original publication. Third, the reader is entitled to know how its

---

1. "To Mrs. Cora B. Millay" (25 May 1927), in *The Letters of Edna St. Vincent Millay*, ed. A. R. Macdougall (New York: Harper & Brothers, 1952), 220. Between these two sentences: "Kathleen is about to publish a book."

2. *The Disciples according to Mark: Markan Redaction in Current Debate*, 2nd ed. (Grand Rapids: Eerdmans, 2012). The first edition was published as JSNTSup 27 (Sheffield: JSOT Press, 1989).

3. "An Evaluation of the Investigative Method and Exegetical Results of Redaction Criticism of the Gospel of Mark: The Role of the Disciples as a Test-Case in Current Research" (Ann Arbor: University Microfilms International [DA8624368], 1986). Immediately before its publication, I was startled to learn that the work had been dubbed *The Disciples according to Mark*: a punchier name that I knew would mislead a reader of the book's contents. Even so, I would never have insisted on the dissertation's title, which would choke a giraffe.

twinned topics—the disciples in Mark and the place of redaction criticism in that gospel's exegesis—fare in academic conversation in 2022, at least in my estimation. Finally, I shall offer some reflections on how my mind has changed, or remained the same, three decades later.

Huntsman, What Query?

> *You always need a springboard.* The Rules of the Game *[1939] . . . arose out of my desire to return to the classical spirit, to leave behind* La Bête humaine *and naturalism and even Flaubert—a desire to return to Marivaux, Beaumarchais, and Molière. It's very ambitious, but I'd like to point out, my dear friends, "When choosing masters, it's best to choose a plump one." It doesn't mean you're comparing yourself to them. It simply means you're trying to learn something from them.*
>
> —Jean Renoir[4]

My earliest seminar in Mark's Gospel was at Duke University forty years ago. Using that opportunity to devour Markan scholarship, its many offhand references to "Mark's redactional technique" confounded me. I had no quarrel with redaction criticism as such. I still do not.[5] Mine was the child's simple question: How do we know? If Mark's Gospel was the earliest written, how can one differentiate what the evangelist wrote from what he borrowed, then edited? The casual confidence, the certainty of received opinion, was the itch that aggravated me. Writing my dissertation was a thirty-month scratch.

With that simple query clutched in my sweaty fist, my biggest problems were those every graduate student must confront. (1) How do you answer it? (2) On what material do you concentrate? Robert Stein's ThD dissertation, "The Proper Method for Ascertaining a Marcan *Redaktionsgeschichte*" (Princeton Theological Seminary, 1968), was my lifeline: its condensation into several articles, published in reputable venues, provided a way into my question.[6] The harder problem was limiting its scope. The project was conceived

---

4. Jean Renoir, introduction to *La Règle du jeu*, for *The Rules of the Game*, directed by Jean Renoir (New York: Criterion Collection, 2004), disc 1.

5. Thus, my later reflections in "Lightfoot, Robert Henry (1883–1953)," *DBI* 2:77–78; "Redaction Criticism," in *Encyclopedia of the Historical Jesus*, ed. Craig A. Evans (New York: Routledge; London: Taylor & Francis, 2008), 491–95; "Redaction Criticism, New Testament," *OEBI* 2:240–51.

6. "What Is *Redaktionsgeschichte*?," *JBL* 88 (1969): 45–56; "The 'Redaktionsgeschichtlich'

as an examination not of Mark but of Markan *scholarship*. By the 1960s, virtually every theological commentary or monograph on the Second Gospel was redaction-critical, and I did not relish the prospect of dissertating into middle age. Comparing different studies of a common topic seemed more manageable and more interesting than haphazard plowing through whole commentaries. By then, Markan Christology had been flogged nearly to death; moreover, from that topic sprang so many tangled offshoots (Messiah, Son of God, Son of Man) that controlling all the variables promised migraines. Mark's presentation of the disciples, especially the Twelve, seemed more feasible and almost as important. In the early 1980s, Theodore Weeden's volume was still churning the waters,[7] and Ernest Best's studies had lately been synthesized.[8] Needing a third interlocutor, ideally one veering starboard of either Best or Weeden, I contemplated Rudolf Pesch's two-volume commentary on Mark.[9] I decided against Pesch for several reasons. Frankly, I feared that my German was not equal to the challenge. Even had it been adequate, my analysis had to test like with like. I knew that a dissertation placing a method under the microscope would lay itself open to keen scrutiny of its own procedure. Placing a thousand-page commentary alongside trim monographs invited comparison of a cornucopia with kumquats. A practical compromise was Robert P. Meye's well-executed *Jesus and the Twelve: Discipleship and Revelation in Mark's Gospel*.[10] With that decided, off I went.

As a model for the kind of study I was attempting, Albert Schweitzer's *Quest of the Historical Jesus* lurked in my subconscious.[11] Mind you, green hubris hadn't made away with common sense. Schweitzer's is immeasurably the more ambitious project, executed with brilliance and decisive results of durable impact. What fascinated me about that survey, which I first read as an

---

Investigation of a Markan Seam (Mc 1.21f.)," *ZNW* 61 (1970): 70–94; "The Proper Methodology for Ascertaining a Markan Redaction History," *NovT* 13 (1971): 181–98.

7. *Mark: Traditions in Conflict* (Philadelphia: Fortress, 1971).

8. *Following Jesus: Discipleship in the Gospel of Mark*, JSNTSup 4 (Sheffield: JSOT Press, 1981); *Disciples and Discipleship: Studies in the Gospel according to Mark* (Edinburgh: T&T Clark, 1986).

9. *Das Markusevangelium*, 2 vols., HTKNT 2 (Freiburg: Herder, 1976, 1977). Pesch's earlier monograph, *Naherwartungen: Tradition und Redaktion in Mk 13*, KBANT (Düsseldorf: Patmos, 1968), was preoccupied more by the gospel's eschatology than by discipleship.

10. Grand Rapids: Eerdmans, 1968.

11. First complete English edition, based on the first (1906), second (1913), and sixth (1950) German editions, ed. John Bowden (London: SCM; Minneapolis: Fortress, 2000). I am dumbfounded to discover no reference to Schweitzer in *Disciples according to Mark*. *Sic transit intentus auctoriti.*

undergraduate, was its probing of the questions beneath the quest: how a way of reading the gospels became reflective of scholars' unexamined assumptions and thereby conventionalized. Tightly compressed, the first two chapters of *Disciples according to Mark* sketch outlines of "the quest of Mark the redactor";[12] my discussions of Meye, Best, and Weeden occupy the strategic positions that Hermann Samuel Reimarus, David Friedrich Strauss, and William Wrede did for Schweitzer's argument.[13] Beyond the prickly burden of a mantle fit only for genius, adopting Schweitzer as my "plump master" entailed costly risks. I could not countenance his imperious tone: those Olympian aperçus, which still make his book such a zesty read, had no business trailing from my pen.[14] (Yes, I drafted my dissertation by hand.) More to the point, Schweitzer's *Quest of the Historical Jesus* is carefully structured to demonstrate that all genuine progress toward a proper conception of its subject inexorably advanced toward his own conclusions. When I began formulating my modest offering, I was unsure where it was headed. By the time that direction was certain, I found myself locked into an argument of my own framing. I reached a point of no return and was virtually compelled by my reading of selected evidence to reckon Markan redaction criticism a failure. To admit otherwise, even had I believed otherwise, would have scuttled my thesis. The burden of devising a foolproof argument vexed me. It still does. Accepting the foolproof will prove you a fool. Unlike Schweitzer, I had no breathtaking pronouncement on which to end my study. That bothered me less than the danger of being trapped inside my own argument. The ironic failure of Schweitzer's *magnum opus* is that he, no less than all his skewered precursors, ultimately discovered a Jesus to his own taste.[15] I now recognize that the deduction drawn at the end of *Disciples according to Mark*'s sixth chapter is similar to Schweitzer's, albeit applied to the

12. This was the title I gave to a revision of *Disciples according to Mark*'s chapter 8 as a freestanding teaser in *JSNT* 10 (1988): 19–39, republished as chapter 3 of the present volume. Professor David Hill of the University of Sheffield was instrumental in Sheffield Academic's acceptance of both that article and my monograph. For his benevolence I remain grateful.

13. Schweitzer, *Quest of the Historical Jesus*, 14–26, 65–109, 296–314.

14. "Hence the fiendish joy with which [Bruno] Bauer snatches away the crutches of this pseudo-science, hurls them to a distance, and makes merry over its helplessness" (*Quest of the Historical Jesus*, 136); "In the end [Wilhelm] Weiffenbach's critical principle proves to be merely a bludgeon with which he goes seal-hunting and clubs the defenceless Synoptic sayings right and left" (196–97). Had I accused Weeden of wresting crutches from the halt or envisioned Best's bludgeoning of baby seals, my *Doktorvater* would have slain such metaphors *tout de suite*.

15. "Thus each successive epoch of theology found its own thoughts in Jesus; that was, indeed, the only way in which it could make him live" (*Quest of the Historical Jesus*, 6).

Second Evangelist: "In the end, the *redaktionsgeschichtlich* analysis of Markan discipleship appears to function less as a critical control . . . [and] more as a conduit, along which the investigator's assumptions can flow, without check or impediment."[16] Unlike Schweitzer, however, I did not finish my book by proposing a better way (in my case, of practicing an interpretive method found unsuited for Mark). I had little idea what to put in its place. With a magisterial flourish, Schweitzer concluded, "He comes to us as one unknown."[17] Whimpering, my argument quit without quite knowing where it had come out. More on this presently.

Since *Disciples according to Mark*'s original publication, I've wondered whether there may have been another, more attenuated influence on it: the dissertation written two decades previously by my director. Substantively, *The Composition and Order of the Fourth Gospel* has nothing to do with Mark or its redaction criticism. Formally, however, both concentrate on a gospel's redaction-critical treatment, rather than on particulars of its exegesis. In his monograph,[18] D. Moody Smith articulates the complicated literary theory on which Rudolf Bultmann's Johannine commentary was predicated: a project, never undertaken by Bultmann, which nevertheless guided his interpretation of that gospel.[19] Based on Bultmann's suggestions, Smith reconstructs in continuous Greek texts the conjectural "revelation discourses" (*Offenbarungsreden*), a signs source, John's passion source, and other traditions. Smith also constructs what Bultmann conjectured had been the evangelist's original text of the Fourth Gospel, which was damaged before its reconstitution by an "ecclesiastical redactor."[20] Smith himself does not evaluate Bultmann's method of identifying and separating sources, though he compiles the critiques of other scholars who had.[21] Without aiming to refute Bultmann's hypothesis, Smith identifies some of its weaknesses: its minimization of John's stylistic uniformity, the plausibility of recovering subterranean sources with such pre-

16. *Disciples according to Mark*, 203.

17. *Quest of the Historical Jesus*, 487.

18. *The Composition and Order of the Fourth Gospel: Bultmann's Literary Theory*, YPR 10 (New Haven: Yale University Press, 1965; repr., with a foreword by R. Alan Culpepper, JMS, Eugene, OR: Wipf & Stock, 2015).

19. *Das Evangelium des Johannes erklärt, mit Ergänzungsheft*, 2 vols., KEKNT 2, 11th ed. (Göttingen: Vandenhoeck & Ruprecht, 1950).

20. *Composition and Order*, 15–56, 179–212.

21. Namely, Joachim Jeremias, Martin Dibelius, Burton Scott Easton, Philippe-Henri Menoud, Ernst Käsemann, Eugen Ruckstuhl, Eduard Schweizer, Bent Noack, Heinz Becker, and Paul Niewalda (*Composition and Order*, 57–117).

cision, and the possibility of restoring the original order of a gospel as seriously disturbed as Bultmann believed it to have been.[22] While sympathetic to Bultmann's intention, Smith reasonably asks which text the exegete is responsible for interpreting: a scholarly reconstruction or the canonical product?[23] With hindsight, it appears that many of the issues Smith raises of John in the hands of its most celebrated redaction critic—style as a slippery redactional indicator, deducing an evangelist's theology by separating redaction from tradition, the practical impossibility of verifying elaborate hypotheses—resurfaced in my deliberation over Markan *Redaktionsgeschichte*. Not once, however, do I recall mention of Smith's *Composition and Order* in the same breath—or until now the same sentence—as *Disciples according to Mark*.

THE BEST WAS YET TO COME

> *This is not a novel to be tossed aside lightly. It should be thrown with great force.*
> —Dorothy Parker[24]

It is a sadly ludicrous truism that doctoral dissertations in the humanities are written for an audience of one (the student's director), at most three to five (a committee). If the dissertation be approved, never again should an author with scholarly aspirations write so much for so few. Should Fortune smile and one's dissertation be accepted for publication, the potential readership is enlarged, though the royalties thereafter are dismal reminders that a cupboard of regular dimensions would accommodate that audience. *Disciples according to Mark* was reviewed far beyond my expectation (that it would vanish without a trace). As far as I know, the book was critiqued in seventeen journals: mostly American or British, though some French and German. I marveled at reviews in Italian and Finnish; I would have fainted dead away had I been able to read them. Compensating for my linguistic deficiencies, I solicited the

---

22. *Composition and Order*, 238–49.

23. Smith's most devastating assessment of Bultmann's procedure is quintessentially understated: "*Das Evangelium des Johannes* is actually a commentary, not upon the canonical Gospel of John, but upon a hypothetical original document which Bultmann constructed out of the materials provided by the traditional book" (*Composition and Order*, 244). In fairness to Bultmann, Smith, and the scholars whose work *Disciples according to Mark* considers, I should note that Mark's Gospel does not exhibit the Fourth's literary aporiae and seeming disarray, which prompted Bultmann's conjectures.

24. *The Algonquin Wits*, ed. Robert E. Drennan (Kensington: Citadel, 1985), 116.

kind offices of native speakers of those tongues to understand what was being said of my work.[25]

What did the book's first critics make of it? General patterns are traceable. Some found its analysis "well-written and provocative" (Muddiman), "trenchant . . . [and] sobering" (Yarbro Collins), "thoroughly researched and eminently readable . . . a model of careful scholarship" (Donahue), a "sustained, penetrating critique . . . accomplished with a measured evenhandedness" (Green), "judicious and systematic" as well as "accurate" (Fowl), clear, orderly, and rigorous with good sense ("con chiarezza, ordine, rigore e buon senso" [Fusco]). One reviewer upheld the book's caution that all methods stand in service of the biblical text—"et non le contraire" (Cuvillier). "It is always fun to attack an established dogma," particularly when the assault jibes with a reviewer's own suspicions (Hooker).[26] One reviewer noted the book's "measure of skepticism about history of traditions work on [Mark]" (Morgan); others regarded its evaluation of *Redaktionsgeschichte* as too severe (Fusco; Taeger; Räisänen). "At the end of the day, Black is probably too negative" (Hooker). The most lavish praise: *Disciples according to Mark* was "a brilliant and necessary critique . . . [so] fine and thought-provoking [that] it should be self-critically pondered by all New Testament scholars. . . . It shows the potential of studying the history of research in order to redraw the contours of biblical criticism" (Morgan). Dear me. That, surely, was the reviewer's estimate of another book, which by editorial snafu got attached to the title of mine. In any event, redrawing the contours of biblical criticism was the farthest thing from my mind. I was trying to complete a degree and, subsequently, find a job.

Mission accomplished? Not a chance. In biblical studies, no mission is ever accomplished for good and all, and *Disciples according to Mark*'s reviewers were quick to blast its shortcomings. Though one scholar reckoned my coverage of

---

25. Ernest Best, *JTS* 41 (1990): 602–7; Edwin K. Broadhead, *PRSt* 17 (1990): 83–84; Adela Yarbro Collins, *CRBR* 4 (1991): 169–71; Étienne Cuvillier, *ETR* 65 (1990): 272–73; John R. Donahue, *PSTJ* 42 (1989): 11–12; Stephen Fowl, *JSNT* 13 (1990): 116; Vittorio Fusco, *Bib* 72 (1991): 123–27; Joel B. Green, *CBQ* 53 (1991): 314–15; William R. Herzog II, *TS* 51 (1990): 513–15; Morna D. Hooker, *EpRev* 18 (1991): 86–87; J. Estill Jones, *RevExp* 87 (1990): 129; Elizabeth Struthers Malbon, *Int* 45 (1991): 82, 84; Robert Morgan, *Theological Book Review* 1 (1989): 12; John B. Muddiman, *ExpTim* (under the title, "The End of Markan Redaction Criticism?") 101 (1990): 307–9; Heikki Räisänen, *TeolT* 96 (1991): 80–81; J.-M. Rousée, *RB* 96 (1989): 474–75; Jens-Wilhelm Taeger, *TLZ* 115 (1990): 590. Addressed in German and Italian to continental audiences, the reviews by Taeger and Fusco reported the book's contents in greatest detail, for which I remain appreciative.

26. This may have been Professor Hooker's idea of fun. For me the experience had all the amusement of a barefoot stroll on broken glass.

German works and unpublished dissertations "thorough indeed" (Malbon), others wanted more attention to European scholarship (Fusco; Taeger), which "would significantly alter Black's findings at various points" (Broadhead). For Malbon, too many scholars were already clambering for attention: "[The book] is, in fact, a book about books. . . . the sense of reading a series of book reviews, even though they are well arranged to present the author's argument, is disappointing." Although some (Fowl; Morgan) were satisfied by its final recommendations for a coherent interpretation of Mark, coordinating historical and literary techniques, most judged those suggestions "too brief" (Donahue), at best programmatic without "deal[ing] adequately with the tensions between these methods of exegesis" (Green) and at worst disappointing (Hooker). "While the detail of Black's study is impressive, the conclusion is not startling. . . . [He] points to . . . a way beyond redactional studies to a new type of gospel criticism . . . but offers no clear, original solutions" (Broadhead). Muddiman interpreted the book as suggesting that "[Markan] redaction criticism cannot evolve; it has to be toppled by revolution." For Donahue, however, that revolution had already come and gone in the work of Pesch and of Donahue's own teacher, Norman Perrin:[27] "Black . . . undervalues 'composition criticism' of Mark . . . which has often yielded more interesting and solidly grounded results, underscor[ing] Mark's creativity in arranging material for theological purposes (e.g. the recurrent threefold passion prediction and subsequent misunderstanding in 8:27–10:45) and in plotting overarching themes which span the whole gospel. . . . [T]he kind of redaction criticism pilloried by Black, while still frequent in German dissertations, never became the dominant approach in the English-speaking world, especially in the United States."[28] Writing in Münster, Taeger also complained of my one-sided conception of the method, observing that close readings of a text could be just as subjective and erroneously opinionated as its redaction criticism.[29] In effect, Taeger called Black's kettle potted.[30]

The jury was hung on the import of *Disciples according to Mark* for reflecting on exegesis appropriate to Mark. For some, the book usefully reopened

---

27. "The Interpretation of the Gospel of Mark," *Int* 30 (1979): 115–24, esp. 120.

28. *PSTJ* (1989): 12. Donahue developed this line of thought in "Redaction Criticism: Has the *Hauptstrasse* Become a *Sackgasse*?," in *The New Literary Criticism and the New Testament*, ed. Elizabeth Struthers Malbon and Edgar V. McKnight, JSNTSup 109 (Sheffield: Sheffield Academic, 1994), 27–57. Donahue's answer to his essay's titular question is that redaction criticism is neither Main Street nor dead end, but rather *Querstrasse*: a crossroad where historical, traditional, literary, and theological methods continue to intersect.

29. *TLZ* 115 (1990): 590.

30. Best notes the same, as we shall see.

the hermeneutical question, "un débat" that will never be closed (Cuvillier), confirming the need of a methodological rethinking of whose urgency many were unaware (Fusco). "No longer can biblical interpreters presume they are engaged in research analogous to the experiments of ordinary science, carefully constructing assured results upon assured results. The task of biblical interpretation is much more akin to work in the social sciences and humanities, where results are relative to many and varied frames of reference, open to dispute and controversy" (Herzog). Another maintained that, though "we [may] never reach consensus" on the extent of Markan priority, the nature of Mark's sources, and our conception of its oral *Vorlage*, "as long as scholars continue to engage in reconstructing the history of the tradition, including the pre-gospel tradition, there will be a place for redaction criticism as defined by Stein" (Yarbro Collins). Still others expressed dismay at the book's concern for reliable and confirmable interpretations. Malbon chastised its failure to appreciate readings that, in all their diversity, were interesting. Räisänen asked how redaction criticism of Mark could be judged unsuitable if the method was not in fact being used, in spite of its practitioners' claims.[31]

Later in this chapter, I shall address some of these criticisms, but the stage must now be cleared for the bow of a featured critic: the redoubtable Ernest Best. Of all *Disciples according to Mark*'s principal interlocutors, only Best responded in print to my treatment of his scholarship. The longest published anywhere, his review sums up and extends the critiques of others. It also generated a private correspondence: I replied to his review through the postal service, and he answered my letter. The conversation was courteous, candid, substantive, and worth replicating here. For the sake of clarity and economy in presentation, I shall quote Professor Best's criticisms, then immediately quote my replies to him in a letter dated 4 April 1991.[32]

The defendant and the plaintiff opened their remarks with the customary though sincere expressions of appreciation.[33] Best thanked Black for a "valu-

---

31. A reviewer who shall remain nameless rendered the critique that most baffled me. Suggesting that mine was "an honest attempt," he opined that my "little faith in the redaction method lay perhaps . . . in the great difficulty of separating Mark's source material from [my] theological presuppositions." Then and now I have held theological assumptions when approaching Mark, though in that book, I remain unaware of how they directly bore on the labors of that gospel's redaction critics. This critic concluded, "The book offers a good exercise in redaction criticism." I lament not having made my position transparent to all.

32. In parentheses I have adjusted all page references to *Disciples according to Mark* in alignment with the new pagination of the second edition (2012). Naturally, Best's references were to the first edition's pagination (1989).

33. I leave for the reader to assign these personae. Years later most of these reviewers

able," "thought provoking piece of writing," whose flaws forbade the conclusion "that the redaction critical method is not a useful tool in the hands of New Testament scholars."[34] Graciously he expressed hope that I might forgive if his review were overly critical, owing to his emotional investment. In return, Black thanked Best "for the depth and care with which you have probed both my work as well as some of the issues that you judge to be implicated by it," and for helping all of us better to understand Mark's Gospel.

First, Best opened by rejecting my misinterpretation of his own work.

> Your reviewer would like to answer some of the criticisms made of him but if he did so this review would turn into a lengthy article. A few examples drawn from p. 130 will suffice. Black says that I regard γρηγορεῖν as Marcan on insufficient evidence. It occurs six times in Matthew, six in Mark, once in Luke, and not at all in John. What he does not notice is that at least five of the six occurrences in Matthew depend on Mark, and that if the word were also Matthean we should in fact (allowing for relative lengths of the two gospels) expect nine independent occurrences. (603)

My epistolary response to Professor Best: "In the matter of γρηγορεῖν, an explanation such as you give . . . could account for a word's being considered 'Markan,' while appearing with the same frequency in Matthew and Mark. However, does that not still leave unresolved for us the puzzle of whether γρηγορεῖν is more than characteristically Markan but *distinguishably* Markan, that is, redactionally so? Given the word's recurrence in various eschatological texts of the NT (e.g., 1 Thess 5:6, 10; Matt 25:13; 1 Pet 5:8; Rev 3:2–3, all of which you helpfully cite in *Following Jesus*, p. 159 n. 47), could not one reasonably infer that γρηγορεῖν was inherited by the Second Evangelist from his traditions, not redactionally imported by him in material such as 13:35? (I should hastily enter the caveat that 'inference' is by no means tantamount to 'proof,' with respect to the character and scope of either pre-Markan tradition or Markan redaction.)"

> When [Black] lists συνάγειν (24 times in Matthew, 5 in Mark) among the words I regard as Marcan favourites he has simply not read the context (*Following Jesus*, p. 49 n. 51) in which I gave the figures; I was not arguing

---

have become friends. I have no scores to settle, nor do I feel spurred to charge or to defend. Here my job is to report.

34. *JTS* 41 (1990): 602, 607. Subsequent citations appear above in the main text.

the word was Marcan but seeking to eliminate it from an argument about Marcan favourite words. (603)

My reply: "I can understand your perplexity with my reading of your comments on συνάγειν in *Following Jesus*. On the other hand, I confess to similar perplexity in attempting to square those comments with your observation (ibid., p. 193) that συνάγειν, though not appearing frequently in Mark, occurs only in redactional seams and, for that reason, could be taken as supporting evidence of the redactional character of Mark 6:30 (p. 192). (At this point I begin to wonder if a third party could criticize both of us, in constructing very different arguments, of pressing equivocal evidence too hard!)"

I cannot find where I claim that θαυμάζειν is a Marcan favourite; what I did claim was that the *theme* of amazement was Marcan. Inaccurate reading of those (I have not examined in detail his study of Meye and Weeden) he is criticizing does nothing to build up confidence in the ultimate result. (603–4)

My answer: "In reading p. 387 of your *NTS* article, 'The Role of the Disciples in Mark,'[35] I was led to conclude that you regarded θαυμάζειν and ἐκπλήσσεσθαι as examples of Markan redactional vocabulary on the strength of (a) their parenthetical citation in support of your claim that 'The amazement of the disciples . . . [was] entirely redactional,' and (b) their immediate collocation with two other words (θαυμάζειν and ἐκπλήσσεσθαι) that elsewhere you judged to be 'Markan word[s]' (*Following Jesus*, pp. 111, 116 n. 20). In short, however mistaken my belief, it seemed to me that you had introduced the disputed terms into the discussion of "amazement" in Markan redactional theology, and that your acceptance of those words as redactional thus was warranted. Nevertheless, if that neither was nor is your intention, then I should simply retract the point and apologize to you for a critical question raised on its basis."

Some of the comparisons drawn are also inaccurate. On p. 91 [Black] lists the words which Meye considers redactional, and on p. 198 says that Meye and I have only six words in common. Had he looked at my work more closely he would have seen that with Meye I also regard διδαχή and κατ᾽ ἰδιάν and some forms of πολύς as Marcan words. (604)

35. *NTS* 23 (1977): 377–401.

My rejoinder: "Returning to pp. 91–92 and 125–27 in my *Disciples*, I see that I recorded both διδαχή and κατ᾽ ἰδιάν in Table 1 (Meye's identification of redactional vocabulary) but neither term in Table 3 (your own such identification). As a result, neither term recurs in my comparative assessment of the redactional vocabulary on which you and Meye agree (p. 198). Evidently, at least these two terms slipped through the net I cast across those of your publications that I examined for this test, and in the interest of accuracy I am happy to have the corrections brought to my attention. The same could be said of 'some forms of πολύς,' if by that you mean something other than the cognate πολλά, used adverbially (which I accounted for in *Disciples*, p. 198, n. 41). Practically, I am not certain that these few additions would materially alter my conclusion, on p. 198, regarding the relatively minimal agreement on Markan redactional vocabulary among representative redaction critics. These additions do position you and Meye exegetically closer to each other than either of you to Weeden, a result that is scarcely surprising."

Second, Best also suggested that I had inadequately conveyed my own critical intentions.

> Black has little difficulty in showing that his three representatives come up with very different answers about the role of the disciples. He does not discuss their answers to the question of discipleship, how Mark expects his readers to behave, which to your reviewer at any rate is the more important question; the other is only incidental to it. I suspect that if he had considered this theme he might not have found his three representatives differed so greatly. At times indeed he does not preserve the necessary distinction between these two themes (e.g. p. 254, n. 2). (603)

My response: "I agree with you that Mark's portrayal of the disciples and Mark's understanding of discipleship can be usefully distinguished, and your criticism of my lapse in conflating them on p. 254, n. 2 of *Disciples* is well-taken. (However, I am less sure that a consideration of representative redaction-critical treatments of 'discipleship,' not 'the disciples,' in Mark would yield, as you suspect, results that were far removed from the ones I document.)"

> Black compares and contrasts [the] results [of his three representatives] and concludes that if such different results appear when the method of redaction criticism is applied it probably indicates a flaw in the method itself. He draws this conclusion a little too hastily. Listing the criteria used in the direction of redaction, he indicates which each scholar has thought most

important. There turns out to be only one which all three used extensively. It may then be the use of different criteria to detect redaction which has led to differing results rather than the use of the method as a whole, for some criteria may be more useful in detecting redaction than others. Until this possibility has been eliminated the method cannot be faulted. (604)

Serve returned: "In fact, on pp. 192–202 of my *Disciples*, I conjured with that possibility and found, on the contrary, that my three representative interpreters effectively *agreed* with one another in the employment of not one but four redaction-critical criteria: Markan modifications of traditional material as discerned through comparison with Matthew and Luke, Markan arrangement of traditional material, the Markan conclusion, Markan vocabulary and style."

[Black] claims these writers [in chapter 7] realized the circularity of the [redaction-critical] method, as if his original three writers had not done so (e.g. see my *Mark: The Gospel as Story* [1983], p. 10), and consciously attempted to overcome this deficiency. (605)

Answer: "I do not recall claiming that you, Meye, or Weeden did not realize the inherent circularity of Markan redaction criticism. On the contrary, on p. 111 of *Disciples*, I quote your own acknowledgement of this circularity (in *Mark: The Gospel as Story*, p. 10); elsewhere (p. 253) I state, 'from the method's inception it has been understood that the rationale and procedure of redaction criticism is fundamentally circular.'"

At one point (pp. 290–91) [Black] does confess that he agrees most closely with the conclusion I reached on the role of the disciples, but goes on to add that it is possible to reach this conclusion by a close reading of the text without resort to redaction criticism. Now Black may be able to do this, but W. H. Kelber's *Mark's Story of Jesus* [1979] uses the kind of approach Black advocates and comes up with an entirely different result! It is not so easy just to read the text and understand it. It is necessary also to say that the realization of the importance of the role of the disciples in the Gospel is a result of redaction critical work." (606)

My response: "Notwithstanding your reservations, I continue to think it demonstrably the case, in recent scholarship, that 'one may arrive at such exegesis [as you propose on redaction-critical grounds] on the basis of a close reading of the text, mindful of its surface subtleties, without ever raising *redak-*

tionsgeschichtlich conjectures into the discussion' (*Disciples*, p. 291). In support of this claim one might recall the recent work of Robert Tannehill and John Donahue, among others. The contrasting interpretation of Werner Kelber may be cited, as you have, as evidence that a literary critic will *not necessarily* arrive at an exegesis like Ernest Best's (especially if such an interpretation has been less than completely 'mindful of Mark's surface subtleties'); that, however, is a very different matter."

Third, other objections raised by Best seemed, as I wrote to him, "not entirely germane to my own project; some from among these, however, are interesting and may be worthy of further pursuit by proponents of Markan redaction criticism." He replied, "Black has also not enquired whether the criteria [for ascertaining Markan redaction] are independent of one another (e.g. the selection of Marcanisms and seams); such independence is important in statistical work" (604).

I replied: "The reason for this is that my research led me to the conclusion that Markan redaction critics themselves either were not conducting such an inquiry or (especially with regard to the method's attempted 'rehabilitators': Chapter 7) had been unsuccessful, in my judgment, in making the case that such criteria *could* be adjudged as independent of one another."

> Black fails to ask whether our theological and other presuppositions affected the way we operated the method. We may be predisposed to look for certain conclusions and manipulate the evidence so that the result [expected] appears. Because I started as a pastor rather than as an academic I may have tended to see Mark's Gospel as pastorally oriented; this would then affect my outlook on the disciples. Doubtless Meye and Weeden have their own presuppositions and these may have affected the way they have looked at the evidence. (604-5).

My answer: "I attempted to treat *in extenso* the methodological presuppositions that avowedly govern the redaction criticism of each of the scholars whose work I examined (especially pp. 69-75, 108-11, 142-49, 179-83). In fact, one of my conclusions (pp. 202-3) was rather similar to what you yourself conjecture: namely, that the exegetical results seem to be affected by the exegetes' varying presuppositions of what they generally expected to find. (For another of your hypotheses, however, I found no clear evidence: namely, that Markan redaction critics were 'manipulating' either the Gospel of Mark or the practice of its redaction criticism [p. 199].) However, I did not think it appropriate to speculate on the personal, professional, or theological reasons for the various presuppositions made by different scholars, inasmuch as (a) such information is generally not in the public domain and for that reason is uncontrollable, and (b) even if such information were publicly accessible, its use could be misconstrued in all manner of ad hominem arguments. If this be a lacuna in my argument, then it is by design and not by accident."

> I have indeed examined more sections of Mark than either Meye or Weeden so it is a priori probable that I will have identified a longer list of Marcanisms. This failure to check the base from which Meye, Weeden and I work seriously flaws Black's conclusions. He may still be correct, but a more rigorous proof is necessary. . . . It is in the light of [distinguishing Mark's theological presentation from the historical life of Jesus] that we can see the importance of Black's failure to list the criteria for determining [pre-Markan] tradition. (604, 607)

Comeback: "With respect to [these] criticisms . . . I can only plead that it was the intention of *this* study to do neither; as stated in different ways on different occasions (e.g., *Disciples*, pp. 33, 64–67, 205), the task that I set for myself was not to propose ways by which Markan *Redaktionsgeschichte* might be rendered more trustworthy, but rather to observe carefully and critically the work of those who have attempted such a project (or who themselves have neglected to execute just such operations as you urge). If the majority of critics were to achieve principled agreement on the extent and material dimensions of Mark's traditional and redactional base, then this would be a considerable step forward in that gospel's redaction criticism (on the assumption of its chronological priority). Although my own study does not suggest that such a critical consensus currently exists, its establishment, as well as the analytical bases on which it may be attained, could be a needful, next stage in the evolution of Markan redaction criticism."

Fourth, the positive yet insufficient proposals in chapter 8 did not escape Professor Best's laser-like penetration.

> Regrettably [Black] gives us no indication how this method [he proposes] would work in practice so that we could see if it in fact would free those who use it from error: the proof of the pudding is in the eating, not in the recipe. . . . Black seems to imagine [circular reasoning] is a danger which appears only in the redaction criticism of Mark. It is a danger to almost all New Testament scholarship. . . . Even the use of five methods or tools will not eliminate the perils of circularity. I am sure that even if all Black's five

methods were to be used scholars would still come up with different answers to the same problems. The whole history of the historical critical method shows how opinions have changed from generation to generation, very often because outside influences have played on the interpreters. (605, 606)

Again, with a heavy sigh, I flagellated myself. "As suggested on p. 291 of *Disciples*, I admit, readily and with my own share of dissatisfaction, that my outline of methodological approaches and their possible correlations is slender and in need of development and practical confirmation; obviously, more work needs to be done, by myself and by others. (Perhaps you can understand and forgive that I did not prosecute this at the end of a work whose text and notes already had extended 296 pages!) However, in response to two comments you make . . . , I wish to emphasize that by no means do I believe it "so easy just to read the text and understand it" (606), or that the hermeneutical circle can be escaped through the sheer accretion of methods. In my constructive methodological comments, I was attempting to suggest, rather, that *no single method*, operating independently of others, is ultimately sufficient for the task of interpreting complex texts. That for which I am groping, though it may prove chimerical, is something like the satisfaction of a 'criterion of coherence,' as observed in the recent quest for the historically reconstructed Jesus: an interpretation of a document like Mark may be accorded greater credibility to the degree that it coheres with the results of exegeses undertaken from different methodological perspectives. Put differently, it seems to me that different indicators, pointing in a consistent direction, may prove to be more critically satisfying than an exegesis that operates only within one methodological framework (such as redaction criticism), no matter how elegantly wrought or defensible on its own terms such an exegesis may be. In any case, I am pleased that you did not charge me (as has another reviewer) with advocacy of a revolutionary toppling of Markan redaction criticism; on the contrary, that method indisputably has enhanced the modern study of that gospel and retains, in my judgment, a significant (albeit chastened) position among the cluster of methods to be coordinated in the interpretation of that gospel (*Disciples*, pp. 267–87)."

Near his review's end Best proffered two "general reflections" I thought worth engaging.

First, he stated:

Studying Mark is like dealing with a document in code which in wartime needs deciphering. More than one solution may be possible but there are some rough tests which may distinguish between them so that the correct one can be chosen. If one solution sets out a dinner menu and another the movement of troops the second may be accepted as correct because it belongs in the context of war. (606)

My riposte: "I wonder if this analogy oversimplifies the critical procedures involved. Can the gospels, or any biblical literature, be 'decoded' in the way you suggest? Given that Mark is a stylized portrayal of the ministry of Jesus, not an overt chronicle of its author's time, place, and circumstances, with what degree of confidence may its cultural context be construed a priori as war-torn, uneasily peaceful, or something else? Modifying your analogy in a fanciful way to make a serious point, I wonder at times if some Markan redaction critics— among whom I would not number Ernest Best—have handed us 'a dinner menu' and have asked us to read it *as though it were* a communiqué concerning troop deployment. It was with some of the dimensions and implications of this problem that *Disciples* was intended to grapple."

Second, he wrote:

> Black appears to operate with the assumption that [redaction criticism] is designed to discover the theology of the evangelists. I would agree that this is a part of its purpose but it is not the whole purpose. In the preface to my first attempt at redaction criticism I expressed the hope that what I wrote would "be useful in some small way in the quest of the historical Jesus" (*The Temptation and the Passion* [1965], p. xii). . . . The only way to Jesus is through the Gospels, but if we are to go that way then we need to know how the evangelists manipulated the tradition which they received; while this will not itself bring us to the historical Jesus it is a necessary first step. How do we shed what Mark has contributed to the material so that we can discover the form of an incident before Mark used it?" (607)

I replied: "As to your reflection on redaction criticism and the search for the Jesus of history, I am not without sympathy. You may recall that, in *Disciples* (pp. 277–86), I recognized both the validity and the needfulness of historical criticism (with respect both to the life of Jesus and to the social location of primitive Christian communities) and the constructive interaction of such historical research with various forms of tradition criticism. Again I should emphasize that my dissertation was intended to elicit, not indiscriminate derision of redaction criticism, but salutary skepticism of its overly ambitious claims and practices with regard to a gospel whose sources are usually considered indeterminate (*Disciples*, p. 67). Conceivably, the recognition and appropriate correction of such claims and practices ultimately could eventuate, not in the abandonment of the critical quest for Jesus, but in more rigorous methods of its pursuit. Whether or not some forms of narrative and rhetorical criticism, now in their infancy, will make enduring contributions to historical investigation as such, only time will tell. It may be, as you suggest, that the work of some literary critics amounts to an evasion of historical research. Except for the more exotic streams of deconstruction, it is less clear to me that, in principle or in practice, such evasion is necessarily implicated in all forms of literary criticism, as Amos Wilder has argued with no little eloquence.[36] My suspicion is that, in the interpretation of texts and contexts, self-styled historical critics and literary critics have much to teach and to learn from one another."

That was not the end of it. Professor Best replied to my missive in a letter, neatly typed with a faded ribbon (29 April 1991). I shall not weary the reader with all of its contents.[37] Let it suffice that he opened with a gracious paragraph in which he expressed hope for no hard feelings in either direction. That hope was fulfilled. At varying length, he responded precisely to several of my points: acknowledging those where, on reflection, he believed he had been inconsistent, pressing others where he thought my argument flabby. Chief among the latter was the "statistical method" I had adopted. Per Best, "In statistical work it is important to ensure that categories and criteria are not interdependent. That you had not done so seemed to me to leave a gap in your work." Fair enough, say I.[38] In Best's assessment, "This is something that needs to be further examined if comparisons are to be made." Agreed. To my knowledge that examination has yet to be undertaken. Neither Best nor I had the appetite for it; by that time, both of us were knee-deep in other projects. Cheerfully he relinquished the metaphor of "decoding" Mark: "I heartily agree with you that this oversimplifies the matter. I was only hoping to provoke discussion; my suggestion was by way of flying a kite." His penultimate paragraph is worth quoting in full: "Finally may I say that I thoroughly enjoyed reading your book. It helped me to understand myself, or rather my work, better. I hope that my review does not stop others from reading what you wrote but will encourage them to examine more deeply the methods, all of them, that we use in our scholarly work."

36. Here I was probably thinking of Wilder's collected essays, *The Bible and the Literary Critic* (Minneapolis: Fortress, 1991).

37. By this time, that reader can only be a member of my family. No—I stand corrected. She put down this book and never returned to it.

38. Before turning to theology, Best had studied mathematics at Queen's University, Belfast. Unawares, I had crossed swords with a samurai. How my makeshift knowledge of statistics in chapter 7 dodged his saber I shall never know.

Affectionately known as "Paddy," Ernest Best was a pastor in Northern Ireland before accepting a lectureship in biblical literature and theology at St Andrews. From 1974 until 1982, he held the chair in divinity and biblical studies at the University of Glasgow and was awarded an honorary DD in 1999.[39] He died in 2004 at the age of eighty-seven. I never met him but wish very much that I had. He was a scholar and a gentleman.

Robert Meye, dean emeritus and professor emeritus of New Testament interpretation at Fuller Theological Seminary, died on 9 August 2020.[40] Again I regret never having had opportunity to meet or to converse with him.

Still with us, thankfully, is Theodore Weeden. In a plot-twist that would raise O. Henry's guffaws, mere months after defending my dissertation, I was teaching in Rochester, New York, and on Sundays attended a United Methodist church whose pastor was—wait for it—the Reverend Dr. Theodore J. Weeden Sr. We enjoyed several friendly lunches together. Not once was my dissertation mentioned. Call me Coward if you like; I prefer Discretion. During one repast I remember asking Ted about his thesis, which in revised form was central to my own monograph's fifth chapter. How had he come to write it? "It was the sixties," he said. I cannot recollect the rest of his explanation well enough for quotation. Its gist was that his own graduate work had been done in an era not only of miniskirts and flower power but also of antiestablishmentarians. What happens if you read Mark's Gospel as a covert assault on Peter's authority? Whatever else, you have an interesting reading—the very thing one reviewer faulted *Disciples according to Mark* for failing to deliver. Best got it right: "Doubtless Meye and Weeden have their own presuppositions and these may have affected the way they have looked at the evidence."[41]

MARKING TIME

> *The only thing anybody today knows about Chesterfield's [Letters] is that Johnson said of it that it taught the manners of a dancing-master and the morals of a whore, and it must be a century since anybody read it to find out whether Johnson was right.*
>
> —Bernard Levin[42]

---

39. On the occasion of his retirement, David Hill published a warmhearted tribute, "Ernest Best: An Appreciation," *JSNT* 5 (1982): 3–6. It is well worth reading.

40. A detailed, heartfelt memorial to Robert Meye may be found on the Fuller Seminary website: https://www.fuller.edu/posts/in-memoriam-robert-p-meye/.

41. *JTS* 41 (1990): 605.

42. *Enthusiasms: Art, Literature, Music, Food, Walking* (New York: Crown, 1983), 41–42.

Since few shall wait for a century's elapse, let's constrict our purview to the past thirty years. The following review cannot be comprehensive, and I tender apologies to all who have published in these areas and are disappointed to find their work undocumented here. I mean to shortchange none. The best I can do is trace some relevant scholarly tendencies since my book first appeared. Extending my story line from 1989, I pose the questions thus: Has Markan scholarship continued down a redaction-critical track? What other paths have been taken? Have the interpretive markers I associated with Meye, Best, and Weeden reappeared in more recent Markan investigation? Has one of their readings proved more popular among professional exegetes? What patterns have lately emerged?

The Continued Quest for Mark's Sources and Traditions

To speak of Mark as redactor implies some kind of assumption about what the evangelist was editing. In *Disciples according to Mark* it was not my original purpose to examine the oral traditions or written sources presupposed by this gospel's redaction critics; nor shall I mount such an investigation here. Yet to ignore the matter entirely is irresponsible, and the reader may benefit from brief comments at this late juncture.[43]

In my view, the most positive reconnaissance of this area in the past three decades has entailed Mark's adaptation of a known, recognizable source: the Greek translation of the Hebrew Scriptures.[44] After Alfred Suhl's pioneering study in 1965,[45] Joel Marcus's *The Way of the Lord* in 1992 most vigorously re-opened the question with special, though not exclusive, attention to the Second

---

43. For more extensive surveys of this subject, consult William R. Telford, "The Pre-Markan Tradition in Recent Research (1980–1990)," in *The Four Gospels 1992: Festschrift Frans Neirynck*, ed. Frans Van Segbroeck et al., BETL 100 (Leuven: Leuven University Press; Peeters, 1992), 2:693–723; Andreas Lindemann, "Literatur zu den Synoptischen Evangelien 1992–2000 (III): Das Markusevangelium," *TRu* 69 (2004): 369–423; Cilliers Breytenbach, "Current Research on the Gospel according to Mark: A Report on Monographs Published from 2000–2009," in *Mark and Matthew I, Comparative Readings: Understanding the Earliest Gospels in Their First-Century Settings*, ed. Eve-Marie Becker and Anders Runesson, WUNT 271 (Tübingen: Mohr Siebeck, 2011), 13–32; repr. Cilliers Breytenbach, *The Gospel according to Mark as Episodic Narrative*, NovTSup 128 (Leiden: Brill, 2021), 377–97.

44. For convenience, I restrict myself to that general denotation, even though the precise or multiple forms of the Septuagint available to the evangelist and other first-century writers is a matter of considerable debate.

45. *Die Funktion der alttestamentlichen Zitate und Anspielungen in Markusevangelium* (Gütersloh: Gütersloher Verlagshaus, 1965).

Gospel's appropriation of Isaiah.[46] Rikki Watts has argued for an even more allusive, pervasive influence of Deutero-Isaiah on Mark's theology and narrative structure.[47] Thomas Hatina presses "a model for reading scriptural quotations and allusions that is sensitive to both the narrative of Mark's Gospel and the historical setting in which it is written."[48] Cilliers Breytenbach widens the scriptural lens by noting Mark's use of Deuteronomy in combination with other pentateuchal books (e.g., Mark 7:10 // Deut 5:16 + Exod 21:17; Mark 12:19 // Deut 25:5–6 + Gen 38:8).[49] Stephen Ahearne-Kroll puts the Psalms back into the picture, arguing (*pace* Watts) that the Davidic suffering king is more influential in Markan theology than the Deutero-Isaianic suffering servant.[50] James M. Neumann tacks in a very different direction: "The argument of this [dissertation] is that Mark portrays Jesus's earthly life as the actualization of Psalm 2: a coronation hymn for the Davidic king that became associated with the victory of the Messiah in Judaism and with Jesus's passion in Early Christianity."[51] New wine is fermenting in old wineskins (cf. Mark 2:22), but at this time it is impossible to know which varietal will prevail. Less influential have been the neo-Griesbachian offerings of Harold Riley and the team formed by David Peabody, Lamar Cope, and Allan J. McNicol.[52] While this research has

46. *The Way of the Lord: Christological Exegesis of the Old Testament in the Gospel of Mark* (Louisville: Westminster John Knox, 1992). Though not restricted to Mark, Donald H. Juel's *Messianic Exegesis: Christological Interpretation of the Old Testament in Early Christianity* (Philadelphia: Fortress, 1988) is another important contribution in this area.

47. *Isaiah's New Exodus in Mark*, WUNT 88 (Tübingen: Mohr Siebeck, 1997; repr., Grand Rapids: Baker Academic, 2001).

48. *In Search of a Context: The Function of Scripture in Mark's Narrative*, LNTS 232 (London: Sheffield Academic, 2002).

49. "Die Vorschriften des Mose im Markusevangelium: Erwägungen zur Komposition von Mk 7,9–13; 10,2–9 und 12,18–27," *ZNW* 97 (2006): 23–43; repr. Breytenbach, *The Gospel according to Mark as Episodic Narrative*, 433–55.

50. *The Psalms of Lament in Mark's Passion: Jesus' Davidic Suffering*, SNTSMS 142 (Cambridge: Cambridge University Press, 2007).

51. James M. Neumann, "The Gospel of the Son of God: Psalm 2 and Mark's Narrative Christology," (PhD diss., Princeton Theological Seminary, 2020), 25–26.

52. Harold Riley, *The Making of Mark: An Exploration* (Macon, GA: Mercer University Press, 1990); David Peabody, Lamar Cope, and Allan J. McNicol, *One Gospel from Two: Mark's Use of Matthew and Luke; A Demonstration by the Research Team of the International Institute for Renewal of Gospel Studies* (Harrisburg, PA: Trinity Press International, 2002). To date, C. S. Mann's *Mark: A New Translation with Introduction and Commentary*, AB 27 (Garden City, NY: Doubleday, 1986), remains the only technical commentary working within this redactional framework. It has now been replaced in the Anchor Bible by Joel Marcus's two-volume commentary, which is based on the two-source hypothesis (see below, n. 102). On Peabody's attempt to refine Markan redaction criticism, see Black, *Disciples according to Mark*, chapter 7.

sensibly concentrated on methodological clarity and justification, its ensuing interpretations of Mark as redactor of Matthew (and Luke) are so remote from the mainstream that most scholars have found them difficult to accept.[53]

"If we are frank," wrote Michael Goulder, "we have no idea whether there was a pre-Marcan Gospel, in the sense of a continuous written account of Jesus."[54] Goulder may not have known, but others have claimed to. One was Marie-Émile Boismard, who reconstructed in Greek and in French an intermediate, or proto-, Mark, which was influenced by intermediary Matthean and Lukan sources.[55] Boismard's is a recondite theory, though it's simple as a stick compared with that of Delbert Burkett, whose *Rethinking the Gospel Sources: From Proto-Mark to Mark* is, hands down, the most heroic measure to resuscitate *Urmarkus*.[56] Burkett posits that none of the canonical gospels used one another as a source. Instead, there was (1) a primitive gospel, Proto-Mark, which was revised by (2) a Proto-Mark A and Proto-Mark B, which yielded (3) Markan C-material, which (4) each of the Synoptic evangelists used independently of one another. In other words, canonical Mark is a fourth generation removed from the oldest Markan source: it is a redaction of a redaction (C) of collateral redactions (A and B). Burkett's argument is stunning in its creativity, diligence, caution, clarity, and (for the most part) logical coherence.[57] Like Boismard, he is on to something true of both Markan redaction and of the Synoptic problem: namely, our evidence implies traditional and literary developments whose complexity far outstrips the explanatory power of a simple two-source theory. My primary question is, How on earth could one verify

---

53. See, for instance, the review of Riley by William O. Walker Jr., *JBL* 110 (1991): 346–48, and of Peabody, Cope, and McNicol by Harry T. Fleddermann in *CBQ* 66 (2004): 498–500. I concur with Craig A. Evans: "It has been recognized over and again that Matthew and Luke make the greatest sense as *interpretations of Mark*. If the Griesbach-[William] Farmer Hypothesis were correct, one would expect major breakthroughs in Markan research. After all, we would know what Mark's sources were. But Farmer's following have not cast significant light on Mark" ("Source, Form and Redaction Criticism: The 'Traditional' Methods of Synoptic Interpretation," in *Approaches to New Testament Study*, ed. Stanley E. Porter and David Tombs, JSNTSup 120 [Sheffield: Sheffield Academic, 1995], 26]).

54. "The Pre-Marcan Gospel," *SJT* 47 (1994): 453.

55. *L'Évangile de Marc: Sa Préhistoire*, EBib, n.s. 26 (Paris: Gabalda, 1994). Boismard's reconstructed texts are presented therein on pp. 243–75. For an assessment, see Frans Neirynck, "Urmarcus Révisé: La Théorie Synoptique de M.-É. Boismard, Nouvelle Manière," *ETL* 71 (1995): 166–75.

56. London: T&T Clark, 2004. This is the first volume in a projected trilogy, whose second installment has appeared at this writing: *The Unity and Plurality of Q*, ECL 1 (Atlanta: Society of Biblical Literature, 2009).

57. More recently, see the same author's *Case for Proto-Mark: A Study in the Synoptic Problem*, WUNT 399 (Tübingen: Mohr Siebeck 2018).

a hypothesis like this? It has no textual basis: that is to say, there's nothing one can recover and identify as an actual Proto-Mark or its recensions A, B, and C. They are all in Burkett's brain.[58] If you grant the probability of a development as complicated as he has proposed,[59] should you be prepared to grant the improbability of its ever being recovered, whether by Burkett or anyone else? A half-century later, Burkett's source-theory for Mark offers a hermeneutical reprise of Bultmann's for John. Even if either scholar were correct, which gospel does one interpret: the canonical document or the theoretical reconstruction by its scholarly exegete?

The Disciples in Mark: Bringing a Survey Up to Date

In *Disciples according to Mark*, I identified as Type I a generally positive assessment of the Second Evangelist's attitude toward history, pregospel tradition, and the role of the disciples in Mark. That point of view has not vanished. Its simplest expression may be reflected by Ekkehard Stegemann, who, in a fundamentally historical essay, suggests that Mark remembered the triumvirate of Peter and the Zebedee brothers as martyrs who, like Jesus, gave their lives for the sake of the good news (Mark 8:35).[60] A more complex account emerges from the comparative study of Mark and Matthew by John Riches, who draws upon Clifford Geertz's cultural anthropology.[61] For Riches, the Second Gospel evinces complementary cosmologies: one, cosmic-dualist, "which [sees] the

58. Burkett is aware of this problem (*Rethinking the Gospel Sources*, 263–66), but it must be faced squarely. Thus, Douglas W. Geyer (*RBL* [2005], https://www.sblcentral.org/home): "Yet it remains difficult to know what one has when one has a conclusion in this area of study. It appears not to be a historical conclusion, although its rhetoric is posturing as such. Source criticism seems to want to sound like it is setting straight the historical record. Outside of corresponding independent testimony, it can do no such thing."

59. By concentrating on literary sources and neglecting vagaries of the gospels' oral transmission, Nicholas H. Taylor finds Burkett's argument *insufficiently* complicated (*JSNT* 28 [2006]: 57–58). *Jesus and the Oral Gospel Tradition*, ed. Henry Wansbrough, JSNTSup 64 (Sheffield: Sheffield Academic, 1991; repr., London: T&T Clark, 2004), is an important collection of essays on that subject from a diverse company of international scholars. In a review of Boismard's *L'Évangile de Marc* (*CBQ* 58 [1996]: 535–36), Craig Evans reminds us that about two centuries elapsed between codices of any of the Synoptics and their original compositions. During that time, a perpetual process of editing and updating surely occurred, which could more simply account for the minor agreements of Matthew and Luke against Mark.

60. "Zur Rolle von Petrus, Jakobus, und Johannes," *TZ* 42 (1986): 366–74.

61. *Conflicting Mythologies: Identity Formation in the Gospels of Mark and Matthew*, SNTW (Edinburgh: T&T Clark, 2000).

origin of evil as residing in the invasion of this world by hostile angelic forces, which enslaved or ensnared men and women"; the other, a forensic view that "attributes evil to human disobedience."[62] Congruent with these models are two different emphases in Mark's presentation of discipleship. Aligned with the dualist view of humanity's plight, the conversionist view "stresses the giving of the mystery of the kingdom through private instruction to an in-group of followers, sharply distinguished from the parent group from which they come." As seen in Mark 3:20–35, "Fictive ties [of discipleship] replace natural ties *as definitive of group membership*." The restorationist view, more exoteric and engaged with the public sphere, is concentrated on "bringing the good news to the wider world and with directly engaging in conflict with the demonic powers."[63] These two emphases are not neatly compartmentalized; instead, they are "different moods and attitudes" that, intermingled, color discipleship in Mark 8:22–10:52. "The darker mood of the [dualist-conversionist] images seems to have cast its spell over the [forensic and] restorationist account."[64] For Riches, Mark's sectarian portrait of Jesus's followers is at bottom positive: disciples are responsible agents who, sadly, are blinded and possessed by demonic forces that can be overcome only by divine rescue.[65]

Equally sensitive to Jewish apocalypticism, yet even more positive, is Suzanne Watts Henderson's interpretation, which proceeds from a blend of *Traditionsgeschichte* and narrative criticism.[66] In six passages from the gospel's first half (1:16–20; 3:13–15; 4:1–34; 6:7–13; 6:32–44; 6:45–52), "Mark predicates true discipleship not on full knowledge of Jesus' precise agenda but rather on his followers' full participation in his kingdom-of-God agenda." When failing to trust "the prevailing promises of God's coming dominion," the disciples fall short; elsewhere, however, "they emulate [Jesus's] paradigmatic exposition of God's rule" because he has empowered them to extend his christological witness.[67] In a redaction-critical spin-off from the notion that biological families

62. *Conflicting Mythologies*, 51. For these formulations, Riches acknowledges his debt to Martinus de Boer's essays on Paul's Jewish apocalyptic eschatology.

63. *Conflicting Mythologies*, 77. "In this respect, one (but only one) of the key markers of Jewish identity is undermined."

64. *Conflicting Mythologies*, 87–89.

65. *Conflicting Mythologies*, 88–102.

66. *Christology and Discipleship in the Gospel of Mark*, SNTSMS 135 (Cambridge: Cambridge University Press, 2006). Like Meye—and in striking contrast with Wrede—Henderson notes that "the chasm between the historical and narrative worlds may not be so sprawling after all: ironically, Mark may preserve, even develop, authentic traditions of Jesus' reticence precisely in service of the evangelist's own Christological purpose" (256 n. 20).

67. *Christology and Discipleship*, 245.

pale in significance before discipleship, Torsten Reiprich argues that Mark's Gospel presents a transformation of Jesus's own parent into an exemplary disciple among the *familia dei*: the previously unbelieving mother of 3:20–21, 30–35 reappears at the crucifixion as the vigilant "Mary the mother of James the younger and Joses" (15:40).[68]

Epitomized by Weeden, Type III interpreters (as I so styled them) envision Mark as operating with a longer leash on antecedent traditions, unafraid to cast the disciples in unremitting gloom. As Robert Fowler comments, "Weeden more than anyone else broke the grip of the strong readings of Mark that had enthralled readers for centuries. By arguing that the reader is led to distance himself from the Twelve instead of identifying closely with them, Weeden broke the ancient spell of the earliest and strongest of Mark's readers, namely, Matthew, Luke, and John. Weeden shattered these corrective lenses for reading Mark, but we will take years to get accustomed to reading Mark with uncorrected vision."[69]

Some have already tossed these glasses aside. Thus, Jeffrey Gibson's literary and theological assessment of the puzzling Mark 8:14–21: what Jesus rebukes here is not (à la Weeden) a heretical Christology but rather a parochial limitation of salvation to Israel. The disciples had conveniently "forgotten" to take loaves because they denied gentiles the salvation Jesus had demonstrated was theirs in the second feeding miracle (8:1–10).[70] Tradition-critically, William Telford refreshes a suggestion Joseph Tyson made in 1961:[71] through the personae of the disciples, Mark assails a primitive Jewish Christianity that accepted the risen Jesus as a Davidic sovereign without according any significance to his cru-

---

68. *Das Mariageheimnis: Maria von Nazareth und die Bedeutung familiärer Beziehungen im Markusevangelium*, FRLANT 223 (Göttingen: Vandenhoeck & Ruprecht, 2008). Sympathetic with this aspect of Riches's monograph, Reiprich makes no reference to it. With Reiprich's revelation of "the Marian secret," one might compare the altogether positive portrayal of women in Mark proposed by Susan Miller in *Women in Mark's Gospel*, JSNT-Sup 259 (London: T&T Clark, 2004). For her, female disciples in this gospel act in a manner befitting God's new creation that the Twelve never manage; "[Mark] records the accounts of women who live their lives in such a way that the kingdom of God is revealed in the earthly context" (199).

69. *Let the Reader Understand: Reader Response Criticism and the Gospel of Mark* (Minneapolis: Fortress, 1991), 256–57. For reasons I shall explain, Fowler's own reading of the disciples in Mark seems to me more exemplary of my Type II category. Still, his is the most lavish encomium of Weeden's contribution in recent scholarly literature.

70. Jeffrey B. Gibson, "The Rebuke of the Disciples in Mark 8:14–21," *JSNT* 9 (1986): 31–47.

71. "The Blindness of the Disciples in the Gospel of Mark," *JBL* 80 (1961): 261–68.

cifixion. "This theory," avers Telford, "has much to commend it, although one has to add that an equally primitive view of Jesus as the exalted, apocalyptic Son of Man shortly to return in glory is in addition being modified by the evangelist in the light of his *theologia crucis.*"[72] In Telford's judgment, Weeden correctly spotted conflicting Christologies in the early church as the tacit nub of controversy in Mark but misidentified the crux: not a high view of Jesus as Son of God (which, Telford believes, the miracle stories enhance) but instead a Jerusalem-based Christianity that sought to control nascent gentile churches.[73]

The most relentlessly negative account of the disciples in recent Markan study may be that of Mary Ann Tolbert.[74] Her monograph adopts a modern narrative approach that acknowledges the techniques of Hellenistic rhetoric and novels (35–126). For Tolbert, the tension between the Markan Jesus and his disciples is not symptomatic of competing Christologies in early Christianity; rather, "Mark's use of disciples to illustrate the rocky ground [4:5, 16–17] thwarts conventional expectations" in antiquity that a teacher's disciples will support him (154–56, 195–211, 218–27 [quotation, 222]).

> The disciples in Mark, as victims of constant and increasingly broad doses of situational irony, become at the same time increasingly removed from the audience's sympathy. If irony serves to bind more closely together the audience and the narrator (and, of course, Jesus, since he shares much of the narrator's status) by underscoring their joint knowledge and point of view, it also serves to distance the audience from the witless victims of irony, whether they be high priests or disciples. The rhetorical effect of irony, then, is twofold: it builds and strengthens community among those with superior knowledge, and it excludes those with inferior knowledge. (103)

Thus, by the evangelist's narrative design, nothing good can be said of Peter and the rest of the Twelve. They are arrogant, grasping, stubborn, fearful, treacherous, miserable, grieving failures (201–2, 206, 211, 218, 226). Why? Such a negative depiction stirs Mark's audience to search for flaws among themselves: "What type of earth am *I*? Will *I* go and tell?" (224, 299). Even

---

72. William R. Telford, *The Theology of the Gospel of Mark*, NTT (Cambridge: Cambridge University Press, 1999), 136.

73. Telford, *Theology*, 88–103, 135–37.

74. *Sowing the Gospel: Mark's World in Literary-Historical Perspective* (Minneapolis: Fortress, 1989). Subsequent citations appear in text.

more, "portraying the *disciples* as failing foils to Jesus manipulates the reader to respond by becoming a *better disciple*. . . . Mark has created in the role of the authorial audience the perfect disciple" (224, 297).

Splitting the difference between I and III, Type II interpretations favor Mark's positive though chastened attitude toward history, tradition, and the role of Jesus's disciples. Over this mediate realm Ambivalence rules. In a socio-theological exegesis of Mark 3:19b–35, John Painter observes that the Twelve (3:13–19a)—like the crowd (3:20–21), Jerusalem's scribes (3:22–30), and the natural family (3:31–35)—are quite fallible followers.[75] Space is thus made for the reader to enter Jesus's family, open to all and based not on this world's social networks but on the eschatological reality created by God's kingdom.[76] The crossing of social boundaries by Jesus's disciples, especially their relinquishment of family (see 10:29–31), also figures in Richard Strelan's comparison of the Second Gospel with a wide range of Jewish apocalyptic literature (including the books of Enoch, Jubilees, 2 Baruch, Philo's *De gigantibus*, and Qumran's Damascus Document). These and other specimens of ancient Jewish literature cite the legend of the fallen watchers (Gen 6:1–4) to point up the sinfulness of the present generation, whose fidelity to God's law is tested. For Strelan, Mark 13:32–37 adapts the same myth for similar purpose: to encourage watchful hope among an unfaithful generation (8:11–13; 9:19; 14:32–42).[77] Analyzing Xenophon's *Memorabilia*, Iamblichus's *Pythagorean Life*, Philostratus's *Life of Apollonius of Tyana*, and the Wisdom of Ben Sira, Whitney Shiner compares their presentations of philosopher-student relationships with Mark's portrait of Jesus and the Twelve. Viewing the gospel in this light, Shiner concludes: "[In contrast to the crowds and his opponents t]he disciples, on the other hand, provide a sympathetic human perspective seriously engaged with Jesus and his meaning. The difficulty that the disciples experience in understanding Jesus, in spite of their positive orientation and commitment, makes the hiddenness of his identity a reality for the listener. . . . The tragedy of Peter's recognizing his own cowardly denial of Jesus makes real the tragedy of humanity's denial of

75. Elizabeth Struthers Malbon's alliterative coinage ("Fallible Followers: Women and Men in the Gospel of Mark," *Semeia* 28 [1983]: 29–48) has entered the scholarly literature as shorthand for a Type II presentation of the disciples in Mark. It aptly marries their durable qualities: though they fail, yet they follow; though they follow, still they fail.

76. John Painter, "When Is a House Not a Home? Disciples and Family in Mark 3:13–35," *NTS* 45 (1999): 498–513.

77. Richard E. Strelan, "The Fallen Watchers and the Disciples in Mark," *JSP* 20 (1999): 73–92.

Jesus. The disciples represent the best human reaction to Jesus. It is that which brings their failures home so tellingly to Mark's listeners."[78]

The mediate readings considered to this point are historical-critical in a classical sense: they regard the Second Gospel within the framework of its social world and religious traditions. A broad swath of other Type II specimens adheres to modern literary criticism. A good example of close reading of the text, sans thick theory, is Larry Hurtado's "Following Jesus in the Gospel of Mark—and Beyond."[79] Hurtado argues that Mark portrays the Twelve as having two roles, both positive and negative, and "it is in this duality that the evangelist's purpose is served and disclosed." That purpose is pedagogical: to warn readers away from the failures of discipleship and to reveal "Jesus [as] the only adequate model of discipleship."[80]

Other literary critics are fascinated by the duality on which Hurtado puts his finger. Thus, Elizabeth Struthers Malbon: "I read the data [Werner] Kelber collects for 'discipleship failure' as evidence of Markan pastoral concern for the difficulty of true discipleship, which affirms both the power and the suffering of Jesus."[81] So stated, that is a neat paraphrase of Ernest Best's exegesis—though not for his reasons. Best and other redaction critics sought to identify the tensions between the Second Evangelist's style and substance from those of their inherited traditions and their cultural situation. Without repudiating such interpretations but allowing them potential to correct her own, Malbon focuses on complicated interrelations of elements within the text. She advocates a reading of Mark that recognizes its techniques for eliciting readers' identification with the disciples and takes as seriously Jesus's predictions of their persecution, arraignment, and possible martyrdom (13:9–13) as their speechless fear at the empty tomb (16:8).[82] "If there is a connotative coloring to Mark's Gospel, the disciples represent neither white nor black but gray. The shading of the Gospel of Mark—and especially of its portrait of the disci-

---

78. Whitney T. Shiner, *Follow Me! Disciples in Markan Rhetoric*, SBLDS 145 (Atlanta: Scholars Press, 1995), 292.

79. In *Patterns of Discipleship in the New Testament*, ed. Richard N. Longenecker (Grand Rapids: Eerdmans, 1996), 9–29.

80. "Following Jesus," 21–27 (quotations, 21, 25).

81. *Narrative Space and Mythic Meaning in Mark* (San Francisco: Harper & Row, 1986), 179 n. 26. The similarity between Kelber and Weeden's readings of Mark are noted in Black, *Disciples according to Mark*, 57–64, 141.

82. Elizabeth Struthers Malbon, "Texts and Contexts: Interpreting the Disciples in Mark," *Semeia* 62 (1993): 81–102; repr., Malbon, *In the Company of Jesus: Characters in Mark's Gospel* (Louisville: Westminster John Knox, 2000), 100–130.

ples—is thus more subtle than that to which a polemical reading is sensitive. And the challenge of being a follower of Jesus is thus more intricately drawn. The Markan Gospel discredits not the disciples, but the view of discipleship as either exclusive or easy."[83]

Paul Danove registers a "a profoundly ambivalent estimation of the disciples for [Mark's] narrative audience" that, unlike Malbon, tilts toward their abject failure and the narrative's deconstruction.[84] "The narrative audience is characterized by conflicting expectations; and cultivated positive and negative elements of the disciples' characterization simultaneously encourage the narrative audience to identify with and distance itself from the disciples."[85] The means by which he arrives at this conclusion is theoretically dense. Danove bifurcates the now commonplace "implied reader" into "the authorial audience" (a narrator's construction of an actual readership with preexistent beliefs, knowledge, and familiarity with literary conventions)[86] and "a narrative audience" (whose beliefs, knowledge, and literary competence are developed by the text).[87] The narrator cultivates the narrative audience's competence through "semantic frames" and in that process modifies preexisting frames assumed by the authorial audience. Such frames provide "(1) points of information about the particular words accommodated by the frame, (2) relationships among these words and references to other frames containing them, and (3) perspectives for apprehending and evaluating the function of these words and expectations for their content."[88] The words in these frames may carry a positive, negative, or ambiguous valance (respectively, in Mark 15:40–41; 16:8, ἀκολουθεῖν, φοβεῖσθαι, and θεωρεῖν).[89] Mark's narrative manipulates these semantic frames to achieve different rhetorical strategies, which Danove styles

83. Malbon, "Texts and Contexts," 93. Variations on this theme may be found throughout Malbon's collection, *In the Company of Jesus*, esp. 41–99, 166–225.

84. "The Narrative Rhetoric of Mark's Ambiguous Characterization of the Disciples," *JSNT* 20 (1998): 36; repr., with elaboration, as "A Rhetorical Analysis of Mark's Construction of Discipleship," in *Rhetorical Criticism and the Bible*, ed. Stanley E. Porter and Dennis L. Stamps, JSNTSup 195 (Sheffield: Sheffield Academic, 2002), 280–96.

85. Paul Danove, *The Rhetoric of the Characterization of God, Jesus, and Jesus' Disciples in the Gospel of Mark*, JSNTSup 290 (New York: T&T Clark, 2005), 126.

86. Such as one finds in Ernest Best, "Mark's Readers: A Profile," in Van Segbroeck et al., *Four Gospels 1992*, 2:839–55; cited by Danove in "Narrative Rhetoric," 23 n. 5.

87. Paul Danove, "The Characterization and Narrative Function of the Women at the Tomb (Mark 15,40–41.47; 16,1–8)," *Bib* 77 (1996): 375–97, esp. 377.

88. Danove, "Narrative Rhetoric," 22; also "Characterization and Narrative Function," 376.

89. Danove, "Characterization and Narrative Function," 394.

as "neutral (the absence of repetition), sophisticating (repetition that builds on the authorial audience's pre-existing beliefs), and deconstructive (repetition that undercuts pre-existing beliefs)."[90] The exegetical payoff: by marching its readers through these strategically arranged semantic fields, "the Gospel as gospel seeks to persuade the original believing community to assume the ideology of the narrative audience and become the believing community proposed by the narration"—notwithstanding the fact "that the formation of the believing community envisioned by the narration is frustrated."[91] My reason for presenting Danove's method in such detail is to note a curious point: by differentiating "positive" and "negative" terms in these strategically distributed semantic frames, Danove has transposed old-fashioned redaction criticism into the newfangled semiotic analysis of Charles J. Fillmore, Menakhem Perry, Umberto Eco, and Peter J. Rabinowitz. Moreover, Danove is well aware of this: he correlates the semantic field attributed to the author's cultivation of his "narrative audience" with the redactional vocabulary ascertained by E. J. Pryke.[92] Dress "tradition" as "authorial audience" and "redaction" as "narrative audience," keep the author firmly centered as "rhetorical strategist" (instead of "redactor"), and, with Danove, you have a reasonable facsimile of Best's technique and much of his exegesis of Mark.

Cédric Fischer closely attends to the oscillating tension, generated by Markan segments (1:16–8:26; 8:27–10:52; 11:1–12:44; 13:3–37; 14:1–16:8), between a *pôle christologique* and a *pôle anthropologique*. Finally, however, his study is less diachronically literary, more synchronically theological.[93] For the disciples in Mark and their real-life counterparts in the Markan community, the incursion of God's unconsummated kingdom creates the paradox of the church's crucified-risen, now absent–still present Lord, mirrored by the disciples' believing infidelity. The evangelist's anthropological determinism gives to his portrayal of the disciples a tragic aspect, correlative with Jesus's own

---

90. Danove, "Narrative Rhetoric," 24. In "The Rhetoric of the Characterization of Jesus as the Son of Man in Christ in Mark," *Bib* 84 (2003): 16–34, Danove applies the same kind of analysis to study of Markan Christology.

91. Danove, "Rhetorical Analysis," 296. That frustration reaches its highest pitch at Mark 16:8: "With the notice that the women never delivered the message and the implication that the disciples never became faithful proclaimers of that message, the parasite kills the host!" (293).

92. Danove, "Rhetorical Analysis," 281 n. 4; 282 nn. 5–6; 286 n. 17; 287 n. 20; 290 n. 31; 292 n. 37. On Pryke, see Black, *Disciples according to Mark*, 233–41.

93. *Les Disciples dans l'Évangile de Marc: Une grammaire théologique*, EBib, n.s. 57 (Paris: Gabalda, 2007), esp. 19–24, 42–49, 142.

tragic destiny; the disciples' incomprehension of Jesus reflects the fragility of the Christian's believing condition.[94] Fischer's exegesis intersects with that of Donald Juel,[95] who emphasizes the disciples' need to be released from the demonic, and with that of Juel's student I. Brent Driggers, who stresses the sheer mystery of God and of God's hardening of the Twelve.[96]

The disciples' ambivalent conduct and the paradox of discipleship are recurring motifs in recent theological studies of the Second Gospel. Interpreters differ, primarily, on whether there is for Mark a pedagogical takeaway—the need for candid reappraisal within the community of faith[97]—or whether (with Juel; Driggers; and Fischer) Mark intends to plunge its readers into what Christopher Burdon describes as "the radiant obscurity" whose "mystery is unveiled but not assimilated."[98] Robert Fowler's exercise in reader-response criticism accepts the didactic option: "Because Mark is willing to put the story and the discourse into tension with each other, he is able to offer a narrative that instructs the naratee in the challenges of discipleship without a full and explicit portrayal of successful discipleship in the story. In Mark the twelve are foils to Jesus at the story level so that at the discourse level the naratee can observe their mistakes and inadequacies and learn to behave differently."[99] James Hanson disagrees that Mark's story and discourse are pedagogically at odds. For him, Mark presents God as heavily invested in disciples who are grasped by Satan; their fate "rests not in their own capacity to overcome their failures, but in God's capacity to break through their unbelief and rescue them from their darkness."[100]

---

94. *Les Disciples*, 107, 110, 171, 193–203.

95. *A Master of Surprise: Mark Interpreted* (Minneapolis: Fortress, 1994), 70–75, and chapter 5 of the present volume.

96. *Following God through Mark: Theological Tension in the Second Gospel* (Louisville: Westminster John Knox, 2007), 99–106.

97. Thus, Cyril Latzoo, "The Story of the Twelve in the Gospel of Mark," *Hekima Review* [Nairobi] 13 (1995): 25–33; P. M. Meagher, "The Gospel of Mark: The Vulnerable Disciples," *Vid* 67 (2003): 779–803.

98. *Stumbling on God: Faith and Vision through Mark's Gospel* (London: SPCK; Grand Rapids: Eerdmans, 1990), 74, 106.

99. Fowler, *Let the Reader Understand*, 259–60. See also Michaelis Christoffel Dippenaar, "The Disciples in Mark: Narrative and Theology," *Taiwan Journal of Theology* 17 (1995): 139–209.

100. "The Disciples in Mark's Gospel: Beyond the Pastoral/Polemical Debate," *HBT* 20 (1998): 137. "Granted, the strong hint in 4:13 that the disciples may prove to be outsiders is borne out in the ensuing narrative; but if the reader's insider status is purchased at the expense of keeping the disciples out forever, the reader's inside status reveals itself as a Pyrrhic victory, for it suggests that human opposition and blindness can have the final word" (154 n. 37).

What then shall we say to these things? Some patterns emerge. Here's what I see.

First, all three types of interpretation of the disciples in Mark, which I categorized over thirty years ago, remain lively options to the present day. None of them has disappeared or supplanted the others. Each is represented by a recent, major monograph: Type I, by Suzanne Watts Henderson (2006); Type II, by Cédric Fischer (2007); Type III, by Mary Ann Tolbert (1989).

Second, of these types, the second, or mediate, position is most heavily represented in the past three decades of Markan scholarship. In the survey just presented, for every Type I or Type III reading, there are three or four among Type II. If one weighs the probabilities, this might be expected. By definition, "mediate" positions are "both/and," recognizing the measure of truth perceived in their more "conservative" or "liberal" counterparts, which tend toward the "either/or."[101] In 1989, I thought—and still I think—that Type II readings of the disciples in Mark claim the strongest exegetical support. If one regards the disciples—whether reckoned as the Twelve or more expansively—altogether positively, then satanic Peter at Caesarea Philippi (8:33) or the mute women at the tomb (16:8) will perplex. If one sees in them nothing but bad, then their abandonment of everything to follow Jesus (10:28) or their faithful ministry to him (15:40–41) will confound. If neither of these exclusive options satisfy, then your reading of Mark is probably somewhere in Type II.

Third, whatever their type, few of the studies I have noted are redaction-critical in character. That is a big difference from mid-twentieth century scholarship. Some still so proceed (Telford; Reiprich); others' exegeses are vestigially *redaktionsgeschichtlich* while conducted on other bases (Stegemann; Henderson). Already we have noted the interesting case of Danove, who offers a semiotic redaction divested of tradition-history. Nevertheless, a majority of inquiries into the disciples in Mark no longer proceed by separating, then weighing, tradition and redaction. No tumbling, please, into *post hoc, ergo propter hoc*: I find no evidence that my monograph made the slightest difference in others' methodological choices. Those still favoring Markan *Redaktionsgeschichte* continue with calm, without qualm. Those inclined toward different approaches haven't needed my encouragement. Continental scholars

---

101. Though I tried to define them precisely, the labels "conservative," "mediate," and "liberal" dissatisfied me in the 1980s (*Disciples according to Mark*, chapter 2, n. 38). They still do, not least because they invite mischievous confusion in the polarized political and religious climate of the United States in the early twenty-first century. Aside from "Types I, II, and III," I still haven't landed on better shorthand. Neither did the book's reviewers. Hope springs eternal.

may display slightly greater propensity for Markan redaction criticism, though that is not universally demonstrable (see Telford and Fischer).[102] What's clear, thirty years on, is that redaction criticism is no longer the automatic default setting in Markan scholarship.[103]

Is there a *different* default setting among Markan exegetes? That question leads to a fourth conclusion that may be drawn from my updated *Forschungsbericht*: methodologically, these studies of the disciples in Mark are all over the map. Irrespective of the ways in which I have typed them, one finds (1) historical and sociological investigations (see Stegemann; Painter; Riches), (2) *traditionsgeschichtlich* (Shiner; Strelan; Henderson) or redactional (Telford) analyses, (3) narrative or rhetorical examinations (Malbon; Tolbert; Dippenaar; Danove [to a degree]), (4) *Tendenzkritik* (Burdon; Juel; Latzoo; Hanson; Meagher; Driggers; Fischer), (5) reader-response exercises (Fowler; Danove [to some extent]), as well as studies that marry two or more of these approaches (most obviously, Gibson; Hurtado; Miller; and Reiprich). It is worth noting that representatives from each of these five converge on a Type II exegesis of Mark resembling Best's, which was undertaken on strenuously redaction-critical premises. From that, one might conclude that the ambivalent portrait of the disciples in Mark is strengthened, or at least for now is most popular among scholars operating in five different methodological theaters.[104] Those are the same five that I mapped in figure 3 of chapter 8 of *Disciples according to Mark*.[105] Many reviewers joined with me in faulting my model for composite

102. Though all cultural differences have not been effaced, the exegetical boundaries among European, British, North African, and North American Markan scholarship seem to me more porous today than they were three decades ago. For instance, Dieter Lührmann's *Das Markusevangelium* (Tübingen: Mohr Siebeck, 1987), which replaced Erich Klostermann's commentary (1926; 4th ed., 1950) in the Handbuch zum Neuen Testament. While sensitive to Mark's traditions, sources, and redaction, Lührmann emphasizes the gospel's narrative flow. The same may be said of Camille Focant's *L'évangile selon Marc*, CBNT 2 (Paris: Cerf, 2004). On the Atlantic's western side, the history and redaction of traditions occupy an important place in the technical commentaries by Adela Yarbro Collins (*Mark: A Commentary*, Hermeneia [Minneapolis: Fortress, 2007]) and Joel Marcus (*Mark 1–8: A New Translation with Introduction and Commentary*, AB 27 [New York: Doubleday, 2000]; *Mark 8–16: A New Translation with Introduction and Commentary*, AB 27A [New Haven: Yale University Press, 2009]).

103. Telford notes: "Redaction criticism is a discipline in tension with itself, seeking to remain an historical method but struggling in particular to come to terms with the literary aspects of its source material" ("Pre-Markan Tradition in Recent Research," 2:708).

104. Again, Telford ("Pre-Markan Tradition," 712): "Results are always strengthened when different methods produce similar conclusions."

105. See p. 283. Best was "sure that even if all Black's five methods were to be used schol-

exegesis. That model, however, has turned out to be reasonably predictive of the various ways my colleagues would proceed. No grove-decimating insight there, either. In 1989, I was offering not a normative prescription of the multiple ways in which Markan scholarship ought to proceed but rather a positive description of how in fact it did and could progress. The fact that it has done so demonstrates only that little, methodologically speaking, has radically changed in the past thirty years.[106] Would one expect otherwise?

That said, (fifth) a change is detectable. It is that which John Donahue charged me with underestimating:[107] redaction criticism's composition-critical dimension. Thirty years ago, and longer, scholars theologically attentive to the Markan text naturally attempted to peel away the evangelist's editorial embellishment from his inherited traditions. That exercise seemed natural, because such exegetes were the children of an antecedent generation of form criticism. In 2022, it seems just as natural for theologically sensitive interpreters to "read Mark in its final form," as a narrative unity. So notes Telford, who is quite sympathetic to Markan *Redaktionsgeschichte*: "Redaction criticism has been giving away, therefore, to a broader composition criticism in its search for Markan fingerprints. . . . There have been growing doubts about our ability to separate source from redaction in Mark, far less identify specific written sources or establish the earlier form of a proposed traditional unit. . . . There has been a growing recognition of the unity of the gospel in its language, style,

---

ars would still come up with different answers to the same problems" (*JTS* 41 [1990]: 606). Of course they have, though at present the results are not as scattered as Best predicted. There is a working, exegetical consensus. Three decades from now, things may look differently.

106. The exception to this assessment would be deconstructive analyses, which relocate the interpretive focus away from the text and onto its interpreter: several of the exercises, e.g., in *Mark and Method: New Approaches in Biblical Studies*, 2nd ed., ed. Janice Capel Anderson and Stephen D. Moore (Minneapolis: Fortress, 2008). This, too, remains a lively option, though not one that has yet taken the field. Most historical and literary critics of Mark have reached rapprochement on the text's centrality, which is where most recent Markan commentaries operate: among others, John R. Donahue and Daniel J. Harrington, *The Gospel of Mark*, SP 2 (Collegeville: Liturgical Press, 2002); M. Eugene Boring, *Mark: A Commentary*, NTL (Louisville: Westminster John Knox, 2006); C. Clifton Black, *Mark*, ANTC (Nashville: Abingdon, 2011). Reviewing Bas M. F. van Iersel's *Mark: A Reader-Response Commentary*, trans. W. H. Bisscheroux, JSNTSup 164 (Sheffield: Sheffield Academic, 1998), I reported surprise by how little exegetical difference it made that van Iersel wrote of "reader response," not "authorial intention" (*CBQ* 62 [2000]: 570–72).

107. *PSTJ* (1989): 12. There Donahue had me dead to rights. Best's spirited defense of the kind of Markan redaction criticism I challenged demonstrates, nevertheless, that the old method still had life in it and remained deeply attractive to some, even in English-speaking scholarship. It still does, as we have witnessed.

composition and theology, and a growing appreciation of its literary coherence at the global level, despite inconsistencies at the micro-level."[108] For most interpreters, this may be more a matter of recalibrated emphasis than of radical departure. Some will always be interested in constructing levels of Markan exposition behind or beyond the text, be they traditional layers or semantic frames. Good on them. There is no inherently correct method of approach to any complex text; some methods are simply better suited than others to address particular questions that interest interpreters. If an approach throws light on a text as obscure as the Second Gospel, then let us embrace it and bless its practitioners' labors. And if in 2053 our reading of Mark as a narrative unity has become tendentious or blasé, we may rest assured that healthy scholarship will have kept pace to restore the balance or refresh the questions.

Sixth, the score of studies surveyed maintain a vibrant interest in the Second Evangelist as theologian, a substantial bequest of redaction criticism.[109] Recent scholarship tends to side more closely with Meye and Best, who construed Mark's aims as pedagogical or pastoral; in general, it shows less sympathy for Weeden's view of Mark as polemicist. An interesting aspect of recent research on the disciples is how much stress Mark's interpreters lay on its apocalyptic eschatology (Tolbert; Burdon; Juel; Shiner; Hanson; Painter; Strelan; Telford; Riches; Miller; Henderson; Fischer; and Driggers). This, to be sure, is no new idea;[110] still, Markan apocalypticism was not highlighted in the scholarship (roughly, 1960–1980) on which I originally concentrated.[111] I am not sure how to account for this; different kinds of cross-fertilization are possible. Juel and Marcus have probed Markan eschatology;[112] predictably, their students would

108. "Pre-Markan Tradition," 707.

109. Yarbro Collins called me out on this characterization: "The category 'evangelist as religious thinker' seems to be straightforward and poses no major problems for those of us who think historically. The category 'evangelist as theologian,' however, has connotations related to the creeds of the church and the history of doctrine and dogma" (*CRBR* 4 [1991]: 171). I appreciate her fear of anachronism. Like most theologians I know, however, I, too, think historically and suffer no fidgets by styling Mark as a theologian. Creedal and dogmatic connotations attend the term only if one chooses to import them, which in this case I do not. The claims (οἱ λόγοι) of this gospel have fundamentally to do with the God (ὁ θεός) whose kingdom Jesus instantiates. Provided that the term is carefully defined, neither do I find "historian" an impertinent description of Mark. See chapter 8 of this volume.

110. Timothy Colani, *Jésus Christ et les Croyances messianiques de son Temps*, 2nd ed. (Strasbourg: Treuttel et Wurtz, 1864).

111. Pesch's *Naherwartungen* (1968) and Howard Clark Kee, *Community of the New Age: Studies in Mark's Gospel* (Philadelphia: Westminster, 1977), were important exceptions.

112. Juel, *Master of Surprise*; Marcus, *Mark 1–8* and *Mark 8–16*. The same is true of Yarbro Collins, *Mark*, though, to my knowledge, none of her students are here represented.

follow their leads (the former, Driggers; the latter, Miller and Henderson).[113] *Wie der Doktorvater, so die Doktorkinder.* Contemporaneous research in Jesus and in Paul has also been apocalyptically preoccupied.[114] The Zeitgeist at the century's turn may have been influential, though that's impossible to prove. For whatever reason, the study of the disciples in Mark coheres with renewed appreciation of that gospel's eschatology. That is an important scholarly development.[115] Coincident with my preoccupations in *Disciples according to Mark*, it is also fitting: among the earliest exercises in Markan *Redaktionsgeschichte* was James M. Robinson's *The Problem of History in Mark* (1957), which posited that Jesus's struggle with Satan shapes the evangelist's perception of history.[116]

Mr. Popper's Falsifiable Penguins

> *You must learn from the mistakes of others. You can't possibly live long enough to make all of them yourself.*
>
> —Attributed to Sam Levenson[117]

What are we doing, and why are we doing it? Trying to answer those questions sums up my reasons for writing *Disciples according to Mark*. The same ques-

---

113. After Juel's death in 2003, Driggers's dissertation was completed the following year under Professor Brian K. Blount's direction.

114. Representative are E. P. Sanders, *Paul and Palestinian Judaism: A Comparison of Patterns of Religion* (Philadelphia: Fortress, 1977); Sanders, *Jesus and Judaism* (Philadelphia: Fortress, 1985); J. Louis Martyn, *Theological Issues in the Letters of Paul* (Nashville: Abingdon, 1997); Dale C. Allison, *Jesus of Nazareth: Millenarian Prophet* (Minneapolis: Fortress, 1998); Allison, *Constructing Jesus: Memory, Imagination, History* (Grand Rapids: Baker Academic, 2010).

115. *Pace* Breytenbach, for whom recent "investigation [of discipleship in Mark] has resulted without significant progress in scholarship" ("Current Research," 25). For Breytenbach, apparently, only that which is new qualifies as progress. I disagree. Especially in the humanities, the testing, corroboration, and refinement of the old can be as valuable as the introduction of novelty. Sometimes the vaunted "cutting edge" cannot dent soft butter.

116. SBT 21 (London: SCM, 1957); repr., *The Problem of History in Mark and Other Marcan Studies* (Philadelphia: Fortress, 1982). Robinson's dissertation was first published in German (*Das Geschichtsverständnis des Markusevangeliums* [Zürich: Zwingli]) in 1956, the same year in which Willi Marxsen's *Der Evangelist Markus* appeared (Göttingen: Vandenhoeck & Ruprecht).

117. Similar counsel is ascribed to Lao Tzu, Eleanor Roosevelt, and Hyman Rickover. In all cases, the source has proven impossible to confirm. Levenson may be the least remembered today, and the witty author of *Everything but Money* (New York: Simon and Schuster, 1966) deserves rescue from obscurity.

tions haunted the execution of my own labors. Even if many Markan exegetes no longer proceed redaction-critically, they operate by some critical light, and of that approach, those questions are still worth raising. A critique of method, especially one's own methods, is like a colonoscopy. You need to know what's in there but wish that you might learn it more comfortably.

In the mid-1980s, I may have heard of Sir Karl Raimund Popper (1902–1994); I knew little of his philosophy. I know only a smidgen now, though what I have learned chimes with my recollection of a dungeon carrel in Duke Divinity School's library.[118] Popper styled his philosophy of science as critical rationalism, "the critical search for error."[119] Theories "are statements which are tested by being submitted to systematic attempts to falsify them."[120] Contrary to the inductive method of classical empiricism,[121] "scientific theories [are] not the digest of observations, but . . . inventions—conjectures boldly put forward for trial, to be eliminated if they [clash] with observations; with observations that [are] rarely accidental but as a rule undertaken with the definite intention of testing a theory by obtaining, if possible, a decisive refutation."[122] Popper argued that corroboration and disproof are logically asymmetrical: one can never verify a theory's validity, no matter how many positive results issue from its testing, though a single negative outcome can demonstrate its falsity.[123] "The criterion of the scientific status of a theory is its falsifiability, or refutability, or testability":[124] not a prejudgment that the theory is bogus or necessarily false but rather its *capability of being shown false*—if it is false—by severe testing. "According to my proposal, what characterizes the empirical method is its manner of exposing to falsification, in every conceivable way, the system to be tested. Its aim is not to save the lives of untenable systems but, on the contrary, to select the one which by comparison is the fittest, by exposing them all to the

118. This is no exaggeration. Ask any graduate student assigned to one ca. 1980 and you're sure to hear the same.

119. Karl R. Popper, *Conjectures and Refutations: The Growth of Scientific Knowledge*, 3rd ed. (London: Routledge & Kegan Paul, 1969), 26–27. See also David Miller, *Critical Rationalism: A Restatement and Defence* (Chicago: Open Court, 1994).

120. Karl R. Popper, *The Logic of Scientific Discovery* (New York: Basic Books, 1959), 313.

121. "Induction, i.e. inference based on many observations, is a myth. It is neither a psychological fact, nor a fact of ordinary life, nor one of scientific procedure" (Popper, *Conjectures and Refutations*, 53).

122. Popper, *Conjectures and Refutations*, 46.

123. Popper, *Logic of Scientific Discovery*, 33. "It must be possible for an empirical system to be refuted by experience" (41, italicized in the original).

124. Popper, *Conjectures and Refutations*, 37 (emphasized in the original).

fiercest struggle for survival."[125] For Popper, the seeming "explanatory power" of a theory proves nothing; "It is easy to obtain confirmations, or verifications, for nearly every theory—if we look for confirmations."[126]

> The rationality of the sciences lies not in its habit of appealing to empirical evidence in support of its dogmas—astrologers do so too—but solely in the *critical approach*: in an attitude which, of course, involves the critical use, among other arguments, of empirical evidence (especially in refutations). For us, therefore, science has nothing to do with the quest for certainty or probability or reliability. We are not interested in establishing scientific theories as secure, or certain, or probable. Conscious of our fallibility we are only interested in criticizing them and testing them, hoping to find out where we are mistaken: of learning from our mistakes; and, if we are lucky, of proceeding to better theories.[127]

In the testing of theories, how does Popper propose we proceed? His basic axiom is *PS1* → *TT1* → *EE1* → *PS2*. "That is, we start from some problem *PS1*, proceed to a tentative solution or tentative theory *TT1*, which may be (partly or wholly) mistaken; in any case it will be subject to error-elimination, *EE1*, which may consist of critical discussion or experimental tests; at any rate, new

---

125. Popper, *Logic of Scientific Discovery*, 42. Robert John Ackermann disputes this Darwinian metaphor: "The real evolutionary metaphor suggests that lots of theories (competing ones) ought to be present in any area of investigation—and that theories, like species, may survive the death of particular individuals that belong to them" (*The Philosophy of Karl Popper* [Amherst: University of Massachusetts Press, 1976], 58).

126. Popper, *Conjectures and Refutations*, 36. "Our propensity to look out for regularities, and to impose laws upon nature, leads to the psychological phenomenon of *dogmatic thinking* or, more generally, dogmatic behaviour: we expect regularities everywhere and attempt to find them even where there are none; events which do not yield to these attempts we are inclined to treat as a kind of 'background noise'; and we stick to our expectations even when they are inadequate and we ought to accept defeat" (49).

127. Popper, *Conjectures and Refutations*, 229. William Warren Bartley's restatement clarifies: "How then are hypotheses or theories to be confirmed? *They are not to be confirmed*. There is no way to confirm—that is, to prove, verify, make firmer, make more probable—any theory of interest. They are and remain forever conjectural. There is no certain knowledge. What *is* done—and what has been mistaken for confirmation—Popper calls 'corroboration.' For a theory to be corroborated is simply *to have been tested* severely and to have passed the test. Such a theory is not made more probable thereby: it may yet fail a more severe test tomorrow" ("A Popperian Harvest," in *In Pursuit of Truth: Essays on the Philosophy of Karl Popper on the Occasion of His 80th Birthday*, ed. Paul Levinson (Atlantic Highlands, NJ: Humanities; Sussex: Harvester, 1982], 264).

problems *PS2*, arise from our creative activity; and these new problems are not in general intentionally created by us; they emerge autonomously from the field of new relationships which we cannot help bringing into existence with every action, however little we intend to do so."[128] Therefore, "the advance of knowledge consists, mainly, in the modification of earlier knowledge."[129] Of decisive importance is the criticism of our conjectures: "by bringing out our mistakes it makes us understand the difficulties of the problem we are trying to solve."[130]

The scientist lives at the intersection of three interactive worlds. World 1 is the physical world of blastulas and wart hogs and galaxies, which science attempts to explain. World 2 is the subjective world of human affect and thought: our feelings, beliefs, and dispositions. World 3 is the world of objective human cognition—language and books, paintings and symphonies, myths and theorems and theories—by which the World 2 mind creates products out of World 1 materials. The knowledge grasped by the individual human mind (World 2) is as indebted to the accumulated fund of human culture (World 3) as to the aggregate sense of experience (World 1).[131]

The mind of the individual scientist is free to acknowledge "that scientific discovery is impossible without faith in ideas which are of a purely speculative kind, and sometimes even quite hazy; a faith which is completely unwarranted from the point of view of science, and which, to that extent, is 'metaphysical.'"[132] What the scientist dare not do is assume that her discoveries are secure foundations for further research: "The empirical basis of objective science thus has nothing 'absolute' about it. Science does not rest upon rock-bottom. The bold structure of its theories rises, as it were, above a swamp. It is like a building erected on piles. The piles are driven down from above into the swamp, but not down to any natural or 'given' base; and when we cease our attempts to drive our piles into a deeper layer, it is not because we have reached firm ground.

---

128. Karl Popper, "Knowledge: Subjective versus Objective," in *A Pocket Popper*, ed. David Miller (Oxford: Fontana, 1983), 70–71.

129. Popper, *Conjectures and Refutations*, 28.

130. Popper, *Conjectures and Refutations*, vii.

131. Karl Popper, *Objective Knowledge: An Evolutionary Approach*, rev. ed. (Oxford: Clarendon; New York: Oxford University Press, 1979); Popper, *Knowledge and the Mind-Body Problem: In Defence of Interaction*, ed. M. A. Notturno (London: Routledge, 1994). Notes Ackermann (*Philosophy of Karl Popper*, 55): "The concept of intellectual evolution and of something like world 3 is not new with Popper. What is important here is Popper's use of these notions to ground an objective notion of the growth of scientific knowledge."

132. Popper, *Logic of Scientific Discovery*, 38.

We simply stop when we are satisfied that they are firm enough to carry the structure, at least for the time being."[133]

Well, then, Sir Karl: how *do* we know? On what basis can we assert any theory? "My answer . . . would be: 'I do *not* know: my assertion was merely a guess. Never mind the source, or the sources, from which it may spring—there are many possible sources, and I may not be aware of half of them; and the origins or pedigrees have in any case little bearing upon truth. But if you are interested in the problem which I have tried to solve by my tentative assertion, you may help me by criticizing it as severely as you can; and if you can design some experimental test which you think might refute my assertion, I shall gladly, and to the best of my powers, help you to refute it.'"[134]

At the age of seventeen, Popper, a member of Austria's Social Democratic Worker's Party, watched while police shot eight, unarmed party comrades. His World 2 revulsion at World 1 atrocity led to his World 3 disavowal of Marxist historical materialism as pseudoscience. That may account, in part, for his plea at age sixty-one:

> What we should do, I suggest, is to give up the idea of ultimate sources of knowledge, and admit that all knowledge is human; that it is mixed with our errors, our prejudices, our dreams, and our hopes; that all we can do is to grope for truth even though it is beyond our reach. . . . If we thus admit that there is no authority beyond the reach of criticism to be found within the whole province of our knowledge, however far it may have penetrated into the unknown, then we can retain, without danger, the idea that truth is beyond human authority. And we must retain it. For without this idea there

---

133. Popper, *Logic of Scientific Discovery*, 111. "The programme of tracing back all knowledge to its ultimate source in observation is logically impossible to carry through: it leads to an infinite regress. (The doctrine that truth is manifest cuts off the regress. This is interesting because it may help to explain the attractiveness of that doctrine.)" (*Conjectures and Refutations*, 23). Alternatively, Popper suggested, investigators cut short that regress by grounding their knowledge on the authority either of reason (the dogmatism of classical rationalism) or of experience (the psychologism of classical empiricism).

134. Popper, *Conjectures and Refutations*, 27. "This answer applies, strictly speaking, only if the question is asked about some scientific assertion as distinct from a historical one. If my conjecture was an historical one, sources (in the non-ultimate sense) will of course come into the critical discussion of its validity. Yet fundamentally, my answer will be the same." "All theoretical or generalizing sciences make use of the same method, whether they are natural sciences or social sciences" (Karl Popper, *The Poverty of Historicism*, 2nd ed. [London: Routledge & Kegan Paul, 1960], 130).

can be no objective standards of inquiry; no criticism of our conjectures; no groping for the unknown; no quest for knowledge.[135]

As best I can judge by Popper's criteria, "strict editorial criticism" of Mark's Gospel has failed and continues to fail.[136] That's the fundamental case I made in *Disciples according to Mark*.[137] I'll reformulate it in Popperian terms. Given the problem of distinguishing the Second Evangelist's editorial hand from his traditions or sources (*PS1*: chapters 1–2), I constructed a tentative theory (*TT1*) that redaction criticism, narrowly defined, was a deeply flawed method for Markan exegesis (chapters 3–6). I subjected *TT1* to the highest level of error-elimination (*EE1*) of which I was capable (at first, chapter 7; later, the book's testing by a jury of peers). The result was a new set of problems (*PS2*)—how Markan exegesis might more fruitfully proceed (chapter 8)—with which my reviewers and I have subsequently grappled. The fact that my outcomes were severely skeptical would be, for a Popperian, expected and even desirable: "The conjectural character of scientific hypotheses lies not so much in the fact that they cannot be shown to be right as in the fact that they are ready to be shown to be wrong."[138]

As best I can judge—and Best helped me reach this judgment—*Disciples according to Mark* also failed, on Popper's terms. Indeed, *it failed in multiple ways*. For brevity's sake, let's consider only three.[139] First, I had begun my study by asking, "How do we know what the Evangelist wrote and what he borrowed from others and then edited?" Popper insists, "There are all kinds of sources of our knowledge; but *none has authority*. . . . Thus the empiricist's questions, 'How do you know? What is the source of your assertion?' are wrongly put.

135. Popper, *Conjectures and Refutations*, 30. Popper favored theories with "verisimilitude"—approximation to truth—rather than claims of Truth with a capital T (233–35). See Miller, *Critical Rationalism*, 194–209.

136. This term is Donahue's, which he suggests in differentiation from "composition criticism" ("Redaction Criticism," 29–34). As we have seen, classical redaction criticism comprised both elements.

137. Nevertheless, I confess that some Markan pericopae (e.g., 7:1–23) are almost impossible for me to understand without theoretical recourse to *Traditions*- and *Redaktionsgeschichte*. See Black, *Mark*, 32–33, 169–77, as well as some reservations lodged in chapter 15 of the present volume.

138. David Miller, "Conjectural Knowledge: Popper's Solution of the Problem of Induction," in *In Pursuit of Truth*, ed. Levinson, 23.

139. Until writing this chapter I could not recall having previously attempted, in print, a convincing refutation of my own argument. I've lost more than Edna Millay's trousers. I'm now almost buck naked.

They are not formulated in an inexact or slovenly manner, but *they are entirely misconceived*: they are questions that beg for an authoritarian answer."[140] As a blockheaded empiricist, I had sought to validate my conjecture, which for Popper is impossible; the best for which I could have hoped was its partial corroboration. Second, from Popper's vantage point, my critics denied me even that. Most of *Disciples according to Mark*'s reviewers took its *PS2*, subjected their own *TT2* to strenuous *EE2*, and arrived at the *PS3* that one or another aspect of my tentative theory was erroneous. Even if a majority of reviewers agreed in the main with my new hypothesis, *all it took was one error*—for instance, my lack of clean statistical separation of categories and criteria—*to falsify it. Quod erat demonstrandum.* Third, I certainly did not stick my neck out and advance a bold alternative for others to test. My representative redaction critics, as well as the method's rehabilitators, were far more courageous than I, though their conjectures could also be falsified. I called it Discretion. Popper might prefer, Cowardice.

Arguably, therefore, Meye, Best, Weeden, their successors—and Black—have *all* failed.

There is yet another possibility: that Popper's brand of critical rationalism is also flawed. I haven't the philosophical or scientific chops to demonstrate that, though I'd bet someone could. John Worrall argues that Popper seriously misidentified the nature of both the scientific process of identifying error and the process by which scientists generate "tentative theories."[141] Physicist and theologian John Polkinghorne agrees: "Science does not in fact progress by continually drawing a bow at a refutable venture. . . . There is clearly much more to be said about science than Popper has been able to articulate."[142]

There is more to be said about *Wissenschaft* than many biblical scholars often admit. Reviewing the last three decades of Markan scholarship, I am struck by how much of our work operates within World 3 while we genuflect

---

140. Popper, *Conjectures and Refutations*, 24–25.

141. "'Revolution in Permanence': Popper on Theory-Change in Science," in *Karl Popper: Philosophy and Problems*, ed. Anthony O'Hear, RIPS 39 (Cambridge: Cambridge University Press, 1995), 75–102. For appreciative critiques of Popper's philosophy, the other essays in O'Hear's volume are well worth consulting, as are Ackermann, *Philosophy of Karl Popper*, and Herbert Keuth, *The Philosophy of Karl Popper* (Cambridge: Cambridge University Press, 2005).

142. *Beyond Science: The Wider Human Context* (Cambridge: Cambridge University Press, 1996), 15–16. Both Polkinghorne and Worrall (see previous note) counterpropose a more gradual process, in which specific new theories are constructed from background theories regarded by scientists as well entrenched. Such a model is more in line with that suggested in chapter 8 of *Disciples according to Mark*.

before World 1. Save for archaeologists or textual critics who can sift physical materials, most of our sociohistorical or literary-theological analysis remains grounded in theoretical construction. If that is unavoidable, perhaps other metaphors for our work would better serve us than the strictly scientific.[143] Are exegetes less akin to chemists with spectroscopes, more like judges applying statutes or pianists playing Chopin? If so, then jurists and musicologists may offer more help in disciplining our minds than we have credited them.[144] If not, Popper sobers and encourages us in a still salubrious humility: "Science has no authority. It is not the magical product of the given, the evidence, the observations. It is not a gospel of truth. It is the result of our endeavours and mistakes. It is you and I who make science as well as we can. It is you and I who are responsible for it. . . . I may be wrong and you may be right, and by an effort we may get nearer to the truth."[145]

143. Attempting to differentiate responsible historical criticism from flat-footed historicism, elsewhere I have made a case for scriptural interpretation as a relationship between the Lover and the beloved, not merely the investigator and her subject matter ("Trinity and Exegesis," in *Reading Scripture with the Saints* [Eugene, OR: Wipf & Stock; Cambridge: Lutterworth, 2014, 2015], 9–36).

144. See Richard A. Posner, *How Judges Think* (Cambridge: Harvard University Press, 2008); Frederick Dorian, *The History of Music in Performance: The Art of Musical Interpretation from the Renaissance to Our Day* (New York: Norton, 1966).

145. Karl Popper, *Realism and the Aim of Science* (London: Routledge, 1983), 259–60; Popper, *The High Tide of Prophecy: Hegel, Marx, and the Aftermath*, vol. 2 of *The Open Society and Its Enemies* (London: Routledge & Sons, 1945), 238.

CHAPTER 5

A Servant of Surprise: Juel Interpreted

Some things have to be believed to be seen.

—Ralph Hodgson

WHEN DON JUEL DIED AT AGE SIXTY-ONE in Princeton, New Jersey, he left in his debt thousands of students and colleagues for a lifetime of ministry, education, and exegesis. The exegesis was devoted primarily to the Gospel according to Mark. Juel's earliest work in the field was assisting his seminary professor (and first cousin) Roy Harrisville in a translation of Willi Marxsen's classic monograph, *Der Evangelist Markus* (1956).[1] In later years, Harrisville's hand upon Juel's scholarship was, by his own admission, more guiding than that of Marxsen.[2] Harrisville regarded Mark as a preacher's sermon.[3] In his last book, Juel nodded toward Saint Augustine by articulating "a rhetorical approach" to the gospel, one that intended "to teach, to delight, and to move."[4] In the vivid terms of his longtime Luther Seminary colleague, Patrick Keifert, Juel had little interest in playing "mind reader" to the Second Evangelist and his community.[5] When undertaking historical excavation of what the text had

---

In memoriam: Donald Harrisville Juel (1942–2003).

1. Willi Marxsen, *Mark the Evangelist: Studies on the Redaction History of the Gospel*, trans. James Boyce, Donald Juel, and William Poehlmann, with Roy Harrisville (Nashville: Abingdon, 1969); German original, *Der Evangelist Markus: Studien zur Redaktionsgeschichte des Evangeliums* (Göttingen: Vandenhoeck & Ruprecht, 1956).

2. Donald H. Juel, *A Master of Surprise: Mark Interpreted* (Minneapolis: Fortress, 1994), vii.

3. Roy A. Harrisville, *The Miracle of Mark: A Study in the Gospel* (Minneapolis: Augsburg, 1967).

4. Donald H. Juel, *The Gospel of Mark*, IBT (Nashville: Abingdon, 1999), 31–32; cf. Augustine, *Doctr. chr.* 4.27.74.

5. Patrick Keifert, "Mind Reader and Maestro: Models for Understanding Biblical Interpreters," *WW* 1 (1981): 153–65.

meant, his heart didn't seem in it.[6] But when conveying the impact of this gospel's truth, his sentences sparkle, for Juel was a consummate "maestro." What follows is a modest appreciation of Donald Juel's exegetical musicianship as an interpreter of Mark.

Reclaiming God from Interpretive Neglect

Juel's reading of the Second Gospel begins and ends with an unwavering conviction of God's life and work through the text. The activity of the living God is the point of departure for Juel's understanding of Mark, for his construal of the evangelist's own means of interpretation, for his adoption and refinement of modern exegetical method, and for his sense of what is ultimately at stake in scriptural interpretation. Juel much appreciated the famous essay by Nils Dahl, his *Doktorvater* at Yale, on "the neglected aspect of New Testament theology"—namely, God—and Juel was determined not to perpetuate that neglect.[7] If one does not recognize its theocentricism, one cannot possibly understand Don Juel's scholarship.

One can watch this fundamental premise at work in his general comments about exegetical method, the choices interpreters make before they even turn to the text in question. "If what moves us to read the Bible is the possibility not just of meaningfulness but of truthfulness, then we have little choice but to weigh anchor and sail out of the harbor into the deep"—that is, beyond the comfortable shallows of allegedly disinterested historical criticism.[8] Even more pointedly, "To whatever extent modern interpretation effectively exorcises God from public imagination, such scholarship is anti-theological, in spite of the intentions of particular interpreters."[9]

This relentless concentration on what God may be up to, as Mark narrates the story of Jesus, is palpable at numerous points in Juel's commentary on that gospel.[10] Of Jesus's perennially baffling explanation for speaking in parables

---

6. See, for instance, Juel, *Master of Surprise*, 123–28, and *Gospel of Mark*, 36–38.

7. Nils Alstrup Dahl, "The Neglected Factor in New Testament Theology," in *Jesus the Messiah: The Historical Origin of Christological Doctrine*, ed. Donald H. Juel (Minneapolis: Fortress, 1991), 153–63.

8. Juel, *Master of Surprise*, 10.

9. Juel, *Master of Surprise*, 9.

10. Donald H. Juel, *Mark*, ACNT (Minneapolis: Augsburg, 1990). Subsequent citations appear in text.

(Mark 4:10–12), Juel acknowledges, "There seems no escape from the implication: God has the sovereign right to determine who will and who will not see and hear—and repent. Jesus claims that right as his own" (71). Accordingly, upon his return home in Mark 6:1–6a, "We know only that Jesus' neighbors remain imprisoned by their unbelief, and, as a result, Jesus does no mighty works in their midst—except, the narrator adds, for a few healings" (92). The God to whom Mark's Jesus introduces us is a promising God. Amid the grim forecast in 13:2–23, "divine necessity is embedded in a promise: the gospel will be preached. Persecution will not silence the preachers. The word will be spread. This is not a command but a declaration of what God will make possible" (177).

Yet this God is also dangerous, as one of Juel's students helped him better to appreciate with respect to the temple veil's rending in the passion narrative. Conceding that the evangelist may be obliquely expressing the claim made in Heb 10:19–22, Juel notes that, at Mark 15:38, "the imagery may as well suggest the removal of protection," which the inner curtain concealing the holy of holies was meant to provide. "The protection is gone and now God is among us, on the loose."[11] "The heavens, understood as a great cosmic curtain that separates creation from God's presence, are in the process of being torn open. . . . Viewed from another perspective, the image may suggest the protecting barriers are gone and that God, unwilling to be confined to sacred spaces, is on the loose in our own realm. If characters in the story find Jesus' ministry threatening, then they may have good reason."[12] While Juel had no quarrel with Anselm of Canterbury's doctrine of the atonement,[13] he doubted that such was what Mark was driving at—which is, instead, how the world appears from the vantage point afforded by the cross. In Juel's view, the evangelist seems less interested in soteriology than in epistemology: "What does Jesus' death disclose about us and our world—and about God?" (217). Juel answers his own question: "[Mark] attempts in narrative form a "theology of the cross"—a glimpse of reality that takes as its point of departure the execution of the King of the Jews. If Jesus is the promised Messiah, this is how the world must be—and this is the only way the story can be told! . . . In the death of the

11. Juel, *Gospel of Mark*, 61.

12. Juel, *Master of Surprise*, 35–36, citing Josephus, *B.J.* 5.212–214.

13. See *Gospel of Mark*, 160–63, wherein Juel draws into conversation *Cur Deus Homo?* (1099; *Why God Became Man, and the Virgin Conception and Original Sin*, trans. Joseph M. Colleran [Albany, NY: Magi Books, 1969]) with C. S. Lewis's *The Lion, the Witch and the Wardrobe: A Children's Story* (New York: Collier, 1950), esp. 138–40, 152, 159–60.

King of the Jews we experience in the most profound way the great surprise God had in store" (224–25).[14]

Equally profound, however, is the end of Mark's narrative: "Jesus' resurrection has exploded the old standards of reality and appearance, truth and absurdity. Those to whom this is revealed and who understand the secret can no longer measure reality and truth by convention, by institutional standards, or even by common sense."[15]

Just there we may understand why so many of Juel's comments on Mark seem almost to have been lifted from anti-Pelagian broadsides. "The yearning to know what God knows is great; the temptation to 'be like God' seems to be inherent in humankind" (184). It is not merely that Juel read Mark through an Augustinian lens, even though he cheerfully acknowledged how Pauline his interpretation of the Second Gospel could be.[16] For Juel, the evangelist (Mark) shared with the apostle (Paul) a comparable theological ecology: God alone is the sovereign source of life, and only God can release humanity from its enslavement. For us, no less than for the rich man in Mark 10:17–22, "eternal life is obviously not a right but a gift" (142).[17] "Yet believers ought not to be naïve about what to expect from a world bound by sin that hung Jesus on a cross" (185). So follows the significance of Jesus's prediction and rebuke of Peter at Caesarea Philippi (8:31, 33): "There must be a clash. The scandal of the cross is not due to slightly flawed scriptural interpretation but to the very nature of things. There must be a confrontation between God and the human race—and we are now told that the encounter will be marked by a cross. Someone must die, even if death will not have the final word. . . . Humans are powerless to break through that barrier; in fact, most are obliged to defend it. For God to reclaim a captive creation there must be a battle. And Jesus will be the casualty" (122–23).

Jesus is no mere victim. Since his baptism (1:9–11), he has been possessed— by God's Spirit.[18] God will also vindicate him by resurrection. Even at his transfiguration (9:2–8), "he is a heavenly being. He will eventually appear in his

14. See also Juel, *Master of Surprise*, 105. Here, the influence of Dahl's thought on Juel's construction of Markan Christology is obvious; see especially Dahl, "The Crucified Messiah," in *Jesus the Messiah*, 27–47.

15. Donald H. Juel, with James S. Ackerman and Thayer S. Wardlaw, *An Introduction to New Testament Literature* (Nashville: Abingdon, 1978), 195.

16. "History's termination marks the birth of a new age. Paul uses the same language in Romans (8:21–33)" (*Mark*, 176; see also *Gospel of Mark*, 134); "In Mark, however, [Christian] reinterpretation [of Jewish messianism] does not obscure the shock: that the offspring of David should be invested and enthroned on a cross, a victim of those from whom he was expected to deliver Israel, is an offense (1 Cor 1:23)" (*Mark*, 126; see also *Gospel of Mark*, 155).

17. In the original, the first two words of this sentence are set in bold font.

18. Juel, *Master of Surprise*, 36.

'glory' (8:38; 14:62). . . . [But] there can be no final glory, no consummation until after the cross. That is the 'necessity' which dominates Jesus' career" (127).

FROM SOLUTION TO PLIGHT

I do not recall Juel's contradicting Marxsen's generally accepted dictum that the Second Evangelist reasoned backward, from the passion to the beginning of Jesus's story.[19] Typically, however, Juel follows the evangelist's own lead by attending to the gospel's narrative sequence, which moves from "solution"— the advent of Jesus as agent and incarnation of God's kingdom (1:14–15)—to "plight": various, increasingly dire representations of the human predicament, manifested by humanity's checkered response to Jesus. It is the severity of that plight in Mark that prompts Juel to give full weight to the gospel's assessment of humanity's hard-heartedness (3:5; 4:10–12; 6:51–52; 8:17–18).

For example, Juel had much to say about Israel, its leaders during the time of Jesus, and the gentiles. To begin with, "Mark is the most careful of the evangelists in distinguishing various groups within the Jewish community. There is no basis for the claim that 'Israel' rejects Jesus" (121).[20] Juel was death on all Jewish stereotyping whose covert objective was (gentile) Christian triumphalism:

> The whole Pharisaic enterprise [is] to sanctify all of life. The tradition of the elders [in Mark 7:3, 5] was not an attempt to bury the commands of God in trivia but to apply the Torah to every facet of life. . . . We do the Pharisees an injustice when we regard them as petty hypocrites. Mark does not portray them as petty. They have a definite view of Jewish identity that differs at points from Jesus', and they ask questions. . . . Judaism cannot be viewed as a decadent religion; it has remained vital throughout the centuries. . . . [Rather] what distinguishes [Judaism and Christianity] is the view of the law and its function. For Judaism . . . , the relationship with God and the world is mediated by the Torah, understood as a structure that orders all of life in terms of holiness. For Jesus' followers, the relationship with God and

---

19. Marxsen, *Mark the Evangelist*, 32.

20. Juel's assessment has lately been upheld by Suzanne Watts Henderson, "Was Mark a Supersessionist? Two Test Cases from the Earliest Gospel," in *The Ways That Often Parted: Essays in Honor of Joel Marcus*, ed. Lori Barton, Jill Hicks-Keeton, and Matthew Thiessen (Atlanta: SBL Press, 2018), 145–68. For Henderson, Mark's Jesus does not supplant Jewish tradition but reorients its ethnic and religious preoccupations toward trust in God's sovereign authority.

the world is mediated by Jesus, whose desire to heal and to save acknowledges no boundaries. (102, 106–7)[21]

For Juel, that assessment's implications were at least twofold. As regards the evangelist's ecclesiology, which comes to a head in Mark 14:53–65, "the church is characterized as a spiritual temple without hands and is viewed as a replacement of the Jewish temple."[22] Second, if gentiles are to be included [among the people of God], it will not be because Jews have been rejected and not given an opportunity to hear the promises of God. Even Paul, whose career was built on the equality of gentiles within the church, insists that the word of God is "to the Jew first and also to the Greek." "[In Mark 7:24–30] Jesus expresses such sentiments without attempting to conceal their offensiveness" (108).[23]

Within that context—Jesus's repugnance to both Jews and gentiles—we are better positioned to understand the evangelist's multilevel political critique. Here, one must tread cautiously, lest Juel be misclassified as a practitioner of what is now styled as political or ideological approaches to biblical texts. Juel was no unreconstructed liberal: a polemicist, traveling under exegetical guise, for causes whose promotion would assure that the church was "behaving itself." In reading Mark, Juel was fascinated by what happened when "the gospel of God" and the impact of God's kingdom (1:14–15) ran headlong against and exposed this world's religious and political conventions as sacred cows by which "the will of God" (3:35) was held at bay or conveniently ignored. "Conformity to the crucified involves such matters as social organization and relations" (149). This theme runs as a scarlet thread throughout Juel's commentary on Mark:

> While [Jesus's pronouncement of forgiveness in 2:5] may not qualify as blasphemy by any known legal code, the religious leaders certainly understand Jesus' willingness to make declarations on God's behalf as the kind of infringement that constitutes a violation of the sacred boundary [constructed by some first-century scribes]. Jesus blasphemes! (47)

> The pronouncement [in Mark 3:33–35] is explosive. Jesus threatens the most fundamental of all structures, the family. Blood relations guarantee nothing.

21. Note also 51: "Jesus would have looked more like a Pharisee than a member of any other of the various groups in the story."

22. Donald H. Juel, *Messiah and Temple: The Trial of Jesus in the Gospel of Mark*, SBLDS 31 (Missoula, MT: Scholars Press, 1977), 57.

23. The quotation of Rom 1:16 and allusion to Rom 9–11 again demonstrate the theological congruence that Juel recognized between Mark and Paul.

What will alone unite, he seems to say, is fidelity to the truth. Those who are troubled by Jesus have good reason to be. He appears as the opponent of structured life—of civilization. . . . "New skins for new wine." But at what cost? Who will be able to pay? (65)

What is frightening about Jesus is that he refuses to leave the world as it is. He transgresses the boundaries and rescues those beyond help. He has the power. Such a person cannot be controlled, only followed. (81)[24]

Jesus' terse explanation [in 7:14–15] undermines the whole enterprise of constructing a system by which the world is structured in terms of pure and impure, clean and unclean. . . . What should be said is that religious Jews found Jesus a threat to their religion. (106–7)[25]

Jesus did not promise peaceful coexistence between Rome and those whose primary allegiance is to the Lord God. The Roman government certainly did not understand Jesus to be politically harmless. (165)

[Mark's] comment [in 15:1–15] ought not to obscure the good intentions both Jewish and Roman leaders had for taking action against Jesus. He was dangerous. (215; see also 89)

Jesus was threatening and God's kingdom, dangerous: the constant refrains. "The world is a dangerous place for the elect" (186).[26] Juel does not interpret the kingdom of God in Mark as a mandate for anarchy, of which Roman thinkers and politicos were understandably fearful (137). "While Jesus' preaching speaks of fidelity to God in a way that threatens the fabric of society, his ultimate goal is not the destruction of human community but the establishment of that community on a firmer foundation. . . . New social units will take the place of the old" (139, 144; see also 133–34). Rather, "the argument that the narrative seeks to make, if we may use such language, is that Jesus must trans-

24. So also Donald H. Juel, "Plundering Satan's House: Mark 5:1–20," *WW* 17 (1997): 278–81.

25. So also 159, on Mark 11:15–19: "The temple is thoroughly corrupt, as was the case once before in the history of Jerusalem [thus, Jeremiah's sermon in 7:2–11]. Evidence of that corruption will be the refusal of its priestly leaders to accept Jesus."

26. "Jesus' [Olivet] discourse . . . addresses a readership whose greatest danger is not a failure of nerve as much as a tired lack of awareness both of the dangers and the possibilities that lie ahead" (Juel, *Master of Surprise*, 88).

gress the bounds of propriety and tradition for the sake of a higher good. . . . Lines must be crossed, curtains torn, the heavens themselves rent asunder in the course of the career of one whose coming can be characterized as good news."[27] On the other hand, "the world's standards of judgment appear to run headlong into God's ways. Jesus does not measure up" (91).

The sauce that gags Jesus's adversaries is equally bitter for his own followers to swallow. Because Juel finds no suggestion that the Twelve in Mark are any less epistemologically fettered than is everyone else—save Jesus—Juel cuts the disciples appreciable slack: "If the problem [in Mark 6:52] were one of will, encouragement could perhaps suffice. If the problem is a hardened heart, something more than exhortation will be required. . . . Deliverance can come only from outside. . . . [The disciples'] problem is not simply attributable to sloth or lack of effort. They are unable to see and hear, blocked from understanding by a malady that requires a cure from outside" (100, 115).

If the "disciples' problem is that they are in the grasp of a power from which they must be delivered" (17), then they are due greater charity than many Markan commentators offer them:[28] "The disciples are not simply foils for readers whose privileged position allows for a certain disdain. It never ceases to amaze me that commentators take a kind of delight in the disciples' failures. There are few readings of the Gospel that elicit any empathy with those whose eyes were very heavy, and fewer still who pick upon the promises of their rehabilitation. While readers cannot identify with the disciples—we are located at a different place from the beginning of the story—something about their plight is instructive."[29]

"Nothing less than an act of deliverance will solve [the disciples'] problem—and the problem of the human race" (197–98). And that is precisely what Juel invites his students to discern in the terrified witnesses' faltering silence at the empty tomb (Mark 16:8, the gospel's true ending):

> Yet the world is not the same. The tomb is empty. Jesus is out, beyond death's reach, on the loose. . . . Turning the completion of the story into an act of human will makes the same mistake as turning the parable of the sower into a statement about a task to be achieved: it turns a gift into a demand. There is hope only because Jesus is no longer imprisoned in the tomb—and because God can be trusted to finish what has been begun. . . . We walk by

27. Juel, *Master of Surprise*, 41.
28. See C. Clifton Black, *The Disciples according to Mark: Markan Redaction in Current Debate*, 2nd ed. (Grand Rapids: Eerdmans, 2012).
29. Juel, *Master of Surprise*, 87.

faith and not by sight. We can only trust that God will one day finish the story, as God has promised.[30]

The heart of Mark's theology, for Juel, lies in Jesus's promise in 10:27: "With mortals it is impossible, but not with God; for with God all things are possible." If in God alone, altogether apart from human effort, there is good reason for hope, then Mark's Gospel ends at 16:8 on a pitch-perfect note: "In Jesus' ministry, God tears away barriers that afforded protection in the past. God cannot be kept at arm's length. Such a possibility that light dawns even on those who inhabit the realm of darkness is disquieting; it means there is no refuge for the cynical any more than for the naive. . . . Jesus has promised an encounter with him against which there is no assured defense. God will be put off neither by our failures, or infidelity, nor by our most sophisticated interpretive schemes."[31]

Of our evasive sophistication, Juel has more to say. Before attending to those caveats, we need to probe with him more deeply Mark's own interpretive strategy and its bearing on our own.

ELLIPTICAL SCRIPTS

Joined at the hip theologically, and consistent with his approach overall, were two hermeneutical dimensions that occupied much of Juel's attention: ancient Jewish exegesis and modern literary approaches.

Messianic Exegesis

On this topic, Juel wrote the book, or at least a major contribution to scholarship's understanding of early Christianity's appropriation of its Jewish Scripture.[32] Juel is careful to differentiate his view of the subject from that of C. H. Dodd and Barnabas Lindars:[33] "'Proof from prophecy' is not the point of the [scriptural] allusions [in 14:17–25 and elsewhere]. The scriptural references indicate that it was impossible to tell the story of Jesus' last days without using the language of the Scriptures. The events made sense, even from earliest times, only within a scriptural framework. The conviction that Christ died "in

---

30. Juel, *Master of Surprise*, 233, 234, 235.

31. Juel, *Master of Surprise*, 63, 120–21.

32. Donald H. Juel, *Messianic Exegesis: Christological Interpretation of the Old Testament in Early Christianity* (Philadelphia: Fortress, 1988).

33. C. H. Dodd, *According to the Scriptures* (London: James Nisbet & Company, 1952); Barnabas Lindars, *New Testament Apologetics* (London: SCM, 1961).

accordance with the Scriptures" is basic—more basic perhaps than individual scriptural arguments (192).

In other words, early Christians like Mark did not plunder Jewish Scripture to prove, to themselves or others, that Jesus was the Christ. Rather, they began from the unshakable if stupefying conviction that God had vindicated Jesus as the crucified Messiah, then repaired to Scripture for resources that would render their faith intelligible. "The Scriptures were mined for material that could help Jesus' followers understand how it could be that the Christ must suffer and be treated with contempt. . . . We are offered [in Mark] a biblical framework within which to locate the drama as it unfolds. . . . The Psalms in particular provided the means by which Jesus' followers made sense of his death. . . . Jesus' story—particularly the account of his passion and resurrection—could not even be narrated without using the language of the Scriptures" (130–31, 121).[34]

In particular, Juel believed that Ps 118—far more than Second Isaiah's Servant Songs (passim)[35]—offered early Christians their primary script for insight into the career of the rejected, crucified, and risen Christ (154).[36] For modern exegetes and theologians who found such interpretive strategies passé, if not reprehensible, Juel offered this riposte: "[Ancient] interpreters viewed the Scriptures as writings, meaning collections of sacred sentences and words, whose meanings were not bound to an immediate historical or literary context. . . . To expect post-Enlightenment arguments from first-century interpreters is a form of imperialism. We must appreciate the scriptural arguments of another age—then find appropriate ways to make them our own for our own time" (168).[37]

Juel's admiration for ancient midrash was honed under the tutelage of Judah Goldin at Yale. What Juel recognized in the works of Erich Auerbach (1892–1957) and Frank Kermode (1919–2010) were contemporary strategies for modern readers to appropriate Markan hermeneutics.

Vision, Irony, and Disappointment

Early on, Juel seemed certain that two ways of reading Mark would lead only to dead ends: psychologizing (the default setting of bad preaching) and con-

---

34. See also 97 (on Mark 6:37), 148 (on 10:35–45), 157–59 (11:11–26), 171 (12:35–37), 181 (13:3–23), 207 (14:62), and 151 (Mark's passion narrative generally).

35. See also Donald H. Juel, "The Image of the Servant-Christ in the New Testament," *SwJT* 21 (1979): 7–22.

36. Juel, *Messiah and Temple*, 73.

37. See also Juel, *Messianic Exegesis*, 15.

ventional redaction criticism (the academic option). The former he held in contempt: "Collapsing the story into psychological categories represents a particular preoccupation—and one might say, disease—of our time that offers little promise as an approach to interpretation" (37; see also 110, 119). While grateful to historical criticism for its enrichment of the reader's experience of the gospel and its adjudication of serious exegetical differences,[38] Juel doubted that reconstruction of the gospel's tradition-history—even if that were possible—could vivify the truth claims vouched by Mark.[39]

> Dissecting Mark's Gospel will not result in a reading of Mark but of something else. . . . As a reader of the Bible, I am not interested principally in the history behind the Gospel, although historical considerations are important[, . . . or] in the communities behind the Gospels nor the intention of the author. . . . I am principally interested in an engagement with the story—with the "world in front of the text"—which may benefit from the various approaches, but is a distinct enterprise. . . . I can imagine no sound reason for interest in study of the Bible if it does not provide for a more lively engagement with the material. . . . If scholarship does not produce better readers, then it is not only a waste of time but also genuinely harmful, and there are good reasons for churches to regard such scholarship with suspicion.[40]

"Earlier European methodological purity" left Juel cold.[41] For him, methods got interesting when Mark's claims upon its modern interpreters—"the interior level of the story . . . at which the events he reports are viewed in light of the resurrection and as a fulfillment of Scripture and as visible in the life of the church"[42]—began to bristle with life and life's questions, in an imaginative manner commensurate with messianic exegesis of the gospel's first-century readers.

In that endeavor, Auerbach's treatment of Mark's "aesthetic vision" afforded Juel considerable help, which he acknowledged throughout his career.[43] Auerbach fortified Juel's conviction that the evangelist "did not respect [antiquity's]

---

38. Juel, *Master of Surprise*, 6.

39. Juel, *Messiah and Temple*, 214; see also *Master of Surprise*, vii.

40. Juel, *Gospel of Mark*, 123–24; *Master of Surprise*, 4–6.

41. Juel, *Master of Surprise*, 23.

42. Juel, *Messiah and Temple*, 47.

43. Erich Auerbach, *Mimesis: The Representation of Reality in Western Literature* (Princeton: Princeton University Press, 1953), 40–49; Juel, *Messiah and Temple*, 45; Juel, *Introduction to New Testament Literature*, 199; Juel, *Gospel of Mark*, 141.

aesthetic conventions because they did not permit him to do with his story what he intended. . . . Mark's goal is to relate the events and persons described to the profound change in the human situation that has come about as a result of Jesus' life, death, and resurrection, and correspondingly, to describe this profound historical moment by narrating the story" (16–17).[44] Thus, Juel marveled at the perdurable power of Mark 4:10–12 to generate within a modern student the very "hardening" to which the text refers: said she, through clenched teeth, "I will not believe in a God who hardens!" "Like most readers," Juel observed, "she was hardened, as Jesus promised. The parable succeeded in keeping her outside."[45]

Equally dazzling is Mark's artfulness in creating "insiders" among his readership, by giving them crucial knowledge of which the narrative's characters were unaware: "'Identifying' with any characters in the story is made difficult when we hear what no one else can and receive explanations unavailable to those in the story. . . . 'Irony' is the appropriate term. Events are unfolding just as Jesus has predicted—and just as the prophets have announced. Characters in the story understand their roles only within their limited spheres and have no idea that they are playing roles assigned to them by God.[46]

Because the reader understands the true meaning of events, beneath the surface at which the story's characters play out their roles to the best of their flawed understanding, dramatic irony runs throughout Mark from stem to stern.[47]

Yet, in a mind-boggling masterstroke, the evangelist trumps his own ironic stance by ensnaring readers—alongside others within the narrative—who reckon themselves insiders. For Juel, "however successful we are at penetrating the secrets of Mark's Gospel, there will always be those dimensions that we cannot probe. We still read as outsiders" (201; see also 156). Mark accomplishes this feat by springing on the knowledgeable reader gaps without plugs and provocations without resolution. Among many others:

> Is there reason to believe Jesus' ministry has anything to do with the glorious kingdom of God? . . . The decision about Jesus will have to be made on evidence from his ministry. There is no escape from the decision that must be made. The tension between Jesus and the tradition will have to be resolved, and Jesus will not do the resolving. (68, 113; see also 72, 87, 99, 117, 156).[48]

---

44. See also Juel, *Messiah and Temple*, 45.

45. Juel, *Gospel of Mark*, 128.

46. Juel, *Gospel of Mark*, 69, 143. See also *Master of Surprise*, 69; *Mark*, 111–12 (on Mark 6:30–44; 8:1–10); 122 (8:31; 9:31; 10:33–34); 154 (11:1–10); *Messiah and Temple*, 56–57 (14:53–65).

47. Juel, *Introduction to New Testament Literature*, 178–79. See also *Mark*, 204 (on Mark 14:53–72), 228 (on 15:39).

48. See also Juel, *Master of Surprise*, 56.

Perhaps Mark, like Matthew, attributes Peter's insight [at Mark 8:29] to inspiration. But inspiration by whom? If Peter and the disciples are addressed as Jesus addresses others who are possessed, perhaps we are to wonder if Peter's insight is not of the same order . . . akin to the confessions of the demoniacs. . . . If that is true, then Peter, and the rest, will have to be set free. Satan will have to be exorcised from their imaginations.[49]

The most revealing moment in [Mark's] story [namely, 14:62] is, paradoxically, the moment at which the darkness seems most impenetrable.[50]

Interpretation [of Mark] must respect the two impressions with which the story concludes: disappointment and anticipation. . . . Loose ends are infrequently tied up in real life; disappointment is the universal human experience. There may be some point to life, but we will never know it. The most we can hope for, as one author so eloquently puts it, is a "glimpse . . . before the door of disappointment closes on us" (233).[51]

At bottom, Mark "portrays a world, and the world it portrays—the world it allows us to experience—is one in which there is far less stability than we may have imagined."[52]

Enter Sir Frank: "If there is one belief (however the facts resist it) that unites us all . . . it is this conviction that somehow, in some occult fashion, if we could only detect it, everything will be found to hang together."[53] Interpreters' resistance to accept, not to explain away, textual aporiae gave Juel some hermeneutical leverage that his approach to Markan theology required: "One of Kermode's great gifts is the ability to unmask interpretive strategies that seek to protect readers against overly difficult and painful insight. He is able to demonstrate the degree to which much scholarship is little more than a way of protecting ourselves from painful or disappointing readings by the employment of cunning and violence. One of Kermode's great contributions

49. Juel, *Master of Surprise*, 74–75.

50. Donald Juel, "The Function of the Trial of Jesus in Mark's Gospel," in *Society of Biblical Literature 1975 Seminar Papers*, ed. George MacRae (Missoula, MT: Scholars Press, 1975), 102; see also Juel, *Mark*, 109.

51. See also Juel, "The Parable of the Mustard Seed," in *Studies in Lutheran Hermeneutics*, ed. John Reumann with Samuel H. Nafzger and Harold H. Ditmanson (Philadelphia: Fortress, 1979), 366.

52. Juel, *Gospel of Mark*, 151.

53. Frank Kermode, *The Genesis of Secrecy: On the Interpretation of Narrative* (Cambridge: Harvard University Press, 1979), 72.

is a willingness to entertain the possibility that there are no satisfying endings—in Mark or in life."[54]

Nevertheless, an unflinching commitment to the God who finally will keep all his promises prevented Juel from capitulating to any postmodern failure of nerve before the truth of the gospel. On that point, Juel rightly challenged Kermode for prematurely closing all possibility of an ending that God, in Mark's Gospel, leaves open.[55]

> Mark's Gospel forbids . . . closure. There is no stone at the mouth of the tomb. Jesus is out, on the loose, on the same side of the door as the women and the readers. The story cannot contain the promises. Its massive investment in the reliability of Jesus' words becomes a down payment on a genuine future. . . . That end is not yet, but the story gives good reasons to remain hopeful even in the face of disappointment. The possibilities of eventual enlightenment for the reader remain *in the hands of the divine actor* who will not be shut in—or out.[56]

AN OPEN QUESTION

By commonplace standards of propriety, Mark's Gospel seems curtailed—it does not end where or as it should. So many have said of the life and career of Don Juel, among this generation's preeminent Markan interpreters. So coherent, so consistent, was his vision of Mark across three decades that it is jarring to recognize in Don's own life and death echoes of a mysterious revelation by that gospel he loved so well and taught us to read with such insight. Before the uncanny, one trembles with awe and terror (Mark 16:8). In life, as in Mark,

---

54. Juel, *Master of Surprise*, 61, 112; see also 29–30 (on Mark 16:1–8).

55. Donald H. Juel, "Christian Hope and the Denial of Death: Encountering New Testament Eschatology," in *The End of the World and the Ends of God: Science and Theology on Eschatology*, ed. John Polkinghorne and Michael Welker (Harrisburg, PA: Trinity Press International, 2000), 180–81. In a personal letter to Juel, received before his death, Kermode conceded his error: "I remember at the time of writing [my studies of Mark] that I found part of my mind rebelling against my own arguments, and in a sense it is a relief that you have been able to dismiss all the more obvious excuses and evasions, stick to the text that ends at 16:8, and still find the door open. And so I find myself trapped by my own Kafkaesque evasions—or by your knight's move, the introduction of all those other open doors" (quoted in Thomas W. Gillespie, "A Case of 'Doctrinal Adhesion,'" *PSB* 24 [2003]: 189).

56. Juel, *Master of Surprise*, 120 (my emphasis); see also *Mark*, 177, 233–34.

things do not hang together. The endings do not satisfy. In the Christian life, as also in Mark, there remain promises from agents of unimpeachable integrity, "good reasons to remain hopeful even in the face of disappointment." All of us—our lives and deaths, our possibilities and prospects—remain in the hands of the same divine actor to whom Christ Jesus and all his servants have entrusted themselves, the one whose "plan for the fullness of time [is] to recapitulate all things in Christ, things in heaven and things on earth" (Eph 1:10). In the meanwhile:

> Truthfulness comes to focus on the character of God. Can we afford to trust the One in whose hand the future lies? Is there a reason to imagine that we can live at the mercy of God—and that in so doing we will live richer, more productive lives? That depends on God's coming to us to accomplish reconciliation and deliverance that are not within our power. It is the testimony of the church that God does indeed come and that Jesus's plantings will ultimately flourish. For us, the truthfulness of the parable [in Mark] must remain to some degree an open question.[57]

57. Donald H. Juel, "Encountering the Sower: Mark 4:1–20," *Int* 56 (2002): 283: the last words of the final article that, to the best of my knowledge, Don Juel published in Markan interpretation.

CHAPTER 6

Markan Studies: Whence and Whither?

I was gratified to be able to answer promptly, and I did. I said I didn't know.

—Mark Twain[1]

WHILE DISCUSSING THE PRESENT VOLUME, my editors suggested that I create a new essay on the future of Markan studies. I'm all for freshness, but I'm no Edgar Cayce.[2] My crystal ball is cracked. I can suggest some topics on which I would be delighted for a new generation of Markan scholars to discourse. If the quality is good, I'd love to read it. In the meantime, I can identify a few currents in Markan scholarship of the last generation, thus executing the maneuver that I've witnessed in thousands of students' papers and exams: "You didn't ask this question, but here's my answer."[3]

---

1. *Mississippi Writings: The Adventures of Tom Sawyer, Life on the Mississippi, Adventures of Huckleberry Finn, Pudd'nhead Wilson*, ed. Guy Cardwell, The Library of America (New York: Library Classics of the United States, 1982), 264 (from *Life on the Mississippi*).

2. Edgar Cayce (1877–1945) was an American clairvoyant. He would fall asleep, go into a trance that he thought elevated him to his higher self, and answer questions about future occurrences. Unlike "the Sleeping Prophet," I have never been introduced to my higher self, spent my waking hours semiconscious, then collapsed, unconscious, into the arms of Morpheus.

3. In pondering and constructing this chapter, I am indebted to Professors Dale C. Allison Jr., Mary Ann Beavis, R. Alan Culpepper, Laura Sweat Holmes, and M. J. P. O'Connor, some of whom graciously commented on earlier drafts in parts or their entirety. They are in no way responsible for its remaining errors of fact and judgment.

WHENCE? (ACROSS THREE DECADES)

The Gospel Train (Get on Board, Children)

The second half of twentieth-century scholarship in the gospels was deeply preoccupied by the most accurate determination of their genre in antiquity.[4] In Markan studies alone, arguments have been constructed for every conceivable possibility: biography, history, aretalogy (accounts of "divine men"), tragedy, romantic novel (sans romance), eschatological monograph, extended apothegm, collected *chriae*, "mythic ontology," an early Christian liturgical calendar, a modified Passover haggadah,[5] even sui generis—a Christian orig-

---

4. By way of reminder, Justin Martyr (ca. 100–ca. 165) is the earliest extant witness to "gospels" as written texts, not "gospel" as an oral proclamation (*1 Apol.* 66.3; cf. 1 Thess 2:2, 8–9; 3:2). In Mark 1:1, I suppose that εὐαγγέλιον refers to the kerygma (see also 1:14; 10:29; 13:10; 14:9; Black, *Mark*, ANTC [Nashville: Abingdon, 2011], 45–46), but that interpretation—like just about everything else in Mark—is debatable.

5. For biography, see, early on, Johannes Weiss, *Das älteste Evangelium: Ein Beitrag zum Verständnis des Markus-Evangeliums und der ältesten evangelischen Überlieferung* (Göttingen: Vandenhoeck & Ruprecht, 1903); Clyde Weber Votaw, *The Gospels and Contemporary Biographies in the Greco-Roman World*, FBBS 27 (Philadelphia: Fortress, 1970; consisting of articles published in *AmJT* 19 [1915]: 45–73, 217–49); history, see Theodor Zahn, "Der Geschichtsschreiber und sein Stoff im Neuen Testament," *ZWKL* 9 (1888): 581–96; James M. Robinson, *The Problem of History in Mark*, SBT 21 (London: SCM, 1957); aretalogy, see Moses Hadas and Morton Smith, *Heroes and Gods: Spiritual Biographies in Antiquity*, RP (New York: Harper & Row, 1965) (Hadas himself acknowledged the lack of any specimens of this alleged genre, so labeled [xiii, 60]: a liability for which other scholars rapped his knuckles); tragedy, see Gilbert G. Bilezikian, *The Liberated Gospel: A Comparison of the Gospel of Mark and Greek Tragedy* (Grand Rapids: Baker, 1977); romantic novel, see Mary Ann Tolbert, *Sowing the Gospel: Mark's World in Literary-Historical Perspective* (Minneapolis: Fortress, 1989), 48–79 (alternatively, dependent on Mikhail Bakhtin's notion of "narrative chronotopes," Michael Vines views the problem of genre by way of the Jewish novel in *The Problem of the Markan Genre: The Gospel of Mark and the Jewish Novel*, AcBib 3 [Atlanta: Society of Biblical Literature, 2002], a study that runs hard on Bakhtin, soft on Mark, Esther, Susanna, and Dan 1–6); eschatological monograph, see Adela Yarbro Collins, *Mark: A Commentary*, Hermeneia (Minneapolis: Fortress, 2007), 42–84; extended apothegm, see J. A. Baird, "Genre Analysis as a Method of Historical Criticism," *Proceedings: Society of Biblical Literature* 2 (Missoula, MT: Society of Biblical Literature, 1972), 385–411; collected *chriae*, see Josef Kurzinger, "Die Aussage des Papias von Hierapolis zur literarischen Form des Markusevangelium," *BZ* 21 (1977): 245–64; Burton L. Mack and Vernon K. Robbins, *Patterns of Persuasion in the Gospels*, FF (Sonoma, CA: Polebridge, 1989); "mythic ontology," see Paul-Gerhard Klumbies, *Der Mythos bei Markus*, BZNW 108 (Berlin: de Gruyter, 2001);

inal, a one-off unto itself.[6] Some readers may consider a few of these inconceivable, save by their conceivers. The alternative that I have always found least persuasive is the last. Strictly speaking, neither Mark nor any document, ancient or contemporary, can be altogether unique yet intelligible: it is only by its satisfaction of particular expectations, created by discernible conventions, that any literary specimen can be understood.[7] Nevertheless, until the 1990s, Mark as sui generis seemed the prevailing point of view, possibly owing to its favor by the Mighty Bultmann, whose dicta have been hard for NT scholars to dismiss.

After the dust had settled by the century's turn, the option reckoned most satisfying by most Markan commentators had shifted to βίος or *vita*. If one defines ancient biography as a prose narrative, comprising multiple literary forms (anecdotes, maxims, whatnot), which selectively depicts the deeds and words of a personage on the historical stage with the intent to teach or incul-

---

liturgical calendar, see Philip Carrington, *The Primitive Christian Calendar: A Study in the Making of the Markan Gospel* (Cambridge: Cambridge University Press, 1952); Michael D. Goulder, *The Evangelist's Calendar: A Lectionary Explanation of the Development of Scripture* (London: SPCK, 1978); and a modified Passover haggadah, see John Bowman, *The Gospel of Mark: The New Christian Jewish Passover Haggadah*, StPB 8 (Leiden: Brill, 1965).

6. Franz Overbeck, "Über die Anfänge der patrischen Literatur," *HZ* 48 (1882): 417–72; Rudolf Bultmann, *The History of the Synoptic Tradition*, trans. John Marsh, rev. ed. (New York: Harper & Row, 1963), 369–94; Bultmann, *Theology of the New Testament*, trans. Kendrick Grobel, vol. 1 (New York: Scribner's Sons, 1951): "a unique phenomenon in the history of literature" (89). "[Mark created] a genre of literature for which, as a whole, there was no precedent" (Howard Clark Kee, *Jesus in History: An Approach to the Study of the Gospels*, 2nd ed. [New York: Harcourt Brace Jovanovich, 1977], 139). More recently and with qualifications suggested by a subtitle, see Eve-Marie Becker, *Das Markus-Evangelium im Rahmen antiker Historiographie*, WUNT 194 (Tübingen: Mohr Siebeck, 2006), 50–52. Acute survey and analysis of these and other proposals may be found in David E. Aune, *The New Testament and Its Literary Environment*, LEC 8 (Philadelphia: Westminster, 1987), 17–45, and Yarbro Collins, *Mark*, 15–84.

7. Frank Kermode: "we can [understand a statement] only because we bring to our interpretation of the sentence a pre-understanding [*Vorverständnis*] of its totality. We may be wrong on detail, but not, as a rule, wholly wrong. . . . We must sense the genre of the utterance" (*The Genesis of Secrecy: On the Interpretation of Narrative* [Cambridge: Harvard University Press, 1979], 70). See also Richard Burridge, *What Are the Gospels? A Comparison with Graeco-Roman Biography*, 3rd ed. (Waco, TX: Baylor University Press, 2018), 247–48.

cate values,[8] then Mark's Gospel qualifies as a biography.[9] If its earliest listeners heard for the first time a coherent arrangement of Jesus's activities in Galilee and Jerusalem, with a denouement at the empty tomb, then the evangelist may have offered them something radically new—though of that we are uncertain, because we cannot verify the degree of cohesion attained by oral traditions about Jesus before their commitment to writing.[10] If a practical consensus has been reached that Mark is a βίος, that hasn't settled the matter: its content seems to transgress acceptable biographical boundaries. Most NT scholars may type Mark as biography, but now they cannot agree on what a βίος is.[11]

Enter Richard Burridge. Few doctoral dissertations are game changers, but Burridge's *What Are the Gospels? A Comparison with Graeco-Roman Biography* qualifies.[12] Here are its conclusions:

8. Here I follow Aune's lead (*New Testament and Its Literary Environment*, 28), augmented by Charles H. Talbert, *What Is a Gospel? The Genre of the Canonical Gospels* (Philadelphia: Fortress, 1977), esp. 17 (cf. *Comp. vit.* 1–3; *Ab urbe cond.* 1.1). With them I concur that "history" in antiquity is elastic and stylized, amenable to fictionalizations; with them I disagree that βίοι and ἱστορίαι need be sharply differentiated. (More on this later; also see chapter 8.) In turn, Aune and Talbert follow Arnaldo Momigliano, *The Development of Greek Biography*, exp. ed. (Cambridge: Harvard University Press, 1993). See also Patricia L. Cox, *Biography in Late Antiquity: A Quest for the Holy Man* (Berkeley: University of California Press, 1983); Tom Thatcher, "The Gospel Genre: What Are We Looking For?," *ResQ* 39 (1994): 129–38.

9. I tend toward the use of βίος in the rest of this section, as a reminder that ancient and modern biographies proceed in accordance with different principles. That said, no biography, then or now, is ever transparent to historical fact; all are exercises in creative interpretation. See R. G. Collingwood, *The Idea of History*, rev. ed., ed. Jan van der Dussen (Oxford: Oxford University Press, 1994), and chapter 8 of the present volume.

10. Francis J. Moloney, *The Gospel of Mark: A Commentary* (Peabody, MA: Hendrickson, 2002), 16–17.

11. Thus, e.g., Cilliers Breytenbach, "The Gospel according to Mark: The Yardstick for Comparing the Gospels with Ancient Texts," in *Modern and Ancient Literary Criticism of the Gospels: Continuing the Debate on Gospel Genre(s)*, ed. Robert Matthew Calhoun, David P. Moessner, and Tobias Nicklas, WUNT 451 (Tübingen: Mohr Siebeck, 2020), 179–200; repr. Breytenbach, *The Gospel according to Mark as Episodic Narrative*, NovTSup 128 (Leiden: Brill, 2021), 41–65.

12. Cambridge: Cambridge University Press, 1992, based on the author's PhD dissertation (1989), directed by P. Maurice Casey at the University of Nottingham; 2nd ed., Grand Rapids: Eerdmans, 2004; 3rd ed., Waco, TX: Baylor University Press, 2018. The book's subsequent editions are distinguished from the first by engaging scholars' approbation or critique of their predecessors (2nd ed: 252–340; 3rd ed.: 1–112). In what follows, I cite the third edition.

[In the Greco-Roman world] *biography is a type of writing which occurs naturally among groups of people who have formed around a certain charismatic teacher or leader, seeking to follow him.* . . . [A] *major purpose and function of βίος is in a context of didactic or philosophical polemic or conflict.* . . . The genre of βίος is flexible and diverse, with variations in the pattern of features from one βίος to another. The gospels also diverge from the pattern in some respects, but not to any greater degree than other βίος; in other words, they have at least as much in common with Graeco-Roman βίος, as the βίοι have with each other. Therefore, the gospels must belong to the genre of βίος. (76, 250)

In themselves these propositions were not all original, as Burridge acknowledged: with different inflections, Votaw, Talbert, Aune, and others had argued much the same (4–6, 79–86, 98–99). What set Burridge's treatment apart was the expanse and depth of evidence collected and the rigor of its analysis: genre criticism among biblical and classical scholars (3–100); generic features of βίος both external (such as scale, structure, and modes of characterization) and internal (style, social setting, authorial intent, and others) (105–23); generic features of Greco-Roman lives both early (e.g., Isocrates, *Evagoras*; Philo, *Life of Moses*) and late (Suetonius, *Lives of the Caesars*; Philostratus, *Apollonius of Tyana*; and others) (124–84); comparison of these features and βίος with the Synoptics and John (185–232). Contrary to his original expectation, Burridge discovered a high degree of correlation between the gospels and their closest analogues in Greco-Roman literature (212), and the same "family resemblance" obtains with John vis-à-vis the Synoptics and non-Christian βίοι (231–32; 253–47). "If genre is the key to a work's interpretation, and the genre of the gospels is βίος, then the key to their interpretation must be the person of their subject, Jesus of Nazareth" (248). *Quod erat demonstrandum.*

There's no need to belabor critique of Burridge's thesis: his monograph's second and third editions accurately, if tendentiously, present that.[13] Upon its original publication, those predisposed to βίος as the most satisfactory genre for Mark's classification considered Burridge's argument compelling.[14] Conducted on classically form-critical premises, Dirk Frickenschmidt's *Evangelium*

---

13. By "tendentiously," I intend no defamation. It is to be expected that Burridge would weigh his work's criticisms in the balance and find them wanting.

14. Notably, Charles H. Talbert, review of *What Are the Gospels? A Comparison with Graeco-Roman Biography*, by Richard Burridge, *JBL* 112 (1993): 714–15; Graham N. Stanton, *Jesus and Gospel* (Cambridge: Cambridge University Press, 2004), 192–93; N.B. 192 n. 3: "I first tackled this topic when it was right out of fashion [1974, 2002]."

als Biographie arrived, five years later, at many of Burridge's conclusions.[15] For the past thirty years, Burridge's thesis has been subjected to intensive debate and has persuaded, if not all, then a majority: as fine a record of confirmation in biblical studies as can reasonably be expected of any hypothesis.[16] Furthermore, other scholarly studies have extended its scope, two of which may be noted as representative. Based on two decades of his own published research, Craig S. Keener's *Christobiography* concludes, "The biographical genre does not automatically answer all our questions about the gospels, but, especially when taken together with studies about ancient memory, it does give us a more historically sensitive approach . . . that these biographies written within living memory of Jesus do in fact succeed in preserving many of Jesus's acts and teachings."[17] After examining the βίοι of Xenophon, Plutarch, and scores of other ancient biographers, Helen K. Bond zeroes in on Mark's passion narrative, because "the moment of transition between life and death was an especially clear window into a person's character."[18] Mark demonstrates that Jesus died as he lived: "turn[ing] all worldly conceptions of honor on their head in favor of a deeply countercultural focus on what contemporary society would usually brand as shameful."[19] Why did Mark situate Jesus at the heart of a biography? "[It was] a bold step in outlining a radical form of Christian discipleship patterned on the life—and death—of Jesus."[20] To regard Mark and the other gospels as βίοι also has in its favor a point so obvious that it usually goes unstated: common sense. For two millennia, Christians have heard Mark as a story about Jesus, though

15. Dirk Frickenschmidt, *Evangelium als Biographie: Die vier Evangeliem im Rahmen antiker Erzählkunst* (Tübingen: Francke, 1997), esp. 65; discussed by Burridge, *What Are the Gospels?*, 285–86.

16. Judith A. Diehl: "Scholarship could continue to debate this issue for another twenty-five years, still looking for a better or more descriptive term for the Gospels' genre, but what would be the cost of doing that?" (review of *What Are the Gospels? A Comparison with Graeco-Roman Biography*, by Richard Burridge, *CBQ* 82 [2020]: 314).

17. *Christobiography: Memory, History, and the Reliability of the Gospels* (Grand Rapids: Eerdmans, 2019), 497. In this chapter's next section, we shall take up "studies about ancient memory" and their bearing on historical accuracy. For now, as Professors Culpepper and O'Connor have remarked to me in conversation, classification of an ancient document as βίος guarantees nothing of its historical accuracy, which is a modern preoccupation.

18. *The First Biography of Jesus: Genre and Meaning in Mark's Gospel* (Grand Rapids: Eerdmans, 2020), 38–77, 121–66, 222–58 (quotation, 222). In abbreviated form, see Bond's "A Fitting End? Self-Denial and a Slave's Death in Mark's *Life of Jesus*," *NTS* 65 (2019): 425–42.

19. Bond, *First Biography*, 231. Bond cites Plutarch, *Cato Minor* 37.1, as another example of cultural subversion: Cato the Younger defied Julius Caesar's clemency by committing suicide (*First Biography*, 44).

20. Bond, *First Biography*, 253.

very few of them have read Suetonius and wouldn't recognize Xenophon if he were raised from the dead and kissed them on the lips.[21]

What, then, has prevented other sensible scholars from boarding the train engineered by Burridge? In general, they have perceived salient aspects of Mark that the category βίος seems inadequate to explain. Allowing for the gospel's biographical elements, Joel Marcus suggests, "Mark's style consciously imitates the OT historical narratives."[22] Viewing the evidence from another angle, Adela Yarbro Collins has long argued that "the primary intention of Mark was to write history" of a peculiar kind: "a narration of the course of the eschatological events," "the combat myth [between Jesus and Satan] in historic and apocalyptic mode."[23] These are valid considerations. Margaret Davies has wondered, "From reading Burridge's list of features, no one would guess that the gospels are theological narratives, and that they set the life of Jesus in the context of what God, the Creator and Sustainer of the world, is achieving through him," which includes "God's dealings with Israel in the past and present, Jesus' resurrection, and the expectation of an imminent end of history."[24] Burridge set himself up for such disapproval by claiming that βίος *must be the key* that unlocks the gospels' interpretation. That's an unnecessary exaggeration, a red rag flapped before the bull's snout. Nothing so irritates scholars as the pressure to concede that one hypothesis, however good, *must* be true.

I conclude this section with two comments: one, specific to Mark; the other, procedural. At day's end, the Second Gospel seems to me more closely analogous to ancient biography than to any of the suggested alternatives. Nevertheless, that genre's limitations and admissibility of variety, as well as the score of generic labels with which it has been tagged, imply that neither Mark nor any of the gospels is *precisely* comparable with other ancient writings but rather ex-

---

21. A possibility so ghoulish that I regret having mentioned it.

22. *Mark: A New Translation with Introduction and Commentary*, AB 27 (Garden City, NY: Doubleday, 2000), 65. I don't know how anyone could climb into the evangelist's consciousness, but phrases like "answered and said" (3:33; 6:37) and "it came to pass in those days" (1:9) are clear reverberations of the OT (e.g., Gen 31:43; Exod 2:11; 1 Sam 4:17; 28:1; Joel 2:19). Whether they are unmistakable indicators of the OT's "historical" style is moot.

23. "Is Mark's Gospel a Life of Jesus? The Question of Genre," in *The Beginning of the Gospel: Probings of Mark in Context* (Minneapolis: Fortress, 1992), 27, 71, based on her 1989 Père Marquette Lecture in Theology; painstakingly developed in *Mark*, 42–84. Yarbro Collins is too intelligent a scholar to equate Mark's genre with that of Qumran's Testimonia (4QTest 5–8) or 1 Enoch (53.6; 69.29), and she is justified in pointing up their religious kinship with Mark.

24. Review of *What Are the Gospels? A Comparison with Graeco-Roman Biography*, by Richard Burridge, *NBf* 74 (1993): 110.

hibits recognizable affinities with many of them. As David Aune observes, the quest for a generically exact analogy is as inconsequential as it is misguided: many Hellenistic compositions are generic composites, and it is fallacious to interpret complex wholes without identifying their constituents.[25] However we identify its bark, Mark is a mongrel: an amalgam of Hellenistic Jewish and Greco-Roman literary types.[26]

Second, without for a moment belittling the extraordinary efforts that Richard Burridge, Adela Collins, and many other sophisticated readers have expended, I wonder whether we in the guild are susceptible to what might be dubbed Aristotelianitis: a taxonomical fixation that diverts as much as it directs. Paul's letter to the Romans is an astonishing adaptation of ancient epistolary conventions, but I have yet to encounter a convincing argument that, at bottom, it isn't a letter. Most of its recipients may never have heard anything like it, but Paul offered them enough conventional handrails that it was intelligible.[27] More than intelligible: dynamically mind-blowing. So, too, Mark and the other gospels: whatever their categorization, they "are history-like witnesses to truths both historical and transcendent." The conviction "that they fundamentally tell us who Jesus was and is . . . emerges both from the persuasive power the stories themselves have on us and from the power we find in a way of seeing and living in the world that presupposes these stories are true."[28]

Speak, Memory

A second current in recent Markan study may be identified as the convergence, in the first century, of memory and oral performance of the traditions

---

25. Aune, *New Testament and Its Literary Environment*, 46.

26. Black, *Mark*, 34. That deduction is consonant with Elizabeth E. Shively's argument for theories of "conceptual blending" that permit interpreters to construe Mark as "multi-generic" and the gospel's audience as capable of receiving it "on different generic levels at the same time": "A Critique of Richard Burridge's Genre Theory: From a One-Dimensional to a Multi-Dimensional Approach to Gospel Genre," in *Modern and Ancient Literary Criticism of the Gospels: Continuing the Debate on Gospel Genre(s)*, ed. Robert Matthew Calhoun, David P. Moessner, and Tobias Nicklas, WUNT 451 (Tübingen: Mohr Siebeck, 2020), 109, 110. In the same volume, see also R. Alan Culpepper, "The Foundations of Matthean Ethics," which highlights the First Gospel's similarity to the Dead Sea Scrolls (359–79).

27. The same may be said of John vis-à-vis the Synoptics: Harold W. Attridge, "Genre Bending in the Fourth Gospel," *JBL* 121 (2003): 3–21.

28. William C. Placher, "How the Gospels Mean," in *Seeking the Identity of Jesus: A Pilgrimage*, ed. Beverly Roberts Gaventa and Richard B. Hays (Grand Rapids: Eerdmans, 2008), 39, 42.

about Jesus. Such investigation is in equal measures fascinating and frustrating. How could it be otherwise? That Jesus's earliest followers and converts remembered and retold his teachings and stories about him for decades before being committed to writing is commonsensical and verified by Paul's letters (ca. 50–58).[29] The processes by which Mark and the other evangelists received these traditions is inherently speculative, because none of us was in Galilee and its environs in the early first century to hear it.

In his presidential address to the Studiorum Novi Testamenti Societas (2002), James D. G. Dunn made a convincing case for "altering the default setting" by which we regard the gospels.[30] Dunn's thesis is that, as children of Gutenberg and Caxton, it is extraordinarily difficult for us to consider the gospels outside of a literary paradigm. We give lip service to oral tradition, then automatically revert to literary explanations for resolving the Synoptic problem. Dunn challenged NT scholars to think intelligently about the conditions of rural Galilee, circa 30–70, 90 percent of whose denizens were illiterate.[31] Some of them heard and remembered things about Jesus by means of an evanescent oral tradition.[32] They likely received those traditions from recognized teachers in communal assemblies (cf. Acts 2:42). Until traditions reached a point of transcription, their every retelling was an "original" performance. Because oral tradition is a remembrance of things past for the benefit of listeners present and to come, it combines "fixity and flexibility, . . . stability and diversity."[33] By his own admission,[34] Dunn aims to chart a medial course between the Scylla of a loose, uncontrolled tradition and the Charybdis of a more regimented, rabbinic model of transmission.[35]

---

29. Rom 1:3; 1 Cor 1:17–2:5, 8; 7:10–11; 9:5, 14; 11:23–25; 15:3–4, 7; Gal 1:4, 19; 2:7–9, 12; 3:1; 4:4; Phil 2:8; perhaps also Rom 12:14; 1 Thess 2:14–16.

30. "Altering the Default Setting: Re-envisaging the Early Transmission of the Jesus Tradition," *NTS* 49 (2003): 139–75; repr. in Dunn, *The Oral Gospel Tradition* (Grand Rapids: Eerdmans, 2013), 41–79.

31. "Altering the Default Setting," 148, relying upon William V. Harris, *Ancient Literacy* (Cambridge: Harvard University Press, 1989); Catherine Hezser, *Jewish Literacy in Roman Palestine*, TSAJ 81 (Tübingen: Mohr Siebeck, 2001).

32. This is presuppositional for all the studies I shall take up in this section. However, we do well to remember that early Christianity exhibits notable interest in textual composition, copying, reading, and distribution: thus, Harry Y. Gamble, *Books and Readers in the Early Church: A History of Early Christian Texts* (New Haven: Yale University Press, 1995).

33. "Altering the Default Setting," 154 (italicized in the original); cf. 150–55.

34. *Oral Gospel Tradition*, 205, also 277–82.

35. Between Bultmann, *History of the Synoptic Tradition*, and Birger Gerhardsson, *Memory and Manuscript: Oral Traditions and Written Transmission in Rabbinic Judaism and Early*

A modern analogy, which Dunn does not cite but seems to me apt, is jazz. In its origins, continuing to the present, jazz is an auditory experience, performed by a musician before a live audience. Only 10 percent of the listeners may be able to read music; by far fewer will have been trained in composition, harmony, counterpoint, and chord progressions. But all can be mesmerized by what they hear. No competent jazz musician plays a song identically every night: the performance always incorporates an established, recognizable melody (say, "St. Louis Blues," by W. C. Handy) with spontaneously inventive improvisations that delight, stretching out the theme with fresh sonic dimensions. Like all analogies, this one is imperfect: music and speech are quite different media of human communication. Gospel traditions assert or imply claims upon human existence, subject to reflection, rejection, or acceptance. Louis Armstrong said, "If you have to ask what jazz is, you'll never know."[36] The similarities, however, are suggestive: by means of a performer's memory, an aural experience is activated for a community that recognizes something familiar yet never heard the same way twice. In effect, Dunn cautions us that NT scholars have reverted to analyzing a musical score when, as Duke Ellington insisted, "It Don't Mean a Thing If It Ain't Got That Swing."[37]

The $64,000 question: how does one assess ancient traditions so influential, which vanished at the moment of utterance? Many proposals have been ventured; only some may be examined here.

First, Birger Gerhardsson's *Memory and Manuscript*, already mentioned, may have done more than any other study of the mid-twentieth century to kickstart investigation of the *Sitz im Leben der antike Kirche* after the skeptical impasse at which Bultmann had left scholars some four decades previously. One can read Gerhardsson's monograph as an erudite reaction against just about everything Bultmann claimed. Instead of fairly free-floating developments of pregospel traditions, few of which can be traced back to the Jesus of history,[38] Gerhardsson asserted just the opposite. Papias, Irenaeus, and the

---

Christianity, trans. Eric J. Sharpe, ASNU 22 (Uppsala: Gleerup; Copenhagen: Munksgaard, 1961). More on this anon.

36. The source of this famous declaration is impossible to ascertain. It's part of North America's oral tradition. Like Jesus, Satchmo probably offered his bon mots more than once.

37. In fact, that may have been said by Ellington's manager and musical publisher, Irving Mills. Before his death in 1985, Mills claimed to have come up with that title, as well as "Mood Indigo" (Terry Teachout, *Duke: A Life of Duke Ellington* [New York: Gotham Books, 2013], 57). That was only thirty-five years ago. Already a nasty problem in tracing oral transmission rears its ugly head.

38. "One can say . . . that Bultmann and his disciples . . . have regarded the synoptic

anti-Marcionite prologues testify to the existence of a pregospel tradition: among them, "there is general agreement that all four Gospels derive from well-known, reliable traditionists who stand at one or two removes from Jesus Christ." Within the NT itself, Paul nods (in Gerhardsson's reading) toward a controlled transmission of authoritative tradition from a collegium in Jerusalem (1 Cor 15:3–7; cf. Gal 1:18–2:2), even as Luke aligns himself with such an assembly (Luke 1:2–3; Acts 1:1; 6:2–4; 15:1–29). "[The apostles] are bearers, not only of the tradition concerning Christ, but also of the correct interpretation of the Scriptures."[39] Ergo, Gerhardsson concludes

> that the leading *collegium* in the Jerusalem church carried out a direct work on ὁ λόγος τοῦ κυρίου (i.e. the Holy Scriptures and the tradition from, and about, Christ). From certain points of view this work resembled the labours of Rabbinic Judaism on דבר יהוה (the Holy Scriptures and the oral Torah) and the work carried out in the Qumran congregation on דבר יהוה (the Holy Scriptures and the sect's own tradition, which was partly oral and partly written). This apostolic work on "the word of God" was thus the most important element in the comprehensive concept ἡ διδαχὴ τῶν ἀποστόλων (Acts 2.42) and the concept ἡ διακονία τοῦ λόγου (Acts 6.4).[40]

Because this tradition and its interpretation were overseen with such care, the evangelists "worked on a basis of a fixed, distinct tradition from, and about, Jesus—a tradition which was partly memorized and partly written down in notebooks and private scrolls, but invariably isolated from the teachings of other traditional authorities."[41]

Sixty years later, many assumptions and arguments in *Memory and Manuscript* have not held up well. "The Jerusalem collegium" in which Gerhardsson places confidence is a hypothetical construct, cobbled out of rabbinic

---

tradition as a post-Easter creation of the early church. My position is that one must proceed on the belief that the synoptic material in principle comes from the earthly Jesus and the disciples who followed him during his ministry, but that one must also do full justice to the fact that this memory material has been marked by the insights and interpretations gradually arrived at by the early Christian teachers" ("The Origins of the Gospel Tradition" [1977]; repr. in Birger Gerhardsson, *The Reliability of the Gospel Tradition* [Peabody, MA: Hendrickson, 2001], 1–58, quotation, 57).

39. Gerhardsson, *Memory and Manuscript*, 194, 193–323, 230 (italicized in the original).

40. Gerhardsson, *Memory and Manuscript*, 331. Gerhardsson's painstaking reconstruction of scribal schools attached to the temple, Qumran's scriptorium, and the rabbinic tradition preserved in the Mishnah, Tosefta, and the Talmuds is presented on pp. 71–189.

41. Gerhardsson, *Memory and Manuscript*, 335.

assemblies that themselves now appear a lot less fixed, stable, and universally authoritative than they once did.[42] (Even if a group of authorities in Jerusalem were regarded as "pillars," Paul shows no hesitation in prioritizing over them the revelatory value of his own experience of the risen Christ: Gal 1:15–2:10.) It is highly unlikely that the rabbinic interpretive process or the Scriptures they engage, mapped by Gerhardsson with such care, had locked into place during the era when the NT writings were composed.[43] Although he recognizes material variations among the gospels, particularly between the Synoptics and John, Gerhardsson tends to downplay their significance.[44] Put differently, if his proposal were intrinsically correct, one would expect the gospels to evince a higher level of similarity, as well as a greater degree of correspondence between their content and the rest of the NT, than can be documented. In addition, Gerhardsson leans perilously close to asserting the *ipsissima verba et facta Jesu* in the gospels, though that is no necessary inference from his analysis.[45] Nevertheless, Gerhardsson staked out a rather lonely claim for the gospels' essential reliability in an era (ca. 1930–80) when scholars had resigned themselves to little more than existentialist interpretations of an eccentric, noneschatological sage who improbably ended up being crucified as a threat to the Jewish hierarchy and Roman imperium.[46]

Second, with modifications, Richard Bauckham's meticulous study, *Jesus and the Eyewitnesses*,[47] renews the basic thrust of Gerhardsson's seminal work (249–71). Instead of a *Collegium apostolorum* as "authoritative guarantors"

---

42. See, e.g., Jack P. Lewis, "Jamnia after Forty Years," *HUCA* 71 (2000): 233–59; Shaye D. Cohen, *The Significance of Yavneh and Other Essays in Jewish Hellenism*, TSAJ 136 (Tübingen: Mohr Siebeck, 2010).

43. In later publications, Gerhardsson backed away from the assumption of rigid memorization in the traditional process: thus, "The Secret of the Transmission of the Unwritten Jesus Tradition," *NTS* 51 (2005): 1–18.

44. See *Reliability of the Gospel Tradition*, 41–58.

45. As recognized by Joseph A. Fitzmyer in his appreciative review of *Memory and Manuscript* in *TS* 23 (1962): 442–57.

46. See Ben F. Meyer, "Some Consequences of Birger Gerhardsson's Account of the Origins of the Gospel Tradition," in *Jesus and the Gospel Tradition*, ed. Henry Wansbrough, JSNTSup 4 (Sheffield: Sheffield Academic, 1991), 424–40. For recent reassessments of Gerhardsson's postulates, see *Jesus in Memory: Traditions in Oral and Scribal Perspectives*, ed. Werner Kelber and Samuel Byrskog (Waco, TX: Baylor University Press, 2009).

47. *Jesus and the Eyewitnesses: The Gospels as Eyewitness Testimony* (Grand Rapids: Eerdmans, 2006), whose subsequent citations appear above in text. A second edition, published by the same press in 2017, adds three new chapters, totaling 107 pages, that engage questions and criticisms raised of the first. Like Burridge, Bauckham is invigorated by his proposals' rejection, taking up hammer and tongs to rebuff all rebuffers. One is reminded of the inter-

of Jesus tradition, Bauckham boldly substitutes the Twelve as those who fulfilled that function (93–113 [quotation, 113], 146).[48] They, alongside named
and unnamed figures in the gospels, were reliable eyewitnesses of what those
documents report. Thus, with respect to Mark, the comments of Papias of Hierapolis (*Hist. eccl.* 3.39.14–16) invite acceptance at face value (12–38, 202–39):
the Second Evangelist acknowledges Petrine testimony by framing his entire
gospel with references to Peter (Mark 1:16–17; 16:7), by presenting Peter as
primus inter pares among the Twelve (e.g., 8:29–33; 9:5–6) and by structuring
the entire narrative in a manner that highlights Peter (124–27, 155–82). Not
only that, personages like Jairus (5:21–23, 35–43), Bartimaeus (10:46–52), and
Simon of Cyrene (15:21) plausibly reported what they saw and heard (51–55).
So, too, did nameless figures, such as the woman who anointed Jesus (14:3–9),
whose identities were left undisclosed to protect them from hostile authorities (183–201).[49] Similar patterns of eyewitness testimony are discernible in
Luke and John, less so in Matthew (108–12, 116–32, 301–2, 390–411). Bauckham
is pushing back against form criticism's assumption of anonymous tradents,
indefinable communities, and alleged laws by which traditions emerge and
develop (240–52, 290–300), as well as hyperskepticism of the gospels' historical veracity (472–508). Drawing on the research of such scholars as Kenneth E. Bailey and Samuel Byrskog (the latter, to be considered momentarily),[50]
Bauckham believes that Jesus's eyewitnesses drew upon a recollective memory
of him that held in tension the objective reality of events that were witnessed,
which stabilized their accuracy, and normal "cognitive structures" that orga-
nized remembrances in meaningful ways (8–11, 252–63, 319–57). "The Jesus
the Gospels portray is Jesus as these eyewitnesses portrayed him, the Jesus of
testimony," and "in the end, testimony is all we have" (472, 490).[51]

As with Gerhardsson, so also Bauckham: brief distillations do injustice to
the erudition of which their monographs are brimful. With that caveat firmly
lodged, a few questions may be raised. In general and in particularities, does

---

rogation of Ivy League students by a certain German professor of religion: "Do you agree,
or do you not yet understand?"

48. As Bauckham notes, Gerhardsson's later work, *Reliability of the Gospel Tradition*
(73–74), gravitates in this direction; see also *Memory and Manuscript*, 329–30.

49. Why Bethany's magnanimous woman would go unidentified but not the Twelve
(Mark 3:16–19), a bigger target for putative altercation, puzzles me.

50. Kenneth E. Bailey, "Informal Controlled Oral Tradition and the Synoptic Gospels,"
Them 20 (1995): 4–11. *Pace* Bauckham, Bailey posits a noninstitutionalized, more fluid transmission of the pregospel testimonies.

51. "All history, like all knowledge, relies on testimony" (5).

a gospel like Mark's substantiate the claims Bauckham makes of it?[52] If Simon Peter or Simon of Cyrene served as antiquity's best evidence, namely on-the-spot "autopsy,"[53] why does the gospel never assert their probity as such? If "it went without needing to be said," then why would Mark present Peter and the Twelve, indeed all of Jesus's disciples, as such incorrigible dunderheads? (Incidentally, Mark's Gospel does not begin with Peter. After Jesus, it opens with John the Baptist: 1:4–11. And the gospel ends not with Peter per se but with the muted women at the empty tomb.) Like Bauckham, the evangelist is well aware that eyewitness testimonies are not *inherently* reliable: Jesus's own mother and brothers, Jerusalem's scribes (3:19b–22), as well as his fellow countrymen (6:1–6a), see what he is doing but are dead wrong in its interpretation.[54] No one disputes that Mark the Evangelist intends to offer a proper interpretation of Jesus. Grant that, however, and something more than eyewitness testimony has intruded into this gospel: namely, subsequent decisions about that testimony's molding and arrangement, be it the staging of Bartimaeus's healing and incipient discipleship on the threshold of Jesus's entry to Jerusalem or a juxtaposition of two "Simons" in the passion narrative (14:72; 15:21).[55] The road from historical realia, however reliably testified, to Mark's interpretation is twistier than Bauckham's arguments sometimes declare.[56] He never denies that Matthew and Luke appropriated *Mark*, who even Papias knows was not an

52. Here I suggest only a partial bearing of Bauckham's argument on Mark. For a more capacious examination, which draws John into the picture, see David Catchpole, "On Proving Too Much: Critical Hesitations about Richard Bauckham's *Jesus and the Eyewitnesses*," *JSHJ* 6 (2008): 169–81.

53. Following Byrskog (*Story as History—History as Story: The Gospel Tradition in the Context of Ancient Oral History*, WUNT 123 [Tübingen: Mohr Siebeck, 2000], 48–91), Bauckham (24) uses this term not in the pathological sense but in the manner coined by Byrskog: the visual means by which "socially involved" historians gathered information. "Eyes were surer witnesses than ears" (Byrskog, *Story as History*, 64, italicized in the original). Note Luke's use of οἱ ἀπ' ἀρχῆς αὐτόπται in 1:2; cf. 1 Cor 9:1; 15:5–8; Gal 1:16; Acts 1:21–22; 10:39–41; John 19:35; 21:24; 1 John 1:1–4.

54. With some justification, Clare K. Rothschild muses, "It almost seems, in Mark, that knowing Jesus before he died was a liability to understand his true purpose" ("'Have I Not Seen Jesus Our Lord?!' (1 Cor 9:1c): Faithlessness of Eyewitnesses in the Gospels of Mark and Paul," *ASE* 31 (2014): 44). To Bauckham's credit, in the book's second edition, he reasserts no plea for "*uncritical* reliance on testimony" (608) or "blind faith" (490).

55. Black, *Mark*, 234–35, based on R. Alan Culpepper, "Mark 10:50: Why Mention the Garment?," *JBL* 101 (1982): 131–32.

56. Jens Schröter: "The category 'eyewitness testimony' can contribute to an understanding of the early Jesus tradition only insofar as it is integrated into a perspective on the Gospels as consciously composed literary and theological Jesus stories" ("The Gospels as

eyewitness to the events he recounts.[57] If Bauckham's basic argument is sound, why would they have done that?[58] What is the evidence in the NT or patristic literature "that the Twelve constituted an *official* body of eyewitnesses"? (96 [my italics]).[59] Bauckham evidently believes that some such agency is necessary for the gospels to be considered trustworthy. Is that really so?[60]

Third, as I have noted, Bauckham depends on the work of Gerhardsson's student, Samuel Byrskog.[61] Like Bauckham, Byrskog argues that early first-century traditions about Jesus were accurately remembered and handled with care. Comparing the gospels with classical practices of historiography (Heraclitus, Herodotus, Thucydides, Polybius, Josephus, and Tacitus), the process of that transmission may have run something like this. (1) Essential elements in the oral tradition of early Christian communities were probably based on the eyewitness testimony ("autopsy") of Peter, some disciples, Mary Magda-

---

Eyewitness Testimony? A Critical Examination of Richard Bauckham's *Jesus and the Eyewitnesses*," *JSNT* 31 [2008]: 208).

57. For that matter, Papias never stresses that *Peter* was an eyewitness.

58. Bauckham answers this question by reasserting, "Mark's Gospel is largely based on the tradition of the Twelve in Peter's version" ("In Response to My Respondents: *Jesus and the Eyewitnesses* in Review," *JSHJ* 6 [2008]: 243). That, in my view, at best finesses the problem; at worst it flirts with *petitio principii*.

59. Bauckham argues that the lists of the Twelve (Mark 3:13–19a; Matt 10:1–4; Luke 6:12–16; Acts 1:12–14) buttress this claim's credibility. In fact, beyond Peter, Andrew, James, John, and Judas, the NT verifies memory of twelve disciples selected by Jesus, whose names the earliest Christians could not keep straight. Bauckham's follow-up article, "The Eyewitnesses in the Gospel of Mark," *SEÅ* 74 (2009): 19–39, concludes that Peter, Simon of Cyrene, and the three named female disciples are Mark's principal eyewitness sources, not the Twelve as such. Has Bauckham substituted an alleged apostolic control for form criticism's alleged laws of traditional development?

60. Early in his *Constructing Jesus: Memory, Imagination, History* (Grand Rapids: Baker Academic, 2010), 1–2, Dale C. Allison Jr. cites Thucydides: "Different eyewitnesses give different accounts of the same events, speaking out of partiality for one side or the other or else from imperfect memories" (*Hist.* 1.22). From that incontestable confession, there's no reason to doubt the occurrence of the Peloponnesian War even if its most famous chronicler got some details wrong (Allison, *Constructing Jesus*, 14). The honesty of Thucydides inclines me to trust him the more in the absence of stronger, conflicting information or its more astute interpretation.

61. *Story as History*, 100–101, 107 n. 72. This volume's precursor is Byrskog's *Jesus the Only Teacher: Didactic Authority and Transmission in Ancient Israel, Ancient Judaism and the Matthean Community*, CBNT 24 (Stockholm: Almquist & Wiksell, 1994), which concludes that the dominical traditions were "careful and controlled" (401), probably by "transmitters highly able and motivated to preserve the tradition faithfully" (400, originally italicized).

lene and other women, and Jesus's family members.[62] (2) To prevent these autoptic elements from being forgotten, oral recollections were transformed into literary accounts (92–144).[63] Having been written, oral materials were not silenced but remained in constant interaction with that which was written in a process of "re-oralization" (138–44, 300–301). (3) For both eyewitness reporters (such as the women at the cross and the tomb) and contemporary inquirers, these acts of memory, report, and reception were ineluctably interpretive (145–98, 301–3). Subject to bias yet sensitive to factual truth, socially engaged oral tradents "sought for the visual images of the past stored in the memory" (165), which, like a wax tablet, had been impressed "with a certain fixity and perpetuity" (162).[64] (4) At the intersection of interpretive reoralization and narrative history, "persuasion and factual credibility were supplementary rhetorical virtues, not contradictory" (223),[65] because "the pastness of history was not entirely swallowed up by the concern of the present" (213, 303). (5) At every level of transmission, "both the event and its meaning are historical facts" (266), because eyewitness report combines "historical truth and interpreted truth" (274). So it follows, "as one produced a story about the past, one narrativized and interpreted not merely history, but essentially one's present existence" (255, 303–4).[66] "While a Petrine influence behind the Markan narrative is likely, in my view, the evangelist, in accordance with the ancient practice, incorporated Peter's oral history into his story by means of

---

62. Byrskog, *Story as History*, 48–91, 300. Subsequent citations appear above in text.

63. Byrskog criticizes (128–38) the tense distinction between the oral and written gospel, proposed by Werner H. Kelber (*The Oral and the Written Gospel: The Hermeneutics of Speaking and Writing in the Synoptic Tradition, Mark, Paul, and Q*, VPT [Bloomington: Indiana University Press, 1997; original ed., Philadelphia: Fortress, 1983]).

64. Citing Aristotle, *De an.* 424a; Quintilian, *Inst.* 11.2.4; Herodotus, *Hist.* 3.17.30; Cicero, *De or.* 2.86.354; 2.88.360; see also Byrskog, "The Transmission of the Jesus Tradition: Old and New Insights," *EC* 1 (2010): 441–48; Byrskog, "The Eyewitnesses as Interpreters of the Past: Reflections on Richard Bauckham's *Jesus and the Eyewitnesses*," *JSHJ* 6 (2008): 157–68, esp. 166–67. That the dominical traditions were committed to a high degree of memorization is not implausible but impossible to verify. It is also plausible—more likely, I think—that by oral remembrance the primitive church in different locales produced multiple performances, whose similarity and variability have left residues in the written gospels (so also Alan Kirk, "Memory," in Kelber and Byrskog, *Jesus in Memory*, 155–72).

65. At this point, Byrskog does not engage the prickly question of whether the gospels were originally heard, read, or both. See the contributions to *The Fourth Gospel in First-Century Media Culture*, ed. Anthony LeDonne and Tom Thatcher, LNTS 426 (London: T&T Clark, 2011).

66. "The truth of the matter, even historical truth, resides nowhere else but in that dialectical synthesis between history and story" (306).

a subtle interchange between the eyewitness testimony and other traditional material available to him, on the one hand, and his personal, selective and interpretative perspective, on the other hand, at the end thus narrativizing his own existence by presenting history as story" (292).[67]

At the risk of tiresome repetition, I have compressed a comprehensive monograph into several sentences. Likewise, my questions must be concise. (1) Though more reserved than Bauckham in conceding the influence of eyewitness testimony in the tradition's development (297),[68] both Byrskog and Bauckham allow precious little difference between history and story. If they are correct, then the quest for the historical Jesus can be concluded, full stop, since the *historische Jesu* (who traipsed the villages of Galilee) seems effectively identical to the *geschichtliche Jesu* (the Christ of the church's faith). I consider that conflation misguided, even though I am a Christian who considers the canonical gospels trustworthy and the only reliable media for reconstructing who Jesus was—and is.[69] (2) Having elsewhere contemplated the testimony of Papias, I needn't repeat that analysis here. To restate my position: according to Papias, Mark offers a faithful recollection of dominical traditions associated with Peter. Because that claim is asserted without evidence, we are in a position neither to dismiss his testimony out of hand nor to swallow it uncritically.[70] (3) In a response aimed at Bauckham but equally pertinent to Byrskog, Judith C. S. Redman has subjected the theory of eyewitness (and "earwitness") testimony to modern psychological analysis.[71] The results do not inspire confidence. Owing to manifold factors—expectations, perceptual accuracy, deterioration in retrieving stored memories, cognitive dissonance,

---

67. Citing the Papias tradition, recalled by Eusebius (272–80), as well as putatively Petrine accents throughout Mark and in Acts 10:34–43 (281–92). See also 304–5.

68. "We have no absolutely watertight criteria for identifying precisely [its] influence" (297). Yet he argues that Jesus's female followers were in all likelihood a reliable source for Peter and other men (73–82). One senses some ambivalence here.

69. Dale C. Allison Jr.: "As with most of the [gospels'] sayings, so it is with most of the stories, including the miracle stories: their origin is not subject to our demonstration" (*The Historical Christ and the Theological Jesus* [Grand Rapids: Eerdmans, 2009], 77). For a healthier *via media*, I recommend Leander E. Keck, *Who Is Jesus? History in Perfect Tense*, SPNT (Minneapolis: Fortress, 2001).

70. C. Clifton Black, *Mark: Images of an Apostolic Interpreter*, SPNT (Minneapolis: Fortress; Edinburgh: T&T Clark, 2001), 82–94.

71. "How Accurate Are Eyewitnesses? Bauckham and the Eyewitnesses in the Light of Psychological Research," *JBL* 129 (2010): 177–97. To restrain a lapse into anachronism, Redman modifies modern psychological models in accordance with what Bailey and others have inferred to be probably valid of ancient oral cultures.

and so forth—Redman concludes that "inaccuracies can, and almost inevitably will, arise in eyewitness testimony before it *becomes* valuable community tradition that is seen to be in need of preservation."

> The existence of many of Jesus' teachings in more than one form across the four Gospels indicates that if, as Bauckham [and Byrskog], following Gerhardsson, suggests, Jesus trained his disciples to remember his teachings as the third-century rabbis taught the Torah (that is, to result in verbatim recollection of text), one of three things has happened: they were far less successful students than the trainee rabbis; the authors of the Gospels did not receive their material from one of these trained disciples; or it has been significantly changed by the author of the Gospel (redacted) to fit the theological purposes of the Gospel. Therefore, regardless of whether the rabbis of Jesus' time were using the method described by Gerhardsson and named as anachronistic by his critics, if it was used by Jesus to train his disciples then [the] contention that eyewitness transmission guarantees accuracy is untenable.[72]

To Byrskog's claim for the probative demonstration of rhetorical devices in Mark,[73] Redman replies: "any good storyteller who is trying to persuade will select information to include and omit in order to achieve his or her objective. A trained rhetorician will simply do this according to a particular set of rules. Byrskog's point about the skewed content of eyewitness testimony is true, but does not require the assumption of the use of formal rhetorical method." *Enfin*, Redman concludes, "The continued presence in Christian communities of eyewitnesses to Jesus' ministry until the time when these events were recorded is a guarantee only of the preservation of the community's agreed version, not of the exact details of the event itself."[74]

Fourth, to this point, the scholarship we have reviewed has intersected with Mark yet intermittently concentrated on it. Not so Sandra Huebenthal's *Das Markusevangelium als kollektives Gedächtnis*.[75] Like other works surveyed to this

---

72. Redman, "How Accurate Are Eyewitnesses?," 192, 193.

73. See also these somewhat repetitive articles by Byrskog, all of which focus on Mark 1:29–39: "Transmission of the Jesus Tradition," 456–66; "The Early Church as a Narrative Fellowship: An Exploratory Study of the Performance of the *Chreia*," *TTKi* 78 (2007): 207–26; "When Eyewitness Testimony and Oral Tradition Become Written Text," *SEÅ* 74 (2009): 41–53; "Memory and Narrative—and Time," *JSHJ* 16 (2018): 108–35.

74. Redman, "How Accurate Are Eyewitnesses?," 195, 197.

75. FRLANT 253 (Göttingen: Vandenhoeck & Ruprecht, 2014); ET *Reading Mark's Gospel*

point, she is much interested in the character of memory and its utilization by remembering communities. More than any, she leads us through the tulgey wood of *Kulturwissenschaftliche Gedächtnistheorie*, "social memory theory," inhabited by Maurice Halbwachs, Aleida and Jan Assmann, Johannes Fried, Harald Welzer, Hans Markowitsch, and others heretofore visited by few NT scholars.[76] The payoff of their research for Huebenthal's own is the notion that, in their processes of self-definition, social organizations exert conventional pressures on their members' memories, whose literary distillates (or, as Huebenthal prefers, "externalizations") evolve from dynamic interaction with those communities' memorial practices. "Long before having access to the different media modernity offers, societies have defined through rites, feasts, the sanctification of places, and the formation of a canon what they deemed worthy of transmission, the very past from which they wanted to gain their identity."[77] In matters of historical fact, Huebenthal concurs with Welzer: "the question of truth is answered by saying that *factuality is replaced by authenticity*. The actual experience is much less important than its significance for a community of narration" (137).[78] "The realization of the past is created in accordance with the needs of the present and thus is not an image of the past, but a perspective-based, selective construction" (147).

> Working on the assumption that the text of Mark's Gospel gives voice to a community of commemoration understanding itself to be carriers of memories about Jesus, I will investigate *what* the community remembers and *how* this memory is structured and presented. . . . The event itself is not represented directly in the text, but its meaning is for the subjects of memory, to whom the text gives a voice. . . . Mark's Gospel is an episodically structured narration with a clear leading or guiding perspective that is oriented toward forms and patterns available in its context(s). Because of

---

as a Text from Collective Memory (Grand Rapids: Eerdmans, 2020). For convenience, I refer to the English version of Huebenthal's monograph and provide subsequent citations above in text.

76. Maurice Halbwachs, *Les cadres sociaux de la mémoire*, BEH 8 (Paris: Michel, 2001; original 1925); Aleida Assmann, *Erinnerungsraüme: Formen und Wandlungen des kulturellen Gedächtnisses* (Munich: Beck, 1999); Jan Assmann, *Das kulturelle Gedächtnis: Schrift, Erinnerung im politische Identität in frühen Hochkulturen*, 5th ed. (Munich: Beck, 2005); Johannes Fried, *Der Schleier der Erinnerung: Grundzüge einer historischen Memorik* (Munich: Beck, 2004); Harald Welzer, *Das kommunikative Gedächtnis: Eine Theorie der Erinnerung*, 2nd ed. (Munich: Beck: 2008); Hans Markowitsch, *Das Gedächtnis: Entwicklung, Funktionen, Störungen* (Munich: Beck, 2009).

77. Nicolas Pethes, *Kulturwissenschaftliche Gedächtnistheorien: Zur Einführung* (Hamburg: Junius, 2008), 65; quoted by Huebenthal, *Reading Mark's Gospel*, 157–58.

78. Citing Welzer, *Das kommunikative Gedächtnis*, 172.

its guiding perspective and narrative gaps, the narration is transparent for its narrating community and invites recipients to become conversant with and fully engaged and part of it. (81)[79]

An exegesis of the gospel leads Huebenthal to conclude that its narrative object—its *what*—is τοῦ εὐαγγελίου ᾽Ιησοῦ Χριστοῦ [υἱοῦ θεοῦ] (Mark 1:1) (189–92). *How* this object of memory is presented is patient of multiple explanations: narrative points of view (193–94), the text's structure (200),[80] gaps in speech or narrative (201–14), cohesive anecdotes (214–22),[81] variations in narrative pace (222–36), mediated images of Jesus (236–46), and depictions of his followers, usually in crisis, with variable degrees of fidelity to Jesus (246–62). Huebenthal then takes a deep dive into Mark 6:7–8:26, deducing its structural patterns (265–346),[82] guiding perspective (347–97),[83] and invitation to the community's engagement (398–509).[84] The community that finds its voice in this text is one not only of commemoration but also of action, realized in the rituals of baptism and the Lord's Supper (510). "Looking back to Jesus and learning from him, getting into contact and beginning relations all become the norm; likewise, their being visible and present to the world" (508–9).

---

79. Following Donald E. Polkinghorne: "The result of narrative cognitive processing is a story that can serve to give an integrating identity to the self and meaning to one's actions and experiences" ("Narrative Psychology and Historical Consciousness," in *Erzählung, Identität, Historische Bewusstsein: Die psychologische Konstruktion von Zeit und Geschichte, Erinnerung, Geschichte Identität 1*, ed. Jürgen Straub, trans. Alexander Kochinka and Jürgen Straub [Frankfurt: Suhrkamp, 1998], 11; cited by Huebenthal, *Reading Mark's Gospel*, 124–25). *Pace* Gerhardsson and others, "memory does not reproduce but creates" (Daniel L. Schacter, *Seven Sins of Memory: How the Mind Forgets and Remembers* [New York: Houghton Mifflin, 2002], 9; cited by Huebenthal, *Reading Mark's Gospel*, 95). Note also her approving citation (98) of Jan Assmann: "The past exists only as a social construct. It is reconstructed as remembered only insofar as it is needed" ("Halbwachs, Maurice," in *Gedächtnis und Erinnerung: Ein interdisziplinäres Lexikon*, ed. Nicolas Pethes and Jens Ruchatz [Hamburg: Rowohlt, 2001], 248).

80. She outlines this as "[Remembrances] In and Around Galilee" (1:16–8:26), "The Way to Jerusalem" (8:27–11:10), "In and Around Jerusalem" (11:11–37), framed by caesurae that focus on Jesus (1:14–15) or his followers (15:38–41), prologue (1:1–13), and epilogue (15:42–16:8).

81. Indebted to Cilliers Breytenbach, *Nachfolge und Zukunftserwartung nach Markus: Eine methodenkritische Studie*, ATANT 71 (Zürich: HTVZ, 1984).

82. N.B. 268 (*formelle organisation*), 284–85 (*konstituierende Gattungen*), 309 (*Intertextualität*).

83. For Huebenthal, the narrative mediates conflict between text-worlds of norms and desires (396–97).

84. Drawing from Mark 6:14–29, 30–44, 7:27, and 8:1–9 special significance for the community's table fellowship (453–66, 509).

By her admission Huebenthal's analytical agenda adopts a "reception-aesthetic perspective," blending narratological and historical methods (175, 526), form-critical categories like *Sprachgeschichte* [slogans], apothegms, novella, miracles, and epiphanies (284–85). Everything, however, is conscripted in the attempt to reconstruct a community whose own construction was founded and rebuilt over time on its remembrance of Jesus. Since, by this method, that community cannot be localized (in Jerusalem, Syria, Rome, wherever) (516–17),[85] one is boxed inside *der theoretisch zweiten Sitz im Leben*, the second social setting between that of Jesus and that of the text's producers.[86] That's precisely where the form critics were content to roam. Huebenthal is leery of leaving "the community of memory" for an editor or author of the text we know as Mark, because the latter is considered unnecessary: the community kept overwriting earlier versions of its remembered stories, as (to use a chirographic analogy she might resist) a computer overwrites previous iterations when its hard drive is backed up. Thus, she speaks of "the narrative voice [that] clearly directs [listeners to] the favored reception" (397). But whose voice is that? Who pressed the back-up button? If one answers, "the community *en masse*," is that sociologically credible? Speaking of form criticism, do the collective recollections and commitments that generated Mark remain any more amenable to recovery than the beliefs of Jesus? While *Kulturwissenschaftliche Gedächtnistheorie* justifiably asserts the indisputable function of memory in an approach that shortchanged it, will most scholars be prepared to jettison *Formgeschichte*'s alleged rules of oral transmission and instead shoulder the heavy hypothetical baggage of the continental memory theorists? It's too soon to say. If the hurdle to be cleared is "the explanatory power of the research," then Huebenthal and the like-minded have a ways to go (519).[87] From the critical importance of Mark's incipit (1:2–15) to "the dynamic ritual setting of the earliest house churches" as powerfully instrumental in the gospel's gene-

---

85. Huebenthal reckons this as a plus: it shifts the critic's attention away from the gospel's speculative origins, which tends toward circular reasoning, to its potential for reception in a particular cultural context (517–18).

86. Adopting the distinction popularized by Willi Marxsen, *Der Evangelist Markus: Studien zur Redaktionsgeschichte des Evangeliums*, 2nd ed. (Göttingen: Vandenhoeck & Ruprecht, 1959), 12; ET *Mark the Evangelist: Studies on the Redaction History of the Gospel*, trans. James Boyce et al. (Nashville: Abingdon, 1969), 23.

87. Citing Lukas Bormann, "Kulturwissenschaft und Exegese: Gegenwärtige Geschichtsdiskurse und die biblische Geschichtskonzeption," *EvT* 69 (2009): 176.

sis,[88] I find surprisingly little in her exegesis of the text that others, bereft of her method, have not already documented or assumed.

Fifth, *that* Mark's Gospel or its constituents were orally recounted is assumed by Gerhardsson and company. *How* it may have been retold is Whitney Shiner's interest.[89] After restating the case for the ancients' preference of oral over literary delivery (11–35),[90] he considers the different types, genres, and audiences of oral performances in the Greco-Roman world (37–56). Based on the assumption that, "in the ancient Mediterranean world oral performance was generally oriented toward emotional impact" (57),[91] Shiner examines those rhetorical techniques best suited to achieve that effect: emotion (57–76), delivery (77–101), memorization (103–25), and gesture and movement (127–42). After considering different religious and philosophical settings, he then attempts to gauge audience response to Mark (143–52), with attention to audience-inclusion (171–90) and applause markers (153–70).[92] Shiner speculates on the evangelist's own competence: "[Mark was] a gifted storyteller," whose "gift was most likely developed through the performance of Gospel stories rather than through the writing of narratives" (4).[93]

88. See Francesco Filannino, *The Theological Programme of Mark*, WUNT 551 (Tübingen: Mohr Siebeck, 2021), and, quoted here, Charles A. Bobertz, *The Gospel of Mark: A Liturgical Reading* (Grand Rapids: Baker Academic, 2016), 199.

89. *Proclaiming the Gospel: First-Century Performance of Mark* (Harrisburg, PA: Trinity Press International, 2003). I flag Shiner's study as representative of so-called performance theories of Mark that emerged in the late twentieth century and are still finding their footing in gospel scholarship. An interesting specimen of this research is distilled by *Communication, Pedagogy, and the Gospel of Mark*, ed. Elizabeth E. Shively and Geert van Oyen, RBS 83 (Atlanta: SBL Press, 2016), whose title indicates its practical, not merely theoretical, interest in performance: that which occurs in the classroom. Subsequent citations of Shiner's *Proclaiming the Gospel* appear above in text.

90. But see my cautionary comment in n. 32.

91. "Because of the embodied nature of speech, it is the perfect vehicle for emotions, which involve visceral reactions of the whole body" (192).

92. On a related subject, see Kelly R. Iverson, "Incongruity, Humor, and Mark: Performance and the Use of Laughter in the Second Gospel (Mark 8:14–21)," *NTS* 59 (2013): 2–19.

93. Along a similar line, Antoinette Clark Wire argues that Mark was composed, whole hog, by several storytellers across time (*The Case for Mark Composed in Performance*, BPC 3 [Eugene, OR: Cascade, 2011]). This proposal has not gained purchase among gospel exegetes. It seems to compel a needless choice between oral tradition and literary composers. Moreover, "there is no Roman-era example of such an extended literary text *composed* in 'performance,' and no basis for positing that Mark was so composed" (Larry W. Hurtado, "Oral Fixation and New Testament Studies? 'Orality,' 'Performance,' and Reading Texts in Early Christianity," *NTS* 60 [2014]: 340).

Commendably Shiner concedes that his investigation deals "with probabilities rather than certainties" (153).[94] Among those uncertainties is how conversant Mark's performers—including witnesses to Jesus and respondents to his earliest followers—would have been with philosophical and practical rhetoric (Plato, Demosthenes, Aristotle, Cicero, Quintilian, and others). A crucial question hovering over this study is implied by Shiner himself: "One's reconstruction of the Markan performance hinges first of all on a determination of whether the Markan narrative is intended primarily as instruction or as drama, as addressing the intellect or the emotions" (89). Shiner assumes that Mark's Gospel is a specimen of epideictic rhetoric, probably executed in house-churches or occasional outdoor settings, which intended, less to convince its listeners, more to reinforce their preexisting values through a primarily emotional appeal (51–52, 153–54). To a point, that may have been the case, though Mark—whether in its oral antecedents or literary transmutation—may also have served missionary purposes,[95] as well as spurred even predisposed audiences to mull over what it had heard, as did listeners to philosophical discourse (*Nigr.* 6–7) (144–45).

This section's "misery memoire" might explain why Jimmy Dunn wrote over one thousand pages on *Jesus Remembered* yet laconically stated,[96] "I do not provide any theory of memory or of remembering or engage in discussion with those who have."[97] He was satisfied to assume that there was a reliable oral dominical tradition that, as judged on the basis of the texts before us, evolved in a fluid yet stable manner. "Memorisation is inadequate to describe the *impact* made by Jesus" on disciples "who had been transformed by that impact."[98] The remembrance of Jesus in Mark, or any of the gospels, was not a

94. Noteworthy among erudite skeptics is Cilliers Breytenbach, "Das Evangelium nach Markus: Verschlüsselte Performanz?," in *Reading the Gospel of Mark in the Twenty-First Century: Method and Meaning*, ed. Geert van Oyen, BETL 301 (Leuven: Peeters, 2019), 87–114; repr. Breytenbach, *The Gospel according to Mark as Episodic Narrative*, 468–97.

95. Jesper Svartvik, *Mark and Mission: Mark 7:1–23 in Its Narrative and Historical Contexts*, CBNT 32 (Stockholm: Almqvist & Wiksell International, 2000).

96. *Jesus Remembered*, Christianity in the Making 1 (Grand Rapids: Eerdmans, 2003).

97. "This is principally because *my concern has always been to understand better why and how the Synoptic tradition came to take the shape which it still has*, with all its commonalities and differences" ("On History, Memory and Eyewitnesses: In Response to Bengt Holmberg and Samuel Byrskog," in *Oral Gospel Tradition*, 206). In characterizing that tradition, Dunn's recurring mantra is "the same yet different" (*Oral Gospel Tradition*, 8, 124, 126, 133, 195, 214, 225, 239, 243, 249, 305, 346, 360).

98. Dunn, *Oral Gospel Tradition*, 201, 240; another theme repeatedly emphasized by Dunn (8, 121, 165, 201, 204, 211, 216–17, 239, 241, 251, 271–73, 315).

bloodless chronicle of events circa 30. It was the church's honor of, and judgment by, its living Lord through recollection of an interpreted past in a present experience.[99] That Jesus, in faith and in fact, re-membered his community, as individuals and as social units. To that extent I am in concord with Huebenthal and her confreres—if my memory serves.

The Empire Strikes Back

The past three decades have also witnessed a resurgence of interest in the larger sociopolitical world from which Mark's Gospel emerged and its exegetical and hermeneutical implications. Much of this research has streamed into two different channels, both stimulating yet susceptible of turbidity.

The primary runnel has entailed scrutiny of resonances of the Roman imperium in this gospel, in shading its narrative or for instilling resistance to Caesar. For instance, Matthew James Ketchum has compared legends and archaeological depictions of spectral emperors with Jesus's ghostly presence on the sea (Mark 6:49), his transfiguration (9:2–8), and his absence from the tomb (16:6–8). "Jesus is no longer there, and appears to be no longer anywhere." Ketchum attributes this common spectrality to "the systemic violence of Rome's Empire."[100] Allan T. Georgia suggests that Mark has coopted the ritual of Roman triumphal processions to subvert Jesus's ignominy on the Via Dolorosa into a presentation of royal majesty.[101] Engaging *De clementia* (ca. 56 CE), "a work in which [Seneca] advocates a political theory in which the many deaths ransom the one life of the Emperor [Nero]," Matthew Thiessen argues that "Mark's Jesus advocates a radically different vision—in which the one Son of

---

99. Dunn, *Jesus Remembered*, 130–32; so also Nils A. Dahl, "The Problem of the Historical Jesus," in Dahl, *Jesus the Christ: The Historical Origins of Christological Doctrine*, ed. Donald H. Juel (Minneapolis: Fortress, 1991), 81–111; C. H. Dodd, *The Founder of Christianity* (London: Collins, 1971); Jens Schröter, *Erinnerung an Jesu Worte: Studien zur Rezeption der Logienüberlieferung in Markus, Q, und Thomas*, WMANT 76 (Neukirchen-Vluyn: Neukirchener Verlag, 1997), N.B. 3–4; Keck, *Who Is Jesus?*

100. "Haunting Empty Tombs: Specters of the Emperor and Jesus in the Gospel of Mark," *BibInt* 26 (2018): 241, 219.

101. "Translating the Triumph: Reading Mark's Crucifixion Narrative against a Roman Ritual of Power," *JSNT* 36 (2013): 17–38. Edward P. Meadors takes a different path: while recalling Isa 40:3, Mark 1:2–3 parr. lampoon Roman imperial ideology by puncturing the imperium's pretentious engineering projects, designed for military expansion and conquest ("Isaiah 40:3 and the Synoptic Gospels' Parody of the Roman Road System," *NTS* 66 [2020]: 106–24).

Man offers his life as a ransom for the many."[102] More pointedly, Michael Peppard revisits the Greco-Roman context for "son of God," with special attention to the early Roman principate, arguing that Mark has transmogrified the imperial eagle and *genius Augusti* into the baptismal dove and Holy Spirit in 1:9–11.[103] Armed resistance against Rome by Jesus's followers at Passover—conjectured by Hermann Samuel Reimarus, revivified by S. G. F. Brandon—has lately been reasserted by Dale B. Martin.[104] The work of Adam Winn may be, to date, the most thoroughgoing endeavor to read Mark as a blatant challenge to Roman imperial propaganda: "Mark presents Jesus as a legitimate world ruler, one who is in all ways superior to the current world ruler, Vespasian."[105]

All these studies are deeply conversant with primary texts, including relevant Hellenistic Jewish sources. While some interpretations are overstated,[106] all perform worthwhile service in situating the Second Gospel in the *Weltanschauung* of the early principate. However, one must beware extrapolating sweeping conclusions from meager evidence. "Caesar" is mentioned only twice

102. "The Many for One or One for the Many? Reading Mark 10:45 in the Roman Empire," *HTR* 109 (2016): 466.

103. *The Son of God in the Roman World: Divine Sonship in Its Social and Political Context* (Oxford: Oxford University Press, 2011), N.B. 94–133.

104. "Jesus in Jerusalem: Armed and Not Dangerous," *JSNT* 34 (2014): 3–24; cf. Hermann Samuel Reimarus, *Fragments*, ed. Charles H. Talbert, trans. Ralph Fraser, LJS (Philadelphia: Fortress, 1972); S. G. F Brandon, *Jesus and the Zealots* (Manchester: Manchester University Press, 1967).

105. *The Purpose of Mark's Gospel: An Early Christian Response to Roman Imperial Propaganda*, WUNT 2/245 (Tübingen: Mohr Siebeck, 2008), 200; Winn, "Resisting Honor: The Markan Secrecy Motif and Roman Political Ideology," *JBL* 133 (2014): 583–601, which puts a political spin on David F. Watson's interpretation, via cultural anthropology, of William Wrede's *Das Messiasgeheimnis in den Evangelien: Zugleich ein Beitrag zum Verständnis des Markusevangeliums* (Göttingen: Vandenhoeck & Ruprecht, 1901); ET *The Messianic Secret*, trans. J. C. G. Greig, LTT (Cambridge: James Clarke, 1971) with respect to ancient Mediterranean principles of honor and shame (*Honor among Christians: The Cultural Key to the Messianic Secret* [Minneapolis: Fortress, 2010]).

106. *Pace* Ketchum, the risen Jesus in Mark is not witnessed but plainly located "somewhere"—*en route* to Galilee (16:7)—and his resurrection is not manifestly connected with systemic imperial violence. Peppard's efforts to align Mark 1:9–11 with Roman propaganda strike me as too subtle by half. For a sympathetic yet systematic dismantling of Martin's proposal, see Paula Fredriksen, "Arms and the Man: A Response to Dale Martin's 'Jesus in Jerusalem: Armed and Not Dangerous,'" *JSNT* 37 (2015): 312–25. Most reviewers of Winn's monograph consider tenuous the evidence for a "messianic" view of Vespasian, on which much of his analysis hinges (e.g., Joseph D. Fantin, review of *The Purpose of Mark's Gospel: An Early Christian Response to Roman Imperial Propaganda*, by Adam Winn, *BSac* 169 [2012]: 499–501).

in Mark: once by Jesus's antagonists (12:14), the other in his response to them (12:17). That is not a wide platform on which to build a secure case of textual reception. Would most of Mark's readers, unlikely to have been well-bred, have picked up so many of the faint political cues suggested? The question is more than hypothetical: "the imperial cult" is a modern scholarly construct, whose burden on the consciousness of everyday listeners of Mark (and the NT generally) is alleged by biblical scholars but regarded with dubiety by some Roman historians.[107] The rebuttal that Mark was forced, for safety's sake, to embed critiques of empire into a "hidden transcript" seems an extraneous argument from silence: the gospel is addressed to believers who shared the author's worldview and could have regarded such issues frankly, had they so wished.[108] Mark shares with Jesus a greater interest in God's kingdom than in any empire of their world.[109] Some of the more ambitious of these studies display a kind of allegorization: Mark 10:46–52 one-ups Vespasian the healer (Tacitus, *Hist.* 4.81), the Zebedee brothers are ciphers for Titus and Domitian, and so forth.

The second rivulet of scholarly interest in Mark and empire is hermeneutical and ideological in attitude. Its main premises are two. (1) The evangelist's readers were submerged in a ubiquitous ideology of the early Roman principate: its assurance of blessings and threats of reprisal against dissent. (2) Mark's

107. See Teresa Morgan's review of *The Son of God in the Roman World: Divine Sonship in Its Social and Political Context*, by Michael Peppard, *JTS* 64 (2013): 216–18. To date, the coinage "imperial cult" is unattested in ancient literature or epigraphy. Because the evidence may be differently interpreted, the subject remains controversial; see Duncan Fishwick, "A Critical Assessment: On the Imperial Cult in *Religions of Rome*," *RelStTh* 28 (2009): 129–74.

108. Ched Myers refers to Mark's "need for a coded discourse of resistance that could elude Roman censors and military intelligence" (*Binding the Strong Man: A Political Reading of Mark's Story of Jesus* [Maryknoll, NY: Orbis, 1988], 419); similarly, Brian J. Incigneri, *The Gospel to the Romans: The Setting and Rhetoric of Mark's Gospel*, BIS 65 (Leiden: Brill, 2003): Mark's use of "cryptic allusion[s] . . . understandable only to insiders" (226). Such a case might be made for the Johannine Apocalypse. However, unless one is determined to demythologize or historicize its apocalyptic and socioeconomic structures (see, e.g., Myers, *Binding the Strong Man*, 222–23; 342), I see no necessity to decode Mark. What is the evidence that the Roman legion were so agitated by followers of *Chresto* (*sic*: Suetonius, *Claud.* 25) in the mid-first century that soldiers engaged in such espionage?

109. Here I am doubly indebted: first, to my colleague, Professor Dale C. Allison Jr., for directing me; second, to the astute essay by John M. G. Barclay, "Why the Roman Empire Was Insignificant to Paul," in Barclay, *Pauline Churches and Diaspora Jews*, WUNT 275 (Tübingen: Mohr Siebeck, 2011), 363–87. Barclay attributes the term "hidden transcripts" to James C. Scott, *Domination and the Arts of Resistance: Hidden Transcripts* (New Haven: Yale University Press, 1990).

Gospel is engaged with imperial propaganda, whether by apologetics, antagonism, transformation, or compromise.[110] Such readings, many of which style themselves as postcolonial, attempt a rapprochement—whether Marxist or neoliberal—of religion and politics, both in reading Mark and in appropriating the gospel for today's allegedly postsecular world. Carefully executed, such approaches to the text can be eye-opening, even poignant. They can also generate interpretive distortion if we straitjacket an ancient text with theory, squeezing Mark to fit our own political assumptions and social aspirations. All biblical interpretation in every era risks anachronism, to some degree.[111] That is no reason to celebrate it or to countenance distortions that mischievously mislead. Unless self-critical caution is exercised, postcolonial readings of Mark can become as provincial and hegemonic as those they would displace. Deconstructing and politicizing Mark seem to me our generation's iteration of *The Peril of Modernizing Jesus*.[112] In both cases, our prejudices can quash an old, strange, and corrective voice very different from our own.

Without disregarding political dimensions, Teresa J. Morgan's *Roman Faith and Christian Faith: Pistis and Fides in the Early Roman Empire and Early Churches* examines early Christian documents with a far wider lens, encompassing social economic and judicial practice and religions of all stripes: Greek,

---

110. For apologetics, see Robert H. Gundry, *Mark: A Commentary on His Apology for the Cross* (Grand Rapids: Eerdmans, 1993); antagonism, see Myers, *Binding the Strong Man*; Herman C. Waetjen, *A Reordering of Power: A Socio-political Reading of Mark's Gospel* (Minneapolis: Fortress, 1989); Laurel K. Cobb, *Mark and Empire: Feminist Reflections* (Maryknoll, NY: Orbis, 2013); transformation, see Winn, *The Purpose of Mark's Gospel*, 40: "[Mark] is advancing the imperialism of both God's kingdom and the one who bears it, Jesus" (see also Winn, *Reading Mark's Christology under Caesar: Jesus the Messiah and Roman Imperial Ideology* [Downers Grove, IL: InterVarsity Press, 2018]); and compromise, see Tat-siong Benny Liew, *Politics of Parousia: Reading Mark Inter(con)textually*, BIS 42 (Leiden: Brill, 1999): "Mark is a strong challenge against the existing (colonial) (dis)order. . . . At the same time, however, Mark's politics of parousia, by promising the utter destruction of both Jewish and Roman authorities upon Jesus' resurrected return, is one that mimics or duplicates the authoritarian, exclusionary, and coercive politics of his colonizers" (149). Where in Mark does one find such threats of political wipeout? The prophecy in 12:9 is limited in scope; nothing in the rest of that chapter, or in the remainder of Mark, propounds a claim so violent.

111. Hans Leander, *Discourses of Empire: The Gospel of Mark from a Postcolonial Perspective* (Atlanta: Society of Biblical Literature, 2013), 15. Leander's monograph argues that Markan scholarship must "uninherit" (why not "disinherit"?) the heritage of nineteenth-century commentaries on Mark, corrupted by European colonialism. As for anachronism, it bears remembering that the evangelists themselves retrojected their communities' interests onto their narratives of Jesus.

112. Henry Joel Cadbury, *The Peril of Modernizing Jesus* (New York: Macmillan, 1937).

Roman, Jewish, and Christian.[113] Morgan attempts to answer "two interlocking questions: how do the attitudes and social practices encompassed by the language of *pistis* and *fides* (complex terms whose central meanings include 'trust', 'trustworthiness', 'faithfulness', and 'good faith') operate in the world of the early Roman empire? And within this world, why is *pistis/fides* (which in this context we often translate 'faith') uniquely important to early Christian communities?" (563).

Roman Faith and Christian Faith overflows with insights, only some of which may be noted here. (1) In the world that cradled infant Christianity, intensity or weakness of πίστις varies with the personages involved. The evidence of one's own senses is regarded as relatively trustworthy, as are family members (including slaves) and experts in a field (39–55). Trust is vested in magistrates, though not in emperors or other sovereigns (85–95, 108–20). Friends may be untrustworthy; accordingly, such instruments as oaths, credit agreements, and legal contracts are executed (55–60, 95–108). "Most strikingly, in almost every human situation, trust is to some degree fragile and contestable, cut with mistrust, doubt, fear, or scepticism."[114] (2) In the religious realm, personal experience (including visions or dreams) and tradition are considered fairly dependable; reason and report less so, owing to their insecure foundations (145–75). The trustworthiness of the gods is reckoned fundamental for social stability. "If the gods are neither able nor willing to help us, nor do they look after us in any way, nor take notice of what we do, nor is it possible that anything comes from them into human life, what makes us give any cult, honours, or prayers to the immortal gods?" (Cicero, *Nat. d.* 1.3; trans. Morgan, 166). As religious practices go, so goes society itself: if the one collapses, so does the other. (3) In Greco-Roman and Hellenistic Jewish religiosity, trust among adherents is a coefficient of divine-human πίστις/*fides* (204–11). Strikingly, this is not attested in early Christianity: "Christians are regularly told to love one another and live in peace with one another, but they are never told, simply as community members, to trust one another."[115] (4) In alignment with

---

113. Teresa J. Morgan, *Roman Faith and Christian Faith:* Pistis *and* Fides *in the Early Roman Empire and Early Churches* (Oxford: Oxford University Press, 2015), 104–16, 123–261. The author's succinct summary of her thesis and argument's procedure is found in "Introduction to *Roman Faith and Christian Faith*," *RelS* 54 (2018): 563–68. Subsequent citations of *Roman Faith and Christian Faith* appear above in text.

114. Morgan, "Introduction," 565.

115. Morgan, "Introduction," 566. This is one of numerous observations by Morgan that takes me by the scruff of the neck, demanding that I sit up and pay attention to texts I've studied all my life.

gentile prophecy and the Septuagint's presentation of Moses, "Christian *pistis* operates in a cascade: God places *pistis* in Christ, Paul, and other community leaders; they channel it to other community members, who *pisteuein* in God, in Christ, and in those entrusted with authority over them by God and Christ" (504; see also 463–98). (5) Exploration of faith's interiority—its linkages with emotion, cognition, and virtue—comes to fruition in Christianity's second through fifth centuries. In the NT as in Greco-Roman and Jewish sources, faith is less propositional but "foundationally trust" (352), "inherently relational and characteristically expressed in action towards other human beings. . . . Interiority, relationality, and action are inseparable wherever *pistis/fides* operates" (472; cf. 212–61). (6) Why the earliest Christians chose to identify themselves as "the faithful" is impossible for us to ascertain. Morgan hypothesizes that the term may be traceable to Jesus's earliest followers and may have solidified in their successors' interactions with Jews and gentiles because of its "complexity and elasticity, together with its familiarity and multidimensional resonance" (239).

Reconstructing earliest Christian πίστις, Morgan examines every NT book. How does she assess Mark? (1) The πίστις of God and of Jesus toward humans is assumed, never explicated. Conversely, human πίστις toward God or his Messiah is "ideally absolute" albeit "a work in progress" (365). "The *apistia* of [the Twelve], it seems, is symptomatic of an ongoing struggle between *pistis*, fear, doubt, and scepticism" (356). (2) Jesus summons human πίστις (1:15; 5:36; 11:22–24), commends its practice (5:34; 10:52), and rebukes its shortfall (4:40; 9:19) (350). (3) Needy vulnerability appears to be a prerequisite for πίστις (9:42) (360). (4) Mark maintains a tension between πίστις based on sight or audition of Jesus (e.g., 5:22–28) and an inevitable ἀπιστία (6:6a; 8:11–13) (358–64). (5) Those who trust Jesus receive more than immediate remedies; they "find themselves in a quite different and much more radically transformative relationship with God" (2:5; 10:52; 11:27–33) (365).

With much in Morgan's exegesis I agree. Faith in this gospel is portrayed as mortals' trust of God or of Jesus, indisputably compromised by doubt (9:19, 24) and fear (4:40; 5:33, 36; 16:8).[116] Mark's depiction, however, seems to me considerably more complex than Morgan allows. Here, as elsewhere, she tends to assign faith's cognitive component—"belief in the good news" (1:15)—to later developments in Christianity's evolution,[117] even though (1) she has

116. Black, *Mark*, 37–40, 133–50, 211–19, 337–62, et passim.
117. A criticism lodged also by Francis Watson and Mark Seifrid, "*Quaestiones disputa-*

granted that propositional beliefs and interpersonal relationships are coinherent and (2) "the gospel" in Mark may allude to the entire complex of God's salvific activity through Jesus and his deputies, not merely to the kerygma (4:14–20; 5:19–20; 6:2b, 5; 10:29; 13:10; 14:9). Morgan acknowledges the failure of the Twelve in Mark but never notes that not once are they said to put trust in Jesus, although some reliance on his authority must be assumed if they responded to his call (1:16–20; 2:14; 3:13–19a) and discharged ministries assigned to them (6:7–13).[118] She does not consider Jesus's own anguish in trusting God (14:32–42; 15:34) and the gospel's stupefying finale, in which those female disciples who held fast longer than the Twelve demonstrate no trust at all (14:50–52, 72; 15:40–41, 47; 16:1–8). Mark may be the exception to a NT rule, but I fail to witness in that gospel a "cascade" of faith from God through Jesus to his followers and supplicants, however much the evangelist or we might wish it so.

As with Hellenistic Judaism, so, too, Greco-Romanism: the social setting of Mark's Gospel invites ongoing investigation, especially of the caliber of Morgan's magnificent study. A practical question, which should concern all who care about the liberal arts, is whether the next generation of biblical scholars will be able to keep that torch aflame. As American universities turn more careerist and departments of classics become less exacting, or shuttered outright, will there be more Teresa Morgans to guide our paths? The outlook is not hopeless, but it does appear ominously darkened.

Before hastening to this chapter's end, I register an irony in the three tendencies of Markan study whose contours I have traced. Despite the fact that all express or imply discontent with early twentieth-century *Formgeschichte*—some, vehemently so—attention to genre, traditional transmission, and social setting is, attitudinally, as *formgeschichtlich* as can be. The questions have been reframed; the scholarly stimuli remain unchanged. New Testament scholars cannot outjump their own shadows. It is futile, arguably ill-advised, to try.

---

tae: Roman Faith and Christian Faith," *NTS* 64 (2018): 243–55, with a response by Morgan, 255–61. Scholars in classics and philosophy have expressed similar concerns: Lindsay G. Driediger-Murphy, "'Do Not Examine, But Believe': A Classicist's Perspective on Teresa Morgan's Roman Faith and Christian Faith," *RelS* 54 (2018): 568–76; Daniel J. McKaughan, "Cognitive Opacity and the Analysis of Faith: Acts of Faith Interiorized through a Glass Only Darkly," *RelS* 54 (2018): 576–85; Daniel Howard-Snyder, "Pistis, Fides, and Propositional Belief," *RelS* 54 (2018): 585–92. Morgan responds to these critics in *RelS* 54 (2018): 592–604.

118. The Twelve's unreliability tallies with Morgan's observation that, in antiquity, friends are not necessarily trustworthy.

What we can learn from our predilections is to be wary of repeating our ancestors' overreach: "what begins as a very tentative guess becomes by repetition an assumed fact and represents 'the consensus of scholarly opinion.'"[119]

WHITHER? (WHO KNOWS?)

In closing, I note some areas of investigation that have been shortchanged and invite investigation.[120]

First, it has been nearly a century since Cuthbert Hamilton Turner (1860–1930) published his seminal "Marcan Usage: Notes, Critical and Exegetical, on the Second Gospel" in the *Journal of Theological Studies*.[121] With perspicacity, E. J. Brill cooperated with J. K. Elliott in republishing in a single volume those miniature classics, to which were appended additional studies on Markan Greek by G. D. Kilpatrick (1939–1956), Nigel Turner (1976), and Elliott himself (1971–1981).[122] John Charles Doudna's *The Greek of the Gospel of Mark*, a careful consideration of deviations from Atticism and unexplained Markan constructions, has been all but forgotten.[123] Beyond these studies, little has

119. Henry Joel Cadbury, "Some Foibles of New Testament Scholarship," *JBR* 26 (1958): 213.

120. Mine is a highly selective, personal list. I doubt that the disputed question of Mark's provenance—whether Syria (Gerd Theissen, *The Gospels in Context: Social and Political History in the Synoptic Tradition* [Minneapolis: Fortress, 1991]), Rome (Incigneri, *The Gospel to the Romans*), the Galilee (Hendrika N. Roskam, *The Purpose of the Gospel of Mark in Its Historical and Social Context*, NovTSup 114 [Leiden: Brill, 2004]), or elsewhere—will go away. With Dwight N. Peterson (*The Origins of Mark: The Markan Community in Current Debate*, BIS 48 [Leiden: Brill, 2000]), I doubt whether that question is answerable. I also doubt how much it finally matters for understanding the gospel. Here we are in much the same position as Pauline scholars find themselves with the origin of a letter like Philippians: Caesarea (cf. Acts 23:33–26:32)? Rome (Acts 28:14–31)? Ephesus (1 Cor 15:30–32)? Even if an airtight argument could be constructed for any of these possibilities, how much light would it throw on the text's interpretation? Very little, I suspect.

121. *JTS* o.s. 25 (1923): 377–86; 26 (1924): 12–20, 145–56, 225–40, 337–46; 27 (1925): 58–62; 28 (1926): 9–30, 349–62; 29 (1927): 257–89, 346–61.

122. *The Language and Style of the Gospel of Mark: An Edition of C. H. Turner's "Notes on Marcan Usage" Together with Other Comparable Studies*, ed. J. Keith Elliott, NovTSup 71 (Leiden: Brill, 1993).

123. John Charles Doudna, *The Greek of the Gospel of Mark*, SBLMS 12 (Philadelphia: Society of Biblical Literature and Exegesis, 1961). Robert A. Guelich, *Mark 1–8:26*, WBC 34A (Dallas: Word, 1989), and Craig A. Evans, *Mark 8:27–16:20*, WBC 34B (Nashville: Nelson, 2001), and Marcus, *Mark 1–8* and *Mark 8–16*, cite Doudna's monograph once apiece. Collins, *Mark*, refers to it not at all.

been done, of which I am aware, and nothing that gathers the threads of what one may reasonably discern on this topic.[124] Craig A. Evans has revisited it, with attention devoted to Mark's characteristic narrative intercalations and its accepted bipartite structure (chapters 1–8; 9–16), but limitations of space precluded an in-depth examination.[125] That is what we need. It would be interesting to see how Markan style and narrative devices now appear this side of four decades of rhetorical-critical inquiry, which has been applied by Alex Damm with fruitful consequences for the Synoptic problem.[126]

Second, building on a foundation laid by Austin Farrer, Ulrich Mauser, Ernest Best, and Hugh Anderson, Markan scholars have come a long way from Alfred Suhl's assessment of a thin scriptural consistency (*Schriftgemässheit*) in the Second Gospel.[127] For heightened sensitivity to Mark's use of Jewish Scripture we are much indebted to the careful scholarship of Joel Marcus, Rikki E. Watts, Marie Noonan Sabin, Stephen P. Ahearne-Kroll, and Adam Winn, to name but a few.[128] Not all of their conclusions cohere, but the fundamental

---

124. Elliott C. Maloney, *Semitic Interference in Marcan Syntax*, SBLDS 51 (Chico, CA: Scholars Press, 1981); John G. Cook, *The Structure and Persuasive Power of Mark: A Linguistic Approach*, SemeiaSt (Atlanta: Scholars Press, 1995).

125. "How Mark Writes," in *The Written Gospel*, ed. Markus Bockmuehl and Donald A. Hagner (Cambridge: Cambridge University Press, 2005), 135–48. Based on his careful study of "Markan Sandwiches: The Significance of Interpolations in Markan Narratives," *NovT* 31 (1989): 193–216, James R. Edwards's commentary, *The Gospel according to Mark*, PNTC (Grand Rapids: Eerdmans; Leicester: Apollos, 2002), is particularly attentive to this device. See also the illuminating study by Cilliers Breytenbach, "Alternation between Aorist, Historical Present and Imperfect: Aspects of Markan Narrative Style," *ETL* 95 (2019): 529–65; repr. in Breytenbach, *The Gospel according to Mark as Episodic Narrative*, 179–219.

126. *Ancient Rhetoric and the Synoptic Problem: Clarifying Markan Priority*, BETL 252 (Leuven: Peeters, 2013), with which I have conversed in *RBL* (2015), https://www.sblcentral .org/home.

127. Among others: Austin Farrer, *A Study in St Mark* (London: Dacre, 1951); Ulrich Mauser, *Christ in the Wilderness: The Wilderness Theme in the Second Gospel and Its Basis in the Biblical Tradition*, SBT 39 (London: SCM; Evanston, IL: Allenson, 1963); Ernest Best, *The Temptation and the Passion: The Marcan Soteriology*, SNTMS 2 (Cambridge: Cambridge University Press, 1965); Hugh Anderson, "The Old Testament in Mark's Gospel," in *The Use of the Old Testament in the New and Other Essays: Studies in Honor of William Franklin Stinespring*, ed. James M. Efird (Durham, NC: Duke University Press, 1972), 280–306; Alfred Suhl, *Die Funktion der alttestamentliche Zitate und Anspielungen im Markusevangelium* (Gütersloh: Mohn, 1965).

128. Joel Marcus, *The Way of the Lord: Christological Exegesis of the Old Testament in the Gospel of Mark* (Louisville: Westminster John Knox, 1992); note also Marcus's "Scripture and Tradition in Mark 7," in *The Scriptures in the Gospels*, ed. C. M. Tuckett, BETL 131 (Leuven: Leuven University Press; Peeters, 1997), 177–96; Rikki E. Watts, *Isaiah's New Exodus in Mark*,

question is whether Mark's own employment of Jewish Scripture and tradition is coherent. On its face, it is less programmatic than Matthew, Luke, or John. The issue that has not been resolved is whether Mark comprises a jumble of OT sources and themes or possesses a scriptural cohesion that has yet to be identified.[129]

Third, an important subject in Mark that is overdue for revisiting is its record of the miracle tradition. Recent studies have explored different aspects of Jesus's δύναμις,[130] but, unless I have overlooked something painfully obvious, a comprehensive assessment of miracles in the Second Gospel has not been attempted since Kenzo Tagawa in 1966.[131] Now is a propitious time to return to that topic, thanks to the trailblazing work of Graham H. Twelftree in *In the*

WUNT 2/88 (Tübingen: Mohr Siebeck, 1997); Marie Noonan Sabin, *Reopening the Word: Reading Mark as Theology in the Context of Early Judaism* (Oxford: Oxford University Press, 2002); Stephen P. Ahearne-Kroll, *The Psalms of Lament in Mark's Passion: Jesus' Davidic Suffering*, SNTSMS 142 (Cambridge: Cambridge University Press, 2007); Adam Winn, *Mark and the Elijah-Elisha Narrative: Considering the Practice of Greco-Roman Imitation in the Search for Markan Source Material* (Eugene, OR: Wipf & Stock, 2010).

129. Note the hermeneutically ambiguous conclusions of Max Botner, "Has Jesus Read What David Did? Probing Problems in Mark 2:25–26," *JTS* 69 (2018): 484–99.

130. Timothy Dwyer, *The Motif of Wonder in the Gospel of Mark*, JSNTSup 128 (Sheffield: Sheffield Academic, 1996); Geert van Oyen, *The Interpretation of the Feeding Miracles in the Gospel of Mark*, CBRA 4 (Brussels: Koninkluke Vlaamse Academie van Belgie voor Wetenschappen en Kunsten, 1999), a *Forschungsbericht* of Mark 6:34–44 and 8:1–11; Wendy J. Cotter, *The Christ of the Miracle Stories: Portrait through Encounter* (Grand Rapids: Baker Academic, 2010), which emphasizes Jesus's restrained, affable kindness in Mark and Luke (cf. Gerard Mackrell, *The Healing Miracles in Mark's Gospel: The Passion and Compassion of Jesus* [Slough: St. Paul, 1987]); Simon Mainwaring, *Mark, Mutuality, and Mental Health: Encounters with Jesus*, SemeiaSt 79 (Atlanta: Scholars Press, 2014), stressing the implications of identity, agency, and dialogue for "the social location of the relational dynamics of persons with poor mental health in contemporary North Atlantic societies" (3).

131. *Miracles et évangile: La pensée personnelle de l'évangéliste Marc*, EHPR 62 (Paris: Universitaires de France); cf. Dietrich-Alex Koch, *Die Bedeutung der Wundererzählungen für die Christologie des Markusevangeliums*, BZNW 42 (Berlin: de Gruyter, 1975). It has been nearly three decades since publication of Howard Clark Kee's *Miracle in the Early Christian World: A Study in Sociohistorical Method* (New Haven: Yale University Press, 1983); four decades since Gerd Theissen's *Urchristliche Wundergeschichten: Ein Beitrag zur formgeschichtlichen Erforschung der synoptischen Evangelien* (Gütersloh: Mohn, 1974); ET *The Miracle Stories of the Early Christian Tradition*, ed. John Riches, trans. Francis McDonagh (Philadelphia: Fortress, 1983). Andrew J. Kelley, "Miracles, Jesus, and Identity: A History of Research Regarding Jesus and Miracles with Special Attention to the Gospel of Mark," *CBR* 13 (2014): 82–106, supplies a helpful *Forschungsbericht* from about 1960 to 2012.

Name of Jesus: Exorcism among Early Christians, Jennifer Eyl's careful study *Signs, Wonder, and Gifts,* Dale Allison's comprehensive *The Resurrection of Jesus: Apologetics, Polemics, History,* and Luke Timothy Johnson's hermeneutically incisive *Miracles.*[132] Although disconcerting to modern sensibilities, the miracle tradition stands at the crossroads of Mark's social world, his apocalyptic worldview, and his assumptions about the kingdom of God and Jesus as mediator of the divine Spirit.[133]

Fourth, in reaction to a long-standing history of interpretation that harmonized the Bible's disparate voices, many twentieth-century scholars argued, then eventually assumed, that the NT's constituent authors hammered out their points of view independently of one another. In the past three decades, the pendulum has begun to swing back in the opposite direction: that the evidence for cross-fertilization among the earliest Christian writers is stronger than we have allowed. With characteristic verve, Richard Bauckham pushed the pendulum to its outermost arc: "Why would Mark, if Mark was the first evangelist, have written merely for a few hundred people, at most, who composed the Christian community in his own city, when the very act of writing a book would naturally suggest the possibility of communicating with Greek-speaking Christians everywhere?"[134] In an influential article published two

---

132. Graham H. Twelftree, *In the Name of Jesus: Exorcism among Early Christians* (Grand Rapids: Baker Academic, 2007); see also *The Cambridge Companion to Miracles,* ed. Graham H. Twelftree (Cambridge: Cambridge University Press, 2011); Jennifer Eyl, *Signs, Wonder, and Gifts: Divination in the Letters of Paul* (New York: Oxford University Press, 2019); Dale Allison, *The Resurrection of Jesus: Apologetics, Polemics, History* (London: T&T Clark, 2021); Luke Timothy Johnson, *Miracles: God's Presence and Power in Creation,* IRUSC (Louisville: Westminster John Knox, 2018).

133. Gregory M. Barnhill's "Jesus as Spirit-Filled Warrior and Mark's Functional Pneumatology," *CBQ* 82 (2020): 605–27, is brief but no less welcome. See also Armand Puig I Tàrrech, "Holy Spirit and Evil Spirits in the Ministry of Jesus," in *The Holy Spirit and the Church according to the New Testament: Sixth International East-West Symposium of New Testament Scholars, Belgrade, August 25 to 31, 2013,* ed. Predrag Dragutinovic et al., WUNT 354 (Tübingen: Mohr Siebeck, 2016), 365–93. In *Miracles and the Kingdom of God: Christology and Social Identity in Mark and Q* (Minneapolis: Fortress, 2018), Myrick C. Shinal Jr. argues that miracles in Q highlight the conquest of God's kingdom over that of Satan, while Markan miracles demonstrate Jesus's divinity. That contrast and its attendant exegesis seem to me overstated, but Shinal's probe merits attention.

134. "For Whom Were the Gospels Written?," in *The Gospels for All Christians,* ed. Richard Bauckham (Grand Rapids: Eerdmans, 1998), 30. A plausible answer to this question: Mark may have originated as an address to a particular community's needs, was subsequently circulated, and eventually found adaptable by the authors of Matthew and Luke,

years later, Joel Marcus argued, *pace* Martin Werner, that Paul and Mark do not represent generally accepted points of view in the early church; instead, Mark's theology of the cross is best explained as dependent on Paul's own, whose force the other gospels attenuated.[135] Marcus also notes that Mark's dismissal of *kashrut* (7:19) tracks Paul's own in Rom 14:20 almost verbatim, a point later developed by Dale Allison.[136] Allison also ponders the flash of Adamic Christology in Mark 1:12–13 (by way of T. Levi 18.10), which Paul expands in Romans (5:12–21) and 1 Corinthians (15:20–22, 45–49). Heidi Wendt contends that "Mark's [motif of] secrecy as a narrative strategy . . . cooperate[s] to privilege Paul as the principal (or only) authority on Christ."[137] The most striking expression of the evangelist's reliance on the apostle that I have encountered is that of Margaret M. Mitchell: while Paul was alive, his gospel was embodied in his "epiphanic presence," conveyed in his letters; after his death that presence and gospel is embodied in Mark's Gospel.[138]

I don't know what to make of all this.[139] As chapters 11 and 12 of this volume indicate, I am more comfortable in comparing Mark's beliefs with those of other NT witnesses at the textual level, prescinding from assumptions of traditional dependence. I am not averse to the latter's possibility; in principle, it seems to me likely. I am confounded by the methodological controls by which such a possibility could rise to the level of proof.[140] Marcus's primary

---

perhaps also John. Support for such a development may be drawn from the origin, circulation, modification, and canonization of Paul's letters.

135. Martin Werner, *Der Einfluss paulinischer Theologie im Markusevangelium: Eine Studie zur neutestamentlichen Theologie*, BZNW 1 (Giessen: Töpelmann, 1923); Joel Marcus, "Mark—Interpreter of Paul," *NTS* 46 (2000): 473–87, esp. 481–84. W. Ernest Moore anticipated something of Marcus's position in "'Outside' and 'Inside': Paul and Mark," *ExpTim* 103 (1992): 331–36.

136. "Mark—Interpreter of Paul," 486–87; cf. Dale C. Allison, "Cyprus and Early Christianity: Did Everybody Know Everybody?," in *Cyprus within the Biblical World: Are Borders Barriers?*, ed. James H. Charlesworth and Jolyon G. R. Pruszinski (London: T&T Clark, 2021), 127–46, esp. 136–37.

137. "Secrecy as Pauline Influence on the Gospel of Mark," *JBL* 140 (2021): 579. Do tell. This would come as a surprise to all the eastern and western fathers of the church, none of whom ventures a claim so audacious—even those who more closely align the Second Gospel with Paul than with Peter. See Black, *Mark: Images of an Apostolic Interpreter*, 75–191, N.B. 149–53, 165–70.

138. "Epiphanic Evolutions in Earliest Christianity," *ICS* 29 (2004): 183–204.

139. Neither do others. See the critically equivocal estimates in *Mark and Paul: Comparative Essays Part II; For and Against Pauline Influence on Mark*, ed. Eve-Marie Becker, Troels Engberg-Pedersen, and Mogens Muller, BZNW 199 (Berlin: de Gruyter, 2014).

140. Richard Last provides reasons, predicated on the character of ancient associations,

criterion is one of dissimilarity: the more that various views held by both Paul and Mark can be shown to disagree with other early Christian writers, the more probable a relationship of interdependence. If someone were able to work out that argument through Mark's entirety, I could be convinced. My reluctance is based on the panoply of major Pauline topoi—God's rectification of sinners, the character of faith, life in the Spirit—that seems compatible with Mark's theological attitude yet inexplicably undeveloped (2:17; 11:22; 13:11).[141] To varying degrees, in divergent ways, all these ideas claimed some purchase on other writers' imaginations: Matthew, Luke, John, Hebrews, and 1 Peter. Is it possible to trace definable arcs of direct dependence?[142] Given the equivocal evidence available to us, I doubt it but am happy to entertain such arguments with an open mind.[143]

Fifth, we also need competent, careful detective work applied to the *Wirkungsgeschichte* of Mark in all of the centuries before the Enlightenment. Truly this is *terra incognita*: partly because premodern exegetes gave Mark shorter shrift than its canonical companions, partly because most NT scholars are not trained in the languages and techniques of patrology. Some preliminary work has been done. The compilation of citations in the volume on *Mark* in the Ancient Christian Commentary on Scripture: NT is slender, to say the least: many have nothing to

---

for diminishing the likelihood that the gospels were written with all Christians in view: "Communities That Write: Christ-Groups, Associations, and Gospel Communities," *NTS* 58 (2012): 173–98.

141. Comparable reserve is expressed in the interesting analysis of Andy Johnson, "The 'New Creation,' the Crucified and Risen Christ, and the Temple: A Pauline Audience for Mark," *JTI* 1 (2007): 171–91.

142. Jesper Svartvik thinks so: "the Gospel of Mark could and should be understood as a Pauline Gospel," the narrative unfolding of an apostolic kerygma that, in David Sim's view, was repudiated and suppressed by Matthew (Svartvik, "Matthew and Mark," in *Matthew and His Christian Contemporaries*, ed. David C. Sim and Boris Repschinski, LNTS 333 [London: T&T Clark, 2008], 27–49; Sim, "Matthew's Use of Mark: Did Matthew Intend to Supplement or to Replace His Primary Source?," *NTS* 57 [2011]: 176–92). R. Alan Culpepper leans in this direction, while citing divergent assessments (*Matthew: A Commentary*, NTL [Louisville: Westminster John Knox, 2021], 3–6).

143. Allison notes, "We need to take great care to separate the issue of theological diversity from the issue of historical connection. One can have diversity of thought because two individuals or groups have developed their ideas independently of one another. But, to state the obvious, individuals and groups who know each other or each other's writings can also hold diverse and conflicting opinions" ("Cyprus and Early Christianity," 130). The same argument can be inverted: individuals and groups who do not know one another's writings can hold similar and corroborative opinions.

do with Mark in particular.[144] Sean P. Kealy's discussion of Markan interpretation in the second through seventeenth centuries is far superior in coverage but
lacks close analysis.[145] Heartily to be welcomed is Michael Cahill's edition of *The
First Commentary on Mark: An Annotated Translation*,[146] an anonymous work
of possibly Irish provenance, which influenced Thomas Aquinas (1225–1274)
and Cornelius à Lapide (1567–1637). The leader in this venture of "chasing the
invisible" is Joseph Verheyden of the University of Leuven, who has drawn a
smart map of how we might proceed, but he could use some help.[147] Brenda
Dean Schildgren has lent a hand, particularly in excavating Mark's role in the
medieval Easter liturgy, but there's more to be said.[148] Such studies are of more
than antiquarian interest. The more we learn about the interpretation of Mark
and the rest of the NT in the patristic and medieval eras, the greater the awareness of our ignorance and the humbler our insights become.

Sixth, in case it has escaped the reader's attention, our era (in 2022) is preoccupied by issues raised by race, ethnicity, gender, sex, class, and the power
dynamics that emerge—sometimes, erupt—at their intersection. Because biblical interpretation never occurs in a cultural vacuum, it is inevitable that some
interpreters would bring such concerns to their readings of Mark and other
ancient texts.[149] An array of approaches so vast is impossible to measure here.
Some are certain to affect Markan interpretation in the foreseeable future;[150]

144. Thomas C. Oden and Christopher A. Hall, eds., *Mark*, ACCSNT 2 (Downers Grove,
IL: InterVarsity Press, 1998).

145. *A History of the Interpretation of the Gospel of Mark: Through the Nineteenth Century*
(Lewistown, NY: Mellen, 2007), 1:41–274. See my review of Kealy's three-volume set in *CBQ*
73 (2011): 391–92.

146. *The First Commentary on Mark: An Annotated Translation* (New York: Oxford
University Press, 1998).

147. "Before Embarking on an Adventure: Some Preliminary Remarks on Writing the
NTP Commentary on the Gospel of Mark," *StPatr* 44 (2010): 145–56; Verheyden, "The
Reception History of the Gospel of Mark in the Early Church: Adventuring in Still Largely
Unexplored Territory," in *Reading the Gospel of Mark in the Twenty-First Century: Method
and Meaning*, ed. Geert van Oyen, BETL 301 (Leuven: Peeters, 2019), 395–428. The phrase
"chasing the invisible" was coined by Verheyden ("Reception History," 404).

148. *Power and Prejudice: The Reception of the Gospel of Mark* (Detroit: Wayne State
University Press, 1998), 72–75. See also Collins, *Mark*, 103–19.

149. See, e.g., Janice Capel Anderson and Stephen D. Moore, eds., *Mark and Method:
New Approaches to Biblical Studies*, 2nd ed. (Minneapolis: Fortress, 2008); *New Testament
Masculinities*, ed. Anderson and Moore, SemeiaSt 45 (Atlanta: Scholars Press, 2003), esp.
93–161.

150. Thus, *A Feminist Companion to Mark*, Amy-Jill Levine with Marianne Blickenstaff

others, in time, may fade away. Although I myself am not consciously wedded to such overtures, I am as willing to learn from the most perceptive of their exponents as I am to be challenged to view Mark through a religious lens altogether different from that to which I am accustomed.[151] My vision is as blinkered as any mortal's; like everyone, I need reminding that the questions one asks control the answers one gets. All I ask of such ventures is that they subject themselves to the self-criticism they rightly expect of me, that they receive in good faith critique as well as approbation, and that they, like me, do their best to hear and represent *Mark's* claims as accurately as they are able, without ventriloquizing our prejudices into it.[152]

In an essay on writing, Shirley Jackson related this anecdote:

> I was playing bridge one evening with a musician, a chemistry teacher, and a painter when, during a particularly tense hand, a large porcelain bowl that we kept on the piano suddenly shattered. After we had all calmed ourselves down, we found four completely individual reactions. Looking at all the tiny scattered pieces, I thought that I had never realized before how final a metaphor a broken bowl could be. The chemistry teacher pointed out that someone had emptied an ashtray into the bowl with a cigarette still burning, and of course the heat had shattered the bowl. The painter said that the green of the bowl was deepened when the light caught the small pieces. The musician said that the sound it made when it broke was a G sharp. Then we went back and finished our bridge hand.[153]

Whose appraisal of the broken bowl was accurate? Maybe everyone's. Which was incomplete? All of them. Owing to differences of perspective, each made a claim about a common object, which was subject to testing. (Had the temperature in itself been sufficient to shatter the bowl, or would a better-built

---

(London: T&T Clark; Cleveland: Pilgrim, 2001).

151. John P. Keenan, *The Gospel of Mark: A Mahayana Reading*, FMFS (Maryknoll, NY: Orbis, 1995).

152. The gruesome alternative is a divisive, narcissistic dogmatism that crushes genuine liberalism, which aims to engage the better angels of our nature by expanding our empathy and sense of fairness toward all. See, if you dare, Helen Pluckrose and James Lindsay, *Cynical Theories: How Activist Scholarship Made Everything about Race, Gender, and Identity—and Why This Harms Everybody* (Durham, NC: Pitchstone, 2020).

153. "Memory and Delusion," *New Yorker*, 31 July 2015, https://www.newyorker.com /books/page-turner/memory-and-delusion.

basin have withstood the heat? Was the resultant color green or turquoise? Was the sound when it burst G sharp or A?) The important thing is that within the range of their respective competence, all responded to an explosive artifact, then stayed at the table to play out their hand.

Seventh, and last, after forty years of studying it, I find the Gospel of Mark surpassingly *weird*. The Johannine Apocalypse is baffling; still, after one learns the conventions of apocalyptic literature, it is, up to a point, intelligible. For all we have learned about the conventions of ancient history and biography, Mark still upends our expectations. Here's an attempt I once made to describe it:

> Mark's genius lies not in telling a story about Jesus, but in creating conditions under which the reader may experience the peculiar quality of God's good news (1:14). . . . The Evangelist hurries one along breathlessly, "immediately" (1:10, 12, 18, 20, 21, 23, 29, 30, and so on), . . . making sure that the reader lurches with the characters into one pothole after another. "What is this new teaching" (1:27a AT) that consorts with the flagrantly sinful (2:15), turning the pious homicidal (3:6), intimates into strangers (3:21; 6:1–6a), and mustard seeds into "the greatest of all shrubs" (4:32a)? What healer is moved by one supplicant (1:40–42) but offers another a cold shoulder (7:26–27)? What pilgrim saunters the temple one day (11:11) and unhinges its operations the next (11:15–16)? What teacher speaks well (12:28), impartially teaching "the way of God in accordance with truth" (12:14a), while spinning riddles intended to blind the sighted and to deafen the hearing, "so that they may not turn again and be forgiven" (4:11–12)? . . . The Twelve are craven, stupid, self-serving, and disobedient (4:40; 8:4; 9:34; 10:32, 35–37, 41; 14:37–40, 66–72) . . . "their hearts were hardened" (6:52; 8:17). Who hardens hearts? God. Should not God's Messiah lift the burdens of those following him? What kind of Christ heads to a cross, handing his disciples another for themselves (8:31–35)? "Do you not yet understand?" (8:21).[154]

I am not alone in my respectful yet bewildered estimate. Others have told me much the same.[155] I know at least three Markan scholars who dedicated their professional lives to its study because, when they were honest with themselves, they found this book irresistibly enigmatic. We scramble for logical explana-

---

154. Black, *Mark*, 38–39.
155. To quote one: "I quite agree too about how perplexing it is to work out what Mark is, and what he's doing. I still find it baffling."

tions, but the narrative's gaps—especially at its end—yawn as gigantically as ever.[156] Mark transcends narrative irony and theological paradox.[157] Something about it is *irreducibly uncanny*. I don't have a clear proposal for studying a wild yet seemingly simple text that all but defies understanding. I do hope that those who come after me appreciate that and try to avoid taming it.

156. David Aune concludes that "Mark is in fact a *parody* of ancient biography" ("Genre Theory and the Genre Function of Mark and Matthew," in *Mark and Matthew I: Comparative Readings; Understanding the Earliest Gospels in Their First-Century Settings*, ed. Eve-Marie Becker and Anders Runesson, WUNT 271 [Tübingen: Mohr Siebeck, 2011], 175). Aune may be onto something, but I place my bet with Kermode: "If there is one belief (however the facts resist it) that unites us all . . . it is this conviction that somehow, in some occult fashion, if we could only detect it, everything [in Mark] will be found to hang together" (*Genesis of Secrecy*, 72). Kermode does not share that conviction. Neither do I.

157. Jerry Camery-Hoggatt, *Irony in Mark's Gospel: Text and Subtext*, SNTSMS 72 (Cambridge: Cambridge University Press, 1992); Laura C. Sweat, *The Theological Role of Paradox in the Gospel of Mark*, LNTS 492 (London: Bloomsbury, 2013).

Part Two

THEOLOGICAL STUDIES

CHAPTER 7

A Conspectus of Markan Theology

> No other gospel, even Matthew with its broad grounding in He-
> braic lore, is quite brave enough to admit that chasm yawning
> between the claims of Jesus and his agonized fate—a fate that may
> well yawn before each one of us, between here and death. Isn't
> that bravery—reckless, unnerving—the source of the pull that
> Mark the writer has exerted through all the life of his story . . . ?
>
> —Reynolds Price[1]

No biblical writing systematizes its theology. While Romans and
Hebrews offer sustained articulations of early Christian faith, the Gospel of
Mark does not. For convenience, one may abstract and coordinate aspects
of Markan theology; in so doing, one betrays the narrative form in which
the evangelist leads the reader on a jagged journey of faith. This essay offers
something like analysis of movements and leitmotifs extracted from their sym-
phonic context. Comprehension of Mark's theology depends on reading the
gospel whole.

The Kingdom of God, Its Agent and Power

Mark opens (1:1), "The beginning of the good news of Jesus Christ, the Son
of God."[2] This theme is recapitulated in Jesus's introductory announcement

---

1. *Three Gospels: The Good News according to Mark; The Good News according to John;
An Honest Account of a Memorable Life* (New York and London: Scribner, 1996), 84.
2. Ancient manuscripts of Mark disagree on whether "Son of God" (ὁ υἱός θεοῦ) was
included in the original text of Mark. Scribes tended to enlarge, rather than to abbreviate,

(Mark 1:15): "The time is fulfilled, and the kingdom of God has come near; repent, and believe in the good news." Within and between these framing assertions, much of this gospel's theology is compressed.

"The good news" (εὐαγγέλιον; see also 1:14; 10:29; 13:10; 14:9) concerns the coming of God's "kingdom" or dynamic sovereignty (βασιλεία) over mortal life and human monarchies. God's mysterious dominion is bursting into the theater of human life (4:11, 26, 30); old structures cannot contain it (2:18–28; 3:31–35; 7:1–23; 10:2–12, 35–45).

Jesus, *God's anointed* (χριστός), *heralds this good news, summoning others to trust it* (1:15). Jesus mediates the kingdom by exercising divine authority to exorcise unclean spirits (1:21–28; 5:1–20; 7:24–30; 9:14–29), to heal infirmities (1:29–34; 3:1–6; 5:21–43; 7:31–37, 8:22–26; 10:46–52), to forgive sins (2:1–12), and to confront others (3:19b–35; 11:15–12:44)—in a moment of crisis even himself (14:36)—with God's will. Where Jesus is, there is God's kingdom.

The kingdom's advent, activated by Jesus, is presaged in *the scriptural prophecy of preparing "the way of the Lord"* (1:2–3; cf. Exod 23:20; Mal 3:1; Isa 40:3), itself personified by John the Baptist in Elijah's guise (Mark 1:4–8; 6:14–29; 9:9–14; cf. 2 Kgs 1:8; Zech 13:4). John's message of repentance (μετάνοια, "turning of the mind") and forgiveness (ἄφεσις ἁμαρτιῶν, "release from sins") anticipates Jesus's proclamation (Mark 1:15). Many of Jesus's astonishing deeds (4:35–41; 6:30–52; 8:1–10) recollect prophetic activity in Israel (2 Kgs 4:8–37, 42–44) and God's own mighty works (Exod 16:4–21; Ps 107:23–30).

The Holy Spirit attends Jesus's baptism (Mark 1:8–11; cf. 3:29; 13:11; 14:38; Isa 42:1–5; Ezek 2:2; 3:12–15). Immediately afterward, the Spirit drives Jesus into the wilderness for forty days of satanic temptation (Mark 1:12–13; cf. Deut 8:2; Neh 9:21). The gospel's remainder is suffused by Jesus's assault of diabolical powers (Mark 3:11, 23, 26; 4:15; 5:12; 6:7), temptations of him and of his disciples to abandon the kingdom's mandates (8:11–13, 31–33; 10:35–41; 14:1–2, 10–11, 29–42, 43–53, 66–72), and apocalyptic foreshadowing of distress and eventual redemption (4:13–20, 26–32; 8:34–9:1; 9:38–50; 10:42–45; 13:1–37; 14:22–28).

From this précis emerge distinguishing features of Markan theology.

---

the beginnings of books. The tendency to clarify through expansion inclines toward the shorter reading's originality, in which "Son of God" is absent from Mark 1:1. On the other hand, a strong combination of diverse witnesses favors the inclusion of a title that is undeniably important in Mark (3:11; 5:7; 12:6; 14:61), occurring at climactic points in this gospel (1:11; 9:7; 15:39). The textual evidence is remarkably well balanced: see Reuben Swanson, ed., *New Testament Greek Manuscripts: Mark* (Sheffield: Sheffield Academic; Pasadena: William Carey International University Press, 1995), 7. If Mark had originally written the longer form, why would later scribes have truncated it?

First, formally, it unfolds as *a brisk narrative*, with Jesus its principal protagonist (1:1). Compared with other gospels (Matt 5:1–7:28; Luke 12:1–18:14; John 13:12–17:26), Mark rarely pauses for Jesus to offer uninterrupted instruction (4:1–32; 13:5–37); by comparison with other Synoptics, the teaching in Mark is more opaque than clarifying (cf. Mark 8:15 = Luke 12:1; Mark 9:13 = Matt 17:12–13).

Second, substantively, *Markan theology is coherent but not systematically coordinated*. Past (Israel's history), present (first-century Judea and Galilee, Mark 1:5, 14; cf. 6:14–29), and future (eschatological completion) are tightly telescoped. As God's beloved Son (1:11), Jesus preaches God's good news on God's behalf (1:14) at the Spirit's behest (1:10–12). While Mark assumes no doctrine of the Trinity, its three "persons" and their dynamic interaction are germinally in play (cf. Matt 28:19; Eph 2:18).

Third, though not an apocalypse in genre, *Mark's Gospel is eschatologically saturated*. The heaven's rending and the Spirit's descent (Mark 1:10), encounters with Satan, wild beasts, and angels (1:12–13) are elements in Hellenistic Jewish apocalypticism (Isa 64:1; Ezek 1:1; 1 En. 72.1; As. Mos. 10.1; T. Naph. 7.7). Though rare, "the kingdom of God" or "of heaven" is also an apocalyptic metaphor (Pss. Sol. 17.1; 3 Bar. 11.2), and some strands of Jewish messianism are eschatological (CD VI, 7–11; Ps. Sol. 17.1–18.13; 4 Ezra 11–12, 40, 72).

Fourth, *unresolved tension* is distinctive of Mark. In its prologue (1:1–15), this trait is conspicuous. The very first word signals the gospel's "beginning" (ἀρχή, v. 1), with no terminus indicated. The identity of the "messenger [sent] to prepare [the] way" (v. 2) is equivocal because it is unclear whether it refers to John or to Jesus. Jesus is addressed from heaven as God's Son, overheard by the reader (v. 11), and intuited by unclean spirits (1:24, 3:11); no one else in Mark is privy to his identity at the start (cf. Matt 3:17; Luke 2:49; John 1:29–34). Unlike Matthew 4:11 (cf. Luke 4:13), Jesus's temptation does not end in obvious triumph (Mark 1:13; cf. 3:27). Jesus does not proclaim that God's dominion has fully arrived; rather, "the time [καιρός] is fulfilled, and the kingdom has come near" (1:15; cf. 9:1; 13:32–37; 14:25). "Belief in the good news" lies in a gap between the kingdom's inauguration and consummation.

God

Mark's forty-eight occurrences of θεός are unique in the NT because they predicate almost nothing about God (9:37; 11:25; 12:27 are exceptions). Attributes of God may be inferred from Mark's fourteen sayings about "the kingdom of God," which is not coterminous with Israel or any geopolitical entity,

neither an inner spirituality nor a utopian dream. God's βασιλεία is anticipated (9:1; 14:25; 15:43) yet secretly erupting in history (4:22; cf. Matt 13:18–23;
Luke 17:20–21). A gift from God, not a human achievement (Mark 4:26–29;
10:23–27; cf. Luke 12:32; John 3:3), the kingdom upends conventional expectations (Mark 4:30–32; cf. Matt 20:1–16; Luke 9:59–60). Its acceptance demands
radical sacrifice (Mark 9:42–50) and infant dependence (10:13–15). The kingdom's ineluctable mystery, simultaneously revelatory and concealing (4:11–12;
cf. Rom 11:25–36; 1 Cor 1:18–2:13), is developed in Jesus's references to God's
transcendence (Mark 11:12–12:34).

To God belongs compassionate but final judgment over Israel, all the nations, and their religious custodians (Mark 11:17–18; 12:1–12; cf. Ps 96:13; Isa 2:4;
Ezek 7:27). Secular power is relativized by God's sovereignty, which encom-
passes all of life without reduction to sectarian theocracy (Mark 12:13–17; cf.
Rom 13:1–13). Through Scripture (Exod 3:2, 6, 15), God affirms his enduring
life and power over death (Mark 12:18–27). No commandment is greater than
Israel's complete love of the one and only God (Deut 6:4–5) and love of neighbor as one's self (Lev 19:18; Mark 12:28–34; cf. Luke 10:27; Rom 13:9; Gal 5:14;
Jas 2:8). Throughout Mark, Jesus's teaching is radically theistic: membership in
Jesus's family is defined as doing "the will of God" (3:35); discipleship to Jesus
turns satanic when Peter sets his mind "not on divine things but on human
things" (8:33); repeatedly, the criterion of Jesus's fidelity is acceptance that "the
Son of Man must [δεῖ] undergo great suffering" because it is God's will (8:31;
cf. 9:31; 10:33–34; 14:36). The resurrection decisively verifies God's own fidelity
to his beloved Son (1:11; 9:7; 14:28; 16:6–7).

Jesus

Because he perfectly represents the one who sent him (Mark 9:37; 12:6; cf. John
5:30; 13:20) and instantiates the kingdom's values, Jesus is uniquely positioned
in Mark to convey God's good news.[3] A key metaphor is *sonship*: used absolutely ("Son": Mark 12:6; 13:32) but more often with predicates of Jesus's likeness
to God (Mark 1:1; 3:11; 5:7; 14:61; cf. Jer 31:20 [referring to Israel]; Sir 4:10c [pro-
tectors of the poor]; Philo, *Spec.* 1.58.318 [the virtuous]). Compared with some
other NT Christologies, Mark's appears functional rather than ontological:
Jesus is God's Son through obedience, not by origin (cf. Matt 1:21–23; Luke 1:35;

3. An important literary analysis that subordinates Christology to theology is Elizabeth
Struthers Malbon, *Mark's Jesus: Characterization as Narrative Christology* (Waco, TX: Baylor
University Press, 2009).

John 5:19–24; Heb 1:2). Although acclamations of Jesus as God's Son occur at critical points in the narrative (Mark 1:11 [Jesus's baptism; cf. Gen 22:2; Ps 2:7; Isa 42:1]; 9:7 [his transfiguration]; 15:39 [his death]), to claim this title's primacy in Mark outruns the evidence. "Son of God" complements other aspects of the evangelist's presentation of Jesus and counterbalances other modes of reference to him, none of which adequately encompasses everything Mark asserts.

Compared with other NT witnesses—especially Luke-Acts, Paul, and Hebrews—Mark rarely refers to Jesus as "Christ" (= "Messiah": Mark 1:1; 8:29; 9:41; 14:61; 15:32) or "Lord" (Mark 1:3; 2:28; 11:3; 12:37).[4] By contrast with Matthew (e.g., 1:1; 21:9, 15), Mark seems leery of "Son of David": only a blind man so addresses him (10:47–48), and Mark 12:35–37 implies that title's inappropriateness for Jesus (cf. Rom 1:3; 2 Tim 2:8; Rev 22:16).

By far, Mark's most common appellation for Jesus is the most enigmatic: "Son of Man." This self-identification carries several connotations: an earthly, authoritative figure who can transgress conventional Jewish piety (Mark 2:10, 28; cf. Isa 56:2, which assumes torah's strictures), an apocalyptic figure to come (Mark 8:38; 13:26–27; 14:62; cf. Dan 7:13–14; 1 En. 69.27–29; Sib. Or. 5.414–33), or—by a ratio of three to one—a figure that must suffer and be vindicated by God (Mark 8:31; 9:9, 12, 31b; 10:33–34, 45; 14:21, 41; cf. Ezek 4:1–5:17; 12:1–28; 24:15–27; Wis 1–6). These three nuances are mutually interpretive, begging coordination with other designations (like "Son of God") within Mark's narrative framework, which presents Jesus as the teacher whose insight is uniquely authoritative (2:23–28; 7:6–15) and the healer whose power over hostile forces will be consummated (1:21–28; 13:26–27; 14:62) only after he has relinquished his life for others (10:45). What sets the Markan "Son of Man" apart from other Jewish apocalypticism is its emphasis on his death, with a redemptive consequence that extends beyond Israel. Significantly, the single point in Mark at which all major ascriptions of Jesus converge is his acceptance of the high priest's oblique affirmation of him as Christ and Son of God, which seals the Son of Man's death warrant (14:61–64).

The Holy Spirit

Compared with Luke-Acts (Luke 1–2; Acts 2:1–42; 10:1–11:18), John (14:15–26; 16:13–15), and the Pauline tradition (Rom 8:1–30; Gal 5:16–6:10; Eph 2:1–22),

---

4. Whether "the Lord" refers to God or to Jesus in 1:3 is a hard question. Elsewhere in the gospel, ὁ κύριος can refer either to the former (5:19) or to the latter (12:37). Possibly the evangelist intends such ambiguity here.

Markan pneumatology is underdeveloped. Nevertheless, the Spirit is the power that propels Jesus's ministry (Mark 1:8, 10, 12), particularly his assault against unclean spirits that plague human life (1:23, 26; 5:2, 8; 7:25; 9:17, 20, 25). To confuse Jesus's healing power with diabolism is an unforgivable blasphemy against the Spirit (3:22–30), presumably because it drives the accuser away from the genuine agent of God's forgiveness (Mark 2:10; cf. 1 John 5:16–17). Beyond the Spirit's presence with Jesus, his persecuted followers may rely on the Spirit to provide them testimony in their hour of trial (Mark 13:11).

RESPONSES TO GOD'S SOVEREIGNTY: DISCIPLESHIP AND RESISTANCE

As Christology and pneumatology follow from the Second Evangelist's view of God, so also is discipleship (incipient ecclesiology) a coefficient of Christology. Discipleship in Mark is "following Jesus" at his command (1:16–20; 2:13–14; 3:13–19a), extending his authority over demonic forces while healing the sick and feeding the hungry (6:7–13, 30–44; 8:1–10). Disciples who abandon family and property for the sake of Jesus and the gospel are reintegrated into a new family around him who does God's will (3:31–35), assured they will receive a hundredfold of all they have lost and, in the age to come, eternal life (10:28–31). With such rewards come persecutions (10:30c): intrafamilial betrayals, beatings, and susceptibility to deceit (13:5–27), all of which must be endured to the end (13:13b, 32–37).[5]

As the Son of Man's vindication depends on giving up his life for others (Mark 8:31–32a; 9:31–32; 10:33–34), so do self-denial and taking up one's cross constitute the essence of discipleship (8:34). Mark reiterates this hard dedication paradoxically: saving one's life by losing it (8:35); becoming first by being last and servant of all (9:35); receiving the kingdom as a powerless child (10:13–16); giving up everything for heavenly treasure (10:17–25); achieving greatness only by self-enslavement (10:43–45); preaching that provokes temporary futility, punishment, and universal hatred (13:10–13a; cf. 4:14–19). Such self-sacrifice is distinguished from masochistic despair by Jesus's insistence that all is done for the gospel's sake (1:15; 8:35; 10:29), united with Jesus's newly inaugurated covenant (14:22–25) and assured of redemption by his own sacrifice (10:45; 14:24) plus the promise of his postresurrection persistence (14:28).

5. An excellent, well-balanced treatment is Cédric Fischer, *Les disciples dans l'Évangile de Marc: Une grammaire théologique*, EBib n.s. 57 (Paris: Gabalda, 2007).

Moral Responsibility

Upon receiving Jesus's word, rootless disciples may jump for joy but, "when trouble or persecution arises on account of the word, immediately they fall away" (Mark 4:17). On the night of their master's arrest, the Twelve are equally glib and traitorous (14:29–31, 50–52, 66–72). Jesus's interpretation of the sower parable (4:3–8) identifies another temptation besetting discipleship: being "sown among the thorns," wherein "the cares of the world, and the lure of wealth, and the desire for other things come in and choke the word, and it yields nothing" (4:18–19). That is the experience of a devout man whose many possessions block his inheritance of eternal life (10:17–22). Though less developed than in Luke (12:15–21; 16:1–13, 19–31; 19:1–10), Mark is pointedly concerned about the danger of wealth, which perverts filial responsibility (Mark 7:6–13; cf. Exod 20:12; 21:17; Lev 20:9; Deut 5:16); eases divorce, whose economic burden fell primarily on the woman (Mark 10:2–9); and encourages fraud (10:19b, seemingly interpolated from Deut 24:14 into the Decalogue's second table [Exod 20:9–17; Deut 5:13–21]). By contrast, the child who owns nothing (Mark 10:13–16), the plutocrat who gives all to the poor (10:21; cf. Deut 15:6–15; 24:10–22), and the poor widow who relinquishes everything (Mark 12:41–44) are models of discipleship. For both OT prophets (Isa 3:13–17; Mic 2:1–2) and Hellenistic moralists (Diodorus, *Bib. hist.* 21; Plutarch, *De cupiditate divitiarum*; cf. Eph 4:19; Col 3:5), avarice is peculiarly pernicious for its rupture of the social fabric. Likewise, Mark is sensitive to malicious conduct that violates communal responsibility (7:20–22; 12:38–40). Written when the Jerusalem temple was on the verge of destruction or had already been destroyed (13:1–2; 15:38), the Second Gospel defines defilement as evil that comes from within (7:14–15, 23) and specifies mutual forgiveness, underwritten by God, as normative among disciples (11:24–25).[6]

The Twelve

More so than any other evangelist, Mark portrays the Twelve severely. Their understanding of Jesus's teaching and intentions deteriorates as the Second

6. Dan O. Via Jr., *The Ethics of Mark's Gospel: In the Middle of Time* (Philadelphia: Fortress, 1985), has been a standard work in this area. For a more recent, comprehensive investigation, see Maurice John-Patrick O'Connor, *The Moral Life according to the Gospel of Mark*, LNTS 667 (London: Bloomsbury T&T Clark, 2022).

Gospel unfolds (e.g., 4:13, 40–41; 5:31; 6:37, 51; 7:17–18; 8:4, 14–21; 9:18c–19, 32, 38–41; 10:13–14, 32). Many of these passages have Synoptic parallels, though Luke (8:45; 9:13, 45; 18:34) and especially Matthew (8:27; 9:20–22; 13:51–52; 14:28–33; 16:7–12; 17:19–20, 23b) soften Mark's presentation. Three times in Mark, Jesus explains the implications of his passion for discipleship (8:31–9:1; 9:31–37; 10:33–34, 42–45); three times the disciples miss or reject the point, bickering among themselves for exalted status (8:32–33; 9:33–34; 10:35–41). None of the Twelve appropriates power available only through prayer (9:28–29); one of them colludes with Jerusalem's chief priests to betray Jesus (14:10–11, 43–46); three sleep during his anguish in Gethsemane (14:32–42); another triply denies knowing him (14:66–72); all forsake him, fleeing at his arrest (14:50–52). Simon Peter, the Twelve's spokesman (1:36; 8:29; 9:5–6; 10:28; 11:21; 14:29–31) and *primus inter pares* (1:16–18, 29; 3:16–19a; 5:37; 9:2; 13:3; 14:33), is singled out most unflatteringly (8:32; 9:5–6; 14:29–31, 37, 66–72). Among all of Jesus's opponents in this gospel, only Peter is addressed as Satan (Mark 8:33); his last words about Jesus are devastating: "I do not know this man you are talking about" (Mark 14:71). The reason Mark gives for the Twelve's incomprehension and miserable failure raises as many questions as it answers: "their hearts were hardened" (6:52; cf. 7:17–18; 8:17). Despite their receipt of "the secret [μυστήριον] of the kingdom of God," they are as blinded and deafened by it as others (4:10–13; 8:18–21).

In the biblical tradition, God hardens hearts (Exod 4:21; 7:3; 10:1, 20, 27; 14:8, 17; Deut 2:30; Isa 6:9–13; John 12:37–41; Acts 28:25–29; Rom 11:7–8, 25), usually for a season until repentance is ripe. Those traditions, however, also emphasize human culpability (Exod 8:15, 32; Pss 36:1; 58:2; Isa 29:13–14; Zech 7:8–14; Rom 1:24–25). The same paradox is crystallized in Mark (14:21): "For the Son of Man goes as it is written of him, but woe to that one by whom the Son of Man is betrayed! It would have been better for that one not to have been born."

The Anonymous

Discipleship in Mark is often demonstrated by shadowy, mostly nameless figures that briefly take the stage before disappearing. These include Simon's mother-in-law, who after being healed by Jesus serves him (1:30–31); sufferers of various infirmities, within Israel and on its frontiers, who approach Jesus with justified confidence that he can cure them (1:33–34b, 40–45; 2:10b–12; 3:1–5, 7–10; 5:18–20; 7:31–38); surrogates for the sick, who demonstrate faith (1:32; 2:1–5; 5:21–24a, 35–36; 7:24–30; 9:14–29); a well-intentioned scribe, who discerns torah's deepest intent (Mark 12:28–34; cf. Lev 19:18; Deut 6:4; 1 Sam 15:22;

Hos 6:6; Mic 6:6–8); a desperately poor widow, who invests in a lost cause (the temple) "everything she had, all she had to live on" (Mark 12:41–44); a woman whose lavish gift to Jesus is a beautiful, anticipatory anointing of his body before its burial, forever remembered in the gospel's universal proclamation (14:3–9); many other female ministers who observe Jesus's crucifixion, death, and burial long after the Twelve have abandoned him (15:40–41, 47; 16:1–2); and Joseph of Arimathea, "a respected member of the council, who was also himself waiting expectantly for the kingdom of God," who boldly asks Pilate for Jesus's body and properly buries it, in the Twelve's absence (15:42–46; cf. John's disciples in 6:29). Mark's central segment, exposing the Twelve's blindness to Jesus's teaching, is framed by tales of faltering yet eventual restoration of visual perception (8:22–26; 10:46–52).

Adversaries

Though Jewish opponents are criticized (Mark 3:6, 22–30; 7:1–13; 10:1–5; 12:9–40), the vitriol occasionally gushed in other gospels toward Pharisees and Jesus's other coreligionists is absent from Mark (cf. Matt 23:1–39; John 8:12–59; Acts 28:17–28). Instead, Mark emphasizes the bottomless irony that Israel's most devout leaders fail to recognize their king and collude with Rome's imperial forces to destroy him (15:25–32). Representative antagonists repeatedly speak the truth of the gospel without intention or comprehension: "You are the Messiah, the Son of the Blessed One?" (14:61: the high priest's quizzical claim); "He saved others; he cannot save himself" (15:31: the chief priests and scribes' paraphrase of 10:45); "Truly this man was God's Son" (15:39: Jesus's gentile executioner). In Mark, Jesus is misunderstood and betrayed by almost everyone: his family (3:19b–21, 31), countrymen (6:1–6a), Jerusalem's crowds (15:11, 13–14), and the Twelve (3:19a; 8:32–33; 10:35–41).

Faith and Fear

Jesus's mighty works are not noteworthy for their happy endings; the miracles performed by Apollonius of Tyana (Philostratus, *Vit. Apoll.*) and Hanina ben Dosa (b. Yebam. 121b, b. Ta'an. 24b) were also successful. Jesus's works are important for what they disclose about disciples' faith. To know Jesus in Mark is to see beneath the Galilean prophet, recognizing him as God's eschatological agent who is retaking the field of a damaged creation from the diabolical forces of its occupation and restoring the ecology of God's sovereignty on earth (Mark 3:7–12; 5:1–20). When Jesus is so regarded, his parabolic teaching becomes intelligible, important, and trustworthy. As in Paul (Rom 4:1–25; 2 Cor 4:13–5:10; Gal 3:1–29), faith is humanity's trust in God in the face of manifestly hopeless situations (Mark 4:35–6:1–6a).[7] Unlike those described in John's Gospel (2:11; 4:46–54), Jesus's mighty works in Mark do not stimulate faith. The sequence flows in reverse: first comes faith, fostering conditions in which God's power to heal, executed by Jesus, can be realized (Mark 5:23, 34a). Neither a cluster of belief (1 Tim 3:9; 4:6; Jude 3) nor an arrow released irrevocably toward its target, faith oscillates: it swings from confidence to panic, caught for a time by weak mortals before slipping from their grasp (Mark 5:33–36; 9:23–24). Because faith is a matter more of volition than of cognition, its opposite is cowardice (4:40) or fear (5:15, 33, 36), which repudiates Jesus's authority to wield God's healing potency (6:3c–4; 11:27–33). Those thinking themselves close to Jesus, friends of the family (6:1–6a) and even the Twelve (4:40; 5:31), are at best imperceptive (5:31), at worst craven (4:40). The powerless tap reservoirs of persistent trust that elude those with commonplace authority (7:24–30). At Gethsemane (14:32–42) and Golgotha (15:21–33), Jesus himself exhibits the depth of trust that activates self-sacrificial service to God for the gospel's sake. At the empty tomb, female disciples, who continued with Jesus longer than all others, flee in fear after learning of his resurrection (16:1–8; cf. the risen Jesus's reassuring appearances in Matt 28:8–20; Luke 24:13–52; John 20:11–21:25; 1 Cor 15:3–8). Mark leaves the reader to ponder the continuing mystery of disciples' fear when confronted by cryptic evidence of Jesus's own fidelity and that of the God who raised him from death.

Concluding Assessments

Owing to its association with Peter and the Roman church, the Second Gospel's normative status was firm and unchallenged from the mid-second century.[8] Yet its canonicity did little to stimulate its use in liturgies, commentaries, and quotations: "present but absent" in the patristic and medieval periods,[9] Mark's distinctive theological voice was submerged beneath those of Matthew and John and by a general tendency to harmonize the gospels. Mark's stature was

7. The most comprehensive general discussion remains Christopher D. Marshall, *Faith as a Theme in Mark's Narrative*, SNTSMS 64 (Cambridge: Cambridge University Press, 1989).

8. See chapters 1 and 2; in greater detail, C. Clifton Black, *Mark: Images of an Apostolic Interpreter*, SPNT (Minneapolis: Fortress; Edinburgh: T&T Clark, 2001).

9. Note Brenda Deen Schildgen's discussion in *Power and Prejudice: The Reception of the Gospel of Mark* (Detroit: Wayne State University Press, 1999).

elevated in the nineteenth century as scholars increasingly accorded it special importance as the earliest gospel.[10] For decades thereafter, exegetes disparaged its shaping of inherited traditions;[11] eventually redaction critics recognized Mark's theological achievement, which became generally acknowledged.[12]

Concentrating on the secret of Jesus's identity, William Wrede was the first modern scholar to give full weight to the early church's "dogmatic" transmission of Mark's sources.[13] Wrede's seminal study proved a mixed blessing. While opening the way for due appreciation of Markan theology, he projected onto the gospel a reading tailored to fit his own hypothetical reconstruction of primitive Christianity while setting generations of critics on the dubious task of differentiating the earliest gospel's redaction of practically irrecoverable traditions (save the LXX)[14] and focusing twentieth-century scholarship almost exclusively on Christology.[15] "The Messianic Secret" is a conventional yet imprecise label for a more complex phenomenon in Mark: only at Mark 8:29–30 is confession of Jesus's *messiahship* rebuked; elsewhere Jesus accepts it (14:61–62). The evangelist lays an obscure trail of suppressing Jesus's identity and activities (1:34–35; 3:11–12; 5:43; 7:36; 8:26; 9:9, 30), which are impossible to hide (5:19–20; 6:14a, 53–56; 7:36–37; 9:14–15). Dramatizing an apocalyptic precept—"For there is nothing hidden, except to be disclosed; nor is anything secret, except to come to light" (4:22)—Mark's narrative situates its characters

---

10. See Albert Schweitzer, *The Quest of the Historical Jesus: First Complete Edition*, ed. John Bowden (Minneapolis: Fortress, 2001), 110–23.

11. For instance: Rudolf Bultmann, *History of the Synoptic Tradition*, trans. John Marsh, rev. ed. (New York: Harper & Row, 1963), 350.

12. Robert Henry Lightfoot, *History and Interpretation in the Gospels* (London: Hodder & Stoughton, 1935); Willi Marxsen, *Mark the Evangelist: Studies on the Redaction History of the Gospel*, trans. James Boyce et al. (Nashville: Abingdon, 1969 [German original, 1956]); Joachim Rohde, *Rediscovering the Teaching of the Evangelists*, trans. Dorothea M. Barton, NTL (Philadelphia: Westminster, 1968 [German original, 1966]).

13. *The Messianic Secret*, trans. J. C. G. Greig, LTT (London: James Clark, 1971 [German original, 1901]).

14. C. Clifton Black, *The Disciples according to Mark: Markan Redaction in Current Debate*, 2nd ed. (Grand Rapids: Eerdmans, 2012); see also chapters 3 and 4. On Mark's adaptation of the LXX, N.B. Cilliers Breytenbach, "Das Markusevangelium, Psalm 110,1 und 118,22f.: Folgetext und Prätext," in *The Scriptures in the Gospels*, ed. Christopher M. Tuckett, BETL 131 (Leuven: Peeters, 1997), 197–222; repr. Breytenbach, *The Gospel according to Mark as Episodic Narrative*, NovTSup 128 (Leiden: Brill, 2021), 246–73; "The Minor Prophets in Mark's Gospel," in *The Minor Prophets in the New Testament*, ed. M. J. J. Menken and S. Moyise, LNST 377 (London: T&T Clark, 2009), 27–37; repr. Breytenbach, *The Gospel according to Mark as Episodic Narrative*, NovTSup 128 (Leiden: Brill, 2021), 456–67.

15. John R. Donahue, "A Neglected Factor in Markan Theology," *JBL* 101 (1982): 563–94.

and readers in that stressfully ambiguous time between the kingdom's arrival and its fulfillment (1:15; 13:13b).

If, as Martin Dibelius suggested, "the historian . . . must endeavor to illuminate and somehow to present the meaning of events,"[16] and if Mark was the earliest of Jesus's ancient biographers, then Mark—not Luke—is long overdue for recognition as Christianity's earliest theological historian.[17] Mark established the basic format for the story of Jesus, the Messiah of Israel and of the nations, as the church chose to remember it: the template to which Matthew, Luke, and John adhered. Moreover, Mark does not simply tell a story about Jesus; he creates conditions under which readers may *experience* the peculiarity of God's good news: hurried into successive exegetical potholes (e.g., 4:1–34; 7:24–20; 8:14–19; 11:11–19), suspended within interlaminated stories of almost unbearable tension (e.g., 3:19b–35; 5:21–43; 14:53–72), stuck with the women in the gospel's final, unresolved chord (16:1–8). Systematic theology coordinates and explains; the Second Gospel hurls one into the kingdom's mystery. After two millennia, Mark's genius may no longer be hidden but is at last coming to light.

---

16. *Studies in the Acts of the Apostles*, ed. Heinrich Greeven, trans. Mary Ling (New York: Scribner's Sons, 1956 [German original, 1951]), 125.

17. See chapter 8.

Mark as Historian of God's Kingdom

Was the Buffalo chicken wing invented when Teressa Bellissimo thought of splitting it in half and deep-frying it and serving it with celery and blue-cheese dressing? Was it invented when John Young started using mambo sauce and thought of elevating wings into a specialty? How about the black people who have always eaten chicken wings? The way John Young talked, black people may have been eating chicken wings in thirteenth-century Spain. How is it that historians can fix the date of the Battle of Agincourt with such precision? How can they be so certain of its outcome?

—Calvin Trillin[1]

UNCERTAINTY BEDEVILS EVERY HISTORICAL ENDEAVOR. Though elicited by inquiry into a humble gastronomic item, Trillin's sober questions strike the bass key that resonates throughout this chapter, and on which it will conclude.

THE FIRST CHRISTIAN HISTORIAN

The historian's art is not limited to collecting and framing traditions, however many he may have at his disposal. He must endeavour to illuminate and somehow to present the meaning of events. He must be impelled by a desire to know and understand. If Luke had more traditions at his disposal, but has linked them together only as he does in the Gospel, he would not qualify

---

1. Calvin Trillin, "An Attempt to Compile a Short History of the Buffalo Chicken Wing," in *The Tummy Trilogy: American Fried; Alice, Let's Eat; Third Helpings* (New York: Farrar, Straus & Giroux, 1994), 275.

for the title "historian." We ascribe this title to him only because he did more than collect traditions. He tried to combine in his own way, into a significant, continuous whole, both the tradition current in the community and what he himself discovered. Secondly, he tried to make clear the meaning which these events contained.

—Martin Dibelius[2]

For those reasons, the mantle of earliest Christian historian has been draped upon Luke. Dibelius does not argue, as he might have, that Luke's status as historian rests on being the first to narrate the development of Christianity in the decades after Jesus. Luke is not *Ur-Eusebius*. Dibelius's *discrimen* for historical reportage is not material, an account of initial steps along "the Way" (Acts 9:2; 19:9, 23; 22:4; 24:14, 22) among gentiles and its parting from Judaism. Instead, the criterion is perspectival: the historian is so recognized for construing the meaning of events, the communication of "a desire to know and understand" what has happened. If that is how the historian's craft is understood, then, standing this side of extensive redactional and literary investigation of the gospels, there is no good reason to reject its expression in the Third Gospel as well. By express testimony (1:1–4), Luke intends not merely to chronicle anecdotes but to arrange them meaningfully, persuasively, and with reliability. No biblical scholar would any longer characterize Luke as a simple collector of traditions. Grant that, however, and there remains no reason to deny that Mark, still reckoned by most as primary among Luke's own sources, also proceeds with historical intent on Dibelius's terms. By arranging antecedent traditions in a manner as sophisticated as it is subtle, Mark is demonstrably interested in the meaning of those events he recounts. Whereas that concern becomes palpable in Mark's celebrated central section (8:22–10:52), the tip-off is present as early as that gospel's first verse (1:1): "The beginning of the good news of Jesus Christ [the Son of God]."[3] From the very beginning, the reader is directed to interpret the *meaning* of what follows as glad tidings of God's own anointed.[4] With commonplace allowance for differences in modus operandi

2. Martin Dibelius, "The First Christian Historian," in *Studies in the Acts of the Apostles*, ed. Heinrich Greeven, trans. Mary Ling (New York: Scribner's, 1956 [German original, 1951]), 125.

3. Adjudicating the text-critical problem in Mark 1:1, the jury remains out. When it will return with a generally acceptable verdict is anyone's guess. See chapter 7.

4. Thus, Francis J. Moloney: "Every element in the [Markan] story is there for a reason, which we will discover only by combing back and forth through the text until it yields its own narrative coherence" (*The Gospel of Mark: A Commentary* [Peabody, MA: Hendrickson,

ancient and modern, Mark has long been acknowledged the first of Jesus's biographers.[5] If βίος or *vita* be recognized as a species of the genus *historia*, then to describe the evangelist Mark as a historian should no longer strain anyone's credulity. And if that be accepted, then Mark—not Luke—may be long overdue for recognition as the first Christian historian, if by the second of those adjectives we mean the earliest account of Jesus's life narrated from a point of view that would soon be accepted as characteristically Christian: history viewed through the confessional lens of Jesus as the Messiah of Israel and of the nations.

It is just here that, in spite of their many intriguing theological intersections, Mark goes his own generic way, with determination and a difference, apart from Paul: for the thing in which the apostle's letters evince virtually no interest—a narrative account, located in time and space, of what Jesus said and did, and what in response to those events was done to him and his followers— is Mark's bread and butter.[6] "Born of woman, born under the law" (Gal 4:4) is inadequate as the story of Jesus's life that Mark, in sharp contrast, very much wants and considers it necessary to tell. We remain uncertain to whom Paul was referring as "the rulers of this age" who "crucified the Lord of glory" (1 Cor 2:8), but apart from Mark and the other evangelists, we would never know that Jerusalem's high priests and Rome's Pontius Pilate (Mark 14:53–65;

2002], 22). To paraphrase Moloney's assertion in Dibelius's terms: The historian's impulse "to know and understand" is revealed in part by the principles of coherence she applies to those traditions available to her.

5. Clyde Weber Votaw, *The Gospels and Contemporary Biographies in the Greco-Roman World*, FBBS (Philadelphia: Fortress, 1970 [original publication, 1915]). With differences in emphasis, Votaw's conclusions are now widely accepted: Charles H. Talbert, *What Is a Gospel? The Genre of the Canonical Gospels* (Philadelphia: Fortress, 1977); David E. Aune, "The Gospels as Ancient Biography and the Growth of Jesus Literature," in *The New Testament in Its Literary Environment*, LEC (Philadelphia: Westminster, 1987), 46–76; Richard A. Burridge, *What Are the Gospels? A Comparison with Graeco-Roman Biography*, 3rd ed. (Waco, TX: Baylor University Press, 2018). See also the discussion of gospel genre in chapter 6 of this volume.

6. For this reason, among others, I remain unconvinced by Joel Marcus's arguments that Mark is demonstrably a Paulinist ("Mark—Interpreter of Paul," *NTS* 46 [2000]: 473–87). While acutely exposing Martin Werner's labored attempts to drive a wedge between apostle and evangelist (*Der Einfluss paulinischer Theologie im Markusevangelium: Eine Studie zur neutestamentlichen Theologie*, BZNW 1 [Giessen: Töpelmann, 1923]), Marcus offers comparatively little to say under "A General Point—The Earthly Jesus" ("Mark—Interpreter of Paul," 476–79); as a scrupulous exegete of Pauline literature, Marcus's sparse comments follow directly from Paul's own. As chapter 12 indicates, I tend toward a more elliptical correlation of Paul and Mark, which for Marcus goes not far enough.

15:1–15) were among the possible candidates. Without Mark and his successors, at least within the canon, the Lord Jesus in Paul's letters could have become— quite apart from the apostle's intention—"a Docetic figure, a figment of pious imagination, who, like Alice's Cheshire cat, ultimately disappears from view."[7] After Mark, that possibility remains but is considerably harder to realize.

THE UNEASY CONSCIENCE OF HISTORIOGRAPHY

> *Throughout the course of his work the historian is selecting, constructing, and criticizing; it is only by doing these things that he maintains his thought upon the* sichere Gang einer Wissenschaft. . . . *So far from relying on an authority other than himself, to whose statements his thought must conform, the historian is his own authority and his thought autonomous, self-authorizing, possessed of a criterion to which his so-called authorities must conform and by reference to which they are criticized. . . . Even if he accepts what his authorities tell him, therefore, he accepts it not on their authority but on his own; not because they say it, but because it satisfies his criterion of historical truth. . . . For the historian there can never be authorities, because the so-called authorities abide a verdict which only he can give.*
>
> —R. G. Collingwood[8]

To speak of Mark and other ancient writers as "historians" in even a sense so highly hedged gives some historical critics the fidgets. It threatens to muddy all those careful distinctions that post-Enlightenment investigators strove mightily to identify and preserve from taint.[9] The usual caveats are invoked. Unlike practicing historians of our day, the ancients (whether Herodotus or Thucydides, Suetonius or Tacitus, Josephus or Mark) favored typical motifs over comprehensive chronologies, didacticism over neutrality, subjectivism and degrees of tendentiousness over a Rankean insistence on "how it essentially was" (*wie es eigentlich gewesen*).[10] The real elephant in the historian's parlor is

7. G. B. Caird, *New Testament Theology*, ed. and completed by L. D. Hurst (Oxford: Clarendon, 1994), 347.

8. R. G. Collingwood, *The Idea of History*, rev. ed., ed. Jan van der Dussen (Oxford: Oxford University Press, 1993), 236, 238.

9. Albert Schweitzer, *The Quest of the Historical Jesus*, trans. W. Montgomery et al. (London: SCM, 2000 [based on the German editions of 1906, 1913, and 1950]).

10. Leopold von Ranke, *The Secret of World History: Selected Writings on the Art and Science of History*, ed. Roger Wines (New York: Fordham University Press, 1981), 21; cf.

the entwined question of transcendence and revelation, a subject so dense that its consideration, however cursory, must be deferred until this chapter's end.

Yet no matter how boldly one marks the borders between historiography ancient and modern, many shades of gray resist suppression. There is little doubt that Mark offers its readers, probably by intent rather than by default, a stylized presentation of Jesus that highlights typical traits. Mark does not offer a complete life of Jesus, either because his sources did not permit such or because the evangelist was interested mainly in what he considered religiously significant. Most likely both reasons were in play. Yet no life of Jesus produced in the past seventy years with hope for a scholarly hearing has fundamentally contradicted most of the materials that Mark's common reader would regard as both typical and suggestive of "how it essentially was": Jesus's alliance with John the Baptist; Jesus's performance of astonishing acts of healing in Galilee's environs; his teaching, in metaphor, about "the kingdom of God"; the confused mixture of acceptance and rejection that his ministry generated; key moments of Mark's passion narrative, especially Jesus's disturbing activity in the temple and some Jewish-Roman collusion precipitating his death in Jerusalem by crucifixion. To accept the historical plausibility of so many narrative traits while damning their selective typicality is a catch-22 that no historian, ancient or modern, could hope to escape. It should be further noted that, for reasons baffling exegetes to this day, Mark also admits into his narrative things that are *atypical* of his own portrait of Jesus, such as the ethnic or religious chauvinism (7:24–30) that flies in the face of his own purported dietary and missionary liberality (7:1–23; 13:10).

At least in principle, ancient historians were not as cavalier with the facts as they are sometimes alleged.[11] It is an equally fine question whether even modern historians play strictly by rules whose disregard among the ancients is oft lamented. It is very hard to read Barbara Tuchman's superb treatments of any subject to which she turned her attention without the impression that in them she saw historical lessons her readers would do well to contemplate.

Burridge, *What Are The Gospels?*, 105–84. In private correspondence (19 October 2007), Professor Marianne Meye Thompson justly reminded me that Ranke's admonition is not principally concerned with the recovery of facts—although he is often so interpreted—but rather to capture the "essence" of what actually happened.

11. Thus, Lucian: "As to the facts themselves, [the historian] should not assemble them at random, but only after much labourious and painstaking investigation. He should for preference be an eyewitness but, if not, listen to those who tell the more impartial story, those whom one would suppose least likely to subtract from the facts or add to them out of favour or malice" (*How to Write History*, vol. 6, trans. K. K. Kilburn, LCL [London: Heinemann, 1959], 60).

Certainly President John F. Kennedy believed that when he required his specially formed executive committee to read *The Guns of August*, Tuchman's study of the causes of World War I, during the thirteen gorge-rising days of the Cuban missile crisis (1962).[12] Didacticism with a heavy hand makes for ponderous reading; still, one wishes that the second Bush administration had read with appreciation Tuchman's *March of Folly* before launching its military adventure in Iraq (2003–2011).[13] While every successive contribution to the vast library of biographies of Abraham Lincoln aims to fill some important gap in our grasp of that figure—be it his alleged religious skepticism, clinical depression, or administrative genius—each also asks us to ponder some trait or set of characteristics that helps us take a more satisfying measure of the man than has been heretofore registered.[14] Because Lincoln scholarship can assume general familiarity of its subject with reasonable comprehensiveness, the would-be PhD or bestselling author now tends toward the selective cameo, not the wall-encompassing mural.

The question of historical stylization also remains a disputed question among practicing historians. In an undergraduate course on Renaissance and Reformation Europe during the 1970s, I read Garrett Mattingly's *The Armada* with no awareness of its drubbing by some experts for its novelistic quality.[15] To the contrary, its sparkling prose and rattling narrative made late medievalism come alive. Is Carl Sandburg's six-volume biography of Lincoln to be pulped, because its author was no professional historian and his poetry kept getting in the way?[16] While retaining unmitigated respect for James McPherson's studies in the American Civil War,[17] for color and spectacle I still pull

12. Barbara W. Tuchman, *The Guns of August* (New York: Ballantine, 1962). This book won the Pulitzer Prize for general nonfiction.

13. Barbara W. Tuchman, *The March of Folly: From Troy to Vietnam* (New York: Knopf, 1984).

14. See, respectively, Richard Lawrence Miller, *Lincoln and His World: The Early Years, Birth to Illinois Legislature* (Mechanicsburg, PA: Stackpole, 2006); Joshua Wolf Shenk, *Lincoln's Melancholy: How Depression Challenged a President and Fueled His Greatness* (Boston: Houghton Mifflin, 2005); Doris Kearns Goodwin, *Team of Rivals: The Political Genius of Abraham Lincoln* (New York: Simon & Schuster, 2006).

15. Garrett Mattingly, *The Armada* (Boston: Houghton Mifflin, 1959). Scholarly reception of Mattingly's award-winning classic is detailed and criticized by Richard J. Evans, *In Defense of History* (New York: Norton, 2000), 122–30.

16. Carl Sandburg, *Abraham Lincoln: The Prairie Years*, 2 vols. (New York: Harcourt, Brace & Company, 1926); *Abraham Lincoln: The War Years*, 4 vols. (New York: Harcourt, Brace & Company, 1939). *The War Years* won for its author the Pulitzer Prize.

17. See, among others, *Battle Cry of Freedom: The Civil War Era* (New York: Oxford

from my shelf Shelby Foote.[18] Are readers like myself simply confused, or do we respect alternative approaches to history for the different values to which they aspire?

The one Rubicon that *die Aufklärer* crossed, from which there appears no turning back, is the control of the historian's imagination by corroborative evidence. As early as 1936, however, Robin George Collingwood (1889–1943), in his lifetime a foremost expert on Roman Britain and the intricate puzzles surrounding Hadrian's Wall, dared to articulate what surely had crossed the minds of other, self-critical critics:

> Historians certainly think of themselves as working from data; where by data they mean historical facts possessed by them ready made at the beginning of a certain piece of historical research. Such a datum, if the research concerns the Peloponnesian War, would be, for example, a certain statement of Thucydides, accepted as substantially true. But when we ask what gives historical thought this datum, the answer is obvious: historical thought gives it to itself, and therefore in relation to historical thought at large it is not a datum but a result or achievement. . . . It is thus the historian's picture of the past, the product of his own *a priori* imagination, that has to justify the sources used in its construction.[19]

Has Collingwood thereby skeptically undercut his own essays in ancient history? No, he replies:

> This is only the discovery of a second dimension of historical thought, the history of history: the discovery that the historian himself, together with the here-and-now which forms the total body of evidence available to him, is a part of the process he is studying, has his own place in that process, and can see it only from the point of view which at this present moment he occupies within it. But neither the raw material of historical knowledge, the detail of the here-and-now as given him in perception, nor the various endowments that serve him as aids to interpreting this evidence, can give

University Press, 1988); *For Cause and Comrades: Why Men Fought in the Civil War* (New York: Oxford University Press, 1997).

18. *The Civil War: A Narrative*, 3 vols. (New York: Random House, 1958, 1963, 1974). Foote began his literary career as a novelist: *Follow Me Down* (1950); *Love in a Dry Season* (1951); *Shiloh* (1952).

19. Collingwood, *Idea of History*, 243–44, 245. Subsequent citations appear above in the text.

the historian his criterion of historical truth. That criterion is the idea of history itself: the idea of an imaginary picture of the past. That idea is, in Cartesian language, innate; in Kantian language, *a priori*. . . . The idea of the historical imagination [is] a self-dependent, self-determining, and self-justifying form of thought. (248, 249)

On its face, this appears to put the historian at least formally on the same plane as the religious believer. That implication Collingwood candidly accepts: "History is thus the believing [of] some one else when he says that he remembers something. The believer is the historian; the person believed is called his authority" (234–35). Asking himself wherein that authority lies, Collingwood reasons his way, without flinching, to the anthropocentric deduction that opened this section: "the discovery that, so far from relying on an authority other than himself, to whose statements his thought must conform, the historian is his own authority and his thought autonomous, self-authorizing, possessed of a criterion to which his so-called authorities must conform and by reference to which they are criticized. . . . Even if he accepts what his authorities tell him, therefore, he accepts it not on their authority but on his own; not because they say it, but because it satisfies his criterion of historical truth" (236, 238). By reckoning with the history of historiography, Collingwood realizes that the root issue is irreducibly theological:

The facts have been obscured by a smoke-screen of propagandist literature, beginning with the "illuminist" movement of the eighteenth century and prolonged by the "conflict between religion and science" in the nineteenth, whose purpose was to attack Christian theology in the supposed interests of a "scientific view of the world" which in fact is based upon it and could not for a moment survive its destruction. Take away Christian theology, and the scientist has no longer any motive for doing what inductive thought gives him permission to do. If he goes on doing it at all, that is only because he is blindly following the conventions of the professional society to which he belongs. (255–56)

From within the historian's own framework, Collingwood, among others, has identified most of the terms for the rest of the argument this chapter will pursue.[20] By now, however, a few things should be painfully obvious. First,

20. Similarly, Martin Buber: "But the philosophical anthropologist must stake nothing

whether one speaks of pre- or post-Enlightenment figures, the durable tension between "faith and history" has obscured their highly porous membranes. From its inception, Christian faith has never been predicated without reference to historical persons and events, just as historical reconstruction has never been conducted apart from faith, whether orthodox or some secularized version in reaction to it.[21] Second, as very likely the first to coordinate literarily the story of Jesus in a meaningful way, to Mark belongs the accolade of "the first Christian historian." Third, if so, then Mark's Gospel is more than a mine of data from which later historians may quarry their own reconstructions of Jesus. To think that is to regard that gospel only as an object for our disposition, whether academic or religious or some admixture of both. To the contrary, Mark is a *subject*, whose own historical and theological integrity makes of him a fully equal partner in conversation and debate with our own subjective biases as historians. To a degree considerably greater than many subsequent, even highly sophisticated constructions of Jesus, Mark poses the question of authority raised by that Galilean and his association with the kingdom of God. By now, it should be clear that such is the fundamental question, not only for Christian faith but also for one's understanding and practice of history.

---

less than his real wholeness, his concrete self. And more: it is not enough for him to stake his self as an *object* of knowledge. He can know the *wholeness* of a person and through it the wholeness of *man* only when he does not leave his *subjectivity* out and does not remain an untouched observer. He must enter, completely and in reality, into the act of self-reflection, in order to become aware of human wholeness" (*Between Man and Man*, trans. Ronald Gregor Smith [London: Kegan Paul, 1947], 124).

21. Just here Martin Kähler's theological critique of the Quest risks a parlous unilateralism (*The So-Called Historical Jesus and the Historic Biblical Christ*, ed. Ernst Wolf, trans. Carl E. Braaten [Philadelphia: Fortress, 1964]). The same might be ventured of our generation's Kähler, Luke Timothy Johnson (*Living Jesus: Learning the Heart of the Gospel* [San Francisco: HarperCollins, 1999]), even though Johnson is little concerned with Kähler's Protestant principle of doubt, not only sin, as the basis for justification by faith. Let those who remember Kähler only as the bête noir of nineteenth-century life-of-Jesus research be reminded that he explicitly "apprais[ed] the development of [historical] criticism as a divine dispensation for the church" (*So-Called Historical Jesus*, 148 n. 25), owing to its chastisement of "abstract dogmatism" (46): the biblically untethered fantasies of both preachers and systematicians (54–57, 67–71). Kähler's battle was waged against not one but two fronts: versus both the practical Arianism of the life-of-Jesus movement (see esp. 102–3) and the Apollinarianism of contemporary dogmatics (78–87). At their least modest, in Kähler's view, both historians and theologians were culpable of a dogmatism for which each needed the other's correction.

Whose Life Is It, Anyway?

As historians of Jesus we are storytellers. We can do no more than aspire to fashion a narrative that is more persuasive than competing narratives, one that satisfies our aesthetic and historical sensibilities because of its apparent ability to clarify more data in a more satisfactory fashion than its rivals.

—Dale C. Allison[22]

Nothing is easier, or offers more perverse satisfaction, than to position one's self against those believed incorrigibly misguided. Rather than choose that nasty path, I beg the reader's indulgence for a brief, cordial argument—stripped of belligerence—with one whose scholarship unfailingly instructs me.[23] In spite of its unfortunately worded subtitle, Dale Allison's *Jesus of Nazareth: Millenarian Prophet* makes important contributions to the current conversation, which I applaud.[24] If not blindingly original,[25] Allison's Jesus, an eschatological prophet, strikes me as far more plausible than some alternatives lately pro-

22. *Jesus of Nazareth: Millenarian Prophet* (Minneapolis: Fortress, 1998), 35–36. I am grateful to Professor Allison for graciously and cheerfully debating with me issues raised by the present chapter.

23. At the time of this essay's original composition, Professor Allison and I served on the faculties of different theological schools. At this writing, we are colleagues at the same institution, where my admiration of his scholarship and gratitude for his friendship have grown beyond all capacity to measure.

24. Allison's use of the term "millenarianism" derives from its technical use among social scientists and students of cross-cultural religious phenomena (*Jesus of Nazareth*, 78–94). Some of its criteria, cited by Allison, correspond to Mark's presentation of Jesus: e.g., imminent catastrophe (13:3–27), promotion of egalitarianism (9:33–41; 10:13–16; 12:41–44; 14:3–9), the shattering of taboos (1:40–45; 2:1–12; 2:23–3:6), the substitution of religious for familial bonds (3:31–35), and unconditional loyalty (8:34–9:1; 9:42–50). Some allegedly millenarian traits are flouted by the Markan Jesus: a fairly exclusive appeal to the disaffected (cf. Mark 1:19–20, 39; 2:13–14; 5:14–17, 22–24, 35–43; 10:17–22; 12:28–34; 15:42–47), unfettered utopianism (cf. 10:29–31), nativism (cf. 7:1–23; 10:2–9; 12:13–27), revelation's authentication by miracle (cf. 1:44; 3:19b–21; 4:35–41; 6:1–6a, 45–51a; 8:11–13; 15:27–32), and a paradisiacal restoration with the return of ancestors (cf. 6:14–29; 9:9–13; 16:6–8). Others are colored in Mark with highly ambiguous hues, such as revivalism (cf. 3:7–12; 15:6–32), political passivity (cf. 11:1–19; 14:43–50; 14:53–65; 15:1–5), and a tendency to divide humanity into camps saved and unsaved (cf. 4:10–12; 6:51b–52; 8:14–21; 10:35–45). Mark's eschatology is a motley affair, defying clear categorization. In any case, nowhere in Mark does Jesus espouse a strictly theological millenarianism (9:1; 13:32–37; cf. Rev 20:1–3).

25. See Johannes Weiss, *Jesus' Proclamation of the Kingdom of God*, trans. and ed. by Richard Hyde Hiers and David Larimore Holland, LJS (Philadelphia: Fortress, 1971 [German original, 1892]); Ben F. Meyer, *The Aims of Jesus* (London: SCM, 1979). Incidentally,

posed,[26] precisely because it squares with the unadorned picture that Mark presents.[27] And more than many "Third Questers," Allison is refreshingly humble about the historian's limitations: "We can do no more than aspire to fashion a narrative that is more persuasive than competing narratives, one that satisfies our aesthetic and historical sensibilities because of its apparent ability to clarify more data in a more satisfactory fashion than its rivals."[28]

The more I ponder this expression of Allison's common sense, the more perplexing it seems. Methodologically, please note in this statement that it is *our* stories that historians are called to fashion. Here Allison tacitly follows Collingwood. Silently we have slipped from the gospels' narratives into our own. The cheerful (or vitriolic) cut-and-thrust of Jesus-research implies criticism not of Mark's narrative but of the different ones *we the historians* construct. The persuasive rhetoric criticized is not the evangelist's but rather that of historians whose competing stories are reckoned more or less plausible.[29] Allison recalls Thomas Kuhn's celebrated notion of a convincing "paradigm," "an explanatory model or matrix by which to order our data. . . . The initial task is to create a context, a primary frame of reference, for the Jesus tradition, a context that may assist us in determining the authenticity of traditions and their interpretation."[30] How else could a historian, operating as a historian, proceed?[31] Just there, however, lies a fundamental problem: why must *our*

"blinding originality" is an overrated academic virtue, as experience demonstrates. All of us have read specimens of highly original scholarship that are simply blind to common sense.

26. Allison, *Jesus of Nazareth*, 39–44, 95–171. Marcus J. Borg, *Jesus, a New Vision: Spirit, Culture, and the Life of Discipleship* (New York: Harper & Row, 1987), whose position is adumbrated in the same author's "An Orthodoxy Reconsidered: The 'End-of-the-World Jesus,'" in *The Glory of Christ in the New Testament: Studies in Christology in Memory of George Bradford Caird*, ed. L. D. Hurst and N. T. Wright (Oxford: Clarendon, 1987), 207–17. Earlier in my career, I rendered a favorable assessment of Borg's *Jesus* (*Int* 43 [1987]: 422–24), which I now recant with some embarrassment. Borg's sapiential, noneschatological, and essentially liberal Protestant Jesus does not adequately account for a perceived threat great enough to nail him on a cross. Rome might as well have executed a Rotarian.

27. Matthew and Luke present essentially the same picture. The message of the Johannine Jesus is no less eschatologically charged, albeit differently tinctured.

28. Allison, *Jesus of Nazareth*, 35–36.

29. Allison, *Jesus of Nazareth*, 51–54, 95–171. I reckon Allison's point representative of that held by most competent historians now laboring in that section of the vineyard.

30. Allison, *Jesus of Nazareth*, 36. See Thomas S. Kuhn, *The Structure of Scientific Revolutions* (Chicago: University of Chicago Press, 1962).

31. I prescind from the procedural debate, conducted between Allison and others, whether it is wiser to proceed from accumulation of particulars to the construction of larger patterns, or vice versa. See Allison, *Jesus of Nazareth*, 45–51.

"aesthetic and historical sensibilities" be satisfied? Since when have *our* paradigms become determinative for authentic interpretation?

Since the Enlightenment's dawning, of course. We need, however, to recall Collingwood's reminder of the wobbly epistemology on which the historical enterprise is based. Because we live in a philosophically confused era—when was it never so?—I should at this point state as clearly as possible that my critique in no way disavows critical historical study as such, nor implies on my part any conversion to a cranky postmodernism that would reduce all reasoned arguments to blatant if disguised power plays. I suspect that much of what currently passes for postmodernism is actually hypermodernism, which, very much like the reactionary stance toward theology adopted in the nineteenth century by "the scientific view of the world," depends on modern values and could not for a moment survive their abolition. Since the Enlightenment, however, some things indubitably have changed. One is Western culture's relationship to the church. Back then, the quest for the historical Jesus promised, without delivering, liberation from the iron fist of ecclesiastical dogma.[32] Except for small pockets in some denominations, that is no longer a problem in the twenty-first-century West. The problem now is the church's general irrelevance to a thoroughly secularized culture, or the church's all but complete cooptation by it. Will Allison's historically reconstructed Jesus—the typically failed leader of a Jewish millenarian movement, interchangeable with the prophet Wovoka of the 1890 Ghost Dance—liberate anybody?[33] I doubt it. I should expect Allison to counter: You're asking the historian to deliver more or other than what the historian can offer. To which I would reply: You bet. More to the point, *so would Mark*, who, operating from different premises, could not more vociferously disagree with the conclusion that Jesus was a utopian prophet finally proved wrong. To paraphrase the apostle, if for this plausible narrative only the historian in Christ has aspired, we are of all people most to be pitied (cf. 1 Cor 15:19).[34]

32. Schweitzer, *Quest of the Historical Jesus*, 3–13, 478–87.

33. Allison, *Jesus of Nazareth*, 78–94, 217–19. This I regard as the weakest aspect of Allison's reconstruction, quite apart from its theological implications. Here he follows Schweitzer and his adversaries into formal psychologism.

34. In fairness to Allison, I should stipulate that nowhere in his *Jesus of Nazareth* does he claim his historically reconstructed Jesus to be the only valid interpretation of that figure. Allison's Jesus, nevertheless, finally bears more than passing resemblance to Schweitzer's, though conspicuously denuded of the latter's heroism: "[Jesus] makes the best of a bad situation: things are not what they seem to be; everything will be OK. . . . Jesus the millenarian prophet, like all millenarian prophets, was wrong: reality has taken no notice of his

I speak of the historian in Christ, who honors the scholarly contributions of Abraham's many children.[35] In that regard, let me mention another heavy hitter whose work commands admiration: John Meier, whose magisterial *Marginal Jew* now runs at 3,521 densely argued pages and at this writing remains incomplete. Meier opens his introduction with ruminations on "the quest for objectivity": "There is no neutral Switzerland of the mind in the world of Jesus research. . . . Whether we call it a bias, a *Tendenz*, a worldview, or a faith stance, everyone who writes on this historical Jesus writes from some ideological vantage point; no critic is exempt. . . . The solution is to admit honestly to one's standpoint, to try to exclude its influence in making scholarly judgments by adhering to certain commonly held criteria, and to invite the correction of other scholars when one's vigilance inevitably slips."[36] Likewise, Allison states, "Maybe our reach for the historical Jesus must always exceed our grasp. . . . Our goal is not to be free of prejudice, but to have the right prejudices."[37]

Who determines, however, which prejudices are the right ones? In common practice, certainly not Mark. By standard operating procedure, the redaction critic can and should limn the evangelist's intention, but under no circumstances should the critic's own *Tendenz* be allowed entrée into the exercise. Once the evangelist's bias has been identified, then, through application of the scalpel-sharp criterion of dissimilarity, that point of view should be factored out of, or at least mitigated in, the critically reconstructed Jesus of history.[38]

---

imagination" (217, 218). By contrast, Mark the historian offers his readers one crucified and vindicated, for whom and for whose followers everything is *not* "OK," a Messiah whose ministry upends what we construe as "reality."

35. It should be needless to add that many responsible historians abjure any correlation of their endeavors with Christian faith. Still others register no such qualms: e.g., N. T. Wright, *Jesus and the Victory of God* (Minneapolis: Fortress, 1996).

36. John P. Meier, *A Marginal Jew: Rethinking the Historical Jesus*, 5 vols., AYBRL (New York: Doubleday; New Haven: Yale University Press, 1991, 1994, 2001, 2009, 2016), 1:5–6.

37. See Allison, *Jesus of Nazareth*, 33, 39. Doubtless Bultmann would have preferred the term "presuppositions" (which for him are inescapable) to "prejudices" (which can and should be left at the door before entering critical interpretation): "Is Exegesis without Presuppositions Possible?," in *New Testament and Mythology and Other Basic Writings*, ed. and trans. Schubert M. Ogden (Philadelphia: Fortress, 1984), 145–93. In common parlance, "presuppositions," "tendencies," and "biases" are virtually synonymous, though "bias" in English veers toward "prejudice," which in the US and the UK carries a pejorative connotation. We might say that a scholarly presupposition is a reasonable bias that has surfaced to the level of consciousness and, having been purged of personal idiosyncrasies by the guild's conventions of chastening, enjoys general acceptance as an argumentative a priori.

38. Reginald H. Fuller: "As regards the sayings of Jesus, traditio-historical criticism eliminates from the authentic sayings of Jesus those which are paralleled in the Jewish tradition

That process I regard as multiply problematic. First, at the outset it eliminates *Tendenzen* possibly shared by both Jesus and the evangelist. Second, it unjustifiably elevates the historian's bias—or, if you prefer, Meier's "adherence to certain commonly held criteria"—over that of the evangelist, as though the latter were in no sense interested in the Jesus of history and whose point of view is self-evidently inferior to our own. Third, it fosters among many historians, and of the students and pastors they teach, an intellectual schizophrenia finally impossible to sustain. In effect, the historian is forced to choose between history and theology even though (1) many historians care about theology, and vice versa, (2) Mark is one historian who operates as though the two are inextricably wedded, and (3) historians as a class are (if we accept Collingwood's analysis) themselves believers—if not in God, then in their own critical powers—whether they acknowledge it or not.[39] Fourth, standard procedure dissolves the tension between faith and history by dismissing confessional considerations *tout court* without entertaining a possibility that exegesis, as Moshe Greenberg suggests, "both edifies the [faith] community and enables it to retain its identity through continuity with its past."[40] Finally, genuine conversation about Jesus or any other subject of consequence will never take place for as long as we bracket out what we believe, as the atheists and agnostics and Jews and Muslims and Christians that we are, while closing ourselves off from the claims made upon us by the traditions we study.[41] To pretend otherwise again sets us at cross-purposes with our source material: however much one might wish it otherwise, *apart from the church's faith, there can be in Mark no access to the Jesus of history*. That figure simply does not exist, save in the flickering figments of our historically conditioned imaginations.

Such is the risk entailed by realigning the historian's relationship to Mark as one of a colleague consulting a specialist, instead of a pathologist carving a cadaver. For the evangelist may pluck the probe from our hand to train it upon

---

on the one hand (apocalyptic and Rabbinic) and those which reflect the faith, practice and situations of the post-Easter Church as we know them from outside the Gospels" (*The Foundations of New Testament Christology* [London: Lutterworth, 1965], 18).

39. Hugh Trevor-Roper: "Objective science has its place in historical study, but it is a subordinate place: the heart of the subject is not in the method but in the motor, not in the technique but in the historian" ("History and Imagination," *TLS*, 25 July 1980, 833).

40. Moshe Greenberg, "Exegesis," in *Studies in the Bible and Jewish Thought* (Philadelphia: Jewish Publication Society, 1995), 367.

41. Hans-Georg Gadamer: "In fact, history does not belong to us; we belong to it" (*Truth and Method*, trans. and ed. Garrett Barden and John Cumming [New York: Crossroad, 1975], 245; see also 321–25).

us. The historian is tempted—indeed, if Collingwood is correct, trained and rewarded by the guild—to adopt the stance of independent investigator. If not a surgeon, then an archaeologist: the historian excavates the Second Gospel for traditional (read: heavily hypothetical) tells of scientifically verifiable data.[42] Mark, I submit, will have none of that; for the very gospel to which he testifies undermines his readers' delusions of autonomy, all pretense to neutrality, human hubris in demanding verification, our naivete or arrogance in thinking ourselves sifters of evidence instead of those being sifted. Be we young students in early stages of perplexity, anxious to reconcile critical study with religious belief, or their more experienced and jaundiced instructors, Mark's Gospel dynamites everyone's intellectual comforts.

THE ECHO IN HARNACK'S WELL

> It is beyond all doubt that Mark wants to emphasise that God's revelation happened in the historical life and death of Jesus, that is, in a real man. . . .
> [Yet] this does not mean that we could see anything which could really help us in the historical Jesus, without the miracle of God's Spirit who, in the word of the witness, opens our blind eyes to the "dimension" in which all these events took place. . . . It is not the historical Jesus that [Mark] proclaims. It is not a Jesus who could be reconstructed and carried over from his time to our time by historians. [Jesus] can only be proclaimed and witnessed to by a believer like Mark.
>
> —Eduard Schweizer[43]

The primary thing we should note about Mark's history of Jesus is that he wrote one at all. Unless we adopt a minority position that might be correct notwithstanding its apparent unlikelihood—that, say, Matthew or John was the first gospel[44]—we have no evidence that Paul, Q, or anyone else prior to Mark produced in literary consecution a story of Jesus's life, death, and their immediate aftermath. The familiar suggestion that Mark was an Easter coda with an overblown overture obscures the thematic coherence of the gospel's

---

42. I have worried over this elsewhere: C. Clifton Black, *The Disciples according to Mark: Markan Redaction in Current Debate*, 2nd ed. (Grand Rapids: Eerdmans, 2012).

43. "Mark's Contribution to the Quest of the Historical Jesus," *NTS* 10 (1964): 423, 431.

44. Matthew (William R. Farmer, *The Synoptic Problem: A Critical Analysis* [New York: Macmillan, 1964]); John (John A. T. Robinson, *The Priority of John* [London: SCM, 1985]).

first eleven chapters with its final five, which nearly seven decades of Mark's composition and literary analysis have now demonstrated beyond reasonable doubt.[45] With Mark, the *recoverable pastness* of Jesus—his consecutive activity, with a discernible character, in an ancient time and place—becomes important. Apart from its procedure in accordance with theistic faith and not a-theistic rationalism—the critical qualification invoked above by Schweizer— Mark could be justifiably regarded as the first who, by his work, sallied forth in quest of the Jesus of first-century Palestinian history, which is *not* synonymous with "the historical Jesus" or "Jesus reconstructed in accordance with modern historical criticism." Mark thus places a question mark beside any attempt, ancient or modern, to reduce Jesus of Nazareth to a religious cipher, a bloodless repository of revealed knowledge (the Gospel of Thomas), or a mythic redeemer of a thousand faces (Joseph Campbell).[46]

Also notable in Mark's narrative is the peculiar manner in which it deals with questions of authority and warrant. The NT's Second Gospel makes no claim of authorship (cf. John 21:24), nor offers any reason for accepting its account's reliability (cf. Luke 1:1–4). When compared with ancient histories or biographies—compared even with literature of other genres in the NT (see Acts 1:1–4; Gal 1:1–2; 2 Pet 1:1; Rev 1:4–11)—Mark's nonchalance regarding its own bona fides makes of this gospel an unusual literary product for its time. The authentication of Mark's Gospel extends no further than its claim to present "the beginning of the good news of Jesus Christ" (1:1); its only supporting corroboration lies in a suggested correspondence (1:2) of the gospel's earliest narrative segment (1:4–11) with Jewish Scripture (Exod 23:20; Mal 3:1; Isa 40:3). One might say that, with this evangelist, we encounter a pure instance of Collingwood's idea of the historical imagination as "self-dependent, self-determining, and self-justifying," save for the fact that the *author* of Mark fades entirely from the scene, present throughout the narrative only as an unidentified narrator. The one figure in the Second Gospel who, indisputably, is self-dependent, self-determining, and self-justifying is God, who privately albeit infrequently acclaims Jesus as his Son (1:11; 9:7).[47] The vital point of

45. Kähler, *So-Called Historical Jesus*, 80 n. 11: "To state the matter somewhat provocatively, one could call the Gospels passion narratives with extended introductions."

46. *The Hero with a Thousand Faces*, 2nd ed. (Princeton: Princeton University Press, 1968). Similarly, Georg Strecker: "the historical concretion of the kerygma in the Gospels means that the Jesus event is attested *extra nos* of faith, as a given which must exclude from itself every [purely] subjective understanding of faith" ("The Historical and Theological Problem of the Jesus Question," *TJT* 6 [1990]: 215).

47. One could argue, of course, that the God of the Second Gospel is nothing more than

intersection between God and Jesus is the subject matter of Jesus's preaching: the kingdom of God (1:14–15), already erupting into everyday life (4:1–34). Nowhere in Mark does Jesus act as an autonomous agent: "doing the will of God" is the only consequential criterion, for Jesus or for others (3:35; 14:36); his answer to questions is based on an intuitive penetration of Scripture's underlying intent (7:6–23; 10:2–9, 17–22; 12:18–37); "the Son of Man goes as it is written of him" (14:21), toward rejection and vindication divinely ordained (8:31; 9:31; 10:33–34; 14:41–42). It is Jesus's refusal of conventional accreditation—due recognition of status, biblical literalism, astral signs—that repeatedly draws the fangs of his coreligionist antagonists (2:6–9, 16–18; 3:1–6; 6:1–6a; 8:11–13; 15:29–32). With typical Markan irony, obsequious entrapment is laced with truth unaccepted and unrecognized: "Teacher, we know that you are honest and don't concern yourself with what others think; for you are no respecter of persons but teach God's way with sincerity" (12:14a).

Here we approach a watershed, cascading to the heart of Mark's testimony and its historical handling. Never has a disinterested life of Jesus been written. With his announcement at 1:1, Mark lays his cards face up on the table before players who prefer to conceal their hands. By declaring his intent as "a beginning of the gospel," Mark calls into question the alternative values of those satisfied with *der sichere Gang einer Wissenschaft* (Collingwood). The distance between first-century scribes and twenty-first-century historians may be shorter than we suppose. For it is Mark's insistence that whenever the investigator approaches Jesus faithlessly, without trust that Jesus's compass is oriented to the magnetic north of God's will, then Jesus can never be understood. That is the fundamental point Schweizer was making in 1964; it remains true today. Ultimately it matters little whether we dress Jesus as the Cynic sage (Borg and Mack), the peasant revolutionary (differently conjured by Brandon, Horsley, and Crossan), the frustrated apocalyptist (Allison, Schweitzer, and Weiss), the "pale Galilean" (Renan), the exemplar of liberal values (Harnack and, in a feminist key, Schüssler Fiorenza), the epitome of God-consciousness (Schleiermacher), the ethical (Kant) or mythic ideal (Strauss and Campbell), the mountebank (Reimarus), the blasphemer (Capernaum's unnamed scribes: Mark 2:7), Satan's wizard (Jerusalem's scholars: Mark 3:22), or in the costume

---

a mask for the autonomous if invisible evangelist. That is Ludwig Feuerbach's claim: the accusation of bad or at best confused faith by no conviction other than that which resides in the autonomous self (*The Essence of Christianity*, trans. George Eliot [New York: Harper & Row, 1957; German original, 1855]).

of countless other roles in which we may cast him.[48] In every case, the rags can be assembled only temporarily before crumbling away, revealing the radical resistance of God's kingdom to all the *wissenschaftlich* evidence by which we might try to measure it. The deep well into which Adolf Harnack was said to have peered, only to see his own face staring back at him,[49] is the same as that which Schweitzer exposed throughout the nineteenth century before gazing into it himself. It is as old as Narcissus, as recent as yesterday's Jesus book.[50] If Collingwood is correct, that well is the historical imagination itself. If Mark is right, it is Jesus, the agent of God's apocalyptic sovereignty, who reveals to us who we really are and whether our motives are misguidedly religious (3:4–5), timorous (5:34–36), disbelieving (8:11–13), or self-delusional bluster (14:30–31).[51] It is no accident that in Mark, the only qualification for "getting Jesus

48. Borg, *Jesus, a New Vision*; Burton L. Mack, *The Lost Gospel: The Book of Q and Christian Origins* (San Francisco: HarperSanFrancisco, 1993); S. G. F. Brandon, *Jesus and the Zealots: A Study of the Political Factor in Primitive Christianity* (Manchester: Manchester University Press, 1967); Richard A. Horsley, *Jesus and the Spiral of Violence: Popular Jewish Resistance in Roman Palestine* (San Francisco: Harper & Row, 1987); John Dominic Crossan, *The Historical Jesus: The Life of a Mediterranean Jewish Peasant* (San Francisco: HarperSan-Francisco, 1991); Ernst Renan, *The Life of Jesus*, 23rd ed., rev. John Henry Allen (New York: Random House, 1927 [French original, 1863]); Adolf Harnack, *What Is Christianity?*, trans. Thomas Bailey Saunders (New York: Harper & Row, 1957 [German original, 1899–1900]); Elisabeth Schüssler Fiorenza, *Jesus: Miriam's Child, Sophia's Prophet: Critical Issues in Feminist Theology* (New York: Continuum: 1994); Friedrich Daniel Ernst Schleiermacher, *The Life of Jesus*, ed. Jack D. Verheyden, trans. S. MacLean Gilmour, LJS (Philadelphia: Fortress, 1975 [German original, 1864]); Immanuel Kant, *Religion within the Limits of Reason Alone*, trans. Theodore M. Greene and Hoyt H. Hudson (New York: Harper & Row, 1960 [based on the 2nd German edition, 1794]); David Friedrich Strauss, *The Life of Jesus Critically Examined*, 4th ed., ed. Peter Hodgson, trans. George Eliot, LJS (Philadelphia: Fortress, 1972 [German original, 1835]); Campbell, *Hero with a Thousand Faces*; Hermann Samuel Reimarus, *Fragments*, ed. Charles H. Talbert, trans. Ralph S. Fraser, LJS (Philadelphia: Fortress, 1972 [German original, 1778]).

49. George Terrell, *Christianity at the Cross-Roads* (London: Longmans, Green, & Co., 1909), 44.

50. Of all reasons to write a book on the Jesus of history, the least apposite is that it will offer *a more historically reliable substitute* than the account presented by Mark. Such a claim, whether explicit or tacit, follows from positivist assumptions of nineteenth-century historicism that, although yet to be verified, automatically discount ways of interpreting Jesus in alignment with traditional Christianity. As Robert Morgan argues, "Purely historical constructions of Jesus are theologically at best defective and probably misleading" ("The Historical Jesus and the Theology of the New Testament," in *Glory of Christ in the New Testament*, ed. Hurst and Wright, 197]).

51. One might protest that I insist only on compliant readers of the gospel, that I accord

right"—which for the evangelist amounts to entrance into God's kingdom—is not more information but *self-renunciation* (10:17–31; also 8:34–9:1). The problem is not that we don't know enough about Jesus. The problem lies in the self of the historian, who may know all that is important but refuse to yield.[52]

An Apocalyptic Finale

> *If we are going to stick to this damn quantum-jumping, then I regret that I ever had anything to do with quantum theory.*
>
> —Erwin Schrödinger[53]

In spite of creative attempts to tackle the problem,[54] for Jesus's historical in-

---

a privilege to Mark's perspective that disenfranchises other reading communities—some resistant—that bring different concerns and goals to the interpretive process. To such a charge I plead not guilty. I am not contending that Mark's perspective be accorded plenary privilege, except of course within communities of faith that have already so consented. My point is that if we regard the evangelist as a *colleague*—a fully equal partner in conversation and debate with our own subjective biases as historians—then Mark's *Tendenz* has a right to be heard and grappled with even if finally repudiated, *as the evangelist himself concedes* (thus, 3:6; 6:3b; 8:17–18; 12:18; 16:7–8). Mark does not obligate any reader to accept his presentation of Jesus; neither do I. That is not the question. At issue, rather, is our respectful invitation to hear the evangelist out before accepting or rejecting his historical assessment.

52. Similarly, Leander E. Keck: "the primary opponent to be overcome [by Jesus's follower] is not an external enemy, as in messianism, but a power internal to the self" (*Who Is Jesus? History in Perfect Tense*, SPNT [Minneapolis: Fortress, 2001], 147). I regard Keck's contribution as one of the few "success stories" within recent *Questliteratur*, precisely because it sidesteps that project's deep flaws and instead offers nuanced rumination on Jesus as presented by the NT. In many ways, Keck's book is a historically sophisticated, *wissenschaftlich*-conversant exercise in contemporary Christology, based on exegesis of Mark by way of Paul (the earliest recorded interpreter of Jesus) and the other Synoptic evangelists (the earliest commentaries on Mark).

53. Quoted in John C. Polkinghorne, *The Quantum World* (London: Longman, 1985), 53.

54. Recently, note Gerd Theissen and Annette Merz, *The Historical Jesus: A Comprehensive Guide*, trans. John Bowden (Minneapolis: Fortress, 1998), 474–511. For Ernst Troeltsch, "On the analogy of events known to us we seek by conjecture and sympathetic understanding to explain and reconstruct the past" ("Historiography," in *Encyclopedia of Religion and Ethics*, ed. James Hastings [New York: Scribner's Sons, 1922], 18). Theissen and Merz reformulate Troeltsch's analogical axiom to leave open, without prospect of historical confirmation, the possibility of Jesus's resurrection by comparison with another mystery whose reality no one doubts: death. I doubt how far that refinement can carry the historian, who on such terms is no more able to corroborate the veracity of Easter claims than reports of

quirers the resurrection remains no man's land, the frontier once occupied by miracle stories. The latter—embraced so ingeniously by rationalists like Paulus, whose explanations Strauss demolished with palpable relish—seem no longer an occasion for academic apoplexy.[55] That is due in large measure to their historical contextualization by Géza Vermes, among others, positioning Jesus alongside other Jewish wonderworkers.[56] In Mark's Gospel, however, Jesus's mighty works are of a piece with his teaching (1:25–27), which includes the Son of Man's death and resurrection (8:31; 9:9) but comes repeatedly into focus on the kingdom of God (1:14–15; 9:1). The big question is not how the historian deals with the resurrection, which in Mark is but the climax of a larger apocalyptic scenario (see 13:3–37). The crucial issue is how we shall address a claim for the irruption of God's kingdom in human history. To date, responses to ἡ βασιλεία τοῦ θεοῦ have been understandably guarded, removed by at least one degree from the phenomenon itself and practically identical to those surrounding resurrection. The scholarly drill is familiar: Document from the pseudepigrapha that some ancient Jews were in various ways convinced of such a thing, then halt because historical reconstruction cannot cope with the validity or spuriousness of religious claims.

Let us entertain a thought experiment. If a historian were bold enough, or sufficiently foolhardy, to attempt even provisional description of the kingdom's intersection with human history, what sort of image might emerge?

It would have to be an ambiguous, even paradoxical picture. At the moment it acquired adequate definition for discursive analysis, the game would be up. Such an image could never be verified as a cluster of activities expressive of God. In theory, it could only be falsified as a human fabrication of what mortals think a divine kingdom ought to look like: namely, *human* goods of an exponential scale beyond reckoning. If it were *God's* kingdom with which the historian were dealing, then it would of necessity be temporally non sequitur (continuous with the past while disrupting it; now but not yet), circumstantially contradictory of normal experience, and impossible to characterize in positive terms that were not absurd.

It would, I suspect, look a lot like the depiction of God's kingdom in Mark's Gospel.

---

near-death or postmortem experiences. The analogy also creaks at a critical point: the real *tertium comparationis* is not one mystery (resurrection) with another (death) but a common human experience (cessation of life) with Christian revelation (death's undoing by God).

55. See Schweitzer, *Quest of the Historical Jesus*, 47–55, 65–90.

56. Géza Vermes, *Jesus the Jew: A Historian's Reading of the Gospels* (London: SCM, 1973); see also E. P. Sanders, *Jesus and Judaism* (Philadelphia: Fortress, 1985), 157–73; Theissen and Merz, *Historical Jesus*, 281–315.

Grant a historian permission even to address transcendence as it may impinge on history, and Mark's achievement appears formidable indeed. In every major aspect of this gospel—Jesus's teaching, couched in riddles (4:1–34; 12:1–12); his works, at once blatant yet secreted, unsatisfying, and inexplicable (3:7–12; 4:35–41; 5:1–20; 6:45–56; 7:31–37; 8:11–21; 11:13–20); a messiahship crowned by contemptuous execution and God's silence (15:22–39), a vindication announced though never witnessed and immediately hushed (15:38; 16:1–8)—ambivalent traces of God's intervention are *acknowledged without rational explanation or any verification whatever.* At day's end, Mark *proves* nothing. It is as though the author realized, as both theologian and historian, that such a kingdom as Jesus presented is intrinsically impatient of proof, even or especially for sympathetic readers.[57] The evangelist toils in the same twilight zone as Calvin Trillin in his quest for the Buffalo chicken wing. To chronicle the history of Jesus as agent of God's reign, Mark must bend Ranke's famous dictum: *Wie es ist und wird werden, das ist wie es eigentlich gewesen,* "How it is and is coming to be is essentially how it was." By intuitive understanding, the historian of God's kingdom attempts to convey the inner being of the future as it has pushed its way into the past.

Such an approach, or any so theologically attuned, the classically trained historian will be tempted to dismiss out of hand. Before doing so, let her remember that, whether consciously or not, she already proceeds from a theological basis: namely, the deistic assumption of a closed system of commonplace cause and effect, subject to the autonomous investigator's analysis and adjudication. Her position is not unlike that of the classical physicist, whose deterministic view of mechanical reality, obedient to Newton and Maxwell's laws, were overturned by Rutherford and Heisenberg's demonstration of the unpredictable instability of a nuclear atom. It was to this now famous uncertainty principle that Schrödinger objected in conversations with Niels Bohr in 1926. Even more viscerally repulsed was Einstein: in 1924 he claimed that, if theories renouncing strict atomic causality were upheld, he would "rather be a cobbler, or even an employee in a gaming-house, than a physicist."[58] Although he never quit the laboratory for boot- or bookmaking, at length Einstein gave up his numerous attempts to undermine the uncertainty principle, which has

---

57. For this reason, the present chapter offers no succor to conservative apologetics, which occasionally plies syllogisms demanding that if God can perform "supernatural" miracles (N.B. the Deist-inspired language), then anything interpretable as intervention in a closed universe must be just that. For help in refining this clarification I am indebted to Professor Markus Bockmuehl.

58. Letter to Max and Hedwig Born, 29 April 1924; quoted in Jürgen Neffe, *Einstein: A Biography,* trans. Shelley Frisch (New York: Farrar, Straus & Giroux, 2007), 335.

become basic in quantum theory. As Kuhn would say, a paradigm, dominant for centuries, has shifted with revolutionary impact.[59]

My last suggestions are offered sans defensiveness or apologetic intent. Adoption of either would betray the gospel I mean to interpret. By all means, let the historian continue to probe ancient Galilee and Jerusalem, Jewish practice and belief in the early centuries of our common era, and the dynamics of imperial Rome with its conquered parties. Time-honored studies in those fields invite ongoing refinement and occasional reconsideration. When carefully executed, they contribute important knowledge that is interesting on its own terms and needs no other justification. If, however, an investigative shift of quantum magnitude is to occur, the publication of yet another life of Jesus will never make it happen. If after more than three centuries of trial and error we have not yet learned this, then either we are cockeyed optimists or we haven't been paying attention. A quantum jump will take place when some historians summon the requisite intellectual and intestinal fortitude to question their hermeneutical assumptions and, as a consequence, reckon humbly with a divine eschatology that explodes modern historiography.[60] As ever, historians will need assistance from experts in other fields: not only in archaeology, epigraphy, and numismatics, but also among philosophers, theologians, and perhaps even poets.[61] Mark, evangelist and historian, stands ready to assist, for he was the first to make such an attempt. The results, impossible to predict, will surely surprise.

59. It should go without saying that I cite this shift in the study of physics for illustrative purpose only. A universe characterized by the radical indeterminacy of quantum mechanics is no more probative for historical procedure or theological veracity than the more predictable conviction that "[The Old One] does not play dice" (Einstein in a letter to Max Born, 4 December 1926, quoted by Abraham Pais, *"Subtle Is the Lord . . .": The Science and Life of Albert Einstein* [Oxford: Clarendon; New York: Oxford University Press, 1982], 443).

60. For provocative reflections in this vein, see Paul S. Minear, *The Bible and the Historian: Breaking the Silence about God in Biblical Studies* (Nashville: Abingdon, 2002), 25–84.

61. Among others: Andrew Louth, *Discerning the Mystery: An Essay on the Nature of Theology* (Oxford: Clarendon, 1983); C. Stephen Evans, *The Historical Christ and the Jesus of Faith: The Incarnational Narrative as History* (Oxford: Clarendon, 1996); Reynolds Price, *Three Gospels: The Good News according to Mark; The Good News according to John; An Honest Account of a Memorable Life* (New York: Scribner, 1996).

CHAPTER 9

The Face Is Familiar—I Just Can't Place It

> Mark's Gospel ends with both hope and disappointment. The
> relationship between the last two verses [16:7 and 16:8] embodies
> the critical tension in the story between blindness and insight,
> concealment and openness, silence and proclamation. The ten-
> sion is not resolved. Why is this so?
>
> —Donald H. Juel[1]

MY LATE COLLEAGUE DON JUEL did not suffer gladly any attempt to dilute
Christian theology's bittersweetness and so betray the gospel. For that reason,
he resisted all efforts of those whom Frank Kermode dubbed "the pleromatists":
those so unnerved by unresolved tension that they are determined to cobble
up filler (πλήρωμα) for narrative gaps.[2] Chief among Markan pleromatists are
the scribal houses that provided us endings beyond Mark 16:8—particularly,
the Textus Receptus that gave us Mark 16:9–20, immortalized in the KJV—
probably on the assumption that the women's terrified silence while fleeing
the empty tomb was no way to end a gospel (cf. Matt 28:8b–20; Luke 24:8–53;
John 20:3–21:25). A shrewd exegete, Juel was adept at unmasking modern
commentators' subtler ways of giving Mark a satisfying conclusion.[3] Pressing
himself for an answer to his own question about Mark's refusal to resolve his
gospel's tension, Juel suggested a literary-based reply immediately transposed
into a theological key, so eloquent that it justifies extended quotation here:

---

1. *A Master of Surprise: Mark Interpreted* (Minneapolis: Fortress, 1994), 116.

2. Frank Kermode, *The Genesis of Secrecy: On the Interpretation of Narrative* (Cambridge:
Harvard University Press, 1979), 72–73; see also Kermode, *The Sense of an Ending: Studies
in the Theory of Fiction* (London: Oxford University Press, 1966).

3. Donald H. Juel, *Mark*, ACNT (Minneapolis: Augsburg, 1990), 230–31; Juel, *The Gospel
of Mark*, IBT (Nashville: Abingdon, 1999), 167–76. See also chapter 5 of the present volume.

Kermode's analysis clearly exposes the human need for closure, structure, and control. One can argue theologically from the same premises that interpretation can become a way of defending ourselves against truths that make a claim on us. . . . Mark's Gospel—and, we might add, the whole Christian tradition—argues that our lack of enlightenment and bondage arise from attempts to box God in or out of experience. All such attempts come to grief in the resurrection of Jesus. He cannot be confined by the tomb or limited by death. In Jesus' ministry, God tears away barriers that afforded protection in the past. God cannot be kept at arm's length. . . . Jesus has promised an encounter with him against which there is no assured defense. God will be put off neither by our failures, or infidelity, nor by our most sophisticated interpretive schemes. And if this "good news about Jesus Christ" is God's work within the intimate realm of human speech, there is reason to hope that our defenses will prove insufficient and that we will not have the last word.[4]

Plucked from the context of Juel's comprehensive exegesis, this formulation seems emphatically anthropological. Taking his cue from Kermode—whose Norton Lectures (1977–1978) descry the foibles and fate of his fellow literary critics—Juel speaks here about *human* need and its disappointment, *human* speech and its undoing, *our* ultimately unavailing stratagems to defend *ourselves*, *our* lack of enlightenment and bondage, *our* failures and infidelity and schemes. To be sure, Mark's Gospel offers abundant testimony to all these things. It does so, however, in persistent, dialectical tension with an element that fascinated Juel as far back as his doctoral dissertation at Yale:[5] the character of the God who has opted to meet Israel and Mark's readers in Jesus Christ. It is not only the case in the Second Gospel that *homo religiosus* is the constant bungler who plays faith false. Neither is it only the case in Mark that "Jesus is out, on the loose" from the tomb, that "God is no longer safely behind the [temple] curtain" rent in twain, that "[all] doors in Mark's Gospel are emphatically open."[6] True as these things are, in Mark's Gospel, it is also—and, to my thinking, more pointedly—the case that God is simultaneously *Deus revelatus atque absconditus*: as Samuel Terrien translates, "God [who] is near, but [whose] presence remains elusive."[7] With this and other cues taken from

4. Juel, *Master of Surprise*, 120–21.
5. Donald H. Juel, *Messiah and Temple: The Trial of Jesus in the Gospel of Mark*, SBLDS 31 (Missoula, MT: Scholars Press, 1977).
6. Juel, *Master of Surprise*, 120.
7. Samuel Terrien, *The Elusive Presence: The Heart of Biblical Theology*, RP 26 (San Francisco: Harper & Row, 1978), 170.

Terrien's seminal contribution to biblical theology, it is my aim in what follows to trace in Mark's Gospel some outskirts of this fundamentally elusive God.

A MULTIVALENT TRIPTYCH

> *That St Mark's thought runs cyclically is a thesis which needs no advocate.*
>
> —Austin Farrer[8]

It may have been Norman Perrin who most sensitively attuned Markan exegetes to the subtle yet unmistakable threefold pattern of predictions concerning the persecuted and vindicated Son of Man, arranged and elaborated in that gospel's central section (8:31; 9:31; 10:33–34).[9] There is, however, another tripartite structure within Mark that, though not neglected, has received less attention: the triptych composed of Jesus's baptism (1:9–11), transfiguration (9:2–8), and death (15:33–41). These episodes have not always been correlated with the interpretive care they invite. Their verbal and conceptual similarities are not quite so obvious as the passion predictions in Mark 8:22–10:45. In addition, these tableaux are more widely separated from one another than the Son of Man sayings concentrated in three contiguous chapters. It may also be that these episodes have triggered the operation of an almost unconscious, form-critical default mode that tends to separate rather than conjoin them: Mark 15:33–41 as the climax of the gospel's passion narrative; 1:9–11, a mythic account of a virtually undisputed event in the life of Jesus; 9:2–8, an epiphany myth.[10] In any event, it seems to me that Jesus's baptism, transfiguration, and death in Mark beg joint consideration as mutually interpretive. Consider:

1. Their location is critical. The transfiguration story is located in almost the dead center of the Second Gospel, whose bookends are the baptism and death of Jesus.
2. All three anecdotes are drenched in imagery that is indisputably apocalyptic or revelatory.
3. As I hope to demonstrate, Mark's intervening narrative provides impor-

8. *St Matthew and St Mark*, 2nd ed. (Westminster: Dacre, 1966), 224.

9. See Norman Perrin, "Towards an Interpretation of the Gospel of Mark," in *Christology and a Modern Pilgrimage: A Discussion with Norman Perrin*, ed. Hans Dieter Betz (Claremont: The New Testament Colloquium, 1971), 1–78.

10. See, e.g., Martin Dibelius, *From Tradition to Gospel*, trans. Bertram Lee Woolf (New York: Scribner's Sons, 1965), 275–79.

tant commentary on how these episodes are interconnected and should be interpreted.

4. The punch line of all three affirms Jesus as God's Son—a comparatively rare claim in this gospel (see also 1:1; 3:11; cf. 5:7; 12:6; 13:32; 14:61).[11]

5. Although the tenor of Mark 15:39 is debatable, the validity of Jesus's divine sonship remains incontestable. In 1:11 and 9:7—and *only* here, in Mark— God is the speaker. Jesus's affiliation with God, by divine decree, could not be more intimate. While these verses have understandably occupied a central place in scholarly constructions of Markan Christology (Jesus as *Son*),[12] they are no less significant for construing Mark's presentation *of God*.[13] While it would be absurd to reduce every aspect of Mark's portrait of Jesus and of God's kingdom to no more than a few verses, by these assertions, the evangelist could not send his readers a clearer signal that theology and Christology are complementary and inseparable. If we want to learn something about God in Mark's Gospel, attention must be paid to him who is identified as God's Son.

In this light, let us stipulate at the outset that Mark 1:9–11, 9:2–8, and 15:33–41 are of an interwoven, interpretive piece. Each merits examination in its own right, but to isolate any of these pericopae from its narrative counterparts risks exegetical misapprehension.

EXALTATION AND SUBSERVIENCE

> *Behold: I send my messenger before your face,*
> *Who will prepare your way.*

—Mark 1:2a[14]

11. The textual evidence for and against the original occurrence of υἱοῦ θεοῦ, "Son of God," in Mark 1:1 is so evenly balanced as to be irresolvable with confidence. See chapter 7, note 2; also consult Adela Yarbro Collins, "Establishing the Text: Mark 1:1," in *Texts and Contexts: Biblical Texts in Their Textual and Situational Contexts; Essays in Honor of Lars Hartman*, ed. Tord Fornberg and David Hellholm, assisted by C. D. Hellholm (Oslo: Scandinavia University Press, 1995), 111–27.

12. See especially Jack Dean Kingsbury, *The Christology of Mark's Gospel* (Philadelphia: Fortress, 1983), 47–155.

13. In this connection, see David Fredrickson, "What Difference Does Jesus Make for God?," *Di* 37 (1998): 104–10; Elizabeth Struthers Malbon, *Mark's Jesus: Characterization as Narrative Christology* (Waco, TX: Baylor, 2009).

14. Here and elsewhere, all translations are my own unless otherwise noted.

Perhaps by the evangelist's design, it is unclear to whose face and whose way Mark's opening epigraph refers. Having read the gospel's title (1:1), which seems aimed at the book's readers, at first one might interpret the conflated quotation from Exod 23:20 and Mal 3:1 as continued address to that audience. Thus, God, whose voice authorizes the prophet, sends his messenger before the reader's face, to prepare the reader's way. While that messenger could refer to Jesus Christ (1:1), 1:3 and especially 1:4 seem instead to identify God's ἄγγελον as John the Baptizer. Reasoning backward, if the one crying in the wilderness (1:3a) is identical to the one who prepares "your way" (1:2c), then "the way of the Lord" (1:3b) appears to be the way of Jesus Christ, before whose face God's messenger is sent (1:2b). Notice how intricate is the web of associations that Mark already is spinning. First, the way of the reader elides into the way of Jesus Christ, a theme the evangelist will expressly develop in terms of discipleship in 8:27–9:1 (N.B. ἡ ὁδός, v. 27; ἀκολουθείτω μοι, v. 34). "Your" (σου) way (1:2c), Mark's apparent adjustment to Mal 3:1 LXX, stresses by repetition both Christ and Christ's follower, before whose face the herald is dispatched. Second, "the way of the Lord" (Mark 1:3b), which in Isa 40:3 originally referred to the Lord God of Israel, apparently retains that sense in Mark (thus, 11:9; 12:9, 11; 12:29–30; 13:20, 35) while at the same time associating "the Lord" with Jesus (thus, 2:28; 5:19–20; 7:28; 11:3; 12:36–37). A similar identification is suggested by the phrase poetically parallel with "your way," πρὸ προσώπου σου, "before your face." In this gospel, the way that Jesus "faces" suggests God's own self-revelation in the OT (Mal 3:1: וּפִנָּה־דֶרֶךְ לְפָנָי [MT]; καὶ ἐπιβλέψεται ὁδὸν πρὸ προσώπου μου [LXX]). Third, the very fact that the reader must reason backward to peel away these layers of meaning provides an important key to Mark's theology: the significance of Jesus in this gospel depends on faith's hindsight not only upon the resurrection and death and life of Jesus but also upon Scripture,[15] which is now regarded as speaking prophetically of him and his gospel (1:2–3). In this light, Scripture also discloses a different aspect on John the Baptizer, who now appears as *Elias redivivus* (1:4–8; cf. 2 Kgs 1:8), the prophet who would precede the day of the Lord, turning minds around (μετάνοια, Mark 1:4; cf. Mal 3:5–6).

Thus, Mark readies us for Jesus's baptism, a denouement no less crucial in this gospel for its early placement. The straightforward description of Jesus's coming from Nazareth to be baptized in the Jordan by John (Mark 1:9)—with its implied subordination of Jesus to the baptizer, which other gospels strive

---

15. Hence, Willi Marxsen's penetrating insight that "Mark composes backward": *Mark the Evangelist: Studies on the Redaction History of the Gospel*, trans. James Boyce et al. (Nashville: Abingdon, 1969), 32.

mightily to undo or at least mitigate[16]—is contrasted with the astonishing phenomena that attend his emergence from the waters: Jesus's vision (εἶδεν) of the heavens' rending (σχιζομένος τοὺς οὐρανοὺς) and the descent of the Spirit upon him (1:10). The imagery is conspicuously prophetic and apocalyptic (see 1 Sam 10:6; Ezek 1:4–21; Rev 1:10; 4:2); unlike John's Gospel (1:32–34) but entirely in accord with the association forged in Mark 1:2–3, only Jesus and the reader are privy to this astounding disclosure by God. This revelation is completed by a rumbling reverberation (בַּת קוֹל) from heaven (1:11), which, unlike Matthew's presentation (3:17), is directed solely to Jesus with the reader as eavesdropper:

A "You are my Son,
B the Beloved,
C in whom I am well pleased."

As in 1:2–3, Mark has adopted a familiar OT formula (there, Isa 40:3; here, Ps 2:7) but has modified that basis in theologically significant ways. First, in poetic stich A, Mark lets stand the climactic announcement of divine adoption for Israel's king in Ps 2, a coronation hymn. This, tied to the imagery of water and spiritual unction, recalls Jesus's identification as χριστοῦ, "anointed one," in Mark 1:1.[17] Second, rather than continuing to quote Ps 2:7c as it appears in the LXX (ἐγὼ σήμερον γεγέννηκά σε, "Today I have begotten you"), in stich B Mark shifts to the appositive ὁ ἀγαπητός, "the Beloved," whose closest Septuagintal counterpart is in Gen 22: Isaac, "the beloved son" (τὸν υἱόν σου τὸν ἀγαπητόν) of Abraham, who is offered up in sacrifice by divine command.[18] Instead of returning to Ps 2, with its saber rattling before the nations of the earth (vv. 8–12), in stich C Mark rounds out the heavenly acclamation with a muffled echo of Isa 42:1a–b, the introduction to the first of Deutero-Isaiah's

16. Matthew (3:13–17) articulates the theological problem and his own resolution of it on the lips of John and Jesus. Luke (3:21) shifts the baptism itself into an adverbial clause. In the Gospel according to the Hebrews (according to Jerome, *Pelag.* 3.2), Jesus flatly resists his family's invitation that he be baptized with them, on the grounds of his sinlessness.

17. As Donald Juel notes in *Messianic Exegesis: Christological Interpretation of the Old Testament in Early Christianity* (Philadelphia: Fortress, 1988), 59–88, both Ps 2 and 2 Sam 7 (Nathan's oracle to David) may have been interpreted messianically by some Jews even before the Christian era.

18. While many commentators correctly note that the christological issue of adoptionism is not in view in 1:11, Mark's decision to depart from Ps 2 LXX at precisely the point of v. 7c (ἐγὼ σήμερον γεγέννηκά σε, "I have begotten you today") might suggest, to the contrary, a decision to avoid any such intimation.

Servant Songs: "This is My servant, whom I uphold / My chosen one, in whom I delight" (NJPS; see also Matt 12:18; 2 Pet 1:17). The same servant, of course, is the one upon whom God's Spirit has been placed (Isa 42:1c), the one "smitten and afflicted by God; . . . wounded because of our sins, crushed because of our iniquities" (Isa 53:4d–5b NJPS).

So familiar is Mark's account of "Elijah's" preparatory address and Jesus's baptism that we might easily overlook a cluster of important, occasionally subversive, claims in this presentation. Jesus is God's anointed, beloved Son, the unique beneficiary of God's own Spirit, on whom divine favor rests; by his conduct, Jesus aligns himself with Scripture's promise of Israel's realignment with the LORD's way. And like all Judea (1:5), Jesus himself implicitly "turns" (μετανοέω), allowing himself to be baptized among sinners. This becomes the occasion *not* for a public announcement of his own authority but rather for a passive acceptance of God's dramatically revelatory acclamation made known only to him (and to us). Precisely in connection with coronation hymns like Pss 2 and 110, Samuel Terrien reminds us of the theological and political perils they courted: "As the adopted son of the Godhead, the [Davidic] king could do no wrong, and autocratic caprice easily trespassed the limits of Yahwistic ethics. Presence as royal adoption represented a deterioration of the Hebraic theology of presence."[19] When such trespass occurred, it was an easy yet catastrophic step to confuse Israel's "rock," the LORD who was the ultimate instrument of the nation's deliverance (Ps 18:1–3, 31–32, 46), with a vigorous, militarily triumphant king (vv. 28–29, 33–34; cf. Pss 2:8–9; 110:1). Repeatedly, Mark's Gospel will undermine such braggadocio by depicting Jesus as a humble servant (9:35; 10:43–45; 11:7–10), ironically echoing the sovereign's own hymnic acknowledgment of God's self-abasement and appearance of weakness (Ps 18:35).[20] The undercutting of presumptions about Davidic lordship is probably suggested by Jesus's "putting of David in his place" in Mark 12:35–37; it is surely at work in Jesus's self-presentation as another, very different rock: the "beloved son" rejected by the builders yet laid by the LORD as cornerstone (Mark 12:6, 10–11, quoting Ps 118:22–23). As the Second Gospel unfolds, Jesus will demonstrate the habits acquired by living in the divine presence—"the will of God," as Mark 3:35

---

19. Terrien, *Elusive Presence*, 294. Likewise, a serious danger attached to the priesthood lay in "the corruptibility of the mediating agent" (400).

20. "The more one knows about the background of the [royal] imagery in Mark, the more striking is the account. . . . Jesus should be among the mighty, in the great city that served David as his citadel, not among sinners who have come to repent for their sins" (Donald H. Juel, "The Origin of Mark's Christology," in *The Messiah: Developments in Judaism and Early Christianity*, ed. James H. Charlesworth [Minneapolis: Fortress, 1992], 457).

sums it—but such conduct will consistently baffle those entrenched in conventional religious and social mores (1:27; 2:1–3:6, 21b–34; 6:1–6a). That stage is set in Mark 1:1–11: God will be God, binding himself, intractably anointing and eventually sacrificing his own beloved Son, in the face of unrepentant humanity's repeated efforts to fabricate a god in human image.

THE PARADOXICAL PROPHET

> . . . and he was transformed in front of them.
>
> —Mark 9:2c.

The transfiguration of Jesus in Mark 9:2–8 has long seemed to me among this mysterious gospel's most mysterious passages—not so much on its own terms, but touching on its function within the evangelist's comprehensive scope. Bultmann assumed that this legend was originally a postresurrection appearance story that had been later relocated into the narrative of Jesus's ministry "to serve as a heavenly ratification of Peter's confession [in 8:29] and as a prophecy of the Resurrection in pictorial form [see 8:31]."[21] Whatever one makes of the tradition-critical assessment, this explanation leaves much unanswered.[22] If Mark did not consider heavenly ratification of a Christian confession and a pictorial dramatization of Jesus's resurrection needful in chapter 16, following discovery of the empty tomb and the herald's announcement that Jesus has been raised, why on earth would Mark think it appropriate in chapter 9? In fact, Mark 9:2–8 directly refers neither to Peter's confession, as such, of Jesus as Messiah nor to the promise of Jesus's resurrection (8:31).

The most obvious narrative clue to this episode's placement just here in the gospel seems to be Jesus's warning, in Mark 8:38, that "the Son of Man [would] come in the glory [ἐν τῇ δόξῃ] of his Father with his holy angels [or messengers: μετὰ τῶν ἀγγέλων τῶν ἁγίων]." This, I think, sets us on a proper footing for interpreting 9:2–8, for the latter passage immediately fulfills two aspects of that promise: on a mountain or in hill country (εἰς ὄρος), the biblical topography of divine revelation (Exod 19:3–25; 24:12–18; 1 Kgs 19:8), Jesus is brilliantly transformed (vv. 2–3) in a manner reminiscent of both the כָּבוֹד or

---

21. Rudolf Bultmann, *The History of the Synoptic Tradition*, trans. John Marsh, rev. ed. (New York: Harper & Row, 1963), 260.

22. Rendering a firmly negative verdict to his article's titular question is Robert H. Stein, "Is the Transfiguration (Mark 9:2–8) a Misplaced Resurrection-Account?," *JBL* 95 (1976): 79–96.

shekinah, God's essential splendor (Exod 16:10; Num 14:10; Pss 104:2; 145:5), as well as of apocalypticism's supernatural imagery (Dan 7:19; 12:3; 2 Esd 7:97; Matt 13:43; Rom 12:2; 2 Cor 3:18; Phil 3:21; Rev 3:5; 4:4; 7:9, 13). Attending the metamorphosed Jesus are figures that intertestamental Judaism surely considered "holy messengers," Elijah with Moses (Mark 9:4; cf. Mal 4:4–6; Sir 45:1–22; 48:1–16; Philo, *Mos.* 2.2; 2.35). In a real sense, then, the glimpse of glory given to Jesus's intimates (Peter, James, John, and us as readers) in 9:2–8 immediately satisfies Jesus's promise in 9:1: "Truly I tell you, there are some standing here who will by no means taste death until they have seen that God's sovereign rule has come with power." Should one counter that 9:1 probably refers to the Son of Man's cataclysmic advent, portrayed by Jesus in Mark 13:24–31, then one must explain (1) why Mark does use an intensive double negative in 9:1 (οὐ μὴ, "by no means"), which, if referring to the final *parousia*, would unnecessarily invite instantaneous disproof; (2) why Mark would later insist that the timing of historical catastrophe is unknown to all—including the Son—but only to the Father (13:32), thus placing Jesus in needless contradiction with himself at 9:1; (3) why, in view of the evangelist's repeated references to God's inbreaking kingdom (1:15; 3:24; 4:11, 26, 30; 9:47; 10:14–15, 23–25; 12:34) and the Son of Man's present activity (2:10, 28; 8:31; 9:9, 12, 31; 10:33, 45; 14:21, 41), Mark must be referring in 9:1 to the final apocalypse. More likely, I think, Mark 9:2–8 invites interpretation within the proximate context of 8:27–9:1 and 9:9–13 as well as with the remote yet kindred declaration in 1:1–11.

Christologically considered, the primary burdens of Mark 9:2–8 in its immediate context are to coordinate and to counterbalance at least three kinds of claims made by the material that frames the passage: the relationship between Jesus and his Israelite precursors, the distinctive identity of Jesus with respect to God, and the point at which such things may be properly declared. Very much as we witnessed in this gospel's opening verses, Mark 9:2–8 seems at pains both to demonstrate the continuity of Jesus's messiahship with scriptural precedent and to show where Jesus surpasses all precedent. Thus, whereas popular opinion mistakenly equates Jesus with Elijah or one of the prophets (8:27–28), Peter identifies Jesus (correctly, from Mark's viewpoint: 1:1) as the Christ (8:29) but is hushed (8:30) and instructed about the Son of Man's God-given destiny (8:31; N.B. the divine agency implied in δεῖ, "it is necessary"). A comparable pattern unfolds in 9:9–13: the disciples are again sworn to secrecy until after the Son of Man's vindication (v. 9), of whose unjust suffering "it has been written" (πῶς γέγραπται, v. 12); in the meanwhile, the disciples' confusion over Elijah's mission must be dispelled, then accurately reassessed (vv. 10–13). Wedged between these disputes (N.B. ἐπετίμησεν, "rebuked," 8:30,

32–33; συζητοῦντες, "arguing," 9:10) is the hilltop revelation, which, at God's direct instigation, obscures even as it clarifies.

The narrative of Jesus's transfiguration reprises, with subtle variations, the same motifs announced in Mark 1:1–11: an apocalyptic vision, a divine declaration, and their scriptural foreshadowing. "After six days" (9:2; an allusion, perhaps, to Moses's ascent of Sinai in Exod 24:16), Jesus leads a trio up (ἀναφέρει) a high mountain (cf. Mark 1:10, "going up [ἀναβαίνων] from the water"). Instead of Jesus's beholding the Spirit's descent from the riven heavens (1:10), this time the disciples have thrust before them (ἔμπροσθεν αὐτῶν) a vision of Jesus's radiance and his conversation with Elijah and Moses (9:2–4). Notice that the key verbs in Mark's narration—μετεμορφώθη, "was metamorphosed" (v. 2), and ὤφθη, "there appeared" (v. 4)—are conjugated as so-called divine passives, indicating God's agency as in the comment that no human fuller could have bleached garments so luminous (v. 3; recall the passive participle, σχιζομένους, "were split," in 1:10). Moses, too, had reflected the divine effulgence when proximate to God's glory over the tabernacle (Exod 34:29–35); like Moses, Elijah had experienced a theophany upon Sinai/Horeb (1 Kgs 19:8–18). Beyond these obvious correspondences, this pair in Mark 9:4–5 is significant in other ways. (1) By the first century CE, a parallelism between the lives and ministries of Moses and Elijah had become so well established in Jewish tradition that Elijah appears as *Mosi redivivus*.[23] (2) Moses and Elijah are explicitly linked, in Mal 4:4–5, as tandem heralds of the LORD's day.

A cloud descended over Sinai (Exod 24:16); a voice spoke to the prophet on Horeb (1 Kgs 19:12–13). So also here: A cloud overshadowed the participants (cf. Luke 1:35); from the cloud comes a בַּת קוֹל, largely reiterating what was uttered at Jesus's baptism—this time, however, addressed to his disciples (Mark 9:7):

A "This is my Son,
B the Beloved:
C Listen to him."

The critical difference between the two heavenly announcements in Mark lies in stich C. This is surely no accident. It is a direct order to pay attention *to Jesus*, quoting from Deuteronomy, in which Moses enjoins Israel's obedience to a forthcoming prophet, like him, whom the LORD God would raise up (18:15).[24]

---

23. For documentation, consult Jerome T. Walsh, "Elijah," *ABD* 2:463–66.

24. See, among others, Joel Marcus, *The Way of the Lord: Christological Exegesis of the Old Testament in the Gospel of Mark* (Louisville: Westminster John Knox, 1992), 80–93.

By emphasizing Jesus alongside Elijah and Moses—only Jesus is transfigured; only he is singled out by the heavenly voice—it now should be clear what the קוֹל בַּת at the baptism suggested: the Son ἀγαπητόν is the Son יָחִיד, "only" or "unique." A father's love for such a son is fathomless, precisely because there is no other.[25] The substance of what Jesus's disciples should obey is left unspecified, therefore all-encompassing. In the gospel's immediate context, what they must heed is God's design for the Son of Man to suffer and be vindicated (8:31), their adoption of his way as theirs (8:34–35), an injunction against reporting what they have seen until after the resurrection (9:9), and an assurance that all proceeds according to divine plan (9:12–13). For those able to see, Elijah has already returned in the person of John the Baptizer, preparing the way (1:2–8; cf. 9:12a); this time, however, he has not escaped the murderous clutches of Ahab and Jezebel *redivivi* (9:13; cf. 6:14–29; 1 Kgs 19:1–3; 21:1–16).

An odd but critical point remains unaccounted for: Peter's confused, frightened suggestion to Jesus transfigured that three tents (τρεῖς σκηνάς) be built for him and his heavenly interlocutors (Mark 9:5–6). On its face, the referent appears to be the Feast of Booths, or Tabernacles (Lev 23:39–43), a popular harvest festival whose relevance here is less than conspicuous. While Josephus and doubtless other Jews remembered such thanksgiving celebrations as occasions for political turmoil (*A.J.* 13.372–373; *B.J.* 6.300–309), three disciples on a hill do not a riot make, not even potentially. Probably underlying Peter's addled proposal is Israel's religious memory of the wilderness tabernacle as the LORD's mobile home (Exod 25:1–31:18; Lev 26:11–12; Rev 21:3) and, by imaginative extension, eternal dwellings for the righteous (Luke 16:9; 2 Cor 5:1). A forerunner and constituent of the Solomonic and Herodian temples, the tabernacle was both liturgical shrine and oracular venue ("the tent of meeting": Exod 27:21; 29:43–44).[26] If Peter intended to encompass divine disclosure by creating sacred dwelling places, that hope is dashed. The evangelist dismisses his proposal (Mark 9:6); the supernatural colloquy evaporates (9:8); the four descend the mount (9:9). Like Elijah from Horeb (1 Kgs 19:15) and Jesus from the Jordan (Mark 1:12–13), the disciples are redirected into the world (9:9–29), having gotten from God something considerably more than Elijah's thick silence (1 Kgs 19:12–13) yet altogether different from that prophet's political marching orders (19:15–18).

---

25. Though the nuance may have been lost on audiences lacking Hebrew, ἀγαπητόν ("beloved") is employed throughout Gen 22 LXX to translate יָחִיד, "only" or "unique" (vv. 2, 12, 16). Margaret E. Thrall, "Elijah and Moses in Mark's Account of the Transfiguration," *NTS* 16 (1970): 305–17, points up Mark's emphasis on Jesus's superiority.

26. See Richard Elliott Friedman, "Tabernacle," *ABD* 2:292–300.

They must pay attention to Jesus: the moving nexus and veiled disclosure of divine mystery that asserts, without clear resolution, a supremacy more radiant than any fuller can bleach and a suffering that overshadows like a cloud.[27] The beloved Son encountered on this mountain is *beyond* glory (δόξα). He is, in the most literal sense, *para*dox.[28]

THE CONFOUNDING CONFESSION

. . . facing him, he beheld that thus he had expired.

—Mark 15:39

In this, the Second Gospel's climax, Mark operates at the peak of his rhetorical and theological powers but with a profound reserve, an exquisite narrative braiding that disavows all blatancy in favor of a completely subliminal statement. In Mark, Jesus's death is a near perfect, albeit macabre, inversion of his transfiguration: every gleam of radiance is now suffocated by darkness, all splendor dissolved into lifeless shame. For Mark's reader, ancient or contemporary, there's nothing heroic about how Jesus dies.[29] Yet the resonance of 15:33–41 extends far beyond 9:2–8, reaching deeply into this gospel's first verses. In its form of expression, it is as though the evangelist were proclaiming: "More than merely the brute fact of what has been repeatedly forecast [in 8:31; 9:31; 10:33–34] is now laid before you. Listen. Look [4:3]. Behold how completely this one's nadir corresponds to his zenith."

As he is wont, the evangelist begins simply by setting the clock: "when it came to be the sixth hour . . . until the ninth hour" (Mark 15:33; cf. 1:9: "And it came to be in those days"; 9:2: "And after six days"). In crucifixion (15:24), Jesus

27. As Morna D. Hooker observes, "on the rare occasions when [Mark] uses the word *doxa* [8:38; 10:37; 13:26], he links it every time with the suffering and death of Jesus' followers" ("'What Doest Thou Here, Elijah?' A Look at St Mark's Account of the Transfiguration," in *The Glory of Christ in the New Testament: Studies in Christology in Memory of George Bradford Caird*, ed. L. D. Hurst and N. T. Wright [Oxford: Clarendon, 1987], 70).

28. The most systematic investigation of paradox in the Second Gospel is now Laura C. Sweat, *The Theological Role of Paradox in the Gospel of Mark*, LNTS 492 (London: Bloomsbury T&T Clark, 2013).

29. *Pace* John J. Pilch, "Death with Honor: The Mediterranean Style Death of Jesus in Mark," *BTB* 2 (1995): 65–70, which argues that "Jesus' [Stoic] death proves that he was reared well."

has been elevated (cf. 15:30, 32: "Come down from the cross"), even as at trans-figuration he ascended a high hill (9:2) and at baptism came up from the water (1:10). At three in the afternoon, the whole land falls under eclipse (15:33)—a weird, contrapuntal composite of Jesus's unearthly radiance on the mount (9:3) with "all of the Judean countryside and the Jerusalemites" that once went out to the Jordan (1:10). In 9:2a, Jesus and his disciples were at first "alone by them-selves" before the appearance of Elijah with Moses (9:4). Similarly, Jesus was at first numbered among a plethora (1:5), then paired with John (1:9), before Mark concentrated our attention on a transaction between Jesus alone with the Spirit (1:10). In chapter 15, there are unnumbered passersby (vv. 29, 31, 35), nar-rowed down to a runner (v. 36) and a centurion on watch (v. 39), and a pair of fellow victims on either side of Jesus (v. 27)—occupying exactly the positions of "honor" that another pair have requested of Jesus before being corrected about "[his] baptism" (10:35–40). In 1:11, there was a heavenly voice (φωνὴ); in 9:7, a voice (φωνὴ) from a cloud; in 15:34 and 15:37, the loud voice (φωνῇ μεγάλῃ) of Jesus himself, who cries out with need (βοάω). Into all three tableaux, Mark carefully reintroduces Elijah: first, as John the Baptizer (1:6–7); later, in the hilltop colloquies (9:4, 11); finally, in the response of hard-of-hearing bystand-ers (15:35–36), whose foolish hope that Elijah may miraculously rescue Jesus is ignorant of the fact that Elijah has already come—and was decapitated for his trouble (6:14–29; 9:12–13). They no more know what they are saying than did Peter in his building proposal (9:6). In his baptism and transfiguration, Jesus has stood out from the rest; so, too, in his crucifixion—though never in his life has Jesus appeared so alone (15:34, 40). Given the many changes that the evangelist is obviously ringing, one wonders whether he has selected with precision the very word for Jesus's death—"expired," ἐξέπνευσεν (15:37, 39)—which of course is cognate with the Spirit (τὸ πνεῦμα) that, at his baptism, literally "came down into him" (καταβαῖνον εἰς αὐτόν, 1:10).[30]

Mark's dense web of repetitions—some minor, others refracted—comes into sharp focus at three critical moments in 15:33–41: the centurion's statement in 15:39, the revelatory sign in 15:38, and Jesus's anguished question in 15:34. To begin with the last, let us not only dispel Jesus's words from the cross in

---

30. Bas M. F. van Iersel suggests that such resonance with 1:10 would explain why, in 15:37 and 15:39, Mark avoids the far more common verb ἀπέθανεν, "he died" (15:44; 1 Cor 15:3–5; *Mark: A Reader-Response Commentary*, trans. W. H. Bisscheroux, JSNTSup 164 [Shef-field: Sheffield Academic, 1998], 477). Though ingenious, Stephen Motyer's proposal that the *velum scissum* amounts to a Markan Pentecost overreaches the textual evidence ("The Rending of the Veil: A Markan Pentecost?," *NTS* 33 [1987]: 155–57).

other gospels but also renounce any exegetical legerdemain that would dull the knife edge of the psalmist's lament (22:1).[31] While the evangelist has manifestly determined to end the story of Jesus as he began it, with scriptural context (cf. Mark 1:2–3), the proffered wine in 15:36 would have sufficed to satisfy mere strategy (Ps 69:21).[32] As Samuel Terrien has noted, of all the laments in the Psalter, Ps 22 most passionately disclaims any sense of the petitioner's sin, from which, as in Ps 51:9, the LORD was typically urged to hide his face.[33] In that psalm the penitent prays not to be expelled from the divine presence (מִלְּפָנֶיךָ/πρόσωπόν σου, "your face" [51:13 MT; 50:11 LXX]). By contrast, in Mark 15:34, Jesus stares with the psalmist into God's unveiled face and asks why the Almighty has left him in the lurch (22:1). By adopting the Hebrew text and opting to translate it with a doubled personal pronoun, in 15:34 the evangelist has intensified the heart-searing question: ὁ θεός μου ὁ θεός μου, "*my* God, my God" (cf. Ps 21:2 LXX: ὁ θεὸς, ὁ θεός μου, "God, my God"). Not only that, Jesus hurls back to the absent God the comparably intense, personal address that the voice from heaven has twice used for the beloved Jesus: ὁ υἱός μου (Mark 1:11), ὁ υἱός μου (9:7). It is as none other than the beloved Son, who faithfully goes as it is written of him (14:21), that the crucified Jesus prays to the God who is absent in his hidden presence.

Whatever else may be signified, surely it is the presence of the elusive God that Mark 15:38 asserts: "And the curtain of the temple [τὸ καταπέτασμα τοῦ ναοῦ] was split in two, from top to bottom." Again note Mark's use of the verb in passive voice, suggesting divine agency of the destruction. Notice, too, that Mark does not say what Matthew does (27:54), which is often smuggled back into Mark: that the centurion witnessed the curtain's rending and, on the basis of this and other extraordinary phenomena, deduced Jesus's sonship. Such a maneuver sometimes constitutes an exegetical basis to differentiate exactly which appointment Mark intends: the outer curtain, covering the Jerusalem temple's entrance from its forecourt (which would have been visible to spectators outside), or the inner curtain, separating the temple's interior from its most sacred precinct, the holy of holies. Complicating interpretation is the fact that the Septuagint and Josephus employ τὸ καταπέτασμα for both (outer curtain: Exod 26:37; 38:18; Num 3:10, 26 LXX, among others; Josephus, *A.J.* 8.75; *B.J.* 5.212; inner curtain, Exod 26:31–35; Lev 21:23; 24:3 LXX, among others;

31. On this point, observe the cautions of Raymond E. Brown, *The Death of the Messiah: From Gethsemane to the Grave*, ABRL (New York: Doubleday, 1994), 2:1049–51.

32. Kenneth E. Bailey highlights, furthermore, the fabric of associations between Mark's crucifixion narrative and the book of Lamentations. See "The Fall of Jerusalem and Mark's Account of the Cross," *ExpTim* 102 (1991): 102–5.

33. Terrien, *Elusive Presence*, 323.

A.J. 8.75). Even if we put aside what was visible from Golgotha—a red her-ring, as Mark says nothing of this—it is questionable that the evangelist would have rigorously discriminated between τὸ καταπέτασμα and τὸ κάλυμμα, the proper name for the entryway's drapery. In any case, the inner curtain is prob-ably the referent in Mark 15:38. So far as we know, the outer curtain had no special religious significance, which probably explains the NT's exclusive use of τὸ καταπέτασμα (here in Mark, plus Matt 27:51; Luke 23:45; Heb 6:19; 9:3; 10:20).[34]

All that said, what does Mark 15:38 *mean*? Characteristically, the evangelist offers no interpretation of the veil's breach: to do so would attempt exposure of the God who remains hidden from us, even from Jesus. Still, for perhaps the only time in this gospel, Mark allows the reader a vision of something unseen by any figure in the story. Does Mark offer us adequate resources to infer its meaning? The traditional exegesis is that "God's judgment has fallen on the temple."[35] In that, there may be truth. Yet it says too little, merely restating Mark 13:1-2 (perhaps also 11:15-19) and leaving the *purpose* of such judgment unspecified. In my view, the simplest answer that squares with evidence avail-able elsewhere in this gospel is that, by God's deliberate intervention, there is no longer any shield between the holy presence and the world around it. (Here we might recall that ναίω, the verbal cognate of ὁ ναός, "temple," fundamen-tally means "to dwell" or "to inhabit.") Even prior to the resurrection, Jesus's death spells the defeat of any human attempt to localize divinity—whether in a religious structure, such as a temple or tabernacle (thus also 9:5-6), or in the religious imagination that would fix God in the heavens—which, like the curtain in 15:38, have been decisively ripped asunder (σχίζω), spiritually penetrated, and cut down, by God (1:10). The expiration of the beloved Son coincides with and is ratified by the apocalyptic release of God's living yet covert, holy presence.

That which remains is the soldier's declaration and the circumstances prompting its utterance (Mark 15:39): "And when the centurion, the bystander facing him, saw that thus he had died, he said,

A 'Truly,
B this man [οὗτος ὁ ἄνθρωπος],
C was God's son [υἱὸς θεοῦ ἦν].'"

34. Cf. David Ulansey, "The Heavenly Veil Torn: Mark's Cosmic *Inclusio*," *JBL* 110 (2001): 123–25, suggesting a correspondence between the heavens in Mark 1:10 and the starry sky depicted on the outer curtain, as Josephus describes it (*B.J.* 5.207).

35. Otto Michel, "ναός," *TDNT* 4:885.

Although the syntactic elements are shuffled, the pattern is the same as in 1:11 and 9:7. The material difference lies in the speaker. In previous verses, the voice has issued from the heavens or from the cloud. Here, for the first and only time in the gospel, the voice acknowledging Jesus as God's son belongs to a human character.[36] Readers familiar with the commentary tradition will immediately spot the exegetical difficulties. Is this statement to be taken at face value, with all its attendant ironies: a gentile recognizes this Jewish victim as faithful ("God's son"), perhaps even the Messiah ("God's Son")?[37] A Roman legionnaire who ludicrously betrays his imperial oath and acclaims a dead Jew as *divi filius*, like unto the divine Augustus?[38] Or is the irony even deeper? Far from making a Christian confession, does the centurion sarcastically utter the last of a long series of taunts, true (from Mark's point of view) though not for one moment believed by their speakers (see also 14:61, 65; 15:2, 9, 12, 17–18, 26, 32)?[39]

Many commentators are determined to slice the Gordian knot, offering reasons for one alternative or the other. If, however, we remain true to the spirit of "the mystery of the kingdom of God" (Mark 4:11), I consider it imperative that the circumstances of this climactic utterance be held firmly in mind while leaving open, to eyes open or shut to faith, its precise significance. The believing reader has been given access, at Jesus's baptism and transfiguration, to faith's evidence that what the centurion says is indeed true—whether *he* knows and believes it or not.[40] The evangelist does not lead us down any path of the centurion's psychology, so there we ought not go.[41] The unbelieving or

36. In 3:11, the wording is exact, but the voice belongs to the unclean spirits. In 12:6 and 13:32, the speaker is Jesus but the wording is only approximate (υἱός ἀγαπητός, ὁ υἱός).

37. Compounding the interpretive problem here is the lack of a definite article for υἱός ("son") in the Greek text. In idiomatic Koine, however, no article is necessary when the predicate precedes the verb "to be" (εἰμί). Consult the discussions in T. Francis Glasson, "Mark xv.39: The Son of God," *ExpTim* 80 (1969): 286, and Philip B. Harner, "Qualitative Anarthrous Predicate Nouns: Mark 15:39 and John 1:1," *JBL* 92 (1973): 75–87.

38. Philip H. Bligh, "A Note on *Huios Theou* in Mark 15:39," *ExpTim* 80 (1968): 51–53; Tae Hun Kim, "The Anarthrous *Huios Theou* in Mark 15,39 and the Roman Imperial Cult," *Bib* 79 (1998): 221–41.

39. Whitney T. Shiner, "The Ambiguous Pronouncement of the Centurion and the Shrouding of Meaning in Mark," *JSNT* 22 (2000): 3–22; Donald H. Juel, "The Strange Silence of the Bible," *Int* 51 (1997): 5–19.

40. A dress rehearsal for this enigmatic confession occurs in Mark 14:3–8, where Jesus—not the woman with the alabaster flask—interprets the suggestion of royal anointing (1 Sam 10:1; 2 Kgs 9:6) as a proleptic funeral preparation.

41. See Earl S. Johnson Jr., "Mark 15,39 and the So-Called Confession of the Roman Centurion," *Bib* 81 (2000): 406–13. For an opposing—in my view, unconvincing—exegesis, see Howard M. Jackson, "The Death of Jesus in Mark and the Miracle from the Cross," *NTS* 33 (1987): 16–37.

undecided reader, however, is put on notice: this side of the kingdom's coming, the only empirical evidence that can truthfully support the claim that Jesus is God's Son is nothing other or beyond that which the centurion regards: that is, a dead Jew ("facing him" or "opposite him," ἐξ ἐναντίας αὐτοῦ) who thus has died (οὕτως ἐξέπνευσεν).[42] "The critical tension" that Juel discerned in Mark "between blindness and insight, concealment and openness, silence and proclamation" is, indeed, "not resolved" with the announcement of Jesus's resurrection at the empty tomb (16:7–8). And neither does Mark resolve it with the centurion's acclamation at the cross (15:39).

"Such a Fast God"

> *"How long till I come and see the face of God?"*
> —Ps 42:2b Smith-Goodspeed

As Christopher Burdon perceptively comments, "Mark's is literally a gospel of 'following,' not of Jesus' 'abiding' as in John's or of his being 'in the midst' as in Matthew's."[43] Through Jesus, God outruns everyone in Mark. Occasionally, to the consternation of later Trinitarian thought, God outstrips even Jesus, his beloved Son (Mark 7:24–30; 13:32; 15:34). Ultimately, if not expressly, that is the point underlying the venerable question of Mark's "theological geography" or, in its more recent reformulation, "boundary-crossings."[44] Arguably, God's self-concealing revelation is the primary element in Mark's presentation of

---

42. Because Mark's description of the centurion is so precise, Brian K. Gamel's suggestion that his statement in 15:39 should be taken at face value, to fill out (with 15:38) an *inclusio* with 1:10–11, seems to me possible though less likely (*Mark 15:39 as a Markan Theology of Revelation: The Centurion's Confession as Apocalyptic Unveiling*, LNTS 574 [London: Bloomsbury T&T Clark, 2017]).

43. Christopher Burdon, "Such a Fast God—True and False Disciples in Mark's Gospel," *Theology* 90 (1987): 94; see also Burdon, *Stumbling on God: Faith and Vision through Mark's Gospel* (London: SPCK; Grand Rapids: Eerdmans, 1990), 42–52.

44. The literature is vast. Representative are Elizabeth Struthers Malbon, "Galilee and Jerusalem: History and Literature in Marcan Interpretation," *CBQ* 44 (1982): 242–55; Gerd Theissen, "Lokalkoloritforschung in den Evangelien: Plädoyer für die Erneuerung einer alten Fragestellen," *EvT* 45 (1981): 481–99; Sean Freyne, "The Geography of Restoration: Galilee-Jewish Relations in Early Jewish and Christian Experience," in *Restoration: Old Testament, Jewish, and Christian Perspectives*, ed. J. M. Scott, JSJSup 72 (Leiden: Brill, 2001), 405–33; William Loader, "Challenged at the Boundaries: A Conservative Jesus in Mark's Tradition," *JSNT* 19 (1997): 45–61; Brian K. Blount, *Go Preach! Mark's Kingdom Message and the Black Church Today* (Maryknoll, NY: Orbis, 1998).

suffering discipleship and its christological corollary, which, somewhat mis-leadingly, has too often been epitomized as "the messianic secret." For when we speak of Mark's Jesus—his baptism, transfiguration, death and resurrection; his gospel of the kingdom and way of discipleship; all of the religious and cultural definitions exploded by the Messiah's apocalypse—are we not probing, at bottom, a particular theology of divine presence and its "mysterious revelation"?[45] Are we not invited by this evangelist to reconsider where God is truly found and, in the process of that search, to discover what the true God looks like—the one whose power is revealed in power's renunciation, whose glory is cloaked in suffering self-abnegation?[46] "Truly, thou art a God who hidest thyself, O God of Israel, the Savior" (Isa 45:15 RSV). Thus did Second Isaiah marvel. The record is clear that the evangelist Mark agreed.

Theology is not an inquiry that pursues the divine as an object. Rather, it is the attempt to clarify and to communicate the inherently mysterious operation by which God pursues and transforms humanity into the *imago Dei*.[47] Writ large across Scripture, exemplified by the Second Gospel, that divine pursuit is utterly free, uncontrollably gracious, ever present yet forever elusive. Aping the Almighty, we seek God in comfortable zones, precincts of power, among the pious; constantly we are startled that God's kingdom already is among us, its Messiah enthroned where we least expect. At our best, we want him enshrined; at our worst, we want him dead. Though elusive, Jesus will not collude with our delusions. He refuses to keep still on a holy hill. He won't stay buried. Roving, relentless, Jesus persists in calling disciples into a Sabbath of which he is Lord (Mark 2:28), along a way he makes sacred though never safe. They follow where glimpses of God's presence are traceable yet intractable, where the Face, made familiar among us, can never be placed.

45. In this connection, T. Alec Burkill, *Mysterious Revelation: An Examination of the Philosophy of St. Mark's Gospel* (Ithaca, NY: Cornell University Press, 1963), remains a worthwhile study.

46. See Dorothy A. Lee-Pollard, "Power as Powerlessness: A Key Emphasis in the Gospel of Mark," *SJT* 40 (1987): 173–88; Claude Wienér, "Voyant Qu'il Avait Ainsi Expiré (Marc 15,39)," in *Pense la Foi*, ed. J. Doné and C. Theobald (Paris: Assas Éditions, 1993), 551–81; William C. Placher, "Narratives of a Vulnerable God," *PSB* 14 (1993): 134–51.

47. Martin Luther: "But one is worth calling a theologian who understands the visible and hinder parts of God to mean the passion and the cross" (*The Heidelberg Disputation* [1518] in *Luther: Early Theological Works*, ed. James Atkinson [Philadelphia: Westminster, 1962], 290–91).

CHAPTER 10

Does Suffering Possess
Educational Value in Mark's Gospel?

Suffering builds character.

—Unknown

SO GOES THE OLD ADAGE. That, in all likelihood, is a conflated paraphrase of Rom 5:3–4. Affliction is a topic so pervasive in Mark that one popular introduction to the NT typifies it as "the Gospel of Suffering."[1] The question before us in this chapter is whether Mark either explicitly or tacitly agrees with Paul on this point. That question may be modestly framed: Does the Second Gospel suggest that suffering carries educational value?

BEARINGS IN RECENT RESEARCH

In a slender yet useful monograph, *Learning through Suffering: The Educational Value of Suffering in the New Testament and in Its Milieu*, Charles H. Talbert has surveyed the NT's literary environment for ancient expressions of the pedagogical value of suffering.[2] In the HB, the phenomenon of suffering is explained in various ways, such as the consequence of sin (e.g., Neh 9:26–27; Ps 73:12–20) or as a vicarious boon for others (Isa 53:2–12; 2 Macc 7:37–38). Talbert's study focuses on a particular biblical view of suffering—namely, "a divine education by which moral and spiritual development are facilitated."[3] Ancient Judaism likened God's merciful discipline of his people to a parent's loving punishment of a child: "Son, do not despise the Lord's discipline [παιδείας]

---

1. Robert A. Spivey, D. Moody Smith, and C. Clifton Black, *Anatomy of the New Testament: A Guide to Its Structure and Meaning*, 8th ed. (Minneapolis: Fortress, 2019), 51–76.
2. Collegeville, MN: Liturgical Press, 1991.
3. Talbert, *Learning through Suffering*, 10; see also 9–13.

229

nor relax his reproof; for the one whom the Lord loves, he disciplines" (Prov 3:11–12a LXX; see also Deut 8:5; Jdt 8:27; Pss. Sol. 10.1–23; 13.7–11; 1QH[a] 8; 4QDibHam[a] 3; Philo, *Congr.* 175, 177).[4] A similar view was later attributed to rabbis like Akiba: "Chastisements are precious" (b. Sanh. 101a; b. Ber. 5a–b). Greek authors regarded suffering as a test of character (Plato, *Resp.* 413D–E; 503A), a struggle that increases the sufferer's stamina (Aeschylus, *Ag.* 176–177; Sophocles, *Oed. col.* 7). That idea was popularized by first-century Stoics, who compared suffering to parental discipline (Seneca, *Prov.* 1.5; 2.5–6) or athletic training (Epictetus, *Disc.* 1.29.33; 3.10.7–8). "Hardships, my friend, are a kind of preparatory astringent to the children with a view to the virtue that will come with full maturity" (Pseudo-Theano, *Letter to Eubule*).[5] "Consequently," observes Epictetus, "when a difficulty befalls you, remember that God, like a trainer of wrestlers, has matched you with a rough young man . . . so that you may become an Olympic champion" (*Disc.* 1.24.1–3).

Such Jewish and Greco-Roman views are blended in 4 Maccabees, wherein martyrs for torah undergo hideous deaths at pagan hands with the noblest equanimity: "And immediately they led [a Jewish martyr] to the wheel, and while his vertebrae were being dismembered upon it he saw his own flesh ripped around and drops of blood flowing from his entrails. When he was about to die he said, 'We, you most abominable tyrant, suffer these things for our godly training and virtue [παιδείαν καὶ ἀρετὴν θεοῦ]; but you, for your impiety and bloodthirstiness, will endure unceasing tortures'" (4 Macc 10:8–11; see also 11:9–12, 20–27; 16:25; 17:11–22).

Talbert identifies Rom 5:3–4 as a conceptual bridge to earliest Christianity from its Mediterranean milieu: "We boast in our afflictions, knowing that affliction produces endurance; and endurance, character; and character, hope. And hope does not disappoint, for God's love has been poured into our hearts through Holy Spirit given to us" (see also 1 Cor 11:32; Rev 3:19; 1 Clem. 56.16).

New Testament documents as various as the Epistle of James, 1 Peter, the Epistle to the Hebrews, and Luke-Acts describe human suffering in a manner analogous with this topos in Mediterranean antiquity. Adversity corrects misdeeds (Heb 12:5–11; Jas 5:13–20), strengthens endurance (Heb 10:32–34; 11:1–12:4, 12–13; Jas 1:2–18), and purifies Christians' faith (1 Pet 1:6–7; 4:1–6, 12–19). Those who temporarily suffer receive God's compensatory blessing now (1 Pet 3:13–14a) and ultimately will be vindicated (5:7–10). While his self-sacrifice was a priestly atonement for sin (Heb 13:11–12), Christ's own obedi-

---

4. Here and throughout, all translations are my own, unless otherwise indicated.

5. Trans. Abraham J. Malherbe; cited by Talbert, *Learning through Suffering*, 19.

ence was perfected through suffering (Heb 2:9–10, 18; 5:8–9; 12:1–4). In Luke-Acts, Jesus's spiritual development, through suffering unto death, is normative for his followers, like Paul. Sharing in Christ's experience may catalyze the conversion of pagans (1 Pet 2:18–25; 3:14b–22). Rejecting a reductionist exegesis that would force all NT reflection on suffering into a single category, Talbert identifies a cluster of pervasive images: "Suffering is the arena in which the Christian can be (1) disciplined, in the sense of training that develops strength; (2) refined, in the sense of the smelting process's use of fire to purify precious metals; and (3) educated, in the sense of learning the right way to live."[6]

Whereas Talbert's investigation does not treat in detail suffering in Mark's Gospel, other studies have done so. Sharyn Echols Dowd considers the theological function of prayer in the Second Gospel, a book she construes as "a didactic biographical narrative whose purpose is to shape the community that takes its identity from the central figure," Jesus Christ.[7] Dowd notes that Mark's longest, most strategically positioned instruction on prayer is 11:22–25 (the withered fig tree as an occasion for faith in God, who can do the impossible); Mark's longest, most strategically positioned modeling of prayer is 14:32–42 (Jesus's petitions for deliverance from the cross, if it be God's will). In Dowd's reading, these texts are sharply contrastive, generating a tension between divine power and human suffering that Mark never resolves but to which prayer is closely related. "What makes discipleship in the Markan community so difficult is not that it involves suffering, but that it involves suffering by those who participate in God's power to do the impossible."[8] Jesus's stress on faith is an implied exhortation, directed to Mark's audience, to persist in believing that for God everything is possible, despite unanswered prayer and relentless challenges to that worldview. Because he entertains no limitation on divine power, the evangelist can provide no rational defense of God, "a solution to the problem of theodicy." What Mark offers his readers, instead, is encouragement in their relation to God, "a way of coping with the tension that pervades their existence as empowered sufferers."[9]

Susan Garrett has explored the trials both of affliction and of seduction that beset Jesus and his disciples (Mark 4:19; 13:33–37).[10] She regards the Second Gospel as a complex precipitate of traditions about testing (πειρασμός) in an-

6. Talbert, *Learning through Suffering*, 92.
7. *Prayer, Power, and the Problem of Suffering: Mark 11:22–25 in the Context of Markan Theology*, SBLDS 105 (Atlanta: Scholars Press, 1988), 16.
8. Dowd, *Prayer, Power, and the Problem of Suffering*, 158.
9. *Prayer, Power, and the Problem of Suffering*, 158–65 (quotations, 162).
10. *The Temptations of Jesus in Mark's Gospel* (Grand Rapids: Eerdmans, 1998).

tiquity, which variously portray God (Deut 8:2–5; Jdt 8:25–27; Sir 4:17; 4 Macc 17:20–22; Pss. Sol. 13.7–11) or Satan (Job 1–2; T. Job 37.5–7; 2 Cor 12:7; 2 Thess 2:9–11; Rev 2:9–29) as agents of πειρασμοί. In Garrett's treatment of Mark, Jesus epitomizes "one who in every respect has been tested as we are, yet without sin" (Heb 4:16).[11] The entire course of Jesus's ministry is subjected to temptation, not merely by Satan in the wilderness (Mark 1:12–13) but by religious adversaries (8:11–13; 12:13–17; 14:43–15:15; cf. Wis 2:12–14) and even his own disciples (Mark 8:17–21, 31–33; 9:34; 10:35–37), all of whom blindly collude to "make a straight path crooked" for God's Messiah (cf. Mark 1:2–3; Acts 13:10).[12] Jesus's life under trial reaches its climax at Golgotha, where for a brief time God stands aside to test his Son (Mark 15:23–34; cf. T. Jos. 2.4–7). Because he was "tried and [proven] true," Jesus's perfectly obedient endurance resulted in God's acceptance of his death as an acceptable sacrifice, ransoming others from sin (Mark 10:45; 14:24) and empowering his followers to see clearly, to think the things of God, to persevere during their own times of trial (cf. Heb 5:7–10; 10:20). "Only after Easter would the disciples be given full sight and brought to singleminded faith" (see Mark 10:39; 14:27–28; 16:5–7).[13]

At important points, the investigations by Talbert, Dowd, and Garrett intersect and, just as significantly, diverge from one another. All three recognize the seriousness with which biblical authors reckon with suffering, whether of Jesus or of his followers. All three acknowledge the Bible's multiple explanations for suffering; all resist any forcing of the evidence into a uniform pattern. All discern in the NT clear echoes of older or contemporaneous Jewish and Greco-Roman thought, while underlining the distinctive adaptation of those beliefs by early Christians.

The differences among these treatments arise from their distinctive aims and from their authors' exegetical intuitions. These three studies are focused on three theologically distinguishable issues: early Christians' adoption of their culture's view of suffering as divine education (Talbert); Mark's emphasis on the endurance of trials to prove purity of faith that is acceptable to God (Garrett); Mark's exhortation to prayer in response to a paradox produced by unswerving belief in God's omnipotence and the incontestable reality of suffering (Dowd). While prayer amid suffering is regarded by Dowd as a practice

11. Garrett, *Temptations of Jesus*, 106–10, discusses theological parallels between Mark and Hebrews.

12. Jesus's ongoing temptation throughout Mark's narrative distinguishes Garrett's exegesis from that of Ernest Best, *The Temptation and the Passion: The Markan Soteriology*, 2nd ed., SNTSMS 2 (Cambridge: Cambridge University Press, 1990).

13. Garrett, *Temptations of Jesus*, 142 (originally italicized).

that shapes the ethos of Mark's community, she does not clearly characterize it as a form of Christian παιδεία; Talbert points up the παιδεία in suffering itself, saying comparatively less about the role of prayer. Although Garrett and Dowd concentrate their energies on Mark—occasionally, with differences of nuance, on prayer in Mark—in a way that Talbert does not, in some respects Garrett's approach and conclusions are closer to Talbert's than to Dowd's.[14] Thus, Garrett's description of Jesus in Gethsemane as momentarily double-minded, experiencing "a conflicted state of being" that is overcome by his vow of obedience to God no matter what, chimes with Talbert's comments about Jesus's own "spiritual growth": "The Lukan Jesus, through prayer, has come to see that he is about to enter a new phase of God's plan for him . . . [in which] he will learn obedience through what he suffers."[15] For Dowd, by contrast, the terror in Gethsemane lies not as something *within Jesus* that might cause him to flee the cup of suffering but in the fact that a God powerful enough to intervene and to prevent that suffering wills otherwise.[16]

As the pieces fall, so emerge the overall patterns. Dowd's reading of Mark leaves unresolved the tension between a mercifully omnipotent God and the suffering unto death of his beloved Son and of those who follow him. In its prayers, the community is "forced to entertain conflicting propositions simultaneously."[17] Whether that conflict would be moderated by Jesus's transfiguration (9:2–8), resurrection (8:31; 9:31; 10:34; 9:9; 16:6), and promise of reunion with his disciples (14:28; 16:7) remains moot in Dowd's study. Garrett's interpretation of Mark is less equivocal and more reassuring: "Jesus [has] made the perfect and once-for-all sacrifice, accepted by God as atonement for the sins of the people."[18] While Mark's readers continue to be genuinely tested, "the Good News is that by his own endurance Christ has empowered followers to persevere in the straight and narrow way of the Lord."[19] One leaves Garrett's book wondering why Mark's priestly Christology and view of discipleship are

---

14. For Garrett, prayer tends to be an activity of the faithful: "Prayer is the means by which persons put doublemindedness behind them, as Jesus demonstrates in his move from distress and grief (14:33–34) to confident obedience (vv. 35–36)" (*Temptations of Jesus*, 98). For Dowd, prayer tends to be an instrument of God, "the vehicle [in Mark 11:22–25] by means of which the God who can do the impossible meets the needs of the Christian community" (*Prayer, Power, and the Problem of Suffering*, 129).

15. Garrett, *Temptations of Jesus*, 98; Talbert, *Learning through Suffering*, 85–86.

16. Dowd, *Prayer, Power, and the Problem of Suffering*, 151–62.

17. Dowd, *Prayer, Power, and the Problem of Suffering*, 162.

18. Garrett, *Temptations of Jesus*, 121.

19. *Temptations of Jesus*, 18; see also 159–63.

considerably more muted than that of Hebrews (9:11–10:14) or of Matthew (16:17–23; 28:16–20). Of Luke-Acts, Talbert says, "Master and disciple learn obedience through what they suffer. In this sense their suffering is part of their divine education."[20] If applied to Mark, it is as hard for me to imagine Garrett's disagreement with that conclusion as to expect Dowd's acceptance of it.

A Triptych of Suffering in Mark

There are many means of approaching the question of suffering's disciplinary import in Mark. One of the least promising paths is that of simple word-study. παιδεία, the term we have witnessed in other Hellenistic documents, never appears in the Second Gospel, though it occurs a half-dozen times elsewhere in the NT (Eph 6:4; 2 Tim 3:16; Heb 12:5, 7, 8, 11).[21] πάσχει ("to suffer") is found forty-two times throughout the NT but only thrice in Mark (5:26; 8:31; 9:12).[22] Although "teaching" is the activity of Jesus most frequently mentioned in Mark,[23] the content of that teaching is sparse in comparison with the other gospels and by no means limited to the topic of suffering. If we want to probe the question of educational suffering in the Second Gospel, we shall have to find a better way.

I propose to examine three Markan pericopae in which suffering is conspicuous: the restoration of Jairus's daughter (5:21–24, 35–43), the healing of a woman with vaginal bleeding (5:25–34), and Jesus's prayer in Gethsemane (14:32–42). These episodes are instructive as much for their representative differences as for their compatibility. The first two are among the lengthiest of those tales of Jesus's healings that occupy so much of the Second Gospel's first half. The account of Gethsemane, some nine chapters later, may be second only to the crucifixion in capturing the anguish of Jesus himself in Mark's second half, dominated by the passion narrative. If asked why I have selected for in-

---

20. Talbert, *Learning through Suffering*, 89–90.

21. The cognate verb παιδεύειν is more frequently attested but, again, never in Mark (see Luke 23:16, 22; Acts 7:22; 22:3; 1 Cor 11:32; 2 Cor 6:9; 1 Tim 1:20; 2 Tim 2:25; Titus 2:12; Heb 12:6, 7, 10; Rev 3:19).

22. Twelve occurrences are in 1 Peter (2:19, 20, 21, 23; 3:14, 17, 18; 4:1 [bis], 15, 19; 5:10), which makes of that letter a principal canonical basis for Talbert's *Learning through Suffering*, 42–57.

23. Jesus as "teacher" (διδάσκαλος): 4:38; 5:35; 9:17, 38; 10:17, 20, 35; 12:14, 19, 32; 13:1; 14:14; "to teach" (διδάσκειν): 1:21, 22; 2:13; 4:1, 2; 6:2, 6, 30, 34; 7:7; 8:31; 9:31; 10:1; 11:17; 12:14, 35; 14:49; "teaching" (διδαχή): 1:22, 27; 4:2; 11:18; 12:38.

vestigation three *narratives*, I would reply, first, that narrative is the evangelist's favored mode of presenting "the beginning of the gospel of Jesus Christ" (1:1). Second, by his intercalation, or sandwiching, of the stories of Jairus and the woman who touched Jesus's garment, Mark could send us no clearer signal that he intends for the stories in his gospel to interpret one another.[24] Third, while we would be blind to ignore instruction that takes up suffering (such as the cycle of passion predictions in 8:31, 9:31, and 10:33–34), it seems to me equally myopic to disregard the pedagogical dimension of Mark's tales and legends.[25] Again the evangelist tips his hand by such wording as we find in 1:27, 4:34, and 7:17: mighty works blend indissolubly into "new teaching" in this gospel, even as Jesus's speech is irreducibly parabolic.

Here, then, is a brief, "trifocal" exegesis of three illustrative excerpts from Mark. Convenience and clarity will be better served if I reproduce these pericopae at this point.

The Synagogue Leader's Daughter

[5:21]And when Jesus had crossed again in the boat to the other side, a great crowd gathered about him, and he was beside the sea. [22]Then came one of the archisynagogues, Jairus by name; and seeing him, he fell at his feet [23]and begged him saying, "My little daughter is at the point of death. Come, lay your hands on her, so that she may be made well, and live." [24]And he went with him. And a great crowd followed him and pressed around him.... [35]While he was still speaking [to the woman: 5:34], some came from the archisynagogue's house who said, "Your daughter is dead. Why are you still troubling the teacher?" [36]But overhearing what they said, Jesus said to the archisynagogue, "Don't be afraid, just keep having faith." [37]And he let no one accompany him but Peter and James and John, James's brother. [38]And they came to the house of the archisynagogue, and beheld an uproar, with great weeping and wailing. [39]And when he had entered, he said to them, "Why all the uproar and wailing? The child is not dead but sleeping." [40]And they laughed at him. But he threw them all out, and took the child's father and mother and those with him, and went in where the child was.

24. See James R. Edwards, "Markan Sandwiches: The Significance of Interpolations in Markan Narratives," *NovT* 31 (1989): 193–216.

25. I use these terms in their classic, form-critical senses. See Martin Dibelius, *From Tradition to Gospel*, trans. Bertram Lee Woolf (New York: Scribner's Sons, 1934), 70–132; Rudolf Bultmann, *History of the Synoptic Tradition*, trans. John Marsh, rev. ed. (New York: Harper & Row, 1963), 214–15, 267–68.

[41]And taking the child's hand he said to her, "*Talitha koum*," which means, "Little girl, I tell you, get up." [42]And immediately the girl got up and walked around, for she was twelve years old. And immediately they were stunned with amazement. [43]And he strictly ordered them that no one should know this, and told them to give her something to eat.

The Woman with Chronic Hemorrhaging

[5:25]And there was a woman who had a flow of blood for twelve years, [26]and who had suffered much under many physicians, and had spent all that she had, and had been in no way helped but rather had grown worse. [27]She had heard about Jesus, and came up behind him in the crowd and touched his coat. [28]For she had said, "If I touch even his clothes, I shall be made well." [29]And immediately the font of her hemorrhage dried up; and she knew in her bones that she had been healed of her affliction. [30]And immediately Jesus, inwardly knowing that power had gone out of him, turned around in the crowd, and said, "Who touched my clothes?" [31]And his disciples said to him, "You see the crowd pressing around you, and you say, 'Who touched me?'" [32]And he looked around to see who had done it. [33]But the woman, in fear and trembling, knowing what had happened to her, came and fell at his feet, and told him the whole truth. [34]And he said to her, "Daughter, your faith has made you well. Go in peace, and be healed of your affliction."

Jesus in Gethsemane

[14:32]And they came to a spot by the name of Gethsemane, and he said to his disciples, "Sit here while I pray." [33]And he took Peter and James and John with him, and he began to be utterly despondent and anguished; [34]and he said to them, "My soul is crushed, even to the point of death. Stay here, and stay awake." [35]And going a little farther, he fell on the ground and prayed that, if possible, the hour might pass from him. [36]And he said, "Abba, Father, all things are possible for you. Divert this cup from me—yet not what I want, but what you want." [37]And he came and found them sleeping, and he said to Peter, "Simon, are you sleeping? Weren't you able to stay awake for one hour? [38]Stay awake and pray that you may not enter into temptation: the spirit is indeed eager but the flesh, weak." [39]And again he went away and prayed, saying the same thing. [40]And again he came and found them sleeping, for their eyes were weighed down, and they did not know what to answer him. [41]And he came the third time and said to them, "Still sleeping? Still at ease? Enough! The hour has come. Look! The Son of Man is betrayed into the hands of sinners. [42]Get up, let's go. Look—here comes my betrayer."

The threads interlacing the stories of the woman and Jairus's daughter are many.

1. Those healed are both women (5:25, 41), referred to as "daughters" (vv. 23, 34, 35) who have experienced something (infirmity or life) for twelve years (vv. 25, 42).

2. The petitioners for healing prostrate themselves at Jesus's feet ([πρὸς] πίπτω: vv. 22, 33).

3. Both sufferers undergo hopeless circumstances: incurable illness (v. 26) or death (v. 35).

4. Both women suffer conditions rendering them unclean—a bloody discharge (vv. 25, 29), a corpse (v. 35)—which would restrict or exclude their movements within cult, home, and society (see Lev 12:1–8; 15:19–30; Num 19:1–22).[26]

5. People oscillate between fear (Mark 5:33, 36) and faith (vv. 34, 36).

6. In both stories, Jesus demonstrates uncommon insight through a statement that is seemingly absurd (vv. 30, 39) and instantly rebuffed (vv. 31, 40a; cf. v. 35).

7. Effected in both cases by touch (vv. 23, 27–28, 41), Jesus's healing contravenes the prior activity of professionals: physicians (v. 26) or mourners (vv. 38, 40b; cf. b. Ketub. 4.4).

8. Both women are restored (σῴζω: Mark 5:23b, 28, 34a),

9. a reality immediately confirmed (5:29a, 42a) and recognized (vv. 29b–30a, 42b).

Most commentators detect in Mark 5:21–43 echoes of two ancient tales of prophetic restoration: Elijah's raising of the Sidonian widow's son (1 Kgs 17:17–24) and Elisha's resuscitation of the Shunammite's son (2 Kgs 4:18–37). While neither of these HB stories should be contorted to fit a Markan mold, both

---

26. See Marla J. Selvidge, "Mark 5:25–34 and Leviticus 15:19–20: A Reaction to Restrictive Purity Legislations," *JBL* 103 (1984): 619–23. Judging Selvidge's assessment overstated, Sharyn Dowd summarizes a wealth of ancient religious and medical evidence for gynecologic disorders (*Reading Mark: A Literary and Theological Commentary on the Second Gospel*, RNTS [Macon, GA: Smyth & Helwys, 2000], 57–58).

share many features I have just itemized: (1) the involvement of women (4) beyond Israel's conventional boundaries (1 Kgs 17:9; 2 Kgs 4:8), (8) revival of their dead children (7) by extraordinary means (1 Kgs 17:17, 21–23; 2 Kgs 4:20–21, 32–35), (6) incomprehension (1 Kgs 17:18; 2 Kgs 4:28) (9) that yields to acclamation (1 Kgs 17:24; 2 Kgs 4:37). Other reverberations seem particularly strong between 2 Kgs 4 and Mark 5: the social standing of the parents (the wealthy Shunammite, 2 Kgs 4:8, 22, 24; Jairus the archisynagogue, Mark 5:22, 35–38), the uncertain condition of two children (whether dead or comatose: 2 Kgs 4:23, 26, 32; Mark 5:39), and prostration before the healer (2 Kgs 4:37; Mark 5:22, 33).[27]

In 1 and 2 Kings, as in Mark, the religious dimensions of these tales quickly bubble to the surface. There are differences, however. Throughout, God or God's agent is acknowledged as source or conduit of health and life (1 Kgs 17:24; 2 Kgs 4:37; Mark 5:23, 28). Only the tale of Elijah and the widow of Zarephath contemplates a connection between a child's death and a parent's sin (1 Kgs 17:18, 20);[28] none of these stories suggests that the suffering of parent or child is invoked by God for disciplinary purposes. Mark reiterates a point that rides on the surface of the Shunammite's assurance to her husband and Elisha's assistant, Gehazi (שָׁלוֹם, "It's all right": 2 Kgs 4:23, 26): namely, that faith—a persistent reaching out toward God or God's Messiah—is *antecedent* to health and structures the context within which infirmity and its relief by God may be properly understood as a sign of divine grace.[29]

The importance of faith for Mark is indicated by the term's almost immediate juxtaposition in Jesus's assurances to the woman and to the archisynagogue (πίστις, 5:34; πιστεύειν, 5:36). Furthermore, faith is underscored by many aspects of the evangelist's account. To a degree greater than Luke (8:40–56) and far more than Matthew (9:18–26), Mark recounts in excruciating detail the woman's desperate straits and Jesus's time-consuming endeavor to find

---

27. In "Jesus and Elisha," *Per* 12 (1971): 85–104, Raymond E. Brown finds a closer analogue for the gospel accounts in the Elisha catena of miracles than in either the Elijah cycle or so-called Greco-Roman aretalogies.

28. Citing 2 Sam 6:6–7, Amos 6:10, Mark 1:24, and Luke 5:8, John Gray refers to "the incompatibility of the Holy and other than holy" (*I and II Kings: A Commentary*, 2nd rev. ed., OTL [Philadelphia: Westminster, 1970], 382). While the gospels do not deny sin and its consequences for judgment, in Luke (13:1–5) and John (9:1–5) Jesus repudiates the assumption that victims of calamity have been specially punished by God.

29. As Joel Marcus notes (*Mark 1–8: A New Translation with Introduction and Commentary*, AB 27 [New York: Doubleday, 2000], 360–61), it is especially at this point that Jesus's mighty works in Mark diverge from other Hellenistic tales of healing, in which miracles stimulate faith (see also 1 Kgs 17:23–24)—not the other way around.

her amid the throng, before she steps forward to tell the whole truth (5:25–33). The time expended in that narration effectively simulates (1) how long she has suffered and (2) the intensifying plight of Jairus, whose daughter is dying as precious minutes dwindle away (cf. 5:35).[30] The greater the sense of hopelessness, the more critical the need for faith. By contrast, nowhere in 5:21–43 does Mark invest such care in describing either the healer's technique or the crowd's acclaim for wondrous works (cf. 7:32–37).[31] Nor should we disregard the narrative context in which Mark has placed these interlaminated tales: immediately following an exorcism (5:1–20) whose terrified witnesses push Jesus away (5:15–17), amid a sequence of mighty works that begins with the stilling of a storm and the disciples' craven lack of faith (4:35–41) and ends with Jesus's own astonishment at the faithlessness (ἀπιστία) among those, back home, whom he cannot heal (6:1–6a; cf. 5:42). The hemorrhaging woman and (at least by implication) the distraught father are enabled to do what eludes so many in Mark: to penetrate their fear with faith, thus allowing wholeness to happen.[32]

Although the terms πίστις and πιστεύειν do not appear in Mark 14:32–42, Gethsemane dramatizes Jesus's own crisis of faith in the Second Gospel. The similarities between this episode and the very different, sandwiched tales in 5:21–43 seem to me more than purely coincidental. They are, in any case, worth pondering.

- All three stories describe a change in location (5:21, 24, 37–38a; 14:32) and attendant shifts in mood (5:23, 30, 38b–40; 14:33). Curiously, different "children" in Mark 5 (v. 39b) and 14 (vv. 37, 40, 41; cf. 10:24 [τέκνα]) are mysteriously asleep.
- Present in all three pericopae are the disciples, notably the inner circle of

---

30. In a classic study, Heinz Joachim Held commented, "Matthew preserves the essential elements of the Markan narrative. What he omits are the descriptive non-essentials" (Günther Bornkamm, Gerhard Barth, and Heinz Joachim Held, *Tradition and Interpretation in Matthew*, trans. Percy Scott, NTL [Philadelphia: Westminster, 1963], 173). I think that mistakes Mark's intent. The plethora of detail, which Matthew (or Held) may have regarded as nonessential, Mark has apparently elaborated to strengthen his theological objectives.

31. The command of secrecy in 5:43 subverts any ploy to compel faith by miracle; "the signs of the kingdom have become signs for faith in Jesus" (M. E. Glasswell, "The Use of Miracles in the Markan Gospel," in *Miracles: Cambridge Studies in Their Philosophy and History*, ed. C. F. D. Moule [London: Mowbray, 1965], 161).

32. For a sensitive reading of Mark 5:21–43 among other Markan tales of "faith and the powerless," consult Christopher D. Marshall, *Faith as a Theme in Mark's Narrative*, SNTSMS 64 (Cambridge: Cambridge University Press, 1989), 75–133.

Simon Peter, James, and John (5:37; 14:32–33). Characteristically, they mis-apprehend or disobey their teacher (5:31; 14:34, 37–38, 40).[33]

- Hopelessness suffuses all these tableaux. The archisynagogue's little daugh-ter is at death's door (ἐσχάτως ἔχει, 5:23a); the woman's chronic bleeding has worsened (5:25–26);[34] Jesus in Gethsemane is tormented, even to death (ἕως θανάτου, 14:34a).

- The protagonists' initial response to crisis is fear (5:33, 36; 14:33), whose source Jesus alludes to as human frailty, "weakness of the flesh" (14:38; cf. Isa 40:6).

- In every case, someone falls to the ground in distress (Mark 5:22, 33; 14:35).

- A bond of familial affection is articulated by an interlocutor, who in two of three cases is the petitioner: "my little daughter" (5:23a), "Abba, Father" (14:36).[35] In the third instance, the one who tenderly refers to the woman as "daughter" (5:34) is himself God's "beloved Son" by heavenly acclamation (1:11; 9:7).

- A forthright plea for relief from distress is offered (5:23b; 5:27–28), with Jesus thus beseeching God three times (14:36, 39, 41). None of the principals expresses nobility in suffering. All are in pain. All want it to stop.

- A peculiar tension is manifest in the will of each protagonist, particularly that of the woman and of Jesus. Like her (5:28, 33a), Jesus knows the way ahead (8:31; 9:31; 10:33–34, 45; 12:1–11). In the critical moment, he, like her, temporarily resists discovery (5:32; 14:36ab). Ultimately, both the Son and the daughter come forward not only to face the truth about themselves but also to tell it (5:33b; 14:36c, 41–42).

- All of these stories are cast in a muted apocalypticism that is intensified toward their endings: Jesus's declaration that the woman depart in peace

33. Here, another echo with 2 Kgs 4:27–31: Gehazi first rebuffs the Shunammite, then later proves himself incapable of reviving her child.

34. Since blood was identified with life in Hebrew thought, incessant menstruation could be reckoned as a literal wasting away of the woman's life. See Hans Walter Wolff, *Anthropology of the Old Testament* (Philadelphia: Fortress, 1974), 19, 60–62.

35. Some of Joachim Jeremias's conclusions regarding Jesus's address to God as "Abba"—in particular, that such address was utterly unique, implying Jesus's self-consciousness as the singular "Son of God"—have been refuted in recent scholarship; see James Barr, "'Abba' Isn't 'Daddy,'" *JTS* 39 (1988): 28–47; Mary Rose D'Angelo, "*Abba* and 'Father': Imperial Theology and the Jesus Traditions," *JBL* 111 (1992): 611–30; C. Clifton Black, *The Lord's Prayer*, IRUSC (Louisville: Westminster John Knox, 2018), 70–73. Nevertheless, there remains in Jeremias's study much of value for the interpreter of Paul (Rom 8:15; Gal 4:6) and Mark (14:36): thus, as Father, "God is the *one who helps in time of need . . .* , when no one else can help" (*The Prayers of Jesus*, SBT, 2nd series 6 [London: SCM, 1967], 11–65 [quotation, 19]).

(5:34); his raising of the little girl (ἐγείρω, ἀνίστημι, 5:41–42; see also 6:14, 16; 8:31; 9:9–10, 31; 10:34; 12:25–26; 14:28; 16:6); later, his references to "the cup" (14:36; see also 10:38–39; Isa 51:17, 22) and to "temptation" (Mark 14:38; see also 1:13) and his repeated rousings (γρηγορέω, 14:34, 37–38; 41a–b) of disciples who sleep (καθεύδω, 14:37, 40, 41), which culminate in announcement that the hour (ἡ ὥρα) has come (14:41c; see also 14:35, 37). These tones acquire greater sonority from the eschatological contexts in which the evangelist has positioned them: the inbreaking of God's kingdom and its concomitant rout of demonic forces in the first half of Mark (1:14–15; 3:22–27; 4:35–41); the kingdom's consummation and its preliminary persecution of believers, predicted on the Mount of Olives in chapter 13 (N.B. ἡ ὥρα, vv. 11, 32; καθεύδω, v. 36; γρηγορέω, vv. 34, 35, 37).

If these observations be accepted, some corollaries follow. First, Mark appears to have blended the genres of tale and legend in such a manner that stories of healing highlight the need for faith, and a crisis in Jesus's faith exposes his own affliction and need of healing.[36] In Mark's apocalyptic view, God may be trusted to restore ruptured wombs, crushed souls, breathless bodies—the collapse of social bodies, as well (10:28)—though that restoration take years (5:25), death be unavoidable (5:35), betrayal inevitable (14:41b–42), and afflictions inescapable this side of the age to come (10:29–30).

Second, Mark seems to align the sufferings of those whom Jesus heals with Jesus's own torment, which can be redeemed only by God (10:45; 14:24). Such a conclusion appears counterintuitive, since the evangelist accents the vindication of martyrs, those who suffer voluntarily and specifically for the sake of Jesus and his gospel (8:34–9:1; 10:28–31, 39b–45; 13:9–13, 24–27). It is unwise, however, to draw too sharply a distinction between "human misery" and "Christian suffering," lest we dismiss Mark's many healing narratives—which account for slightly less than one-third of the gospel—or distort his presentation of "the good news." Nowhere in Mark does Jesus leave demoniacs in thrall to Satan, or refuse to heal the afflicted, on the grounds that their suffering was not provoked "for the gospel's sake." To the contrary, God is God not of the dead but of the living (12:27). "The glad tidings of God's sovereignty" (1:14–15) carry no provisos. By drawing together Jairus and Jesus, menorrhagic woman and dead

---

36. So also William C. Placher: "Mark uses every strategy to say two things at once: yes, this is the Messiah, the greatest of miracle workers, the Son of God, but, no, that does not mean at all what you thought it meant" ("Narratives of a Vulnerable God," *PSB* 14 [1993]: 146).

child and crucified Messiah, Mark suggests that physical torment and spiritual anguish are different dimensions of an interconnected whole, which humans can alleviate but only "Abba, Father," a loving God, can ultimately restore.[37]

Third, in Gethsemane—and later, at Golgotha—Jesus evinces what, for Mark, is the sufferer's appropriate response: faith manifested by prayer. This ought not surprise us: throughout Mark, Jesus is portrayed as a prayerful person (1:35; 6:46; 11:24, 25; 13:18) who encourages and honors faith in God (1:15; 2:5; 4:40; 5:34, 36; 9:23, 42; 10:52; 11:22–24, 31). Still it confounds us, whenever we smuggle into the Second Gospel images of Jesus foreign to it: whether that of the tragic hero, abused child, or deluded fanatic.[38] The Markan Jesus is none of these things. Finally, he is God's Son, as obedient as he is beloved, a little child able to enter the kingdom (10:13–16), the servant and disciple of divine sovereignty that none of his own disciples proves to be (9:33–37). As in his mighty works, so also in his plaintive cries: Jesus faithfully enacts Scripture. If the prophet is transparent through Jesus the healer, the psalmist's lament bleeds through Jesus the sufferer: "My soul is heavy within me" (Pss 42:5, 11; 43:5 LXX; Mark 14:34), "My God, my God, why have you forsaken me?" (Ps 22:1; Mark 15:34).[39]

A Summing Up

We opened this chapter by reviewing several book-length considerations of biblical suffering by other NT investigators. A comparison of my outcomes with theirs is a fitting note on which to conclude.

First, this study has found little to support Susan Garrett's suggestion of a peculiar theological affinity between Mark and the Epistle to the Hebrews. In Heb 5:5–10, I hear an echo of the Synoptic portrayal of Jesus in Gethsemane; in

---

37. See also C. Clifton Black, "The Persistence of the Wounds," in *Lament: Reclaiming Practices in Pulpit, Pew, and Public Square*, ed. Sally A. Brown and Patrick D. Miller (Louisville: Westminster John Knox, 2005), 47–58. On the broader scriptural background in which God is said to suffer with and for the people, see Terence E. Fretheim, *The Suffering of God: An Old Testament Perspective*, OBT (Philadelphia: Fortress, 1984), esp. 127–48.

38. The perceptive, zesty account by Charlotte Allen, *The Human Christ: The Search for the Historical Jesus* (New York: Free Press, 1998), traces these and other misconceptions.

39. Commentators frequently observe that, contrary to customary expectation, Jesus's contact with perpetual menstruation (Mark 5:27–29) and a corpse (5:41–42) does not defile him (cf. 7:15a, 18b) but rather purifies both women (see, e.g., Marcus, *Mark 1–8*, 367–68). Less often noted is that, by his own prayers at Gethsemane (14:36, 39) and Golgotha (15:34), Jesus utters the rest of his revisionist definition of *kashrut*: that "clean" and "unclean" are *from within* and come *out of* a person (7:15b, 20).

Mark 10:45 or 14:24, I can imagine that theological acorn from which a mighty oak like Hebrews might have grown.[40] It is harder for me to perceive that development having already occurred in the Second Gospel. In Mark, Jesus sends someone to a priest (1:44) and announces the obliteration of the temple (13:1–2; see also 11:15–19; 15:38). The replacement of that temple by another, heavenly or otherwise, is a matter of perjured testimony (14:58) or ridicule (15:29b–30); Jesus himself is no superior priest by virtue of what he suffered (cf. Heb 5:5–10; 8:1–10:39).[41] On the other hand, like Garrett's study, this essay has identified in Mark's Gospel a christologically articulated view of suffering that is a complex precipitate of particular ancient, especially scriptural, conceptions.

Second, does Mark ever reconcile the paradox, described by Sharyn Dowd, between an omnipotent God and relentless suffering? This study suggests an affirmative response that is neither, to be sure, a philosophical formulation nor, *pace* Dowd, a means by which Christians cope with affliction. The resolution, I think, is revealed at Gethsemane and Golgotha, where, in unimaginable anguish, Jesus steadfastly prays to "Abba, Father," "my God," whose will is done at that moment when his mercy is invisible. It is one thing to ask whether God can make a mountain unmovable by divine hands.[42] The more interesting question is why Jesus *refuses to ask* God to move that mountain that must remain fixed (cf. 11:22–24).[43] By the time Mark's readers have reached the climax of the passion narrative, they can intuit an answer: Through prayer, Jesus has been formed into a child that can lose his life for the gospel, if God's will demands—for only by doing so can his life be made whole (8:35–37).[44] The evan-

---

40. While the point is much debated, I can further imagine that underlying both Mark and Hebrews is a tradition of a human's metaphorical self-sacrifice as a sin offering, which may extend as far back as Isa 53:12. On the evolution of that tradition, consult George Foot Moore, *Judaism in the First Centuries of the Christian Era* (New York: Schocken, 1971), 1:546–52.

41. I concede the possibility that Mark intimates its original community's supplanting Jerusalem's temple, which the evangelist may have known to have been destroyed: thus, Francis J. Moloney, *The Gospel of Mark: A Commentary* (Peabody, MA: Hendrickson, 2002), 226, 302–3, following Donald H. Juel, *Messiah and Temple: The Trial of Jesus in the Gospel of Mark*, SBLDS 31 (Missoula, MT: Scholars Press, 1977). At most, however, that is only an intimation. Mark's Gospel is never so explicit in this matter as, say, Paul's use of the cultic metaphor in 1 Cor 6:19.

42. On the Hellenistic debate over divine omnipotence and intervention, see Dowd, *Prayer, Power, and the Problem of Suffering*, 78–94.

43. *Pace* Dowd: "Now, however, God's will is different from the will of the petitioner" (*Reading Mark*, 151). In the light of Mark 14:36c, to say nothing of the resurrection's fulfillment (16:1–8) of Jesus's repeated predictions (8:31; 9:31; 9:9; 10:33–34), is it *finally* so?

44. With the benefit of other canonical and liturgical resources, later Christian theology, pondering the interwoven mysteries of God's humanity and Christ's divinity, could develop Mark's abbreviated implications: God was in Christ, allowing the death of his beloved Son

gelist emphasizes that conclusion with another, sharply etched intercalation: at precisely the moment Jesus acknowledges who he is (14:53–65), Peter lies not merely about his master but about his own identity (14:66–72). Nowhere in Mark is there a more transparent case of one who, by seeking to save his own life, utterly loses himself. But then, nowhere in Mark has Peter or any of the Twelve ever demonstrated faith or besought God in prayer (cf. 9:28–29).

Third, and finally, does suffering possess educational value in Mark's Gospel? In the terms used by Charles Talbert to characterize that view within and beyond the NT, I do not think so. Nowhere does the Second Evangelist suggest that God afflicts mortals for the purposes of training their obedience, refining their faith, or teaching them endurance (cf. 1 Pet 1:6–9; 2:19–25; 4:12–19). Contrary to Akiba, chastisements in Mark are not precious; God is no punishing agent, and affliction is terrifying. No one in Mark ever faces death with heroic dignity; between the last words of elderly Eleazar (4 Macc 5:1–6:35) and Jesus of Nazareth (Mark 15:34–37) lies a world of theological difference.[45] In another sense, however, the sympathetic reader of Mark does learn something through the pain of its protagonists, particularly Jesus. What is learned is subtler than didacticism, less utilitarian. In the Second Gospel, God does not employ suffering to enhance human virtue. Rather, it is only at the cross that one can recognize God's Son (15:39) or construe adherence to the Messiah (8:34) or understand what prayer is and why faith saves. By affliction, our moral or spiritual faculties are not expanded or disciplined. Instead, from the cross, what disciples learn is *how to learn*: how to discern reality as it truly is, how to distinguish Holy Spirit from Beelzebul (3:22–29), how to discriminate things of θεός from things of ἄνθρωπος (8:33). Of the Second Evangelist, I believe, one can justly say what J. Louis Martyn has helped us to understand about Paul, and for the same apocalyptic reasons: "The cross is *the* epistemological crisis for the simple reason that while it is in one sense followed by the resurrection, it is not replaced by the resurrection."[46] If that be so, then in Mark's Gospel,

---

for the world's redemption; Christ was of God, cooperating with his dear Father in the same work of healing love. For a somewhat Pauline interpretation of the thorny relationship in Mark between Jesus's death and God's will, see Donald H. Juel, *The Gospel of Mark*, IBT (Nashville: Abingdon, 1999), 157–65.

45. See Adela Yarbro Collins, "From Noble Death to Crucified Messiah," *NTS* 40 (1994): 481–503, who correctly points out that, like Eleazar, Jesus does offer his own life for the benefit of many (Mark 10:45; 14:24).

46. J. Louis Martyn, "Epistemology at the Turn of the Ages: 2 Corinthians 5.16," in *Christian History and Interpretation: Studies Presented to John Knox*, ed. W. R. Farmer, C. F. D. Moule, and R. R. Niebuhr (Cambridge: Cambridge University Press, 1967), 286.

suffering is fundamentally not educational but *epistemic*—in much the way that another parent who surrendered a child to death so eloquently expressed: "So suffering is down at the center of things, deep down where the meaning is. Suffering is the meaning of our world. For Love is the meaning. And Love suffers. The tears of God are the meaning of history. . . . When God's cup of suffering is full, our world's redemption is fulfilled. Until justice and peace embrace, God's dance of joy is delayed. The bells for the feast of the divine joy are the bells for the shalom of the world."[47]

47. Nicholas Wolterstorff, *Lament for a Son* (Grand Rapids: Eerdmans, 1987), 90–91.

CHAPTER 11

Mark: John's Photographic Negative

> John, last of all, aware that the bodily facts [τὰ σωματικὰ] [of Jesus] had been set forth in [Mark and] the other gospels, was urged on by his disciples, and divinely moved by the Spirit, composed a spiritual gospel [πνευματικὸν εὐαγγέλιον].
>
> —Eusebius of Caesarea, *Historia ecclesiastica* 6.14.7 (AT)

So reckoned Clement of Alexandria (155–215 CE) and other elders of the ancient church. One can understand such an interpretation: the Synoptics record nothing like John's claim, "It is the spirit that gives life; the flesh is useless. The words that I have spoken to you are spirit and life" (6:63, NRSV here and throughout; cf. 3:34). In John, Jesus is the Spirit's unique dispenser, because he comes from heaven in a manner unprecedented in the Synoptics: "I have come down from heaven, not to do my own will, but the will of him who sent me" (6:38; cf. 3:31; 6:51). Even so, Clement and his predecessors knew that the Holy Spirit is present in the Synoptics (Matt 1:18, 20; 4:1; 12:32; Mark 3:29; Luke 1:35, 41, 67; 4:1; 10:21, among others), and the Johannine Jesus is bodily enough to weep (John 11:35), be troubled (12:27; 13:21), and die (19:30).[1] Broadly serviceable, Clement's appraisal lacks precision.

Having devoted much of his career to unraveling the relationship between John and the Synoptics, D. Moody Smith (1931–2016) concluded, "John clarifies or makes explicit what is implicit or inchoate in the other Gospels or elsewhere in the New Testament."[2] Supporting Smith's judgment is the Q aphorism in

---

1. See Marianne Meye Thompson, *The Humanity of Jesus in the Fourth Gospel* (Philadelphia: Fortress, 1988).

2. D. Moody Smith, *The Theology of the Gospel of John*, NTT (Cambridge: Cambridge University Press, 1995), 64.

Luke 10:22 (= Matt 11:27): "All things have been handed over to me by my Father; and no one knows who the Son is except the Father, or who the Father is except the Son and anyone to whom the Son chooses to reveal him" (cf. John 3:35; 6:44; 8:19b; 14:7a). While agreeing that John invites construal along-side the Synoptics, I have grown less sure that Mark is more christologically rudimentary than John or is as exactly implicative of the Fourth Gospel as Smith supposes. Instead, Mark's theology impresses me as an inverted *Doppel-gänger* of John's. The metaphor that seems most apt is drawn from the science of photography: although both gospels capture the same subject, Jesus, John presents the darker areas lighter; Mark, the lighter areas darker. That is the thesis I intend to test, with concluding reflections on its theological consequences.

Two Narrative Frameworks

Let us begin by comparing items of John's narrative framework (a–f) with those of Mark (a'–f').

(a) John's prologue is the overture that announces many of this gospel's major themes: the incarnation of the divine Logos in Jesus Christ (1:1–4, 14a, 17; cf. 17:3; 20:31). Jesus is the true light that irradiates a darkened and recalcitrant world that was created through him (1:5, 9–10; cf. 3:19; 8:12; 12:46), the fullness of grace and truth (1:14, 17; cf. 8:40, 45–46; 14:6), the unique prism through which God may be seen (1:18; cf. 6:46; 14:9), the reflector of glory "as of the only Son of the Father" (1:14b; cf. 8:54; 13:32; 17:5, 24), the enactment of God's will (1:13; cf. 4:34; 5:30; 6:39–40), and the empowerment of believers to become children of God (1:12; cf. 6:29, 40, 69; 11:25–26, 52; 12:36; 14:1, 11; 17:20–21; 20:31).

(b) John the Baptizer (1:6–8, 15) serves chiefly to bear witness against him-self and for Jesus: "He must increase, but I must decrease" (3:30; cf. 1:19–35; 3:25–29; 5:33).

(c) Punctuated by three trips to Jerusalem (2:13; 6:4; 11:55), the first half of John's narrative exhibits a regular pattern: an encounter with Jesus, sometimes, though not always, provoked by a mighty work (3:1–15; 4:7–12; 5:1–9a; 6:1–15, 22–24; 9:1–8; 10:22–24; 12:20–22), excites extended debate with a heavily mono-logical Jesus (3:16–21; 4:13–38; 5:9b–47; 6:25–65; 9:9–10:18; 10:25–39; 12:23–50). In the raising of Lazarus, conversation (11:1–42) precedes miracle (11:43–44).

(d) Following a lengthy farewell to and prayer for his disciples (13:1–17:26), (e) the passion narrative unfolds with Jesus's arrest (18:1–11), interrogations (18:12–14; 18:33–19:11), crucifixion (19:17–27), death, and burial (19:28–42). Over all of these circumstances, Jesus presides masterfully, as he predicted: "No one takes [my life] from me . . . I have power to lay it down, and I have power to take it up again. I have received this command from my Father" (10:18).

(f) John ends with four appearances of the risen Jesus: to Mary Magdalene (20:1–18), most of his disciples (20:19–23), Thomas (20:24–29), and eight of his disciples by the Sea of Tiberias (21:1–23).

Mark turns inside out most of John's story line.

(a') The Second Evangelist's incipit (1:1) is terse—"The beginning of the good news of Jesus Christ, [the Son of God]"—and its scriptural epigraph (1:2–3 // Exod 23:20a; Mal 3:1a; Isa 40:3) is equivocal.[3] Precisely who are "my messenger" (Jesus or John) and "the Lord" (God or Jesus)? What does it mean to ascribe messiahship or sonship to Jesus? Apart from the baptizer's assurance that his successor will baptize with the Holy Spirit and a celestial announcement that Jesus is well pleasing to God (1:11), these questions are not clearly answered.[4] From Mark, the reader receives only faint clues about Jesus's identity and mission. John spells out everything, upfront, withholding little of significance. The reader of the prologue knows almost as much about Jesus as Jesus will later say of himself.[5]

(b') In Mark, the baptizer acclaims Jesus without naming him (1:4–8); after baptizing him (1:9), John's role is to foreshadow Jesus's arrest and execution (1:14a; 6:14–29). In the Fourth Gospel, John's arrest is mentioned in passing (3:24), his baptism of Jesus is intimated, not narrated (1:32), and his testimonies to Jesus go on and on (1:15, 26–36; 3:25–30; 5:33; 10:41).

(c') John's typical arrangement of healing, controversy, and christological disquisition is missing from Mark. Its few approximations are tightly com-

---

3. If, as a number of ancient witnesses attest, "Son of God" was absent from the original manuscript, then Mark's incipit is even more succinct.

4. The reference is metaphorical, since in Mark neither Jesus nor his disciples baptize anyone. In 10:38–39, Jesus mentions a seemingly sinister baptism he and his followers must undergo. John 4:1–3 is more straightforward but in its own way oblique: "Now when Jesus learned that the Pharisees had heard, 'Jesus is making and baptizing more disciples than John'—although it was not Jesus himself but his disciples who baptized—he left Judea and started back to Galilee."

5. Almost, though not quite everything: ὁ λόγος, for instance, appears as an appellation for Jesus only in 1:1–18. Nevertheless, "The prologue offers a breathtaking vista of God's work in the world from the beginning of time to the full realization of God's purposes" (R. Alan Culpepper, "The Prologue as Theological Prolegomenon to the Gospel of John," in *The Prologue of the Gospel of John: Literary, Theological, and Philosophical Contexts; Papers Read at the* Colloqueum Ioanneum *2013*, ed. R. Alan Culpepper, Udo Schnelle, and Jan G. van der Watt, WUNT 359 [Tübingen: Mohr Siebeck, 2016], 24).

pressed (Mark 2:1-12; 3:1-6) or radically redesigned: thus, in 7:31-37, Jesus's healing evokes astonished approbation, which he attempts to silence. The most characteristic healings in Mark, exorcism of unclean spirits (1:21-28; 3:11; 5:1-20; 6:7; 7:24-30; 9:14-29), are altogether absent from the Fourth Gospel, though John reports others' accusations of *Jesus* as having a demon (7:20; 8:48-49, 52; 10:20). Healings of the lame and blind are the only therapeutic overlaps between Mark and John, recounted in tales that do not tally (Mark 2:1-12; 8:22-26; 10:46-52; John 5:1-12; 9:1-41). The most astounding of Jesus's miracles in John, which precipitates the plot for his execution, is the raising of Lazarus (11:1-53). Its closest analogue in Mark is the raising of Jairus's daughter (5:35-43), which ends on an offbeat (5:43) that Jesus himself downplays: "Why your racket and crying? The little girl isn't dead but only sleeping" (5:39 AT; cf. John 11:11-14). In Mark, Jesus's ransacking of the temple (11:15-19) during a single visit to Jerusalem (11:1) provokes his final confrontation with the Jewish officialdom (11:27-12:27; 14:1-2). In John (2:13-22), the temple episode *inaugurates* Jesus's hostilities with "the Jews."

(d') Jesus's *Abschiedsrede* in Mark (13:1-37) is a mere breath beside the long-winded Farewell Discourse and priestly prayer in John (13:31-17:26). Even though both prepare the disciples for tribulation (Mark 13:8-23; John 15:18-19; 16:2-3, 20-22, 32-33), Mark highlights the unknowability of the climactic hour (ἡ ὥρα: 13:7-8, 32-37) even as John contends, "The hour is coming, indeed it has come" (16:32; also 16:2, 4, 25; 17:1). Mark (13:11) brushes lightly over the Holy Spirit; John (14:16-17, 25-26; 15:26-27; 16:7-15) expatiates on the Paraclete. The Second Gospel stresses endurance (13:9-13, 18-20, 28-31), which the Fourth implies (18:19); love (13:34-35; 14:21-24; 15:9-17; 17:26) and joy (15:11; 16:22-24; 17:13), the Johannine Jesus's admonition and promise, are absent from Mark 13.[6] Mark encourages readers to hold fast for a decisive event that, for John, has already come in Jesus.[7]

(e') Because the subject remains the same as in John, Mark narrates Jesus's arrest (14:43-53), trials (14:55-65; 15:1-15), execution (15:21-38), death (15:39-41), and burial (15:42-47). Jesus's demeanor in Mark, however, reverses that

---

6. "Love" (ἀγαπάω) appears only four times in Mark (12:30-31, 33), all in references to Deut 6:4-5 and Lev 19:18. "Joy" (ἡ χαρά) occurs only once (Mark 4:16), with an ambivalent intimation.

7. Paul W. Meyer: "[In John] eschatology has been replaced by *protology*. Jesus stands in no need of an eschatological vindication. He does not need to come again 'in power.' He is 'right' because God is 'the Father who has sent me'" ("'The Father': The Presentation of God in the Fourth Gospel," in *Exploring the Gospel of John in Honor of D. Moody Smith*, ed. R. Alan Culpepper and C. Clifton Black [Louisville: Westminster John Knox, 1996], 265).

in John: he is not a victor but a victim, who says little (Mark 14:48–59, 62; 15:2, 34) or nothing (14:60–61a; 15:5).

(f′) John presents four scenes of the risen Christ. The earliest manuscripts of Mark present none.

Amid such a blizzard of parallel details it is easy to lose one's focus. To reiterate what I see, John's narrative is no more "spiritual" than Mark's is "bodily." Neither does John draw to the surface what Mark has submerged. At fundamental points, whether by accident or by design, the outer surface of John's plotline is turned inward in Mark, and vice versa. For further clarification of this phenomenon, we proceed to the central subject of both gospels.[8]

Two Presentations of Jesus

In both John and Mark, Jesus is a baffling figure, but the bewilderment cuts in reverse fields.

---

8. My ankle feels the caress of a bear-trap's clamps. It is a good question whether "the central subject" of any NT document is Jesus or God: the very caution issued years ago by Nils A. Dahl when noting that God is "the neglected factor in New Testament theology" (originally published in 1975; reprinted in *Jesus the Christ: The Historical Origins of Christological Doctrine*, ed. Donald H. Juel [Minneapolis: Fortress, 1991], 153–63). Limited space precludes my giving this subject its due in the present chapter. If Marianne Meye Thompson is correct, as I believe she is, that John "always directs its readers' attention to God" (*The God of the Gospel of John* [Grand Rapids: Eerdmans, 2001], 239), then surely the same may be said of Mark (see Elizabeth Struthers Malbon, *Mark's Jesus: Characterization as Narrative Christology* [Waco, TX: Baylor University Press, 2009]). Yet the differences between these gospels' theologies, strictly speaking, are genuine. In John, "[Jesus's] nature is . . . never understood until his origin and destiny with God is truly comprehended" (D. Moody Smith, "The Presentation of Jesus in the Fourth Gospel," in *Johannine Christianity: Essays on Its Setting, Sources, and Theology* [Columbia: University of South Carolina Press, 1984], 236). Jesus's nature vis-à-vis God, with which so much of John is preoccupied, is a rare question in Mark (2:7; 4:41; 14:61; cf. 6:48–50) and never actually debated. Mark's forty-eight occurrences of ὁ θεός are unique in the NT because they predicate almost nothing about God (the exceptions being 9:37, 11:25, and 12:27). In Mark, controversies are driven not by the veracity and import of Jesus's claims to be "the Son sent by the Father" but over his reliability as an index to "the kingdom of God," which he proclaims and instantiates. The character of that kingdom intersects with "eternal life" (Mark 10:17, 30; cf. John 3:15 and 3:36 other occurrences): both imply a quality of life, appropriable by believers, structured in accordance with God's own values. Predictably John's predications about "life" tend to revolve around belief in Jesus as such, in a manner muted by Mark.

Comportment

John uninhibitedly portrays Jesus as a regal figure. As early as 1:49, a disciple says of him, "Rabbi, you are the Son of God! You are the King of Israel!"—an exclamation repeated by the great crowd upon Jesus's climactic entry to Jerusalem (12:13). Far from repudiating such acclamations, he exhorts Nathanael to watch for things even greater (1:50), and the narrator confirms Jesus's royalty (12:14–15) by way of Scripture (Zech 9:9). After feeding a multitude with paltry resources (6:1–14), they were "about to come and take him by force to make him king" (6:15a). Mary of Bethany extravagantly perfumes and anoints his feet (12:1–8). Jesus's prediction of his being lifted up from the earth (12:32) associates his cross with a throne: "He said this to indicate the kind of death he was to die" (12:33). Ascriptions of him as king, seriously or ironically, abound in various conversations with Pilate before and during Jesus's crucifixion (18:33, 37, 39; 19:12, 14, 19–21). Jesus addresses his accusers with majestic bearing: "You say that I am a king" (18:37); "You would have no power over me unless it had been given you from above" (19:11). He is crowned with thorns, dressed in purple (19:2), and carries his own crossbeam to Golgotha (19:17).[9] Supported by an entourage beneath him (19:25b–27), Jesus knows that his life is finished and affirms his end with equanimity (19:28–30). His body is given a royal burial: "a mixture of myrrh and aloes, weighing about a hundred pounds" (19:39). Jesus is no common revolutionary; otherwise, "my followers would be fighting to keep me from being handed over to the Jews" (18:36). His kingdom is not of this world (18:36), yet Jesus is sovereign over the only realm that ultimately matters.

In his account of the crucifixion, Mark employs some of the same irony: "Let the Messiah, the King of Israel, come down from the cross now, so that we may see and believe" (15:32; see also vv. 9, 12, 18, 26). In Mark, however, the language of kingship at Golgotha does not characterize Jesus's conduct but sharpens the incongruity between himself and Barabbas, a genuine insurrectionist who is released only because Jesus is hanged (15:6–15). Bartimaeus beseeches Jesus as David's son (10:47–48), but his vision is none too clear (cf. 12:35–37). Finally, Mark does not portray Jesus as a figure of sovereign majesty: of all the gospels,

---

9. Some commentators might add John 19:13, inferring that Pilate sat (ἐκάθισεν, transitively) Jesus on the judgment seat instead of (intransitively) seating himself on it (see George L. Parsenios, *Rhetoric and Drama in the Johannine Lawsuit Motif*, WUNT 258 [Tübingen: Mohr Siebeck, 2010], 38–39). Grammatically either is possible; a case can be made for both. The intransitive use seems to me burdened with fewer difficulties (Raymond E. Brown, *The Gospel according to John (xiii–xxi)*, AB 29A [Garden City, NY: Doubleday, 1970], 880–81). I worry that the alternative fits my argument too conveniently.

Mark's description of the triumphal entry is least concentrated on Jesus himself (11:9–10; cf. John 12:13; Matt 21:9; Luke 19:38). Jesus exercises unconventional authority over unclean spirits (1:21–27; 3:15; 6:7) and religious practice (2:1–12; 7:1–23; 11:27–33). Unusual power attends his healings (5:30; cf. 6:5). Most impressive, however, is the degree to which Jesus renounces his power while reinforcing the necessity of his suffering in the stark, carefully situated predictions of his death and resurrection in 8:31, 9:31, and 10:33–34—none of which is paralleled in John. There is nothing remotely Johannine about Mark's tormented Jesus, prostrate and disregarded by companions in Gethsemane (14:32–42). Indeed, the Johannine Jesus overrides his Markan counterpart: "Now my soul is troubled. And what should I say—'Father, save me from this hour'? No, it is for this reason that I have come to this hour. Father, glorify your name" (John 12:27–28a). That magisterial Jesus receives instantaneous confirmation: "Then a voice came from heaven, 'I have glorified it, and I will glorify it again'" (12:28b). When Mark's crucified Jesus, abandoned by friend and foe alike (14:66–72; 15:29–32), cries, "My God, my God, why have you forsaken me?" (15:34)—a question unimaginable on the lips of the Johannine Jesus, whose Father always hears him (John 11:41–42; 17:1–5)—there is no answer but silence. Once again, in one gospel, the darkest areas are lightest; in the other, the lightest areas are darkest.

An addendum to this section is prompted by one of Mark's most mysterious passages, which lacks equivalent in John: the transfiguration of Jesus (9:2–8). Jesus is momentarily glimpsed in heavenly radiance: perhaps a window onto "the kingdom of God . . . come in power," promised in 9:1, surely a warrant to "listen to him!" (9:7). His immediate instruction, delivered bluntly and strictly, is dedicated to self-renunciation unto death, endorsed by God through resurrection (8:30–38; 9:9–13). Jesus transfigured is a prolepsis of the glory promised those who endure persecution like his own (8:38; 13:26), bypassing painless privilege (10:35–45). In John, the legend of the transfiguration would be redundant: its Jesus, from start to finish, *is* "the true light" of "the world" (John 1:9; 8:12; 9:5; 12:46) that exposes evil and gives life (3:19–20; 8:12). The glory of the Johannine Jesus never evanesces: it is beheld by believers (1:14; 11:40; 17:24), revealed by his signs (2:11; 11:4), culminated in the hour of his death (12:23; 17:4), and ratified by the Father (12:28; 13:32; 16:14; 17:1, 5). C. K. Barrett grasps the nettle: "The paradox of the Son of man [in John 3:13] is that even when on earth he is in heaven; the mythical—or historical—descent and ascent is of such a kind that effectively the Son of man is in both places at once: the top and the bottom of the ladder."[10]

---

10. C. K. Barrett, "Paradox and Dualism," in *Essays on John* (Philadelphia: Westminster, 1982), 110–11.

Titles

Limitations of space preclude extended examination of the titles attributed to Jesus in the Second and Fourth Gospels, but for our purposes, such is unnecessary. In both, "Son [of God]" and "Son of Man" predominate as designations of Jesus. In John, Jesus usually refers to himself as "the Son" (3:16–17, 35–36; 5:19–23, 26; 6:40; 8:36; 14:13; 17:1 ["your Son"]), which corresponds with his characteristic reference to God as "the Father [who] loves the Son and has placed all things in his hands" (3:35).[11] Like "Son of God" (seven times in John, three of which are Jesus's self-references [5:25; 10:36; 11:4]), this metaphor's primary connotation is Jesus's distinctively filial relationship to God: "The Father and I are one" (10:30). That, of course, is the gravamen of his antagonists' complaint that Jesus was "making himself equal to God" (5:18). Jesus also refers to himself as "Son of Man" (1:51; 5:27; 6:27, 53, 62; 8:28; 9:35; 12:23; 13:31); as in the Synoptics, this designation issues only from Jesus's lips.[12] Its precise nuance is disputed; I am inclined to agree with those who argue that, in John, "Son of Man" essentially restates the incarnational claim in 1:14: "the Word became flesh."[13]

Mark moves in a different direction. Only twice in the Second Gospel does Jesus speak of himself as "the Son" (12:6; 13:32). Others address him as "Son of God": demons, who recognize in him a superior enemy (1:24; 3:11; 5:7); the high priest, who asks, "Are you the Messiah, the Son of the Blessed One?" and receives a positive answer (14:61–62); the centurion at the cross (15:39); and, of supreme significance, the heavenly voice (בַּת קוֹל) at Jesus's baptism (1:11) and transfiguration (9:7). In the latter passages, conflating several OT texts (Gen 22:2; Ps 2:7; Isa 42:1; 53), Mark's theology intersects with John's:

---

11. By my count, Jesus denotes God as "the Father," "my Father," or "your Father" 105 times in John.

12. The exceptions: "The crowd answered him, . . . 'How can you say that the Son of Man must be lifted up? Who is this Son of Man?'" (John 12:34); "Truly, I say to you, all sins will be forgiven the sons of men, and whatever blasphemies they utter" (Mark 3:28 RSV).

13. Francis J. Moloney, *The Johannine Son of Man*, BSR 14, 2nd ed. (Rome: Libreria Ateneo Salesiano, 1978), esp. 213; Douglas R. A. Hare, *The Son of Man Tradition* (Minneapolis: Fortress, 1990), 111; Craig R. Koester, *The Word of Life: A Theology of John's Gospel* (Grand Rapids: Eerdmans, 2008), 97; Marianne Meye Thompson, *John: A Commentary*, NTL (Louisville: Westminster John Knox, 2015), 55–58. "It is as Son of man that Jesus forms the connecting link between the earthly and heavenly spheres; his earthly existence is the place where heavenly things become visible, and also the place where heavenly things are rejected by mankind" (C. K. Barrett, *The Gospel according to St. John: An Introduction with Commentary and Notes on the Greek Text*, 2nd ed. [Philadelphia: Westminster, 1978], 212).

God reveals a uniquely intimate, familial relationship with Jesus.[14] Yet Mark's principal appellation for Jesus is "Son of Man," which occurs thirteen times, always by Jesus as an oblique form of self-reference.[15] The phrase conveys different, mutually interpretive senses in Mark: Jesus as possessing extraordinary authority on earth (2:10, 28), an apocalyptic figure who will return at history's climax (8:38; 13:26; 14:62), and one who will be vindicated for having suffered ignominy and death for others (8:31; 9:9, 12, 31b; 10:33–34, 45; 14:21, 41). Mark accents the last of these three undertones: references to the suffering and vindicated Son of Man outnumber the others by a ratio of three or four to one.

To sum up these findings, in both John and Mark, "Son of God" and "Son of Man" are important, complementary modes of expressing aspects of Jesus's significance, but their comparative weights vary in roughly inverse proportion. In the Fourth Gospel, "Son of Man" is secondary, serving "the Son [of God]" as a way of saying that enfleshed in this man, Jesus, is the Word that saves the world (John 3:16; 4:42). In the Second Gospel, "the Son [of God]" is secondary, serving "Son of Man" as a way of saying that God has accredited and will vindicate this one, who "give[s] his life as a ransom for many" (Mark 10:45; cf. 1:11; 9:7).[16] Put differently, John's readers are invited to take their interpre-

---

14. Mark and John's uses of Scripture are mare's nests beyond solution here. In general, both evangelists assume reciprocity between the comprehensibility of the Christian witness and Scripture's intelligibility. Mark's Jesus upholds the law with an authority superior to Moses's (7:10; 10:2–9; 12:18–27); his teaching and death amplify the prophets and psalms (7:6–7; 14:62; 15:24, 34). John more boldly insists that the Scriptures testify to Jesus, apart from whom their fulfillment is impossible and their intent is bound to be misunderstood (5:39). For this reason, citations of "your law" defend Jesus against charges brought against him (8:17; 10:34; cf. 7:22–23, 51).

15. Whether, in Mark 8:38, 13:26–27, and 14:62, Jesus indicates a figure other than himself is a matter of dispute. Read in their respective contexts, these verses suggest that Mark believes that Jesus, and no one else, is the Son of Man (C. Clifton Black, *Mark*, ANTC (Nashville: Abingdon, 2011], 201). Referring to John 3:13, Culpepper identifies another christological inversion germane to our analysis: whereas Mark refers to the Son of Man's return in glory, "in John, [the Son of Man] has come from above (descent) and will return to his Father (ascent)" ("The Christology of the Johannine Writings," in *Who Do You Say That I Am? Essays on Christology*, ed. Mark Allan Powell and David R. Bauer [Louisville: Westminster John Knox, 1999], 76).

16. In Mark, Jesus publicly confirms his identity as "Son of God" only once: in frank acceptance of the high priest's incredulous acclamation of him as such (14:61–62). This, by no mere coincidence, pulls the trigger for the Son of Man's deliverance to death by the hands of sinners (8:31; 9:31; 10:33–34). By contrast, various interlocutors throughout John address Jesus as "the Lamb of God [who takes away the sin of the world]" (1:29; cf. 1:36), the "Messiah" (4:25–26), the "Holy One of God" (6:68–70a), "the Son of Man" (9:35–38),

tive cue from its prologue; Mark's readers, from the passion. These opposite narrative orientations—one at the beginning, the other at the end—obversely attract and correlate their gospels' dominant titles for Jesus.

Discourse

Relevant to this inquiry is Jesus's speech, which may be considered on two fronts. The *style* of the Johannine Jesus is elevated, redundant, even pretentious.[17] He is remarkably loquacious and "congenitally incapable of giving a straight answer."[18] After healing a paralytic at a pool by Jerusalem's Sheep Gate, Jesus answers his critics in 520 uninterrupted Greek words (5:19–47). On the last day of the Feast of Tabernacles, he delivers another address of 704 words (8:12–58, with brief interventions by others). Interrupted seven times by his disciples, Jesus's parting words to them (13:31–16:33), which elide into a closing prayer (17:1b–26), weigh in at around 2,140 words. At 14:31b, he inserts what has been dubbed "a delayed dramatic exit" characteristic of classical tragedies—"Get up, let us go from here" (AT)—then keeps right on talking.[19] In 16:12, he says, "I still have many things to say to you, but you cannot bear them now." Although John probably intends poignancy, many commentators have heaved a sigh of relief—while Jesus continues to elaborate. By contrast, the speech of Mark's Jesus tends to be abruptly clipped: "Follow me" (2:14). "Let anyone with ears to hear listen!" (4:9, 23). "Do you not yet understand?" (8:21: posed of his disciples after a Q and A of non sequiturs that explains nothing [8:17–20]). "Salt is good; but if salt has lost its saltiness, how can you season it? Have salt in yourselves, and be at peace with one another" (9:50). Normally the Markan Jesus keeps his comments crisp and shuts others up (1:34, 44; 3:12; 7:36; 8:26, 30; 9:9; 11:33; 12:17; 15:2).[20] John and Mark offer their readers a choice in how they shall be confused: by a Jesus too prolix, or one who is too laconic.

"the Messiah, the Son of God, the one coming into the world" (11:27), and even "My Lord and my God!" (20:28). Jesus refuses none of these designations, because the Father has granted such belief to those who apply them (6:29, 40, 65).

17. On John's use of rhetorical grandeur, deemed suitable for sublime subjects, see C. Clifton Black, "'The Words That You Gave to Me I Have Given to Them,'" in *The Rhetoric of the Gospel: Theological Artistry in the Gospels and Acts*, 2nd ed. (Louisville: Westminster John Knox, 2013), 83–99.

18. R. Alan Culpepper, *Anatomy of the Fourth Gospel: A Study in Literary Design* (Philadelphia: Fortress, 1983), 112.

19. George L. Parsenios, *Departure and Consolation: The Johannine Farewell Discourses in Light of Greco-Roman Literature*, NovTSup 117 (Leiden: Brill, 2005), 55–70.

20. The longest, usually interrupted, discourses of Jesus in Mark are 4:3–32 (the parable

Whether sympathetic or adversarial, Jesus's audiences in both gospels misunderstand his words (Mark 7:18; 8:21; 9:32; John 3:10; 10:6; 12:16). The causes of their incomprehension, however, are mirror images that involve his teaching's *substance*. Mark's Jesus characteristically speaks in parables: "dark sayings" (מְשָׁלִים; cf. Ps 78:2), vivid metaphors that cryptically liken the irruption of God's sovereignty, "the kingdom of God" (Mark 1:15), to aspects of everyday life (4:1–34). Repeatedly Jesus points to that kingdom (9:1, 47; 10:14–15, 23–25; 14:25); rarely does he talk of himself, and, when doing so, the references are elliptical (2:10, 28; 8:31; 12:6; 13:32). In John, the circumstances are reversed virtually point for point. Only twice does Jesus mention the kingdom of God (John 3:3, 5); only the aphorisms of a grain of earth (12:24) and a woman in labor (16:21) approximate Mark's parables in form. Instead, the Johannine Jesus proclaims, "*My* kingdom is not from this world" (18:36, emphasis added) and persistently speaks of himself from a post-Easter perspective as the defining fulfillment of human need: "I am the bread of life" (6:35, 48; cf. 6:41, 51); "I am the true vine" (15:1; cf. 15:5); "I am the light of the world" (8:12; 9:5); "I am the gate for the sheep" (10:7); "I am the good shepherd" (10:11, 14); "I am the way, and the truth, and the life" (14:6); "I am the resurrection and the life" (11:25). These ἐγώ εἰμι sayings may allude to the name of Israel's God (Exod 3:14; Isa 43:11), a likelihood that emerges in John 8:58 and 18:5 to the enragement (8:59) or flooring (18:6) of Jesus's opponents. The grounds for his execution, blasphemy, are implausibly pronounced in Mark 14:64;[21] the stronger case is made in John 10:33: "It is not for a good work that we are going to stone you, but for blasphemy, because you, though only a human being, are making yourself God." The unbelieving world (ὁ κόσμος) cannot understand the Johannine Jesus, because he is from above and not of this world (8:23).

Again, the Fourth Gospel's presentation is the Second's turned backside forward. Mark offers a Jesus very much of this world who riddles *to engender* obscurity (4:11–12). The assertions of the Johannine Jesus are so blatant—"the Father is in me and I am in the Father" (10:38)—that their acceptance is impossible apart from belief. In Mark, the truth about Jesus is temporarily withheld (1:34; 3:12; 5:43; 7:36; 8:30; 9:9, 30): "For there is nothing hidden, except to be disclosed; nor is anything secret, except to come to light" (4:22). In John (3:19), "this is the judgment, that the light *has come* into the world, and people loved

---

chapter), 7:6–23 (on defilement), and 13:5–37 (the eschatological address on the Mount of Olives).

21. In Mark 14:62, Jesus employs a circumlocution, "the right hand of the Power," to avoid pronouncing the divine name. Having ears to hear, the high priest has not heard (4:12; 8:18).

darkness rather than light because their deeds were evil." The true light already enlightens the world (1:9); those unable to behold his glory, as could Isaiah (1:14; 12:41), hate the light (3:20) and are blinded by it (12:40). Jesus "came into this world for judgment so that those who do not see may see, and those who do see may become blind" (9:39).

Deeds

Intimately connected with these evangelists' converse outlooks are their estimations of Jesus's marvelous works. The miracle at Cana (John 2:1–11) and the healing of the official's son (4:46–54) as well as others who are sick (6:2) are "signs" (σημεῖα) that reveal Jesus's glory and are capable of kindling faith (2:11, 23; 4:48; 10:40–42; 12:37). Though somewhat in the dark (coming to Jesus by night), Nicodemus glimpses the truth: "Rabbi, we know that you are a teacher who has come from God; for no one can do these signs that you do apart from the presence of God" (3:2). Those seeking Jesus in Capernaum ask for a sign, that they may see it and believe him; he offers them true bread from heaven, for which they plead (6:32–34). After receiving sight from Jesus, a man who had been blind from birth declares his faith and worships the Son of Man (9:1, 6, 38). Another sign, the raising of Lazarus, stimulates a crowd to welcome Jesus to Jerusalem (12:17–18). Although "the Jews," who by definition do not believe (7:1; 8:48, 52; 9:22; 10:31; 11:8; 19:12), react to Jesus's signs with incomprehension (2:18–21) or fear (11:47–48), many of them do believe on the basis of what they have seen (8:31; 11:45; 12:11): "When the Messiah comes, will he do more signs than this man has done?" (7:31; cf. 9:16). For John, that question is rhetorical. "Now Jesus did many other signs in the presence of his disciples, which are not written in this book. But these are written so that you may come to believe that Jesus is the Messiah, the Son of God, and that through believing you may have life in his name" (20:30–31).

Mark would likely concur with that testimony, with one reservation: the probative value of signs. The Second Evangelist evinces no reluctance in detailing Jesus's exorcisms and healings (1:21–34; 1:40–45; 3:7–15; 5:1–43; 6:53–56; among others). By linking faith with restoration (4:35–41; 5:34, 36; 9:14–29) and vicious misapprehension of Jesus's power with unbelief (2:6–7; 3:1–6; 3:22; 6:1–6a), Mark rhymes with John. Yet Mark is noticeably skittish about construing "power" (5:30; 6:14) or "mighty works" (6:2, 5; 9:39) with σημεῖα.[22] Dispu-

---

22. Mark 13:26 may constitute an exception: the advent of "the Son of Man with great power [δυνάμεως πολλῆς] and glory." True, Mark does not identify this occurrence as a

tatious Pharisees who ask "for a sign from heaven, to test him," are rebuffed as spokesmen of "this [faithless] generation" (8:11–13; cf. 8:38; 9:19). Likewise, "false messiahs and false prophets will appear and produce signs and omens, to lead astray, if possible, the elect" (13:22).[23] Such a position is no making patent of what is latent in John. This is retroversion of Johannine theology.

DISCIPLES AND DISCIPLESHIP

The disciples in John exhibit a capacity to change their minds and grow in understanding.[24] As early as John 1:46, Nathanael, "an Israelite indeed, in whom is no guile" (1:47 RSV), wonders whether anything good can come out of Nazareth. Moments later, he has hyperbolically reversed his opinion of Jesus (1:49). Similarly, Martha of Bethany begins by lamenting Jesus's delay in rescuing her brother but, with Jesus's help, promptly entrusts herself to him (11:20–27). Though initially befuddled by the rabbi's teaching (3:1–10), Nicodemus makes surprise reappearances to defend Jesus and to anoint his remains (7:50–51; 19:39). Like the disciples generally (4:27, 31–34), at first the Samaritan woman is not tuned into Jesus's frequency to understand him (4:1–15), but her awareness develops into credible evidence to her fellow citizens (4:28–30, 39–42); likewise, Mary Magdalene, the earliest witness and first evangelist of her risen Rabbouni (20:11–18). Even though Jesus's teaching perplexes members of the Twelve (6:60; 11:16; 14:5, 8, 22), eventually they tumble to the truth: "Now we know that you know all things, and do not need to have anyone question you; by this we believe that you came from God" (16:30). Early on, Simon Peter professes that his Lord has "the words of eternal life" (6:68), receives his master's washing (13:6–9), denies him (18:15–27) as foretold (13:36–38), is ultimately absolved (21:7, 15–19), and with his fellows is authorized to perpetuate the risen Jesus's mission (20:19–23). Shorn of doubt (20:24–27), Thomas utters the climactic declaration: "My Lord and my God!" (20:28). Only two disciples remain unwavering: Judas Iscariot, the betrayer destined to be lost (6:71; 12:4; 13:2, 26–30; 17:12; 18:2–5), and the Beloved Disciple (13:23; 19:26; 20:2; 21:20–23),

---

"sign"; nevertheless, it offers a reliable, albeit delayed, response to distressed disciples who, in 13:4, have asked Jesus to point them toward a σημεῖον of the final judgment. For a detailed argument along this line, see chapter 14.

23. Among the considerable intrinsic evidence against the authenticity of Mark 16:9–20 is its easy association of "signs" with faith and evangelism (vv. 17, 20).

24. See Susan E. Hylen, *Imperfect Believers: Ambiguous Characters in the Gospel of John* (Louisville: Westminster John Knox, 2009).

the first to understand the import of the empty tomb (20:8; cf. 21:7) and the Johannine community's paradigmatic witness (21:24).

The disciples in John enjoy special benefits. Because the Father has irrevocably entrusted them to the Son in whom they believe (6:38–45; 10:27–29; 17:6–12, 20–24), they do "not come under judgment, but [have] passed from death to life" (5:24). They abide in Jesus, as branches are nourished by the vine (15:1–8), and are sustained by the Paraclete, Jesus's postmortem proxy and continuing presence (14:16–17, 25–27; 15:26–27; 16:17–25). They enjoy post-Easter hindsight (2:22; 12:16; 13:7).

The Twelve in Mark enjoy almost none of these advantages, and their fortunes deteriorate as that gospel plays out.[25] They accept Jesus's initial call (1:16–20; 2:14; 3:13–18a), giving up everything to follow him (10:28–31), fulfill their first missionary assignment (6:7–13), obey the teacher's ludicrous demands (6:30–44; 8:1–10; 11:1–8), catch glimmers of his identity (8:29; 9:2–8), and prepare his final Passover (14:12–16). Meanwhile they are never able to shake off their fear (4:35–41; 6:46–52; 9:32; 10:32; 16:8). Not once in Mark does a member of the Twelve "believe" or demonstrate the faith detailed or suggested by such needy nobodies as a paralytic's entourage (2:5), the chronic menstruant (5:34), the Syro-Phoenician woman (7:24–30), the father of an epileptic child (9:14–29), blind Bartimaeus (10:46–52), Jerusalem's poor widow (12:41–44), or the anointer memorialized in Bethany (14:3–9). Repeatedly the Twelve ignore or reject Jesus's plain training in cross-bearing discipleship, bickering among themselves for exalted status (8:32–33; 9:33–34; 10:35–41). None of them appropriates power available only through prayer (9:28–29). One colludes with Jerusalem's chief priests to betray Jesus (14:10–11, 43–46). Three sleep during his anguish in Gethsemane (14:32–42; cf. 13:33–37). Another triply denies knowing him (14:66–72). All forsake him, fleeing at his arrest (14:50–52). Despite their receipt of "the secret [τὸ μυστήριον] of the kingdom of God," they are as blinded and deafened by it as others (4:10–13; cf. 6:52; 8:17–21). Among all of Jesus's opponents in this gospel, only Peter is addressed as Satan (8:33; cf. John 8:44; 13:27). His last words about Jesus are devastating: "I do not know this man you are talking about" (Mark 14:71). Redemption by the risen Jesus awaits him and his confreres in Galilee (16:7), but, since the remaining female followers flee the empty tomb in fear, speechless of the Easter message, one never reads of the message's delivery (16:1–8).

The disciples in John become stronger; their Markan counterparts fade away. Of course this topsy-turvy has another involution: the Second Gospel

---

25. The Holy Spirit's support of beleaguered believers in Mark 13:11 is analogous to John 16:8–13.

suggests a denser approach to faith and a more developed account of moral agency than does the Fourth. In Mark, faith oscillates, swinging from confidence to panic, caught by weak mortals before slipping from their grasp (5:33–36; 9:23–24). Because faith is more a matter of volition than of cognition, its antipode is cowardice (4:40) or fear (5:15, 33, 36), which repudiates Jesus's authority to wield God's potency (6:3c–4; 11:27–33). At Gethsemane (14:32–42) and Golgotha (15:21–33), Jesus himself reveals the depth of trust that activates self-sacrificial service to God for the gospel's sake. At Easter, God's own fidelity is validated (16:6). John's articulation of faith risks reduction to "believing in Jesus" or believing in God as revealed by Jesus (e.g., 6:29, 40; 12:44; 14:1; 17:21).[26] That decision entails genuine peril (9:22; 12:42; 16:2), but, apart from 9:1–41, one rarely witnesses its cost.[27] As for disciples' moral responsibility, Mark warns that "the cares of the world, and the lure of wealth, and the desire for other things come in and choke the word, and it yields nothing" (4:19). A devout man's possessions block his inheritance of eternal life (10:17–22); the kingdom of God belongs to the child with nothing (10:13–17). Avarice ruptures the social fabric, perverting filial responsibility (7:6–13; cf. Exod 20:12; Deut 5:16), easing divorce, whose economic burden fell primarily on the wife (Mark 10:2–9), and encouraging fraud (10:19b; cf. Deut 24:14). To all of these points, John says nothing. In Mark, accountability resolves itself in unfettered love of God and neighbor (12:28–34; cf. Deut 6:4; Lev 19:18). In John, love is centripetal: "love one another" (13:34–35; 15:12, 17).

Light Sensitivity

If there be value in this essay's experiment, I shall leave to others its *traditionsgeschichtlich* or literary-critical implications. Consonant with the attitudes of the biblical authors, I am more interested in this study's theological upshot. Many years ago, Raymond Brown (1928–1998) concluded, "With Käsemann, we agree that the church did not make a mistake in taking the Fourth Gospel into the canon, but it would have been a mistake if it had not placed the

---

26. The noun πίστις never occurs in John; the verb πιστεύειν, ninety-nine times.

27. Yet Leander E. Keck is correct that, at least by implication, Johannine dualism evokes "a decision: either to deny the validity of Jesus' construal of one's condition (and thereby to remain determinedly in it) or to affirm that Jesus is right and so have the grounding of one's existence reconstituted, a change so radical that the appropriate metaphor for it is being 'begotten by God'" ([John 1:12b–13]; "Derivation as Destiny: 'Of-ness' in Johannine Christology, Anthropology, and Soteriology," in Culpepper and Black, *Exploring the Gospel of John*, 284).

Gospel According to Mark alongside the Gospel According to John."[28] With all due respect to that *magister in sacra pagina*, I think the language of error puts our assessment of these writings on a wrong footing. For Christian faith, the Second and Fourth Gospels are more than canonical complements. In my view, these gospels are, in general aspect and many matters of detail, nearly diametrical opposites whose attraction, each to the other, binds the tensive, insoluble elements of the Christian confession: "The place of weakness, when it is also the place of obedience to God, is the place where the power of God is made known and exercised."[29] This keynote, as old as Phil 2:5–11, must be reclaimed by the church in every generation, tempted to abstract one of the Christ hymn's stanzas to the other's excision. Detached from his resurrection, Jesus's crucifixion is tragic farce. Divorced from his crucifixion, Jesus's resurrection is grotesque Fantasyland. Let John be John. Let Mark be Mark. Reading the one while simultaneously sensitive to the other's rejoinder develops a portrait of the gospel neither bleached nor blackened but properly exposed.

28. Raymond E. Brown, "The Kerygma of the Gospel according to John: The Johannine View of Jesus in Modern Studies," *Int* 21 (1967): 400, referring to Ernst Käsemann, *The Testament of Jesus: A Study of the Gospel of John in the Light of Chapter 17* (London: SCM, 1968), 74–78.

29. Edwyn Clement Hoskyns and Francis Noel Davey, *Crucifixion-Resurrection: The Pattern of the Theology and Ethics of the New Testament* (London: SPCK, 1981), 130.

CHAPTER 12

Christ Crucified in Paul and in Mark

Coincidences . . . are a spiritual sort of puns.

—G. K. Chesterton[1]

UNTIL JOEL MARCUS REOPENED THE QUESTION with a sharp critique of Martin Werner's best-known monograph, four score and three years after its publication, the matter of Mark's relationship with Paul had largely lain moribund.[2] Perhaps that's not surprising. Mark's most salient characteristic, its narrative of Jesus, is manifestly lacking in Paul's letters, which offer only the tiniest droplets of information about "the Lord" (e.g., 1 Cor 9:5, 14; 11:23–25; 15:3–7; Gal 1:19; 4:4).[3] Conversely, those letters' most distinctive aspect—their author's creative engagement with the vicissitudes of early Christian communities—is, if extant in the Second Gospel, for the most part cloaked. For centuries, Paul has been elevated alongside John as earliest Christianity's seminal thinker, the NT's theological titan. Mark, by contrast, has been stereotyped as little more than a rube storyteller whose interests were more historical, or historicist, than theological. Unlike Ignatius, Mark acknowledges no direct Pauline influence (Ign. *Eph.* 12.2; *Rom.* 4.3); nor does that gospel articulate many of the apostle's preeminent theological concerns, such as the justification of sinful humanity

---

1. *Irish Impressions* (London: Collins Sons & Co., 1919), 203.
2. Joel Marcus, "Mark—Interpreter of Paul," *NTS* 46 (2000): 473–87; cf. Martin Werner, *Der Einfluss paulinischer Theologie im Markusevangelium: Eine Studie zur neutestamentlichen Theologie*, BZNW 1 (Giessen: Töpelmann, 1923). For further reflections on this subject, see chapter 6 of the present volume.
3. Consult Victor Paul Furnish, *Jesus according to Paul*, UJT (Cambridge: Cambridge University Press, 1993), esp. 19–65.

by grace through faith (Rom 1:17; 3:21–26) and Jesus's post-Easter enthronement as Lord and Son of God (Rom 1:4; Phil 2:9–11).[4]

CLEARING THE TABLE

The distance between Paul the apostle and Mark the Evangelist has not always
been perceived as great. In Christian tradition, links between them have long
been forged and persist in some sectors, despite their loosening by historical
criticism.[5] Within critical scholarship by the mid-nineteenth century, at least
two rapprochements between the Pauline epistles and the Markan Gospel were
possible: one, theological; the other, historical; both, with hindsight's benefit,
problem-fraught. An irreversible torrent has washed over the exegetical dam
in the one hundred sixty-three years since Gustav Volkmar proposed that
Mark was an allegorization of Pauline teaching, that gospel being a life not
of Jesus but of Paul.[6] Such a position now appears eccentric on its face. Indeed, Volkmar's assumptions about traces of Paulinism in Mark were weighed
and found wanting by Werner, who found within that gospel an indebted-
ness, shared with Paul, to early Christian beliefs but virtually nothing of that
apostle's distinctive interests.[7] Werner's assessment has since been refined, in
some quarters questioned; whether it has by now been overturned is a subject
for debate.[8]

A more oblique yet seemingly more propitious strategy for relating Paul
and Mark was to regard that gospel and the other Synoptics as later exemplars
of a Jesus tradition to which, it was assumed, Paul occasionally alluded (cf.,
e.g., Mark 9:42; and parr. = Rom 14:13; Mark 10:11–12; and parr. = 1 Cor 7:10–11;
Mark 14:22–24; and parr. = 1 Cor 11:23–26). Rumbling not far beneath the
search for parallel passages in the Pauline letters and the gospels is, of course,

---

4. The surely secondary ending of Mark at 16:9–20 (A C D K X Δ Θ Π *f*[13] vg syr[c, p, h,]
pal cop[sa, bo, fa] et al.) appears inclined toward these Pauline *theologoumena* (N.B. vv. 16, 19).

5. Consult C. Clifton Black, *Mark: Images of an Apostolic Interpreter*, SPNT (Minneapolis: Fortress; Edinburgh: T&T Clark, 2001), esp. 50–60, 149–56, 165–71, 183–91.

6. Gustav Volkmar, *Die Religion Jesu* (Leipzig: Brockhaus, 1857).

7. Werner, *Der Einfluss paulinischer Theologie im Markusevangelium*.

8. See, among others, Vincent Taylor, *The Gospel according to St. Mark: The Greek Text
with Introduction, Notes, and Indexes* (London: Macmillan, 1952), 125–29; Kazimierz Romaniuk, "Le Problème des Paulinismes dans l'Évangile de Marc," *NTS* 23 (1977): 266–74;
Andreas Lindemann, *Paulus im ältesten Christentum: Das Bild des Apostels und die Rezeption
der paulinischen Theologie in der frühchristlichen Literatur bis Marcion*, BHT 58 (Tübingen:
Mohr Siebeck, 1979), 151–54.

the heavily disputed question of Paul's relation to Jesus. Victor Furnish's land-mark survey of that controversy arrived at this conclusion: "the Jesus-Paul debate has not ever been significantly advanced, nor will a solution of the Jesus-Paul problem ever be finally achieved, by locating parallel passages in Paul and the Gospels."[9] Viewed in the light of subsequent research, Furnish's appraisal remains apt, and for precisely those reasons that he underscored: the subjectivity of criteria for ascertaining Pauline allusions to Jesus's teachings and the problem of establishing linear development from even demonstrable parallels. So far as I can tell, the nature and degree of continuity between Jesus and Paul appear at present as unresolved as ever, throwing the related ques-tion—whether any traditions link the letters and the gospels—into a veritable stalemate.[10] If some intersection of Paul and Mark once appeared to open up a *Hauptstrasse* for exegetical traffic, now more than ever their intersection

9. Victor Paul Furnish, "The Jesus-Paul Debate: From Baur to Bultmann," *BJRL* 47 (1964–1965): 342–81, rev. repr. in *Paul and Jesus: Collected Essays*, ed. A. J. M. Wedderburn, JSNTSup 37 (Sheffield: JSOT Press, 1989), 17–50 (quotation, 44).

10. Among the participants in this reinvigorated debate, see especially Franz Neirynck, "Paul and the Sayings of Jesus," in *L'Apôtre Paul: Personalité, style et conception du ministère*, ed. A. Vanhoye, BETL 73 (Leuven: Leuven University Press; Peeters, 1986), 265–321; James D. G. Dunn, "Jesus Tradition in Paul," in *Studying the Historical Jesus: Evaluations of the State of Current Research*, ed. Bruce Chilton and Craig A. Evans, NTTS 19 (Leiden: Brill, 1994), 155–78; David Wenham, *Paul: Follower of Jesus or Founder of Christianity?* (Grand Rapids: Eerdmans, 1995); James G. Crossley, "Mark, Paul and the Question of Influences," in *Paul and the Gospels: Christologies, Conflicts and Convergences*, ed. Michael F. Bird and Joel Willitts, LNTS 411 (London: T&T Clark, 2011), 10–29; Michael F. Bird, "Mark: Interpreter of Peter and Disciple of Paul," in Bird and Willitts, *Paul and the Gospels*, 39–61; Michael Kok, "Does Mark Narrate the Pauline Kerygma of 'Christ Crucified'? Challenging an Emerging Consensus on Mark as a Pauline Gospel," *JSNT* 37 (2014): 139–60; Oda Wischmeyer, Da-vid C. Sim, and Ian J. Elmer, eds., *Paul and Mark: Comparative Essays Part I; Two Authors at the Beginnings of Christianity*, BZNW 198 (Berlin: de Gruyter, 2014); Eve-Marie Becker, Troels Engberg-Pederson, and Mogens Müller, eds., *Mark and Paul: Comparative Essays Part II; For and against Pauline Influence on Mark*, BZNW 199 (Berlin: de Gruyter, 2014); Margaret M. Mitchell, "Mark, the Long-Form Pauline εὐαγγέλιον," in *Modern and An-cient Literary Criticism of the Gospels: Continuing the Debate on Gospel Genre(s)*, ed. Robert Matthew Calhoun, David P. Moessner, and Tobias Nicklas, WUNT 451 (Tübingen: Mohr Siebeck, 2020), 201–17. It seems to me that the question of Paul's knowledge and use of Je-sus traditions parallels, in some interesting ways, the debate concerning John's knowledge and use of the Synoptics. In both cases, the evidence is ambiguous and admits of varying, plausible interpretations; in both cases, the way forward may lie in thinking afresh about, and perhaps reframing, the kinds of questions that may be most fruitfully addressed to the limited primary data at our disposal.

looks like a *Sackgasse*. Why bother to reopen it? There are, I think, at least three reasons for doing so.

First, and most basically, Pauline theology needs location not only in the variegated worlds of Judaism and Hellenism but also within the narrower swath of primitive Christianity. Written probably less than twenty years after Paul's extant letters, Mark's Gospel should offer some help, though of a general sort, in "putting Paul in his place."[11] And those letters can surely return the favor for Markan interpretation. The impulse to situate the Second Gospel within one or another of the religious exigencies of Paul's letters, which in the twentieth century may have reached its apex with the work of Theodore Weeden, has not been wrongheaded, though at times it has proceeded to an improbable extreme.[12] Working as responsible historians with a proper sense of chronology, Pauline exegetes have been understandably chary of reaching beyond Paul's letters to later Christian documents for interpretive help. The price they have paid for that scrupulous self-confinement, however, has typically been exacted in one or another mirror-reading: conjectural inversions of Paul's surface concerns, pressed (with varying degrees of plausibility) into foils for his letters' interpretation.[13] As C. K. Barrett observed, "There is all too little evidence to inform us about the Christian tradition, oral and written, in the first Christian century, and we cannot afford to neglect any of it."[14] Comparative study of Pauline and Markan theologies should prove instructive, even if the result be little more than a demonstration of broad bands of similarity amid proliferative variety.

Another reason for renewing this investigative lease involves some angles of vision on Mark and Paul adopted by their modern interpreters. On one

---

11. Victor Paul Furnish, "On Putting Paul in His Place," *JBL* 113 (1994): 3–17.

12. Weeden's construction of the Markan community (in *Mark: Traditions in Conflict* [Philadelphia: Fortress, 1971]) draws heavily from Dieter Georgi, *Die Gegner des Paulus im 2. Korintherbrief*, WMANT 11 (Neukirchener-Vluyn: Neukirchener Verlag, 1964). For a critique of Georgi's method and proposal, see Jerry L. Sumney, *Identifying Paul's Opponents: The Question of Method in 2 Corinthians*, JSNTSup 40 (Sheffield: JSOT Press, 1990), 49–61; on Weeden, consult C. Clifton Black, *The Disciples according to Mark: Markan Redaction in Current Debate*, 2nd ed. (Grand Rapids: Eerdmans, 2012), 141–77.

13. On the disputed purpose of Romans, consult Karl P. Donfried, ed., *The Romans Debate*, rev. ed. (Peabody, MA: Hendrickson, 1991). On the perils of mirror-reading in Galatians and 1 Thessalonians, see George Lyons, *Pauline Autobiography: Toward a New Understanding*, SBLDS 73 (Atlanta: Scholars Press, 1985), esp. 75–121, 176–227.

14. C. K. Barrett, "The Parallels between Acts and John," in *Exploring the Gospel of John in Honor of D. Moody Smith*, ed. R. Alan Culpepper and C. Clifton Black (Louisville: Westminster John Knox, 1996), 163.

side, the Second Evangelist's stock as a creative interpreter of Jesus traditions was given a powerful boost by William Wrede's classic study of the messianic secret in the gospels.[15] Reinforced by the pioneering redaction criticism of R. H. Lightfoot and Willi Marxsen,[16] Mark's theological achievement has since been corroborated by a number of literary critics who recognize in that gospel's convoluted narrative religious insights that unintentionally comment on our own disjointed age.[17] To dust off an old metaphor: if Mark wielded scissors and paste on the tradition at his disposal, it was with a collagist's artistry, not the drudgery of a printer's devil.[18] While Mark's way of doing theology is very different from Paul's, for most exegetes, it now appears beyond doubt that theology, among other things, is what Mark is doing.[19] Interestingly, on the Pauline side of the critical ledger, a story of Jesus, or a story of Israel for which Jesus is climactic, is currently being viewed by some as an infrastructure for Paul's nonnarrative, theological formulations.[20] Whether scholars will attain

15. William Wrede, *The Messianic Secret*, trans. J. C. G. Greig, LTT (Cambridge: James Clarke, 1971 [German original, 1901]).

16. R. H. Lightfoot, *History and Interpretation in the Gospels* (London: Hodder & Stoughton, 1935); Willi Marxsen, *Mark the Evangelist: Studies on the Redaction History of the Gospel*, trans. James Boyce et al. (Nashville: Abingdon, 1969 [German original, 1956]).

17. For example, Robert C. Tannehill, "The Disciples in Mark: The Function of a Narrative Role," *JR* 57 (1977): 386–405, repr. in *The Interpretation of Mark*, ed. William Telford, SNTI (Edinburgh: T&T Clark, 1995), 169–95; Frank Kermode, *The Genesis of Secrecy: On the Interpretation of Narrative* (Cambridge: Harvard University Press, 1979); Donald H. Juel, *A Master of Surprise: Mark Interpreted* (Minneapolis: Fortress, 1994).

18. The comparison of the Second Gospel with a collage was drawn by Ernest Best, "Mark's Preservation of the Tradition," in *L'Évangile selon Marc: Tradition et redaction*, ed. M. Sabbe, BETL 34 (Leuven: Leuven University Press, 1974), 21–34, repr. in Telford, *Interpretation of Mark*, 153–68.

19. The intelligibility of this claim depends considerably on what is meant by "theology." Arguably, Mark would not qualify as a theologian if, as Victor Furnish has suggested, theology is appropriately understood as "critical reflection on the beliefs, rites, and social structures in which an experience of ultimate reality has found expression" ("Paul the Theologian," in *The Conversation Continues: Studies in Paul and John in Honor of J. Louis Martyn*, ed. Robert T. Fortna and Beverly R. Gaventa [Nashville: Abingdon, 1990], 25, originally italicized). If I rightly understand Furnish's view, theology is a second-order consideration of the gospel's proclamation, which is a first-order religious activity. Yet one wonders if this sharp differentiation between kerygmatic and theological discourse is either necessary or warranted as regards Paul, Mark, or other Christian authors of the first century. Further, would not the demonstration of such a finely honed distinction in Paul's thought and practice stand in tension with Furnish's prudent observation that Paul is not a systematic theologian in the medieval or modern sense?

20. Richard B. Hays, *The Faith of Jesus Christ: An Investigation of the Narrative Substruc-

the same level of comfort in speaking of "Pauline narrative" as in referring to "Markan theology" remains to be seen. In any event, recent considerations of Mark's Gospel or Paul's letters tend to locate their theologies in a common solar system, for all of the undeniable variance in their orbital paths.

A third reason for revisiting the rapport between Paul and Mark lies in our heightened awareness of their inclusion within Christian Scripture and our sensitivity to the hermeneutical consequences of their canonization. Although historical critics of the Bible have rightly disciplined themselves to filter out the voices of all save that of a particular text under examination, throughout history the church has heard the voices within its Scripture as mutually confirmatory and corrective, with the canon functioning as a theologically trustworthy resonating chamber. Furthermore, through the peculiar canon-logic by which segments of the NT came to be compiled (Gospels, Acts, Epistles, Apocalypse), the church has tended to hear Paul's letters—which antedate the canonical gospels by two to five decades—as theological and ethical commentary on a foundational story of Jesus Christ, differently inflected by Mark, Matthew, Luke, and John.[21] If I correctly understand the interpretive project attempted by Brevard S. Childs and others, this historically anomalous but theologically intelligible tendency is not so much to be lamented, scorned, or throttled as it should be clarified, refined, and deepened.[22] For this process, Robert W. Wall suggests an attractive metaphor: "A canonical approach to the New Testament's pluriform subject matter envisages a conversation that is more complementary than adversarial. In one sense, the *intercanonical* [*sic*] conversation is very much like an intramural debate over the precise meaning of things generally agreed to be true and substantial. The purpose or outcome of debate is not to resolve firmly fixed disagreements among members of the

---

ture of Galatians 3:1–4:11, 2nd ed. (Grand Rapids: Eerdmans, 2002); N. T. Wright, *The Climax of the Covenant: Christ and the Law in Pauline Theology* (Minneapolis: Fortress, 1992). Such reassessments may be viewed as exegetical tributaries of some broader currents in theology, for whose appraisal, see George W. Stroup, *The Promise of Narrative Theology: Recovering the Gospel in the Church* (Atlanta: John Knox, 1981).

21. See Albert C. Outler, "The 'Logic' of Canon-Making and the Tasks of Canon and the Tasks of Canon-Criticism," in *Texts and Testaments: Critical Essays on the Bible and Early Church Fathers*, ed. W. Eugene March (San Antonio: Trinity University Press, 1980), 263–76.

22. Thus, Gerald T. Sheppard: "Just as the semantic force of words is not secured solely by appeal to their etymologies but gains specific import within the context of a particular sentence, so the context of scripture inevitably influences how earlier traditions come to make sense as a part of scripture" ("Canonical Criticism," *ABD* 1:862). See also Brevard S. Childs, *Introduction to the Old Testament as Scripture* (Philadelphia: Fortress, 1979), and Childs, *The New Testament as Canon: An Introduction* (Philadelphia: Fortress, 1985).

same community or panel as though a normative synthesis were possible; rather, more often it is the sort of debate that clarifies the contested content of their common ground."[23]

There are four aspects of this analogy that I find appealing. First, it does not evade but presumptively welcomes temperate historical exegesis of those points of view expressed by "members of the biblical panel"—without which, be it noted, the pluriformity of the NT's witness could not be adequately recognized.[24] Methodologically, this seals off the Volkmar option: we are no more licensed to read Mark as an allegorization of Pauline life and thought than to construe Romans as an epistolary bedecking of the Olivet Address in Mark 13. Second, Wall's approach, like that of Childs, resists shackling the texts' *Sachen* to the particular circumstances of their historical origin or the accidents of their evolution. A real theological exchange can occur between Paul and Mark, in their canonical distillates, without smuggling into the affair dubious assumptions of Mark's genetic dependence on the letters or labored arguments for Paul's knowledge of that gospel's preliterary traditions. (The Jesus-Paul debate is well worth convening, but not in every time and place; neither is it the only intracanonical show in town.) According to this model, third, a carefully structured exercise in "mutual criticism" (Wall) of the positions adopted by Paul and Mark is, for now, an end that is good and sufficient in itself. Areas of common ground can be identified without collapsing their views into a specious homogeneity that well serves neither; points of dispute between them can be sharpened apart from strategies calculated to pronounce the one as theologically superior to the other. Fourth, by conceiving the exercise as a conversation of complements, instead of an adversarial contest, this interpretive paradigm reminds us of a more general quality essential to both the church and its canon: each remains in dynamic conversation within itself and with each other.[25]

23. Robert W. Wall, "Reading the New Testament in Canonical Context," in *Hearing the New Testament: Strategies for Interpretation*, 2nd ed., ed. Joel B. Green (Grand Rapids: Eerdmans, 2010), 384. Similarly, see James D. G. Dunn and James P. Mackey, *New Testament Theology in Dialogue: Christology and Ministry* (Philadelphia: Westminster, 1987).

24. On the tension between historical and theological considerations in Childs's own canonical approach, see D. Moody Smith, "Why Approaching the New Testament as Canon Matters," *Int* 40 (1986): 407–11.

25. Throughout this essay, I use the metaphor of an intracanonical conversation heuristically. Considered historically, I doubt that the authors of 1 Corinthians and the Second Gospel were literally in dialogue with each other. To speak strictly, it is the church that has conversed with Paul's letter and Mark's Gospel, both prior and subsequent to their canonization. As a consequence of that canonical process, however, the church has not regarded

Enough of prolegomena. It is time to turn to some interlocutory texts. But which ones? To compare the whole of Mark's presentation with Pauline theology in its entirety, or even the theology within a particular Pauline letter, is, in a single chapter, manifestly out of the question.[26] We must narrow the scope. For our purposes, two passages of reasonable length may be invited into mutual conversation: 1 Cor 1:18–2:16 and Mark 15:16–41. Needless to say, these passages have not been selected willy-nilly; they are peculiarly promising for the task at hand. There is, to begin with, an intuitive sense of fit between them, borne out by exegetes who draw both texts into a common interpretive arena, often as jointly exemplary of a theology of the cross.[27] For the documents in which they occur, both passages are recognized by most commentators as *cruces interpretum* in more ways than one. Structurally, 1 Cor 1–2 is Paul's introductory point of orientation for the balance of that letter, while Mark 15 is the climax toward which the whole of Mark's narrative builds. Substantively, the crucifixion of Jesus is central in both passages. Not only does the cross constitute the chief point of material correspondence between these texts; in no other Markan or Pauline passages do these authors concentrate at such length and with such intensity on the cross, as such, as they do here. Prior to the passion narrative, there are, of course, general references throughout Mark to Jesus's death (e.g., 3:6; 8:31; 9:9, 31; 10:33–34, 45; 12:7–8); nevertheless, almost all of Mark's references to Jesus's cross or crucifixion occur in 15:16–41 (vv. 20, 21, 24, 25, 27, 30, 32; cf. 15:13–15; 16:6). In Paul's letters, only Gal 6:12–15 approaches 1 Cor 1:18–2:16 as a sustained, albeit more cursory, reflection on the theological significance of "the cross of Christ"; elsewhere in Galatians (2:19; 3:1, 13; 5:11, 24) or in the other undisputed letters (Rom 6:6; 2 Cor 13:4; Phil 2:8; 3:18), Paul's

---

the apostle's and evangelist's witnesses as detached from each other or as amenable to comparison by mere happenstance. Rather, these and other canonical voices have been heard by the church as to some degree theologically interpenetrative and in some sense mutually interpretive (hence, the exegetical principle of antiquity, *Scriptura Scripturae interpres*). The figure of a conversation—between two or more of the Bible's varied constituents, as well as between the church and the Bible as a whole—seems to me, therefore, a reasonable characterization of some religiously important relationships, so long as that trope not be asked to support more weight than any metaphor can bear. For further reflections in this vein, see C. Clifton Black, "Trinity and Exegesis," in *Reading Scripture with the Saints* (Eugene, OR: Wipf & Stock; Cambridge: Lutterworth, 2014, 2015), 9–34.

26. This more ambitious feat has been attempted, with debatable results, by J. C. Fenton, "Paul and Mark," in *Studies in the Gospels: Essays in Memory of R. H. Lightfoot*, ed. D. E. Nineham (Oxford: Blackwell, 1955), 89–112.

27. See, for instance, Ulrich Luz, "Theologia crucis als Mitte der Theologie im Neuen Testament," *EvT* 34 (1974): 116–41.

references to crucifixion or the cross are surprisingly rare, in comparison with his more widespread mention of Jesus's death and its significance.[28] Placing 1 Cor 1:18–2:16 in conversation with Mark 15:16–41 allows us entrée to two of the NT's most profound expositions of "the word of the cross."

LISTENING TO THE PANELISTS

1 Corinthians 1:18–2:16: Primary Claims of Paul's Argument

Paul's comments in 1 Cor 1:18–2:16 are prompted by partisan strife within the Corinthian church (1:10–11; 3:3), each clique aligning itself with one apostolic leader to the denigration of others (1:12; 3:4, 21; 4:6). Within this context "1:18–2:16 stands as a kind of excursus,"[29] which, as Peter Lampe notes, "at first glance, has *nothing* to do with the Corinthian parties."[30] On further reflection, however, this passage is only apparently digressive, having *everything* to do with the Corinthians' factiousness; for, as Paul understands it, a misconstruing of the gospel lies at the heart of their dysfunctional religiosity. A confusion whose root is *theological* must first be addressed before its social aberrations can be put right. Until then, any counsel that Paul could possibly offer would be misapprehended by the Corinthians as a self-interested move on his part (cf. 1:13–15), which would only exacerbate the problem by playing into the hands of both his detractors and his supporters.

While the structure of Paul's theological response, centered on "the word of the cross" (1:18),[31] is patient of different analyses, Victor Furnish's suggestion of a bipartite structure is sensible.[32] First, in 1:18–2:5, Paul considers God's ostensibly foolish but soteriologically purposeful wisdom (1:18–25), confirmed by the

28. For a careful sifting of the relevant evidence, consult Charles B. Cousar, *A Theology of the Cross: The Death of Jesus in the Pauline Letters*, OBT (Minneapolis: Fortress, 1990), N.B. 21–24.

29. Victor Paul Furnish, "Theology in 1 Corinthians," in *1 and 2 Corinthians*, vol. 2 of *Pauline Theology*, ed. David M. Hay (Minneapolis: Fortress, 1993), 64 (hereafter cited as "Theology in 1 Corinthians").

30. Peter Lampe, "Theological Wisdom and the 'Word about the Cross': The Rhetorical Scheme in 1 Corinthians 1–4," *Int* 44 (1990): 118.

31. All translations are my own, except where otherwise indicated.

32. Furnish, "Theology in 1 Corinthians," 64–67. In "Theology in 1 Corinthians: Initial Soundings," *Society of Biblical Literature 1989 Seminar Papers*, ed. David J. Lull (Atlanta: Scholars Press, 1989), N.B. 250–33 (hereafter cited as "Initial Soundings"), Furnish proposes a quinquepartite analysis (1:18–25; 1:26–31; 2:1–5; 2:6–16; 3:1–4).

Corinthians' own circumstances (1:26–31) and by the substance and style of Paul's preaching (2:1–5). Since a critical aim of the apostle's response is to foreclose the possibility that human beings can reason their way to God's wisdom (1:21), in 2:6–16 Paul unfolds the epistemological consequences: that wisdom, which remains hidden (2:7) and incomprehensible by the standards of an age that is passing away (2:6, 8, 14), is revealed by God through the Spirit (2:9–10, 12–13).[33]

From this framework, some "pivotal theological conceptions" arise, only a few of which may be identified here.[34] To begin with, 1 Cor 1:18–2:16 is nothing if not testimony to the stupefying power and salvific purpose of God. Throughout this passage, God is the sole seat of wisdom (1:21; 2:7) and the active, predestining agent (2:7; 2:9b), whether for empowerment (1:18; 2:5) or abrogation (1:28). God is the thwarter of human cleverness (1:19b; cf. Isa 29:14; Ps 33:10), the transmuter of this world's wisdom into foolishness and of this world's strength into weakness (1 Cor 1:20b, 25; cf. 1:19a), the elector of the foolish, the weak, and even "things that are nothing" to the tasks of shaming and nullifying the wise, the strong, and "things that are" (1:27–28). It is God who saves believers by means of the foolishness of apostolic preaching (1:21) and bestows on them the Spirit, by which God's thoughts and gifts may be known (2:10–12). It is God who is the source of believers' life, who has made Christ their wisdom, rectification, sanctification, redemption, and glorification (1:30–31; 2:7). It is hard to imagine a more uncompromising, tightly focused understanding of God's freedom, sovereignty, and restorative power than what Paul offers here. From these conceptions, grounded in ὁ θεός, correlative aspects of Paul's anthropology and soteriology are articulated in 1:18–2:16.

Next we may note the presentation of human beings in 1 Cor 1:18–2:16—not because anthropology is central to Paul's argument but because, in this particular case, its dimensions inevitably emerge in sharp contrast to his depiction of God's sovereign activity. In this passage, the emphasis falls both on a perishing

---

33. Furnish's summary of this second movement in Paul's argument—"the hiddenness of God's wisdom"—seems to put the accent on a topic that is minimally developed (only at 2:7 and 2:9a [the latter citing Isa 64:4]). The flow of Paul's thinking may be better captured by Robin S. Barbour's proposal that 1:18–2:5 is centered on the hidden power of God, 2:6–16 on the knowledge of God's hidden purpose ("Wisdom and the Cross in 1 Corinthians 1 and 2," in *Theologia Crucis—Siglum Crucis: Festschrift für Erich Dinkler zum 70. Geburtstag*, ed. Carl Andresen and Günter Klein [Tübingen: Mohr Siebeck, 1979], 66). Pressing the point, I prefer to describe 2:6–16 as Paul's pneumatological reflections on "*how* God's hidden purpose is known."

34. The category is Furnish's ("Theology in 1 Corinthians," 67–69); my comments are informed by but not restricted to his analysis.

humanity's blindness and folly, predicated on any norm of wisdom other than the radically contradictory standard revealed by God through the cross, and on the restoration of those who have entrusted themselves to the strange power of God, to whom the preached word of the cross bears testimony (1:18, 21–23; 2:5, 8–10; also 2 Cor 4:3). Viewed in context, "Jews [who] demand signs and Greeks [who] seek wisdom" (1 Cor 1:22) are typical instances,[35] not of noble but inadequate human attempts to trace God's designs in this world, but rather of the flat incapability of all, whether Jew or gentile, "[to know] the mind of the Lord so as to instruct him" (2:16a; cf. Isa 40:13; Wis 9:13); of that centripetal human egoism that projects its own self-interest onto the sovereign God, whose thoughts and ways are not our own (1 Cor 1:20, 27–29, 31; cf. Rom 1:22–25; Isa 55:8–9; Jer. 9:23–24); of presumptuous human faithlessness in demanding that God produce authenticating warrants before any mortal bar of judgment (1 Cor 1:23). Because the distance between God and humanity is not a matter of degree, Paul does not belabor the superiority of God's wisdom or strength to our own. Rather, by clashing the wisdom of God's *foolishness* and the strength of God's *weakness* (1:25), Paul's proclamation of "the mystery of God" (2:1) effectively anticipates a Barthian "infinite qualitative difference" between the divine and human norms by which wisdom and folly, strength and weakness, are properly construed (thus, 1:20).[36] The fact that such construing is closed to our sophisticated efforts is further and consistently underlined by the fittingness of human nadir—expressed preeminently in the cross of Christ (1:24; 2:2) but also in the foolishness of preaching (1:21), the church's mean status (1:26), and the apostle's weakness (2:1, 3–5; also 1:17; 2 Cor 10:10)—as the medium through which God's alien yet authentic wisdom and power are revealed. For the same reason, Paul stresses the unqualified dependence of human beings upon God for their calling to faith (1:24, 26; also 1:2; Rom 8:28), for their progressively restored life in Christ (1 Cor 1:18, 21, 30) and its consummation (2:7; cf. Rom

35. In Jewish and pagan writings of Paul's day, there is no single or uniform meaning for "signs" (τὰ σημεῖα) or "wisdom" (ἡ σοφία). Plausible foils for his critique of the demand for signs might include such connotations of σημεῖα as we find in Philo, as argumentative proof (*Fug.* 204; *Mos.* 2.48), and in Josephus and at Qumran, as confirmation by sight or other sensory perception (*B.J.* 6.68; *A.J.* 10.28–29; 1Q27 1 I, 5 [האות]). Among the Stoics, σοφία was defined as "knowledge of things both divine and human" (ἐπιστήμη θείων τε καὶ ἀνθρώπειων πραγμάτων [Aetius, *Placita* 1.2]). See Karl H. Rengstorf, "σημεῖον, κ.τ.λ." *TDNT* 7:200–269, and Ulrich Wilckens and Georg Fohrer, "σοφία, σοφός, σοφίζω," *TDNT* 7:465–528.

36. Karl Barth, *The Epistle to the Romans*, trans. E. C. Hoskyns (London: Oxford University Press, 1933 [German original, 1919]), 10. As Barth notes, the phrase is traceable to Kierkegaard.

8:18–21; 2 Cor 3:18), upon "the Spirit that is from God" for discernment and interpretation of the gifts of God's bestowal (1 Cor 2:11b–16; also 4:7). For those who love him, everything is prepared *by God* and is categorically inaccessible to the spiritually unendowed eye, ear, or heart (2:9; cf. Isa 64:4; 52:15).

At the nexus of these reflections on the saving God and a hubristic humanity is the soteriological value of, or transvaluation indicated by, "Jesus Christ and him crucified" (1 Cor 2:2). In 1:30, to be sure, Paul brushes over what later would become the classical vocabulary of atonement, which elsewhere he also adopts though does not explain: "righteousness" (6:11; Rom 3:21–26; 5:17–21; et passim; Phil 3:9), "sanctification" (1 Cor 1:2; 6:11; Rom 6:19, 22; 1 Thess 4:3; 5:23; cf. Lev 22:32), "redemption" (1 Cor 6:19–20; 7:23; Rom 3:4; 8:23; Gal 3:13; 4:5). Examined within the context of 1 Cor 1:18–2:16, however, these metaphors in 1:30 constitute a chord whose keynote is surely σοφία: "It is due to him [God] that you are in Christ Jesus, who was made wisdom for us by God." To Job's question, "Where shall wisdom be found?" (28:12),[37] Paul's tacit reply is that σοφία—the core of reality, the essential framework of meaning and value implanted by God in creation—is disclosed with restorative power only in the proclamation of Christ crucified (cf. 1 Cor 1:18–25). Accordingly, for Paul, Jesus is not the purveyor of wise teaching par excellence but *wisdom itself.* As Leander Keck puts it, "In making Christ our wisdom, God made Christ the framework for our understanding of God."[38] Such understanding, which Paul describes here as "the mind of Christ" (1 Cor 2:16; cf. Rom 12:2), is itself a critical dimension of the salvation accomplished by God for believers through the foolishness of preaching (1 Cor 1:21).

The implications of this cruciform epistemology are both profound and far-reaching. First, for Paul, it means that the cross of Christ is not a discrete historical datum but *a transformative eruption within the fabric of history*: an occurrence that has recast the character of the divine-human relationship, the way in which we can know and are known by God (cf. 1 Cor 8:3; 13:12). Second, from his description of that event—in terms of mysterious wisdom imparted (2:6–7), a turning of the aeons (1:20; 2:6–8), Christ's death and resurrection (1:23; 2:2; 15:3–28), God's judgment of every human claim and healing of every human aspiration (1:18–31)—it is clear that Paul conceives it altogether *apoca-*

37. Here I am indebted to Furnish's intriguing suggestion that 1:18–2:16 is in a sense propelled by the meditations in Job 28 and other sapiential texts ("Initial Soundings," 254–55). See also Barbour, "Wisdom and the Cross," 62–64.

38. Leander E. Keck, "Biblical Preaching as Divine Wisdom," in *A New Look at Preaching*, ed. John Burke, GNS 7 (Wilmington, DE: Glazier, 1983), 153.

lyptically.[39] Third, Paul's understanding of the cross is *radically eschatological* in the sense of a once-for-all, divine invasion whose impact pulses without surcease into God's present and future with us. As Furnish has suggested, this conviction is subtly yet vividly captured in 1 Cor 1:18–2:16 by Paul's careful use of Greek verbs in perfect tenses to characterize certain punctiliar events in the past whose effects are related to the present:[40] thus, "we speak of God's *wisdom that remains hidden in mystery*" (σοφίαν ἐν μυστηρίῳ τὴν ἀποκεκρυμμένην [2:7]); "to know nothing among you except Jesus Christ, *who indeed continues to be the one crucified*" (καὶ τοῦτον ἐσταυρωμένον [2:2; also 1:23]). "The Risen and Exalted One remains the Crucified One."[41] Because "Christ has been raised from the dead" (again the perfect tense, ἐγήγερται [15:20; also 15:4, 12, 15]), he continues by God's vivification to be *the Christ*; but because God's raising of Jesus has not eradicated his crucifixion but has vindicated this one and no other, "Christ *crucified*" remains the unremitting focus of Paul's preaching (2:2), the ineluctable scandal for human pretensions to power and wisdom (1:23), the indispensable criterion for human knowledge of God's still hidden power and mysterious wisdom (1:24; cf. 2 Cor 13:4a).[42]

Mark 15:16–41: Primary Themes of Mark's Narrative

Mark's account of Jesus's mockery, crucifixion, and death comes near the conclusion of a narrative that has been expressly hurtling toward this precise moment. From its beginning, the reader has been privileged with three critical pieces of information that are either unknown, unappreciated, or disregarded by all of the story's figures save Jesus (and God). First, Jesus is the Christ and Son of God (1:1, 9–11; 8:29–30; 9:2–8, 41; 13:32; 14:36–37, 61–65; cf. 3:21; 4:41; 5:17; 6:1–6a; 12:6; 15:2–11), the Son of Man who must suffer many things (8:31, 33; 9:12, 31–32; 10:33–34; 14:21; cf. 12:7–8, 12; 14:62–65). Second, much as they have already arrested and murdered John the Baptist (1:14a; 6:14–29; 9:11–13; 11:30–33a), the religious and political forces of Israel and Rome are busily scheming to snare and to destroy Jesus (3:6, 22; 7:5; 8:11, 15, 31; 10:2, 33; 11:18, 27–28; 12:6–8, 12–13; 14:1–2, 10–11, 53–65; 15:1, 10–15), in paradoxical

---

39. On the importance of apocalypticism in Paul's worldview, see J. Christiaan Beker, *Paul the Apostle: The Triumph of God in Life and Thought* (Philadelphia: Fortress, 1980), esp. 16–19, 135–81, 351–76.

40. Furnish, "Theology in 1 Corinthians," 68, 81.

41. Ernst Käsemann, *Jesus Means Freedom*, trans. Frank Clarke (London: SCM, 1969 [German original, 1968]), 67.

42. See the judicious assessment by Cousar, *Theology of the Cross*, 103–8.

fulfillment of God's foreordination (1:15; 8:31; 9:12, 31; 10:33–34; 12:10–11; 14:21, 27, 36, 49b). The reader of this intricately entwined plot has also received a third puzzle-piece, equally critical though less emphatically recurrent: once the divinely accredited Son of Man has suffered the full extent of universal contempt, he will arise from the dead after three days (8:31; 9:9, 31; 10:33–34; 14:28). So deeply pervasive of the Second Gospel are these ideas that Martin Kähler's famous characterization of Mark and the other gospels as "passion narratives with extended introductions" is an exaggeration that nevertheless contains a measure of truth.[43] At the heart of the passion proper is Mark 15:16–41, whose structure consists simply of (1) the Roman guard's scornful abuse of the condemned Jesus (15:16–20), (2) the humiliating crucifixion of Jesus (15:21–32), and (3) the death of Jesus (15:33–41).

What pivotal theological conceptions might be inferred from this narrative? Perhaps the most striking dimension of this text is its portrayal of a human depravity that flouts the mysterious sovereignty of God (ἡ βασιλεία τοῦ θεοῦ) to which Jesus has rendered testimony (Mark 1:15; 4:11, 26, 30; 9:1, 47; 10:14–15, 23–25; 12:34; 14:25). While 15:19 mentions Jesus's physical abuse by the Roman guard, none of the torture of crucifixion itself is detailed in 15:21–41. The ultimate punishment is captured by Mark with stark concision: "And they crucified him" (καὶ σταυροῦσιν αὐτὸν [15:24a], the verb in the historical present).[44] Even Jesus's anguish goes unmentioned until the very end (15:34; cf. 15:37). The account dwells, instead, on the heinous conduct of his execution's agents and audience, including even Jesus's fellow victims (15:32b; cf. Luke 23:39–43): their cruelty (15:15–20, 24, 29–32a) and derision (ἐβλασφήμουν [cf. 2:7; 3:28–29; 7:22; 14:64]),[45] their garbling of what Jesus has said (15:29 [cf. 11:15–17; 13:1–2; 15:58]; 15:34–36),[46] their blindness to the ironically placarded charge that he

43. Martin Kähler, *The So-Called Historical Jesus and the Historic Biblical Christ*, ed. Ernst Wolf, trans. Carl E. Braaten (Philadelphia: Fortress, 1964 [German original, 1892]), 80 n. 11.

44. Of Gavius of Messana, "as he was hanged on his cross," Cicero declares that "he hung there, to suffer the utmost extreme among tortures inflicted upon slaves. To bind a Roman citizen is a crime; to whip him, an abomination; to slay him, practically an act of murder; to crucify him is—what? There is no apposite word that can possibly describe a deed so horrendous" (*Verr.* 2.5.66 [LCL 293:654–57]); see also Cicero, *Rab. Perd.* 3.10; 5.16).

45. Jesus's mockery in Mark is not only public but outrageously excessive: "the whole (military) cohort" (ὅλην τὴν σπεῖραν [15:16]) was a battalion ranging in number from two hundred to six hundred.

46. In a context so dark, the offer of sour wine (ὄξος) to the dying Jesus is probably not to be read as a merciful act. Rather, it is humanity's last attempt, uncomprehending of what Jesus has said (ελωι, not Ἠλία), to pump a sign from heaven (see also 8:11; for later instances of the legend that Elijah would return to rescue the righteous, see b. Ber. 58a; b. B. Qam.

is "the King of the Jews" (15:26; cf. Mark 4:10–12; 8:18a), their deafness to the truth that is veiled in their own taunts—"Hail, King of the Jews" (15:18; also 15:2, 9, 12; cf. 1:11; Ps 2:7), "The Christ, the King of Israel" (15:32; cf. 1:1, 11; 8:29; 9:41; 14:61–62), "Others he saved; himself he cannot save" (15:31; cf. 8:35; 10:45). In Mark, the crucifixion of Jesus exposes a bankrupt presumptuousness that feeds on gross demonstrations of power and self-aggrandizement: "Let him now come down from the cross, so that we may see and believe" (15:32).[47] This grim anthropological landscape is relieved by only few streaks of light. One is the centurion, "who stood facing him [and] saw that in this way he breathed his last" and, on that basis, confesses Jesus to be truly God's Son (15:39).[48] Viewing from a distance (cf. Ps 38:11), from among many other women, are Mary Magdalene, Mary the mother of James and Joses, and Salome, disciples who had followed (ἠκολούθουν [see 1:18; 2:14; 6:1; 8:34; 10:21, 28]) and served (διηκόνουν [see 1:31; 9:35; 10:43]) Jesus while in Galilee (15:40–41).[49] Though neither is exonerated as such, from the Markan standpoint, these women and the gentile commander—minor characters at best—appear to be not far from "the mystery of the kingdom of God" (4:11; 12:34; 15:43). The ultimate outsider,

---

60b; b. ʿAbod. Zar. 17b, 18b). That gambit is, of course, utterly futile, since already "Elijah has come, and they did to him whatever they pleased" (9:13; cf. 6:14–29).

47. The final clause, ἵνα ἴδωμεν καὶ πιστεύσωμεν, is without verbal parallel in the other gospels' crucifixion accounts. As Christopher D. Marshall notes, this phraseology "reverses the pattern established throughout [Mark's] entire story where faith is the presupposition of miracle, not its inevitable consequence" (*Faith as a Theme in Mark's Narrative*, SNTSMS 64 [Cambridge: Cambridge University Press, 1989], 205). In support of Marshall's assessment, see Mark 1:15; 2:5; 5:34, 36; 9:23–24; 10:52; 11:22–24.

48. Some commentaries contend that the centurion was convinced of Jesus's identity by the rending of the sanctuary veil, whether by God (Raymond E. Brown, *The Death of the Messiah: From Gethsemane to the Grave*, ABRL (New York: Doubleday, 1994), 2:1144–46) or by the power of Jesus's superhuman shout (Robert H. Gundry, *Mark: A Commentary on His Apology for the Cross* (Grand Rapids: Eerdmans, 1993), 943–79). At least two difficulties attend this interpretation. First, it leaves unexplained why, under equally miraculous circumstances on the Mount of Transfiguration (Mark 9:2–8), only the voice from heaven—and not Jesus's three close confederates—had acclaimed him "[God's] Son." (On the relation of faith and miracles in Mark, see the preceding note.) Second, at 15:39, the centurion is clearly positioned as ὁ παρεστηκὼς ἐξ ἐναντίας αὐτοῦ, "the one who stood facing him"—not the temple. In Mark, what the centurion saw, explicitly and emphatically, was "that [Jesus] *thus expired*—unlike either Matthew (27:54) or Luke (23:47), who in different ways relax the Markan paradox that revelation is mediated through *concealment* (4:11–12, 21–25).

49. *Pace* Brown, *Death of the Messiah*, 2:1155–57, these women's role as disciples is further suggested by their association with Jesus's burial (15:47; 16:1–2), a task performed by John's disciples for their slain leader (6:29). In Mark, as Brown acknowledges (2:1156), the disciples of Jesus are not coterminous with the Twelve (2:15; 3:7, 9, 13–14; 4:10, 34; 8:34; 9:35).

evincing the last full measure of devotion, is the dying Jesus, who submitted himself entirely to his Father's will (14:36, 39; 15:23),[50] whose last words—a prayer addressed to "my God" (15:34)—implicitly maintained a bond with the one who had seemingly left him in the lurch.[51]

Of the presentation of God in this passage, what, indeed, may one say? If 1 Cor 1:18–2:16 appears to have been animated by Job 28:12, Mark 15:16–41 almost registers as an oblique meditation on Isa 45:15: "Truly, you are a God who hides himself, O God of Israel, the Savior." ὁ θεός occurs only three times in this Markan section: twice, in the last cry of Jesus (15:34); once, in the centurion's acknowledgment of whose Son Jesus was (15:39). The earlier occurrence is especially significant, as it is a bell-like resonance of the biblical lament, Ps 22. Gripped by the despondency of Mark's tableau, exegetes have wondered whether, upon hearing that psalm's opening plea (v. 1) on the lips of the dying Jesus, the reader is invited to inject hope within Mark 15 by fast-forwarding to the concluding praise for the psalmist's vindication in Ps 22:22–31.[52] This question distracts us from Mark's verifiable appropriation of Scripture, not only in 15:34 but throughout this passage: it is *allusive*, not explicit. Unlike its Johannine parallel (19:24b, 28, 36–37) and Mark's occasional technique elsewhere (1:2–3; 7:6–7, 10; 10:5–8a, 19; 11:17; 12:10–11, 26, 36; 14:27; cf. 9:12–13; 14:21, 49), Mark 15:16–41 is riddled with details, drawn particularly from Ps 22 (vv. 6–7 // Mark 15:29; v. 18 // Mark 15:24) but also from Pss 38 (v. 11 // Mark 15:40–41) and 69 (v. 21 // Mark 15:23, 36), which suggest without directly demonstrating that, in precisely this manner of Jesus's dying, God's will is being fulfilled.[53] Such a pattern of scriptural intimation tallies not only with Mark's earlier use

50. If the wine mixed with myrrh had analgesic properties (see Prov 31:6–7), its refusal by Jesus might suggest his acceptance of undiminished pain.

51. For Mary Ann Tolbert, "Jesus (in Mark 15:34) is forsaken by God, and at the same time God is available to be called upon" (*Sowing the Gospel: Mark's World in Literary Historical Perspective* [Minneapolis: Fortress, 1989], 283). Surely this inverts Mark's point: God is not "available" to the crucified Jesus, but neither is Jesus abandoned by God (15:38; 16:6; cf. 8:31; 9:31; 10:33–34).

52. This possibility, among others, for softening the cry of dereliction is considered and rejected by Brown, *Death of the Messiah*, 2:1044–51.

53. Missing from the earliest and best manuscripts of both the Alexandrian and Western families (א A B C D X Ψ *Lect* it[d, k] syr[s] cop[sa, bomss, fayvid] Eusebian Canon[txt]), Mark 15:28 is regarded by most exegetes as a later scribal interpolation, prompted by Isa 53:12 (and perhaps also Luke 22:37). By contrast, indirect biblical corroboration is typical of Mark: e.g., Mark 1:6 // 2 Kgs 1:8; Mark 1:11 // Ps 2:7; Isa 42:1; Mark 4:12 // Isa 6:9–10; Mark 4:35–41 // Ps 107:23–30; Mark 7:37 // Isa 35:5–6; Mark 8:18 // Jer 5:21; Mark 11:9 // Ps 118:25–26; Mark 12:1 // Isa 5:1–2; Mark 13:14, 19, 24–26 // Dan 9:27; 12:1; Isa 13:10; Mark 14:18 // Ps 41:9). On Mark's scriptural

of passive verbs implying divine agency in the Son of Man's destiny (8:31 [δεῖ, "must"]; 9:31 [παραδίδοται, "is to be handed over"]; 10:33 [παραδοθήσεται, "will be handed over"]) but also with the apocalyptic trappings of the present text (Mark 15:33 // Ezek 32:7–8; Amos 8:9; Mark 15:38 // Isa 64:1; Ezek 1:1) and the paradoxical warrant for the centurion's acknowledgment of Jesus's identity as "God's Son" (υἱὸς θεοῦ [15:39], an anarthrous construction itself patient of connotations both mundane and exalted). Throughout the crucifixion of Jesus—even in 15:38, whose blatancy Mark leaves ambiguous (cf. Matt 27:51–54; Luke 23:44–48)—the outskirts of God's ways are traceable, but only with the fingers of faith (cf. Job 26:14).[54]

Last, the Christology of this passage invites comment. The classical approaches to this topic, with their monocular concentration on the functions or titles ascribed to Jesus, may mislead us in analyzing Mark 15:16–41, since (1) Jesus seems to perform here no function other than to die in ignominy,[55] and (2) his acclamation as "God's Son" is neither self-defining nor, for that matter, unprecedented in Mark (see 1:11; 3:11; 5:7; 9:7; 14:61; cf. 12:6; 13:32). If, taking Keck's advice, we inquire into the pattern of correlations expressed or implied in this text between (on the one side) Jesus and (on the other) God and the human condition, the results, though provisional, are more promising.[56] With respect to the world, what Jesus does in Mark's account of the crucifixion is to subject himself completely to the misery, degradation, and abandonment that he has previously alleviated in others (e.g., 1:21–28; 5:1–43; 9:14–29). Jesus's self-subjugation is at the same time an act of supreme obedience to the divine will (14:36): an expression, within the heart of faithless darkness, of that

interpretation in general, see Joel Marcus, *The Way of the Lord: Christological Exegesis of the Old Testament in the Gospel of Mark* (Louisville: Westminster John Knox, 1992).

54. Timothy J. Geddert summarizes no fewer than thirty-five different interpretations of Mark 15:38 in the scholarly literature (*Watchwords: Mark 13 in Markan Eschatology*, JSNTSup 26 [Sheffield: JSOT Press, 1989], 141–43). Within the Markan context (see esp. 11:12–18; 13:1–2, 14), the veil's rending probably suggests a divine judgment on the temple that amounts to nothing less than the rupture of its holiness (cf. Ezek 10:1–22; 11:22–25; 2 Apoc. Bar. 6.7; 8.2). This suggestion, however, is only intimated by the evangelist, not explained.

55. The clearest expressions of "functional Christology" in Mark appear at 10:45 and 14:24, which, respectively, draw on the analogies of redemption (cf. Lev 25:47–52; Num 3:45–51) and covenant-ratification (cf. Exod 24:6–8; Jer 31:31) as interpretations of Jesus's death (both activities said to be "for many": ἀντὶ/ὑπὲρ πολλῶν). Neither of these, however, is explicitly coordinated with the other, and both metaphors are absent from Mark 15:16–41.

56. Leander E. Keck, "Toward the Renewal of New Testament Christology," *NTS* 32 (1986): 362–77, esp. 370–74.; repr. in Keck, *Why Christ Matters: Toward a New Testament Christology* (Waco, TX: Baylor University Press, 2015), 1–18.

kind of faith in a hidden God that finds salvation to issue most strangely yet assuredly from loss of life for the sake of the gospel (8:35). Dying in this way (οὕτως [15:39]), Jesus's resemblance ("sonship") to God (his Abba, Father) can be acknowledged by a sinfully implicated human being—for the first and only time (within Mark), publicly and in truth (ἀληθῶς). Of all the equally accurate acknowledgments of Jesus's affinity with God, throughout the gospel, here and only here can humanity *truly* recognize and proclaim Jesus as God's Son: because only at his crucifixion do the antinomies around which Mark pivots—the authority and vulnerability of Jesus (10:42–45), his life and his death (8:34–9:1), the cross of the unexpected Christ and the germination of God's mysterious kingdom (4:10–12, 26–32)—converge without simple resolution, yet with the tensive integrity of narrative paradox.[57] The most apt commentary on 15:16–41 may be that of the Markan Jesus, courtesy of the psalmist: "A stone that the builders rejected—this has become the main cornerstone: this was the Lord's doing, and it is amazing in our eyes" (Mark 12:10–11 // Ps 118:22–23 LXX). The Second Evangelist demonstrates a superb aptitude for "negative capability" some seventeen centuries before Keats extolled that quality in Shakespeare: "when man is capable of being in uncertainties, Mysteries, doubts, without any irritable reaching after fact & reason."[58]

TALKING POINTS

Aspects of Convergence

For all of their ineffaceable differences, both formal and material, 1 Cor 1:18–2:16 and Mark 15:16–41 intersect, with impressive frequency and depth, on at least four theological issues of fundamental importance.

57. The soundness of Keck's procedure (see above) is illuminated by a passage such as Mark 15:39. With its ambient connotations of political legitimation (2 Sam 7:13–14; Ps 89:26–27; 4Q174 I, 7–12; Dio Chrysostom, *Orat.* 4.21), righteousness (Sir 4:10; Wis 2:18; Jub. 1.24–25), and kinship with all humankind (Epictetus, *Diatr.* 3.24.14–16), the title "Son of God" does not so much define Jesus in Mark's Gospel as Jesus redefines what "God's sonship" truly (ἀληθῶς) means. On the generative tensions within Mark's narrative theology, see M. Eugene Boring, "The Christology of Mark: Hermeneutical Issues for Systematic Theology," *Semeia* 30 (1984): 125–53; on paradox in Mark generally, consult Laura C. Sweat, *The Theological Role of Paradox in the Gospel of Mark*, LNTS 492 (London: Bloomsbury T&T Clark, 2013).

58. "Letter to George and Thomas Keats, 22 December, 1817," in John Keats, *The Complete Poetical Works and Letters of John Keats*, Cambridge Edition (Boston: Houghton, Mifflin and Company, 1899), 277.

First, *both Mark and Paul situate the cross of Jesus within a larger apocalyptic outlook.* Though the language of 1 Cor 1–2 and the imagery of Mark 15 are not identical, both draw from a deep reservoir of apocalyptic metaphor ("this age" [1 Cor 1:20; 2:6, 8]; "in mystery" [2:7]; "that which has been hidden" [2:7] and "revealed" [2:10]; "darkness upon the whole of the earth" [Mark 15:33]; the rending of the temple-curtain (15:38]). Further examples can be multiplied across the pages of 1 Corinthians (especially 15:3–58) and Mark (especially 4:1–34; 13:3–37). To be sure, the theological syntax by which such concepts are differently coordinated in Mark and in Paul, their theologies' approach to and divergence from the apocalypticism of their era, and even a satisfying definition for the phenomenon of "apocalyptic" itself are all notoriously complicated questions that cannot be pursued here.[59] In any case, for both Mark and Paul, the cross of Jesus is a historical event of transhistorical significance, which exposes a radical split—quite literally so, in Mark 15:38—between "the rulers of this age" (1 Cor 2:8) and "the reign of God" (Mark 1:15).

Second, *both Paul and Mark concur that the actual though recondite agent behind the cross of Jesus is God.* Of the two, Paul is far more explicit on this point: "the word of the cross . . . is the power of God" (1 Cor 1:18; 2:1–5), however incognizant of this secret and hidden wisdom "the rulers of this age" have proved to be (2:7–8). The cross is the ineradicable stamp of God's radical freedom and sovereignty to judge and to save in a way that overthrows all human expectation and common sense (1:19–21, 27–31). For Paul, the cross is not God's *ex post facto* retrofit of human perversity. Such an interpretation would make of the cross nothing more than a fantastic instantiation of the cloying cliché, "making lemonade out of life's lemons." Quite the contrary, for Paul, "Christ crucified" is God's hidden wisdom, shrouded in mystery and foreordained before the ages, for the confounding of this world's wisdom and the salvation of those who are called to believe and who love him (1:18–25; 2:2, 7–9). Similarly, in Mark, Jesus avers, "The Son of Man goes as it is written about him" (14:21; cf. 8:31; 9:31; 10:33–34), and the circumstances of his crucifixion are, by their tacit fulfillment of Scripture (15:23, 24, 29, 34, 36, 40–41), disguised indicators of God's purpose. Nowhere does the evangelist approximate Paul's nuanced reflections on God's cruciform wisdom, which transcend Mark even

---

59. The secondary literature on these topics is vast. For this essay's concerns, excellent places to begin are Joel Marcus, "Mark 4:10–12 and Marcan Epistemology," *JBL* 103 (1984): 557–74, and Leander E. Keck, "Paul and Apocalyptic Theology," *Int* 38 (1984): 229–41; repr. in Keck, *Christ's First Theologian: The Shape of Paul's Thought* (Waco, TX: Baylor University Press, 2015), 75–87.

in their degree of scriptural explicitness (γέγραπται γάρ [1 Cor 1:19]; ἀλλὰ καθὼς γέγραπται [2:9]). Yet, precisely by leaving such matters allusive and undiscussed, Mark strangely captures if not surpasses the apostle's emphasis on the secrecy and concealment of God's activity in the cross.[60]

Third, *both Mark and Paul agree that at the cross of Jesus humankind not only knows but is known by God.* Paul epitomizes Christ crucified as scandalous to Jews and moronic to Greeks (1 Cor 1:23); Mark dramatizes that insight to a harrowing degree (15:16–20, 28–32, 35–36; see also 14:53–72; 15:1–15). Evangelist and apostle concur that all of humanity falls under the judgment of the cross, at the very moment when it fatuously considers itself judge of the crucified Jesus (cf. Mark 14:27; 1 Cor 1:26–29). Such presumption is embedded in a misunderstanding and abuse of power that, measured κατὰ σάρκα (1 Cor 1:26), mistakes life-giving self-sacrifice for fatal impotence (Mark 15:29–31; also 8:35–36; 10:42–45). And that cognitive/volitive confusion stems from starvation of faith, manifested in an appetite for signs (1 Cor 1:22): precisely the demand hurled at the crucified Jesus by onlookers (Mark 15:32, 36) who cannot comprehend that mighty acts are an evangelical outcome of trust in God (2:5; 5:34; 10:52; 11:22–24; cf. Rom 15:18–19; 2 Cor 12:9b–12), not magic tricks that in themselves could ever compel belief (Mark 6:1–6a). By contrast, the faith of which Paul speaks (1 Cor 1:21; 2:5) is implicitly and ironically articulated in Mark by one who wields power κατὰ σάρκα, yet—with patent foolishness that transcends human wisdom—truly acknowledges God's Son on seeing Jesus's impotence *in extremis* (15:39; cf. 1 Cor 1:25; 2:3; 2 Cor 4:7–12; 12:5–10; 13:4). Such faith is no function of human potential, which would ultimately amount to misplaced faith in oneself. Explicitly in 1 Cor 1–2 and implicitly in Mark 15, it is faith *in God*, who empowers faith among those called to exert it (1 Cor 1:24, 26–28; 2:5, 7, 10; cf. Mark 4:11, 25; 11:22–24; 13:11, 20, 22, 27; 15:34).

Fourth, *both Paul and Mark concur that at the cross, Jesus is the peculiar pointer to the ineffable character of God.* Although Mark and Paul adumbrate some later developments (Mark 10:45; 14:24; 1 Cor 1:30; also 5:7; 11:25; 15:3), neither the evangelist nor the apostle elaborates medieval theories of atonement concerning the cross. The preoccupation of Mark 15 and 1 Cor 1–2 is more obviously christological, and of a distinctive kind. Unlike Luke's presentation of the crucified Jesus as a valorous martyr (23:13–16, 27–31, 34, 40–43, 46–48) or John's understanding of Jesus's death as consummately revelatory of God's glory (12:16, 23–25, 32–33;

---

60. On the theistic ground of Jesus's teaching throughout Mark, and its emphasis on God's mystery and transcendence, see the now classic corrective by John R. Donahue, "A Neglected Factor in the Theology of Mark," *JBL* 101 (1982): 563–94.

13:31–32; 17:1, 4–5), Mark's portrait of Jesus's suffering fidelity to God's will is, without trace of heroism or triumph, "nothing . . . but Christ and him crucified" (1 Cor 2:2; see also 2 Cor 13:4; Phil 2:8).[61] Jesus's identity within the community as the one both crucified and raised, which we observed in 1 Corinthians (1:23; 2:2; 15:4, 12, 15), is also suggested in Mark's description of Jesus's crucifixion and postresurrection activity with verbs in the present or perfect tense (σταυροῦσιν αὐτὸν, "they crucify him" [15:24]; τὸν ἐσταυρωμένον, "the one who has been crucified" [16:6]; προάγει, "He is going ahead" [16:7]). Indeed, Mark's entire narrative is "the beginning of the good news of Jesus Christ, the Son of God" (1:1), whose theological center of gravity is the Son of Man slain and vindicated (8:31; 9:31; 10:33–34). Although the evangelist does not identify Christ as God's power and wisdom (cf. 1 Cor 1:24), in Mark (15:39), the crucified Jesus is the prism through which humanity truly recognizes not only Jesus but also the God whose Son Jesus is. In that sense, Charles Cousar's comment about 1 Cor 1–2 could be made as well of Mark 15: "The crucified one becomes the foundation for epistemology."[62] And because human understanding is subject to restoration by God at the cross as nowhere else, Mark's account at least implies a soteriological claim, which Paul makes more bluntly in 1 Cor 1:18, 21.[63]

Areas of Complementarity

No single text, not even one so rich as 1 Cor 1:18–2:16 or Mark 15:16–41, can comprehend the significance of the crucified Christ for Paul, the Second Evangelist, or subsequent Christian theology. To speak, therefore, of these texts' complementarity is to imply not only their significant divergences from each other but also the capacity of each to assist in rounding out the other's point of view. Here I can merely touch on three such areas.

First, *with respect to the cross, the material emphases of Paul and Mark offer important counterweights.* Given the need to extricate the Corinthians from

61. On Paul's and Mark's critiques of heroism, see, respectively, Keck, "Biblical Preaching as Divine Wisdom," 138–49, and Adela Yarbro Collins, "From Noble Death to Crucified Messiah," *NTS* 40 (1994): 481–503. Among the canonical gospels, Matthew's account is closest to Mark's, although Matthew contains unique elements that correspond to Luke's accent on Jesus's righteousness (Matt 27:19) and John's realized eschatology (Matt 27:51b–53).

62. Cousar, *Theology of the Cross*, 35. Also pertinent is J. Louis Martyn's observation: "The cross is *the* epistemological crisis for the simple reason that while it is in one sense followed by the resurrection, it is not replaced by the resurrection" ("Epistemology at the Turn of the Ages: 2 Corinthians 5.16," in *Christian History and Interpretation: Studies Presented to John Knox*, ed. W. R. Farmer, C. F. D. Moule, and R. R. Niebuhr [Cambridge: Cambridge University Press, 1970], 286).

63. I owe this observation to Professor Ellen T. Charry.

their religious solipsism, Paul in this passage explicates the word of the cross "from above." The flow of 1 Cor 1–2 is expressly theocentric, its argument radiating from Paul's core convictions about what God has done and continues to do for humankind through Christ crucified. For this approach—principled, strategic, and entirely understandable—a theological price must be paid: even to speak of "God's wisdom, secret and hidden" (2:7 NRSV) is to risk compromising its intrinsic mystery and concealment. Paul's claim to have "the mind of Christ" (2:16) might appear to constitute an even further intrusion upon this mystery. Any tendency toward hubris in such an argument is firmly counteracted (1) by Paul's treatment of things held in the world's scale of values to be base and worthless as the inescapable locus of God's wisdom, most patently manifest (1:26–2:5), and (2) by Paul's express acknowledgment that "the mind of the Lord" is permanently inaccessible to human striving and requires for its disclosure God's own gift of the revelatory Spirit (2:10–16).[64] Yet the risk of encroachment on the depths of God arguably remains and may be an unavoidable by-product of the starting point of the apostle's analysis. Viewed intracanonically, Mark 15:16–41 effectively offers a response to this theological problem by approaching the cross just as steadily (and, one assumes, just as deliberately) from the other end of the field: "from below," accenting the human grotesqueries of Jesus's trial and execution that are only beginning to yield to the force of the cross in the words of the incipiently perceptive executioner (15:39). Yet the evangelist's approach carries its own cost: so muted is God's presence in Mark 15 (N.B. 15:34) that, even with the passion predictions in Mark 8–10 but lacking Paul's more explicit treatment in 1 Cor 1–2, Christian theology would be hard-pressed to discern *God's* wisdom within the centurion's cryptic comment. Paul's appraisal of what has happened at the cross is more profound than Mark's: this world's wisdom has been not merely exposed as folly but *made into foolishness*, "moronized" (ἐμώρανεν) by God (1 Cor 1:20). Mark's contribution is to point up, with a presentation more anthropologically animated, just how scandalous that claim of the cross really is.[65]

This leads to a second area of complementarity between these texts. Paul insists (1 Cor 2:2) that among his readers he "decided to know nothing except Jesus Christ and him crucified." If it applies to his discussion in 1 Cor 1:18–2:16 as well as to his earlier preaching (see 2:1), this remark is obviously hyperbolic.

---

64. A most valuable exegesis of Pauline χάρις, coordinating its coherently particular and general senses within the context of Hellenistic Judaism, is that of John M. G. Barclay, *Paul and the Gift* (Grand Rapids: Eerdmans, 2015).

65. I appreciate Professor Paul W. Meyer's help in clarifying some points made in this paragraph.

Beyond its mere assertion, "nothing but Jesus Christ and him crucified" is, in a way, a more fitting description of what we find in Mark 15, whose interpretation of that event is so embedded within a realistic narrative that many generations of Christians (and scholars) have failed to recognize Mark's account as the theological interpretation that it is. Regarded within the context of 1 Cor 1–2, what Paul apparently (and naturally) intends by his comment in 2:2 is that the *significance* of Jesus, the crucified Christ—such as Paul articulates it in these chapters and as it has become manifest in his own life—is the center of his speech and his proclamation (2:3–4). Just here, as I have suggested, 1 Corinthians offers explicitly *theo*logical guidance to the canonical interpreter of Mark. Yet Paul does more than this. By exploring the work of the Spirit, which discerns spiritual things for the benefit of those who have received the Spirit that is from God (1 Cor 2:10–16), Paul provides an explanation for *why* an observer (perhaps, Mark's centurion; surely, the evangelist's audience) is able to recognize "spiritual truths" beyond "the spirit of the world," to judge this one crucified to be God's Son on bases altogether contradictory of "matters taught by human wisdom" (2:12–13). In a word, *where Mark elaborates the empirical opacity through which faith must penetrate, Paul amplifies the epistemological means by which faith "can know the gifts bestowed on us by God."*

Finally, *Paul's and Mark's formal approaches to the cross effectively bolster a canonical counterbalance.* Paul's way of doing theology—discursively, in a pastoral letter to an actual church—appears to offer modern, biblically informed theologians advantages over Mark's more oblique technique, which obscures the presumably ecclesial audience for whom his narrative was created. Manifesting its author's attempt to illuminate particular facets of "the truth of the gospel" (Gal 2:5, 14), 1 Corinthians unintentionally helps us not only in tracing the contours of Paul's own thought but in elucidating some cognate convictions of other early Christian thinkers, like the author of Mark's Gospel. In that sense, there emerges a canonical Mark, whose message acquires a clarity, distinctiveness, and fullness when heard in conjunction with Paul's "word of the cross" (1 Cor 1:18). Yet, when read alongside the Second Gospel, the apostle's proclamation enjoys a different kind of perspicuity and resonance. Focusing on the cross as a climactically salvific event with theologically discriminative implications, Paul's analysis in 1 Cor 1–2 tends to minimize the very dimension that Mark's cruciform story of Jesus maximizes: the character of the one to and through whom that event occurred.[66] To

---

66. For thoughtful comments in this vein, see Donald T. Rowlingson, "The Moral Context of the Resurrection Faith," in *Christ and Spirit in the New Testament in Honour of Charles Francis Digby Moule*, ed. Barnabas Lindars and Stephen S. Smalley (Cambridge: Cambridge University Press, 1973), 415–25.

acknowledge this is not, as Bultmann concluded, tantamount to an existentially anxious, theologically invalid attempt to legitimate the kerygma by appeal to the Jesus of history.[67] To the contrary, if Mark's kerygmatic narrative demonstrates anything, it is the indispensability of faith: the vast majority at Golgotha, historically closer than anyone else to Jesus, were stunningly post-deaf and bat-blind to what the evangelist believes was actually happening.[68] At issue is not the credibility of the kerygma but its intelligibility: for without attention to the lifelong passion of *this one* crucified and vindicated, such as Mark provides, "the cross" is liable to shrinkage into a detached cipher of the sort that Paul himself would never have countenanced.[69] The potential for trivialization is perilous on both sides. Cut off from Paul's propositional incisiveness, the emotive story in Mark 15 could be misread as some moralistic news from a Judean Lake Wobegon.[70] Isolated from Mark's narrative texture, the trenchant claims of 1 Cor 1–2 could be misconstrued as the chance legacy of a surprisingly lucky Jew who won the Almighty's eschatological jackpot. To say it more straightforwardly: if Paul's theological method sharpens the disclosure point of "the one crucified" along the horizon of God's eternity, Mark's deepens its irrefragable "this-worldliness," as defined by Jesus Christ.[71]

67. Rudolf Bultmann, "The Primitive Christian Kerygma and the Historical Jesus," in *The Historical Jesus and the Kerygmatic Christ: Essays on the New Quest of the Historical Jesus*, ed. Carl E. Braaten and Roy A. Harrisville (Nashville: Abingdon, 1964), 15–42. As is well known, Paul and John stood, for Bultmann, as the twin peaks of NT theology; the Synoptics, as an aspect of doctrinal development toward the ancient church (*Theology of the New Testament*, trans. Kendrick Grobel [New York: Scribner's Sons, 1955], N.B. 2:119–54).

68. Thus, Eduard Schweizer: "First, it is beyond all doubt that Mark wants to emphasize that God's revelation happened in the historical life and death of Jesus, that is, in a real man. . . . Second, this does not mean that we could see anything which would really help us in the historical Jesus, without the miracle of God's Spirit who, in the word of the witness, opens our blind eyes to the 'dimension' in which all these events took place" ("Mark's Contribution to the Quest of the Historical Jesus," *NTS* 10 [1963–1964]: 431).

69. See also Luz, "Theologia crucis als Mitte der Theologie," 135–39.

70. Cf. Garrison Keillor, *Lake Wobegon Days* (New York: Viking, 1985), a compilation of that humorist's popular radio monologues.

71. Apropos of these reflections, see E. Cyril Blackman, "Is History Irrelevant for the Christian Kerygma?," *Int* 21 (1967): 435–46; Paul W. Meyer, "The This-Worldliness of the New Testament," *PSB* 2 (1979): 219–31, repr. in Meyer, *The Word in This World: Essays in New Testament Exegesis and Theology*, ed. John T. Carroll, NTL (Louisville, Westminster John Knox, 2004), 5–18; William C. Placher, *Narratives of a Vulnerable God: Christ, Theology, and Scripture* (Louisville: Westminster John Knox, 1994), esp. 27–52, 87–108.

CHAPTER 13

Endzeit als Urzeit:
Mark and Creation Theology

The world's creation has a beginning from the world's point of view, not from God's.

—Rowan D. Williams

ONE THING ON WHICH VIRTUALLY ALL Markan exegetes agree is its apocalypticism. Among the first to identify that *Tendenz* was Timothy Colani in the nineteenth century.[1] During the twentieth, Willi Marxsen, James M. Robinson, and Howard Clark Kee concentrated our attention on it.[2] The twentieth century's commentaries have cemented its significance.[3] N. T. Wright's assessment is representative: "Mark has written a Christian apocalypse, in which the events of Jesus' life . . . form the vital theatre in which Israel's history reaches its moment of 'apocalyptic' crisis."[4] Presented the consensus contract, I too have signed on the dotted line and don't intend to renege: evidence of apocalypticism in Mark seems to me irrefutable.[5] Nevertheless, "the assured results of scholarly investigation" have always unsettled me, and R. Barry Matlock's critique of apocalypticism in recent Pauline study does nothing to steady my

1. *Jésus Christ et les Croyances messianiques de son Temps*, 2nd ed. (Strasbourg: Treuttel et Wurtz, 1864).
2. Willi Marxsen, *Mark the Evangelist: Studies on the Redaction History of the Gospel*, trans. James Boyce et al. (Nashville: Abingdon, 1969); James M. Robinson, *The Problem of History in Mark*, SBT 21 (London: SCM, 1957 [German original, 1956]); Howard Clark Kee, *Community of the New Age: Studies in Mark's Gospel* (Philadelphia: Westminster, 1977).
3. Among others, Adela Yarbro Collins, *Mark: A Commentary*, Hermeneia (Minneapolis: Fortress, 2007), esp. 42–44; Joel Marcus, *Mark 1–8: A New Translation with Introduction and Commentary*, AB 27 (New York: Doubleday, 2000), esp. 71–73.
4. N. T. Wright, *The New Testament and the People of God* (Minneapolis: Fortress, 1992), 396.
5. Most recently, *Mark*, ANTC (Nashville: Abingdon, 2011), passim.

nerves.[6] Whenever our interpretations become flat, our conclusions pat, revisiting them is a good idea.

My aim in this chapter is to readjust the exegetical lens and ask, What if we consider the Gospel from a different angle? Specifically, I want to consider the evidence for rudiments of a theology of creation in Mark. Though that subject has not vanished from the scholarly radar in the past seventy years, its salience has been obscured with at least two lamentable results.[7] Left underinterpreted, sociological typing of Mark as apocalyptic (or, more misleadingly, millenarian) minimizes that identification's *theological* consequences. When that happens, the exegete may become preoccupied with the end in spite of the evangelist's view of that eschaton in the light of its *beginnings*: multiple aspects of the goodness of God's creation. Creation and apocalypticism should not be posed as alternatives, even less as opposites; an enhanced regard for the former in no way diminishes the latter's theological value. To the contrary: a theology of creation *inheres* in Mark's apocalyptic outlook. The same can probably be said for many specimens of ancient Jewish and Christian apocalyptic theology, though I'll leave that suggestion for others to probe.

BIBLICAL BELIEFS ABOUT CREATION

Bernhard W. Anderson has identified five overlapping yet distinguishable dimensions of "biblical creation faith."[8] We proceed from what is evidently oldest to youngest in attestation.

First, *creation of a people*. Adopting a Ugaritic image of cosmological triumph (see below, the fourth dimension), the Song of the Sea (Exod 15:1–18)

---

6. *Unveiling the Apocalyptic Paul: Paul's Interpreters and the Rhetoric of Criticism*, JSNTSup 127 (Sheffield: Sheffield Academic, 1996).

7. Often hurriedly compiled, subject indexes can mislead. Still, it is safe to say that recent commentaries have not attended as studiously to creation (*la création*; *die Schöpfung*) as to apocalyptic or Son of Man. Notable exceptions include Camille Focant, *L'évangile selon Marc*, CBNT 2 (Paris: Cerf, 2004), 127–29, 373–76; M. Eugene Boring, *Mark: A Commentary*, NTL (Louisville: Westminster John Knox, 2006), 51–59, 369–73; Marcus, *Mark 1–8*, 168–71; Marcus, *Mark 8–16*, 703–7, 883–907. Especially attentive is Dan O. Via Jr., *The Ethics of Mark's Gospel: In the Middle of Time* (Philadelphia: Fortress, 1985), 27–32, 45–50.

8. "Introduction: Mythopoeic and Theological Dimensions of Biblical Creation Faith," in *Creation in the Old Testament*, ed. B. W. Anderson, IRT 6 (Philadelphia: Fortress; London: SPCK, 1984), 1–24, repr. Anderson, *From Creation to New Creation: Old Testament Perspectives*, OBT (Minneapolis: Fortress, 1994), 75–96. "Biblical creation faith" grates on my ear, but repeated gulps of *biblisches Schöpfungstheologie* inflict even worse things on my digestion.

accents Israel's formation as a covenant people: "while the people whom you made [קָנִיתָ] your own passed by" (15:16e REB). The root קנה connotes "acquisition" (NRSV), "purchase" (RSV), or "redemption" (NJPS). That fundamental idea recurs in the Song of Moses (Deut 32:1–43) and Ps 100:

> Is not He the Father who created you [קָנֶךָ],
>> Fashioned you and made you endure! (Deut 32:6c–d NJPS)

> He made us [עָשָׂנוּ] and we are His.
>> His people, the flock he tends. (Ps 100:3b–c NJPS)

Gerhard von Rad noted that redemption sometimes swallows Israel's understanding of creation; "this soteriological interpretation of the work of the creation [is] the most primitive expression of Yahwistic belief concerning Yahweh as Creator of the world."[9]

Second, *creation and order.* Anderson's second aspect taps traditions that stress an analogy, variously expressed, between the cosmic and social orders. Recalling 2 Sam 7:12–17, Ps 89 marries cosmology with the Davidic dynasty: God's cosmos stabilizes the throne.

> I will set [my servant David's] hand on the sea
>> and his right hand on the rivers.
> He shall cry to me, 'You are my Father,
>> my God, and the Rock of my salvation!'
> I will make him the firstborn,
>> the highest of the kings of the earth.
> Forever I will keep my steadfast love for him,
>> and my covenant with him will stand firm. (vv. 25–28 NRSV; cf.
>> Ps 74:1–17)

In Ps 96, the LORD's enthronement, not the Davidic covenant as such, undergirds Zion:

> For great is the LORD and much praised,
>> awesome is He over all the gods.

---

9. "The Theological Problem of the Old Testament Doctrine of Creation," in Gerhard von Rad, *From Genesis to Chronicles: Explorations in Old Testament Theology,* ed. K. C. Hanson (Minneapolis: Fortress, 2005), 183.

For all gods of the peoples are ungods,
> but the Lord has made the heavens. (vv. 4–5 Alter; cf. Ps 93:3–4)

Third, *creation and creaturely dependence.* Psalm 104 refers neither to the sociopolitical order nor even to Israel. Anderson's exegesis of its view of creation merits extended quotation:

> In contrast to the Genesis creation story (and Psalm 8), this psalm puts all creatures, including human beings, on a plane of equality in the wonderful order of God's creation (see Ps. 104:27–30). . . . Every creature is assigned its proper place and time, and all function harmoniously in the wondrous whole. . . . Moreover, the poetic language also indicates . . . the radical dependence of all creatures upon the Creator. . . . The cosmos is not an autonomous whole, governed by its own laws, but is completely dependent on the God who transcends it. Moment by moment it is held in being by the sovereign will of the Creator.[10]

Mountains and trees, springs and grasslands, beasts and birds, seafarers and Leviathan:

> All of them look to You
> > to give them their food in its season.
> Give it to them, they gather it up;
> > open Your hand, they are well satisfied;
> Hide your face, they panic;
> > withdraw their breath, they perish
> > and turn again into dust;
> Send back Your breath, they are created,
> > and You renew the face of the earth. (Ps 104:27–30 NJPS, adapted)

Fourth, drawing on elements just described, *creation as origination* is a relative latecomer in the OT. Specifically, its home is the Priestly tradition, which adapted Babylonian tropes into the distinctively Hebraic בְּרִית עוֹלָם (God's covenant with Israel in perpetuity),[11] inaugurated by the creation narrative in Gen 1:1–2:3 and succeeded by the Noachic (Gen 9:8–17), Abrahamic (17:1–21),

---

10. Anderson, "Introduction," 12–13.
11. Gen 9:16; 17:7, 13, 18, 19; Exod 31:16; Lev 24:8; Num 15:15; 18:19.

and Sinaitic covenants (Exod 31:12–17).[12] The Priestly accent is on creation's aesthetic suitability to God's intent (Gen 1:31), the eruption of violence that must be purified (6:11–12), creation's radical dependence on its Creator (7:11), and a promise of consummation (8:1–2; 9:1–17).

Fifth, gathering all other aspects, Deutero- and Trito-Isaiah unfold *creation as new creation*:

> The LORD is the everlasting God,
>> the creator of the ends of the earth. . . . (Isa 40:28b–c NRSV)

> Stop dwelling on past events
>> and brooding over days gone by.
> I am about to do [= make (הִנְנִי עֹשֶׂה)] something new;
>> this moment it will unfold. . . .
> Even through the wilderness I shall make a way,
>> And paths in the barren desert.
> The wild beasts will do me honour, . . .
> For I shall provide water in the wilderness
>> And rivers in the barren desert,
> Where my chosen people may drink,
> This people I have formed for myself,
> And they will proclaim my praises. (43:18–19b, 19d–20a, 20c–21 REB)

> For behold, I create new heavens and a new earth;
> And the former things shall not be remembered
>> or come into mind. (65:17 RSV)

Some deductions are in order. First, creation in the OT elides time and space. Texts of origin—of all things, of a particular people—are not locked into a cell "back then"; revivified in worship, such confessions stretch across a durable covenantal lineage.[13] Likewise, a vertical dynamism: God calls Israel

---

12. The classic study is Hermann Gunkel, *Schöpfung und Chaos in Urzeit und Endzeit: Eine religionsgeschichtliche Untersuchung über Gen 1 und Ap Joh 12* (Göttingen: Vandenhoeck & Ruprecht, 1895), 2–120.

13. See Ben C. Ollenburger, "Israel's Creation Theology," *ExAud* 3 (1988): 54–71, and, earlier, Rudolf Bultmann, "Der Glaube an Gott den Schöpfer," *EvT* 1 (1934–1935): 175–89; ET *Existence and Faith: Shorter Writings of Rudolf Bultmann*, ed. Schubert M. Ogden (Cleveland: World, 1960), 171–82. I thank Professor M. Eugene Boring for reminding me of Bultmann's expressly Lutheran, tacitly anti-Nazi sermon.

and the world into an ongoing creation that implies traffic between heaven and earth. Second, the OT does not observe sharp distinctions among creation, redemption, and sustenance.[14] God's creative activity describes an arc along which travels an alternating current: new creation recapitulates and conjugates afresh all creative antecedents. Third, biblical creation is inherently relational: congress among creatures with the God who made them.[15] Israel's LORD does not stand aloof but unilaterally instigates a covenant that allows human response to impinge on the execution of divine power. "God remains transcendent in His immanence, and related in His transcendence."[16]

DIMENSIONS OF CREATION IN MARK

First, to encounter creation imagery in the Second Gospel, one needs read no farther than its first fifteen verses. In various ways, they revivify and readjust Priestly interest in *creation as origination*.

(1) Mark's very first word, ἀρχή, fixes the key signature in which the rest of his gospel's symphony is set: a "beginning of the good news of Jesus Christ" (1:1). Significantly, two of Mark's three other references to "beginning" are conjoined with "creation" (ἀπὸ δὲ ἀρχῆς κτίσεως [10:6; 13:19]); the remaining ἀρχή in Mark (13:8) is of the initial "birth pangs" (ὠδίνων) of the last days.

(2) Like its P archetype, that evangel erupts *in medias res*: a new thing resonant of the old. Thus, the announcement of Jesus's messiahship (1:2-3) is heralded in Hebrew Scripture (Exod 23:20; Mal 3:1), particularly "as written in Isaiah the prophet" (Isa 40:3; cf. the sequence of covenants God establishes with Israel in Gen 1:1–2:3; 9:8–17; 17:1–21; Exod 31:12–17).

(3) Introducing the "baptizer in the wilderness" (1:4), Mark tells us nothing of his background and sympathies (cf. Matt 3:1, 7–10, 12, 14–15; Luke 1:5–80; John 1:6–8, 19–26, 29–40; 3:22–30). Instead, Mark distills the OT character of John's ministry:

Table 1: Old Testament Allusions in Mark 1:4-8

| "in the wilderness" | Mark 1:4a | Exod 23:20; Mal 3:1; Isa 40:3 |

---

14. So also Patrick D. Miller, "The Poetry of Creation: Psalm 104," in *God Who Creates: Essays in Honor of W. Sibley Towner*, ed. William P. Brown and S. Dean McBride Jr. (Grand Rapids: Eerdmans, 2000), 87–103, esp. 97.

15. This is the fundamental thesis of Terrence E. Fretheim, *God and World in the Old Testament: A Relational Theology of Creation* (Nashville: Abingdon, 2005).

16. Abraham Heschel, *The Prophets* (New York: Harper & Row, 1982), 486.

"baptism"	Mark 1:4b	Lev 14:5–6, 30–32; Num 19:13, 20–21
"preaching . . . repentance	Mark 1:4c	Isa 1:10–20 (N.B. v. 16); 55:7;
for the forgiveness of sins"		Hos 6:1; Joel 2:12–14; Zech 1:4
"dressed in camel's hair"	Mark 1:6a	2 Kgs 1:8
"in Holy Spirit"	Mark 1:8	Isa 11:1–2; Joel 2:28–32

Likewise, when returning to John in a flashback that describes his gruesome death, Mark grounds that legend in allusions to Eleazar (2 Macc 6:18–31; cf. Mark 6:20), Elijah, Ahab, Jezebel (1 Kgs 18:17–19; 19:1–3; 21:1–26; cf. Mark 6:15a, 19, 24), and Ahasuerus (Esth 5:2–3; 7:1–2; cf. Mark 6:22b–23).

(4) Momentarily deferring consideration of the epiphany in 1:9–11, we note Mark's decision to link the story of Jesus's baptism with his expulsion into the wilderness for a forty-day satanic trial with angelic ministrations (1:12–13; cf. Exod 34:28; 1 Sam 22:4; 23:29; 24:1, 22; 1 Kgs 19:5, 7–8; 1 Chr 21:1; Ps 91:11–13). Mark 1:12–13 is a miniaturized *Chaoskampf*, historicized and christologized: in place of Marduk's cosmological triumph over Tiamat,[17] the evangelist offers a cameo of Jesus, newly acclaimed as God's Son (1:11), in contest with suprahuman forces that immediately threaten the anointed one's fidelity. The outcome of that cosmic combat is equivocal: Mark's version does not end on Matthew's decisive victory (Matt 4:10a: "Begone, Satan!"). John's arrest (Mark 1:14a) and the imminent return of demonic forces (1:21–18) and even Satan himself (8:33) suggest an open ending like that of Luke 4:13 (the devil's departure until "an opportune time" [RSV]).[18] Still, Jesus is supported by angels (Mark 1:13c) and undeterred from announcing a fulfillment of the season (ὁ καιρός) in which God's dominion breaks through (1:14b–15). Mark's enigmatic presentation of Jesus in the desert "with the wild beasts" (1:13b) leans toward a restoration of primordial harmony before the fall (Gen 1:28; 2:19–20; Ps 91:9–14; Isa 11:6–9; 65:17–25) without quite depositing us at that destination. More on this anon.

(5) Within this context, Mark's claims for the "freshness" or "newness" of Jesus's ministry are not vacuous commendations; within the gospel's theological framework, they make sense. Because his appearance, initial trials, proclamation, and (as we shall note presently) anointing are all creative events, grounded in Israel's *Heilsgeschichte*, others can recognize his authority as unconventional (1:27). Jesus contrasts the freshness (τὸ καινόν) of his teaching

---

17. See James B. Pritchard, ed., *The Ancient Near East: An Anthology of Texts and Pictures* (Princeton: Princeton University Press, 1971), 31–39; E. A. Speiser, *Genesis*, AB 1 (Garden City, NY: Doubleday, 1964), 9–13.

18. Contra Ernest Best, who reads Mark 1:12–13 as Jesus's defeat of the devil (*The Temptation and the Passion: The Markan Soteriology*, 2nd ed., SNTSMS 2 [Cambridge: Cambridge University Press, 1990], xviii, 3–60, 190).

to the old (τὸ παλαιόν [2:21–22]) and points to his postmortem participation (ὅταν αὐτὸ πίνω καινόν) in God's kingdom (τῇ βασιλείᾳ τοῦ θεοῦ [14:25]).

Second, of all aspects of creation derivative from the OT, *creation as ordered restoration* is predominant in Mark. The reason is simple, though its expressions manifold and complicated: here the evangelist's fundamental theological, christological, and soteriological claims converge.

(1) Following Anderson, I have suggested that Pss 89, 74, and 93 crystallize Israel's conviction that its stability is maintained either by the Davidic monarchy or by the LORD's own enthronement. Predictably for a writing that locates "God's good news" in Jesus Christ (1:1, 14), Mark modifies that conviction by narrating Jesus's coronation by the Spirit at his baptism (1:9–11): God's first act of plenipotentiary ministry for the beloved Son on whom divine favor rests. Recasting this baptism as a christologized realization of Ps 2:7 and Isa 42:1, Mark extends the originative nuance of creation. The differences, however, are important: the true heir (12:6–7, 10–11) is Jesus, neither a Davidid (cf. Mark 12:35–37) nor corporate Israel (12:1–9). Unlike God's declarations in the Psalms and Deutero-Isaiah, Jesus's anointing is not publicized: only he and Mark's audience see and hear God's intervention at the baptism (cf. Matt 3:17; John 1:32–34). This veiled acclamation of God's Son is no one-off: Jesus's baptism is the first panel of a mysterious triptych, constructed by the evangelist, which includes Jesus's transfiguration (9:2–8) and death by crucifixion (15:33–41). All three are drenched in biblical imagery (Gen 22:2; Deut 18:15; Pss 2:7; 22:1; 38:11; 57:5, 11; 69:21; Isa 42:1) with apocalyptic resonance (Isa 64:1; Ezek 1:1; Amos 8:9–10; Dan 7:19; 12:3; 4 Ezra 7.87). Entwining these climactic episodes is similar, sometimes identical, wording.[19] Designed to complement one another, Mark's beginning, middle, and end confront its audience with oblique revelations of this Jesus as the Son of this God. In the Jordan, on a mount, and at Golgotha, Mark 1:9–11, 9:2–8, and 15:33–39 present inextricable dimensions of the evangel's vanguard—Jesus's anointing, transfiguration, and wretched death—that suggest a creation stabilized by *Deus praesens atque absconditus* (cf. Isa 45:15).[20]

(2) Nowhere in Mark does Jesus assert himself as God's Son.[21] His recurrent self-reference is as "the Son of Man" (ὁ υἱὸς τοῦ ἀνθρώπου): a literal rendering

19. Specific "days" (1:9a; 9:2a) or "hours" (15:33); "coming up" (1:10a; 9:2b) or "down" (1:10b; 15:36b); "light" (9:3) and "dark" (15:33); "seeing" (1:10b; 9:8; 15:36c), a "voice" (1:11a; 9:7b; 15:34a); the recurrence of "spirit" (1:10b; 15:37b) and "Elijah" (9:4; 15:35a, 36c; implied in 1:6 [2 Kgs 1:8; Zech 13:4]; cf. 9:13); Jesus as "God's Son" (1:11b; 9:7b; 15:39b). For further discussion, see Black, *Mark*, 335–36.

20. See chapter 9.

21. Jesus silences the unclean spirits' confession of him as such (3:11–12); on only one

of the Aramaic *bar nāshā*, whose most basic meaning is a human being (בֶּן־
אָדָם; cf. Ps 8:5).[22] It is commonplace to group Mark's presentation of Jesus as
"Son of Man" into three categories: an authoritative figure on earth (2:10, 28),
one who must suffer for others and be vindicated (8:31; 9:9, 12, 31b; 10:33–34;
14:21, 41), and an apocalyptic agent to come (8:38; 13:26–27; 14:62). The evangelist probably intends for these different connotations to be mutually interpretive; certainly, he gives us no reason to think otherwise. One may press this
observation farther: all the different nuances of "Son of Man" in Mark correspond to different connotations of "Son of God." The earthly authority of God's
Son, disclosed at his baptism, is exerted by his exorcisms and healings (1:21–28,
29–34, 39, 40–45) and exercised in his controversies with scribes and Pharisees
(2:10, 28). The transfigured Son of God anticipates the powerful Son of Man
who will come in glory (13:26–27; 14:62); indeed, the events on the mount in
9:2–8 immediately fulfill Jesus's prediction of that Son of Man in 8:38. The
Son of Man who must suffer with horrendous humiliation—the most pervasive nuance in this gospel—coheres with the centurion's acclamation (whether
faithfully or in ridicule) "when, facing him, he saw that [Jesus] had died in this
way" (15:39).[23] In Mark, "Son of God" and "Son of Man" interpret each other:
this peculiar "Man" points to and interprets God, whose unique Son Jesus is.

(3) If this be the case, do Mark's theology and Christology imply a renewed
anthropology? Bluntly stated, does the evangelist suggest for Jesus a coherence,
if not equation, among the concepts "Son of God," "Son of Man," and "Adam"
(אָדָם/ὁ Ἀδάμ)? The best evidence for that possibility lies in Mark 1:13, which
Joachim Jeremias places on the same theological plane as Paul's references to
Christ the ἑνὸς/ἔσχατος Ἀδάμ, "one"/"last Adam":

> Adam is the antitype of Christ in M[ar]k 1:13; R[om] 5:12–21; 1 C[or] 15:22,
> 45–49. The account of the temptation in Mark (1:13) shows how Jesus as the
> new man (υἱὸς τοῦ ἀνθρώπου) overcame the temptation which overthrew
> the first man. Jesus, like Adam, is tempted by Satan. Again, as Adam was once
> honoured by the wild beasts in Paradise according to the Midrash [*Apoc.*

---

occasion—which will seal his death warrant—does he accept that acclamation by the high
priest (14:61–63).

22. In Mark 3:28, the aphoristic reference to τοῖς υἱοῖς τῶν ἀνθρώπων, "people" carries
that simple connotation.

23. Mark 15:39 caps the evangelist's redirection of "gospel" and "power" away from the
norms of Roman imperial ideology, which identified renewed creation with the *pax romana*.
See T. Ryan Jackson, *New Creation in Paul's Letters*, WUNT 272 (Tübingen: Mohr Siebeck,
2010), 60–80.

Mos. 16], so Christ is with the wild beasts after overcoming temptation. He thus ushers in the paradisial state of the last days when there will be peace between man and beast (Isa 11:6–8; 65:25). As Adam in Paradise enjoyed angels' food according to the Midrash [b. Sanh. 59b; LAE 4.2], so the angels give heavenly food to the new man. Jesus reopens Paradise closed to the first man.[24]

This reading is riddled with non sequiturs. First, it begs the fundamental question: that Mark, like Paul, regards Jesus as "the new man." Nowhere does the gospel develop this idea; the evangelist never mentions "Adam." Second, Mark 1:13 says that wild beasts were "with" (μετά) Jesus, nothing of their honoring him. Third, a comment about the angels' ministry (διηκόνουν) to him is far short of claiming that they gave "heavenly food to the new man" (cf. the menial service stipulated in 1:31b; 10:45a; 15:41). Fourth, where in this gospel does Jesus usher in a paradisial age (cf. Luke 23:43)? Nowhere that I can see. To the contrary, demon-possessed swine provoke terror at Gerasa (5:11–16), and things generally will deteriorate before improving (13:1–39; 15:20b–16:8). Seized by Paul's articulation of Christ as "new Adam," Jeremias has skewed his Markan exegesis into a fabulous midrash of his own.

That said, Jeremias is on to something that invites temperate explanation. Like "Adam," "Son of Man" is an elliptical idiom whose interpretation depends mightily on its context. Genesis 1:26–28 (P) describes humanity in toto as אָדָם (so also 8:21); in 5:3–5 (P), the term refers to an individual, with children and a limited lifespan, though in 2:4b–4:25 (J) to a particular human representative of humanity. Jump to Philo in the first century CE: "As now formed, *adam* is perceptible . . . , by nature mortal; but, made in accordance with God's image, *adam* was an ideal or a genus or a seal, perceptible by intellect alone . . . , by nature imperishable" (*Opif.* 134).[25] So, too, "Son of Man": even its contrast with the LORD in Ps 8:3–8 suggests qualified exaltation, absent from the simpler אִישׁ ("man") and אִשָּׁה ("woman"). The same ambiguity colors God's address

24. J. Jeremias, "Ἀδάμ," *TDNT* 1:141; with equal confidence, Hans-Josef Klauck, *Vorspiel im Himmel? Erzähltechnik und Theologie im Markusprolog*, BTS 32 (Neukirchener-Vluyn: Neukirchener, 1997), 55–60. Consonant with this interpretation, though more restrained, are Eduard Schweizer, *The Good News according to Mark*, trans. Donald H. Madvig (Atlanta: John Knox, 1970), 42–43; Robert A. Guelich, *Mark 1–8:26*, WBC 34A (Dallas: Word, 1989), 37–40; Francis J. Moloney, *The Gospel of Mark: A Commentary* (Peabody, MA.: Hendrickson, 2002), 38–40.

25. Philo conflates "son of God" with Adam: "Though there is not as yet one worthy to be called a son of God, still let us sincerely strive to be adorned to suit his first-born word . . . : humanity befitting God's image" (*Conf.* 146).

to Ezekiel as בֶּן־אָדָם (ninety-three times): the name simultaneously places the prophet on par with all mortals while recognizing him as a divine delegate. The key passage from which evolves the convoluted בֶּן־אָדָם in subsequent apocalyptic literature, Dan 7:13, describes the figure that approaches the Ancient of Days as "one *like* [כְּ] a son of man": a heavenly creature of human semblance. "Adam" and "Son of Man" thus appear to be conceptual cognates, both rich in lapidary connotations.[26] Apparently Paul took the "Adam" track, educing anthropological (Romans) and eschatological (1 Corinthians) implications from one aspect of his Christology. Probably in closer alignment with early remembrances of Jesus's self-reference,[27] Mark travels the "Son of Man" line, correlating its multiple connotations while leaving underdeveloped its tacit anthropological or cosmological consequences.[28] As Son of Man, the Markan Jesus *begins* the reclamation of God's creation from chaos (4:35–41; 6:48–52), sin (2:5, 10; 10:45), and diabolical corruption (1:21–28; 5:1–20; 7:24–30; 9:14–29), even though this new creation is not yet fully realized.[29] "The end is not yet" (13:7b); much remains to do (13:10, 33–37) and to be endured (13:8–13). Perhaps for that reason, Mark resists asserting in 1:12–13 all that the Testament of Naphtali (8.4; ca. 105 BCE) promises and Jeremias presumes of the gospel as a fait accompli: "The devil will flee from you; wild animals will be afraid of you; and the angels will stand by you" (see also T. Benj. 5.2; T. Iss. 7.7). Until God's dominion crosses the threshold from "near" (ἐγγύς [1:15b]) to "now" (νῦν [2 Cor 6:2]), *Paradise Regain'd* is perfectly Miltonic but more than Mark appears comfortable to claim.

26. Likewise, Morna D. Hooker: "there is a very close resemblance between the figures of Adam and the Son of man—a connection whose cause, however, appears to lie in Hebrew ideas regarding creation, election and corporate personality, rather than in foreign speculations about a primal or heavenly man" (*The Son of Man in Mark* [Montreal: McGill University Press, 1967], 72).

27. Like everything else associated with "Son of Man," this is debatable. On balance, I think it likelier than not to be true: the idiom is so inexplicit that it's hard for me to imagine the early church having handed it down unless Jesus had used it. See Douglas R. A. Hare, *The Son of Man Tradition* (Minneapolis: Fortress, 1990), 213–82.

28. Similarly, regarding a *theologia crucis* that Paul articulates (in 1 Cor 1:18–2:16) but to which Mark only alludes (15:21–39), see chapter 12. Marcus denies the gap that I find: "For Mark as for Paul, then, Jesus is the firstborn of a new humanity" (*Mark 1–8*, 170); see also Herman C. Waetjen, *A Reordering of Power: A Socio-political Reading of Mark's Gospel* (Minneapolis: Fortress, 1989).

29. See Michael F. Bird, "Tearing the Heavens and Shaking the Heavenlies: Mark's Cosmology in Its Apocalyptic Context," in *Cosmology and New Testament Theology*, ed. Jonathan T. Pennington and Sean M. McDonough, LNTS 355 (London: T&T Clark, 2008), 45–59.

Third, once God (creation's maker: 10:6) and his Messiah (its redeemer: 10:45) are theologically in place, the apocalyptic prospect of *renewed creation* takes shape in this gospel: "new wine in fresh skins" (2:22; cf. Isa 43:19). The plainest clue of its character lies in Jesus's reply to the question of divorce: "From creation's beginning [God] made them male and female. . . . such that no longer are they two, but one flesh; thus, whatever God has conjoined, let no one separate" (Mark 10:6, 8b–9; cf. Gen 1:27; 2:24).[30] *Wholeness* recovers creation at its genesis and stamps its restoration. Jesus makes *all* foods clean (7:19b; cf. Lev 17–26), opens wide "a house of prayer for *all* the nations" (11:17b; cf. Isa 56:7), and mandates evangelism "to *all* the nations" (13:10). Unfettered sacrifice for the gospel will be fulfilled a hundredfold (10:29–30; cf. 4:20). The Lord God, who is one, requires of Israel love with unmitigated wholeness (ἐξ ὅλης) of heart, soul, mind, and strength (12:29–30; cf. Deut 6:4–5). Jesus's healings create unity from internal divisions: exorcism of demons that wrench humans apart (Mark 1:24–25; 5:2–8; 9:22a, 25–26a); release from paralysis and sin (2:5, 11); bestowal of ability to "gaze clearly upon all" (8:23–25; cf. 10:51–52); conferral of life to those apparently dead (5:25–29, 39–42a; 9:26b–27; N.B. 12:27a: "God of the living"). Nowhere in Mark's apocalyptic scenario (13:3–37) are the unrighteous damned; those whose sin is eternal put themselves beyond the pale by confusing Jesus with Satan, whose kingdom is fractured (3:22–30). Constantly, mortals resistant to this creation aborning are antagonists and intimates torn among or within themselves (2:6–8; 3:19b–22; 4:15–29; 6:2–3; 8:16; 9:10, 33–34; 10:17, 22, 35–37, 41; 11:31; 14:29–31, 50–52, 56, 66–72). With equal constancy, at the cross, Jesus remains faithful to God (15:34; cf. 14:32–42); at the tomb, God keeps faith with Jesus (16:6; cf. 14:28); at his story's open ending, Mark returns the reader to its beginning (16:7–8; 1:1). The gospel's form, a Möbius band, mimics God's ongoing creation: a beginning (ἀρχή) still pulsing toward completion.

Fourth, the earliest and most pervasive aspect of creation in Hebrew Scripture, *God's making of a people*, is present in Mark though least developed. Israel's past and future are acknowledged (12:1–11, 28–31; 15:32); Galilee and Judea make up the theater of the kingdom's breakthrough (1:5, 9, 14, 28, 39; 3:7–8; 10:1; 11:1, 11). Though its association with twelve tribes (Num 1:4–16; 13:1–16) is not as clear as in Q (Luke 22:30 = Matt 19:28), in Mark the nucleus of Jesus's followers are twelve "whom he wanted . . . and made [ἐποίησεν], . . . to be with him and to be sent

---

30. Via (*Ethics of Mark's Gospel*, 108–9) argues that Jesus's assertion of indissoluble marriage depends on his assuming "the role of the Creator" in Mark 4:35–41. That's farther than I would go, though I agree with Via that the evangelist presents Jesus as struggling with chaos that is both cosmic and social.

out to preach and have authority to cast out demons" (3:13–15; also 6:7). As in Deutero-Isaiah (45:22b), Mark's soteriological scope encompasses "all the ends of the earth" (13:27); thus, all are summoned to repentance and salvation (Isa 45:22a; Mark 1:15). Practically, as we have seen, this means that Israel's emblematic differentiations—sabbath (2:23–28), kashrut (7:1–23), the temple (11:12–21; 13:1–2; 15:38)—are universally exploded by the kingdom Jesus proclaims. Commensurately, conventional markers of social identity are overturned (1:16–20; 2:13–17); replacing old ones governed by *patres familias*, new families gather around Jesus on the sole basis of doing God's will (3:31–35; 6:1–4; 10:28–31). Within this context, a child becomes the exemplary disciple (9:33–50; 10:13–27): only one so helplessly dependent can enter a realm in which nothing is possible without faith in God's graceful provision (4:11–12, 25; 6:5–6a; 8:35–37; 9:23–24; 10:27; 11:24–26; 12:41–44; 14:32–42).[31] Psalm 104's efflorescent images of mortal contingency on the creative God—master of deep waters (vv. 5–9), maker of light and darkness (vv. 19–20), giver of food in due season (vv. 27–28), the one who hides his face yet gives life anew (vv. 29–30)—rhyme with many of Mark's most memorable episodes (4:35–41; 6:30–52; 8:1–10; 13:24–25; 15:33–34; 16:2–6).

WHY IT ALL MATTERS

Mark does *not* present a systematic doctrine of creation, any more than it systematizes a doctrine of any other theological topic. The Second Gospel *does* offer a view of the subject that is internally coherent and consanguineous with that of the OT. To this aspect of the gospel's theology, Mark's exegetes should pay closer attention: unless we are careful, we risk domesticating its apocalypticism into a *sozialreligionsgeschichtlich* phenomenon (otherwise known as millenarianism) or neutering it as an academic cliché. Eschatology does not dangle free in biblical ether; it is a coefficient of ktisisology, just as soteriology follows from harmatology and Christology is correlative to theology.[32]

Such interconnections are detectable in other apocalyptic literature around the time of Mark. The book of Jubilees (second century BCE) offers an instructive comparison. Appealing to divine revelation (1:27, 29; 2:1; cf. Mark 4:10–12), Jubilees, like Mark, intends to redirect its readers onto the LORD's way in a season of

31. Katherine Joy Kihlstrom Timpte, *The Transformational Role of Discipleship in Mark 10:13–16: Passage Towards Childhood*, LNTS 650 (London: T&T Clark, 2021).

32. Compare the conclusions of John R. Donahue's "A Neglected Factor in the Theology of Mark," *JBL* 101 (1982): 563–94, published in a day when preoccupation with Markan Christology had all but ignored God.

apostasy under gentile pressure ("the sinners of the nations": Jub. 23.23a).[33] More explicitly than in Mark, Jubilees's apocalypticism rewrites the stories of Israel's creation (Gen 1–Exod 24): thus, *lex talionis* (Exod 21:24; Lev 24:19–20; Deut 19:21) was in force at the time of Cain and Abel (Jub. 4.31–32); Noah and Abram observed the Festival of Weeks (6:17–22; 15:1–2; cf. Exod 23:16; 34:22; Lev 23:15–20; Num 28:26). Israel's only hope for rescue and restoration is to double down its obedience to the law, which is eternal and immutable (Jub. 3.10, 31; 6.17; 15.25; 16.28–29).

> And in those days, children will begin to search the law,
> and to search the commandments
> and to return to the way of righteousness. . . .
> And all of their days they will be complete
> and live in peace and rejoicing
> and there will be no Satan and no evil [one] who will destroy. . . .
> And then the LORD will heal his servants,
> > and they will rise up and see great peace.
> And they will drive out their enemies,
> > and the righteous ones will see and give praise,
> > and rejoice forever and ever with joy;
> > and they will see all of their judgments and all of their curses
> > among their enemies (Jub. 23.26, 29a–c, 30).[34]

Like Jubilees, Mark's Gospel summons repentance and promises wholeness among a faithless generation that lives in a world populated by angels and demons. Disparate adaptations of God's creative purpose shape these books' eschatologies. Conspicuously Jubilees is preoccupied with Israel's cleansing, its cleaving to all of the commandments and fitness to be called "sons of the living God" (1.24–25a). The gentiles can go to hell, because that's where their wickedness belongs. Mark's creational-eschatological view is more expansive; instead of retrojecting the Sinaitic covenant into primeval history, as Jubilees is inclined, Mark tends to contextualize the Israelite covenant within God's earlier covenants with all humankind "from creation's beginning" (10:6): Adam and Eve (10:7–8) and Abraham (12:26–27).[35] The other obvious difference be-

---

33. On the different *Sitze im Leben* of Jubilees and Mark, consult George W. E. Nickelsburg, *Jewish Literature between the Bible and the Midrash: A Historical and Literary Introduction* (Philadelphia: Fortress, 1981), 73–80; C. Clifton Black, *Mark: Images of an Apostolic Interpreter*, SPNT (Minneapolis: Fortress; Edinburgh: T&T Clark, 2001), 224–50.

34. Trans. O. S. Wintermute, *OTP* 2:101–2.

35. The Noahic covenant (Gen 9:8–17) does not appear in Mark, though it, too, is on this wavelength.

tween Jubilees and Mark is God's soteriological instrument: in the earlier book the LORD promises to create for his people a purifying, holy spirit that prevents their perpetual stubbornness (Jub. 1.23c–d). A messiah is never mentioned; evidently one is not needed. In the Second Gospel, the Messiah is indispensable, without whom Scripture cannot be properly obeyed and sin cannot be redeemed (2:25–28; 7:1–13; 10:17–22; 10:35–45; 12:10–37; 14:22–24).

In Mark, the coming of Jesus Christ spells this world's invasion by God's βασιλεία, a dominion that creates as well as exposes fissures within and beyond the human heart (2:22; 4:10–12; 7:14–23; 8:11–21; 11:27–12:34; 13:1–37; 14:22–72). That's true, but it's not the whole truth.[36] The Second Evangelist also underscores continuity: Christ's repair of the ruptured (10:2–9, 45), his insistence on forgiveness and redemption, not dissolution and abandonment (1:4; 2:5, 9–10; 3:28–29; 11:25; 14:22–31; 16:1–8). "Divine suffering," notes Lois Malcolm, "is ultimately creative—bringing justice out of oppression, life out of death, health where there is disease."[37] The wedding of these antipodes is graphically rendered in Mark 9:42–50: the necessity of amputation to enter the kingdom whole. The physician must cut in order to heal (cf. 2:17). Salt is for sacrifice (Lev 2:13; Ezek 43:24) and preservation (Num 18:19; cf. Luke 14:34 = Matt 5:13; Col 4:6). "Have in yourselves salt, and be at peace among one another" (Mark 9:50b). Though the term καταλλαγή never appears in Mark, reconciliation lies near its heart,[38] even as reconciliation—the first and last act of God's self-giving freedom—nestles in the bosom of *creatio continua* as Scripture understands it.[39]

36. In this connection, consider the parallel debates of Pauline apocalypticism, whether it is better understood within a *heilsgeschichtliche* framework (J. Christiaan Beker, *Paul the Apostle: The Triumph of God in Life and Thought* [Philadelphia: Fortress, 1980]) or as "a disjunctive dualism of the ages" (J. Louis Martyn, *Theological Issues in the Letters of Paul* [Nashville: Abingdon, 1997], 178). Does the answer to that question partly depend on which letter the interpreter focuses his exegesis, Romans or Galatians?

37. "The Crucified Messiah and Divine Suffering in the Old Testament," in *"And God Saw That It Was Good": Essays on Creation and God in Honor of Terence E. Fretheim*, ed. Frederick J. Gaiser and Mark A. Throntveit, WWSup 5 (Saint Paul: Luther Seminary, 2006), 144.

38. Christoph Schwöbel perceptively correlates divine reconciliation with creation in "Reconciliation: From Biblical Observations to Dogmatic Reconstruction," in *The Theology of Reconciliation*, ed. Colin E. Gunton (London: T&T Clark, 2003), 13–38.

39. For their acute criticisms of an earlier version of this study, I am grateful to Professor M. Eugene Boring and the late Professor Patrick D. Miller.

CHAPTER 14

An Oration at Olivet

The loveliest thing we can experience is the mysterious. It is the basic feeling that stands at the cradle of true art and science.

—Albert Einstein[1]

MARK'S IS A MYSTERIOUS GOSPEL, and no portion of it bristles with more mysteries than the so-called Synoptic apocalypse in chapter 13.[2] Beyond discrete exegetical problems posed by its verses, interpreters have long pondered the material's derivation, either from the historical Jesus or from some Jewish or Jewish-Christian prototype, and the degree, if any, to which that material may properly be regarded as apocalyptic.[3] Curiously, few have studied one of Mark 13's most obvious features: its character and function as a rhetorical event.

Precisely at this point, George Kennedy's rhetorical approach offers help.[4] Accordingly, in this chapter, I essay an assessment of the rhetoric of Mark 13, beginning with particular presuppositions. First, in line with what may be reckoned as the current scholarly consensus, I regard this chapter to be eschatolog-

---

1. "Wie ich die Welt sehe," in *Mein Weltbild*, 2nd ed. (Amsterdam: Querido, 1934), 16 (AT).

2. For the chapter's modern history of exegesis, see George R. Beasley-Murray, *Jesus and the Last Days: The Interpretation of the Olivet Discourse* (Peabody, MA: Hendrickson, 1993).

3. Beasley-Murray (*Jesus and the Last Days*, 350–76) is highly optimistic in tracing the discourse back to Jesus himself. First proposed by Timothy Colani, *Jésus Christ et les Croyances messianiques de son Temps*, 2nd ed. (Strasbourg: Treuttel et Wurtz, 1864), the theory of a "little apocalypse" underlying Mark 13 has fallen on hard times in recent Synoptic study. The hypothesis was notably revived by Rudolf Pesch, *Naherwartungen: Tradition und Redaktion in Mk 13*, KBANT (Düsseldorf: Patmos, 1968), 207–23, and just as notably rejected by Adela Yarbro Collins, *The Beginning of the Gospel: Probings of Mark in Context* (Minneapolis: Fortress, 1992), 73–91.

4. George A. Kennedy, *New Testament Interpretation through Rhetorical Criticism* (Chapel Hill: University of North Carolina, 1984), 3–38.

ically oriented but not an apocalypse as such.[5] If we accept a helpful distinction drawn by John Collins, we needn't worry that Mark 13 fails to conform to the literary genre of an apocalypse (as the book of Daniel so obviously does).[6] It is enough to recognize that Mark adopts an apocalyptic *perspective*, awaiting a cataclysmic end of the present age. A second assumption, analyzing Mark 13 in accordance with Greco-Roman rhetorical conventions is appropriate, owing to rhetoric's pervasiveness throughout Mediterranean antiquity.[7] Third, questions attached to the sources and authenticity of the Olivet Discourse, while interesting, are immaterial to the question of its rhetorical effectiveness.[8] It is with the discourse in its canonical literary form, as presented by the Markan Jesus to the Second Evangelist's early Christian community, that I am concerned.[9]

5. Thus, Elisabeth Schüssler Fiorenza, "The Phenomenon of Early Christian Apocalyptic: Some Reflections on Method," in *Apocalypticism in the Mediterranean World and the Near East: Proceedings of the International Colloquium on Apocalypticism, Uppsala, August 12–17, 1979*, ed. David Hellholm, 2nd ed. (Tübingen: Mohr Siebeck, 1989), 295–316; Christopher Rowland, *The Open Heaven: A Study of Apocalyptic in Judaism and Early Christianity* (New York: Crossroad, 1982), 9–72, 351–57. Dissenting and reasserting this pericope's formal apocalypticism is Egon Brandenburger, *Markus 13 und die Apokalyptik*, FRLANT 134 (Göttingen: Vandenhoeck & Ruprecht, 1984), 21–42.

6. John J. Collins, "Towards a Morphology of Genre," *Semeia* 14 (1979): 2–20.

7. James L. Kinneavy, *Greek Rhetorical Origins of Christian Faith: An Inquiry* (New York: Oxford University Press, 1987), 56–100, conveniently summarizes the evidence.

8. Broadly conceived, the question of sources is not, however, entirely irrelevant. As we shall see, the *ēthos* of Jesus and the use of Septuagintal allusions enhance Mark's rhetorical force.

9. That community's geographical and social location remains debatable. Joel Marcus mounts a serious case for Mark's Syrian provenance in "The Jewish War and the *Sitz im Leben* of Mark," *JBL* 111 (1992): 441–62; Marcus, *Mark 1–8: A New Translation with Introduction and Commentary*, AB 27 (New York: Doubleday, 2000), 25–39. With equal vigor, H. N. Roskam, *The Purpose of the Gospel of Mark in Its Social and Religious Context*, NovTSup 114 (Leiden: Brill, 2004), argues that Mark's audience was a persecuted community situated in Galilee after the climax of Israel's revolt against Rome in 70. Elsewhere I have suggested that the Second Gospel's traditional association with first-century Rome in the 60s is not implausible, though not exactly for the reasons traditionally given: see C. Clifton Black, *Mark: Images of an Apostolic Interpreter*, SPNT (Minneapolis: Fortress; Edinburgh: T&T Clark, 2001), 224–50, and chapter 1 of the present volume.

A Rhetorical Analysis of Mark 13

The Rhetorical Unit

For defining the limits of the speech in Mark 13, the markers of *inclusio* are obvious. At 13:5a, a common Markan formula, "And Jesus began to say to them," introduces Jesus's discourse, which commences at 13:5b.[10] At 14:1, the narrator intervenes, shifting the time, characters, and circumstances. Accordingly, 13:37 may be regarded as the oration's end. Between these points lies an unbroken address of thirty-three verses (5b–37), a unit of considerable magnitude. This is the longest uninterrupted speech presented by Jesus in the Second Gospel.[11]

The Rhetorical Situation

According to Lloyd Bitzer, a rhetorical situation may be defined as that "natural context of persons, events, objects, relations, and an exigence which strongly invites utterance; this invited utterance participates naturally in the situation, is in many instances necessary to the completion of situational activity, and by means of its participation with [the] situation obtains its meaning and its rhetorical character."[12] Does this complex state of affairs obtain in Mark 13?

Though its verification depends on closer inspection of the rhetoric of verses 5b–37, a provisional case can be made for its rhetorical situation.

First, as described by Mark, the audience is appropriate for the rather esoteric discourse that will follow. After a period of public instruction within the temple (11:27–12:44), the dramatis personae are reduced, first to Jesus and his disciples (13:1–2), then quite abruptly to Jesus and a quartet from among the Twelve (13:3). While reflecting that conjunction, evidenced in various rabbinic texts, of "public retort and private explanation,"[13] such a progression is characteristic of Mark's narrative: repeatedly therein, a small group of Jesus's intimates are permitted instruction or disclosures that are denied the general

---

10. See also Mark 1:45; 4:1; 5:20; 6:2, 34; 8:31; 10:32; 12:1.

11. The only discourses of comparable length are Mark 4:3–32 and 7:6–23, both of which are repeatedly interrupted by the narrator (4:10–11a, 13a, 21a, 24a, 26a, 30a; 7:9a, 14a, 17a, 18a, 20a).

12. Lloyd F. Bitzer, "The Rhetorical Situation," *PR* 1 (1968): 5. On the concept of "exigence," the circumstances that exert pressure for an oral response, see 6–7.

13. David Daube, *The New Testament and Rabbinic Judaism* (Salem, NH: Ayer, 1984), 141–50.

populace (see 4:10–34; 7:17–23; 9:28; 10:10–12). On three occasions in Mark other than that recounted in 13:3, Peter, James, and John participate in events closed to others, even to the rest of the Twelve (5:37; 9:2; 14:33).[14] Thus, Jesus's oration in 13:5b–37 is privately addressed (κατ᾽ ἰδίαν, "by themselves" [v. 3]) to a privileged inner circle, three of whom have been informed of their teacher's identity as Messiah (8:29; 9:41) and Son of God (9:7; note also 8:31, 38; 9:9, 31; 10:33, 45).[15]

Second, by the beginning of Mark 13, a number of related events have converged in a manner that would render the ensuing speech natural, if not inevitable. In response to a disciple's comment on the temple's rock-solid stability (13:1),[16] Jesus's prophecy of its annihilation (13:2) overtly proclaims Judaism's cultic destruction, which has been foreshadowed in Jesus's prophetic activity (11:12–21) and subversive teaching within the temple precincts (11:27–12:44). Jesus's own destruction is also imminent: immediately after the Olivet Discourse, the plot for his arrest and crucifixion is hatched in earnest (14:1–11; cf. 3:6; 8:31; 9:31; 10:33–34; 12:12). In terms of both narrative and rhetorical logic, Jesus's address is appropriately situated at Mark 13:5b–37: its sheer length and gravity, laden with images and phraseology that will be echoed in chapters 14–15,[17] correspond with the dark hues and conspicuous deceleration of narrative speed in Mark's passion narrative.[18] Occurring on the eve of Jesus's execution, Mark 13:5b–37 is reminiscent of an *Abschiedsrede*: a "farewell address of a great man before his death," of which there are numerous specimens in Semitic and Greek literature.[19]

14. Recall that Simon Peter, Andrew, James, and John are the first disciples summoned by Jesus in Mark (1:16–20).

15. The audiences for this address seem incrementally enlarged in Matthew (24:3) and Luke (21:5–7).

16. Cf. Josephus, *A.J.* 15.380–425; *B.J.* 5.184–247. Brandenburger (*Markus 13 und die Apokalyptik*, 91–115) may be right that Mark 13:1–2 originated as an independent "pronouncement story." Nevertheless, in their present literary position these verses open the address in vv. 5b–37.

17. Consult C. Clifton Black, *Mark*, ANTC (Nashville: Abingdon, 2011), 276–338.

18. See further R. H. Lightfoot, "The Connexion of Chapter Thirteen with the Passion Narrative," in *The Gospel Message of St. Mark* (Oxford: Clarendon, 1950), 48–59. For insight into the "narrative deceleration" created by Mark 13, I am indebted to W. S. Vorster, "Literary Reflections on Mark 13:5–37: A Narrated Speech of Jesus," *Neot* 21 (1987): 203–24, esp. 212.

19. Cf. Gen 41:21–49; 49:1–33; Deut 31:1–33:29; Josh 23:1–24:30; 1 Sam 12:1–25; 1 Kgs 2:1–9; 1 Chr 28:1–29:5; Tob 14:3–11; 1 Macc 2:49–70; John 14:1–17:26; Acts 20:18b–35; 2 Tim 1:1–4:22; 1 En. 91–105; Jub. 23.9–32; Plato, *Apology, Crito, Phaedo*; Xenophon, *Mem.* 4.7.1–10; and the pseudepigraphical Testaments of the Twelve Patriarchs. In *Prophecy in Early Christianity*

Third, for Bitzer, an "exigence" refers to an actual or potential imperfection, marked by urgency, which is amenable to positive modification by discourse. The exigence that occasions the speech in Mark 13 is indicated by potential imperfection (v. 2: Jesus's prediction of the temple's toppling) and implied urgency (v. 4: the quartet's inquiry about the realization of these things). Implicit in both these aspects is an intricate web of rhetorical associations. The prophecy in verse 2 tacitly locates Jesus among prophets who announced the temple's desolation.[20] While seemingly detached from the proclamation of a singular catastrophe, the query in verse 4 (πότε ταῦτα ἔσται ... ὅταν μέλλη ταῦτα συντελεῖσθαι πάντα, "When will these things be; ... when are all these things to be accomplished?") echoes the wording of Dan 12:7 LXX (συντελεσθήσεται πάντα ταῦτα, "all these things will be accomplished"). By this choice of Danielic expression, Mark suggests that the disciples' reaction to the possibility of the temple's destruction was colored by a degree of eschatologically generated excitement.[21] Delivered at a venue with eschatological associations (Zech 14:1–5), Jesus's response will attempt in part to bolster the confidence of an audience whose "soul" is reckoned to be agitated (Plato, *Phaedr.* 271a–d; Aristotle, *Rhet.* 2.5 [1382a–1383b]).

As far as I can tell, rhetorical criticism of Mark 13 cannot in itself resolve the vexed question of whether the tragedy of 70 CE has already occurred. If Mark knew that the temple had already fallen, a *vaticinium ex eventu* (a prophecy sprung from a known event) to that effect would have amplified the *ēthos* of Jesus (a rationale seemingly at work in Luke 19:41–44; 21:20–24).[22] On the other hand, a more precise statement of cultic collapse, reflecting the post-

---

and the Ancient Mediterranean World (Grand Rapids: Eerdmans, 1983), 186, 399–400 n. 93, David E. Aune observes that the introduction of Mark 13 reflects a complex entwining of various ancient literary genres: the peripatetic dialogue (13:1–2), the solicitation of an oracular response (13:3–4), and the *Tempeldialog* (13:1–4). All such *Abschiedsreden* display superior elegance but inferior pith to the last words of botanist Luther Burbank (1849–1926): "I don't feel good."

20. Mic 3:10–12; Jer 7:14; 26:6, 18; Mark 14:58; 15:29; John 2:19; Acts 6:13–14; 1 En. 90.28; B.J. 6.300–309; b. Yoma 4.1.39b.

21. Jewish reaction to the events of 70 CE was anything but uniform, though some associated the temple's fall with divine judgment (2 Bar. 7.1; 80.1–3; Sib. Or. 4.115–27) or eschatological hopes for Jerusalem's re-creation (2 Esd. 11.1–12.3). For further discussion, consult G. W. H. Lampe, "A.D. 70 in Christian Reflection," in *Jesus and the Politics of His Day*, ed. Ernst Bammel and C. F. D. Moule (Cambridge: Cambridge University Press, 1984), 153–71.

22. Here and throughout this chapter, I use transliterations of the standard modes of persuasion—*ēthos* (ἦθος), *pathos* (πάθος), and *logos* (λόγος)—because they have become conventional in biblical as well as classical scholarship.

70 reality, could have heightened the very eschatological tension that, as we shall see, Mark 13:5b–37 seems designed to relax. Rhetorical analysis cannot arbitrate this classic exegetical stalemate.[23]

Assessing this material's rhetorical situation does offer help in adjudicating another, no less contentious, scholarly debate. On grounds both stylistic and substantive, the very existence of the Olivet Discourse in its present location has appeared intrusive to some scholars.[24] Quite the contrary: if the foregoing analysis be accepted, one may conclude that Mark 13 is propitiously, even powerfully, situated, however obtrusive it may seem to some modern literary sensibilities.

The Rhetorical Problem

Scholars have long puzzled over the raison d'être of Mark 13. How might a rhetorical interpretation of this passage clarify the principal issues at stake?

First, presupposing an association of the temple's destruction with the end of all things, the four disciples' questions in 13:4 invite neither a forensic evaluation of past facts nor a deliberative assessment of actions that might be expedient for future performance. Essentially, their questions pivot on proper belief ("When will these things be?") and evidence that might substantiate that belief ("What is the sign when these things are all to be accomplished?"). Jesus's address in 13:5b–37 responds to these issues of belief and their validation: certain virtues are implicitly or explicitly extolled (wariness, endurance, preparedness, perspicacity), while specific, corresponding vices are censured (cf. Aristotle, *Rhet.* 1.9 [1366a–b]; *Rhet. Her.* 3.6.10–3.8.15; Augustine, *Doctr.*

23. Vicky Balabanski presents a guarded interpretation of Mark 13 as cognizant of Jerusalem's destruction: *Eschatology in the Making: Mark, Matthew and the Didache*, SNTSMS 97 (Cambridge: Cambridge University Press, 1997), 55–100. In "The Apocalyptic Rhetoric of Mark 13 in Historical Context," *BR* 41 (1996): 5–36, Adela Yarbro Collins refers to Bitzer's theories of "rhetorical situation" and "exigence" to introduce an argument that the Olivet Discourse is best understood as a specific response to the first Jewish war against Rome in the summer of 66 CE, after Menachem, a son or grandson of Judas the Galilean (Acts 5:37), emerged as a messianic leader (Josephus, *B.J.* 2.430–440). Like Balabanski, Yarbro Collins acknowledges and responds to alternative proposals for the sociohistorical setting of Mark 13; to engage that debate in this chapter is not integral to my task. I would note, however, that what Yarbro Collins offers is a sophisticated traditio-historical analysis, which is not dependent on rhetorical-critical premises. Her references to Bitzer are lagniappe for her argument, not requisite for it.

24. See, e.g., Pesch, *Naherwartungen*, 48–73; Kenneth Grayston, "The Study of Mark XIII," *BJRL* 56 (1974): 371–87.

chr. 4.4.6). Therefore, from among the various species of rhetoric,[25] epideictic most accurately describes the type of oration that we find in Mark 13:5b-37.

Even if this judgment be accepted, it requires trimming with some qualifications. First, by typing the Olivet Discourse as epideictic, I intend no suggestion that here Jesus is engaged in oratorical display, calculated chiefly to please his audience (thus, Aristotle, *Rhet.* 1.3 [1358b]; Cicero, *De or.* 2.84.340-85.349). By 300 CE, Menander Rhetor analyzed and systematized a rhetorical reality that had long existed: the complexity of epideictic as a rhetorical species.[26] When viewed in the light of Menander's categories, Mark 13:5b-37 begins as a kind of *lalia*, or informal talk (Menander, 2.4); as the speech progresses, it entwines the concerns of *paramythetic*, or consolation (2.9), with *proemptic*, a speech for one departing on a journey (2.5). If our earlier conclusions about this material be upheld, then the Olivet Discourse also functions *syntactically*, as a speech of leave-taking (2.15). I would not argue that Mark 13:5b-37 fits snugly into any of these oratorical pigeonholes of late antiquity, since the speech does not precisely accord with the topics, germane to these types, presented by Menander. My point, rather, is that the presiding functions of this oration may be defensibly described as epideictic, construed broadly with respect to ancient norms.[27] Jesus intends neither to dazzle nor to delight his auditors but to bolster their confidence and to instruct them in modes of conduct that are essential in an eschatological age.

A second qualification: as is often the case in epideictic discourse, portions of Mark 13:5b-37 shade into deliberative rhetoric: an undeniable concern is

---

25. Among the standard classical discussions of this topic are Aristotle, *Rhet.* 1.3 (1358b-1359a); Cicero, *Inv.* 1.5.7; *Rhet. Her.* 1.2.2; Quintilian, *Inst.* 3.4.1-16; 3.6.80-85.

26. *Menander Rhetor*, ed. with trans. and commentary by D. A. Russell and N. G. Wilson (Oxford: Clarendon, 1981).

27. Yarbro Collins disagrees that the resemblance between Mark 13 and epideictic is as close as I suggest ("Apocalyptic Rhetoric of Mark 13," 10-13). In response, I reiterate that those similarities seem to me real but should not be forced in ways that would violate the manifest intent of either Mark or the rhetoricians. While Yarbro Collins is obviously correct that, on the narrative plane of Mark 13, Jesus has not yet died or otherwise departed from his disciples (12), "on another level . . . the evangelist indirectly provides his audience with an interpretation of the first Jewish war with Rome" (6)—and, I would add, an interpretation construed in the light of that audience's experience of the living voice of Jesus, crucified and raised. If Mark 13 "does not explicitly address [Jesus's] impending death or departure" (13), then neither does that speech expressly refer to Menachem's uprising, his royal pretensions, or those specific Jewish-Roman hostilities in the summer of 66 CE to which, as Yarbro Collins argues, the Olivet Discourse alludes (see above, note 23). Beyond this reply, I leave to the reader's adjudication whether Yarbro Collins or the present author presents a more satisfying rhetorical assessment of Mark 13.

manifested for the disciples' actions in the future (vv. 10–11, 14–16). Both theoretically and practically, this is tolerable within epideictic. Classical theorists acknowledged fluidity among rhetorical species, granting that considerations of past and future often converge in epideictic (Aristotle, *Rhet.* 1.3 [1358b]; see also Quintilian, *Inst.* 3.4.15–16; 3.7.28). Within Mark 13:5b–37, Jesus responds in terms of circumstances to come, inasmuch as the exigence triggering the oration is oriented toward the future (vv. 2, 4; see Quintilian, *Inst.* 3.8.25). Nevertheless, Jesus ultimately denies that the course of the future, while providentially assured, can be locked into a timetable (vv. 32–37). Nor, on the basis of expedience or self-interest, can one prepare beforehand for the upcoming distress (v. 11). Overall, this speech—even the climactic exhortation of verses 14–16—relativizes without preempting activity, emphasizing equanimity during that stressful period when "the gospel must first be preached to all nations" (v. 10).[28] Though tinctured with deliberative elements that carry persuasive weight, the center of gravity remains, I believe, epideictic: an attempt by Jesus to instill and to enhance in his listeners particular attitudes and feelings in the present regarding things to come, as well as to denounce or to extirpate the converse of those values and inclinations.

Second, another approach to the question of this unit's primary rhetorical problem is by means of stasis theory: identifying the point on which the speech pivots and to which the audience's attention is directed (Quintilian, *Inst.* 3.6.9, 12, 21). Though the discussion of stasis in antiquity was complex, at times chaotic,[29] our purposes are adequately served by Cicero's and Quintilian's simpler parsing of the alternative rational questions that discourse attempts to answer: fact or conjecture (*an sit*, whether a thing is), definition (*quid sit*, what it is), and quality (*quale sit*, of what kind it is).[30] Which of these stases captures the main question at issue in Mark 13?

28. Similarly, see Grayston, "Study of Mark XIII," 378–79, who arrives at this judgment independently of rhetorical premises. Obviously, such an interpretation throws doubt on the exegesis of Mark 13 by Willi Marxsen, *Mark the Evangelist: Studies on the Redaction History of the Gospel*, trans. James Boyce et al. (Nashville: Abingdon, 1969), 151–206: namely, that Mark is a Galilean gospel summoning Christians to flee to Pella for the Lord's parousia. On the other hand, utter passivism is foreclosed by evangelization (κηρυχθῆναι τὸ εὐαγγέλιον), which is a form of revolutionary engagement: thus, Brian K. Blount, "Preaching the Kingdom: Mark's Call for Prophetic Engagement," *PSB* 15 (1994): 33–56; Brian Blount, *Go Preach! Mark's Kingdom Message and the Black Church Today* (Maryknoll, NY: Orbis, 1998).

29. Among numerous treatments, see Cicero, *Inv.* 1.8–14; 2.4.14–54.177; Cicero, *De or.* 2.24.104–26.113; Quintilian, *Inst.* 3.6.63–82; *Rhet. Her.* 1.11–16; Raymond Nadeau, "Hermogenes' *On Stases*: A Translation with an Introduction and Notes," *SM* 31 (1964): 361–424.

30. Cicero, *De or.* 2.25.104–9; 2.30.132; Quintilian, *Inst.* 3.6.66–67, 86. Nevertheless,

Evidently, for this audience, the facts concerning which Jesus prophesies are not at issue. That the temple will totter—and, by extension, that the other calamities foretold by Jesus will come to pass—appears intelligible to the disciples. Neither do their questions in Mark 13:4 deny the veracity of Jesus's pronouncements. Nor is the quality of these occurrences in dispute: whether God is justified in so designing or permitting this eschatological scenario is never broached. The principal question to which Jesus's oration is addressed concerns the proper definition of facts whose reality is, or will be, conceded: when bogus prophets arise, when wars and rumors of wars circulate, how shall they be interpreted? Will they constitute the final consummation, or will they be merely preliminary to it? Jesus maintains the latter interpretation. After the prophecy in 13:2, the disciples ask for more facts (v. 4). Jesus complies with their request, yet raises the discussion to another level: the proper definition or faithful interpretation of those facts (*quid sit*).

The Arrangement of the Olivet Address

The classical *taxis*, or *dispositio*, of an epideictic address consists of three major components: the *proemium* (or *exordium*), a narration (*narratio*) of various topics, and the *peroratio* (or *epilogos*). Mark 13:5b–37 exhibits general conformity with, as well as creative adaptation of, this typical taxis.

First, a textbook *exordium* prepares the audience by informing it of the object(s) of the discourse and by disposing the listeners to be receptive to what will be said (Aristotle, *Rhet.* 3.14 [1415a]; *Rhet. Her.* 1.4.6–7; Quintilian, *Inst.* 4.1.1–79). If Mark 13:5b is considered the introduction of the Olivet Discourse (as appears to be the case, since the first of the oration's topics is presented in 13:6), then the minimalism and abruptness of "Beware that no one lead you astray" seemingly flout the criteria for an appropriate *proemium*. Despite its unconventionality, a case can be made for the suitability and effectiveness of this *exordium*. Admittedly, 13:5b does not attempt to ingratiate the speaker to his audience. For that, however, there is no need. This oration is intended to be heard within, not detached from, the context of the gospel's previous twelve chapters, from which has emerged Jesus's commanding yet mysterious authority. Nor need the orator at Olivet solicit his listeners' attention: he knows that he has it, as they have already invited his response (vv. 3–4). No statement of the discourse's objects is necessary, since they have already been

---

among classical theorists, there is no consensus on the exact divisions among stases (thus, Aristotle, *Rhet.* 3.17 [1417b]; Cicero, *Inv.* 1.8.10; *Rhet. Her.* 1.11.18–15.25; 2.12.17).

proposed in the disciples' questions: "When will these things be?" (a question of time) and "What will be the sign?" (a question of attendant circumstance). On the other hand, the sudden, authoritative command in 13:5b does satisfy the one indispensable requirement of a *proemium*: to capture the audience's attention for the ensuing discourse (Quintilian, *Inst.* 4.1.5). Conjoined with the questions of time and circumstance in verses 4a and 4b, Mark 13:5b economically and effectively accomplishes all that is needed to prepare this audience for this speech.[31]

Second, the bulk of the address, Mark 13:6–36, is a *narratio*, comprising specific topics that appear to have been carefully grouped for their fitness with the *exordium*, their internal coherence, and their maximum amplification. Although none of these characteristics may be thoroughly analyzed here, all invite brief comment.

(a) Notice, to begin with, a chiastic relationship between the implied objects of the *proemium* (the questions in v. 4) and the kinds of topics treated in the *narratio* (vv. 6–36). The disciples' second query ("What is the sign?") is addressed by roughly the first three-quarters of the *narratio* (vv. 6–27). The remainder, Mark 13:28–36, takes up their first question ("When will these things be?"). Thus, the observation of the fifth-century commentator, Victor of Antioch, is not quite apt: "They asked one question; he answers another."[32] In fact, they asked *two* questions. Jesus responds to both, but in such a way—disproportionately and in inverse order—that realigns the disciples' assumptions of their inquiries' force and significance.

(b) Another thing to notice in the arrangement of Mark 13:6–36: the topics therein are formally repetitive but materially progressive. Aside from the pathetical lament and petition in 13:17–18, Jesus's statements in this *narratio* assume one of four basic forms, which recur in varying juxtapositions throughout this address:

1. Exhortation, usually to vigilance (vv. 9a, 10, 23a, 28a, 33a, 35a);
2. Prediction of future occurrences (vv. 6, 8a, 9b, 12–13a, 19, 22, 24–27);

31. With Mark 13, one may compare the majority of the speeches in Acts, the length of whose *exordia* is one sentence or less: 1:16; 2:14b; 3:12; 4:8b; 5:35b; 7:2a; 10:34–35; 13:16b; 15:7a, 13b; 17:22b; 19:35; 22:1; 24:10a; 25:24a; 27:21; 28:17b. Four speeches in Acts contain an extended *proemium* (4:24b–26; 20:18–27; 24:2–4; 26:2–3); three, no *proemium* at all (5:29–32; 11:4–18; 25:14–21).

32. Cited by Dennis E. Nineham, *The Gospel of St Mark*, PGC (Baltimore: Penguin Books, 1963), 343–44.

3. Commission or prohibition, preceded by a temporal or relative conditional clause (vv. 7a, 11, 14–16, 21, 28b–29);
4. Authoritative pronouncement (vv. 7b, 8b, 10, 13b, 20, 23b, 30–32, 33b–34, 35b–36).

Concentrations of one form or another occur at certain points: thus, verses 24–27 are uninterruptedly predictive; verses 30–36, nearing the end of the address, are predominantly pronouncements, peppered with exhortations. Most striking, however, is the high degree of recurrence and braiding of these four forms throughout the speech. As regards rhetorical effect, their repetition implicitly offers the listeners some consistent and regular points of orientation in grappling with equivocal occurrences and uncertain responsibilities in an eschatological age.

For all of their formal repetitiveness, the topics in Mark 13:6–36 are substantively distinguishable and logically progressive. Responding to his disciples' question of "the sign" attending the eschatological consummation (Mark 13:4b), Jesus arranges four topics:

1. General earthly calamities to be experienced by all (vv. 6–8);
2. Particular earthly calamities to be experienced by believers (vv. 9–13);
3. Particular human responses to the calamitous "great tribulation" (vv. 14–23);
4. Particular supernatural responses to the "great tribulation" (vv. 24–27).

In reply to the question of the time of "these things" (13:4a), two topics are addressed:

5. Predictable imminence and assurance of the time (vv. 28–31);
6. Unpredictable suddenness and ignorance of the time (vv. 32–36).

The formal regularity of these six topics assists in reassuring the disciples, who receive a more complex response than their simplistic questions may have envisioned or invited.

(c) A third aspect of this *narratio* warrants mention: its arrangement of eschatological topics escalates to a climax. Jesus does not mention random "troubles"; rather, they advance from more familiar, abstract disturbances—which are but the beginning of the world's labor contractions (vv. 6–8)—through more intense, personal suffering (vv. 9–13), ultimately culminating in breathtaking, cosmic turbulence (vv. 24–27). This rhetorical technique is known as ἀπ' ἀρχῆς ἄρχι τέλος: a progression that moves "from beginning to end."[33] With the completion of circumstantial topics, at 13:27, the speech has reached its emotional climax. From there until the end, the address unfolds with somewhat quieter, thoughtful caution. This is more characteristic of Greek than of Roman oratory, which tended to reserve its full passion until the conclusion.[34] Doubtless this arrangement also reflects one of Mark's theological convictions: the need for Christians' grace under eschatological pressure. The *narratio* of this address exemplifies Quintilian's standards of lucidity, brevity, and plausibility (*Inst.* 8.2.1–2). The latter criterion is better satisfied by the oration's invention and style, to which we shall turn momentarily.

Third, although a one-sentence conclusion is unusual in classical rhetoric, that's just what we find in Mark 13:37.[35] On the other hand, by Aristotelian standards (*Rhet.* 3.19 [1419b–1420b]; see also Quintilian, *Inst.* 6.1.1–55), verse 37—"And what I say to you I say to all: Watch!"—does just what needs to be done. The repetition of "I say" encourages the audience's favorable estimation of the orator and, by implication, discourages its trust in those "false messiahs and false prophets" (v. 22) who might attempt to vitiate his pronouncements. The extension of Jesus's address, from "you" to "all," amplifies the force of his points, broadening their significance beyond a small coterie of disciples to the larger Markan community. The audience's emotions are suitably stirred by the final command, "Watch!" Although Mark 13:37 does not summarize the various arguments of the discourse, it forcefully recapitulates the oration's principal refrain: "Beware" (βλέπετε: vv. 5, 9, 23, 33). One could argue that, at 13:37, Mark skillfully accomplishes several rhetorical objectives in one sharp stroke. He rivets the reader's attention to the passion narrative, immediately following, which will detail the consequences for disciples who fail "to watch" (14:32–42). The abrupt command on which Jesus's speech concludes in 13:37 (γρηγορεῖτε, "watch") formally and substantively balances the equally pointed imperative in 13:5b (βλέπετε, "Beware"), which opened the address. The form and content of this *peroratio* are utterly apposite: the speech ends just as sud-

33. Hermogenes, "On Invention" 3.10, in *Invention and Method: Two Rhetorical Treatises from the Hermogenic Corpus*, trans. George A. Kennedy, WGRW 15 (Atlanta: Society of Biblical Literature, 2005), 107–13.

34. As noted by Kennedy, *New Testament Interpretation*, 48.

35. Alternatively, one might classify Mark 13:32–37 as the *peroratio*. Such an assessment is problematic: it all but relegates the critical issue of time (v. 4a) to the *epilogos* without the topic's having been previously developed in the *narratio*. Moreover, vv. 32–37 restate nothing that has preceded them, other than what v. 37 adequately recapitulates: the admonition to "watch."

denly and without warning as "the master of the house" will come (vv. 35–36). While disturbing some classical sensibilities, this curt conclusion mirrors others: with "emphatic concision" (βραχυλογία: *Rhet. Her.* 4.54.68), Mark 13:37 preserves the "internal economy" of the address (Quintilian, *Inst.* 7.10.16–17) and dramatically leaves its audience at the threshold of decision (Aristotle, *Rhet.* 3.18 [1420b]; *Rhet. Her.* 3.10.18).

What does the foregoing analysis contribute to the larger scholarly conversation, conducted from different critical premises, about the arrangement of Mark 13:5b–37? In general, rhetorical criticism provides some standards, roughly contemporaneous with the biblical material, by which competing scholarly assessments of a passage's literary structure may be adjudicated. Mine is by no means the only possible rhetorical analysis of the arrangement of Mark 13. I suggest only that such principles, and the sort of interpretive outcome to which they lead, may be used to corroborate and to refine results reached by other interpreters, primarily on the basis of form and composition criticism.[36] By attempting to construe the Olivet Discourse as a literary whole, not as a patchwork arising from its composite origins, rhetorical analysis may throw light, in specific cases, on the persuasive function of problematic or seemingly ill-fitted verses.[37]

Rhetorical Invention in Mark 13

"Among the . . . tasks of the orator, invention is the most important and the most difficult" (*Rhet. Her.* 2.1.1 AT). Equally challenging is the analysis of *inventio*, the devising of arguments, or proofs, that lend conviction to a case. The inventional strategies inherent in Mark 13:5b–37 are of sufficient intricacy that only some of their more conspicuous features may be noted here.

First, "inartificial" (ἄτεχνοι) proofs, not created by the speaker (including such things as laws, contracts, witnesses, and oaths), appear to have been

36. Cf. the reconstructions by Jan Lambrecht, *Die Redaktion der Markus-Apokalypse: Literarische Analyse und Strukturuntersuchung*, AnBib 28 (Rome: Pontifical Institute, 1967), 285–97; B. H. M. G. M. Standaert, *L'Évangile selon Marc: Composition et genre littéraire* (Brugge: Sint Andreisabdij, 1978), 231–53; Brandenburger, *Markus 13 und die Apokalyptik*, 13–20.

37. For instance, if the prediction concerning usurpers of Christ (v. 6) falls within the purview of "general earthly calamities," then it probably does not allude to some intramural, Christian aberration. Moreover, the putatively intrusive pronouncement regarding universal preaching of the gospel is surely to be coordinated with the particular persecutions that believers will undergo (cf. vv. 9–13). Thus, I think, Morna D. Hooker ("Trial and Tribulation in Mark XIII," *BJRL* 65 [1982]: 78–99, esp. 85–88) has correctly intuited the evangelist's intentions in both of these cases, for which my rhetorical analysis offers theoretical support.

more characteristic of judicial rhetoric (Aristotle, *Rhet.* 1.15 [1375a]); thus, their general absence in the Olivet Discourse is understandable. If, however, "law" be broadly understood as any testament, record, or document, to which appeal is made for the substantiation or refutation of a claim,[38] then the numerous Septuagintal allusions throughout this address function as inartificial proofs of Jesus's position.[39]

Scholars have long recognized the scriptural echoes reverberating within Mark 13. Noteworthy in this regard is Lars Hartman's thesis that the chapter is a midrash on Daniel.[40] Whatever we make of that proposal, insufficient attention has arguably been paid to *the rhetorical effect* of such biblical appropriation in this discourse. Here I venture two opinions. First, to hint at such a range of Scripture without explicit citation pays tacit tribute to the biblical literacy of one's audience, if the listeners' recognition of those allusions was presupposed. Second, and more important, enlisting Scripture to assist in construing disruptive and threatening prospects could generate considerable consolation among Mark's anxious auditors.

Second, surely "artificial" proofs (ἔντεχνοι), which the rhetor constructs from circumstances of the case (Aristotle, *Rhet.* 1.2 [1355b–1356a]; *Inst.* 3.8.15), bear the brunt of the persuasive task in Mark 13. As is typical of epideictic, neither inductive nor deductive logic looms large in this oration. The various events, recounted by Jesus in the first four topics (vv. 6–8, 9–13, 14–23, 24–27), are roughly analogous to Aristotle's historical arguments by "examples" (παραδείγματα);[41] however, because Jesus's topics are couched as predictions of the future, not yet actual history, the analogy is imprecise. Closer to the Aristotelian model are examples in the last two topics (vv. 28–31, 32–36): the

38. Thus Edward P. J. Corbett, *Classical Rhetoric for the Modern Student*, 2nd ed. (New York: Oxford University Press, 1971), 142.

39. The following catalog, drawn from Mark 13, is illustrative: v. 7 ("this must take place"), cf. Dan 2:28–29; v. 8a ("nation against nation"), cf. 2 Chr 15:6; v. 8b ("birth pangs"), cf. Isa 26:17; 66:8; Jer 22:23; Hos 13:13; Mic 4:9–10; v. 9c, cf. Ps 119:46; v. 12, cf. Isa 3:5; 19:2; Ezek 38:21; Mic 7:6; v. 14a ("the abomination of desolation"), cf. Dan 9:27; 11:31; 12:11; 1 Macc 1:54; 6:7; v. 14c ("let them head for the hills"), cf. Gen 14:10; v. 19, cf. Dan 12:1; v. 22, cf. Deut 13:1–3; vv. 24–25, cf. Isa 13:10, 13; 34:4; Ezek 32:7–8; Joel 2:10, 31; 3:15; Hag 2:6; v. 26, cf. Dan 7:13–14; v. 27 ("from the end of the earth to the end of heaven"), cf. Deut 13:7; 30:3–4; Zech 2:6, 10.

40. Lars Hartman, *Prophecy Interpreted: The Formation of Some Jewish Apocalyptic Texts and of the Eschatological Discourse Mark 13 Par.*, ConBNT (Lund: Gleerup, 1966), esp. 145–77. More recently, see Aage Pilgaard, "Apokalyptik als bibeltheologisches Thema: Dargestellt an Dan 9 und Mark 13," in *New Directions in Biblical Theology: Papers of the Aarhus Conference, 16–19 September 1992*, ed. Sigfried Pedersen, NovTSup 76 (Leiden: Brill, 1994), 180–200.

41. *Rhet.* 2.20 (1393a); see also Quintilian, *Inst.* 5.10.125–11.44; *Rhet. Her.* 4.3.5; *Rhet. Alex.* 7–8 (1428a17–1430a13).

image of the fig tree (vv. 28–29) is an "illustrative parallel" (*Rhet.* 2.20 [1393b]; = *similitudo*, Quintilian, *Inst.* 5.10.1);[42] the story of the traveler (vv. 34–36), a "fable" (Aristotle, *Rhet.* 2.20 [1393b–1394a]).[43] Although these παραδείγματα are intended to persuade (v. 28a: "from the fig tree learn the parable"), in fact they do not prove anything. And while this speech evinces careful arrangement, as we have seen, it does not proceed in accordance with the dictates of deductive or enthymematic logic.[44] On the other hand, the address has been partially motivated by a logical fallacy: that of confusing fallible signs (persecutions and spurious prophecies) with infallible signs (that will demonstrably attend the parousia of the Son of Man; cf. Aristotle, *Rhet.* 1.2 [1357b]). Thus, the force of Jesus's argument, while not rigorously logical, does aim to expose that logical fallacy.

To that end, it is worth observing that Mark 13:5b–37 employs, in effect if not by design, several of Aristotle's general lines of argument, or "commonplaces" (κοινοὶ τόποι: *Rhet.* 2.18–19 [1391b–1393a]; *loci*: Quintilian, *Inst.* 5.10.20–125). Against various misapprehensions concerning the time and circumstances of the end, Jesus constructs the following conventional arguments:

1. *The division of genus into species:* Against a mistakenly or prematurely realized eschatology, Jesus introduces a "periodized tribulation." He deflects attention away from "the end," generically conceived, onto various species of eschatological events (general calamities, believers' trials, the great tribulation, the coming Son of Man).[45]

42. Mark 13:28–29 should be correlated with 11:12–21, on which see William R. Telford, *The Barren Temple and the Withered Tree: A Redaction-Critical Analysis of the Cursing of the Fig-Tree Pericope in Mark's Gospel and Its Relation to the Cleansing of the Temple Tradition*, JSNTSup 1 (Sheffield: JSOT Press, 1980), esp. 213–18.

43. Alternatively, the ὡς ("as") clause in 13:34 can be taken as a simile (Quintilian, *Inst.* 8.3.72–76). On the tradition-history of 13:34–36, consult Beasley-Murray, *Jesus and the Last Days*, 470–74.

44. Mark 13:20b contains the speech's only enthymeme. Although it can be syllogistically reconstructed, its major and minor premises would not be considered probable, much less universally true, by those not already disposed to accept the validity of Jesus's definitions:
Those human beings who will be saved are the elect.
God shortened the days for the sake of those who will be saved.
Therefore, God shortened the days for the sake of the elect.
On enthymemes, see Aristotle, *Rhet.* 2.22–23 (1395b–1400b); 2.25 (1402a); Quintilian, *Inst.* 5.10.1–6; 5.14.1–35; 8.5.9–11.

45. A similar strategy is adopted by the author of 2 Thess 2:1–12, rhetorically analyzed by Glenn S. Holland, *The Tradition That You Received from Us: 2 Thessalonians in the Pauline Tradition*, HUT 24 (Tübingen: Mohr Siebeck, 1988). N.B. 134–39 of Holland's monograph for a comparison of 2 Thess 2:1–12 with Mark 13.

2. *The relationship of antecedent and consequence:* The species of events into which the eschatological genus is divided occur not haphazardly but in a particular chronological order, with certain consequences following specific antecedents (thus, v. 8c: "This is [only] the beginning of the birth pangs").

3. *The relationship of contradiction:* Against antagonists who would short-circuit God's appointed chronological progression with illegitimate claims that the end is either imminent or calculable, Jesus invokes contradictory propositions ("the end is not yet" [v. 7b]; "you do not know when the time will come" [v. 33; see also v. 35]).

4. Jesus contends, not that the end is indefinitely delayed (cf. v. 30), but that all the penultimate conditions must become manifest before the final reclamation of God's elect. This is one form of *the circumstance of future fact:* if the antecedents of something are present, then the natural consequences will occur (Aristotle, *Rhet.* 2.20 [1393a]).

A common form of rhetorical argument is exploited not once in this discourse: the interrogation of one's opponents. While constructions from silence are always hazardous, the accepted use of question and answer in classical rhetoric (Aristotle, *Rhet.* 3.17 [1419a]; *Rhet. Her.* 4.15.22–16.24), as well as the prevalence of this technique by Jesus elsewhere in Mark (some fifty-seven occurrences), may confirm our earlier assessment of the rhetorical situation of Mark 13. This speech resonates not as an apologetic rejoinder within an already schismatic situation in the Markan community but as pedagogical, even pastoral, consolation for uneasy Christians.[46]

Either in practice or by assumption, *logos* is only one of the modes of internal persuasion evident in this address. Of far greater persuasive power are *pathos*, the emotions stirred among the audience, and *ēthos*, the rhetor's character.[47] Incorporated within Jesus's eschatological scenario are sobering, even fearsome occurrences (wars, persecutions, familial infighting, cosmic ruptures, and so forth), for which an effective counterfoil is the arousal of pity for those especially vulnerable (expectant and nursing mothers [v. 17], endangered travelers [v. 18];[48]

46. Similarly, Grayston, "Study of Mark XIII," 375–76; contra Theodore J. Weeden, *Mark: Traditions in Conflict* (Philadelphia: Fortress, 1971), 52–100.

47. For both Cicero (*De or.* 2.43.182–46.194) and Quintilian (*Inst.* 6.2.7–27), *ēthos* and *pathos* can constitute varying degrees of similar proof.

48. With Rudolf Pesch (*Das Markusevangelium*, 2nd ed., HTKNT 2 [Freiberg: Herder, 1980], 2:293), I take the reference χειμῶνος ("in winter") to refer to the season of heavy rains, when passage across the wadis would have been impeded.

see Aristotle, *Rhet.* 2.8 [1385b–1386b]; Cicero, *De or.* 2.52.211). So vividly rendered are these images that they might be considered examples of ἐνάργεια (Quintilian, *Inst.* 4.2.63–64; 8.3.61–67; cf. *Rhet. Her.* 4.55.68–69) or *visiones* (*Inst.* 6.2.29–36; Longinus, *Subl.* 15.1–12): graphic exposition that excites the imagination and stirs the emotions. If the exigence and situation of this address have been properly construed, we may wonder what purpose is served by depiction of such horrifying prospects. Tacitly, the answer seems to lie in the recurrent assurances and exhortations to endurance in Mark 13:7, 11, 13b, 20, 23, 27, and 30–31: the bolstering of confidence presupposes, and to some degree is dependent on, a clear-eyed acknowledgment of fearful potentialities (thus, Aristotle, *Rhet.* 2.5 [1382a–1383b]). By rhetorically creating in his listeners' minds the experience of terrors to come, Jesus can now reassure "the elect" of the ultimate triumph of God's providence, while equipping them for future trials and tribulations (see *Rhet.* 2.5 [1383a]).

Implied in this address, indeed throughout the Second Gospel (1:27–28; 4:41; 9:14–15; 12:32), is an estimation of Jesus "as [one] possessing genuine wisdom and excellence of character" (Quintilian, *Inst.* 4.12.1 [trans. H. E. Butler, LCL]; see also 1.Pr.9–12; 1.2.3; 2.15.33; 12.1.1–45). The *ēthos* of Jesus lends considerable persuasive weight to this oration's various pronouncements (13:9 ["for my sake"], 13a ["for my name's sake"]; see also 13:23b, 26, 31, 37). Even the self-professed qualification of his knowledge (v. 32) redounds to the Son's credit, insofar as it magnifies the surpassing knowledge of God. So powerful is Christ's *ēthos* that it can backfire on gullible believers: when suborned by pseudochrists and fake prophets, that *ēthos* can be wielded as an instrument of deceit (vv. 5–6, 21–22), whose potential damage can be thwarted only by authoritative forewarnings of the authentic Christ (vv. 5b, 23). On balance, it is probably the case that the *logos* and *pathos* of the Olivet Discourse depend ultimately upon the *ēthos* of its orator.[49]

Rhetorical Style in the Oration at Olivet

Kindred to the invention and arrangement of this address is its *elocutio*: "the fitting of the proper language to the invented matter," as Cicero puts it (*Inv.* 1.7.9 [trans. H. M. Hubbell, LCL]). The observations that follow are categorized in

---

49. Aristotle (*Rhet.* 1.2 [1356a]) considered *ēthos* to be internal to a speech. However, as Kennedy notes (*New Testament Interpretation*, 15), the speaker's authority was brought to the rhetorical occasion, such that *ēthos* in the Bible functions largely as an external means of persuasion.

accordance with the four virtues of style, proposed by Theophrastus: correctness, clarity, ornamentation, and propriety.[50]

First, for classical theorists, correctness (ἑλληνισμός, *purus*) seems to have referred mainly to appropriate grammar (e.g., Cicero, *De or.* 3.40). If Atticism be taken as grammatical touchstone, as was the case in Roman oratory of the mid-first century BCE,[51] then Mark 13:5b–37 would be regarded as deficient at several points. The Olivet Discourse harbors grammatical constructions that by classical standards would be considered inelegant: ὅτι ("that") recitative following λέγειν ("to say"; vv. 6, 30); the use of εἰς ("into") in constructions where ἐν ("in") would be favored (vv. 9, 10); the impersonal use of a plural verb, with no subject expressed (vv. 9, 11); the solecistic conjunction of an attributive participle in the masculine case with a neuter noun (v. 14); the use of ἄν (a particle indicating contingency in subjunctive constructions) followed by a verb in the indicative mood (v. 20); various Semitisms (redundant pronouns [vv. 11c, 19]; the use of εἰμι, ["I am"] followed by a participle [vv. 13a, 25a]; the substitution of an impersonal plural for a passive verb [v. 26]); and probably at least one Latinism (v. 35c). There are also various instances of asyndeta, the absence of connecting particles (vv. 5b–6, 7b–c, 8a–d, 23a–b, 33a).[52] Matthew and Luke may have considered some of these constructions infelicitous; that would account for their alteration of Mark's grammar in the Synoptic parallels.[53]

On the other hand, in defense of the overall correctness of Markan style in chapter 13, one may offer the following rejoinders. First, with respect to Markan Koine Greek, an ideal standard of Attic purity is as unrealistic as it is unsuited. Second, the line of demarcation between classical and semitiz-

---

50. Theophrastus's four virtues were anticipated by Aristotle (*Rhet.* 3.2 [1404b–1405b]) and later taken up by Cicero (*Or.* 75–121; *De or.* 3.9.37–39; 3.52.199), Quintilian (*Inst.* 1.5.1; 8.1–11.1; 12.10.58), and Hermogenes (*Per. id.*). For discussion, see George A. Kennedy, *The Art of Persuasion in Greece* (Princeton: Princeton University Press, 1963), 273–90.

51. Kennedy, *Art of Persuasion*, 330–40.

52. In some of these instances, Matthew Black imputes to Mark the adoption of an Aramaic pattern (*An Aramaic Approach to the Gospels and Acts*, 2nd ed. [Oxford: Clarendon, 1954], 42).

53. Among others: Mark 13:6 // Matt 24:5; Luke 21:8 (both delete ὅτι); Mark 13:9 // Matt 10:17 (εἰς συναγωγὰς ["in synagogues"]); cf. Luke 21:12; Mark 13:10 // Matt 24:14 (ἐν ὅλῃ ["throughout (the) whole"]); Mark 13:11c // Matt 10:19; Luke 21:15 (both delete the *casus pendens* followed by τοῦτο ["this"]); Mark 13:14 // Matt 24:15 (ἑστηκότα ["standing" (neut.)]); Mark 13:25a // Matt 24:29 (πεσοῦνται ["will fall"]); Mark 13:35 // Matt 24:42; Luke 12:38, 40 (both delete Mark's allusion to Roman "watches"). However, Matthew and Luke agree with Mark in preserving some impersonal plurals (Mark 13:9, 11 = Matt 10:17 = Luke 21:12; Mark 13:26 = Matt 24:30 = Luke 21:27) and the phrase, λέγω ὑμῖν ὅτι ("I say to you that") (Mark 13:30 = Matt 24:34 = Luke 21:32). Note also Matthew's preservation of the conditional ἄν plus the indicative mood (24:22a = Mark 13:20a).

ing Greek is scarcely hard and fast: for example, the construction of a *casus pendens* with a resumptive pronoun (cf. Mark 13:11c) is not unknown in classical Greek,[54] and (as we shall presently see) asyndeta need not be automatically identified as Semitisms.[55] Third, assuredly in the case of Mark 13:19 (cf. Dan 12:1) but possibly elsewhere, the Semitic flavor of this address owes much to Mark's inventional mimicry of the LXX. Fourth, Mark 13:5b–37 lacks many of the syntactical excesses often attributed to that evangelist (the heaping of participles, prepositions, and adverbs; excessive use of the historical present and double negatives).[56]

On balance, the syntax of Mark 13:5b–37 betokens, if not classical purity, then the direct simplicity of Koine Greek. If it does not exhibit the elegance of the Epistle to the Hebrews, then neither does it manifest the linguistic barbarism of Revelation.

Second, for Quintilian (*Inst.* 8.2.22), the primary stylistic virtue is clarity (*perspecuitas*, τὸ σαφές). Here the oration at Olivet merits high marks. In Mark 13:6–36, most of the referents, if not in every case their precise significations, are clear enough. The παραδείγματα ("examples") in verses 28, 34–36a are less obscure than the parables in Mark 4:3–32 (cf. *Inst.* 8.6.52). Verse 14 presents a glaring exception to this assessment. As we shall see, however, its obscurity may be calculated.

Third, it is with respect to ornamentation (*ornatus*, τὸ μεγαλοπρεπές) that the style of Mark 13 holds the greatest surprise. Classical theorists divided style into two parts. First, there is *lexis* (diction), the choice of words for forceful expression, including metaphors and tropes ("turnings," in which one word is substituted for another). Second, synthesis: verbal compositions that manipulate clusters of sounds or words ("figures of speech") or ideas ("figures of thought") in striking or unexpected ways.[57] Although not exhaustive, the

---

54. See James H. Moulton, *Prolegomena*, vol. 1 of *A Grammar of New Testament Greek*, 3rd ed. (Edinburgh: T&T Clark, 1957), 69–70, and the Attic evidence cited therein.

55. On the slippery subject of Semitisms (linguistic infiltrations of classical and Koine Greek from Semitic languages), consult the balanced treatment in C. F. D. Moule, *An Idiom Book of New Testament Greek*, 2nd ed. (Cambridge: Cambridge University Press, 1959), 171–91.

56. For a good précis of Markan vocabulary, syntax, and style, see Vincent Taylor, *The Gospel according to St. Mark: The Greek Text with Introduction, Notes, and Indexes*, 2nd ed. (New York: Macmillan, 1966), 44–66.

57. The standard classical treatments of ornamentation include Aristotle, *Rhet.* 3.1–12 (1403b–1414a); *Rhet. Alex.* 22–28 (1434a35–1436a13); Longinus, *De sublimitate*; Demetrius, *De elocutione*; Cicero, *De or.* 3.37.149–42.168; 3.54.206–8; Quintilian, *Inst.* 8.6.1–76; 9.1.1–3.102. Heinrich Lausberg, *Handbook of Literary Rhetoric: A Foundation for Literary Study*, trans. Matthew T. Bliss, ed. David E. Orton and R. Dean Anderson (Leiden: Brill, 1998), 242–411, offers the most detailed, modern examination of classical canons of style.

following catalog offers a conspectus of the diction and composition employed in Mark 13:5b–37.[58]

Tropes

A. Metaphor (*translatio*): the transference of a word, applying to one thing, to another that is similar (*Rhet. Her.* 4.34.45):

> "if the Lord hadn't cut short the days" (v. 20a);
> "from the fig tree learn the parable" (v. 28a);
> "he is near, at the very gates" (v. 29);
> "for you do not know when the lord of the house is coming" (vv. 35b–36).

B. Synecdoche (*intellectio*): the suggestion of the whole or genus of something by its part or species (Quintilian, *Inst.* 8.16.19):

> "for my name's sake" (v. 13a).

C. Metonymy (*denominatio*): the substitution of some attribute or suggestive word for what is actually meant (*Rhet. Her.* 4.32.43):

> "all flesh" (v. 20a);
> "my words" (v. 31).

Figures of Speech

A. Parallelism: the collocation of related words, phrases, or clauses of similar structure:

> "and . . . you will be flogged [δαρήσεσθε] and . . . you will be made to stand [σταθήσεσθε]" (v. 9b–c);
> "he cut short the days . . . he cut short the days" (v. 20a–d);

---

58. In the following tables, I have translated excerpts from Mark 13 as literally or as freely as necessary to convey, in English, those stylistic features present in the Greek. Where a play on words or sounds exists in the original that can be rendered in English only clumsily, if at all, I have reproduced the corresponding Greek words or phrases.

"let those in Judea flee . . . , let the one on the roof not descend . . . , let the one in the field not turn back" (vv. 14–16);
"the sun . . . the moon . . . the stars . . . the powers" (vv. 24b–25b).

B. Homoeoptoton (*exornatio*): the appearance, in the same sentence, of two or more words with like terminations (*Rhet. Her.* 4.20.28; cf. Quintilian, *Inst.* 9.3.78):

"he will send out the angels [ἀποστελεῖ τοὺς ἀγγέλους] and he will gather together the elect [ἐπισυνάξει τοὺς ἐκλεκτοὺς]" (v. 27).

C. Reduplication (ἀναδίπλωσις): immediate repetition of one or more words of identical syntax, for the purpose of amplification (*Rhet. Her.* 4.28.38; Quintilian, *Inst.* 9.3.28):

"as soon as . . . you know that [it] is near . . . as soon as . . . you know that [he] is near" (vv. 28b–c, 29b–c).

D. Transplacement (*traductio*): the reintroduction of a word used in various functions (*Rhet. Her.* 4.14.20–21; Quintilian, *Inst.* 9.3.41–42):

"that he watch. . . . watch" (vv. 34d, 35a).

E. Polyptoton: establishing a contrast by variation in a word's declension or inflection (Quintilian, *Inst.* 9.3.37):

"you may hear [ἀκούσητε] wars and rumors [ἀκοὰς] of wars" (v. 7a);
"of creation which he created" (v. 19);
"the elect whom he elected" (v. 20b).

F. Epanaphora: repetition of the same word at the beginning of successive clauses (*Rhet. Her.* 4.13.19):

"there will be . . . , there will be" (v. 8b–c);
"Look . . . , look" (v. 21b–c).

G. Antistrophe (ἐπιφορά): repetition of the same word at the end of successive clauses (*Rhet. Her.* 4.13.19):

"will pass away, . . . will pass away" (v. 31a–b);
"to you I say, to all I say" (v. 37a–b).

H. Homoeopropheron: syllabic correspondence in the beginning of two or more words in close succession (cf. *Rhet. Her.* 4.12.18):

"pseudomessiahs and pseudoprophets" (v. 22a).

I. Homoeoteleuton: syllabic correspondence in the ending of two or more sentences (Quintilian, *Inst.* 9.3.77):

"Be wary [βλέπετε], be chary [ἀγρυπνεῖτε]" (v. 33a).

J. Epanalepsis: repetition of a word at the beginning and end of a clause (Quintilian, *Inst.* 8.3.51):

"nation against nation and kingdom against kingdom" (v. 8a);
"brother will betray brother" (v. 12a).

K. Asyndeton (*dissolutio*): absence of connecting particles (Quintilian, *Inst.* 9.3.50):

"Beware . . . ; many . . ." (vv. 5b–6);
"don't be alarmed: this must happen" (v. 7b–c);
"There will rise up . . . ; there will be . . . ; there will be . . . ; [the] beginning" (v. 8a–d);
"But you beware; I've told you everything beforehand" (v. 23a–b);
"Pay attention—stay alert" (v. 33a).

L. Polysyndeton: superfluity of connecting particles (Quintilian, *Inst.* 9.3.50–52):

καί-parataxis (redundant "and" in successive clauses) in verses 9c–13a and 24c–27a–b;
"no one . . . , neither . . . nor . . ." (v. 32a–b);
"whether" (ἤ) . . . "or whether" (ἤ) . . . "or whether" (ἤ) . . . "or whether" (ἤ) (v. 35bc).

M. Alliteration: repetition, in adjacent words, of initial or medial consonants (cf. *Rhet. Her.* 4.12.18):

δοὺς τοῖς δούλοις: "vesting the vassals" (v. 34b).

N. Assonance: repetition, in adjacent words, of similar vowel sounds conjoined with different consonants (*Rhet. Her.* 4.12.18):

Μὴ θροεῖσθε—δεῖ γενέσθαι: "be not dismayed; plans have been made" (v. 7b–c);
ἐξουσίαν, ἑκάστῳ τὸ ἔργον: "power, to each person a performance" (v. 34b–c).

O. Hyperbaton: transposition of word order for emphasis (*Rhet. Her.* 4.32.44; Quintilian, *Inst.* 8.6.62–67):

"[the] beginning of the birth pangs, these" (v. 8d);
"very near is summer" (v. 28c).

P. Chiasmus (cf. *commutatio*: *Rhet. Her.* 4.28.39): the reversal of grammatical structures in adjacent phrases or clauses:

"they will betray you to sanhedrins, and in synagogues you will be flogged" (v. 9b);
"and a father, [his] child, and . . . children against parents" (v. 12a–b);
"now if he hadn't cut short . . . , all flesh would not have been saved; but for the sake of the elect . . . he cut short . . ." (v. 20a–d).

Q. Antithesis: juxtaposition of contrary ideas (*Rhet. Her.* 4.15.21; *Rhet. Alex.* 26 [1435b]):

"This must happen, but the end is not yet" (v. 7c–d);
"Don't be anxious beforehand what you will say, but . . . say that" (v. 11b–c);
"For it's not you who are speaking, but rather the Holy Spirit" (v. 11d);
"And you will be hated . . . , but the one who endures . . . will be saved" (v. 13a–b);
"Heaven and earth will pass away, but my words will by no means pass away" (v. 31);
"no one knows, . . . except for the Father" (v. 32ac);
"Therefore, watch—for you do not know" (v 35a–b).

R. Parenthesis (*interpositio*): the interruption of the flow of discourse by the insertion of a remark (Quintilian, *Inst.* 9.3.23):

"And in all the nations the good news must first be preached" (v. 10);
"Let the reader understand" (v. 14b).

S. Ellipsis: deliberate omission of a word, which is implied by the context (Quintilian, *Inst.* 9.3.58):

"and kingdom [will rise up] against kingdom" (v. 8a);
"and father [will betray unto death his] child" (v. 12a).

T. Apposition: juxtaposition of coordinate elements, the second of which modifies the first:

"the powers, those in the heavens" (v. 25b);
"no one . . . , neither the angels in heaven nor the Son" (v. 32a–b);
"to the slaves [he gave] authority, to each his assignment" (v. 34b–c).

Figures of Thought

A. Aposiopesis: the incompletion of a thought (*Rhet. Her.* 4.30.41; 4.54.67; Quintilian, *Inst.* 9.2.54–57; 9.3.60–61):

"As a fellow on a journey . . . he charged the porter to keep watch" (v. 34).

B. *Controversia*: ambiguous phraseology designed to excite suspicion or entice discovery (Quintilian, *Inst.* 9.2.65–95):

"When you see the sacrilege that desecrates, standing where he ought not be . . ." (v. 14a).

C. *Ecphrasis*: vivid description (*Rhet. Her.* 4.38.51):

"and then you will see . . . from the four winds, from earth's end to heaven's end" (vv. 26–27);
"when the lord . . . comes, . . . perhaps early" (v. 35b–c).

D. Arousal (ἀνάστασις): the stirring of emotion (*Rhet. Her.* 4.43.55–56):

"Pray that it not happen in winter!" (v. 18).

E. Pleonasm: emphatic superfluity (Quintilian, *Inst.* 9.3.46–47):

> "But you—watch yourselves" (v. 9a);
> "But you—pay attention" (v. 23a).

F. Simile: comparison of implicitly similar figures (*Rhet. Her.* 4.49.62):

> "as a fellow on a journey . . . [so also, you]" (vv. 34–35).

Confident of neither my auditory nor visual acuity, I assume that the preceding lists are incomplete—which only makes so sweeping a range of ornament in a speech of moderate length the more striking. Equally impressive is the skill with which the tropes and figures have been blended into the address: they do not attract to themselves undue attention; most would probably be missed by those who silently read the speech but did not hear it recited aloud. At the time of the oration's performance, even its auditors would not have been entirely conscious of this panoply of ornament; at a subliminal level, however, the various techniques would register with persuasive effect (Cicero, *De or.* 3.50.195). The diction and composition of Mark 13 are not merely decorative. They are functional devices, integral to the purpose of securing an audience's agreement in matters of faith that are beyond deductive, logical proof.[59]

The fourth of Theophrastus's virtues, propriety (τὸ πρέπον, *decorum*), refers to the appropriateness of the style to the circumstances of the speech, the *ēthos* of the orator, the mood of the audience, and the character of the address. In these respects, the Olivet Discourse would likely have been judged successful by a rhetorician of Mark's age. From among the Ciceronian levels of style,[60] "the middle way" (*medius et quasi temperatus*: Cicero, *Or.* 621; *De or.* 3.45.177) tends to control Mark 13: befitting a "cautious" or "restrained" eschatology, the argument and diction are neither majestically grandiloquent (cf. *De or.* 5.20) nor tepidly plain (cf. *Or.* 6.20). Although its precise rhythm, based on metrical quantities in pronunciation, is probably irretrievable,[61] overall this oration

---

59. On the interplay of figures and argument, see Quintilian, *Inst.* 9.1.19, 21; note also the more recent discussion in Chaim Perelman and Lucie Olbrechts-Tyteca, *The New Rhetoric: A Treatise on Argumentation*, trans. John Wilkinson and Purcell Weaver (Notre Dame: University of Notre Dame Press, 1969), 167–79.

60. Cicero, *Or.* 5.20–6.21; 21.69–29.101; *De or.* 3.52.199–200; 3.45.177; see also *Rhet. Her.* 4.8–11; Quintilian, *Inst.* 12.10.58–72; Augustine, *Doctr. chr.* 4.19.38; 4.24.54–26.56.

61. As Kennedy observes (*New Testament Interpretation*, 30), the analysis of prose rhythms in NT literature is precluded by the apparent lack of systematic differentiation be-

evinces a style that is more "free-running" than disjointedly "periodic" (cf. *Rhet.* 3.9 [1409a–b]; Quintilian, *Inst.* 9.4.19–147). While that would be expected in a didactic presentation, a "running" style seems especially appropriate, moreover, for an address that counsels cautious discernment of a lengthy train of eschatological occurrences: the longer the phrases and clauses (*commata* and *cola*), such as we find here, the less hurried and more deliberate the rhetorical effect (*Rhet. Her.* 4.19.26–20.28).[62] The already masterly character of the rhetor would be enhanced by his command of ornament, whose varying clarity and obscurity are congenial with an eschatological scenario that can be broadly forecast (Mark 13:23) yet not pinpointed (13:32).

When compared to studies of its arrangement and "logical" argument, the style of Mark 13:5b–37 has been relatively neglected in recent scholarship. Here is another area in which Greco-Roman rhetoric may throw fresh light on familiar texts: the classical theory and practice of rhetorical style afford us a useful set of conceptual tools with which to frame some new inquiries, as well as to reexamine some perennial problems of interpretation.

A case in point is the notorious *crux interpretum* at Mark 13:14: τὸ βδέλυγμα τῆς ἐρημώσεως, "the desolating sacrilege." Beyond a general consensus on its allusiveness to a similar phrase in Daniel and 1 Maccabees, commentators have despaired of precisely identifying to what or to whom Mark intends for this epithet to refer.[63] In all likelihood, rhetorical criticism will be equally unable to answer the question of reference. That, however, is neither the sole nor arguably the most productive question to be raised of this phrase. Within a rhetorical framework, the significance of τὸ βδέλυγμα τῆς ἐρημώσεως resides largely in its provocative mystery and its concomitant resistance to clear interpretation. The technique is known as *controversiae*, much admired by clever declaimers in the first century CE, "whereby we excite some suspicion to indicate that our meaning is other than our words would seem to imply; but our meaning is not in this case contrary to that which we express, as is

---

tween long and short syllables in the pronunciation of Koine Greek. Still, the Olivet address exhibits some almost poetic features: μὴ θροεῖσθε / δεῖ γενέσθαι ("fear not / this must be," v. 7a–b); καὶ τότε ἀποστελεῖ τοὺς ἀγγέλους / ἐπισυνάξει τοὺς ἐκλεκτοὺς ("and then he will send the angels / he will gather together the chosen," v. 27a).

62. In *Inst.* 9.4.83, 91, Quintilian speaks of the different effects created by short and long syllables, rather than by phrases and clauses of varying lengths. Such clauses and phrases, however, are implied in Demetrius's discussion of the degrees of elevated diction (*Eloc.* 2.36–52).

63. See, e.g., Beasley-Murray, *Jesus and the Last Days*, 408–16; Pesch, *Naherwartungen*, 139–44.

the case in irony, but rather a hidden meaning which is left to the hearer to discover" (Quintilian, *Inst.* 9.2.65).

However unsafe or unseemly it might have been for Mark to speak more plainly at 13:14, for him to have done so would have been assuredly less provocative, even pleasurable, for his audience. This approach may help, moreover, to explain the presence in that same verse of the parenthetical admonition, "Let the reader understand." As rhetorically inept as it might first appear, that equally mysterious injunction may have been intended to seize the imaginations of those in Mark's community who are overhearing this oration, to tease them into an attempted unraveling of the secret of "the desolating sacrilege who [*sic*] stands" (cf. Quintilian, *Inst.* 9.2.78).[64] That the evangelist's rhetorical strategy at this point was indeed successful is confirmed by the captivated creativity that has been exercised by generations of the gospel's exegetes.

Evaluating Mark 13 in Accordance with Ancient Rhetorical Norms

Judged by first-century standards, does the Olivet Discourse constitute "good rhetoric"? As is the case in any form of criticism, the answer depends on the weighing of various criteria. The bobtailed *proemium* and *peroratio* of Jesus's address in Mark 13, as well as its grammatical roughness, probably would have jarred most classical rhetoricians. Moreover, those, like Aristotle, who esteemed the persuasive value of closely reasoned proof would probably have found this speech disappointing. Judged in strict accordance with such canons as these, Mark 13:5b–37 is a flawed declamation.

On the other hand, this discourse is by no means bereft of rhetorical effectiveness and sophistication. It seems appropriate to its situation and exigence: while directly responsive to their queries, the speech encourages its listeners to ponder related questions of a higher order. It is less concerned with dispensing and verifying abstruse information than with allaying anxiety, bolstering confidence, and instilling vigilance among timorous disciples. To those ends, both the form and substance of the address are tailored: the audience is afforded not only an anticipatory, vicarious experience of the vicissitudes and rescue to come but also the reassurance and stability tacitly conveyed through familiar, rhetorical conventions. Having been immediately established, audience contact is maintained by a chiastic, coherent, and climactic narration. Upon an implicitly logical substructure, a speech of powerful *pathos* and *ēthos* has been crafted, whose wide-ranging stylistic devices are not merely decora-

---

64. Daube, *New Testament and Rabbinic Judaism*, 426, adumbrated this proposal.

tive but deftly functional. Characteristic, perhaps, of one disposed to open or equivocal conclusions (see 15:39; 16:8), the evangelist does not say how Jesus's original audience reacted to the oration at Olivet. While Mark is no Cicero, one wonders whether in every respect Quintilian would have disapproved.

FINAL REFLECTIONS

En route to my own *epilogos*, I have ventured judgments on the contributions and limitations of a rhetorical analysis, assessed within the context of other scholarship on Mark 13. Whether those judgments will hold, only time and continued investigation into Mark's Gospel will tell. In any case, the following seem to me appropriate points on which to end this chapter.

First, methodologically, much scholarship on the Olivet Discourse has gravitated toward either the reconstruction of its tradition history or the analysis of its literary composition. Regarding the latter, the usefulness of Greco-Roman rhetorical theory, particularly on the subject of *taxis* or *dispositio* (arrangement), should be evident. From the vantage point of tradition history, rhetorical study may seem largely irrelevant; throughout most of the history of exegesis, however, precisely the reverse of this assessment would have been more common. Indeed, it is highly unlikely that the Second Evangelist and his original audience would have envisioned, much less favored, an interpretation of the address on Olivet through the discrimination of its antecedent traditions from its subsequent redaction. Later generations of listeners and readers have made intelligible sense of Mark 13, and similar passages, by appropriating the material in the rhetorical manner in which it is patently presented.[65] Furthermore, framing our interpretive questions of Mark 13 redaction-critically may as often play us false as true: discrepancies that modern exegetes have construed as evidence of Mark's use of composite sources may have stemmed instead from the evangelist's need to provide significant oral and aural clues to a gospel that was originally heard, not read.[66] Rhetorical theory provides

---

65. Analogously, since 1863, Lincoln's Gettysburg Address has been profoundly moving to North Americans, most of whom have known nothing of its traditional antecedents, which stretch back through the oratory of Edward Everett (1794–1865) to the Greek funeral orations of Pericles and Gorgias. See Gary Wills, *Lincoln at Gettysburg: The Words That Remade America* (New York: Simon & Schuster, 1992), 211–59.

66. See Paul J. Achtemeier, "*Omne verbum sonat*: The New Testament and the Oral Environment of Late Western Antiquity," *JBL* 109 (1990): 3–27, esp. 26–27; Antoinette Clarke Wire, *The Case for Mark Composed in Performance*, BPC (Eugene, OR: Cascade, 2011).

some excellent guidelines from antiquity for understanding and articulating the power of ancient address *as* address.

Second, on the other hand, modern reclamation of classical rhetoric requires correction by, and coordination with, other interpretive perspectives. This is necessitated by the complexity of biblical texts, which have been molded by a broad array of historical, literary, and religious pressures. Thus, as we have witnessed, rhetorical criticism of Mark 13 entails a candid recognition of the degree to which the Olivet Discourse creatively adapts or even flouts rhetorical norms, owing to its location within the larger narrative of Mark's Gospel and its subjection to not one but many generic constraints.

Third, if the essence of this essay's argument be accepted, then a reconsideration of Mark's rhetorical versatility seems in order. As acknowledged earlier, in content and format, Mark 13 is like nothing else in that gospel, which at points actually deprecates the power of verbal persuasion (see 4:10–12; 8:14–21).[67] Nevertheless, in chapter 13, Mark modifies his customary approach and attacks the problems and prospects raised by an apocalyptic eschatology with extraordinary directness, depth, and rhetorical sophistication. As far back as Papias (130 CE: Eusebius, *Hist. eccl.* 3.39.15) and as recently as George Kennedy, the construction of Mark's Gospel has paled alongside those of the other evangelists.[68] May we justly conclude that the Second Gospel's narrative rhetoric is uniformly "fairly crude," as Mary Ann Tolbert has suggested?[69] Alternatively, does Mark remain for us, rhetorically as well as theologically,

67. In this connection, recall Mark 13:11, where the value of practiced rhetorical endeavor seems undercut by Jesus's admonition that his disciples not rehearse their apologia but leave all persuasion to the Holy Spirit in the moment of crisis (see also Exod 4:1–17; Num 22:35; Jer 1:6–10; contrast Quintilian, *Inst.* 11.2.1–51). For very different reasons, Plato exhibits a similar paradox: the rhetorician who distrusts rhetoric (*Phaedr.* 257b–258e; 275d–276a).

68. For Kennedy, Mark's Gospel tends toward "radical Christian rhetoric," a form of "sacred language" that presupposes the believer's immediate and intuitive apprehension of truth without assistance from the art of persuasion (*New Testament Interpretation*, 97–113, esp. 104–7). For deeper analysis of Kennedy's reading of Mark, see C. Clifton Black, *The Rhetoric of the Gospel: Theological Artistry in the Gospels and Acts*, 2nd ed. (Louisville: Westminster John Knox, 2013), 102–17; also Black, "Kennedy and the Gospels: An Ambiguous Legacy, A Promising Bequest," in *Words Well Spoken: George Kennedy's Rhetoric of the New Testament*, ed. C. Clifton Black and Duane F. Watson, SRR 8 (Waco, TX: Baylor University Press, 2008), 63–80.

69. Mary Ann Tolbert, *Sowing the Gospel: Mark's World in Literary-Historical Perspective* (Minneapolis: Fortress, 1989), 59, 78. The outcomes of Tolbert's perceptive study seem to me critically ambivalent: for all of the evangelist's touted lack of literary sophistication, Mark's Gospel remains, in her view, a work of extraordinary composition, subtlety, and power (311–15 and throughout; see my review of Tolbert's book in *CBQ* 54 [1992]: 382–84).

"a master of surprise," an evangelist who relentlessly brings his interpreters up short just when they think they have his little gospel pinned down?[70]

Fourth, if this chapter's analysis has treated Mark 13 accurately and with fairness, it may also be worth pondering the possibility that, in the address at Olivet, the Second Evangelist has created a miniature rhetorical masterpiece. Apocalypticism strikes most moderns along today's religious mainline as essentially brazen, irrational, and primitive. Mark, as always, bewilders us with a very different point of view. The unexpected care with which the Olivet Discourse has been crafted is, in a sense, congruent with the equally off-putting significance of apocalypticism in Markan theology.[71] In chapter 13, Mark administers his audience an unadulterated dose of apocalyptic pastoral care: the healing of a distraught Christian community by revitalizing a vision that sweeps all affairs of heaven and earth under God's mysterious, faithful, restorative dominion.[72] That pastoral objective, pervasive throughout Mark's Gospel, is achieved nowhere with greater clarity, finesse, and power than that which we and the disciples experience in an oration at Olivet.

70. Thus, Donald H. Juel, *A Master of Surprise: Mark Interpreted* (Minneapolis: Fortress, 1994).

71. Among others, see Joel Marcus, *The Mystery of the Kingdom of God*, SBLDS 90 (Atlanta: Scholars Press, 1986); Yarbro Collins, *Beginning of the Gospel*, 1–38.

72. For further reflections in this vein, see Black, *Mark* (passim) and chapter 16 of the present volume.

CHAPTER 15

The Kijé Effect:
Revenants in the Markan Passion Narrative

> I'm reminded of the governess in "The Turn of the Screw," who
> arrives at her new posting and is delighted to discover that her
> room has two full-length mirrors, an unimaginable luxury and a
> clever bit of narrative forecasting; she will soon encounter mir-
> rors of a different sort in the form of two ghosts (or are they?)
> haunting her young charges.
>
> —Parul Sehgal[1]

THIS ESSAY IS AN EXERCISE in composition criticism, prompted by a phenomenon I noted while writing a commentary on Mark but had not the space to
develop therein.[2] As an aid for reading that gospel's passion narrative, I suggested an analogy drawn from the twentieth century's orchestral repertoire:
Sergei Prokofiev's *Lieutenant Kijé* (1934).[3] Its final movement, "The Burial of
Kijé," opens with the same wistful cornet fanfare that announced a soldier's

---

1. "The Ghost Story Persists in American Literature. Why?," *New York Times*, 22 October
2018, https://www.nytimes.com/2018/10/22/books/review/ghost-stories.html.
2. C. Clifton Black, *Mark*, ANTC (Nashville: Abingdon, 2011), 276–338. For their manifold assistance, I tender sincere thanks to Dr. R. Matthew Calhoun and Professors Dale C.
Allison Jr., Edward McMahon, Elizabeth Struthers Malbon, M. J. P. O'Connor, and George L.
Parsenios.
3. Prokofiev's suite (opus 60) rearranged excerpts from a soundtrack he had composed
for Alexander Feinzimmer's motion picture of the same name (1933). Kijé is a fictional character in more ways than one. In a story by Yuri Tynanonov on which the film is based, the
Tsar misunderstands *Parutchik je* ("the lieutenant, however") for *Parutchik Kije* ("Lieutenant
Kijé"). Owing to an unthinkable correction of the Tsar's error and a rigid bureaucracy, a
clerk dutifully enters "the lieutenant"'s name into the military register, which, in turn, leads
to a fabrication of "Kijé"'s life, marriage, distinguished service, and valiant death. Prokofiev's
music captures the comedy. Mark's story expresses something else.

birth in the first movement. As the last movement unfolds, it symphonically superimposes most of the suite's principal themes. Arranged as a military dirge, Kijé's leitmotif, introduced in the first movement by warm woodwinds, is restated in the low registers of clarinet and saxophone. Then follows a melancholy recapitulation by strings of the second movement's ballad, "Romance." Sorrow yields to Kijé's theme, counterpointing a wedding melody from the third movement. Little remains but a final, distant reprise of the cornet's call. Prokofiev has orchestrated the musical equivalent of a dying man's life as it flashes before his eyes, to be forever closed.

Something very much like this is, I propose, what Mark 14–16 achieves: interlaced memories of the gospel's previous chapters that wander in and out of the listener's ear. The Markan passion narrative is haunted by literal revenants: figures, characterizations, events, names, and statements that "come back" from the gospel's previous chapters, reminding us, often subliminally, of what has gone before.[4] Study of Markan foreshadowing is nothing new;[5]

4. "Come back," from the French *revenir*: *un esprit qui revient*, "a ghost that walks." Although I use the term "ghost" metaphorically, it is worth noting that the word crops up in Mark: in 6:49 (par. Matt 14:26), the disciples think that in Jesus, walking past them on the sea, they have seen a φάντασμα. Most commentaries on Mark (including my own) say little about this. The most extensive investigation of the subject I know is that of Douglas W. Geyer, *Fear, Anomaly, and Uncertainty in the Gospel of Mark*, ATLAMS 471 (Lanham, MD: Scarecrow, 2002), 241–67. Geyer cites a wealth of primary sources pertaining to chthonic apparitions, such as Homer's *Odyssey* 11.222: "souls . . . like images appearing in mirrors, . . . images of [the] mortal dead" (τὰς ψυχὰς τοῖς εἰδώλοις τοῖς ἐν τοῖς κατόπτροις φαινομένοις ὁμαίας . . . βροτῶν εἴδωλα καμόντων). Amid many terrifying images evocative of God's judgment in Wis 17:4, 14 are τὰ φαντάσματα and their cognate, τὰ θάσμα; cf. Job 4:15–16; 20:8. Deuteronomy 18:11 proscribes pagan necromancy. Valerie M. Hope, ed., *Death in Ancient Rome: A Sourcebook* (London: Routledge, 2007), 236–47, collects brief ghost stories from burial inscriptions, Plautus, Plutarch, Cicero, Suetonius, Horace, Lucian, Propertius, Pliny the Younger, and Cassius Dio.

5. Among other studies, see Joanna Dewey, "Mark as Interwoven Tapestry: Forecasts and Echoes for a Listening Audience," *CBQ* 53 (1991): 221–36. Dewey's article aims at a different target: the refutation of a single linear structure in Mark. Although focused on a specific theological issue (ἡ βλασφημία), Joel F. Williams's study of Markan flashbacks and flashforwards crisscrosses my offering here ("Foreshadowing, Echoes, and the Blasphemy at the Cross (Mark 15:29)," *JBL* 132 [2013]: 913–33), as do Elizabeth Struthers Malbon's "Echoes and Foreshadowings in Mark 4–8: Reading and Rereading," *JBL* 112 (1993): 211–30, and Peter G. Bolt's *Jesus' Defeat of Death: Persuading Mark's Early Readers*, SNTSMS 125 (Cambridge: Cambridge University Press, 2003). Gérard Genette's *Narrative Discourse: An Essay in Method* (Ithaca, NY: Cornell University Press, 1980), 33–85, offers a fundamental study of the techniques of analepsis and prolepsis.

indeed, that gospel's explicit, extensive use of the technique (1:2; 2:20; 3:19b; 4:25; 8:31; 9:9, 31; 10:28, 31, 33–34, 39; 12:9; 13:1–2, 5–37; 14:9, 13, 18, 27–30, 62) commends its examination. Although some parallel incidents will be noted in what follows,[6] my attitude is *retrospective* and primarily focused on the more understated, curiously doubled elements of which the Markan passion narrative is compounded.[7] For that narrative's attentive listener, or reader, the death of Jesus weirdly recalls much of his life.

For the reader's convenience, I assemble in table 2 sixteen elements in Mark 14–16, each of which will be considered in detail appropriate to its intricacy.[8]

6. In this vein, the seminal research is by Robert Alter, *The Art of Biblical Narrative* (New York: Basic Books, 1981), Peter Miscall, *The Workings of Old Testament Narrative* (Philadelphia: Fortress, 1983), and Meir Sternberg, *The Poetics of Biblical Narrative: Ideological Literature and the Drama of Reading* (Bloomington: Indiana University Press, 1985).

7. In a sense, I am moving in a direction opposite that proposed by Jerry Camery-Hoggatt: "Story elements work synergistically to predispose the reader's reactions *to what follows.* . . . Mark's reader encounters . . . story elements in this particular sequence" (*Irony in Mark's Gospel: Text and Subtext*, SNTSMS 72 [Cambridge: Cambridge University Press, 1992], 179; my italics). I do not consider his observation wrong or wrongheaded; in this essay, I simply reverse the direction of the spyglass and its field of vision. I concur with Camery-Hoggatt's opinion "that indirect allusion may effect reactions in the reader which are less directly conscious, but for that reason more psychologically potent" (70). As should become immediately evident, the kind of doubling I have in mind is not of the strictly linguistic sort (such as pleonasms and verbal repetitions, double questions and antithetical parallelism) scrutinized by Frans Neirynck, *Duality in Mark: Contributions to the Study of the Markan Redaction*, BETL 31 (Leuven: Leuven University Press, 1988).

8. With most commentators (e.g., Vincent Taylor, *The Gospel according to St. Mark: The Greek Text with Introduction, Notes, and Indexes*, 2nd ed. [New York: Macmillan, 1966], 524; Joachim Gnilka, *Das Evangelium nach Markus*, EKKNT 2/2 [Neukirchen-Vluyn: Neukirchener Verlag, 1979], 2:216–17; Morna Hooker, *The Gospel according to Saint Mark*, BNTC [London: A & C Black, 1991], 324–25; Edwin K. Broadhead, *Prophet, Son, Messiah: Narrative Form and Function in Mark 14–16*, JSNTSup 97 [Sheffield: Sheffield Academic, 1994]; Craig A. Evans, *Mark 8:27–16:20*, WBC 34B [Nashville: Nelson, 2001], 351–53; Adela Yarbro Collins, *Mark: A Commentary*, Hermeneia [Minneapolis: Fortress, 2007], 620; R. Alan Culpepper, *Mark*, SHBC [Macon, GA: Smyth & Helwys, 2007], 479; Joel Marcus, *Mark 8–16: A New Translation with Introduction and Commentary*, AB 27A [New Haven: Yale University Press, 2009], 924–31; Mary Ann Beavis, *Mark*, Paideia [Grand Rapids: Baker Academic, 2011], 206–9), I reckon 14:1 as the passion narrative's beginning. Were one to start the clock at 14:32 with Raymond E. Brown (*The Death of the Messiah: From Gethsemane to the Grave*, 2 vols., ABRL [New York: Doubleday, 1994]), the following analysis would lose little in substance.

Table 2: Doubled Figures and Leitmotifs in Mark's Passion Narrative

1. Jesus's Anonymous Anointer (14:3–9)	9. On the *Via Dolorosa*: An Unexpected Simon (15:21)
2. The Disciples' Preparation for Passover (14:12–16)	10. At Golgotha: "Those Who Were Crucified with Him" (15:27, 32b)
3. Bread and Cup at the Last Supper (14:22–25)	11. The Taunt: "Others He Saved; Himself He Cannot Save" (15:31)
4. Jesus in Gethsemane (14:32–42)	12. Waiting for Elijah (15:35–36)
5. A Hostile Multitude (14:43, 48; 15:8, 11)	13. A Third Rip/A Third Pronouncement (15:38–39)
6. Jesus and Peter on Trial (14:53–72)	14. The Ministering Women (15:40–41)
7. Pilate's Interrogation, Sentencing, and Execution of Jesus (15:1–5, 16–32)	15. Joseph of Arimathea (15:42–47)
8. Barabbas (15:6–15)	16. A Young Man in the Empty Tomb (16:5–7)

ANALYZING THE EVIDENCE

1. Jesus's Anonymous Anointer (Mark 14:3–9)

Bethany's magnanimous devotee of Jesus, who anointed his head from an alabaster jar with pure nard, worth more than three hundred denarii and, thus, "quite expensive" (πολυτελοῦς [14:3, 5]), is a spiritual sister of the destitute widow in Mark 12:41–44, who gave her entire livelihood (ὅλον τὸν βίον αὐτῆς [12:44]). Both are anonymous: the evangelist focuses not on who they are but on what they have done. Both are incredibly generous, more so than any male figure in this gospel save Jesus himself (6:30–44; 8:1–10). Both are contrasted with others more privileged than they, whose contributions to the proceedings pale by comparison with theirs (the many rich donors who throw much into the temple's treasury [12:41b]; the chief priests and scribes, who bribe one of the Twelve to assist them in capturing Jesus [14:1b, 10–11]). The religious causes to which both women have committed themselves—Jerusalem's temple and God's Messiah—will soon appear irretrievably lost (13:1–2; 14:8b).[9] There's not the slightest hint

9. In 14:7, Jesus's reminder of the καιρός—"but you will not always have me"—recalls the foreshadowed bridegroom to be taken away (2:19–20; cf. Eduard Schweizer, *The Good News according to Mark*, trans. Donald H. Madvig [Atlanta: John Knox, 1970], 289). As Donald Senior notes, "'Timing' is an important feature of Mark's Gospel" (*The Passion of Jesus in the Gospel of Mark* [Wilmington, DE: Glazier, 1984], 46).

that either is aware of the full import of her donation; both "[have] done what [they] could" (cf. 14:8a) in spite of their seemingly wasted benevolence. In both cases, Jesus alone can assay their gifts' genuine value and interpret it for others. Each is not only the other's *Doppelgänger*; both are doubles for Jesus himself, who will pay for others the ultimate price (10:45). "For what can one give in exchange for his very self?" (8:37).[10] Bethany's benefactor also plays Jekyll to Judas's Hyde: both did the most of which each was capable. For their antithetical acts, wherever the gospel is preached (14:9) neither has ever been forgotten.[11]

2. The Disciples' Preparation for Passover (Mark 14:12–16)

Mark 14:12–16 varies his pattern of doubling. In this instance, two unnamed disciples are dispatched by Jesus to prepare for a consequential event, the Passover's celebration. Their instructions are enigmatic: they are to go into the city, meet a householder carrying a water jug, say what is needed, then follow him to a large upper room strewn and readied for the ritual (vv. 13–15). All transpires as Jesus predicted, and those disciples do their duty (v. 16). In essence, all this duplicates Jesus's directives, again addressed to two unidentified disciples, to go into the village opposite Jerusalem and fetch a colt for Jesus to ride into the city (11:1–2; cf. 1 Sam 10:1–8; 1 Kgs 17:8–16). Then, as later, Jesus demonstrates preternatural knowledge of what his emissaries will encounter: the bystanders' question of why they are doing this (11:3–5). Like the householder, the village onlookers are satisfied that "the Lord has need of it" (11:3). The discovery of both beast and room is "just as [Jesus] told [his disciples]" (14:16b; cf. 11:6). More than five decades ago Vincent Taylor tabulated exact verbal consistencies between these stories, which, with annotation, I reproduce in table 3.[12]

Table 3: Two Missions of Two Disciples

Narrative Element	Mark 11:1–6	Mark 14:13–16
1. Jesus's commission to his agents	ἀποστέλλει δύο τῶν μαθητῶν αὐτοῦ (v. 1)	ἀποστέλλει δύο τῶν μαθητῶν αὐτοῦ (v. 13)

10. For further consideration of these twin benefactors, see Laura C. Sweat, *The Theological Role of Paradox in the Gospel of Mark*, LNTS 492 (London: Bloomsbury T&T Clark, 2013), 109–10.

11. Between this reading and that of Francis J. Moloney, *The Gospel of Mark: A Commentary* (Peabody, MA: Hendrickson, 2002), 280–82, there are points of contact, though (to the best of my recollection) we arrived at our similar conclusions independently of each other.

12. *Gospel according to St. Mark*, 536.

2. His directive	καὶ λέγει αὐτοῖς· ὑπ-άγετε εἰς τὴν κώμην (v. 2)	καὶ λέγει αὐτοῖς· ὑπ-άγετε εἰς τὴν πόλιν (v. 13)
3. Preparatory discovery	καὶ ... εὑρήσετε ... (v. 2)	καὶ ... ἀπαντήσει ὑμῖν ... (v. 13)
4. Preparatory request	εἴπατε· ὁ κύριος ... (v. 3)	εἴπατε· ὁ διδάσκαλος ... (v. 14)
5. The disciples' mission	καὶ ἀπῆλθον (v. 4)	καὶ ἐξῆλθον ... (v. 16)
6. Their discovery	καὶ εὗρον ... (v. 4)	καὶ εὗρον (v. 16)
7. Consonance with Jesus's clairvoyance	καθὼς εἶπεν ὁ Ἰησοῦς, καὶ ... (v. 6)	καθὼς εἶπεν αὐτοῖς καὶ ... (v. 16)

Another parallel point is noteworthy. In both cases, Jesus's disciples prepare what he needs (11:7; 14:16) for a ceremony: in the first, a celebratory entrance into Jerusalem (11:8–10); in the second, the Passover itself (14:16c). Though not identical, these observances are analogous. Both imply Israel's blessed redemption from enslavement: the Passover, inherently so; the entry, "the coming kingdom of our father David" (ἡ ἐρχομένη βασιλεία τοῦ πατρὸς ἡμῶν Δαυίδ [11:10]; cf. ἐν τῇ βασιλείᾳ τοῦ θεοῦ [14:25]). As David Catchpole has reminded us, the so-called triumphal entry replicates a type-scene in Hellenistic Jewish depictions of Israel's conquerors who enter a city with popular pomp and ritual circumstance (1 Macc 4:19–25; 5:45–54; 13:43–48, 49–51; Josephus, A.J. 11.325–339, 342–345; 12.312, 348–349; 13.304–306; 16.12–15; 17.194–239, 324–329 et al.).[13] The uniquely Markan touches to these legends are Jesus's involvement of two disciples in fulfilling elliptical commands. Both stories present seemingly extraneous details: after all, neither Jesus's entry to Jerusalem nor his celebration of Passover required their narration. Mark not only includes these oblique details; he mirrors them, with precise verbal replication, in a pair of different stories.[14]

13. "The 'Triumphal' Entry," in *Jesus and the Politics of His Day*, ed. Ernst Bammel and C. F. D. Moule (Cambridge: Cambridge University Press, 1984), 319–34, N.B. 319–21. See also chapter 16 of the present volume.

14. Commentators disagree on the precise relationship between 11:1–11 and 14:12–17. Taylor (*Gospel according to St. Mark*, 536) regards the stories as doublets; Culpepper (*Mark*, 488–89) thinks the evangelist used one as a template for the other's construction; Evans (*Mark 8:27–16:20*, 369–70) ascribes their likenesses to Mark's "tendency to be formulaic and repetitive." Whatever the explanation, Hooker is correct that 14:13 contains eleven consecutive words identical with those in 11:1–2 (*Gospel according to Saint Mark*, 332).

3. Bread and Cup at the Last Supper (Mark 14:22–25)

However one resolves the vexed question of whether Jesus's final meal with the Twelve was, as Mark indicates, a Passover (14:12, 14, 16),[15] it is impossible to hear Jesus's actions and words "on the night he was betrayed" (1 Cor 11:23) without recalling the feeding miracles narrated in 6:30–44 and 8:1–10. The parallelism is displayed in table 4. In place of the fish (δύο ἰχθύας [6:38c, 41a–d, 43]), which recede in the second feeding (ἰχθύδια ὀλίγα [8:7]), the final supper has the goblet (τό ποτήριον), presented in like manner as the bread (λαβὼν . . . εὐχαριστήσας ἔδωκεν αὐτοῖς [14:23]). In Mark, "the cup" has been presaged both positively and negatively: as that which is commendably offered to those "who bear the name of Christ" (9:41); as that which Jesus must drink (10:38b, 39b), would bypass if only he could (14:36), and must also be quaffed by disciples who think themselves capable but are clueless of its peril (10:39; cf. Ezek 23:32–34; Ps 75:8). In 14:24, the cup's sacrificial connotation is unmistakable: "This is my blood of the covenant, which is poured out for many." The bread (or "loaves") is also multiply symbolic with varying valence. In 7:27–28, it signifies blessing, first to Israel's children, then to a gentile; in 8:14–21, it suggests a superabundant providence (the baskets of leftovers [6:43; 8:8]) that the disciples cannot comprehend; in 6:52, their inability to understand the loaves is correlated with comparable failure to grasp Jesus's power, owing to their "hardness of heart." Finally, in 14:22, the bread he offers is to be taken by his disciples as his body (τὸ σῶμα μου), his very self, on the verge of being sacrificed (v. 25). As with the loaf, so, too, the chalice: they may not understand its significance, but all drink from it (v. 23)—including, presumably, the teacher's impending repudiator (vv. 27–31) and his betrayer as well (vv. 18–21).

Table 4: The Three Meals in Mark over Which Jesus Presides

The Feeding of Five Thousand (6:30–44)	The Feeding of Four Thousand (8:1–10)	The Seder with the Twelve (14:17–18, 22–26)
1. Temporal indication: ἤδη ὥρα πολλή (v. 35)	Temporal indication: ἤδη ἡμέραι τρεῖς προσμένουσίν μοι (v. 2)	Temporal indication: καὶ ὀψίας γενομένης (v. 17)

15. Joachim Jeremias, *The Eucharistic Words of Jesus*, trans. Norman Perrin (London: SCM, 1977), 15–88; cf. Brent Pitre, *Jesus and the Last Supper* (Grand Rapids: Eerdmans, 2015), 374–443.

2. References to eating: ἀγοράσωσιν ἑαυτοῖς <u>τί φάγωμεν</u> (v. 36); δότε αὐτοῖς ὑμεῖς φαγεῖν (v. 37); <u>καὶ</u> δώσομεν αὐτοῖς <u>φαγεῖν</u>; (v. 37); <u>καὶ ἔφαγον</u> πάντες (v. 42); <u>καὶ</u> . . . οἱ <u>φάγοντες</u> (v. 44)	References to eating: καὶ μὴ ἐχόντων <u>τί φάγωσιν</u> (v. 1); <u>καὶ</u> οὐχ ἔχουσιν τί φάγωσιν (v. 2); <u>καὶ ἔφαγον</u> (v. 8)	Reference to eating: <u>καὶ ἐσθιόντων</u> (vv. 18, 22)
3. The recipients' position: <u>ἀνέπεσαν</u> (v. 40)	The recipients' position: <u>ἀναπεσεῖν</u> (v. 6a)	The recipients' position: <u>ἀνακειμένων</u> (v. 18)
4. Jesus's taking bread: <u>καὶ λαβὼν τοὺς</u> . . . <u>ἄρτους</u> (v. 41a)	Jesus's taking bread: <u>καὶ λαβὼν τοὺς</u> . . . <u>ἄρτους</u> (v. 6b)	Jesus's taking bread: <u>λαβὼν ἄρτον</u> (v. 22a)
5. His blessing: <u>εὐλόγησεν</u> (v. 41b)	His blessing: <u>εὐχαριστήσας</u> (v. 6b)	His blessing: <u>εὐλογήσας</u> (v. 22a)
6. His breaking: <u>κατέκλασεν</u> (v. 41b)	His breaking: <u>ἔκλασεν</u> (v. 6b)	His breaking: <u>ἔκλασεν</u> (v. 22a)
7. His giving to his disciples: <u>καὶ ἐδίδου τοῖς μαθηταῖς</u> (v. 41c)	His giving to his disciples: <u>καὶ ἐδίδου τοῖς μαθηταῖς</u> αὐτοῦ (v. 6b)	His giving to his disciples: <u>καὶ ἔδωκεν αὐτοῖς</u> ([sc. <u>τῶν δώδεκα</u> v. 17] v. 22a)

While the sense of the deeds and words in Mark 14:22–25 is intelligible, much as Paul assumed for the Corinthians (1 Cor 11:23–25), in Mark they acquire density of meaning by their recollection of the feeding miracles in chapters 6 and 8.[16] For a third time, Jesus has hosted a supper in which his followers partake and others will benefit. In this prandial trio, Jesus offers simple elements in a ritualized manner, identically worded, in settings (Passover; the wilderness [Mark 6:31–32, 35; 8:3–4] of Israel's wandering [Exod 16:15, 32]) associated with God's singular nurturance of his chosen people. That providence was ratified by blood in the Sinaitic covenant (Exod 24:3–8); in Jer 31:31–34, that covenant had been renewed, even as it is revitalized in Mark 14:24 by the blood of the compassionate Shepherd, stricken for his scattered sheep (6:34; 8:2; 14:27; cf. Num 27:15–17; Ezek 34:1–31; Zech 13:7). By closing the Last Supper with Jesus's confidence that he will drink "the fruit of the vine afresh in

16. Doubtless those tales acquired eucharistic connotations in their traditional retelling (Schweizer, *Good News according to Mark*, 140), but for my purposes that is beside the point. The reader of Mark 14:22–25 hears the bells of 6:30–44 and 8:1–10, just as other events and sayings of the passion narrative resonate with harbingers earlier in the gospel.

the kingdom of God" (14:25; cf. Isa 25:6; Hab 3:17), Mark invites listeners to revisit their interpretations of the feedings of the five and four thousand. No longer are these tales solely reminders of earlier prophets' sustenance of others with meager resources (1 Kgs 17:8–16; 2 Kgs 4:1–7, 42–44). Now they are also foretastes of an eschatological banquet to come (Isa 25:6–8; 1 En. 62.12–14; 2 Bar. 29.5–8; 1QSa II, 11–22; Luke 14:16–24 = Matt 22:1–10).[17]

4. Jesus in Gethsemane (Mark 14:32–42)

Throughout Mark, Jesus has compassionately responded to others in terrible distress (e.g., 1:21–34; 2:1–12; 5:1–43; 6:30–56; 7:24–37; 8:22–26; 9:14–29; 10:46–52). At Gethsemane, Jesus himself—"barely in control, on the verge of panic"—pours out the grief that others have displayed.[18] In table 5 I take the liberty of reproducing from my own commentary a comparison of the evangelist's meticulously detailed account of Jesus's dark night of the soul with the intercalated tales of Jairus's daughter (5:21–24a, 35–43) and the hemorrhaging woman (5:24b–34).[19]

Table 5: Four Sufferers in Mark: Jairus, His Daughter, the Menorrhagic Woman, Jesus

Narrative Element	5:21–24a, 35–43	5:24b–34	14:32–42
1. Jesus's shift in location	v. 21 (sea crossing)	v. 24b (following Jairus)	v. 32 (to Gethsemane)
2. Presence of "children"	vv. 39–40 (Jairus's child)		vv. 40–41 (cf. 10:24, τέκνα)
3. Peter, James, and John	v. 37		vv. 32–33
4. Obtuseness	v. 40a (mourners' laughter)	v. 31 (disciples' protest)	vv. 34, 37–38, 40–41 (slumber)

17. Many commentators have argued—none more vigorously than Charles A. Bobertz (*The Gospel of Mark: A Liturgical Reading* [Grand Rapids: Baker Academic, 2016])—that Mark conveys a discernible progression from salvation to the Jews (6:30–44), then to gentiles (8:1–10), finally to all—"Jews and Gentiles, men and women, . . . present as the body of Christ to eat the one loaf and to drink the one cup" in 14:22–24 (*Gospel of Mark*, 164). That is a plausible reading. If so intended by the evangelist, I wish he had made it clearer: plain enough, at least, to bolster my exegetical confidence.

18. M. Eugene Boring, *Mark: A Commentary*, NTL (Louisville: Westminster John Knox, 2006), 397.

19. Black, *Mark*, 295. See also chapter 10 of the present volume.

5. Hopelessness	vv. 23a, 35 (death)	vv. 25–26 (bleeding)	v. 34a (grieved unto death)
6. Fear	v. 36 (Jairus: φοβοῦ)	v. 33 (the woman: φοβηθεῖσα)	v. 33 (Jesus: ἐκθαμβεῖσθαι καὶ ἀδημονεῖν)
7. Falling to the ground	v. 22 (Jairus: πίπτει)	v. 33 (the woman: προσέπεσεν)	v. 35 (Jesus: ἔπιπτεν)
8. Familial language	v. 23 ("little daughter")	v. 34 ("daughter")	v. 36 ("Abba, Father")
9. Plea for relief	v. 23b	vv. 27–28	vv. 36, 39, 41
10. Perception of the way forward	v. 36 (Jesus's encouragement)	vv. 28, 33a	[8:31; 9:31; 10:33–34]
11. Withdrawal and advance	vv. 38a, 40 (mourners/Jairus)	vv. 32, 33b (the woman)	vv. 36, 41–42 (Jesus)
12. Apocalyptic ambience	vv. 41–42 ("get up": ἔγειρε)	v. 34 ("peace")	vv. 36 ("cup"), 41 ("hour")

The legend of Jesus in Gethsemane is peppered with many elements foreshadowed in Mark: Jesus, the prayerful person (14:32, 35–36, 39; cf. 1:35; 6:41, 46; 8:6), in contrast with disciples who do not pray (9:28–29) but sleep when they should stay awake and alert (14:37–38, 41a; 13:33–37); the doleful cup (14:36; cf. 10:38–39; 14:23–24); addlepated members of the Twelve (14:40; cf. 6:51b–52; 8:14–21; 9:5–6, 32, 35–41); the Son of Man who steps forward to confront his destiny (14:41b–42; cf. 8:31; 9:31; 10:33–34; 14:21–22, 24). Yet so polished is Mark's mirror of chapters 5 and 14, so many are the reverberations in characterization and speech, that here, I believe, we cross the threshold from allusions into actual replication. In Mark 14:32–42, Jesus himself has become a *Doppelgänger*—in fact, a *Dreifachgänger*—of two earlier suppliants, all at their wits' ends. By entwining Jesus and Jairus, hemorrhaging woman and dead child and crucified Messiah, Mark suggests that physical torment and spiritual anguish, flesh and spirit (14:38), are different dimensions of a braided whole, which humans can alleviate but only a loving God—"Abba, Father"—can finally restore.[20] In Galilee, Jesus encourages others in hopeless circumstances. At Gethsemane, he himself demonstrates the sufferer's appropriate response: faith, evoked by prayer, which penetrates anguish. Mark's Jesus is God's Son, as obedient as he is beloved, a little child able to enter the kingdom (10:13–16),

---

20. Cf. Paul's similar contextualization of the cry, "Abba, Father," in Rom 8:15 and Gal 4:6.

the servant of divine sovereignty that some petitioners but none of his disciples proves to be (9:33–37).

5. A Hostile Multitude (Mark 14:43, 48; 15:8, 11)

As Cuthbert Hamilton Turner noted nearly a century ago, Mark visualizes "a crowd" or "multitude" as a single entity: a comprehensive character, as it were.[21] Mark refers to [ὁ] ὄχλος thirty-eight times, allowing for their comparative lengths, a frequency greater than either Matthew (fifty occurrences), Luke (forty-one), or John (twenty). Mobs are by nature volatile. Depending on their narrative context, the connotations of ὁ ὄχλος in Mark are variable: sometimes positive (2:13; 6:34; 7:14; 8:1 [cf. 6:34], 2, 6 [bis], 34; 9:17; 10:1; 12:37), sometimes negative (2:4; 3:9, 20, 32; 5:24b, 27; 9:14; 11:32; 12:12; 14:43; 15:8, 11, 15), sometimes neutral or ambivalent (4:1 [bis], 36; 5:21, 30, 31; 6:45; 7:17, 33; 9:15, 25; 10:46; 11:18; 12:41).[22] The occasionally sinister quality of ὁ ὄχλος in Mark is impressive: "the crowd" impedes the progress of both Jesus (1:45 [unidentified, but implied]) and of those in desperate straits (2:4; 5:24b, 27, 38 [ὁ θόρυβος; 10:48 [οἱ πολλοί]), can be aligned with those who radically misunderstand him (3:32 [cf. 3:21]), are fractious (9:14), and intimidating to those who mean Jesus harm (11:32; 12:12). Mark's narrative displays a pronounced dynamic of Jesus's attempt to withdraw and the multitude's prevention of that endeavor (1:35–36, 45; 4:35–36; 6:30–33; 6:45, 53–55; 7:24, 36), however well intentioned its members may be. At two points early in Jesus's ministry, the crowd is so oppressive that it prevents Jesus from eating (3:20) and threatens to crush him (3:9)—both characterizations absent from Matthew and Luke's parallel passages. These portents are fully realized in Mark's passion narrative, all of whose references to ὁ ὄχλος are to parties hostile to Jesus (15:8, 15), some in overt collusion with the chief priests (14:43; 15:11). More so than in any other gospel, the multitude in Mark return, with malice, to haunt Jesus's final hours.[23]

---

21. *The Language and Style of the Gospel of Mark: An Edition of C. H. Turner's "Notes on Marcan Usage" Together with Other Comparable Studies*, ed. J. Keith Elliott, NovTSup 71 (Leiden: Brill, 1993), 49. Turner's notes were originally published in *JTS* 1924–1927. In only one instance (Mark 10:1) does the plural ὄχλοι occur. When ὁ ὄχλος is modified, it is usually by the adjective πολύς (5:21, 24; 6:34; 8:1; 9:14; 12:37), alternatively by πλεῖστος (4:1) and ἱκανός (10:46). The idiom πᾶς ὁ ὄχλος occurs four times (2:13; 4:1; 9:15; 11:18).

22. Marcus (*Mark 8–16*, 1036–37) expresses such mystification at the crowd's turn against Jesus in 15:1–15 that he imports "the influence of malignant spirits" to explain it. Mark 15 says nothing of this, but the evangelist has planted plenty of clues that the multitudes cannot be trusted to safeguard Jesus's well-being.

23. Matthew (26:47; 27:15, 20, 24) and Luke (22:6, 47a; 23:4) generally follow Mark's lead. Luke tempers the crowd's cruelty by shifting from ὁ ὄχλος to ὁ λαός, incited by their

6. Jesus and Peter on Trial (Mark 14:53-72)

Even more conspicuously than in the tales of Jairus's daughter (5:21–24a, 35–43) and the hemorrhaging woman (5:24b–34), the interrogations of Jesus and Peter at the high priest's court comprise a traditional intercalation in which the principal figures double each other for maximum narrative impact.[24] Unlike the pericopae we have previously examined, here we encounter not the reminiscence of an event from earlier in Jesus's ministry but rather an immediately juxtaposed, intricately entwined composite of *Doppelgängers* within the passion narrative itself. See table 6.

Table 6: Two Trials on the Night of Jesus's Arrest

Narrative Element	The Interrogation of Jesus (14:55–65)	The Interrogation of Peter (14:53–54, 66–72)
1. Settings	The council chamber (v. 53)	The council court-yard (v. 54)
2. The defendants	Jesus (vv. 55–65)	Peter (vv. 53–54, 66–72)
3. Proximity of accusers	Within striking distance (cf. v. 65)	"at a distance . . . with the guards" by a fireside (v. 54); later, backing away to the forecourt (v. 68b)
4. Interrogators	Chief priests and the high priest (v. 55a)	One of the high priest's maids; other bystanders (vv. 66, 69, 70b)

---

leaders (23:5, 13, 14; see also Matt 27:1, 25, 64) and by uniquely reporting the multitude's guilty remorse at Jesus's death (Luke 23:48; cf. v. 27). None of John's twenty references to ὁ ὄχλος (5:13; 6:2, 5, 22, 24; 7:12 [bis], 20, 31, 32, 40, 43, 49; 11:42; 12:9, 12, 17, 18, 29, 34) occurs in that evangelist's passion narrative: one (12:9) precedes Jesus's entry to Jerusalem, which thrice notes "the multitude's" presence (12:12, 17, 18); the remaining and final two uses of ὁ ὄχλος occur in that pericope's aftermath (12:29, 34).

24. For a catalog of Mark's other intercalations, see Black, *Mark*, 88. Luke suggests either an originally separate sequencing of Peter's nocturnal denials (22:54–62) and Jesus's diurnal trial (22:66–71) or a deliberate disruption of Mark's interpolation of the latter into the former.

5. Repeated accusations	Impeachable testimony (vv. 55b–56); divergent charges regarding the temple's destruction (vv. 57–59)	"You, too, were with the Nazarene" (v. 67b); "This one is one of them" (v. 69)
6. Defendants' responses	Silence (vv. 60–61b)	"I don't know or understand what you are saying" (v. 68a); "But again he denied it" (v. 70a)
7. Direct confrontation of defendants	"You are the Christ, the Son of the Blessed" (v. 61b)	"Absolutely you are one of them, for you are a Galilean" (v. 70b)
8. The defendants' pleas	"I am, and you will see the Son of Man [τὸν υἱὸν τοῦ ἀνθρώπου]" (v. 62)	"I don't know this man [τὸν ἄνθρωπον] you are talking about" (v. 71b)
9. Curses	"You have heard the blasphemy" (v. 64a)	"He began to curse and to swear" (v. 71a)
10. Verdicts	The death penalty (v. 64bc)	"And right then, for the second time, a cock crowed" (v. 72a)
11. Prophetic fulfillments	[Implied by 8:31; 9:31; 10:33–34]	"And Peter remembered the thing Jesus had said to him" (v. 72b)
12. The defendants' responses	[None narrated]	"And he broke down [ἐπιβαλών] and burst into tears" (v. 72c)
13. The accusers' response	Abuse: spitting, blindfolding, repeated beatings, taunts to "prophesy" (v. 65)	[None narrated]

That there were not one but two trials on the night of Jesus's arraignment has become a commonplace in Markan interpretation. However, only after analyzing the elements of both legends in the Second Gospel can one appreciate just how subtly they have been recounted—quite an accomplishment for an evangelist who, in the estimate of the twentieth-century's most celebrated NT exegete, "is not sufficiently master of his material to be able to venture on a systematic construction himself."[25] The *Doppelgängers* in 14:53–72 spill over one another in simultaneous waves: inside versus outside, Jesus versus Peter, the high priest versus his maid, the entire Sanhedrin versus a gaggle of bystanders, false charges versus accurate identifications, silence versus sputtering, truth-telling versus flagrant lies, Jesus's alleged cursing of God versus Peter's cursing (whether of his questioners, Jesus, or himself is unclear), wild abuse versus tacit dismissal.[26] As Mark tells these stories, each turns the other inside out: under enormous pressure, Jesus stands fast, acknowledging his identity for the first and only time in this gospel at the precise instant that will seal his death warrant (14:62–64; cf. 8:29–30, where he invokes silence of his followers regarding his messiahship). Meanwhile, at that very moment, the principal among those disciples keeps his distance (14:54) and actually retreats (14:68b), all the while lying through his teeth about any association with his teacher. Jesus seizes his destiny as the Son of Man who must suffer, while Peter, who would save his life, utterly loses it (8:35a).[27] The irony is all but unbearable: at the very moment that Jesus is mocked by unbelieving abusers to prophesy (14:65), all of his prophecies about himself (8:31; 9:31; 10:33–34) and Peter and

25. Rudolf Bultmann, *History of the Synoptic Tradition*, trans. John Marsh, rev. ed. (New York: Harper & Row, 1963), 350. So symmetrical is the structuring of these intercalated narratives that my agnosticism about the degree of Markan redactional activity has become duly chastened (*The Disciples according to Mark: Markan Redaction in Current Debate*, 2nd ed. (Grand Rapids: Eerdmans, 2012]). To think that all of these coincidences lie only at the traditional level, untouched by an authorial hand, is, for me if not for Humpty Dumpty, one thing too impossible to believe before breakfast.

26. See Helmut Merkel, "Peter's Curse," in *The Trial of Jesus: Cambridge Studies in Honour of C. F. D. Moule*, ed. Ernst Bammel, SBT 2nd series 13 (London: SCM, 1970), 66–71. Matthew (26:72, 74) builds Peter's curse to a climax; Luke and John retain Peter's denials but eliminate his curse. Tom Shepherd suggests another way of viewing the curses in Mark 14:53–72: "Where Peter called on God as his witness that he was telling the truth (which he was not), the high priest utilized his sense of God's position and honor to call down an imprecation on Jesus' claim (in the Markan story also incorrect)" ("The Irony of Power in the Trial of Jesus and the Denial by Peter—Mark 14:53–72," in *The Trial and Death of Jesus: Essays on the Passion Narrative in Mark*, ed. Geert van Oyen and Tom Shepherd, CBET [Leuven: Peeters, 2006], 24).

27. Such an exegesis may lend more gravity to Peter's circumstances than is merited. As Schweizer notes, none of the comments directed to him have anything to do with his religious profession as such (*Good News according to Mark*, 331–32). Peter caves in at the *merest whisper* of a *potential* accusation.

the rest of his disciples (14:29–31) flourish to their fulfillment. This transcends cleverness. It is narrative theology at its pinnacle.

7. Pilate's Interrogation, Sentencing, and Execution of Jesus (Mark 15:1–5 + 16–32)

Internal to the passion narrative are some notable correspondences between Pilate's interrogation of Jesus (15:1–5) and its surrounding episodes. After Jesus's transfer to Roman jurisdiction (15:1), the prefect says to Jesus, "[So] you're the King of the Jews" (15:2a). That sentence's construction in Greek is the same as in 14:61: an ironically accurate though faithless affirmation that in context may be punctuated as a question. This is the first of five occurrences of "King of the Jews" in Mark (see also 15:9, 12, 18, 26).[28] It recalls Mark's five references to Jesus as the Messiah (1:1; 8:29; 9:41; 12:35; 14:61): a valid attribution, even if some who make it, like Peter (8:29) or the high priest (14:61), cannot understand its implications. Roman overlords, Pilate (15:2a, 9, 12) and his cohort (15:18, 26), call Jesus "King of the Jews," in contrast to Jesus's coreligionists, who as insiders mock him as "Israel's king" (15:32). The charge of "blasphemy" (14:64) has evaporated: Pilate would have cared nothing about Jewish religious sensibilities but would have been interested in Jesus as a threat to the imperium (15:26). Jesus's words to Pilate, "[So] you say" (σὺ λέγεις [15:2b])—both more cryptic and more ironic than his reply to the high priest (14:62a)—are his last until just before his death (15:34).

Expressing perplexity, Pilate vehemently questions the defendant. "Do you *not* have *nothing* to answer?" (οὐκ ἀποκρίνῃ οὐδέν): in Greek, an emphatic double negative (15:4), which recalls the chief priest's identical question, almost identically articulated (14:60: οὐκ ἀπεκρίνατο οὐδέν). With equivalent force, "Jesus *no* longer answered *nothing*" (οὐκέτι οὐδὲν ἀπεκρίθη [15:5a]; cf. 14:61: οὐκ ἀπεκρίνατο οὐδέν). Pilate marvels (θαυμάζειν [15:5b]), as have others in Mark (5:20; 6:6a; 12:17). Jesus's silence before the prefect is patient of multiple interpretations. It may have been customary for Jews in Roman custody to say nothing to their accusers, lest their rebuttal implicate fellow Jews. If that be the case here, then Jesus refuses to expose and incriminate the chief

---

28. For detailed analysis, consult Frank J. Matera, *The Kingship of Jesus: Composition and Theology in Mark 15*, SBLDS 66 (Chico, CA: Scholars Press, 1982).

priests.[29] Mark may also allude to Israel's Suffering Servant (Isa 53:7 LXX: καὶ αὐτὸς διὰ τὸ κεκακῶσθαι οὐκ ἀνοίγει τὸ στόμα . . . οὕτως οὐκ ἀνοίγει τὸ στόμα αὐτοῦ). Whatever the motivation, by recalling the defendant's silence before the chief priest (14:61a), Mark juxtaposes Jesus's two trials before two magistrates—one Jewish, the other Roman—both, unable to recognize the king they are judging.

Mark 15:6–32 comprises three balanced, interlocking pericopae:[30]

     A. Pilate's sentencing of Jesus (vv. 6–15)
       B. The soldiers' abuse of Jesus (vv. 16–20)
     A.'The soldiers' execution of Jesus (vv. 21–32)

Whether these segments constitute a final Markan intercalation is a good question. Normally the same characters and activities of the framing pericope (A) are interrupted by interlaminated material (B). Substantively, 15:6–15 and 15:21–32 deviate from that pattern. Structurally, however, the component elements do mirror one another:

- The principal theme is ironic rejection of Israel's true yet hidden king.
- The central pericope (vv. 16–20) amplifies Jesus's abuse by the Sanhedrin (14:65). The humiliation is rendered in greater detail; its agents are gentiles (cf. 9:31).
- The primary agents of Jesus's destruction are now Rome's prefect (15:8–10, 12, 14–15) and provincial military (vv. 21–28), provoked by Jewish officialdom (vv. 10, 11, 31) and Jerusalem's rabble (vv. 8, 11, 13, 15, 29).
- Pilate's mockery of Jesus as "the King of the Jews" (vv. 9, 12) foreshadows comparable taunts at the crucifixion (vv. 26, 32).
- The release of a known, murderous bandit (vv. 7, 15: on which, more momentarily) is answered in verses 27 and 29b by the innocent Jesus's execution between a pair of revolutionary bandits (again, more to come).

---

29. Ernst Bammel, "The Trial before Pilate," in Bammel and Moule, *Jesus and the Politics of His Day*, 415–51, N.B. 421–22.

30. In 15:16–39, Mark may be a turning inside out the type-scene of a Roman triumphal procession, which included the victorious general's acclamation, his procession through a captured city with trophies of conquest, and a culminating offer of religious sacrifices (Cassius Dio, *Hist. rom.* 6.23; 58.11; 64.20–21; cf. 2 Cor 2:14–15; thus, T. E. Schmidt, "Mark 15:16–32: The Crucifixion Narrative and the Roman Triumphal Procession," *NTS* 41 [1995]: 1–18). Although this inversion might be reckoned a wraithlike revisiting of Mark 11:1–11, its allusions may be too elusive to qualify.

- The faux regalia in which the cohort first clothe, then undress, Jesus (vv. 17, 20a) anticipate their callous disposition of his garments after crucifixion (v. 24).
- The savagery of this tableau intensifies from the demand for Jesus's crucifixion (vv. 13–14) to his physical abuse (v. 19) to the ultimate penalty, crucifixion (vv. 24a, 25).

This segment of the passion narrative is ghost-ridden. Jesus's trial and sentencing by Pilate do not stand alone in this gospel. They comprise the last of three trials narrated in rapid succession, accompanied by Jesus's threefold anguish in Gethsemane (14:35–36, 39, 41a), three attempts to awaken his disciples (vv. 37–38, 40, 41b–42), and Peter's trio of denials (vv. 68, 70a, 71). The first trial was of Jesus by the Sanhedrin (vv. 55–65); the second, that of Peter in the high priest's courtyard (vv. 66–72). Each of these proceedings has blended veracity ("You are the Christ"; "[Peter,] you are one of them"; "You are the King of the Jews") with mendacity (false witness; denials of discipleship; the chief priests' enmity). Each has fitfully escalated to its conclusion. Initially the Sanhedrin cannot pin anything on Jesus; Peter keeps retreating until he crumples; Pilate's amazement is trumped by another convict's release. Each trial ends furiously, with physical abuse (14:65b; 15:15) or emotional collapse (14:72). At every point, justice is miscarried: the Son of Man goes as it is so written, but woe betide those who collude (14:21a).

Responsibility for Jesus's death lies finally with Pilate, who has his own spectral *Doppelgänger*: Herod Antipas (6:14–29). Oddly, Mark opened that legend with the comment that, on hearing of Jesus, Herod believed him a revenant: John the Baptist, raised from the dead (vv. 14, 16). Ostensibly describing the death warrants of two "righteous and holy" men (6:20; 15:14), both 6:14–29 and 15:1–15 are actually stories about weak authorities who bungle their objectives while being outfoxed. The king no more wants to kill John (6:20) than the prefect wants to execute Jesus: it is *Pilate's* idea to release him (15:9). But their adversaries (6:19, 24; 15:3, 10, 11) possess malicious wit to turn custom against political superiors: irrevocable oaths (6:26b), a Passover privilege (15:6). The manipulators get their way by using pawns who demand grisly deaths: Herodias's daughter for John's head (6:22–25); Jerusalem's crowds for Jesus's crucifixion (15:11, 14b). Neither politico gets what he wanted. Herod paints himself into the corner of beheading John (6:26–28); Pilate suckers himself into executing an innocent (15:15) by releasing a manifestly guilty felon back into Judea's social and political turmoil (v. 7).[31]

---

31. In *Mark*, 153–63, I have suggested that not only 8:1–10 but also (and more immediately) 6:14–29 is an uncanny doublet of 6:30–44: two parallel banquets, reflecting the mores

8. Barabbas (Mark 15:6–15)

Jesus's trial before Pilate climaxes with the release of Barabbas (15:6–15), which Mark describes as customary (vv. 6, 8). While our knowledge of provincial trial law in this era is spotty, by the first century CE Roman authorities may have reviewed some cases among their subjects to assure just sentences and to reverse egregious decisions (cf. 15:9–10).[32] Although 15:7 does not identify a particular revolt, Luke (13:1; Acts 5:36–37) and Josephus (*B.J.* 2.167–177, 228–257; *A.J.* 18.55–62; 20.113–124, 208–210) refer to Jewish insurrections against Rome in the early first century. Mark characterizes Barabbas as one among other rioters (μετὰ τῶν στασιαστῶν) who had committed murder during "the uprising" (ἐν τῇ στάσει [Mark 15:7]). The evangelist repeats, without translating, this rebel's offbeat Aramaic name (vv. 7, 11, 15): "Son of the Father." By contrast, the name "Jesus" is mentioned only once, after judgment has been pronounced (v. 15). Twice Pilate refers to him as "the King of the Jews" in solicitous, highly ironic questions addressed to the rabble (v. 9: in effect, "Why not seize your opportunity?"; v. 12: "Would you like to reconsider your decision?"). As previously noted, "the crowd" (ὁ ὄχλος) in Mark, at times disposed toward Jesus (2:13; 3:32; 4:1; 8:1; 12:37), are not to be trusted. The multitudes have turned on their leaders (11:18, 32; 12:12); in 15:11, they do the same against Jesus. Insisting on Barabbas's release, the crowd is even more determined that "the King of the Jews" be crucified (vv. 13, 14b), despite the fact that Rome's prefect, who alone exercised authority to execute, acquits him (v. 14a). Pilate capitulates: releasing Barabbas, he has Jesus flogged, then "hands over" (παρέδωκεν [v. 15; cf. 1:14]) the condemned to crucifixion.

Mark 15:1–32 is a weird ghost story, with Barabbas as Jesus's *Doppelgänger*. Saying and doing nothing, Jesus is but vaguely present, much talked about before being whipped and transferred for execution. He and Barabbas are opposite subversives. Barabbas opted for violent revolution (15:7). Jesus proclaimed an alternative kingdom structured by repentance and forgiveness (1:15; 11:25). Barabbas has taken one life (15:7); Jesus has restored another's (5:35–43).

---

of two different kingdoms, which culminate in either vicious murder or compassionate nourishment.

32. Ernst Bammel, "Die Blutherichtsbarkeit in der römische Provinz Judaä vor dem ersten jüdischen Aufstand," *JJS* 25 (1974): 39–49; Yarbro Collins, *Mark*, 715–17. For discussion of the historical problems attending the Passover amnesty, consult Brown, *Death of the Messiah*, 2:814–20. Boring, *Mark*, 420, presents a trenchant argument against its historical likelihood (cf. Josephus, *A.J.* 20.215); Evans, *Mark 8:27–16:20*, 479–80, 485–86, gives us precisely the opposite.

The most blatant irony in 15:6–15 lies in the evangelist's tacit contrast between one "Son of the Father," a convicted murderer, and another "Son" of a different "Father" (1:11; 9:7; 13:32; 14:36 [Abba]) who, as his executioner concedes, has done no evil (15:14). "The criminal escaped; Christ was condemned" (Augustine, *Tract. Ev. Jo.* 31.11). "The Son of Man came not to be served but to serve and to give his life for others' release" (10:45). In 15:6–15, such redemption is dramatized before the reader's very eyes.

9. On the Via Dolorosa: An Unexpected Simon (Mark 15:21)

A condemned prisoner like Jesus was forced to carry his own *patibulum* (Plutarch, *Mor.* 554a–b); the gibbet waited at the place of execution. Into the story flits another character who will vanish as fast as he appears: a passerby named Simon. Cyrene (Acts 6:9; 11:20; 13:1) was a city in what is now Libya. It is hard to determine significance in the detail of Simon's "coming in from the country" (or "field": ἀπ᾽ ἀγροῦ), unless (perhaps) Mark is juxtaposing a single follower of Israel's soon-to-be-crucified king with those who cut "leaves from the fields" (στιβάδας κόψαντες ἐκ τῶν ἀγρῶν) while welcoming the advent of "the kingdom of our ancestor David" (11:9–10). When Jesus entered Jerusalem, the cry was *Hosanna*, "Lord, save" (11:9–10); he exits to a very different cry—"Crucify" (15:13–14)—and the one who most obviously needs saving is Jesus himself. Presumably, Mark's audience would have recognized Simon's sons (15:21), as Matthew's (27:32) and Luke's (23:26) readers would not.[33] The evangelist's introduction of another Simon at this point is intriguing.[34] Mark mentions no motive for the soldiers' pressing him "to carry his cross" (15:21). In context, "his cross" refers, of course, to Jesus's; still, after Simon Peter refused the Son of Man's ordained suffering and death (8:31–32), the teacher insisted that those coming after him "take up their cross and follow me" (8:34). Sheer coincidence? Perhaps—though it is strange that one Simon does as another Simon was instructed but refused.[35] Like Barabbas in

---

33. A certain "Rufus, chosen in the Lord," is among many at the church in Rome whom Paul greets (Rom 16:13). It is impossible to confirm that Mark refers to the same person.

34. Given the name's popularity in antiquity, the inclusion of many other Simons in Mark's narrative is no surprise (the Cananaean, 3:18; a brother of Jesus, 6:3; a leper, 14:3). In 15:21, timing, like context, is everything.

35. Helen K. Bond rightly notes that the Cyrenian's act is not voluntary but compulsory (ἀγγαρεύουσιν [15:21]): "Paragon of Discipleship? Simon of Cyrene in the Markan Passion Narrative," in *Matthew and Mark across Perspectives: Essays in Honour of Stephen C. Barton and William R. Telford*, ed. Kristin A. Bendoraitis and Nijay K. Gupta, LNTS 538 (London:

15:6–15, Cyrene's Simon is another revenant, reminding one of a key disciple who lost himself in a terrified attempt to save himself (8:35a), with miserable consequences (14:70–72).

10. At Golgotha: "Those Who Were Crucified with Him" (Mark 15:27, 32b)

Mark's description of the "malefactors" (οἱ κακοῦργοι [Luke 23:32, 33, 39]) with whom Jesus is crucified has been doubly foreshadowed in this gospel.[36] First, they are characterized as δύο λῃστάς: likely, political insurrectionists (freedom fighters, from their viewpoint). Jesus is no such revolutionary (cf. John 18:33–40), but, following Jeremiah (7:11 LXX), he castigated the temple as "a bandits' lair" (σπήλαιον [Mark 11:17c]) and noted the irony that he had been arrested ὡς ἐπὶ λῃστήν (14:48) when he could easily have been apprehended on any of the days he was teaching in the temple (14:49a).[37] Even more ironic is Mark's explicit positioning of those crucified with Jesus: "one on the right and one on his left" (ἕνα ἐκ δεξιῶν καὶ ἕνα ἐξ εὐωνύμων αὐτοῦ [15:27]), an almost verbatim quotation of the Zebedee brothers' petitions to bask in Jesus's reflected glory (δὸς ἡμῖν ἵνα εἷς σου ἐκ δεξιῶν καὶ εἷς ἐξ ἀριστερῶν καθίσωμεν ἐν τῇ δόξῃ σου [10:37]).[38] On that occasion, Jesus has warned James and John that they've no idea what they are asking (10:38; cf. 10:36: "We want you to do for us whatever we ask of you"), that the cup he must drink will someday be theirs, too (10:39b), even though he doesn't want it (14:36) and they are fools to think that they do (10:38b–39a). For Jesus, as for all others, events unfold as they have been divinely prepared (ἀλλ᾽ οἷς ἡτοίμασται [10:40]).

Bloomsbury T&T Clark, 2016), 18–35 (so, too, Hugh Anderson, *The Gospel of Mark*, NCB [London: Marshall, Morgan & Scott, 1976], 340). One needn't claim that Simon the Cyrenean is the paradigm of discipleship in Mark that only Jesus proves to be. One need only note that *another Simon* fades in and out of Mark's passion narrative at a climactic moment (probably, as Bond suggests, to heighten the auxiliary legionaries' ridicule of Jesus).

36. Although I choose not to consider them here, Marcus (*Mark 8–16*, 1046) tabulates items that constitute doublets in Mark's description of Jesus's crucifixion (15:23–24, 29–30, 34–36b) and death (15:25, 31–32, 36a, 37).

37. Only Matthew (27:38, 44) follows Mark in identifying the other victims at this crucifixion as οἱ λῃσταί.

38. In 20:21 and 27:38, Matthew intensifies the verbal coincidence with Mark 15:27: εἷς ἐκ δεξιῶν σου καὶ εἷς ἐξ εὐωνύμων σου. For pointing this out to me, I thank Professor Dale Allison.

11. The Taunt: "Others He Saved; Himself He Cannot Save" (Mark 15:31)

Again returning to the passion narrative after multiple wrangles (2:6, 16; 3:22; 7:1, 5; 9:14; 11:18, 27; 12:38; 14:1, 10; cf. 8:31; 10:33) with Israel's king whom they cannot recognize (cf. 4:12a), the chief priests and scribes ridicule the crucified Jesus in precisely those terms he has accepted as the Son of Man's destiny: "not to be served but to serve and to give his life for the sake of many" (10:45).[39] Once more: "Whoever would save his life would lose it" (8:35a). Like the high priest and Pilate, the chief priests and scribes unwittingly affirm faith in Jesus with blind ignorance and utter faithlessness.

12. Waiting for Elijah (Mark 15:35–36)

Early in the gospel, Jesus warned listeners, "Watch what you hear" (4:24a). Usually they have failed to do so (4:12; 8:14–21). So it goes to the end. Quoting Ps 22, Jesus *cries*, ελωι, ελωι, "My God, my God"; what some in his audience *hear* is Ἐλίας (cf. Matt 27:46). Perhaps extrapolating from 2 Kgs 2:9–12 by way of Mal 3:5–6 and Sir 48, some Jewish traditions envisioned Elijah as protector of the righteous in distress.[40] A sponge is sopped with vinegar, stuck on a stick, and offered to Jesus on the chance that Elijah may return to remove him from the cross (Mark 15:36). The irony of this act is so multilayered that it sets one's head spinning. (1) Before crucifixion, Jesus refused refreshment (v. 23). Why would he accept this now? (2) The previous offering was probably a painkiller; this is vinegary wine (τὸ ὄξος), extended on a cane (ὁ κάλαμος) of the sort the soldiers used to club him (v. 19). (3) The runner fulfills Scripture by unwittingly mimicking another lament (Ps 69:21). (4) That Mark intends this action to be taken as torment, not an errand of mercy, is suggested by the context, coupled with 8:11–12: A faithless generation seeks a sign—even one so gruesome as the spectacular rescue of a tortured innocent. "Truly I tell you, no sign will be given to this generation" (8:12b). (5) Mark's listeners *know* that no sign is forthcoming, because in John the Baptist, Elijah already has returned "and they did to him whatever

---

39. For an acute analysis of Jesus's death from this vantage point, see Helen K. Bond, "A Fitting End? Self-Denial and a Slave's Death in Mark's *Life of Jesus*," *NTS* 65 (2019): 425–42.

40. Unfortunately for our purposes, regard for Elijah as vigilant protector of the innocent and protector in evil times cannot be confidently documented until the talmudic era (e.g., b. 'Abod. Zar. 18b; b. Šabb. 33b; b. B. Meṣ. 84a). See Louis Ginzberg, *The Legends of the Jews: Bible Times and Characters from Moses in the Wilderness to Esther*, trans. Henrietta Szold and Paul Radin (Philadelphia: Jewish Publication Society, 2003), 2:1000–1023.

they pleased" (9:13)—namely, decapitation (6:27–28). (6) During his life, very few have understood Jesus. At his death, still others perpetuate that stupidity.

13. A Third Rip/A Third Pronouncement (Mark 15:38–39)

As practically all modern commentators acknowledge, in Mark Jesus's death recapitulates earlier events in his life: his baptism (1:9–11), transfiguration (9:2–8), and the high priest's verdict (14:62–63). Beyond these evident points of resonance, all the details in Mark 15:38–39 are so exegetically controversial that any hope of resolving them here is both futile and, for my purposes, irrelevant.[41] Of consequence are the particular actions and words that lie in the immediate aftermath of Jesus's death (15:37). They stand among a series of climactic ruptures:

- the rending (σχιζομένου) of the heavens at Jesus's baptism (1:10),[42] which mirrors
- the tearing (διαρρήξας) of the high priest's tunic (14:63), as well as
- a complete split (ἐσχίσθη) of the temple's curtain (15:38), unseen by all save Mark's reader.

These ruptures are conjoined with assertions about Jesus's identity:

- "You are my Son, the Beloved, in whom I take delight" (the בַּת־קוֹל in 1:11, reiterated with an injunction at the transfiguration [9:7]: "This is my Son, the Beloved: listen to him");
- "I am [the Christ, the Son of the Blessed]" (Jesus's acceptance of the high priest's quizzical affirmation: 14:61b–62a);
- "Truly this man was the Son of God" (the centurion's response to Jesus's death: 15:39).[43]

---

41. For detailed discussion, see Black, *Mark*, 330–33.

42. *If* Mark knew that the Herodian temple was draped by several curtains, and *if* he knew that the tapestried details of its outermost drapery "portrayed a panorama of the heavens" (as Josephus describes in *B.J.* 5.207–214), then 15:38, like 1:10, 13:24–25, and 15:33, might allude to astral disturbances of one or another sort (thus, David Ulansey, "The Heavenly Veil Torn: Mark's Cosmic *Inclusio*," *JBL* 110 [1991]: 123–25). This, however, pitches us into one of the many thorny features of Mark 15:33–39, which cannot be resolved here (if ever).

43. The intent of the centurion's statement—whether it be a treasonous affirmation of faith by one who has pledged fealty to Caesar Augustus as *divi filius* or the last sarcastic nail driven into an ironic coffin—may be left open-ended. Sweat's assessment is well tem-

To listeners primed for scrupulous observance of folklore's rule of three (cf. 14:30, 41, 72), one would anticipate a third בַּת־קוֹל in 15:33–39, to close the circuit opened at 1:11 and continued at 9:7. That expectation is frustrated: in answer to the crucified Messiah's cri de coeur (v. 34), there is (first) silence from heaven, (second) a supernatural event seen by the reader alone (v. 38), and (third) a truthful testimony by the least likely human witness, based on evidence most daft (v. 39; cf. 1 Cor 1:23).

14. The Ministering Women (Mark 15:40–41)

Unlike Luke, who early on informs his readers of the presence of women among Jesus's Galilean entourage (8:1–3), Mark withholds this information as a surprise until the narration of Jesus's death and resurrection. Unlike the mother of Jesus and other women in John's narrative, who stand by the cross of the dying Jesus (John 19:25), his female cohort in Mark have beheld the spectacle from afar (ἀπὸ μακρόθεν [Mark 15:40]).[44] Yet there is no question that they are true disciples: they "followed him" (ἠκολούθουν), as expected of all of Jesus's disciples (1:18; 2:14–15; 6:1; 8:34; 10:52);[45] many of them (ἄλλαι πολλαί) did so all the way to Jerusalem (15:41); they persevered with their teacher longer than any of the Twelve, to the point of witnessing his burial (15:47). They are shades of another woman in Mark: like Peter's mother-in-law, they *ministered* to him (διηκόνουν αὐτῷ [15:41; cf. 1:31]). Besides these women, the only figures described by Mark as ministering to Jesus—who defines the Son of Man as the one who ministers (διακονῆσαι [10:45])—are the angels in the wilderness, following his satanic temptation (1:13). Two of the women at the crucifixion are named Mary: Magdalene, and the mother of James the

---

pered: "God continues to work through Jesus' opponents to the very end, prompting even the person who could have been the greatest 'outsider' in the passion narrative to confess Jesus' identity at this crucial point. Yet this revelation is concealed, as the ambiguity of the centurion's words leaves open the possibility that his proclamation is in line with the other mockers at the cross.... God is hidden but active, revealing a mystery at the cross that is not understood" (*Theological Role of Paradox*, 143–44).

44. Simon Peter also followed Jesus ἀπὸ μακρόθεν into the high priest's courtyard (14:54): a vague suggestion that the women's staying power may ultimately prove no greater than his.

45. The standard treatment is Ernest Best, *Following Jesus: Discipleship in the Gospel of Mark*, JSNTSup 4 (Sheffield: JSOT Press, 1981). Best never identifies the women in 1:29–31, 15:40–41, or 16:1–8 as Jesus's disciples, though in one essay ("Mark's Use of the Twelve") he acknowledges that "15:40f. (the women) implies the existence of a wider group [of disciples] than the twelve" (*Disciples and Discipleship: Studies in the Gospel according to Mark* [Edinburgh: T&T Clark, 1986], 157).

younger and of Joses (15:40). Are they revenants of Jesus's mother, named as Mary only once in Mark (6:3)? Is the other Mary in 15:40, mother of James and Joses, in fact, Jesus's own mother? Probably not. If she were, why would not Mark have identified her as *Jesus's* mother? Moreover, these women followed him while he was in Galilee (15:41). Mark has made no such claim for Jesus's own mother and, indeed, has cast doubt on how well she understood her son (3:21, 31).[46] For the present study, precise identification is immaterial. What's important is Mark's gathering, at his conclusion, of precursory threads.

15. Joseph of Arimathea (15:42–47)

From out of nowhere also appears Joseph of Arimathea, who does for Jesus's body what John's disciples did for their teacher's: properly inter it in a tomb (6:29).[47] Beyond that plain yet signal observation, there are four, perhaps five, other shadows of things past in this gospel. First, the corpse of neither John nor Jesus was buried by members of his family. Second, and most quicksilverish, Joseph is identified as "a councilor of good standing" (εὐσχήμων βουλευτής [15:43]), an identification and modifier appearing nowhere else in Mark. On what council he sat, Mark does not say. Unless the evangelist was overcome by his well-known hyperbole, Joseph appears not to have been numbered among the Sanhedrin, *all* of whose members concurred with the high priest's death sentence (14:64b; cf. 14:55: ὅλον τὸ συνέδριον).[48] Third, Joseph was "awaiting

46. See also R. T. France, *The Gospel of Mark: A Commentary on the Greek Text*, NIGTC (Grand Rapids: Eerdmans; Carlisle: Paternoster, 2002), 664; cf. William C. Placher, *Mark*, Belief (Louisville: Westminster John Knox, 2010), 237.

47. Though tempted, one cannot argue that this Joseph does for Jesus what another—his father—might have done for his dead son. Jesus is identified as "the son of Mary" in 6:3. Mark is the only gospel in which Jesus's father is never named.

48. Brown's argument that Simon "was a distinguished member of the Sanhedrin" lacks conviction (*Death of the Messiah*, 2:1214). As Brown himself notes (2:1213), ἡ βουλή could refer to the council of any city or town. If Mark had intended to identify Simon as a Sanhe-drinist, why did he not say so? Yarbro Collins (*Mark*, 777) notes that the wording is suffi-ciently ambiguous to allow for Joseph's seat on an *Arimathean* council; Dennis E. Nineham (*The Gospel of St Mark*, PGC [Baltimore: Penguin Books, 1963], 434) opines that Mark's audience may not have taken εὐσχήμων βουλευτής "to mean any more than a man of high official standing" (so also Schweizer, *Good News according to Mark*, 362). With Elizabeth Struthers Malbon, I agree that Mark depicts both Joseph and Jairus the ἀρχισυνάγωγος (Mark 5:22, 35–36, 38) as men of stature who part company from the religious establishment ("The Jewish Leaders in the Gospel of Mark: A Literary Study of Markan Characterization," *JBL* 108 [1989]: 259–81). One might also add that both are also associated with Markan death scenes (cf. 5:35–43).

the kingdom of God" (15:43)—making him the only figure, apart from Jesus, of whom such is said in Mark. Fourth, Joseph "dared" (τολμήσας) to petition Pilate for the body of Jesus (15:43). After Jesus's riposte to a scribe "not far from God's kingdom," no one dared (ἐτόλμα) further questioning of Jesus in the temple (12:34b). The Twelve in Mark dare nothing; Jesus calls them cowards (δειλοί [4:40]).[49] Fifth, Mark mentions twice in 15:46 that Joseph wrapped Jesus's corpse in a σινδών, linen fabric used as a winding sheet. As far as funerary rites go, there's nothing exceptional in that.[50] However, apart from the Matthean (27:59) and Lukan parallels (23:53), the only other occurrence of ἡ σινδών in the NT is in Mark 14:51–52: the mysterious tale of the young man who flees naked on the night of Jesus's arrest, leaving only a tunic in his would-be captor's clutches.[51]

16. A Young Man in the Empty Tomb (16:5–7)

The last of the revenants in this passion narrative is, by Mark's own account, flabbergasting (ἐξεθαμβήθησαν): "a young man [νεανίσκος], seated on the right [καθήμενον ἐν τοῖς δεξιοῖς], wrapped [περιβεβλημένον] in a white robe," who proclaims to three women—whose attempt to embalm a body was pre-empted by yet another woman (14:8)—that Jesus has been raised from death and, as promised, will meet Peter and the disciples in Galilee (16:5–7; cf. 14:28). The other evangelists' interpretation of this herald at the empty tomb is surely correct: this is an interpreting angel (Matt 28:2, 5; Luke 24:23; John 20:12; cf. Dan 7:15–18; 8:15–26; 9:21; 10:2–14; 1 Macc 3:26, 33; Josephus, *A.J.* 5.276–284), whose accoutrements are traditionally white (Dan 7:9; 2 Macc 11:8–10; Acts 1:10; Rev 1:14; 2:17; 3:4–5, 18; 4:4; 6:2, 11; 7:9, 13; 14:14; 19:11, 14; 20:11). One wonders why Mark does not so identify him. Elsewhere he easily speaks of angels on earth (1:13) or in heaven (8:38; 12:25; 13:27, 32). Eerily, the figure who

---

49. More so than many patristic interpreters, John Chrysostom expatiates on Joseph's courageousness (*Homilies on the Gospel of Saint Matthew* 88 [*NPNF*[1] 10:522]).

50. Byron R. McKane, *Roll Back the Stone: Death and Burial in the World of Jesus* (Harrisburg, PA: Trinity Press International, 2003).

51. Yarbro Collins (*Mark*, 778) develops this detail: "Whereas the young man escaped death by fleeing at the time of his arrest and shamefully leaving the σινδών behind, Jesus did not flee when arrested, but endured humiliation, suffering, and death, so that, at the end of his ordeal, his body was wrapped in a σινδών." To fashion such a pinpoint contrast, Yarbro Collins atypically ventures beyond the textual evidence: while, in context, κρατοῦσιν (14:51) may well imply official "arrest," Mark 14:51–52 says nothing to the effect that the young man's life was in jeopardy. Hooker's formulation (*Gospel according to Saint Mark*, 353) is more accurate: "Jesus dies alone, and it is *he* who is wrapped in a 'linen cloth' (σινδών) in 15:46!"

confronts the women seems a doubled proxy, both for the gospel's only other νεανίσκος περιβεβλημένος—the strange fugitive in Mark 14:51–52—and the gospel's only other figure in white: the transfigured Jesus (9:3), who sits at the right hand of David's Lord (κάθου ἐκ δεξιῶν μου [12:36c; cf. 14:62; Ps 110:1]) and who will come as the Son of Man seated at the right hand of Power (ἐκ δεξιῶν καθήμενον τῆς δυνάμεως [14:62c]).[52] Mind you, I no more suggest that the risen Christ should be *identified with* or considered *symbolic of* either the streaker in 14:51–52 or the young man at the tomb, or that the two unnamed figures are identical, than I regard Herod and Pilate as one and the same.[53] I do wonder whether the visitant whom the women encounter is a kind of *Doppeltdoppelgänger*. Were he so, that would be no more bizarre than the rest of the doubles swirling throughout this unsettling gospel's passion narrative.

ANALYZING THE ANALYSIS

What shall we say of these things? Has the Second Evangelist proved a more sophisticated narrator than he has often been credited? Or have my gentle readers been subjected to overinterpretation by a doddering reader whose response has run amok? I submit that, if only 50 percent of my exegesis were accepted, the listeners of Mark 14–16 would demonstrably remain in the hands of a masterly storyteller. Appreciation of that possibility has been inhibited by the usual questions that have generated modern commentary on the Markan

---

52. Adela Yarbro Collins further notes that only two figures in Mark are "seized": Jesus in 14:46 (καὶ ἐκράτησαν αὐτόν) and the young man in 14:51–52 (καὶ κρατοῦσιν αὐτόν): "Mysteries in the Gospel of Mark," in *Mighty Minorities? Minorities in Early Christianity—Positions and Strategies: Essays in Honour of Jacob Jervell on His 70th Birthday, 21 May 1995,* ed. David Hellholm, Halvor Moxnes, and Turid Karlsen Seim (Oslo: Scandinavian University Press, 1995), 11–23 (N.B. 19 n. 15). If pressed, I am inclined to consider Mark 14:51–52 as an intensified, albeit baffling, depiction of the disciples' scattered panic (*Mark*, 300; cf. Harry Fleddermann, "The Flight of a Naked Young Man," *CBQ* 41 [1979]: 412–18)—but, to be frank, I really do not know.

53. Moloney, *Gospel of Mark*, 345, is able to go a step farther than I am comfortable in taking: "[God's messenger in 16:5–6] recalls the parable on [*sic*] the disciples who abandoned their crucified Messiah (14:51–52). As God has transformed the death of Jesus by raising him from the dead, discipleship may be reestablished and nakedness covered." On the other side, Brown (*Death of the Messiah,* 1:303) is on to something in his exegesis of 14:51–52: "Here with 'the last disciple' the irony is even more biting. In Mark 10:28 Peter described to Jesus a model of discipleship that Jesus praised: 'We have left all things and followed you.' This young man has literally left all things to *flee from* Jesus" (emphasis added).

passion narrative: its historicity, the degree to which the story has been informed by Jewish Scripture, and attempted reconstructions of a pre-Markan passion narrative.[54] All these questions are reasonable and important. All, however, are deeply controversial for the simple if frustrating reason that we have neither the tools nor the lumber with which to construct their answers— as the most honest of our expert carpenters invariably concede. The majority of scholars concur that, however stylized their presentation, the gospels' accounts of Jesus's final days have their basis in fact: a Roman prefect authorized Jesus's crucifixion, likely in collusion with some of his politically influential coreligionists. Jesus's earliest followers tried to make sense of that occurrence with the only practical resource available to them: the synagogue Bible.[55] That they waited forty years after the facts for someone to pull things together defies common sense: surely the earliest Christians told and retold the story of Jesus's death, as well as the events immediately preceding and following, before Mark committed them to writing.

In the details, however, lurk the devils. Some of our best evidence for the particulars of first-century Jewish jurisprudence and imperial protocols are embedded in the gospels themselves, which instantly sucks us into circular reasoning. Corroborative, contemporaneous evidence is spotty. Josephus's reports and mishnaic codification are too late, too equivocal, or too tendentious to serve as adequate controls. Likewise, the scriptural substructure of Mark's passion narrative is contested. In my view, only seven (or eight) biblical quotations or allusions in Mark 14–16 are incontrovertible:[56]

---

54. For critical summaries of the *status quaestionum*, consult Brown, *Death of the Messiah*, 1:13–57; Yarbro Collins, *Mark*, 621–39; Marcus, *Mark 8–16*, 923–31.

55. See Mark Goodacre, "Scripturalization in Mark's Crucifixion Narrative," in van Oyen and Shepherd, *Trial and Death of Jesus*, 33–47. Overall Bas M. F. van Iersel's view of Scripture in Mark rings true to me: "reference and allusions to the Old Testament are not used to demonstrate the fulfillment of the promise or even the credibility of a specific event or of what the Jesus movement stands for. Their function is . . . [to] give the story an Old Testament colouring, and thereby visualize the continuity between the story of Jesus and the stories and prophecies of the Old Testament" (*Mark: A Reader-Response Commentary*, trans. W. H. Bisscheroux, JSNTSup 164 [Sheffield: Sheffield Academic, 1998], 440).

56. Mine is a conservative reckoning. Cf. Joel Marcus, *The Way of the Lord: Christological Exegesis of the Old Testament in the Gospel of Mark* (Louisville: Westminster John Knox, 1992), 157, 174–75, 189, which postulates a far more expansive range of scriptural allusions: Mark 14:1 // Ps 10:7–8; Mark 14:10–11, 18, 21, 41–42, 44; 15:1, 10, 15 // Isa 53:6, 12 // Ps 41:9; Mark 14:24–26, 28 // Isa 53:12 // Zech 9:11; 13:7–9; 14:4, 9; Mark 14:34 // Ps 42:5, 11; 43:5; Mark 14:41 // Ps 140:8; Mark 14:55 // Ps 37:32; Mark 14:57 // Ps 27:12; 35:11; Mark 14:61, 65; 15:4–5, 39 // Ps 35:13–15 // Isa 50:6; 52:15; 53:7; Mark 15:6–15 // Isa 53:6, 12; Mark 15:30–31 //

14:27	Zech 13:7	πατάξω τὸν ποιμένα, καὶ τὰ πρόβατα διασκορπισθήσονται
14:62	Ps 110:1;	ὄψεσθε τὸν υἱὸν τοῦ ἀνθρώπου ἐκ δεξιῶν καθήμενον τῆς δυνάμεως
	Dan 7:13	... ἐρχόμενον μετὰ τῶν νεφελῶν τοῦ οὐρανοῦ
15:24	Ps 22:18	διαμερίζονται τὰ ἱμάτια ... βάλλοντες κλῆρον ἐπ᾽ αὐτά
15:29	Ps 22:7;	κινοῦντες τὰς κεφαλάς
	109:25	
15:34	Ps 22:1	ὁ θεός μου ὁ θεός μου, εἰς τί ἐγκατέλιπές με;
15:36	Ps 69:21	ὄξους ... ἐπότιζεν

Six decades of reconstructed pre-Markan passion narratives have led me to conclude that this endeavor, undeniably erudite in their executions, is a mug's game. Commentators swing between the poles of Rudolf Pesch, who contended that the evangelist adopted, with little or no editing, a preexisting narrative embracing everything from Mark 8:27 through 16:8,[57] and the Perrin school, whose exponents argued that Mark used next to no tradition but fabricated 14:1–16:8 by himself.[58] Between these extremes Marion Soards tabulated thirty-four scholars' meticulous reconstructions of pre-Markan tradition.[59] Raymond Brown summarized the result: "not only are the reconstructions different, but there is scarcely one verse that all would assign to the same kind of source or tradition. . . . None [of these reconstructions] has won wide, enduring agreement."[60] Compared with the historical and *traditionsgeschichtlich* enterprises that have long preoccupied our study of Mark 14–16, the inquiry presented in this chapter has the merit, at least, of reference to a stable text, available to all, on whose interpretation we may agree to disagree.

Ps 22:8; Mark 15:32 // Ps 22:6; Mark 15:40 // Ps 28:11. That the Markan passion narrative was colored by confluent streams from Zech 9–14, Dan 7, and psalms of the righteous sufferer (perhaps also Deutero-Isaiah's Servant Songs) is clear enough. The question is whether discrete narrative details—"the Mount of Olives," "spitting and slapping," "looking on at a distance"—merely coincide with detached biblical phrases. A further question: even if such coincidences were more than merely coincidental, how confidently may they be sorted into pre-Markan and Markan piles (Marcus, *Way of the Lord*, 175–79)?

57. *Das Markusevangelium*, 2nd ed., HTKNT 2 (Freiburg: Herder, 1980), 2:1–27.

58. Werner H. Kelber, ed., *The Passion in Mark: Studies on Mark 14–16* (Philadelphia: Fortress, 1976).

59. "Appendix IX: The Question of a PreMarcan Passion Narrative," in Brown, *Death of the Messiah*, 2:1492–1524.

60. *Death of the Messiah*, 1:55.

That said, I leave my own analysis discontent.[61] To pose my dubiety in the sharpest terms: where, in ancient narratives of a figure's death, does one encounter a phenomenon like that which I have descried in Mark's passion narrative? Such would be a salutary curb on the imagination. I am no expert in either classical or Hellenistic Jewish literature and welcome needful corrections by those who are. To the best of my limited knowledge, I have yet to discover exact analogues for the peculiar way in which Mark relates Jesus's last days and hours. The primary sources are extensive; my space is limited. Only a half-dozen among oft-cited parallels may here be called as witnesses.

1. The Death of Socrates

In four dialogues—*Euthyphro, Apology, Crito,* and *Phaedo*—Plato (ca. 425–347 BCE) details the last days of Socrates. Since none of the Platonic dialogues presents a βίος of its principal figure, any comparison with Mark is bound to be inapt. Still, these works present a composite portrait of Socrates that jibes with his *exitus*: the proper understanding of piety (τὸ ὅσιον) looms large in both the *Euthyphro* (4b–16a) and the *Apology* (34c–35d); in both, Meletus recurs as a dim though dangerous prosecutor (*Euthyphr.* 2b; *Apol.* 25d–26a). The *Crito* probes a different issue (contractual obedience to an unjust law) with a different interlocutor (a wealthy, well-respected friend); the *Phaedo*, yet

61. I would be reassured if premodern commentators noted the literary phenomenon I have described. Perhaps some do, and I have yet to discover them. Of all the gospels, Mark received least attention in the patristic period and Middle Ages. The issue preoccupying most of them was reconciling discrepant details among four diverse passion narratives. Thus, Chrysostom wrestles with Luke's story of the repentant bandit (23:40) and comments by Matthew (27:44) and Mark (15:32) that Jesus's fellow victims mocked him. The problem is soluble: both began badly; upon witnessing the events described in Matt 27:51–53, the penitent "recognized the crucified One and acknowledged his kingdom" (*Paralyt.* 3 [*NPNF*[1] 9:124]). Augustine (*Cons.* 3.21.58 [*NPNF*[1] 6:207–8]) reconciles Matt 27:55–56 = Mark 15:40 with John 19:25 by a simple expedient: the women shifted their locations. How many angels awaited the women at the empty tomb? Two (Luke 24:4; John 20:12). Matthew reports one at the entrance (28:2); Mark, another inside (16:5; Augustine, *Cons.* 3.24.63 [*NPNF*[1] 6:209–20]). Albertus Magnus (ca. 1193–1280), a scriptural concordance incarnate, tended to retrieve verbal and conceptual parallels from the OT, not from within Mark itself (B. Alberti Magni, *Opera Omnia: Ennartiones in Mattheum (XXI–XXVIII)–in Marcum,* ed. S. C. A. Borgnet [Paris: Apud Ludovicum Vives, 1894], 21:687–735). In modern scholarship, Dale C. Allison Jr. has identified phenomena in the First Gospel similar to what I detect in the Second ("Foreshadowing the Passion," in *Studies in Matthew: Interpretation Past and Present* [Grand Rapids: Baker Academic, 2005], 217–36).

another subject (the soul's immortality) addressed to fellow philosophers. All of these dialogues unfold in Plato's usual argumentative fashion (τὸ ἔλεγχος; ἡ διάλεξις) with the condemned Socrates well in control of the proceedings. None of them presents Mark's flitting phantoms or *Doppelgängers*. The same may be said of Xenophon's *Memorabilia* (ca. 370 BCE), which ends with unadulterated encomium: "How then, could a man die more nobly? . . . To me he seemed to be all that a truly good and happy man must be" (4.8.3, 11).[62]

2. Hellenistic Jewish Martyrs (Second Century BCE–Second Century CE)

Often compared with the gospels' passion narratives are legends of pious Jews martyred for their obedience to God's law:[63] Daniel, Shadrach, Meshach, Abednego (Dan 3:1–30; 6:1–28), nameless women and their infants (2 Macc 6:7–17), Eleazar (2 Macc 6:18–31; 4 Macc 5:1–7:23), a nameless mother and her seven sons (2 Macc 7:1–42), Razis (2 Macc 14:37–46; 4 Macc 8:1–17:1), Taxo and his seven sons (T. Mos. 9.1–10.10), and the collective suicides at Masada (Josephus, *B.J.* 7.389–406).[64] Because we are first introduced to these noble victims on the verge of death,[65] nothing in their executions can recall previous person-

---

62. For general comparison of this work with Mark's Gospel, see Whitney Taylor Shiner, *Follow Me! Disciples in Markan Rhetoric*, SBLDS 145 (Atlanta: Scholars Press, 1995). Lest the Socratic *exeunt*, whether in Plato or Xenophon, be assumed typical of death scenes for memorable figures, we do well to remember that the *Life of Aesop* (ca. first-century CE), *Life of Homer* (ca. late third century CE), and *Life of Alexander* (ca. early fourth century CE) all end ignominiously for their estimable protagonists. See Tomas Hägg, *The Art of Biography in Antiquity* (Cambridge: Cambridge University Press, 2012), 99–147.

63. Thus, Michael E. Vines, "The 'Trial Scene' Chronotype in Mark and the Jewish Novel," and Kelli S. O'Brien, "Innocence and Guilt: Apologetic, Martyr Stories, and Allusion in the Markan Trial Narratives," in van Oyen and Shepherd, *Trial and Death of Jesus*, 189–203, 205–28. Following Tessa Rajak ("Dying for the Law: The Martyr's Portrait in Jewish-Greek Literature," in *Portraits: Biographical Representation in Greek and Latin Literature of the Roman Empire*, ed. M. J. Edwards and Simon Swain [Oxford: Clarendon, 1997], 39–67), I refrain from using the term "martyrologies," since in the early imperial era it is unclear whether such stories defined an independent genre or were (as Rajak believes) amalgams of many different genres. The same caution may be advisable not only in the case of the passion narratives but also in the gospels of which they are constituent.

64. Jan Willem van Henten and Friedrich Avemarie, eds., *Martyrdom and Noble Death: Selected Texts from Graeco-Roman, Jewish and Christian Antiquity* (London: Routledge: 2002), 42–87, offer a convenient compilation.

65. Eleazar in 1 Macc 6:43–46 is an exception.

ages or occurrences in life.[66] Some motifs in these stories tally with Mark's passion narrative: irresistible provocation by gentile authorities, indictments, trials, verdicts, tortures, capital punishment, and eventual vindication.[67] In important ways, Mark's passion narrative differs from them: whereas Jesus says next to nothing in 14:53–15:39, the Jewish martyrs are loquaciously eloquent in defense of their εὐσέβεια. Like Socrates, they confront excruciating death with poise; in Gethsemane, Jesus is terrified (14:33). His crucifixion is simply stated (15:24a), sans the gory details recounted in the Maccabean corpus.[68] His vindication is real but elliptical (16:1–8).[69] Death as atonement is muted in Mark (10:45; 14:24), not proclaimed as by the mother and her son: "If our living Lord is angry for a little while, to rebuke and discipline us, he will again be reconciled with his own servants" (2 Macc 7:33 RSV). "I, like my brothers, give up body and life for the laws of our fathers, appeal[ing] to God . . . through me and my brothers to bring to an end the wrath of the Almighty which has justly fallen on our whole nation" (2 Macc 7:37–38 RSV).

Although I cannot discern in them the revenants that haunt Mark's passion narrative, these stories plainly adhere to a common pattern or sequence of events that can be variously identified.[70] In their repetition of motifs, episodic escalation, and conciliatory climax, the stories of Hellenistic Jewish martyrs seem more reminiscent of Luke's parallel accounts of the executions of Jesus (4:16–30; 22:47–23:46) and of Stephen (Acts 6:8–8:1a).[71]

---

66. Another exception: Daniel, Shadrach, Meshach, and Abednego are all rescued from grisly deaths and receive political appointments by their would-be assassins.

67. George W. E. Nickelsburg, "The Genre and Function of the Markan Passion Narrative," *HTR* 73 (1980): 153–84. Recall that, in Mark 13:9, τὸ μαρτύριον is predicted of disciples under formal trial.

68. Among others: incineration (Dan 3:15–22), skillet-frying and cauldron-boiling (2 Macc 7:3), scalping and other mutilations (2 Macc 7:4), the rack (2 Macc 6:28b; 4 Macc 5:3), and self-evisceration (2 Macc 17:45–46).

69. In a carefully reasoned examination, Niels Willert concludes that the "many martyrological motifs in the [Synoptics'] passion narratives . . . [do] not allow us to define these texts [generically] as martyrdom accounts" ("Martyrology in the Passion Narratives of the Synoptic Gospels," in *Contextualizing Early Christian Martyrdom*, ed. Jakob Engberg, Uffe Holmsgaard Eriksen, and Anders Klostergaard Petersen, ECCA 8 [Frankfurt am Main: Lang, 2011], 15–43).

70. Jan Willem van Henten, *The Maccabean Martyrs as Saviours of the Jewish People: A Study of 2 and 4 Maccabees*, JSJSup 57 (Leiden: Brill, 1997), 8; cf. Nickelsburg, "Genre and Function," 157–62.

71. N.B. ὁ δὲ Ἰησοῦς ἔλεγεν· πάτερ, ἄφες αὐτοῖς, οὐ γὰρ οἴδασιν τί ποιοῦσιν . . . ὁ Ἰησοῦς εἶπεν· πάτερ, εἰς χεῖράς σου παρατίθεμαι τὸ πνεῦμά μου (Luke 23:34, 46); καὶ λέγοντα· κύριε Ἰησοῦ, δέξαι τὸ πνεῦμά . . . κύριε, μὴ στήσῃς αὐτοῖς ταύτην τὴν ἁμαρτίαν (Acts 7:59, 60).

3. Plutarch's Lives *(Early Second Century CE)*

When approaching antiquity's virtuoso biographer, it is hard to decide the greater injustice: to treat Plutarch (ca. 45–ca. 120 CE) summarily or to ignore him altogether. The latter is scholarly obscene. Here only a few points may be registered.

While a cursory review of his *Parallel Lives* has not disclosed to me the Kijé effect I find in Mark's passion narrative, in some ways, Plutarch's craft both counters and resembles the evangelist's. On the one hand, Mark is much less methodical than Plutarch, whose introductions and epilogues tend to announce, then recapitulate, compositional elements elucidated throughout his narratives.[72] Moreover, Mark narrates in a linear sequence; at the beginning of his *Lives*, Plutarch favors previews of his subjects' conduct as adults.[73] On the other hand, between these authors lie some deep similarities. In constructing his *Lives*, Plutarch's aim is didactic rather than historical or strictly biographical; he wishes to cultivate particular virtues.[74] The same is certainly true of

Subsequently the same pleas and exculpations were remembered among the last words of Christian martyrs: Pamfilus (Papylus), 2.4; the martyrs of Lyons, 5.2; Pionius, 10.21; Julius the Veteran, 19.4 (*The Acts of the Christian Martyrs*, ed. Herbert Musurillo [Oxford: Clarendon, 1972], 35, 83, 165, 265). "Behind every description of [Christian] martyrdom lay the example of Jesus" (Arthur J. Droge and James D. Tabor, *A Noble Death: Suicide and Martyrdom among Christians and Jews in Antiquity* [San Francisco: HarperCollins, 1992], 156). The fruition of such *imitatio Christi* may be witnessed in the hagiography of Martin of Tours (ca. 317–397); see Danny Praet, "The Divided Cloak as *Redemptio Militiae*: Biblical Stylization and Hagiographical Intertextuality in Sulpicius Severus' *Vita Martini*," in *Writing Biography in Greece and Rome: Narrative Technique and Fictionalization*, ed. Koen de Temmerman and Kristoffel Demoen (Cambridge: Cambridge University Press, 2016), 133–59.

72. Hartmut Erbse, "Die Bedeutung der Synkrisis in den Parellelobiographien Plutarchs," *Hermes* 84 (1956): 398–424, esp. 406; Chrysanthos S. Chrysanthou, *Plutarch's Parallel Lives: Narrative Technique and Moral Judgement*, TC 57 (Berlin: de Gruyter, 2018), 8–15.

73. Mark Beck, "Plutarch," in *Narrators, Narratees, and Narratives in Ancient Greek Literature: Studies in Ancient Greek Narrative 1*, ed. Irene J. F. de Jong, René Nünlist, and Angus Bowie, MnemSup 257 (Leiden: Brill, 2004), 397–411, esp. 403–6. Luc Van der Stockt argues that Plutarch typically presents matters in chronological sequence, interrupted by flashbacks and flashforwards to break monotony and to heighten the reader's interest ("Compositional Methods in the *Lives*," in *A Companion to Plutarch*, ed. Martin Beck [Malden, MA: Wiley-Blackwell, 2014], 321–32, esp. 325–26).

74. A. B. Bosworth, "History and Artifice in Plutarch's *Eumenes*," in *Plutarch and the Historical Tradition*, ed. Philip A. Stadter (London: Routledge, 1992), 56–89, N.B. 79–80; Timothy E. Duff, *Plutarch's Lives: Exploring Virtue and Vice* (Oxford: Clarendon, 1999); David Konstan and Robyn Walsh, "Civic and Subversive Biography in Antiquity," in de Temmerman and Demoen, *Writing Biography in Greece and Rome*, 26–43, N.B. 31.

Mark's Gospel. Plutarch's signature technique is that of comparison (σύγκρισις, "placing side by side"):[75] obviously so in his *Parallel Lives*, which portray in tandem Greek and Roman personages, but in other works as well.[76] The Kijé effect is a subspecies of *comparatio*, whereby one narrative element mirrors another, although Mark, unlike Plutarch, does not create biographical diptychs. More to the point, both Mark and Plutarch are interested not merely in their subjects' grand achievements but in those tiny details that reveal the subject's soul. Plutarch spells out what is implicit in the Markan passion narrative:

> It is not so much histories [ἱστορίας] that I am writing, but lives [βίους]. And in the most illustrious deeds a virtue or vice is not always manifest. To the contrary, a slight thing—a saying, a joke—often reveals more of a character than battles where thousands fall, or the greatest armaments, or the conquest of cities. Just as painters capture likenesses [τὰς ὁμοιότητας] from [their subject's] face and the expression of the eyes by which character is suggested [ἐμφαίνεται] but pay scant attention to the body's other parts, so I must be permitted to probe the signs of the soul [τὰ τῆς ψυχῆς σημεῖα] and through these to shape the life of each man, leaving to others the signal accomplishments [τὰ μεγέθη] and great contests (*Alex.* 1.2–3 AT).

Like Plutarch's *Lives*, Mark's passion narrative attains a sublime balance of ἐνάργεια—palpable, vivid illustration, "a sense of presence"—and that subtlety by which true artistry may be concealed.[77]

4. Suetonius's Lives of the Caesars *(Early Second Century CE)*

In presenting its twelve subjects, *De Vita Caesarum* seems as straight-ahead as Mark's rendition of Jesus.[78] Although Suetonius (ca. 69–ca. 122 CE) recounts

75. A commonplace rhetorical device: Quintilian, *Inst.* 2.4.21; 6.3.66; 7.2.22; 8.4.3, 9; 8.5.5; 8.6.9. On Plutarch's use of this technique, consult Duff, *Plutarch's Lives*, 243–86; J. Boulogne, "Les συγκρίσεις de Plutarque: Une rhétorique de la συγκρίσεις," in *Rhetorical Theory and Praxis in Plutarch*, ed. L. van der Stockt, CEC 11 (Leuven: Peeters, 2000), 32–44.

76. Hägg, *Art of Biography*, 239–44, 280; Maarten De Pourcq and Geert Roskam, "Mirroring Virtues in Plutarch's Agis, Cleomenes, and the Gracchi," in de Temmerman and Demoen, *Writing Biography in Greece and Rome*, 163–80.

77. Quintilian, *Inst.* 6.2.33–36; 8.3.61–71, 88–89; Demetrius, *Eloc.* 4.209–20.

78. Richard C. Lounsbury proffers a deeper appreciation in *The Arts of Suetonius: An Introduction*, AUSS 3.3 (New York: Lang, 1987).

none of the deaths of Rome's first twelve emperors with the modulated verve of Mark's passion narrative, in some curious respects his technique intersects with the evangelist's. First, both evince interest in portents. "[Julius] Caesar's impending murder was foretold to him by unmistakable signs [*evidentibus prodigiis*]": his horses wept and refused to graze; having flown into Pompey's Hall, a tiny kingbird was shredded by other birds in hot pursuit; the night before his assassination, both he and his wife Calpurnia foresaw it in a dream; and, of course, the soothsayer's warning of the Ides of March (*Jul.* 81). An ominous lightning bolt, unexpected diarrhea, and unsettling torchlight by a friend's tomb prompted Augustus, on his last day, to invite an ovation from his friends as he prepared to leave life's stage (*Aug.* 98–99). The murder of the "monster" (*Cal.* 22) Caligula was forecast by laughter erupting from a statue of Jupiter, the god to whom all mortal souls would return (Macrobius, *Saturn.* 1.10.16) and whose effigy Caligula had ordered destroyed (*Cal.* 57). The mausoleum doors of another monster, Nero, flew open by themselves, and a voice from within summoned him (*Nero* 46; cf. 40–41). So things run for another eight *principes*, bad or good (e.g., *Claud.* 46; *Galb.* 18–19; *Vit.* 9; *Tit.* 10; *Dom.* 23), one of whom even quipped, "O dear: methinks I'm turning into a god" (*Vespasian* 23). Suetonius reports such omens as dryly as he describes their victims' military record, civil policy, sexual exploits, diet, and eye color. The variances between his and Mark's approaches are the auguries' blatancy and disconnection from their subjects' lives. "When beggars die there are no comets seen; / The heavens themselves blaze forth the death of princes" (Shakespeare, *Julius Caesar* 2.2).

In three other literary respects, however, Suetonius's *Lives* and Mark's Gospel converge to some degree. First, as Tristan Power has demonstrated, Suetonius employs with delicate subtlety a range of rhetorical devices: ring compositions, as well as endings that recall earlier beginnings, whether of a life or of its constituent book or of another life.[79] Second, for both Suetonius and Mark, a man's character was stamped by the manner in which he died. Augustus leaves life in peace, with piety (*Aug.* 100); Caligula, as a crazed suicide (*Cal.* 49); Jesus, as the obedient suppliant of a God he can no longer see (Mark 15:34). Third, and most provocative for my essay's argument, Suetonius seems sensitive to a different company of "revenants."[80] Postmortem, Tiberius

---

79. "The Endings of Suetonius's *Caesars*," in *Suetonius the Biographer: Studies in Roman Lives*, ed. Tristan Power and Roy K. Gibson (Oxford: Oxford University Press, 2014), 58–77. On Mark's application of rhetoric, see chapter 14 of the present volume.

80. The very term used by Cynthia Damon in "Death by Narrative in Suetonius' *Lives*,"

slayed others, "as though the tyrant's cruelty persisted even after his death" (*quasi etiam post mortem tyranni saevitia permanente* [*Tib.* 75.3]). Caligula returns to haunt the story of his life: first, as a ghost; later, as the cause of his wife and daughter's ghastly murders; last, as the possible creator of his own death narrative (*Cal.* 59–60). "In the house where he was slain not a night passed without some frightening apparition, until at last the house itself was consumed by fire" (*in ea quoque domo, in qua occubuerit, nullam noctem sine aliquo terrore transactam, donec ipsa domus incendio consumpta sit* [*Cal.* 59]). Suetonius mentions or narrates the story of Domitian's death not fewer than four times (*Dom.* 14.1; 16.2; 17.2, 3). Arguably, Julius haunts all the assassination scenes of successive Caesars.[81] Cynthia Damon notes that an important element of an emperor's identity was his residual power: "it was hard to terminate a Caesar."[82] Slaying Jesus, "king of the Jews," was easy. Quelling his divine endorsement was not.

5. Apollonius of Tyana (ca. 225 CE)

Philostratus's *Life of Apollonius* is rich in colorful details about this itinerant wonderworker, who excels in embodying the Greek heritage of such worthies as Socrates (1.2; 4.25, 46), Heracles (2.33; 6.11), and Alexander (2.9, 20–21). None of them and none of Apollonius's serene ruminations on death (7.14–8.12) return at his own end—"if, indeed, he did die" (εἴγε ἐτελεύτα [8.29]). Philostratus concludes his life with four anecdotes of his subject's demise, each tossed away in several desultory sentences (8.29–30) before hastening to his real interest: the transfiguration of Apollonius, "which caused such amazement [that] nobody dared deny that he was immortal" (8.31). In the late fourth century, Eunapius of Sardis opined that Philostratus's *Life of Apollonius* might better have been entitled, *A God Visiting Mankind* (*Lives of the Philosophers and Sophists* 454). What would Eunapius have made of Mark's good news that God's Son had been raised from death after crucifixion?

---

in *Ancient Biography: Identity through* Lives, ed. Francis Cairns and Trevor Luke, ARCA Classical and Medieval Texts, Papers and Monographs 55 (Prenton: Francis Cairns, 2018), 107–27, N.B. 124–25.

81. John Henderson, "Was Suetonius' *Julius* a Caesar?," in Power and Gibson, *Suetonius the Biographer*, 81–110; Rhiannon Ash, "'Never Say Die!' Assassinating Emperors in Suetonius' *Lives of the Caesars*," in de Temmerman and Demoen, *Writing Biography in Greece and Rome*, 200–16.

82. "Death by Narrative," 125.

6. *Lives of the Eminent Philosophers*

Diogenes Laertius (early third century CE) compiled for posterity the only comprehensive album of Greek and Hellenistic philosophy: ten books depicting over eighty figures. Entire books are devoted to Plato (3.1–109) and Epicurus (10.1–154); Cebes, a pupil of Socrates, receives exactly eleven words (2.125). Diogenes revels in quirky details: Aristotle lisped (5.1). Zeno liked green figs and sunbathing (7.1). When Alexander the Great offered Diogenes whatever he desired, the Cynic replied, "Get out of my light" (6.38). When it comes to death scenes, Laertius is usually crisp, sometimes confused. Epimenides lived to be 157. Or was it 239? Maybe 154 (1.111). Pherecydes wrote a friend, "I'm crawling with vermin; I've got a boiling fever and shivering fits" (1.121). Lice-infestation killed Plato (3.41). Diogenes died either from eating raw octopus, from dog-bite, or by holding his breath (6.76–77). Voluntary asphyxiation seems to have been in vogue: that, too, is how both Metrocles (6.95) and Zeno croaked (7.28).[83] Cleanthes starved himself to death (7.176). Arcesilaus drank himself to death (4.44). So did Lacydes of Cyrene (4.61). And Chrysippus (7.184). Calculus disease took out Epicurus (10.15). For fortitude in the midst of unquiet quietus, Anaxarchus of Abdera stands out: when his enemy Nicocreon, "tyrant of Cyprus," had him thrown into a mill with iron grinders, the victim calmly commented, "Pulverize the sack of Anaxarchus, but Anaxarchus you do not pulverize." When the despot ordered his sassy victim's tongue cut out, Anaxarchus bit it off and spat it on Nicocreon (10.58–59). The death of Mark's Jesus lacks both Diogenes's mundanity and exuberance.

ANALYSIS *ULTIMUM*

The final cornet has been sounded at Kijé's funeral. If this study has been rightly conducted, one may conclude that Mark continues to surprise us as a stylist of considerable ability. In the passion narrative, he more than holds his own beside not only the other evangelists but also such classical worthies as Plutarch and Suetonius. Like them, with exquisite care, Mark has molded

---

83. My flippancy may be ill-advised. Eleni Kechagia suggests that self-suffocation may have been regarded as a fitting death by Stoics who were determined to quench their πνεῦμα, the constituent element of cosmic vitality ("Dying Philosophers in Ancient Biography: Zeno the Stoic and Epicurus," in de Temmerman and Demoen, *Writing Biography in Greece and Rome*, 181–99, esp. 189).

historical and traditional materials for the sake neither of artistry nor of entertainment but rather to convey what he believes to be true: a truth surpassing empirically observable reality.[84] That truth is composed of multiple elements, which the evangelist himself epitomizes. Only in his last days do all the motley pieces of Jesus's life fall into place and make Christian sense. "To you has been given the mystery of God's sovereignty, but to those outside all things come in parables" (4:11 AT). God's truly anointed Son could be vindicated in no way other than as the Son of Man who, parabolically, must suffer the ultimate repudiation of crucifixion (8:31; 9:31; 10:33–34). One index of God's signature upon his Son's life, death, and resurrection is their completion of what Scripture was driving at: "the Son of Man goes as it is written of him" (14:21a). As the Second Gospel was heard and pondered over decades, then centuries, its listeners came to conclude—possibly by its author's design—that their Lord's advance to Golgotha, under his Father's aegis, recapitulated that which Mark himself had written of him in chapters 1–13.

Lucian of Samosata (ca. 125–180 CE) insisted, "History . . . cannot tolerate the least fragment of untruth, any more than the windpipe, or so the doctors tell us, tolerates objects that enter it when swallowed. . . . Truth is the only goddess to whom the potential historian has to sacrifice; he need not trouble with anything else" (*How to Write History* 6, 40). Lucian seems to have believed that facts speak for themselves, requiring only their clarity and smoothness of arrangement (50–55).[85] Among other ancient writers, Mark seems to have realized that no fact is self-interpreting, that in the very composition and arrangement of happenings the historian or biographer serves as a prism through which the mystery of a figure's life is brought into focus.[86] A specific

---

84. I consider this at greater length in chapter 8. For comparable assessments, see De Pourcq and Roskam, "Mirroring Virtues," 178 (on Plutarch); James A. Francis, "Truthful Fiction: New Questions to Old Answers on Philostratus' *Life of Apollonius*," *AJP* 119 (1998): 419–41; Kechagia, "Dying Philosophers," 198–99 (on Diogenes Laertius).

85. Here Lucian seems on the same wavelength as Dionysius of Halicarnassus (ca. 60 BCE–ca. 5 BCE): "The science of composition . . . observe[s] which [verbal] combinations are naturally likely to produce a beautiful, attractive, and unified effect. . . . [But] all adornments must be qualified for their suitability [ὁ περὶ τοῦ πρέμον]. Indeed, if any other function fails to meet this requirement, it fails to attain the most important goal" [*Comp.* 6, 20 AT].

86. Thus, Xenophon, Plutarch, Suetonius, Porphyry, and Eusebius, as assessed by Patricia L. Cox, *Biography in Late Antiquity: A Quest for the Holy Man* (Berkeley: University of California Press, 1983), N.B. 8–15, 65–77, 107–12. I am indebted to Cox for the metaphor of author as prism (145–49).

narrative *form*, whether ancient or modern, conveys a particular *meaning.*[87] "Biographical myth," notes Patricia Cox, "is the story of a face reflected in many mirrors, the kind of history whose shadings and nuances reveal a divine *telos*, as Eusebius thought."[88] The *telos* to which the entirety of Mark's narrative drives is the hidden revelation of Jesus Christ as the liberating, self-donative Son of Man who is abandoned, crucified, and vindicated (10:33–34, 45; cf. 4:22–23).[89] In the same manner as Mark's scriptural allusions, and possibly summoned for the same purpose, the revenants of earlier figures and episodes in Mark 14–16 mysteriously disclose the character not only of Jesus but also of God's elusive presence.[90] More so than those biblical reverberations, the ghosts that waft throughout the Markan passion narrative are unexpected and uncanny. They, like the gospel they haunt, refuse to be caged by scholarly analysis. True to the Messiah whose story he tells, Mark performs on his readers an unheimlich maneuver.[91]

87. See Ian Rutherford, *Canons of Style in the Antonine Age: Idea-Theory in Its Literary Context* (Oxford: Clarendon, 1998), 31–36; de Jong, Nünlist, and Bowie, *Narrators, Narratees, and Narratives*, xii.

88. Cox, *Biography in Late Antiquity*, 147.

89. Broadhead, *Prophet, Son, Messiah*, 259–96; Geert van Oyen, "The Meaning of the Death of Jesus in the Gospel of Mark: A Real Reader Perspective," in van Oyen and Shepherd, *Trial and Death of Jesus*, 49–68.

90. See Samuel Terrien, *The Elusive Presence: Toward a New Biblical Theology*, RP 26 (San Francisco: Harper & Row, 1978), and chapter 9 of the present volume.

91. I have pilfered this phrase from John J. Miller, describing the disturbing, dreamlike tales of Robert Aickman, collected by Victoria Nelson in *Compulsory Games and Other Stories*, New York Review Books (New York: New York Review of Books, 2016), viii.

Part Three

HOMILETICAL STUDIES

CHAPTER 16

Priming the Pump:
Exegetical Studies for Preachers

> Mark writes a sermon which is a gospel.
>
> —Willi Marxsen[1]

SINCE 2008, I'VE BEEN INVITED to contribute brief essays to the website *Working Preacher*, created and produced by faculty members at Luther Seminary in Saint Paul, Minnesota. I've never turned down an invitation, and the reasons are simple. First, I have been an ordained clergyman for almost forty-five years, longer than my employment as a professional scholar. My allegiance and responsibility to the church are every bit as resolute as those to the academy. Second, *Working Preacher* encourages novice and veteran preachers as they interpret Scripture every Sunday from pulpits across the globe: a primary, thankless task. In one twelve-month period (2020–2021), that website hosted 5.2 million sessions from 2.7 million users in more than two hundred countries and territories.[2] I can dedicate months on an article that possibly thirty scholars will read and footnote once in a while. I can invest a day or so in a thousand-word essay that may reach upward of two million people, some of whom send me personal thanks by email.

Most of my contributions to *Working Preacher* have been homiletically oriented studies of portions of Mark, in conformity with the gospel texts demarcated for Year B by the Revised Common Lectionary.[3] Occasionally I've

---

1. *Mark the Evangelist: Studies on the Redaction History of the Gospels*, trans. James Boyce, Donald Juel, and William Poehlmann, with Roy A. Harrisville (Nashville: Abingdon, 1969), 138 (emphasis removed).

2. https://www.workingpreacher.org/about-working-preacher.

3. The Revised Common Lectionary (RCL), originally released in 1994, is a product of the North American Consultation on Common Texts and the International English Language Liturgical Consultation. Based on the Roman Catholic Ordo Lectionum Missae

offered thematic essays of comparable length on the Second Gospel. Most of these are collected, with some adaptation, in the following pages.

I regard these studies as neither filler nor fluff. Centuries of Christian interpreters knew, and modern biblical scholars eventually came to understand, that the evangelist Mark was, first and foremost, a preacher. The church has always been that gospel's native habitat; the academy, a secondary passenger. The history of biblical interpretation demonstrates that most of Christianity's most accomplished theologians—Origen, Chrysostom, Augustine, Aquinas, Luther, among scores of others—produced some of their finest work from the pulpit.[4] If in my far more modest endeavors I have been able to jostle the imaginations of fellow preachers and their congregants on a given Sunday, then I have fulfilled a portion of my vocation.

Preaching from Mark's Gospel: Fasten Your Seat Belts

Regarding the gospels, many lectionary preachers may approach Year B in the Revised Common Lectionary with less than uplifted hearts. Gone are Matthew's barbed directions and Luke's breathtaking parables. At best, Mark is deceptively simple; at worst, lean, odd, and hard. The church has long regarded it so.

Yet, as one who has inhabited this gospel for four decades, I say unto you: Fasten your seat belts, ye preachers of Mark. This gospel is a wild ride, piloted by Jesus with befuddled passengers who try to hang on yet keep falling off.

Mark's Jesus does not merely tell parables; as God's crucified and risen Messiah, Jesus *is* a parable of the kingdom he preaches. To that end, Mark has tailored his gospel into a magnificent parable itself.

As you approach Year B, be ready to take some intelligent risks from the pulpit. Dare to follow this evangelist's announcement of good news that teases and offends, perplexes and provokes, in the same way that Jesus does by action and deed.

"What new teaching is this?" (1:27)

(Order for the Readings for Mass, 1969), the RCL offers a three-year cycle of recommended texts from the OT and NT for interpretation in Sunday worship, consonant with the church's liturgical year: Advent, Christmas, Epiphany, Lent, Easter, and Ordinary Time.

4. C. Clifton Black, *Reading Scripture with the Saints* (Eugene, OR: Wipf & Stock; Cambridge: Lutterworth, 2014, 2015). For opening my eyes to the riches of patristic and medieval exegesis, I am indebted to the late David C. Steinmetz (1936–2015), under whose tutelage I was privileged to study while a graduate student at Duke University (1981–1986).

"Who, then, is this?" (4:41b)

"Where did this man get all this?" (6:2)

When you reach the end of this year of Mark, perhaps you'll find that this gospel remains indispensable for the church's heritage, worthy of its embrace, and incumbent on preachers to preach. Here's why.

1. No gospel is more intensely concentrated than Mark on the crucified heart of Christian faith.

Every gospel canonized culminates in Jesus's death and resurrection—but, if Mark was the earliest, then it was the first to frame the entire story of Jesus as a passion narrative, in which his life's last week occupies forty percent of the book. Precisely because it lacks Matthew's and Luke's abundance of church instruction and John's extended christological meditations, Mark focuses our attention on the foolishness of the cross, which makes this world's wisdom moronic (1 Cor 1:18–2:16). The suffering, vindicated Son of Man is Mark's constant refrain (8:31–33; 9:30–32; 10:33–45).

This is of vital importance. No other religion, ancient or postmodern, professes its most patent contradiction as its most fundamental belief. Other believers venerate their founders, extol their achievements, and construct honorable ways of life modeled on their conduct. Only Christianity professes a crucified Messiah as the agent by whom this tortured world is being set to rights. Far from transporting its adherents out of this world's vapor or viciousness, only Christian faith continuously drives them back to its most despicable mockery—the shame of the cross—and dares to proclaim that there, and nowhere else, has the God of the living acted incognito to restore all of creation. Lose that, and we've lost the unique testimony God has entrusted to us as Christians. It's not merely a good idea to dedicate a lectionary year to preaching the Gospel according to Mark; it is *essential* to the clarity of the church's self-understanding and its vision of mission in this world. Throughout Year B, the preacher is summoned to remember and to remind others that we are servants of Christ and stewards of God's mysteries (1 Cor 4:1; cf. Mark 8:34–9:1).

2. No gospel draws us more deeply into the mystery of Jesus Christ and the kingdom he proclaimed.

Mark's genius lies not in telling a story about Jesus but in creating conditions under which the reader may *experience* the peculiar quality of God's good news. The evangelist hurries us along breathlessly, "immediately," making sure that we lurch with the characters into one pothole after another. "What is this new teaching" (1:27) that consorts with the outrageously sinful (2:15), turning the pious homicidal (3:6), intimates into strangers (3:21; 6:1–6a), and mustard seeds into "the greatest of all shrubs" (4:32)? What pilgrim saunters into the temple one day and unhinges its operations the next (11:11, 15–16)? What teacher speaks well, impartially teaching "the way of God in accordance with truth" (12:14, 28), while spinning riddles intended to blind the sighted and to deafen the hearing, "so that they may not turn again and be forgiven" (4:11–12)? What healer routs disease and demonic possession more powerfully and more secretively, only to have that cover constantly blown (3:10–12; 6:53–56; 7:36–37)? Jesus, the Savior of others, cannot save himself (8:35; 10:45)—and the religious and theological elite are blind to the truth of their own ridicule (15:31).

"To you has been given the μυστήριον of God's kingdom" (4:11). That mystery keeps bumping into disclosure by demoniacs, whose testimony is incredible (1:23–24), and antagonists like the high priest (14:61) and Pilate (15:2), who do not realize they are telling the truth. "There is nothing hidden, except to be disclosed; nor is anything secret, except to come to light" (4:22). Even when dawn breaks and things come to light—God emptied Jesus's tomb, as promised (10:33–34; 16:4–6)—Mark leaves the tension unresolved to the very end: disciples flee the tomb, hiding faith's good news, "for they were afraid" (16:8). This evangelist is the church's original master of suspense: a companionable guide for Christians still living in the tension that stretches from Easter to the Son of Man's final return (13:24–37). The prudent preacher, sensitive to this evangelist's masterly technique, will not scurry to fill this gospel's many gaps. Mark never explains the kingdom's mystery. Scripture does not expect us to answer life's most excruciating questions. It challenges us to live them, sometimes praying to the silent God who has apparently left us in the lurch (15:34).

3.   No gospel is more radically countercultural than Mark—be it Mark's culture or our own.

Good news in the first century included extolling Caesar's empire. The gospel preached by Jesus defies imperial values and propaganda. The structures of God's kingdom are neither partisanship nor piety, neither wealth nor prestige, neither patronage nor abusive power (9:38–41; 10:17–31, 35–43). It's easier for a camel to slide through a needle's eye than for Elon Musk to enter the kingdom of God (10:23–25): only if he and we become as a child, helpless and dependent, shall any of us inherit eternal life (10:13–16). Repeatedly Jesus's disciples are stunned by his words (10:24, 26, 32); if we speak them truthfully, so, too, will our congregants. Mark exposes our culture's pervasive fear—of terrorism, disease, and death—and demands of us, "Why are you afraid? Have you no faith?" (4:40). If we accept Jesus's assurance that with God all things are possible—salvation in particular (10:26–28)—then why don't we call the bluff of political and media hucksters who profit from frightening us and send them packing? "Pay attention: I've told you everything beforehand" (13:23).

4. No gospel balances more exquisitely the cost of discipleship, the disciples' tendency to fail, and God's determination to make all things right.

In Mark, following Jesus requires prayerful, voluntary self-sacrifice for the gospel's sake (8:34–35; 11:22–25; 12:41–44); at Gethsemane, the beloved Son demonstrates how hard the complete yielding of oneself to God really is (14:32–42). While getting some things right (1:16–20; 6:7–13; 10:28), the Twelve are notoriously craven, stupid, hard-hearted, self-serving, and disobedient (4:35–41; 6:45–52; 8:14–21; 14:17–31, 66–72). Most congregations would benefit from the preacher's steady holding of Mark as a mirror in which they may recognize themselves. We have met the Twelve, and they are us. We fall into the same traps as they, because Jesus doesn't feed our delusions. Shouldn't God's Messiah lift the burdens of those who follow him? What kind of Christ heads to a cross, handing his disciples another for themselves? "Do you not yet understand?" (8:21). More often than not, we don't. If we do, we'd rather not be reminded of our failures.

The church must face its sin. If it refuses, it will continue its pretense that it is healthy, without need of a physician (2:15–17). We can become so sick that we even fantasize ourselves our own healers. Mark's entrance exam for discipleship is an honest confession of illness and a correct answer to Jesus's question, "What do you want me to do for you?" (10:51). No offer of grace could be clearer.

Mark ends with mysterious confirmation that God and Jesus have kept faith and have done just what they promised (16:6–7). There, perhaps, lies the brilliance of this gospel's open ending (16:8). Mark is a book about God's shattering of human expectations; Mark *as* a book blows apart everything its readers thought they understood, including our assumptions of how a gospel should end. Reaching deep into Gen 17–18, Paul articulates what Mark narrates: a summons to "[trust] in God, who makes the dead live and calls things that are not into things that are" (Rom 4:17). In Mark's case, those things are a crucified Messiah, raised by God to indestructible life, who promises a reunion with those who failed him (14:28) and a mission for them to fulfill (13:10). In the meantime:

"Listen. Look." (4:3)

"Don't be afraid." (16:6)

"Watch." (13:37)

25 November 2014

MARK 1:9–15

This Sunday's lection comprises three episodes: Jesus's baptism (Mark 1:9–11), his temptation (1:12–13), and his inaugural preaching (1:14–15).

The preacher could justifiably dedicate a sermon to any of these. I suggest an alternative: so tightly has Mark stitched these episodes together that one could also preach a straight-line sermon that entwines all three. Mark offers us the organizing point (1:15a): "the kingdom of God has come near."

As the preacher knows but congregants need reminding, "the kingdom of God" is *the* announcement in the Synoptics around which the rest of Jesus's words and deeds revolve. In Mark, "God's kingdom" is mentioned fourteen times: its coming (1:15; 9:1; 14:25; 12:34; 15:43), its peculiarities (4:11, 26, 30), to whom it belongs (10:14–15), and impediments to its entry (9:47; 10:23–25). God's kingdom—alternatively, "kingship," "reign," "sovereignty"—is not a place but a power. It is God's dynamic potency to put right all that is wrong in this world.

In all the gospels, this eschatological dominion, invading time and space, is active in Jesus himself. God *has* ruled (Pss 93:1; 97:1; 99:1). In Jesus, that rule *is* mysteriously irrupting (Matt 10:7 = Luke 10:9; Matt 12:28 = Luke 11:20). The resurrection, the dawn of a new age, warrants that God *will* rule (Luke 1:33; Acts 1:3; 1 Cor 15:24, 50; Rev 11:15). In Mark 1:15, that kingdom "is at hand" (RSV), "is upon you" (NEB), or "has come near" (NRSV).

Mark 1:9–14 offers us clues to this kingdom's character.

At *Jesus's baptism*, the kingdom's end-time features are front and center. Emerging from the Jordan, Jesus "saw the heavens torn apart" (Mark 1:10). That is a classic apocalyptic image, signifying divine disclosure (15:38; see also

Isa 64:1; Ezek 1:1; Acts 7:56; Rev 4:1). The Spirit's descent upon (literally, "into" [εἰς]) Jesus recalls the prophets' promise that Israel would be reinfused by the Spirit in the last days (Isa 11:1–2; Joel 2:28–32; Acts 2:17–22). Jesus alone (Mark 1:11; cf. Matt 3:17) hears the heavenly voice addressing him, "You are my Son, the Beloved; with you I am well pleased": a scriptural embrace interweaving Ps 2:7, Gen 22:1, and Isa 42:1.

Flashes of God's kingdom illuminate *Jesus's temptation*, which Mark narrates more crisply (1:12–13) than either Matthew (4:1–11) or Luke (4:1–13). Unlike the other gospels, in Mark, the Spirit "immediately drove" Jesus (literally, "threw [him] out": ἐκβάλλει) into the wilderness for forty days of temptation (see also Exod 24:18; 1 Kgs 19:8). The desert is a place of arduous testing (1 Sam 22:4; 23:24–25; 24:1, 22) and divine deliverance (Exod 19–24; Hos 2:14–15). In Jewish apocalypticism by the time of Mark's composition, Satan personifies evil as the demons' ringleader. Mark will refer to Satan's continuing battle against the heavenly kingdom Jesus advances (3:23–27; 4:14–15; 8:32–33); Jesus himself will attack Satan's minions, the unclean spirits (1:21–28, 32–34, 39; 3:11; 7:24–30; 9:14–29). Angelic ministration during Jesus's trial harmonizes with 1 Kgs 19:5, 7, and Ps 91:11–13. "The wild beasts" could be threats but might themselves be threatened: "The devil will flee from you; wild animals will be afraid of you; and the angels will stand by you" (T. Naph. 8.4, written around 100 CE). The main point: under the Spirit's aegis, Jesus stands at the center of God's inbreaking kingdom as both beneficiary (at his baptism) and wrestler (at his temptation).

"Now after *John was arrested*" (Mark 1:14a) is no throwaway clause. It casts a long shadow over John's superior successor, Jesus (1:4–8), who will also be "betrayed" (3:19; 9:31; 14:10–11, 18, 21, 41, 42), "arrested" (14:44), and "handed over" (10:33; 15:1, 10, 15). All of these English words translate the same Greek verb (παραδίδωμι) referring to the baptizer in 1:14a. Like John, Jesus, too, will die by the hand of a weak overlord who is outwitted by others' schemes (6:14–29; 15:1–15). The kingdom proclaimed by Jesus clashes against mortal principalities and powers that do not gracefully yield to God's governance (Eph 6:12).

If we pay close attention to it, Mark 1:9–15 has the potential to redraw the contours of the liturgical period that begins this Sunday. The time before Easter has long been associated with penitent self-abnegation. That befits Jesus's preparation for his own sacrifice, to be detailed in coming Sundays. Along the way, however, the church has sometimes extended Passion Week into six weeks of mourning and has confused surrender with easy self-deprivation ("giving up chocolate for Lent").

Mark points us in a different direction. "The time is fulfilled" (1:15a). This time is not χρόνος, measured by calendar or clock. It is καιρός—the time of critical decision: not every day, but D-Day (Ezek 7:12; Dan 7:22; Gal 4:4; Eph 1:10; Rev 1:3b). This καιρός is filled to fullness: the cup has been topped up, its contents brimming to overflow. Lent is to Easter as Advent is to Christmas: God has set the kingdom into motion, which will soon go into turbo-drive. As with Advent, so also with Lent: the suitable response is to "repent, and believe in the good news" (Mark 1:15b).

Repentance is not feeling miserable over our sins or regretting that we haven't been more religious. To repent (μετανοεῖν) is to turn our minds Godward: a 180-degree swing-around from kingdoms of our own fabrication toward God's rectifying power (Mark 8:33). "Belief" in Mark is not creedal or even particularly cognitive: πίστις is trust, lying less in the head and more in the gut (2:5; 5:34, 36; 9:24; 10:52; 11:22–24). After unfurling our sails to catch the Spirit's current, we rely on God's ability to carry us beyond the squalls (4:35–41; 6:45–52; 13:9–13, 22–27). And God *is* able—to forgive our sins (2:1–12), to retrieve us from waywardness (2:15–17), to cast out diabolical powers we cannot control (5:1–20), to restore us from years of wretchedness (5:24b–34), to hold onto us tightly when we turn tail and run away (14:27–28; 16:1–8). As Jesus demonstrates, God's power is propelled by mercy. That is good news: the best anyone could hope to hear. Lent is the season to ponder that.

18 February 2018

Marklarkey: Parabolic Tomfoolery in the Second Gospel

Humor from the pulpit is a delicate thing. Some deem it impertinent: preaching the gospel is serious business. Nevertheless, it is the preacher's job to hold listeners' attention for longer than fifteen seconds in a culture whose sound bites are the most we have been conditioned to consume. Theologically regarded, a gospel eviscerated of mirth is no gospel at all—a harangue at worst; at best a dull drone. Properly injected, laughter unites preacher and congregation with a joyful God. But is there anything funny in Scripture?

I come bearing witness that Mark's Gospel is a hilarious book. Yes, Mark: that somber story of the suffering Messiah. But Mark's is a wry, understated humor whose recovery relies partly on the same discipline of patient, careful reading that is *sine qua non* for good exegesis.

I write from New Jersey, known as the Garden State because it's a great place to live if you're a carrot, so Mark's parable chapter (4:1–34) is an old favorite. According to the NRSV, "As [the sower] sowed, some seed fell on the path"

(v. 4). I'm not sure that's where it fell. The Greek reads παρὰ τὴν ὁδόν, "*beside the path*," which is just where you'd expect to stumble over rocks and thorns (vv. 5, 7). With such an easygoing, not to say idiotic, approach to agriculture, no wonder 75 percent of the sown seed went south (vv. 3–7). That makes the thirty-, sixty-, and hundredfold yield of the remaining 25 percent worth sitting up and noticing (vv. 8–9). Apparent carelessness and subsequent devastation are no indication of how God's kingdom, where it takes root, blasts off (a fairly literal translation of another seed's sprouting in v. 27: βλαστᾷ).

We may hurriedly consider Mark 4:10–12, because its absurdity is so well known: "For those outside everything comes in parables, so that, though they see, they may see and not perceive and, though they hear, they may hear and not understand, lest they turn around and be forgiven" (AT). Recognizing the origin of Jesus's parabolic discourse in Isaiah (6:9–10), Matthew (13:13–15) tinkers Mark's "so that" (4:12a) into "because." Luke (8:10) simply jettisons the razor-edged predestination of "those outside" who "may not turn again and be forgiven" (Mark 4:12d). If the First and Third Evangelists couldn't take the Second straight, no chaser, no wonder most of my students can't. On the other hand, they have an advantage over Matthew and Luke: Princeton Seminary is swarming with Presbyterians. When Calvinist knickers get twisted over Mark 4, you know you're onto something. Maybe it's onto you.

The capper lies in Mark's parable of the mustard seed (4:30–32). If we recall the other Synoptics—for that matter, if we observe folktale logic—we know that the proper contrast between an inauspicious beginning and a stupendous outcome should be illustrated with "the smallest of all the seeds" (Matt 13:32) and "a tree" (δένδρον), even "a huge tree" (δένδρον μέγα, in some manuscripts of Luke 13:19). Not in Mark. There, the birds of heaven come to roost in the shade of big branches of the greatest of the . . . vegetables (λαχάνων, 4:32). Christians with stained-glass eyes may want their kingdom of God as a mighty oak. The Second Evangelist hands them a head of lettuce.

Who can forget the plea of Loretta Young's character to Richard the Lion-hearted in the Turner Classic Movie, *The Crusaders* (1935): "You just gotta save Christianity, Richard! You gotta!" Too many of Mark's commentators, scholars and pastors, have tried too hard to save Mark. This gospel doesn't need saving. It needs attention. It's one thing to stand beside the Twelve and be assured, "To you has been given the mystery of the kingdom of God" (4:11a). It's another thing to expect that Jesus will then *disclose* the kingdom's mystery to us.

That's not how things pay out in this gospel's economy. What we're promised is a mystery, and a mystery is just what we get. So it is with the parables in chapter 4; it is equally true of the parable-spinner, Jesus himself, in all sixteen chapters. If his disciples' hearts have been hardened, if they are bat-blind and stone-deaf (8:17–18), by what right should we expect to come off as Andy Einstein? A truculent atheist, Thomas Edison said, "Religion is all bunk"; but on one point Mark might have agreed with him: "We don't know a millionth of one percent about anything."

The more I study this gospel, the stronger my conviction that its obscurities are not clumsy accidents but deliberate, perversely insightful, and probably premeditated. Mark is unspooling good news that creates for us as readers what Jesus's parables did for his listeners: confusion. "For there is nothing hidden, except to be disclosed; nor is anything secret, except to come to light" (4:22). If God has given us a genuine mystery, then we'll never be able to figure it out ourselves. God will have to reveal to us the secret that lies behind the curtain (15:38). From God we'll receive faith to discern that Jesus was never more the Messiah than when he died on a cross, whether his executioner realized the truth in what he said, or not (15:39). Nothing succeeds like failure. If you believe that, then who needs the kingdom dressed as a sequoia? A zucchini does the job a lot better.

13 September 2010

Mark 5:1–20

The second, longest, and most complex of this gospel's narrated exorcisms (cf. Mark 1:21–28; 7:24–30; 9:14–29), Mark 5:1–20 is a tale of terror.

Jesus encounters a demoniac who horrifies his neighbors by howling among tombs (vv. 2–3a, 5a), commandeered by diabolical powers that provoke him to appalling self-abuse, impossible to restrain (vv. 3b–4, 5b). For Jewish listeners, other details reek of religious impurity. In the Levitical tradition (Lev 22:4b–6a; 11:7–8; Num 5:2; 6:6; 9:6), contact with corpses defiles. More pointedly, "[those] who sit inside tombs, and spend the night in secret places, who eat swine's flesh" (Isa 65:4; see Lev 11:7–8; Mark 5:11) typify a stubborn nation that rebels against the LORD's holiness.

The demon's name, "Legion" (Mark 5:9), referring to a Roman regiment of six thousand soldiers, is at once a petrifying depiction of this sufferer's trauma and a reminder of Israel's oppression by pagan colonials. Although the precise location of this episode has long been disputed (see also "Gadara" [Matt 8:28]; "Gergesa" [some manuscripts of Luke 8:26]), Mark's identification of the Decapolis (5:20) specifies a federation of ten, equally profane gentile cities (*Nat.* 5.16, 74).

Drenched in vilest degradation, menaced and menacing, the victim in Mark 5:2–5 is possessed by abominable forces of such magnitude as to defy any cure.

Unlike disobedient Israel, insisting that the LORD keep his distance from them (Isa 6:5), the man with the unclean spirit runs to Jesus and kneels before him (Mark 5:6). The demoniac's condition is consonant with what modern psychiatry might diagnose as multiple personality disorder: he simultaneously submits to Jesus while holding him at bay (Mark 5:6–7a), confusing healing with torment (v. 7b), referring to himself in both the first-person singular (vv. 7, 8) and plural (vv. 9, 12). While, in Isaiah, the LORD promises to punish an idolatrous Israel (65:5a–10), Jesus receives this hideously tormented figure (Mark 5:2, 8–13a). As in 1:23–25, a contest ensues between unclean spirit and its exorcist (5:7–9); as in 1:26, Jesus vanquishes the demons (5:10), who bargain for a measure of preservation by transferal into other creatures (v. 12). Jesus accedes in an equivocal way: at their begging (παρεκάλεσαν), the demons are driven into thousands of unclean pigs, which thunderously hurl themselves into chaotic waters that drown both hosts and parasites (v. 13). Observant Jews might cheer such a spectacle. Having just lost their livelihood, gentile herdsmen might be less sanguine: they fast report, throughout town and country, what's just happened (vv. 14a, 16).

Here the preacher might pause and ask, How far I am prepared to follow Mark's belief in the demonic? We are sophisticated women and men, as are our parishioners. We can Google dissociative and obsessive-compulsive disorders, varieties of self-mutilation, and manifold chemical addictions, then cluck our tongues at Scripture's primitive explanations. Before mounting our high horses, we might ask just how much farther the American Psychiatric Association's *DSM* carries us.[5] Diagnostic interpretations vary in every era, but a mysterious residuum always remains. Over the course of a pastor's life, or as recent as one's glance at this morning's news, an X factor of ravaging evil is not so easily dismissed.

We've witnessed its ghastly overpowering of persons, cliques, gangs, and so-called civilized Christian nations that facilely justify daily bigotry and homicide, even the extermination of entire ethnic populations. The first step in capitulation to diabolism is our refusal to *see* it. The first step in resistance is our embrace of the Lord who masters it. To ask for the coming of our heavenly Father's kingdom is to repel the reign of the Evil One. For what else do Christians pray when begging for deliverance from evil?

---

5. *Diagnostic and Statistical Manual of Mental Disorders*, 5th ed. (Washington, DC: American Psychiatric Publications, 2013).

Returning to Mark 5:15–20—Act 2 of this Sunday's drama—we might expect the townsfolk and villagers to celebrate Jesus's treatment of the untreatable, and the one treated to join Jesus's entourage with open arms. None of this happens. "They came to Jesus and saw the demoniac sitting there, clothed and in his right mind, . . . and they were afraid" (5:15). Exactly what they fear is unexpressed, though by now in Mark we've learned that fear is the opposite of faith (4:40–41). Here we have a curious case of antievangelism: eyewitness messengers report what they have seen Jesus do (5:16), whose proof is as plain as day (v. 15), and the listeners neither repent nor revel but start begging (παρακαλεῖν) Jesus to get out of town (v. 17). He complies (v. 18a). "Pay attention to what you hear. . . . For to those who have, more will be given; and from those who have nothing, even what they have will be taken away" (4:24–25).

The one who was cured begs (παρεκάλει) Jesus to accompany him: a primary qualification for discipleship (3:14). Now it is Jesus's turn to refuse (5:19a), but not without giving the man a mandate: to return home and tell his friends how much the Lord has done for him (5:19b). The man obeys, and then some: he preaches (see 3:14) not merely at home but throughout the Decapolis, what *Jesus* had done for him (5:20a). That comment laminates another layer of ambiguity: in Mark "the Lord" can refer either to God (12:11, 29–30, 36; 13:20) or to Jesus (1:3; 2:28; 7:28; 11:3, 9; 12:37; 13:35). "And everyone was amazed" (5:20): a notch above repudiation (v. 17), perhaps, but not tantamount to faith (see 1:27; 12:17; 15:5).

To point to Jesus as the calm center in a cyclone of terror (Mark 5:6–9, 13, 15), who authorizes proclamation of the Lord's merciful healing amid chaos and rejection (v. 19), may be the very thing a congregation needs to hear this Sunday. Beware, however, of sandpapering Mark's rough edges. The cure may carry adverse side effects (vv. 13b, 16b). Many beg Jesus; their requests are denied (v. 19a) or granted with unpredictable results (vv. 12–13). To be so affronted by Jesus that we drive him away (vv. 17–18a) may be the greatest terror of all. His gospel does not coerce acceptance. He'll not stay where he is unwanted.

26 January 2020

MARK 5:21–43

Last Sunday's gospel lection, Mark 5:1–20, recounted a tale of terror. This Sunday, a tale of two pities. The predicaments in Mark 5:21–43 are so poignant that they would make a stone weep. Using his trademark technique of intercalation (for another, see 14:53–72), Mark sandwiches one story (5:24b–34) inside another (5:21–24a and 5:35–43). Each complements and amplifies the other with mirrored details so subtle that most would register with Mark's listeners subliminally, if at all.

- Two suppliants, a named synagogue benefactor (ἀρχισυνάγωγος [v. 22]) and an anonymous pauper (v. 26), seek or are sought by Jesus (vv. 22a, 32) before prostrating themselves before him (vv. 22b, 33b).
- Both stories revolve around two "daughters": one, actual (v. 23); the other, figurative (v. 34).
- Both women are in dire straits. One, twelve years of age, lies at death's door (vv. 23a, 42b); the other, a victim of chronic menstruation for twelve years (v. 25). Absent healing, neither will ever experience the joy of childbirth (Ps 113:9).
- Their cases are manifestly hopeless. One "spent all that she had" on ineffectual treatments that aggravated her life's seepage (Mark 5:26): "for the blood is the life" (Deut 12:23). The other is dying (Mark 5:23) and eventually will be pronounced dead (v. 35a).
- Professionals—physicians (v. 26a) or hired mourners (v. 38; see also Jer 9:17–20)—have proved useless. Spectators react stupidly (Mark 5:31), callously (v. 35), or derisively (v. 40a). With cryptic remarks (vv. 30, 39), Jesus responds by rejecting (vv. 32, 36) or ejecting them (v. 40b).
- Perpetual bleeding and death are ritually defiling, impossible to purify, and socially alienating (Lev 15:19–20; Num 19:11–13). By touch—either the sufferer's (Mark 5:27–28) or the healer's (vv. 23, 41)—the polarity of contamination is reversed. Two of Israel's daughters are fully restored to their proper homes, from which they have been horribly estranged.
- The Greek verb for their restoration is identical: "made well" (σωθῇ [v. 23]; σέσωκέν [v. 34]).
- In both cases of healing, the prerequisite is πίστις: the "faith" (v. 34a) or "belief" (v. 36b) that recognizes in Jesus a trustworthy agent of God's curative power (vv. 23, 27–28).
- In both cases, the greatest challenge to such trust is fear (φοβηθεῖσα [v. 33b]; φοβοῦ [v. 36b]).

Random chance could account for a couple of these correspondences. More than a dozen indicate deliberate craftsmanship. Mark has twinned these tales with reverberating details. Notice, too, how much longer Mark's account runs: 377 Greek words, compared with 292 in Luke 8:40–56 and 139 in Matt 9:18–26. Commentators lambasting Mark for verbosity have missed something important: digesting this narrative sandwich takes a lot more time in the Second Gospel—and time is of the essence.

Unlike Matthew's version, in which Jairus's daughter has just died (Matt 9:18), in Mark she is on death's verge, dangling by a thread (Mark 5:23). That starts a ticking clock. The obstructive crowd, the woman's case history and desperate maneuver, Jesus's standstill and search for her, the rehearsal of everything implied by "the whole truth" (v. 33): all these details in verses 24–34 devour precious minutes as a child's life dwindles away. With the heartless report in verse 35, the bomb explodes: "Your daughter is dead." We are emotionally whipsawed by contesting emergencies. For twelve long years, that poor woman's life had bled out of her. When power flowed from him (v. 30)—a miracle occurred for both the healer and the healed—Jesus gave this daughter more attention than she wanted (vv. 32–34). But what of Jairus's daughter? After a dozen years, would an hour's delay have mattered to the menstruant? It certainly does for Jairus. For his child, it's too late now. Or is it?

Here shines Mark's genius as a gospeler. He doesn't merely spin miracle stories. He hooks us into these characters' lives, *creating within us* the awful oscillation between fear and faith. Mark knows that trust in God comes hard. We grasp it. We lose it. We reach again. We trust—God, replenish our lack of trust (Mark 9:24). After years of suffering, we reach our tether's end. The flame is snuffed. If you want to know how hard faith is in Mark, listen, over a long night in Gethsemane, while Jesus prays for escape from the inescapable (14:32–42). At three o'clock one afternoon on Golgotha, listen as he shrieks his abandonment by an apparently absent God (15:34). When Jesus took the hand of a little girl and whispered, "Arise, little lamb" (ταλιθα κουμ, a Greek translation of the Aramaic טְלִיחָא קוּם.), he did exactly what his heavenly Father would do for him at Easter. ἔγειρε: "Get up!" (Mark 5:41). ἠγέρθη: "He has been raised" (Mark 16:6b).

I tell my students that Mark 5:21–43 is so exquisitely wrought that it almost preaches itself. That's an overstatement, yet the power of two voices sensitively reading these entwined stories should not be underrated. Might one structure a sermon-sandwich of interlocking components, thus preaching a scriptural word in a scriptural way?[6] Were I to run a highlighter across this Markan passage, the line would fall on the battle for faith against fear (Mark 5:33–36). That, not the healings in themselves, is where I believe the evangelist's primary interest lies.

---

6. Leander E. Keck. *The Bible in the Pulpit: The Renewal of Biblical Preaching* (Nashville: Abingdon Press, 1978).

God knows that our congregations need all the support we can offer them in resisting a devilish anxiety that now pervades our culture 24/7. Some fears are reasonable. Others are manufactured by politicians and other powermongers for no reason other than to secure for themselves even more wealth and control. Typically, they present themselves as saviors of the populace they frighten. That's a lie. Mark redirects us to the true Savior, who subverts fear and fortifies faith. Trust in God, not paralyzing terror, is bedrock for all of Abraham's children, Jewish, Christian, and Muslim alike.

From the Qur'an, Surah Al-Ma'idah 5:69:

> For whoever believes in Allah and the Last Day, and does what is right—Jews, Sabaeans, or Christians—no fear shall come upon them; neither shall they grieve.

In Isaiah's words (12:2),

> Surely God is my salvation;
> I will trust and will not be afraid.

2 February 2020

Mark 6:1–13

This Sunday's pairing of Mark 6:1–6 and 6:7–13 kindles the preacher's imagination.

The first passage—"Where did this man get all this?" (6:2)—closes a section that began with Mark 4:35–41: "Who then is this?" (4:41). Likewise, 6:12 ("So they went out") opens a door that isn't shut until 6:30 ("The apostles gathered around Jesus, and told him all that they had done and taught"). What happens when the interpreter listens only to the juxtaposition of Jesus's return to his hometown with his sending of the Twelve? We may hear each story rhyme with its mate.

First, the mission of the Twelve parallels Jesus's own mission. In Mark 3:13–15, Jesus assembled the Twelve to extend his ministry of preaching and exorcism (1:21–28; 3:7–12). That extension occurs in 6:12–13, after Mark has made it clear that "his disciples [have] followed him" (6:1). At 6:7a, Jesus takes the initiative: "*he* called the Twelve and began to send them out" in pairs (perhaps for safety and corroboration: Deut 19:15; Matt 18:16; Acts 13:2–3). Their authority derives from Jesus's power over unclean spirits (Mark 6:7b). The implications for Mark's listeners should be clear. Jesus's disciples are not passive beneficiaries of their teacher; he gives them a mandate to witness and to heal, replicating his own public ministry (cf. 1:14–15; 6:5). Jesus's adherents are not self-authorizing; they receive orders from their commander and can execute them because he has given them ἐξουσίαν—authoritative power—to do so.

Second, the equipment for such ministry is astonishingly meager. Some first-century street preachers carried at least a pair of shirts, a staff, and a beggar's bag. In Mark 6:8–9 the Twelve are forbidden the bag and change of tunics; they must live hand to mouth while on the road. In a way, their paltry resources echo Jesus's own, which so astound his listeners in Galilee. This hometown boy is only a τέκτων: a carpenter or stonemason (6:3a). (Celsus, Christianity's second-century critic, mocked the religion's founding by a blue-collar worker [*Cels.* 6.34].) "Where did this man get all this" power to teach and to heal (6:2)? To scoff at the disciples'—and our own—equipment for ministry is to take offense just as those in the synagogue did: literally, "they stumbled over him" (6:3b; cf. 4:17). Later, the Twelve will be perplexed by the magnitude of human need compared with their paltry resources; yet, with our master's blessing, it's amazing how much you can do with so little (6:35–44).

Third, offers of ministry can be accepted or refused, and we see both responses in these twinned tales. Empowered by Jesus, traveling disciples cast out demons, anointed many and cured the sick (Mark 6:13; cf. Jas 5:14; Rev 3:18). Even in hostile environs, Jesus laid his hands on a few sick and cured them (Mark 6:5b). Yet among his own kin, he was dishonored, and that rejection short-circuited his ability to do a mighty deed among them (6:4–5a). So, too, for his disciples (6:11). Shaking dust off the feet appears to have been a prophetic demonstration: from those who repudiate the kingdom's herald, nothing should be received—not even their dirt (see Neh 5:13; Acts 13:51). No one, neither the Christ nor his followers, can ram the gospel down anyone's throat. If people repent—turn their minds Godward—the conditions for healing are satisfied (Mark 6:13). If they refuse to entrust themselves to the good news, delivered by unlikely agents, then Jesus can do little but marvel at their faithlessness (6:6a). Those who expect nothing from Jesus are not disappointed (6:5b).

Fourth, rejecting Jesus and his faithful emissaries isolates; welcoming them creates community. It's easy to miss, but this pair of stories in Mark illumines the social consequences of faith or unbelief in the good news. The aphorism about the prophet honored everywhere but at home recalls the saying in Mark 2:17b: Jesus calls not the familiar righteous but rather alien sinners.

More than any other evangelist (see Matt 13:57b; Luke 4:24; John 4:44), Mark highlights the poignancy in 6:4: God's prophet is dishonored in homeland, among kin, and in his own house. The last item is an explicit link with 3:25–27: the divided house, exemplified by Jesus's own family who think him mad (3:21, 31–32). Another hint of division within Jesus's family may underlie his description as "the son of Mary" (6:3). Unlike Matthew (1:16–24), Luke (3:24; 4:22), and John (1:45; 6:42), nowhere in Mark is Jesus called "the son of Joseph." Does Mark 6 imply that Joseph had died? If Jesus was the eldest son of a widowed mother, then abdication of her support while he practiced itinerant ministry would have been scandalous, though consistent with his teaching elsewhere (Mark 10:29–30). Rejected at home in the synagogue (where Jews assemble for prayer [1:21]), Jesus directs his emissaries—those "appointed to be with him" (3:14)—to outsiders in surrounding villages (6:6b). For shelter, Jesus's deputies are instructed to stay in one house until leaving it for another (6:10), dependent on the kindness of strangers. It is a notable feature of early Christianity that so many of its adherents, ostracized by their kin (Mark 13:12; John 9:18–23), found support among surrogate families in house-churches (Rom 16:5; 1 Cor 16:19; Col 4:15; Phlm 2).

Mark has braided the two stories in 6:1–13 with common themes. Rather than cataloging them, as I have done here, the evangelist shows the attentive preacher how these tales may be twisted for today's listeners. After days at sea and on the road, Jesus astounds his hometown (Mark 6:1–2). Familiarity breeds contempt (6:3). Jesus expects that (6:4) but can't do a thing for them (6:5a) save, incidentally, heal a few sick folk (6:5b). While such tales usually culminate in an audience's astonishment (1:27; 2:12; 4:41; 5:20b, 42), now Jesus is the one flabbergasted—by an unfaith so impenetrable (6:6a). Rejection catalyzes fresh ministry (6:6b–7) by empty-pocketed dimwits (4:13, 35–41; 5:31; 6:8–11) who get the job done (6:12–13). In Mark, there's no stopping the good news (13:10)—but no telling how it breaks through (16:1–8).

5 July 2015

MARK 6:14–29

The preacher of this text for this Sunday's sermon receives my congratulations for originality and guts. Who preaches on the death of John the Baptist? Except for special occasions, who speaks of politics from the pulpit even when the Bible authorizes it?

Years ago, or only yesterday, the *Washington Post* quoted a lavishly paid lobbyist: "There are only two engines that drive Washington: One is greed, and the other is fear." That's a fine description of Herod's birthday party. You recall Herod Antipas (ca. 21 BCE–ca. CE 40): tetrarch of Galilee and Perea, answerable to the emperor Tiberius. Most historians remember him as maladroit and weak. When it comes to our governors, some things never change.

Mark tells of a warped triangle: Herod, his wife Herodias, and John the Baptist, whose arrest was the last we heard of him (Mark 1:14). Defying torah (Lev 18:13–16; 20:21), Herod had married his sister-in-law. John had called them out (Mark 6:18). Believing him righteous and holy, Herod admired his accuser (6:20). Nursing a grudge, Herodias wanted John dead (6:19). Herod compromised: he arrested and jailed under protective custody the threatening preacher to whom he enjoyed listening (6:17, 20). His wife's opportunity came at a state dinner, at which her young daughter "danced and pleased Herod and his guests" (6:21–22). The lecherous fool promised her whatever she asked (6:22–23). After consulting her mother, the girl sprang the trap: "I want John's head on a salver—right now" (6:24–25). Herod was caught. Saving face was an issue (6:26); worse, defaulting on an oath could be reckoned tantamount to taking God's name in vain (Philo, *Spec.* 2:9–10). Birthday morphed into deathday: John's head was delivered to Mother by a ghoulish bucket brigade (Mark 6:27–28).

Ghastly though it be, this tale is told with masterly understatement. "It is Elijah" (6:15a): another prophet who collided with another weak king manipulated by another murderous wife (1 Kgs 18–21). "A righteous and holy man" (Mark 6:20a): just like elderly Eleazar, refusing to compromise Jewish principles to avoid state-sanctioned death (2 Macc 6:18–31). "What is your request? It shall be given you, even to the half of my kingdom." That's the promise of King Hesperus to Queen Esther (Esth 5:3, 6; 7:2). "John, whom I beheaded, has been raised" (Mark 6:16): the dead has returned with awesome power (6:14), but haunted Herod has misidentified the risen one (16:6). "The king was deeply grieved" (6:26): a fat lot of good that does John. Herod is so feckless that the executioner delivers the victim's head not to the king as ordered (6:27) but *to the girl* (6:28). What's on her mind? *She's* the one who demands the head "on a platter" (6:25). Without help, most congregations would miss these details. The larger issue, however, is how well Mark teaches us to tell a story. Hook listeners' imaginations to fill in some blanks, and a sermon can come alive—because they have been invited to help you preach it.

But *why* does Mark tell this story—the longest of the gospel's anecdotes and its only flashback? Aside from the Golgotha plot (Mark 14:1–2, 10–11) and discovery of the empty tomb (16:1–8), this is the only tale in which Jesus never appears. Its villains never reappear (cf. Luke 23:6–12). It's a strange story about John in which the baptizer himself never appears. Even stranger, beneath this story of John is the story of Jesus. The flashback is a flashforward. Mark tips us off in 6:14–16: the confusion over agency for Jesus's mighty works (cf. the identical refrain in 8:27–29). Herod foreshadows Pilate in the same way that John presages Jesus (1:1–15; 9:9–13; 11:27–33). The two prefects are nominally in charge. Like Antipas, Pilate is amazed (6:20; 15:5) by circumstances surrounding an innocent prisoner (6:17, 20; 15:1, 14a), swept up in events that fast spin out of his control (6:21–25; 15:6–13), and unable to back down after being publicly outmaneuvered (6:26–27; 15:15). Like John, Jesus is passive in his final hours (6:14–19; 15:1–39), faces with integrity his moment of truth (6:21: ἡμέρας εὐκαίρου, "an opportunity came"; 12:2: τῷ καιρῷ, "the season came"), and is executed by hideous capital punishment (6:27–28; 15:24–27), dying to placate those he offends (6:19, 25; 15:10–14). John's disciples give their teacher a proper burial (6:29). What will become of the Twelve after Jesus's death (14:27, 50–52; 15:40–47)? That's a pertinent question: Mark has embedded 6:14–29 in the middle of their successful mission (6:7–13), about which they will offer Jesus a jolly report "of all they [have] done and taught" (6:30). Fatal intrigue casts a shadow over the routing of demons and healing of the sick (6:13).

Where's the good news in Mark 6:14–29? There may be none. The drive shafts of corrupted politics torque this birthday party. Everywhere greed and fear whisper: in Herod's ear, among Galilee's high and mighty, behind the curtain between mother and daughter, in a dungeon prison. When repentance is preached to this world's princes, do not expect them to relinquish their power, however conflicted some may be. The righteous die for reasons both valorous and vapid. "As the fishes that are taken in an evil net, and as the birds that are caught in the snare; so are the sons of men snared in an evil time" (Qoh 9:12 KJV). Mark is no more a fool than Qoheleth.

Neither is the evangelist cynical. Herod's banquet is only the first of two in Mark 6. Jesus hosts the second, in the middle of nowhere for thousands of nobodies with nothing to offer save five loaves and two fish. At that feast, greed and fear have no place. There all are fed to the full, with leftovers beyond comprehension (6:30–44).

In the high heat of summer, Mark 6:14–29 beckons you to preach the mystery of Good Friday before the Easter of 6:30–44 next Sunday. Do you have the guts to try?

12 July 2015

Mark 7:24–37

Mark has juxtaposed stories in 7:24–30 and 7:31–37 as mirror images of each other. Both focus on unfortunates suffering infirmities that isolate them from society (vv. 25a, 32a). Something from within the daughter and the deaf man incapacitates them: a demon (v. 30), ear-stoppage (v. 33b), speech-blockage (v. 35). Proxies intercede on their behalf, kneeling before (v. 25) or begging (v. 32) Jesus. The tale of the Syro-Phoenician woman begins with Jesus's failed attempt to escape notice (7:24b); the tale of the deaf man ends with Jesus's defeated order to tell no one (7:36a). The harder secrecy is pressed, the more widely the good news is broadcast (v. 36b): a contradiction pervading Mark (1:44–2:2; 6:31–33) and triply ironic for an account that ends with defiance of a gag order against reporting Jesus's removal of a speech impediment (7:35b–36). The references to Tyre (v. 24), Syro-Phoenicia (v. 26), Sidon, and the Decapolis (v. 31) are important: Jesus is traversing gentile territory, despised by Jews (Ezek 26:1–28:19; Joel 3:4–8). In 2022, xenophobic reactions to border-crossings make worldwide headlines. Some things never change.

The differences between these tales are telling. Mark 7:33–34 itemizes Jesus's therapeutic technique: private treatment, palpation, spitting, looking to heaven, sighing, pronouncing the cure. Its confirmation is particularized: literally, "[the man's] hearing was opened up, and his tongue's shackle was released, and he spoke straight" (7:35). Beyond Jesus's declaration of the child's healing (v. 29) and its subsequent confirmation (v. 30), Mark 7:24–30 recounts no details of the exorcism. The little girl's healing takes place far removed from Jesus. The last verse in 7:31–37 is its punch line: ironically, gentiles acclaim Jesus with an OT paraphrase (Isa 35:5–6). Verse 30 is anticlimactic in Mark 7:24–30, whose interest lies in the thrust and parry between Jesus and the woman in 7:27–29.

She is a gentile, "a Greek" (Rom 1:16; Gal 3:28). Unconventionally for a woman in antiquity, she approaches Jesus for her daughter's exorcism. Nowhere in Mark has Jesus refused such assistance; exorcisms characterize the overthrow of Satan's kingdom by God's Son (1:21–28; 3:11–12, 23–27; 5:1–20; 9:14–29) and his disciples (6:7, 13). In 7:14–23, Jesus's teaching has abolished traditional distinctions between clean (Jews) and unclean (gentiles). Therefore, Jesus's reply to this mother is disturbing. While not ignoring her (cf. Matt 15:23), he suggests a delay in her petition's fulfillment based on ethnic priority ("let the children be fed first") and the ignobility of "taking the children's bread and pitching it to the dogs" (7:27 AT). For one who has just spoken of defilement that emerges from within (v. 23), it is *Jesus* who appears ignoble. There's no escaping the ethnic slur built into "dogs" (τοῖς κυναρίοις [cf. 1 Sam 17:43; Rev 22:15]). The Jesus of history may have had little interaction with gentiles for the reason given in Matt 15:24: "I was sent only to the lost sheep of the house of Israel." Both Matthew (5:47; 6:7; 18:17) and Paul (Gal 2:15) take a dim view of gentile conduct, even though they, like Mark and other NT authors, are dedicated to gentile evangelization (Matt 28:19; Acts 13:46; Gal 1:16; Col 1:27).

What does the preacher do with Mark 7:27–29? Commentators repeatedly try to get Jesus off the hook, somehow, usually by imputing to Mark 7:27–29 a sweetener without textual basis. ("'Little puppies' aren't offensive.") That not only strains credulity; it undermines Mark, who, had he been as embarrassed as some of his interpreters, could have excised the pericope entirely. (Luke did just that.) Others suggest that Jesus was testing the woman's faith. While not out of character for the Markan Jesus (6:37–38), other possibilities are suggested by 7:27. Jesus does not flatly refuse the woman's request but does prioritize "the children" (τῶν τέκνων: presumably, Israel) as primary beneficiaries. In antiquity, a child occupied a station of claimless vulnerability. Even children, however, are fed before lapdogs. While we reel from this affront, the Syro-Phoenician woman executes some comedic jujitsu, twisting Jesus's maxim to deliver the retort best suiting her situation: "Sir [κύριε], even housedogs under the table scarf down the kids' bitty scraps" (7:28 AT). Her acknowledgment of Jesus's superiority, the implied acceptance of his insult, the lowering of self beneath the table, the subtle shift in Greek from one term for "children" to another (τὰ παιδία) that blends immaturity and servanthood, acceptance of crumbs: all these elements anticipate Jesus's own definitions of discipleship (9:33–37; 10:13–16), congruent with the Son of Man's self-condescension (8:31; 10:41–45). That is what makes "this word" so apt and so convincing (7:29). Jesus more than concedes the quick-witted moxie of a female foreigner. He ratifies her claim to the gospel on the very grounds that he himself will explain in 10:28–31. She is not disappointed (7:30).

In the context of Mark 7:1–23, this Sunday's lection proves that Jesus's *offensiveness* is a fact we must face. A conservative congregation will be affronted by Jesus's claim that defilement comes from within, not from without (7:15, 23). Liberal Christians resist the notion that a socially progressive Jesus would say what Mark ascribes to him in 7:27 or, worse, that the woman so insulted would accept the put-down (7:28). The deeper question is whether we can follow a Christ so repulsive as to die by crucifixion (15:22–41). Jesus flummoxes everyone who boxes him into conventional expectations: the pious (2:1–3:6; 7:1–23), his family (3:19b–21), his disciples (8:33), and even some petitioners (7:24–30).

If we, too, are not gobsmacked, it's a safe bet that we have domesticated Jesus and have neutered the gospel.

5 September 2021

MARK 8:31–38

Mark Twain worried, "It ain't those parts of the Bible that I can't understand that bother me, it is the parts that I do understand."[7]

Meet this Sunday's lection. Jesus speaks "quite openly" (Mark 8:32a). There's little in this teaching that requires deep-sea exegesis. It is plain, hard, and inescapable.

In Mark 8:29, Simon Peter has tumbled to the truth about his teacher: "You are the Messiah." Whatever glorious aspirations the Twelve may have associated with that honorific, Jesus shuts them down (8:30): ἐπετίμησεν, a verb used elsewhere in Mark for silencing unclean spirits and savage forces (1:25; 3:12; 4:39). In 8:31, Jesus shifts to what the Son of the Man must endure by the hands of "the elders" (senior lay leaders), "the chief priests" (cultic officials), and "the scribes" (authorities on scriptural tradition). Their modern counterparts are the church's own lay leaders, tall-steeple preachers, and biblical scholars. To what will the establishment subject Jesus? Rejection, suffering, and death. After the full measure of this fatal disgrace has been exacted, he will rise again after three days. None of this is accidental: the Son of Man must (δεῖ) undergo it by God's design.

Peter will have none of it (Mark 8:32b). Taking Jesus aside, Peter rebukes him: ἐπιτιμᾶν ("Shut up!"), the same harsh verb as in 8:30. Regarding all his disciples, Jesus lashes back (ἐπετίμησεν) against Peter (8:33a). Jesus puts him and all followers back in their proper place: "Get behind me!" The stakes are so high that he addresses Peter as "Satan," the tempter (1:12) and thief of the preached word (4:15). Peter is the only figure in Mark whom Jesus addresses so heatedly. Why? "You are setting your mind not on divine things but on human things" (8:33b). Peter has arrogated to himself an authority that is not his to wield. In fact, it's devilish. This is no gentlemanly disagreement. Mark dramatizes a life-and-death clash between the divine and the diabolical.

Then Jesus opens his teaching beyond the Twelve to the overhearing crowd (including us): "If any want to become my followers, let them deny themselves and take up their cross and follow me" (8:34). Self-denial implies taking one's

---

7. This is another of those quips whose literary source eludes me. If Twain didn't say this, he should have.

stand "on the side of God, [not] of men" (RSV). To take up the cross is neither pious sentiment nor temporary disappointment. Crucifixion was the most humiliating, torturous execution the Romans could devise. The cross is Jesus's destination (15:12–39). There his followers must follow him.

To render a gender-inclusive translation, the NRSV generalizes Jesus's blunt admonitions in Mark 8:35–38 into third-person plurals: "those," "their," "them." More closely adherent to the Greek, the RSV sharpens the gravity of individual decisions: "For whoever would save his life [or "self": ψυχὴν] will lose it; and whoever loses his life for my sake and the gospel's will save it" (8:35). "For the sake of the gospel" is a crucial qualification. One may give one's life for no good purpose. To give one's life for the sake of the good news instantiated by Jesus is the valid reason for self-sacrifice. In the economy governed by the gospel, the only way to be made whole is to let go of everything society reckons most valuable. There is no benefit in gaining the entire world—values and aspirations as people define them—if in so doing, one forfeits one's deepest soul.

Ultimately nothing in this world is worth exchanging for one's very center, the self that is claimed by the gospel and accountable to God (Mark 8:36–37). The only shame that should concern a true disciple is desertion of the Son of Man and his words "in this adulterous and sinful generation," which is no arbiter of honor and shame as the gospel redefines them (8:38). The reverse is equally true: self-renunciation for the gospel's sake is neither futile nor masochistic. The faithful disciple who transcends this generation's wickedness and corruption may expect vindication, like that of the slain Son of Man after his resurrection.

The Twelve do not want to hear this. They continue to bumble (Mark 9:33–34; 10:35–41); Jesus repeats the message over and again (9:35–37; 10:42–45). Neither do we want to hear it. Every day, all of us are tempted by worldly standards of prestige and reputation. At critical moments, something punches us in the gut: attracted to "human things" (8:33), we know that they flout what God intends.

For preachers and congregants the most satanic of these desires come coated with a religious veneer. At Caesarea Philippi, that was the trap Peter stepped into. Under pressure in the high priest's courtyard (14:54), he collapsed like a cardboard suitcase. His last words in this gospel: "I do not know this [Jesus] you are talking about" (14:71). Jesus predicted that (14:26–31) but never gave up on him, even at Easter (16:7).

Christian faith is not a lifestyle choice. It is a vocation to never-ending struggle. By lying about Jesus and the truth of the gospel, we deny the truth about ourselves. Rejecting the Son of Man, desperately trying to save our own lives, we lose ourselves—just as he assured us we would (8:35–37). Only by giving ourselves to others as Jesus gave himself for us (10:45) will we ever find ourselves.

While challenging us to consider the caliber of our discipleship, today's gospel lection invites us to pray both for ourselves and for Christians in parts of the world who have internalized this text and are paying dearly for their fidelity. Persecution of Christians *because they are Christians* did not end in the fourth century. North Korea, Somalia, and Afghanistan are only some of the countries where Christian worship is criminal today. Those arrested may be jailed, raped, sold into slavery, and murdered. They are this Sunday's most credible witnesses: for Christ they have given up everything. In so doing, they are totally free to receive God's guardianship and peace, which surpasses all understanding (Phil 4:7).

25 February 2018

MARK 8:27–38

> *Brother, afar from your Savior today,*
> *Risking your soul for the things that decay,*
> *Oh, if today God should call you away,*
> *What would you give in exchange for your soul?*

—F. J. Berry and J. H. Carr (1912)

Mark 8:27–38 is this gospel's most verbally abusive passage. Three times Jesus or Peter tells the other to "shut up" (ἐπιτιμάω)—the same verb that stifles demons and a gale (1:25; 3:12; 4:39; 9:25). Its first occurrence: smothering the disciples' correct ascription of messiahship to Jesus (see 1:1; 14:61–62). For the first and only time in Mark, Peter and peers recognize their teacher, but Jesus commands them to say nothing to anyone (8:30; see also 1:34; 3:12). After Jesus plainly explains to them all that the Son of Man must suffer, Peter shuts him up (8:31–32). "Turning and seeing his disciples, he shut up Peter: Get behind me, Satan. You're setting your mind not on divine things but on human things" (8:33 AT). Only here in Mark does Jesus address an adversary as Satan—and it's the first of the Twelve whom he summoned (1:16).

The language grates not just because the stakes are life and death but because *Jesus upends everything we expect a messiah to be and to do for us.* First-century Jewish messianic hopes varied, but none of them expected a messiah *crucified* by elders (lay leaders), chief priests (tall-steeple preachers), and scribes (biblical scholars). Writings like 4 Ezra (11–12), 2 Baruch (40, 72), and Qumran's Damascus Document (VI, 7–11) dreamt of idealized rulers who would judge the wicked and restore Israel's righteous. None of these messiahs handed their followers a cross to be shouldered en route to their own Golgothas. In no gospel does Jesus say, "It is my responsibility to die for you, while you applaud my heroism." Instead: "The Son of Man is ordained by God to suffer, die, and be raised. And so are his followers. Are you coming?"

One of the ways modern Christians sashay around this question is to trivialize the cross. Crucifixion was an instrument designed for its victims' utter degradation and excruciating torture: capital punishment so vile that it appalled even tough-minded politicos. "To bind a Roman citizen is a crime; to flog him, an abomination. To slay him is virtually an act of murder. To crucify him is—what? No fitting word can possibly describe a deed so horrible" (*Verr.* 2.66.170). Fast-forward to Manhattan in 1993, when the *New Yorker* reported on Macy's Cross Culture: a boutique, purveying "trend-type crosses." Here you could shop for a fist-size cross covered with gold hobnails or "one with a cameo in the center surrounded by purple, green, blue, and pink semiprecious stones . . . with an extra-long antiqued-silver chain, so it can be slung, shoulder to hip, bandolier style, which, by the way, happens to look great with a crushed-velvet cat suit and little biker boots." A sales associate said, "Occasionally, people stop and say, 'Where are the Stars of David? What about equal time?' and I say I understand but also, hey, that's not the fashion. . . . We have one of the best selections in New York City, but, honestly, I'm a little low on crosses right now. They're flying out the door."[8]

"For whoever would save her life will lose it; and whoever loses his life for my sake and the gospel's will save it. For what does it profit a person, to gain the whole world and forfeit one's life? For what can a person give in return for one's life?" (Mark 8:35–37 AT). "Life" is an imperfect translation of the Greek term ἡ ψυχή: "the creature's center; one's inmost self." A thought experiment for this Sunday: in what ways do we pretend that Jesus didn't mean this, or try to be our own messiahs and save ourselves? On what do we stake our lives? In what do we ultimately place our trust? Our bank accounts? (See Luke 12:16–20.) Achievements? (Matt 7:21–23.) Prestige? (Mark 12:38–40.) Politicians? (Mark 12:13–17.) Guns? (Matt 26:51–52.) Run down the entire list of familiar evasions and remember how Jesus locks every escape hatch. Doctrinal

---

8. Anonymous, "God, However, Remains in the Details," *New Yorker*, 18 October 1993, 43–44.

confusion is not the Christian's fundamental problem. Instead, it is disobedience: our refusal to accept Christ's authority over our lives.

Lay your ear upon Mark's page and listen for the wail of lament: the steep price paid for following Jesus. What you won't hear is the yammering of prosperity televangelists who prostitute the Bible with phony assurances of health and wealth if you'll mail them a check every week.

Psychotherapists help clients sort out the many hues of shame. In Mark 8:38, the only guilt suffered by a true disciple is being ashamed of Christ: abandoning his way for the values of "this adulterous and sinful generation," "setting one's mind on this world's things." In the gospel's light, honor and shame are altogether redefined (Rom 1:16–17; Phil 3:3–11).

We are privileged to know everyday folks who have so internalized this quality of discipleship that, in the critical moment, they know what to do. There's Arland D. Williams Jr., the passenger aboard Air Florida Flight 90 on 13 January 1982, which after takeoff crashed into Washington's Fourteenth Street Bridge, then into the icy Potomac River. Fighting a lifelong fear of water, clinging to twisted wreckage, he handed over to the five other survivors one life vest after another. When all but Williams had been pulled ashore, the helicopter returned to the site to save him. He was gone.[9]

Most of us may never master such integral calculus of charity, but failure needn't be the enemy of aspiration. We know the way. Other disciples walk it with us. Jesus remains in the lead.

> More than the silver and gold of this earth,
> More than all jewels the spirit is worth.
> God the Creator has given his word.
> What would you give in exchange for your soul?

12 September 2021

Mark 9:2–9

Most congregations would drown in this text's cascade of details. "Six days later." "A high mountain apart." "Elijah with Moses." "Let's make three dwellings." "A cloud overshadowed them."

---

9. Roger Rosenblatt, *The Man in the Water: Essays and Stories* (New York: Random House, 1994).

Each of these items chimes with the OT. In earlier eras, preachers were expected to explain everything. We are not Aquinas or Luther or Wesley; our audiences do not live in the thirteenth, sixteenth, or eighteenth centuries. My advice is to bracket out, at most brush over, most of these allusions. Save them for an hour of solid Christian education. This Sunday, find your focus and hold it tight. Mark's climax, I believe, lies in 9:7: "This is my Son, the Beloved; listen to him!"

"This is my Son": the second of three decisive acclamations of Jesus's unique identity in Mark. The first is at his baptism (1:11); the last, at his death (15:39). In all three episodes, the atmosphere is apocalyptic in the strict sense: revelatory. The curtain is drawn away from normal appearances, allowing us a glimpse of God behind them. Of these epiphanies, Mark 9:2–8 may be the weirdest. It is the least public, farthest removed from the commonplace (9:2). Events are literally beclouded (9:7). Jesus—he alone (contrast Luke 9:30–31)—is "transfigured": metamorphosed in raiment that is "dazzling white" (Mark 9:3). No one on earth looks like this: such radiance, כָּבוֹד, is God's very essence (Exod 16:10; Num 14:10b; Ps 63:2). Only those judged righteous "will shine like the sun in the kingdom of their Father" (Matt 13:43; see also Dan 12:3; Phil 3:21). Here Mark is dramatizing what the Fourth Gospel claims of Jesus: "The light shines in the darkness, and the darkness did not overcome it" (John 1:5; also 8:12; 9:5; 12:46).

"This is my Son, the Beloved" (Mark 9:7). The speaker is God (1:11; see also Deut 4:36; 2 Sam 22:14; John 12:28; Acts 11:9). In Mark, no one else is designated "God's Son." Not Moses. Not Elijah. Not John the Baptizer. None of Galilee's other itinerant preachers or exorcists (Mark 6:7, 12–13; 9:38). Only Jesus is the beloved (ἀγαπητός) Son, as Isaac was to Abraham (Gen 22:2, 12, 16): "unique," "one of a kind." A father's love for such a son is fathomless, precisely because there is no other.

"Listen to him!" (Mark 9:7). For the first and only time in Mark, the voice from heaven orders Jesus's disciples. This command recollects Moses's directive: Israel should heed a prophet whom the LORD God would raise up (Deut 18:15). In Jesus, God has done this; Israel's successors should respond appropriately. To what should Jesus's disciples pay attention? Presumably, everything in Mark that Jesus says and does. Immediately it refers to God's design for the Son of Man's suffering and vindication (Mark 8:31), the adoption of cross-bearing discipleship (8:34–35), keeping mum about what has been seen until after the resurrection (9:9), and assurance that all proceeds according to the divine plan (9:11–13). These are the very things that his disciples find so hard to understand, to accept, and to obey (9:31–34; 10:32–37; 14:26–31, 50,

66–72; 16:1–8). As suddenly as it struck, the mountaintop vision fades: a handful of disciples are alone with Jesus (9:8).

From this point, the preacher must decide what theological issue most needs development this Sunday for this congregation. Here are only three from among many possibilities.

1. *Who is Jesus, for us and for the world?* Many Protestants are virtual Ebionites: they have lost any appreciation of Jesus's divinity by the canons of orthodox Christianity. It's easy to regard Jesus as a sage, hero, scamp, or fool. Some among our congregants hide out with the History Channel's Jesus and never come out. Mark 9:2–9 uncages a Jesus so tamed. A sermon along this line is unlikely to change fixed minds. It may begin to unsettle them, or at least to set them wondering. If Jesus is nothing more than an oddball Jew from antiquity, to whom does the church bear witness? If the church has so little to confess, why on earth are we here?

2. *Who, in fact, is the Son of God?* The nation Israel was sometimes characterized as God's sons (Exod 4:22–23; Jer 31:9, 20; Hos 1:10). Israel's king was ceremonially regarded as "Son of God" (2 Sam 7:13–14; Ps 2:7). Caesar Augustus acclaimed himself *divi filius*, "deified son" (thus, an inscription on Rome's Porta Tiburtina). If Mark's witness is credible, if God reckons Jesus alone as "the beloved Son," then no one else qualifies. Needful to say, equally disqualified are today's church and presidents and potentates who yearn for such adoration and power. The devil tempted Jesus to self-reliance, political dominion, and civil religion (Matt 4:1–11 = Luke 4:1–13). When last I noticed, Satan hasn't quit trying to seduce us—often with frightening success.

3. *Are we listening?* Igor Stravinsky said, "To listen is an effort, and just to hear is no merit. A duck hears also."[10] If this is true of music, how much more does it bear on Jesus's commands? It is one thing to admire the Messiah; to obey him is something else. "Follow me" (Mark 1:17; 2:14). "Pay attention to what you hear" (4:24). "Do not be afraid, only believe" (5:36; 6:50). "You give them something to eat" (6:37). "It is what comes out of a person that defiles" (7:20). "Deny [yourself] and take up [your cross] and follow me" (8:34). "But many who are first will be last, and the last will be first" (10:31). "Whoever wishes to be first among you must be slave of all" (10:44). "Whenever you stand praying, forgive, if you have anything against anyone" (11:25). That's only from Mark; Matthew, Luke, and John offer more. Anyone who thinks Christian faith is a retreat from reality is clueless.

10. Interview, ca. 1957, with Deborah Ishlon, publicity director for Columbia Records.

Whatever direction your sermon takes, invite your listeners into its mystery. Like Christmas and Easter, Jesus's transfiguration is uncanny. Moralism abounds, but well-placed wonder is in short supply. Peter and his confreres were terrified and tongue-tied (Mark 9:6). When we stand before God, that's a proper response.

11 February 2018

Mark 9:30–37

Mark 8:27–38 jabs three sharp barbs:

1. Jesus's prediction of his suffering, murder, and resurrection (8:31);
2. Peter's repudiation of Jesus's destiny (8:32);
3. Jesus's rebuttal of Peter and command that his followers take up their crosses (8:33–38).

In Mark 9:30–37, the same pattern recurs:

1. Jesus's prediction of his betrayal, murder, and resurrection (9:31);
2. The disciples' incomprehension of their teacher's teaching (9:32–34);
3. Jesus's correction of the Twelve with a surprising definition of discipleship (9:35–37).

In case Mark's audience has failed as miserably as the Twelve to get the point, the same scheme unfolds in chapter 10: prediction (vv. 33–34), misunderstanding (vv. 35–39a), readjustment (vv. 39b–45).

Why this repetition? Two reasons. First, discipleship in Mark is hard to accept. Second, in this gospel, Jesus's closest followers are so dense that light bends around them. Both themes pervade Mark 9:30–37. This lection offers the preacher three options: dwell on one of these twinned subjects, or, as the evangelist has done, creatively interlace them for your listeners.

Dopey Disciples

"But they did not understand [Jesus's] saying [in 9:31], and they were afraid to ask him" (9:32). What's not to understand? Jesus has already said much the same in 8:33–38. But the Twelve in Mark's Gospel *never* understand Jesus

(4:13; 6:52; 8:17, 21). In fact, the last words uttered by Peter, last of the twelve hangers-on, is, "I neither know nor understand what you mean" (14:68). This claim, asserted outside the house where Jesus is betrayed by his countrymen, is a chicken-hearted lie that captures the ironic truth. As for the disciples' fear to ask (9:32), that, too, is true to form: throughout Mark, they are scared spitless (4:40–41; 6:50; 9:6; 10:32; 16:8). Those with faith in Jesus have nothing to fear (4:40–41; 5:33–34, 36), but not once does Mark ever attribute faith to the Twelve. (Compare the usually nameless nobodies in 2:5; 5:34; 9:24; 10:52.) *Immediately after* Jesus has reminded them of his impending humiliation, his followers are shamed to silence: they've been quarreling over which of them is tops in their own pecking order (9:33–34). Given antiquity's preoccupation with social status—not so very distant from our own—that debate is predictable. But in Mark's context, it's nonsensical, since Jesus is superior to them all. Disregarding the general, these foot soldiers bicker over their respective ranks. The picture is clear: those with greatest benefit of Jesus's instruction set for themselves low standards and consistently fail to achieve them.

The Child Embraced

Jesus's teaching in 9:35–37 is as complex as it is concise: an aphorism (v. 35b), followed by a pronouncement story in which the summons of a child (v. 36) sets up two punch lines, the second (v. 37b) an extension of the first (v. 37a). The hinge holding everything together is παιδίον, "little child" (vv. 36, 37a), which in Greek has the double meaning of "immediate offspring" and "slave." It is analogous to a "servant" (διάκονος [v. 35b]): an assistant who mediates for a superior. Jesus's rejoinder to bickering over rank is a paradoxical assertion that parallels 8:35 (from last week's lection) by turning social assumptions inside out: just as the saving of one's life requires its sacrifice for the gospel's sake, so, too, does primacy in discipleship demand taking a place last of all, as everyone's servant (9:35). Matthew 20:16 and 23:11–12 drive home the same idea. (So did the rabbis, though their self-subjugation was to torah: thus, b. B. Meṣ. 85b.)

Beware of sentimentalizing 9:36. A child epitomizes the most subservient human in ancient society, one with slightest status. In Jesus's presence, a little child literally has "standing" (ἔστησεν [Mark 9:36a: obscured in the NRSV but clear in the NIV]). Jesus's embrace (v. 36b) recalls his compassion for another child's father (9:14–29) and Jesus's own standing, at the mount of transfiguration, as God's beloved Son (9:7). Jesus's embrace also captures a peculiar nuance in the doubled saying in 9:37, which reiterates the importance of δέχομαι:

"receiving," "welcoming," or "approving" one such child in my name and, indeed, Jesus himself. Like self-sacrifice for the gospel's sake in 8:34–35, these qualifications for acceptance in 9:37 are important, steering interpretation away from sentimentality: the "last of all and servant of all" (v. 35) is received "in my name" as a disciple of Jesus who evinces the teacher's own belittlement by betrayal (9:31). Welcoming such an ambassador of Jesus is tantamount to receiving Jesus, who himself is a mediating emissary of the one who has sent him (9:37; see also Matt 10:40; Luke 10:16; John 12:44–45; 13:20).

Children will return in Mark as exemplary of discipleship (10:13–16), but the stress in 9:33–37 is different. Here Mark concentrates our attention not on the child's receptivity (cf. 10:15) but on the necessity of a disciple's welcoming other children in Jesus's name. That's the positive counterpoint of both Jesus's rejection, emphasized in 9:31, and the Twelve's aspersions cast on one another. In other words, the top-to-bottom reversal of rank in 9:35 realigns how listeners should receive those whom they have mistakenly regarded as beneath them (9:34, 36–37): a detail reiterated in 9:38–41 and developed in next Sunday's gospel lection.

This Sunday, whichever approach is taken with this lection, our work is cut out for us. Shall we consider with fellow followers our own stupid rejection of Jesus's demonstrations of discipleship? Shall we reexamine the bogus bases of prestige that we or our communities confer on us? Neither prospect is appealing, but neither is surgery nor radiation nor chemotherapy when treating cancer. "The healthy have no need of a physician, but those who are sick. I came to call not the virtuous but sinners" (2:17 AT). If we can look without flinching at the X-ray Scripture affords, we'll find the doctor ready to stand us before him, before taking us in his arms.

19 September 2021

MARK 9:38–50

I hear groans from preachers reading this Sunday's gospel lection. It contains most things that drive the conscientious into a slough of despond: exorcisms (v. 38); multiple disturbances in the Greek text, footnoted in responsible English translations (vv. 42, 44, 45, 46, 49); hard sayings of Jesus (vv. 39–41) that are logically incoherent (vv. 48–50) or manifestly outrageous (vv. 42–47). No brief essay can disentangle all these knots. For that, a reliable commentary is mandatory. Here I can only paraphrase Mark's intent, as best I can, respond to its repugnant aspects, and suggest why I believe such Scripture deserves a hearing from the pulpit.

What Is Mark Driving At?

Mark 9:38–10:31 presents this gospel's most concentrated cluster of moral teaching: vignettes of discipleship expressed within the believing community (9:38–50), the family (10:1–16), and a larger social sphere (10:17–31). This Sunday, Mark considers the church's boundaries and internal responsibilities. The radical character of discipleship is focal, consistent with last Sunday's mandate that each of Jesus's followers become "last of all and servant of all" (9:35).

Mark 9:38–41 encourages a broad-minded attitude toward those who provide relief but operate outside the disciples' circle: "Whoever is not against us is for us" (9:40). Here Jesus commends in strongest terms ("Truly I tell you"; see 3:28; 8:12; 9:1) the reward due anyone who quashes diabolical forces in his name (3:23–27)—whether they are "following us" (9:38: our way of being church) or another who offers a simple cup of water to disciples "because you are Christ's by name" (9:41 AT). Adhering to the spirit of 9:35–37, 9:38–41 stresses gracious reception of *anyone* whose action, bold or modest, genuinely conforms to Jesus's character. If that's something you think your congregants need to hear this Sunday, and no more, I say: Go for it.

> "For whoever offers you a cup of water because you bear Christ's name" (9:41 AT).

> "But whoever trips up one of these little ones who believe" (9:42 AT).

The contrast established in 9:39–41 and 9:42–50 is that between nurturance of Christian believers and infliction of injuries that cause them to lose their faithful footing. The primary meaning of the Greek word σκάνδαλον is a trap for catching a live animal (Josh 23:13; Ps 140:5), which shades into a metaphorical pitfall (Rom 11:9; 1 John 2:10). The cognate verb σκανδαλίζω (NRSV: "put a stumbling block before" [Mark 9:42] or "cause to stumble" [9:43, 45, 47]) conveys the sense of tripping up someone for downfall. While Matthew often employs the term (10:42; 11:11; 18:6, 10, 14), only in 9:42 does Mark use "little ones" (τῶν μικρῶν) to refer to one's fellow believers. It is conceptually related to the child (τὸ παιδίον) who should be received "in my name" (9:36–37). Harming "one of these little ones" invites punishment worse than being hurled into the sea with a huge grinding stone "hung around your neck" (9:42).

In Mark 9:43, 45, and 47, the image of stumbling recurs. Here the self is the apparent victim. Yet the aphorisms' content implies social responsibility: one may trip up oneself through conduct harmful to others. The foot can take you places you dare not go. The hand can reach where it shouldn't. The eye can gaze with malicious intent. A limb's amputation may be required to save the whole body; drastic surgery is necessary in emergencies if one hopes "to enter [eternal] life" (9:43, 45; 10:17) or "the kingdom of God" (9:47). If one suffering gangrene, whether of body or of soul, pretends to have health, the outcome is hell. "Gehenna" (9:43, 45, 47) was a ravine south of Jerusalem notorious for pagan infanticide (2 Chr 28:1–4), envisioned by later Jews as the place of the wicked's final judgment (Luke 12:5). Undying worm and unquenched fire (Mark 9:48) were stock images for the destruction of evil (Isa 66:24; Jdt 16:17). Mark 9:49–50 hearkens back to 8:34–37. "Salt is good": like cross-bearing discipleship, a sacrificial preservative prevents the church from insipidity (9:50a–b; cf. Lev 2:13; Num 18:19). "Salt," self-sacrifice for the gospel, promotes communal peace that quells self-centeredness and one-upmanship (9:50c; 9:33–34, 38).

Why Does Jesus Speak So Grotesquely?

Repeatedly Mark's Jesus heals bodies diseased and deformed (1:31–34, 40–41; 2:1–12; 3:1–6; 5:1–43; 7:31–37; 8:22–26; 10:46–52). Because "he did not speak to them except in parables" (4:33), he cannot be literally advocating self-mutilation in 9:43, 45, or 47. These are stark remarks, intended to grab us by the scruff of the neck and shake us to our senses of the grim consequences that disciples invite when they abuse one another or anyone else. "When you can assume your audience holds the same beliefs you do, you can relax a little and use more normal means of talking to it; when you have to assume that it does not, then you have to make your vision apparent by shock—to the hard of hearing you shout, and for the almost-blind you draw large and startling figures."[11]

Today's preachers might ponder that and, with judiciousness, consider its practice. Shock only for its own sake is juvenile, unbecoming a Christian preacher. But let's face facts. With the exception of the African American church, a lot of contemporary preaching is so anodyne, so colorless, that it may put God to sleep. In Mark 9:42–50 Jesus uses shock treatment to jolt his followers out of smug self-complacency or shameless indecency.

---

11. Flannery O'Connor, *Mystery and Manners: Occasional Prose*, ed. Sally and Robert Fitzgerald (New York: Farrar, Straus & Giroux, 1961), 33–34.

Why Should Scripture Like Mark 9:38–50 Be Preached?

Let's take a hard look at our treatment of little ones who believe in Jesus. Are we supporting them as they totter, or strewing rocks and fences and walls that break them down? Jesus's family is expansive (Mark 3:31–35); the church faces a reckoning. If a bacterial soul isn't disinfected now, its treatment later will be a helluva lot worse.

26 September 2021

MARK 10:17–31

The late Texas governor Ann Richards (1933–2006) once said, "You can put lipstick and earrings on a hog and call it Monique, but it's still a pig."[12]

Read this Sunday's gospel lection. Meet Monique. But make it fast. I'm removing the Estée Lauder and Harry Winstons and going whole hog. It won't be pretty.

Mentioned only four times in this gospel (Mark 9:43, 45; 10:17, 30), "[eternal] life" is not one of Mark's preoccupations, but it overlaps "the kingdom of God" (Mark 9:45; 10:23–25). Nor has the OT much to say about eternal life (Prov 9:6; Job 19:25; Dan 12:2). The concept of indestructible life, transcendent blessedness as God knows it, gathers steam in Jewish literature between the testaments (Wis 5:15; 4 Macc 15:3; Pss. Sol. 3.16). Second Maccabees 7:9 is representative: "The King of the universe will raise us up to an everlasting renewal of life, because we have died for his laws."

Like Mark 10:30, some NT writings distinguish this life from that of future blessing (1 Thess 2:19; 2 Tim 2:10; Rev 20:4–5); for others, the two converge (Col 3:3–4; 1 Tim 6:12, 19; 2 Tim 1:1). Especially in John is the latter true: "Anyone who hears my word and believes him who sent me has eternal life, and . . . has passed from death to life" (John 5:34 and sixteen other verses).

Unlike others in Mark (12:13–15), Jesus's questioner in Mark 10:17 sounds sincere. Even though Jesus rebuffs the compliment (v. 18), "good teacher" seems respectful, not sycophant. There's no reason to suppose this man is disingenuous in claiming that he has kept God's commandments all his life

---

12. "Quotes from Ann Richards," *New York Times*, 14 September 2006.

(v. 20; see Exod 20:12–16 = Deut 5:16–20; Lev 19:3), to which Jesus selectively refers (Mark 10:19).

Jesus regards this fellow lovingly (Mark 10:21a): a unique reaction in this gospel, reminiscent of his embracing little children (Mark 9:36; 10:16). His inquirer's countenance turns to that of "one appalled [στυγνάσας], . . . mournfully [λυπούμενος]" (v. 22a AT). An honest conversation about communal faithfulness instantly turns funereal.

Why? Because the one thing this man lacks is the ability to accept Jesus's directive: to divest his earnings as donations for the poor (v. 21a). Why? This fellow owned a lot (v. 22b). Instead of following Jesus, as invited (v. 21b), he walks away (v. 22a).

Peter insists that the Twelve have done what the rich man could not: they "have left everything and followed" Jesus (v. 28, see Mark 1:16–20). Unlike the disciples' other protests (e.g., Mark 8:32b; 10:13), this one Jesus ratifies. Peter is solemnly assured ("Truly I tell you") that whatever is relinquished "for my sake and for the sake of the good news" (see Mark 8:35) will be munificently reimbursed in kind (Mark 10:29b–30a). Their future recompense will be qualitatively superior: "in the age to come eternal life" (v. 30b)—the very thing Jesus's questioner sought (Mark 10:17).

What is noteworthy in Jesus's pledge of recompence for faithful disciples (Mark 10:29–30)?

- Fulfillment *does* await those who have left all to follow Jesus (also Mark 8:35b; 9:41; 13:13b, 27). Discipleship is hard, but it is not futile.
- Compared to those envisioned elsewhere in Jewish apocalypticism, the rewards promised in Mark are modest, lacking the grandeur of 2 Esdras's seven orders of blessedness (2 Esd 7:88–99) or Matthew's vision of the Twelve enthroned as Israel's judges (Matt 19:28).
- Sacrifices and compensations are *familial*: "house or brothers or sisters or mother or father or children." Those, like the Zebedee brothers (Mark 1:18–20) and Jesus himself (Mark 3:21, 31–33), who have suffered rupture from their families for the gospel's sake, will be reintegrated into other families that dispense with the supposedly indispensable member: a new father. In Jewish and Roman law, extraordinary power was vested in the paterfamilias.[13] In the new family

---

13. In Roman culture, *patria potestas*, paternal power, extended over property and even children's life and death. See Susan Treggiari, *Roman Marriage: Iusti Coniuges from the Time of Cicero to the Time of Ulpian* (Oxford: Clarendon, 1991), 15–16.

promised by Jesus, there is no such figure, because there is no place for such "great ones" who "are tyrants over" others (Mark 10:42–43a; see Matt 23:9).

- While the age to come promises eternal life, in this age, "persecutions" remain among the abundant rewards for sacrificial disciples (Mark 10:30).

Only in Mark 10:24 does Jesus address his disciples as τέκνα: children, like those whose approach to Jesus they had hindered (10:13). Mark asks us to ponder two absurd claims, cheek by jowl:

"Whoever does not receive the kingdom of God as a little child will never enter it." (10:15)

"How hard it will be for those who have wealth to enter the kingdom of God." (10:23)

A child lacks that power of the rich to make things happen. In the subversive economy of God's kingdom, the child's *advantage* is the helplessness to do what only God can do for it (Mark 10:27). While gaining the whole world (Mark 8:36), the man with possessions becomes incapacitated: because *they* possess *him*, he forfeits the eternal life he seeks (Mark 10:17; see Mark 4:18–19).

Only a camel can be threaded through a needle's eye, only the helpless can enter eternal life, because things divine, not human, propel *God's* kingdom (Mark 8:33b): "For mortals it is impossible, but not for God; for God all things are possible" (Mark 10:27). So, it follows: "Many who are first will be last, and the last will be first" (Mark 10:31).

The problem with dismissing Jesus's teaching as utopian is its actual practice in real life. For twenty-nine years, Agnes Gonxha Bojaxhiu (1910–1997) ministered to the poorest of Calcutta's poor. Under a new name, Mother Teresa, she began in 1948 with a one-dollar sari, no funds, and persistent begging for food and medical supplies. By the 1960s, Pope Paul VI gave her a limousine, which she raffled for her Missionaries of Charity. Accepting the Nobel Peace Prize in 1978, she refused its gift and gala, redirecting Oslo's $192,000 to relieve India's poor. When the Nobel Committee asked her what others should do to promote peace, she replied, "Go home and love your family."

Some among your listeners will walk away from this. That happened to Christ. Beside Mark, you speak for those who stake their claim with Mother Teresa: "As to my heart, I belong entirely to the Heart of Jesus."

1 March 2020

MARK 10:32–52

This pericope comprises three interrelated but separable units. All constitute the third revolution of a quadripartite cycle, begun at 8:27–9:1 and repeated in 9:30–37.

Table 7: The Tripartite Structure of Mark 8:27–10:45

Location	Prediction of the Son of Man's Destiny	The Disciples' Misunderstanding	Teaching about Discipleship
Mark 8:27	8:31	8:32–33	8:34–9:1
Mark 9:30	9:31	9:32–34	9:35–37
Mark 10:32	10:33–34	10:35–41	10:42–45

The entire cycle is bookended by Mark's only stories of the healing of the blind (Mark 8:22–26; 10:46–52). That cannot be accidental. As in John 9:1–41, blindness is a metaphor for inability or refusal to acknowledge Jesus for who he truly is; vision, a trope for acceptance of him and of his teaching.

Part 1. Jesus's Third Prediction of His Destiny (vv. 32–34)

"On the road" or "way" (ὁ ὁδός) refers to a path both geographical (Mark 1:2) and theological (1:3). In Mark (3:22; 7:1; 10:33), Jerusalem is a source of hostility; thus, those following Jesus may be "amazed" and "afraid." Of the three prophecies in this central Markan cycle, Mark 10:33–34 is the most detailed: an epitome of the passion narrative (chapters 14–16). Compared with Mark 8:31 and 9:31, Mark 10:33–34 draws out the collusion between Jewish and gentile authorities and catalogs the Son of Man's abuse before his death and resurrection.

Part 2. Discipleship Bogus and Bona Fide (vv. 35–45)

Mark's implied motto for the Twelve is "If at first you don't perceive, fail, fail again." In Mark 8:32–33, Peter rebuked Jesus's teaching; in turn, he was rebuked as "Satan," diverting his teacher from the way that must be trod. In Mark 9:33–34, the Twelve bickered over rank. In Mark 10:35–37, James and John's insinuation with Jesus is multiply inappropriate.

- Their plea is unqualified (v. 35), detached from faithful prayer upon which Jesus insists (Mark 9:29; 11:22–25) and inconsistent with the attitude of others who seek his help (2:5; 5:34; 9:23–24).

- This is a flagrant petition for patronage, which Jesus has granted nowhere in Mark.
- A request to be seated on either side of Jesus "in [his] glory" (Mark 10:37) disregards everything he has emphasized in the Son of Man's destiny to suffer (8:31; 9:31; 10:33–34).
- By paraphrasing Herod's disastrous impetuosity to Herodias's daughter (Mark 6:22–23), the Zebedees ape the way this world's rulers throw their weight around (see also 10:42). Worse, they appeal for places of supreme honor—"at your right hand"—to which only the LORD's regents are entitled (Ps 110:1; Mark 14:62).
- Those positions on Jesus's "right and left" will soon be assumed by faithless rebels crucified with Jesus (Mark 15:27, 32) after the Twelve have vamoosed (14:27, 50–52).

Repudiating Jesus as the suffering Son of Man, the Twelve continue to jockey for his favoritism.

Putting matters mildly, Jesus replies that they know not what they ask (Mark 10:38a). He inquires of their ability "to drink the cup that I drink, or be baptized with the baptism that I am baptized with" (Mark 10:38b). In Scripture, a "cup" may symbolize either joyful salvation (Pss 23:5; 116:13) or woebegone judgment (Ps 11:6; Isa 51:17).

Very early, both baptism and the Lord's Supper were interpreted as participation with Jesus in his death (Rom 6:3–4; 1 Cor 11:25–26). The wires are crossed: salivating over blessings that accompany exaltation with Jesus in glory (Mark 10:37), James and John assert their capability (v. 39a). Jesus refers to a cup and a baptism with baleful consequences (v. 38; see also Mark 9:12–13; 14:38). He does not deny for his followers suffering for the gospel's sake, like Jesus's own (10:39b; 8:34–35; 13:9–23). What he refuses them are places of honor. These are not his to grant; they are God's prerogatives (10:40). To the very end, Jesus refuses any authority not consigned to him by God (Mark 9:37b; 12:6–7; 14:21a), whose will is absolutely final (3:35; 10:6–9; 12:17a; 14:36).

Predictably, the others in Jesus's entourage take umbrage at the Zebedees' maneuvering (Mark 10:41). He reunites all Twelve for teaching about authentic discipleship (vv. 42–45). This world's construction of authority, which James and John have projected onto the end time (v. 37), is altogether fallacious. Status relations determined by the Son of Man upend conventional expectations (v. 43). In Mark 9:36–37, the "servant" is aligned with "a little child." In Mark 10:44, the "servant" slides into "everyone's slave" (πάντων δοῦλος): a self-derogation even more offensive.

Although slavery in antiquity carried varied connotations, it was generally considered a miserable form of life. In Mark 10:44, the status of slavery has become radically *normative* for Jesus's disciples, because the Son of Man came not to be served but to serve. Jesus is not a new master. Instead, as "a ransom [λύτρον] for many," he releases others from their enslavement (Mark 10:45; see also Mark 14:24; Exod 21:30; Lev 25:47–52; Num 3:44–51).

Part 3. Bartimaeus (vv. 46–52)

At Jericho, twenty miles northeast of Jerusalem, Jesus encounters Bartimaeus, blind and begging (v. 46; certainly not "lording it over" anyone [v. 42]). Repeatedly he cries out, "Jesus, Son of David, have mercy on me" (Mark 10:47–48). David was considered the LORD's special regent (2 Sam 7:4–17; Ps 89:3–4); therapeutic powers were associated with David's son (Matt 9:27–31; 12:22–23).

Mark adroitly remodels a miracle story into a vignette of discipleship. The crowd's stern rebuke (ἐπετίμων) of the needy (Mark 10:48a) is a flashback to the disciples' rebuke (ἐπετίμησαν) of little children (10:13); now as then Jesus insists on receiving a needy petitioner (vv. 14, 49). "Throwing off his cloak" (v. 50a) recalls those encumbrances that Jesus's disciples should shed (6:8–9; 13:16).

Jesus's question to Bartimaeus (Mark 10:51a) is identical to that which he asked James and John (v. 36). They blindly plumped for glory (v. 37); Bartimaeus insightfully pleads, "My teacher, let me see again" (v. 51). Unlike the Twelve (vv. 38a, 41), this fellow knows what he is asking; his appeal springs from restorative faith, as Jesus acknowledges (v. 52a). Bartimaeus's request is immediately fulfilled: he regains sight (10:52b). He moves from the wayside (v. 46b) *onto* "the way," following Jesus (v. 52b): Mark's capsule metaphor for discipleship (1:18; 2:14; 8:34; 10:21; 15:41).

The sightless see; the sighted are blind (see also John 9:39). This is a hard saying. Who can listen to it?

8 March 2020

More Marklarkey:
Or, A Funny Thing Happened on the Way to the Temple

In a previous essay (13 September 2010), I proposed that the Second Evangelist may be the NT's unsung comedian. Exhibit A of my case was Mark 4:1–34: a collection of Jesus's teaching in parables. I've intended to try sneaking another essay in this vein before now, but I've been laughing too hard.

So let's consider another example: Mark 11:1–11, the classic lection for Palm Sunday. What some preachers may not appreciate, and no parishioner could be expected to know, is that underlying this text is a type-scene common in antiquity: "Hail the conquering hero." First Maccabees 5:45–54 recounts such a story with a straight face: the return of Judas Maccabeus to Israel following a triumphant massacre. In ancient Jewish literature, the details vary, but the format is predictable. Amid cheering throngs, a military victor enters a city and offers thanksgiving at a religious shrine. This kind of tale was as familiar to Mark's audience as our sagas of the two-fisted marshal who canters into Tombstone, outdraws Bad Brad on Main Street, and strides into the saloon for a shot of rotgut.

Mark 11:1–11 twists the Maccabeus story into a pretzel. There's no blood on Jesus's sword. (He doesn't carry one.) Jesus rides in not on Champion the Wonder Horse but on somebody's ass. The crowds do not hail him as "the Son of David" (Matt 21:9), "the King who comes in the Lord's name" (Luke 19:38a), or even "the King of Israel" (John 12:13). Mark plays his trump card at the story's end, when we expect our hero to do something dramatic. It's time for the general to head for the shrine and offer sacrificial thanks to God for having slaughtered hundreds. Not in Mark 11:11. "Then he entered Jerusalem"—that's right—"and went into the temple"—here it comes—"and when he had looked around at everything, as it was already late, he went out to Bethany with the Twelve." *What?*

Get the picture? We expect Jesus to march into the house of the Lord and do the religious thing. What we get is Jesus the tourist, looking the place over. Well, it's late. Let's pack it in, fellows. What would the Twelve make of that? How about the exuberant multitudes? Do they pick up their garments and leafy branches with a shrug? "I guess the party's over."

The entertainment, such as it is, is postponed until tomorrow (Mark 11:12). Even then, however, people won't get what they anticipate (vv. 13–19). Jesus curses a fruitless fig tree out of season—in itself pretty zany—then returns to the temple, where he does something other than we expect of Commander Pious. Mark, I am sure, knows exactly what he's doing. He leads readers through all the clichés up to the great climax, before pulling the rug out from under us.

As we pick ourselves up, wondering where the denouement went, Mark flips the story again with Jesus the Mad Horticulturalist. And while we're trying to figure *that* out, there's the final fillip: Jesus not only turns the tables on legitimate money changers and religious vendors but also "would not allow anyone to carry anything through the temple" (v. 16). Jesus is not there to offer any sacrifice. Moreover, he won't allow anyone else to do so. The fig tree isn't feeling well, either (v. 20).

Were this story less familiar, we might suppose we had wandered into Monty Python. If you know what the evangelist is lampooning—even if you don't, but are willing to read it with a sense of humor—Mark 11:1-11 frolics in one non sequitur after another. The comedy is there not for its own sake but to lower our defenses long enough for the truth to get through. This Jesus, whom we think we know, is not your everyday liberator. He doesn't act the way he's supposed to. Judge him by ordinary conventions of what God's anointed should be and do, and you will get him wrong every time. The joke is on us.

For this we may thank God: If ever we managed to pen Christ in, there would be no gospel, only the stale clichés with which we keep trying to build a sermon or a life. Mark's genius lies in conveying good news in a way that doesn't merely say that. We *experience* it—laughing all the way into God's upending grace. Does this teach us anything about the craft of preaching?

13 September 2010

Mark 11:1-11 and Mark 14:3-9

Familiarity breeds complacency: the challenge facing the preacher this Sunday.

If we read Mark carefully, the evangelist himself restores to these texts a sense of mystery and surprise.

Jesus's entrance to Jerusalem (Mark 11:1-11) seems straightforward, but the evangelist implants some twists. The significance of securing "a colt that has never been ridden" (11:2) is obscure. A young donkey suggests a humble king's conveyance (Zech 9:9); its never having been ridden is reminiscent of unyoked beasts consecrated for God (Num 19:2). Congruent with Samuel's commission for a pair of asses to confirm Saul's anointing as "ruler over his people Israel" (1 Sam 10:1-8), Mark 11:2-4 suggests an acknowledgment of Jesus's authority and prophetic prescience. In verses 3-6, all unfolds as Jesus predicted. When Israel's hidden Messiah enters the royal city, he does so in a manner no one would expect unless they were tuned into a particular scriptural frequency. Apart from that, a simple act is clothed in secrecy.

A family of ancient Jewish stories details the arrival of a heroic figure following military victory (1 Macc 4:19-25; 5:45-54; 13:43-51). Details vary, but the format is the same: after conquest, a military champion enters a city, joyously acclaimed, then offers cultic thanksgiving. This Messiah's entry to Jerusalem warps this pattern. In place of military conquest is Jesus's ministry of peace (Mark 4:39; 5:34; 9:50). While a festive aura surrounds the spreading of cloaks and branches (11:8; cf. 2 Kgs 9:13; 2 Macc 10:7), in this gospel no adulation is heaped upon Jesus himself (cf. Matt 21:9; Luke 19:38; John 12:13b). In Mark 11:10, the object of praise is general: "Blessed is the coming kingdom of our ancestor David"—a kingdom Jesus has proclaimed without bellicose connotations (Mark 1:15; 4:11, 26, 30). The sucker punch lands in Mark 11:11: instead of performing a customary ritual, Jesus strolls around the temple but does nothing more than "look around at everything" before exiting. Far from flexing his royal muscles, Jesus plays sightseer. On close inspection, Mark has not narrated a "triumphal entry"; he has lampooned it. Such narrative subversions match the character of the gospel Jesus preaches (10:13–31, 42–45). God's reign is erupting with Jesus as its matchless vanguard—but neither that kingdom nor its Christ is at all what we expected.

More surprises pop from the tale of *Jesus's anointing (Mark 14:3–9)* in Bethany, two miles southeast of Jerusalem (John 11:18). As in the present day, benefaction in antiquity was publicly venerated. Rare is the philanthropist who refuses credit for the foundation she has established or for the buildings he has funded. Mark 14:3–9 upsets the way its listeners evaluate fame. Bethany's most generous of women is forever remembered, although she remains anonymous. She was an object of scorn not because she was presumed louche (cf. Luke 7:37) but because of the wealth her onlookers believed her to have squandered (Mark 14:4–5). The estimated value of her balm would have covered a day laborer's wages for nearly a full year. Defending the woman's gift, Jesus interprets all she has done for him: anticipating his burial (14:8), a beautiful thing (14:6) that will endure in memory (14:9).

Neither here nor in Mark 10:21 does Jesus dismiss the needy poor (cf. Deut 15:7–11; Ps 82:3–4; Jas 2:5–6). He qualifies that imperative by coordinating its practice to primary recognition of himself as the kingdom's herald in a unique time: "You will not always have me" (Mark 14:7). Every moral injunction in this gospel is subject to deeper penetration of God's intent (Mark 3:1–6; 7:1–13; 10:2–9). It is fitting that the bridegroom be so honored, for he is soon to be taken away (Mark 2:18–22). The horrible irony is that Jesus's anointing is embedded inside a conspiracy for his arrest (Mark 14:1–2, 10–11). At the very moment that Jesus commends this female disciple, reproached for her extraordinary generosity, one of the Twelve is bribed into a murderous plot against his teacher that delights his conspirators. She is embalming the body that Judas will deliver.

The woman in Mark 14:3–9 is a spiritual sister of the nameless widow in 12:41–44, who "put in more than all [others] contributing; . . . out of her poverty [she] put in everything she had, all she had to live on." Not merely are both incredibly benevolent. The causes to which they committed themselves—Jerusalem's temple and God's Messiah—will soon appear irretrievably lost (13:1–2; 14:8; 15:37). Nor is there the slightest indication that either woman is conscious of the full import of her donation. Both have done what they could (14:8); in both cases, only Jesus can assay the gift's genuine value and interpret it for his followers.

So it goes in this gospel. "What are you [disciples] doing?" (Mark 11:5). "Why was the ointment wasted in this way?" (14:4). In Bethany, as in Jerusalem, "they may indeed look, but not perceive, and may indeed listen, but not understand" (4:12). The throngs who shout "Hosanna" ("Lord, save") and "Blessed" (11:9–10) are the same that, in a matter of days, will cry for crucifixion of the one who has come in the Lord's name (15:13–14). Though we never learn the name of the woman who did for him "what she could," Jesus declares that what she has done will be remembered wherever the gospel is preached (14:9). Thanks to Mark, it has been. Judas also did what he could. For that, neither has he ever been forgotten.

20 March 2016

MARK 14:22–42

Jesus's fidelity and the Twelve's faltering: these cables bind the Last Supper and Gethsemane in Mark.

In a large upper room (Mark 14:22–31): Previously Jesus presided over two other banquets during which he "took, blessed, broke, and gave bread" (6:31–44; 8:1–10), anticipating a messianic banquet envisioned in the age to come (Isa 25:6–8; Matt 22:1–4). What he has done for the multitudes he now does for the Twelve—with important differences. In Mark 14:22, Jesus identifies a loaf with his own body. σῶμα is a flexible metaphor: "my personality" or "my essential selfhood" may capture some nuances here (cf. 1 Cor 10:17). Previously Jesus spoke of his self-sacrifice for many (Mark 10:45). Here it is reiterated for his followers' sake.

Predictably at Passover, Jesus gives thanks over a cup and gives it to all his companions (Mark 14:23). Unpredictably he associates its contents with "my blood of the covenant, which is poured out for many" (14:24): a reminder of Jesus's description of the Son of Man's service as a self-sacrifice for others' freedom (10:45). Jesus's blood, a proxy for Israel's life (cf. Lev 16:1–34), is implicitly correlated with the Passover sacrifice (cf. 1 Cor 5:7). His sacrifice is "poured out" just as the woman in Bethany lavished on Jesus her fragrant ointment (Mark 14:3).

Bookending these explanations are Jesus's final predictions of the Twelve's desertion (Mark 14:17–21, 27–31; cf. 9:42–47). All his closest followers will "stumble" or "fall away" (cf. Zech 13:7), just as the rootless fold under pressure (Mark 4:17) and his countrymen have stumbled over him (6:3). Twice Peter repudiates Jesus's prediction of his threefold defection before the cock has twice crowed that very night (14:29–31a). Peter's peers also defy this prophecy (14:31). Jesus holds fast to his forecast, promising his own postmortem fidelity in Galilee (14:28). The mind reels at the interlocking ironies: Jesus's injunction that his followers must deny themselves (8:34); their reckless refutation of their imminent denials of Jesus; Jesus's denial of himself—the giving of his life—out of enduring loyalty to those who will presently prove traitorous.

The scene shifts to *Gethsemane (Mark 14:32–42)*. Throughout Mark, Jesus is presented as a man of prayer (1:35; 6:41; 8:6; 11:23–25; 13:18); neither in 14:32–42 nor anywhere else does the evangelist show the Twelve praying. Jesus invites Peter, James, and John (cf. 5:37; 9:2; 13:3) to remain with him, "to stay awake" (14:33–34), just as he exhorted them during a previous visit to Olivet (13:33, 35, 37). Rabbi Akiba was remembered as teaching, "Chastisements are precious" (b. Sanh. 101a); Jewish history is filled with stories of heroic martyrdoms (among others, 4 Macc 10:8–11). By contrast, Mark 14:32–42 renders with harsh clarity this critical hour (14:35, 37, 41; cf. 13:32) in Jesus's faith—"distressed and agitated," "deeply grieved" (14:33–34), reminders of earlier stories that presented tormented humanity's need for faith (5:32–36; 9:24). "For you all things are possible" (14:36a): a reminder of Jesus's teaching to the epileptic child's father (9:23) and to the Twelve (10:27; 11:23). "Remove this cup from me" (14:36b) evokes the cup from which Jesus must drink (10:38). "Yet, not what I want, but what you want" (14:36c): God's will must finally override all others' (11:22, 24). Jesus repeats this prayer (14:39, 41). Gethsemane is a rehearsal for Golgotha, where, wretched and isolated, Jesus cries out to an intimate yet distant "Abba, Father" (14:36), "My God, my God" (15:34). These are the only times in Mark we are privy to the content of Jesus's prayers.

Three times Jesus returns to a waiting trio. Each time, he finds them asleep (Mark 14:37a, 40a, 41a) when they ought to have been watchful in "the time of trial" (14:37–38a; cf. 13:33–37). An eager spirit, which Peter has expressed (14:29), is no match for human frailty ("the flesh"), starved of prayer (14:38b). On his final return, Jesus announces that "the hour" has arrived for the Son of Man's ultimate betrayal (14:41–42). Another premonition of Golgotha: in the persons of Peter, James, and John, the Twelve have begun falling away from their teacher, just as he foretold (14:27; cf. 14:50–52).

Mark 14:22–42 encapsulates much of this gospel's theology. *Theologically*, as conveyed through Scripture, all proceeds as required by God's ordination (14:27). *Christologically*, Jesus reveals himself perfectly prescient and aligned with that plan (14:22–24, 27, 30, 36). *Soteriologically*, the goal of Jesus's self-sacrifice is a liberating atonement for sin (14:24). *Ecclesially*, Jesus's adherents prove themselves unreliable. Though they bluster (14:29, 31), after having conspired to betray him outright (14:10–11, 17–21), neither here nor elsewhere does Jesus's fidelity to his followers depend on their faithfulness to him (14:28; cf. 16:7). *Eschatologically*, Jesus's reminder at supper of the kingdom of God (14:25)—the heart of his preaching in Mark (1:14–15; 4:11, 26–32; 10:14–25)—casts events to come in an apocalyptic context (cf. 13:1–37).

While the preacher may legitimately pursue any of these trails, the juxtaposition of Mark 14:22–31 with 14:32–42 grabs my attention at one particular point: on the night of his betrayal, Jesus proved himself the faithful disciple that none of his own disciples could be. At supper, he made good on his repeated promises to be the cross-bearing Son of Man (8:31; 9:31; 10:33–34); by offering his body and blood in the kingdom's covenant, he did for the many what Paul realized personally: "[Christ] loved me and gave himself for me" (Gal 2:20). At Gethsemane, he demonstrated the disciple's appropriate response to suffering: faith, expressed in prayer, which penetrates anguish. As obedient as he was beloved, Jesus was the complete servant of God's will (Mark 14:36), which all his disciples proved themselves incapable of obeying (9:33–37). Jesus became the little child able to enter the kingdom (10:13–16). Only by doing so could his life be made whole, and ours as well (8:34–38). At Mark 14:22–42, a sleeping church is reawakened to its lesson at Caesarea Philippi (8:33–38): self-sacrifice for the gospel's sake defines discipleship to Jesus Christ, from whom the cup could not pass and who finally wanted it no other way.

24 March 2016

Mark 15:16–39

Unvarnished and raw: that's how Mark recounts Jesus's death. More than any other evangelist, Mark drives the church into the heart of its gospel in all its horror and wonder. Every temptation to prettify it should be resisted.

Attraction to Jesus is hyperbolic in Mark (1:28, 45; 3:7–8); 15:16–20 reverses the polarity by spotlighting a huge gang's enmity. Easy on the sadism, Mark magnifies Jesus's humiliation: draped in royal purple, crowned with thorns (15:17) with the reed as a faux scepter (15:19), and a faithless "Hail [to] the King of the Jews" (15:18). "Bending [of] their knees" (15:19 AT) compounds their sarcasm. Here we have the photographic negative of Paul's hymn to Christ (Phil 2:5–11), whose last stanza thunders Christ's exaltation, with every knee bowed and every tongue confessing. Mark recasts that image in a stridently minor key, accenting the Messiah's descent into shameful self-abasement.

Golgotha (Mark 15:21–32) answers Jerusalem (11:1–11). When Jesus entered David's city, the cry was "Hosanna," "Lord, save" (11:9–10). He exits to a very different cry—"Crucify" (15:13–14)—and the one most obviously needing salvation is Jesus himself. After Peter refused the Son of Man's ordained suffering and death (8:31–32), the teacher insisted that those coming after him "take up their cross and follow me" (8:34); in 15:21, Simon of Cyrene does as Simon Peter was instructed. Previously in Mark (14:3, 8), a myrrh-like ointment was a perfume, associated by Jesus with his death. At his crucifixion, myrrh is offered to him mixed with wine (15:23b), probably as a painkiller (Prov 31:6). Jesus's refusal of it has been foreshadowed: he has chosen a different cup (10:38b).

"It was nine o'clock in the morning when they *crucify* him": the Greek historical present tense places us smack at the scene of Jesus's impaling onto a stake and crossbar. The evangelist omits all the gruesome details of harrowing death by crucifixion. Instead, he encourages readers to listen for the event's biblical resonances, "how then is it written about the Son of Man" (Mark 9:12). Psalm 22 provides the soundtrack for Mark's portrayal of Jesus's death (note the paraphrases of Ps 22:7 and 22:18 with Mark 15:24 and 15:29a). Scripturally disclosed, all proceeds in accordance with God's will.

The placard worn by the victim points up the political aspect of Jesus's death: he was executed for sedition, as "the King of the Jews" (Mark 15:26; cf. 15:2, 9, 12, 18). For Mark, this is socially preposterous (14:48) yet religiously valid (12:35–37). On either side of Jesus, two genuine malefactors are executed (15:28), mirroring the sons of Zebedee who had requested seats "one at your right hand and one at your left" (10:35–37). Jesus replied that his disciples didn't know what they were asking (10:38). Now the reader understands that answer's import.

In contrast with Luke (23:39–43) and John (19:25–27), in Mark *everyone* ridicules the crucified Jesus: random bystanders (15:29), the chief priests (15:31), even those crucified with him (15:32b). "The destroyer of the temple and its rebuilder in three days" (15:29b) recalls the spurious charge against Jesus before the Sanhedrin (14:57–59). "Having come down from the cross, save yourself"

(15:30) perverts Jesus's requirement that his disciple take up the cross and relinquish life for the gospel (8:34–35). "He saved others; he cannot save himself" (15:31) stupidly paraphrases Jesus's interpretation of the Son of Man's own duty (10:45). The challenge, "Let [him] come down from the cross now, so that we may see and believe," reverses the sequence of faith and mighty works in this gospel, wherein faith has proved the condition of restoration, not its outcome (2:5; 5:34, 36; 6:5–6a). Amid all this irony, Mark's emphasis remains transparent: Jesus has been abandoned, bereft of consolation. To die crucified, *altogether alone*, is a vision of hell.

At high noon (Mark 15:33), "darkness came over the whole land": an apocalyptic image of divine judgment and human mourning (Amos 8:9–10). At three in the afternoon (Mark 15:34), Jesus howls in distress. His last articulate words are scriptural (Ps 22:1–2): Jesus stares into God's veiled face and asks why ελωι ελωι, "My God, my God," has left him in the lurch. The beloved Son (Mark 1:11; 9:7) persists in praying to the God who, like everyone else, has evidently deserted him. His audience misunderstands this as a cry to Ἠλίας, Elijah, protector of the tormented righteous. By offering refreshment to Jesus on the chance that Elijah may rescue him (15:36), this faithless generation still seeks a sign (8:11–12). During his life, few have understood Jesus (4:12; 8:14–21); at the moment of his death, their foolishness persists. With a second shriek, Jesus dies.

Two reactions are narrated; Mark offers us clear interpretation of neither. The rending of the temple curtain (Mark 15:38) suggests divine agency of cultic destruction (cf. 1:10; 13:1–2). *God is present yet remains hidden.* A "sign from heaven" has been granted, which no one, save the reader, has witnessed. At 15:39, for the first and only time in Mark, a mortal correctly identifies Jesus as "God's Son." Whether the legionnaire believes what he says is irresolvable and ultimately inconsequential. The reader who faithfully accepts the Son of Man's self-assessment (8:31; 10:45) can judge the accuracy of the centurion's verdict and the basis on which it is reached: no miracle of any kind (contrast Matt 27:54), only direct confrontation of one who has thus died (15:39).

So densely layered is Mark 15:16–39 that the preacher should beware of attempting too much in a single sermon. Choices must be made. This, however, cannot be disregarded: Jesus is remembered as *Christ crucified*. His death was no accident; nor did he live to a ripe old age. He was executed by the most barbarous means his contemporaries could devise. It was this, yoked to the confession of Jesus as Messiah, that Paul acknowledged as scandalous for Jews and moronic to gentiles (1 Cor 1:23). That scandal endures. The church dare not forget it.

25 March 2016

MARK 16:1–8

"They said nothing to nobody—they were afraid, you see."

That's a fairly literal, inelegant English rendering of Mark 16:8. Could the evangelist have ended his gospel like this? What kind of victor is vindicated from death, yet no one gets to see it? You might as well ask, What kind of Messiah dies crucified? (15:16–39).

Although various manuscripts add endings to Mark (including 16:9–20, best known from the KJV), there's no question that our earliest Greek texts of this gospel end at 16:8. Did the author continue beyond 16:8 with an ending that was lost? Did he intend something beyond 16:8 but was prevented from writing it? Neither alternative is impossible, but both are speculative: they lack any biblical or traditional basis for verification. Is it preposterous that Mark deliberately ended his gospel at 16:8? Some think so. I think not.

Visiting the tomb at dawn after the Sabbath (Mark 16:1) is the same female trio who beheld Jesus's crucifixion and death at a distance (15:40). Two witnessed his burial (15:47). Long after the Twelve fled the scene (14:50, 72), these are among many women who followed and ministered to Jesus (15:41). Though well intentioned, the mission of these three is superfluous and futile: Bethany's anonymous female benefactor has already anointed their teacher's body for burial (14:3–9). Soon we shall learn that the tomb is empty.

Mark 16:3–4 refers to the stone-stopper Joseph of Arimathea used to seal the tomb (15:46). Elsewhere in this gospel, "looking up" (ἀναβλέπω) describes Jesus's regard of heaven before performing mighty works (6:41; 7:34) and restoration of sight after two blind men have encountered him (8:24; 10:51–52). The verb "behold" (θεωρέω) connotes wondrous apprehension (3:11; 5:15, 38; 12:41). The stone's removal from the tomb's mouth is expressed with a verb conjugated in the passive voice: its unseen mover must have been God, "for this was a very big rock" (16:4b).

The stage is set for a revelation, but Mark's description (16:5) is more restrained than that of Luke (24:4), John (20:12), and especially Matthew (28:2–4). "Sitting on the right side" was favored in antiquity (Mark 10:37, 40), especially if seated beside the right hand of power (1 Kgs 2:19; Ps 110:1; Mark 12:36; 14:62). Other than Jesus at his transfiguration (9:3), this "young man" is the only character in Mark who wears white, the color of apocalyptic glorification (Dan 7:9; 12:3; Matt 13:43; Rev 7:9, 13). Mark foregoes supernatural pyrotechnics, but this vision is enough to leave the tomb's visitors flabbergasted.

The declaration to the women—and, this day, to us—contains four important elements.

- "Don't be alarmed."
- "You are looking for [ζητεῖτε]." Repeatedly in Mark (11:18; 12:12; 14:1, 55), those searching for Jesus are up to no good. While intending nothing ill, these women, like others (3:21, 32; 8:11–13), have mistaken what they found because of what they were looking for: a dead Jew instead of a living Messiah.
- Because of God's direct intervention, "Jesus, the Nazarene [1:24; 10:47; 14:67], the one crucified, has been raised," no longer in the place where they laid him. This is one of the NT's primary claims (Acts 4:10; Rom 4:24; 1 Cor 15:3–4; 2 Tim 2:8).
- The women are entrusted with a message for his disciples, among whom Peter is singled out (cf. Mark 14:66–72). The risen Jesus has gone before them to Galilee, where he awaits. Again, as throughout this gospel (6:45; 10:32), Jesus is in the lead, and others must hurry to catch up. The return to Galilee indicates a fresh start, for it was there that Mark's narrative began (1:14). Jesus will appear to his disciples: alongside the resurrection itself, the other basic Easter confession (John 21:14; Acts 2:32; 1 Cor 15:5–8). This announcement is "just as he said" (to the Twelve at their last supper: Mark 14:28). At the empty tomb, two promises of fidelity are validated: God's final vindication of Jesus, and Jesus's continuing dedication to his disciples.

A final, ironic twist: the women flee the tomb, tremulous and bewildered (Mark 16:8). They who had followed Jesus longer than all others fall short from fear, as Jesus's disciples have typically done (4:40–41). The time has now come to speak in faith (cf. 8:29–30; 9:9)—and the proclaimers are muted by fear.

Mark's Gospel ends with a mysterious confirmation that God and Jesus have kept faith and have done just what they promised (16:6–7; cf. 8:31; 9:31; 10:33–34; 14:28). For this gospel to have ended on another's triumphant flourish would have undermined everything this evangelist has said about God's kingdom, its Christ, and his subjects. Mark is a book about God's shattering of human expectations. Mark *as* a book shatters everything its readers thought it understood—even the conventions of how a gospel should end. "The good news must be preached to all nations" (13:10): if Jesus commanded that, then it shall happen. But when it does, it is likely to occur as much *in spite of* his disciples as because of them. Reaching into Gen 17–18, Paul articulates what Mark's narrative suggests: a summons to "[trust] in God, who makes the dead live and calls things that are not into things that are" (Rom 4:17)—both life and speech.

Back to the beginning are sent the women and Peter and the disciples and all of us on Easter Sunday. We start anew, follow Jesus to the end, then repeat

419

over and again a process by which imperfect disciples are being reformed. Mark has tailored his entire gospel into a parable: a testimony of good news that perplexes and provokes us in the same way Jesus does by deed and word. The evangelist offers us that message, for delivery to others this Easter Sunday. With Jesus, the crucified-risen Christ, God's kingdom has secretly exploded into this world. No matter how often we fall off, we ride that missile of salvation, inviting others aboard to hold on tight.

27 March 2016

CHAPTER 17

Ministry in Mystery: One Evangelist's Vision

I'm going to speak my mind because I have nothing to lose.

—S. I. Hayakawa

THE LATE JOSEPH SITTLER, Lutheran theologian and preacher, reported his mother's frustration with the sometimes arrogant clericalism of the town in which he grew up. Once, a district president, a particularly pompous man, came to preach at a conference. It was Sittler's turn to babysit with their large family so that his mother could go to church. When she returned, young Sittler asked, "What did he say?" She replied, "Nothing—for thirty minutes."[1]

With that anecdote ominously in mind, I was readying myself to address a group of visiting clergy. As part of my preparation, I had conferred with various acquaintances engaged in pastoral ministry. The last consultation was the most difficult. The connection was garbled, the narration roundabout, but, as best I could, I listened as a pastor spoke of his congregation, a minnow in an urban ocean. Of suffering, death, even despair, its members had received their portion. The survivors had been left wondering whether the battle was worth the fighting.

Though understandably reticent to rehearse fine details, the minister described the tearful joy of faith, the fragile resilience of hope, the painful fidelity to Christ under circumstances at worst grim, at best ambiguous. As with most of our stories, his did not so much conclude as simply end, straining for a resolution yet to come. He assured me that God remains at work, despite all

---

Originally delivered at an alumni luncheon during Ministers' Week, Perkins School of Theology, Southern Methodist University, February 1990.

1. *The Eloquence of Grace: Joseph Sittler and the Preaching Life*, ed. James M. Childs Jr. and Richard Lischer, IPS (Eugene, OR: Wipf & Stock, 2012), 97.

appearances to the contrary, and that our mission is wrapped in riddle, our ministry cloaked in mystery. This message, from the evangelist Mark, I relayed to my audience.

Mark is not a book ordinarily associated with guidelines for ministry. Unlike the forthright statements about pastor-parish relations in 1 and 2 Corinthians, the Second Evangelist and his congregation stand offstage, hidden almost entirely in the shadows. Unlike the first Christian missionaries, whose rousing adventures are recounted in the Acts of the Apostles, Mark's prototypical pastors, the Twelve, emerge for many readers as certifiable chowderheads who sink into an ever-thickening morass of misunderstanding and betrayal.

And yet, as this evangelist repeatedly emphasizes, appearances may mislead, if not outrightly deceive. To ponder Mark and ministry at a level so superficial is like gauging a woman's interest in horticulture by her careful selection of roses for her husband's funeral. In biblical interpretation, as in pastoral care, there are texts and subtexts. For those with ears to hear, some silences scream.

Certain knowledge of the undercurrents that flow beneath Mark's Gospel is unattainable. That evangelist never identifies where he is writing, or for whom. The original readers did not need to be told. Various scraps of information both within the gospel and in patristic testimony seem to point to Rome, in the middle of the first century, when a conflagration had consumed much of the imperial capital.[2] Rumors were rife that the emperor himself had ordered it, to enlarge his palace complex:

> Therefore, to scotch the rumor, Nero substituted as culprits, and punished with the utmost exquisite cruelty, a class loathed for their abominations, whom the crowd styled Christians. . . . Accordingly, arrest was first made of those who confessed [to being Christians]; next, on their disclosures, vast numbers were convicted, not so much on the count of arson as for hatred of the human race. Every sort of derision was added to their deaths: they were wrapped in wild beasts' skins and dismembered by dogs; or they were fastened on crosses, and, when daylight failed were burned to serve as lamps by night. (*Ann.* 15.44)

When we place our ears to the pages of Mark's Gospel, can we hear the cries in the darkest night? Can we taste the tears?

---

2. See chapter 1 and note its cautions that, while genuine persecution of Roman Christians lurks in Mark's background, specific connections with a *particular* imperial event or amalgam of events are considerably more speculative than my own ruminations here suggest.

Had I been the pastor in such a situation, I do not know how I would have responded. I know I would not have exercised the pastoral sensitivity and theological insight demonstrated by this evangelist. I would have been tempted to fog the circumstances with bromides. "Tough times never last." "Something good is going to happen to you." In its Grammy award-winning expression (1988), "Don't Worry, Be Happy." In short, I could have easily lied to that church about the very reality confronting it.

Mark refused this gambit. Instead, he told the truth as he understood it: "Look: we are going up to Jerusalem, and the Son of Man will be handed over to the tall-steeple preachers and the biblical scholars, and they will condemn him to death; then they will hand him over to non-Christians; they will mock him, and spit on him, and whip him, and kill him; and after three days he will rise again" (10:33–34 AT). For a beleaguered community, Mark did not deflect pain but seized it with both hands, boldly proclaiming that, even as the Messiah can never be understood apart from his crucifixion, so, too, the cross stands not on the periphery of Christian experience but squarely at its center.

Had I been the pastor of Mark's congregation, I would have been tempted to reduce the issues to their purely personal or political dimensions. I could have designed a series of sermons called "Why Bad Things Happen to Good People" or "When You Feel Punished by a Loving and Righteous God" or "Ten Demands for Peace with Justice That Caesar Must Meet." I easily could have diminished those issues by distorting their significance. Instead, Mark kept his vision steadily on the larger theological ramifications of the crisis before him, and their implications for disciples of Jesus: "If any want to become my followers, let them deny themselves and take up their cross and follow me. For those who want to save their life will lose it, and those who lose their life for my sake, and for the sake of the gospel, will save it" (8:34–35 NRSV). Mark neither denied the injustice of their plight, their hunger for status and power, nor did he magnify it beyond proper proportion. He dared to transmute rejection and suffering as the inevitable outcome and authentication of service in Jesus's name.

Had I been the pastor of Mark's congregation, I would have been tempted to an ecclesial amnesia, seduced by fashion and fad from recognizing and appropriating the fundamentals of Christian faith. Instead, Mark realigned his community's sights christologically by focusing on "the beginning of the good news of Jesus Christ, the Son of God" (1:1). Mark's Gospel is nothing less than a narrative meditation on the ancient hymnic and creedal affirmations known to us from Paul's letters: concerning Christ Jesus, "who . . . did not regard equality with God as something to be exploited, but emptied himself, taking the form of a slave. . . . humbled himself and became obedient to the point of death—even death on a cross" (Phil 2:6–8 NRSV); "[who] died for our sins in accordance with the scriptures, . . . [who] was buried, . . . [who] was raised on the third day" (1 Cor 15:3–4 NRSV). Mark offered his church the kind of consolation that only the Christian confession can give.

Had I been the pastor of Mark's congregation, I would have been tempted to apply Scripture like a Band-Aid on congregational wounds. Had I remembered my appointed rule as traditionist, I might simply have pitched "the story" at people, under the naive assumption that it would automatically stick, like religious Velcro. Instead, while firmly grounded in the classical credo, Mark displayed extraordinary virtuosity in its re-creation. For infant Christians, buffeted by powerlessness, faltering faith, and senseless suffering, Mark attempted some daring narrative feats: relocating Jesus's sovereignty at Golgotha; deconstructing the disciples in their poignantly fallible following; and reconstructing their hope at an empty grave with a pregnant promise. For a wayworn people, Mark faithfully interpreted the Christian story, carefully tailoring it to the experience of those in desperate need.

Precisely because Mark was that sort of pastor, writing that kind of gospel, we must exercise extraordinary caution in moving from his place and time to our own. To pillage this evangelist's proclamation for disembodied precepts or slick recipes serves no one well. For that, Mark's Gospel is too temporally conditioned, too circumstantially shaped—and so are our congregations. To demand that Mark be instantly relevant to us is to treat his gospel as a lush uses a lamppost: for support, not illumination. Yet even as the seasoned judgment of colleagues whose pastorates have been very different from ours may enlarge our perspectives, so, too, may Mark's vision throw light on our own.

At first blush, we might not believe that. Mark's vision, the overall framework within which he weaves the story of Jesus, is nothing if not queer. Here we have Jesus who comes from out of nowhere, whose teaching is calculated to confound, not to clarify, whose disciples are thoroughly briefed yet completely stupefied, whose true identity is hidden, yet exposed by all sorts of characters who either fail to recognize or refuse to accept the truth they spout, whose godly sonship is revealed on a criminal's cross, and whose vindication is verified by sepulchral emptiness and frightened silence. The greater one's familiarity with Mark, the less sense it seems to make. Small wonder that John Donahue has concluded that Mark does not merely contain parables: this gospel *is* a parable.[3] It is not so much a statement as a question that invites an answer, a riddle that teases our response.

3. "Jesus as the Parable of God in the Gospel of Mark," *Int* 32 (1978): 369–86.

Some interpreters attribute Mark's mystery and mystification to his and his community's apocalyptic bent. Such an interpretation is unlikely to render Mark more congenial to most of us: card-carrying apocalypticists tend not to matriculate at mainline seminaries. And yet, on further reflection, it may be precisely at this point of "mysterious revelation" that Mark and our ministries most piquantly intersect.[4] For many of its modern practitioners, ministry is a vocation of whose significance they are firmly convinced, despite precious little evidence to support that conviction. Perhaps you have visited an old, tube-swathed woman in a ten-thousand-dollar-a-day IC unit who wants you to explain to her why the doctors won't let her die. Maybe you have met the new pastor in a suburban boom parish, whose desk, once graced by Niebuhr and Gutiérrez and von Balthasar, is now covered with blueprints, spreadsheets, and samples of asphalt tile. Can you sympathize with a young minister who yearns to leave suburbia for inner-city ministry to the homeless and marginal, much to the astonishment of certain senior colleagues—more than one of whom has made a pass at her— who wonder why she won't "climb the ladder"? Do you understand how, upon receiving a prestigious award, Robert Frost could say to his audience, "I'm an old man. It's a strange world. I don't understand a damn thing"?[5]

For those who live amid a welter of loose ends, Mark's apocalypticism may help in gathering the threads. For too long we have allowed the lunatic fringe to mislead us. Apocalypticism does not suck us out of reality but redefines reality while driving us back into it. In its weird loveliness, the Markan vision grasps the half-sense and nonsense of our lives and callings and dares to suggest that precisely there, contrary to all expectation, the power and presence of God await us. Mark's is the gospel of the concealed kingdom, sown by scattering, germinating in ignorance, outrageously fruitful in the soil of obscurity. His is the gospel of the dumbfounded disciples, pilgrims of the past imperfect, clay jars in whom treasure has been entrusted, "so that it may be made clear that this extraordinary power belongs to God and does not come from us" (2 Cor 4:7 NRSV). Mark's is the gospel that invites us up to Golgotha, there to witness messianic dynamism, hanging dead from a cross.

By what intellectual legerdemain did we come to suppose that our ministry ever could appear more credible than that of the Christ we honor? You may remember the story, recounted by Paul Tillich, of the witness in the Nuremberg trials who had lived for a time in a Jewish graveyard in Poland—the only place

---

4. T. Alec Burkill, *Mysterious Revelation: An Examination of the Philosophy of St. Mark's Gospel* (Ithaca, NY: Cornell University Press, 1963).

5. I have been unable to run this quotation to earth.

where he, with others, could safely hide after escaping the gas chamber. In a grave nearby, a young woman gave birth to a boy, with the help of an eighty-year-old gravedigger. As the newborn uttered his first cries and sucked the tears of his milkless mother, the old man prayed, "Great God, hast Thou finally sent the Messiah to us? For who else than the Messiah Himself can be born in a grave?"[6]

The Jesus of Mark's Gospel does not teach simply in parables. He is *himself* a parable of the God whose sovereignty is manifested in the brokenness of the crucified Christ.[7] It is because Mark is so relentlessly truthful about God's kingdom and Messiah that we may look with equal honesty upon our ministry in Christ's name. Our assignment is to take up not Jesus's cross but our own. In our cruciform life and service is hidden the resurrectionary power of God. This we can do only through the vision with which God graces us: the eyes of faith that, as Karl Barth said, are like "the cat's eyes that can manage in the dark."[8] Such perception is never acquired without pain. Though real, so is the gloom it penetrates: those endless nights of the soul when, as F. Scott Fitzgerald lamented, "It is always three o'clock in the morning, day after day."[9] But if we or those we serve feel ready to embalm our ministry, then Mark reminds us that the entombment is premature. The one who was crucified has been raised and goes before us to Galilee and to Kenosha and to San Diego and to Johannesburg and to Hong Kong. We may trail in prayerful praise or in stunned silence. But we go with the promise that Christ is already there. He's waiting for us.

6. *The Shaking of the Foundations* (New York: Scribner's Sons, 1948), 165.

7. Donahue, "Jesus as the Parable of God."

8. *Theology and Church: Shorter Writings, 1920–1928,* trans. Louise Pettibone Smith (New York: Harper & Row, 1962), 62.

9. *The Crack-Up* (New York: Scribner's Sons, 1931), 74.

Acknowledgments

THE AUTHOR AND PUBLISHER are grateful to the following publishers.

Abingdon Press for kind permission to reprint the introduction, originally published under the title, "Mark," in *The New Interpreter's Bible: One-Volume Commentary*, ed. Beverly R. Gaventa and David L. Petersen (Nashville: Abingdon, 2010), 658–78, © 2010 by Abingdon Press. All rights reserved.

Baylor University Press for kind permission to reprint chapter 13, "*Endzeit als Urzeit*: Mark and Creation Theology," originally published in *Interpretation and the Claims of the Text: Resourcing New Testament Theology*, ed. Jason A. Whitlark, Bruce W. Longenecker, Lidija Novakovic, and Mikeal C. Parsons (Waco, TX: Baylor University Press), 89–101, 230–33, © 2014 by Baylor University Press. All rights reserved.

E. J. Brill Publishing for kind permission to reprint chapter 11, "Mark: John's Photographic Negative," originally published in *Anatomies of the Gospels and Early Christianities: Essays in Honor of R. Alan Culpepper*, ed. Mikeal C. Parsons, Elizabeth Struthers Malbon, and Paul Anderson, Biblical Interpretation Series (Leiden: Brill, 2018), 111–26, © 2018 by Koninklijke Brill NV, Leiden, The Netherlands. All rights reserved.

The Catholic Biblical Association of America for kind permission to reprint, in revised form, chapter 8, "Mark as Historian of God's Kingdom," originally published in *Catholic Biblical Quarterly* 71 (2009): 64–83.

The editors of *The Christian Century* for kind permission to reprint chapter 17, "Ministry in Mystery: One Evangelist's Vision," in revised form, from *The Christian Ministry* 22 (March–April 1991): 15–18, © 1991 by The Christian Century Foundation. All rights reserved.

Luther Seminary for kind permission to reprint an earlier version of chapter 5, "A Servant of Surprise: Juel Interpreted," originally published in *Word & World: Theology for Christian Ministry* 26 (Winter 2006): 47–60, © 2006 by Luther Seminary, Saint Paul, MN. All rights reserved.

Mohr Siebeck GmbH & Co. KG for kind permission to reprint chapter 15, "The Kijé Effect: Revenants in the Markan Passion Narrative," originally published in *Modern and Ancient Literary Criticism of the Gospels: Continuing the Debate on Gospel Genre(s)*, ed. Robert Matthew Calhoun, David P. Moessner, and Tobias Nicklas, WUNT 451 (Tübingen: Mohr Siebeck, 2020), 273–305, © 2020 by Mohr Siebeck, Tübingen, Germany. www.mohrsiebeck.com. All rights reserved.

Oxford Publishing Limited for kind permission to reprint, in revised form, chapter 7, originally published as "Mark," in *The Oxford Encyclopedia of the Bible and Theology*, ed. Samuel E. Balentine (New York: Oxford University Press, 2015), 2:71–77. Reproduced with permission of the Licensor through PLSclear, © 2015 Oxford University Press. All rights reserved.

SAGE Publications for kind permission to reprint earlier versions of chapter 3, "The Quest of Mark the Redactor: Why Has It Been Pursued, and What Has It Taught Us?," *Journal for the Study of the New Testament* 10 (1988): 19–39, © 1988 Sheffield Academic Press / SAGE Journals; chapter 1, "Was Mark a Roman Gospel?," *Expository Times* 105 (1993): 36–40, © 1997 The Expository Times / SAGE Journals; and chapter 2, under the title, "The Evangelist Mark: Some Reflections out of Season," *Theology* 99 (January–February 1997): 35–42, © 1997 The Society for the Promotion of Christian Knowledge / SAGE Journals. All rights reserved.

Westminster John Knox Press for kind permission to reprint earlier versions of chapter 9 in *The End of Mark and the Ends of God: Essays in Memory of Donald Harrisville Juel*, ed. Beverly Roberts Gaventa and Patrick D. Miller (Louisville: Westminster John Knox), 33–49, © 2005 Westminster John Knox Press; chapter 10 in *Character Ethics and the New Testament: Moral Dimensions of Scripture*, ed. Robert L. Brawley (Louisville: Westminster John Knox, 2007), 3–17, © 2007 Westminster John Knox Press; and chapter 14 in C. Clifton Black, *The Rhetoric of the Gospel: Theological Artistry in the Gospels and Acts*, 2nd ed. (Louisville: Westminster John Knox, 2013), 43–66, © 2013 C. Clifton Black. All rights reserved.

Chapter 4 was originally published under the title "Afterword: Mark's Disciples and Markan Redaction after Twenty-Five Years," in C. Clifton Black, *The Disciples according to Mark: Markan Redaction in Current Debate*, 2nd ed. (Grand Rapids: Eerdmans, 2012), 297–340, © 2012 C. Clifton Black. All rights reserved.

Wipf & Stock Publishers, Eugene, OR, for kind permission to reprint chapter 12, originally published under the title "Christ Crucified in Paul and in Mark: Reflections on an Intracanonical Conversation," in *Theology and Ethics in Paul and His Interpreters: Essays in Honor of Victor Paul Furnish*, ed. Eugene H. Lovering Jr. and Jerry L. Sumney (Nashville: Abingdon, 1996), 184–206, © 2017 Wipf & Stock Publishers. www.wipfandstock.com. All rights reserved.

The editors of *Working Preacher*, workingpreacher.org, for kind permission to reprint the commentaries and essays that constitute chapter 16, first published on the website https://www.workingpreacher.org, © 2020 Luther Seminary, Saint Paul, MN. All rights reserved.

Bibliography

Achtemeier, Paul J. "*Omne verbum sonat*: The New Testament and the Oral Environment of Late Western Antiquity." *JBL* 109 (1990): 3–27.

Ackermann, Robert John. *The Philosophy of Karl Popper*. Amherst: University of Massachusetts Press, 1976.

Ahearne-Kroll, Stephen. *The Psalms of Lament in Mark's Passion: Jesus' Davidic Suffering*. SNTSMS 142. Cambridge: Cambridge University Press, 2007.

Aickman, Robert. *Compulsory Games and Other Stories*. Edited by Victoria Nelson. Introduction by John J. Miller. New York Review Books. New York: New York Review of Books, 2016.

Aland, Kurt, ed. *Synopsis Quattuor Evangeliorum*. 10th ed. Stuttgart: Deutsche Bibelstiftung, 1978.

Allen, Charlotte. *The Human Christ: The Search for the Historical Jesus*. New York: Free Press, 1998.

Allison, Dale C. *Constructing Jesus: Memory, Imagination, History*. Grand Rapids: Baker Academic, 2010.

———. "Cyprus and Early Christianity: Did Everybody Know Everybody?" Pages 127–46 in *Cyprus within the Biblical World: Are Borders Barriers?* Edited by James H. Charlesworth and Jolyon G. R. Pruszinski. London: T&T Clark, 2021.

———. *The Historical Christ and the Theological Jesus*. Grand Rapids: Eerdmans, 2009.

———. *Jesus of Nazareth: Millenarian Prophet*. Minneapolis: Fortress, 1998.

———. *The Resurrection of Jesus: Apologetics, Polemics, History*. London: T&T Clark, 2021.

———. *Studies in Matthew: Interpretation Past and Present*. Grand Rapids: Baker Academic, 2005.

Alter, Robert. *The Art of Biblical Narrative*. New York: Basic Books, 1981.

Anderson, Bernhard W. "Introduction: Mythopoeic and Theological Dimensions of Biblical Creation Faith." Pages 1–24 in *Creation in the Old Testament*.

Edited by B. W. Anderson. IRT 6. Philadelphia: Fortress; London: SPCK, 1984. Repr., pages 75–96 in Bernhard W. Anderson, *From Creation to New Creation: Old Testament Perspectives*. OBT. Minneapolis: Fortress, 1994.

Anderson, Hugh. *The Gospel of Mark*. NCB. London: Marshall, Morgan & Scott, 1976.

———. "The Old Testament in Mark's Gospel." Pages 280–306 in *The Use of the Old Testament in the New and Other Essays: Studies in Honor of William Franklin Stinespring*. Edited by James M. Efird. Durham, NC: Duke University Press, 1972.

Anderson, Janice Capel, and Stephen D. Moore, eds. *Mark and Method: New Approaches in Biblical Studies*. 2nd ed. Minneapolis: Fortress, 2008.

———. *New Testament Masculinities*. SBLSS 45. Atlanta: Scholars Press, 2003.

Anonymous. "God, However, Remains in the Details." *New Yorker*. 18 October 1993, 43–44.

———. "In Memoriam: Robert P. Meye." https://www.fuller.edu/posts/in-memoriam-robert-p-meye/.

———. "Quotes from Ann Richards." *New York Times*. 14 September 2006.

Anselm of Canterbury. *Why God Became Man, and the Virgin Conception and Original Sin*. Translated by Joseph M. Colleran. Albany, NY: Magi Books, 1969.

Ash, Rhiannon. "'Never Say Die!' Assassinating Emperors in Suetonius' *Lives of the Caesars*." Pages 200–216 in *Writing Biography in Greece and Rome*. Edited by Koen de Temmerman and Kristoffel Demoen. Cambridge: Cambridge University Press, 2016.

Assmann, Aleida. *Erinnerungsraüme: Formen und Wandlungen des kulturellen Gedächtnisses*. Munich: Beck, 1999.

Assmann, Jan. *Das kulturelle Gedächtnis: Schrift, Erinnerung im politische Identität in frühen Hochkulturen*. 5th ed. Munich: Beck, 2005.

Attridge, Harold W. "Genre Bending in the Fourth Gospel." *JBL* 121 (2003): 3–21.

Auerbach, Erich. *Mimesis: The Representation of Reality in Western Literature*. Princeton: Princeton University Press, 1953.

Aune, David E. "Genre Theory and the Genre Function of Mark and Matthew." Pages 145–75 in *Mark and Matthew I: Comparative Readings: Understanding the Earliest Gospels in Their First-Century Settings*. Edited by Eve-Marie Becker and Anders Runesson. WUNT 271. Tübingen: Mohr Siebeck, 2011.

———. "The Gospels as Ancient Biography and the Growth of Jesus Literature." Pages 46–76 in *The New Testament in Its Literary Environment*. LEC. Philadelphia: Westminster, 1987.

———. *The New Testament and Its Literary Environment*. LEC 8. Philadelphia: Westminster, 1987.

———. *Prophecy in Early Christianity and the Ancient Mediterranean World.* Grand Rapids: Eerdmans, 1983.

Bailey, Kenneth E. "The Fall of Jerusalem and Mark's Account of the Cross." *ExpTim* 102 (1991): 102–5.

———. "Informal Controlled Oral Tradition and the Synoptic Gospels." *Them* 20 (1995): 4–11.

Baird, J. A. "Genre Analysis as a Method of Historical Criticism." Pages 385–411 in *Proceedings: Society of Biblical Literature* 2. Missoula, MT: Society of Biblical Literature, 1972.

Balabanski, Vicky. *Eschatology in the Making: Mark, Matthew and the Didache.* SNTSMS 97. Cambridge: Cambridge University Press, 1997.

Bammel, Ernst. "Die Blutherichtsbarkeit in der römische Provinz Judaä vor dem ersten jüdischen Aufstand." *JJS* 25 (1974): 39–49.

———. "The Trial before Pilate." Pages 415–51 in *Jesus and the Politics of His Day.* Edited by Ernst Bammel and C. F. D. Moule. Cambridge: Cambridge University Press, 1984.

Barbour, Robin S. "Wisdom and the Cross in 1 Corinthians 1 and 2." Pages 57–71 in *Theologia Crucis—Siglum Crucis: Festschrift für Erich Dinkler zum 70. Geburtstag.* Edited by Carl Andresen and Günter Klein. Tübingen: Mohr Siebeck, 1979.

Barclay, John M. G. *Paul and the Gift.* Grand Rapids: Eerdmans, 2015.

———. "Why the Roman Empire Was Insignificant to Paul." Pages 363–87 in John M. G. Barclay, *Pauline Churches and Diaspora Jews.* WUNT 275. Tübingen: Mohr Siebeck, 2011.

Barnhill, Gregory M. "Jesus as Spirit-Filled Warrior and Mark's Functional Pneumatology." *CBQ* 82 (2020): 605–27.

Barr, James. "'Abba' Isn't 'Daddy.'" *JTS* 39 (1988): 28–47.

———. "Biblical Theology." Pages 104–11 in *IDBSup.*

Barrett, C. K. *Essays on John.* Philadelphia: Westminster, 1982.

———. *The Gospel according to St. John: An Introduction with Commentary and Notes on the Greek Text.* 2nd ed. Philadelphia: Westminster, 1978.

———. "The Parallels between Acts and John." Pages 163–78 in *Exploring the Gospel of John in Honor of D. Moody Smith.* Edited by R. Alan Culpepper and C. Clifton Black. Louisville: Westminster John Knox, 1996.

Barth, Karl. *The Epistle to the Romans.* Translated by E. C. Hoskyns. London: Oxford University Press, 1933. German original, 1919.

———. *Theology and Church: Shorter Writings, 1920–1928.* Translated by Louise Pettibone Smith. New York: Harper & Row, 1962.

Bartley, William Warren. "A Popperian Harvest." Pages 249–89 in *In Pursuit of*

Truth: Essays on the Philosophy of Karl Popper on the Occasion of His 80th Birthday. Edited by Paul Levinson. Atlantic Highlands, NJ: Humanities; Sussex: Harvester, 1982.

Barton, John. *Reading the Old Testament: Method in Biblical Study.* Philadelphia: Westminster, 1984.

Bauckham, Richard. "The Eyewitnesses in the Gospel of Mark." *SEÅ* 74 (2009): 19–39.

———. "For Whom Were the Gospels Written?" Pages 9–48 in *The Gospels for All Christians.* Edited by Richard Bauckham. Grand Rapids: Eerdmans, 1998.

———. "In Response to My Respondents: *Jesus and the Eyewitnesses* in Review." *JSHJ* 6 (2008): 225–53.

———. *Jesus and the Eyewitnesses: The Gospels as Eyewitness Testimony.* Grand Rapids: Eerdmans, 2006.

———. *Jesus and the Eyewitnesses: The Gospels as Eyewitness Testimony.* 2nd ed. Grand Rapids: Eerdmans, 2017.

Beasley-Murray, George R. *Jesus and the Last Days: The Interpretation of the Olivet Discourse.* Peabody, MA: Hendrickson, 1993.

Beavis, Mary Ann. *Mark.* Paideia. Grand Rapids: Baker Academic, 2011.

Beck, Mark. "Plutarch." Pages 397–411 in *Narrators, Narratees, and Narratives in Ancient Greek Literature: Studies in Ancient Greek Narrative 1.* Edited by Irene J. F. de Jong, René Nünlist, and Angus Bowie. MnemSup 257. Leiden: Brill, 2004.

Becker, Eve-Marie. *Das Markus-Evangelium im Rahmen antiker Historiographie.* WUNT 194. Tübingen: Mohr Siebeck, 2006.

Becker, Eve-Marie, Troels Engberg-Pederson, and Mogens Müller, eds. *Mark and Paul: Comparative Essays Part II; For and against Pauline Influence on Mark.* BZNW 199. Berlin: de Gruyter, 2014.

Beker, J. Christiaan. *Paul the Apostle: The Triumph of God in Life and Thought.* Philadelphia: Fortress, 1980.

Best, Ernest. *Disciples and Discipleship: Studies in the Gospel according to Mark.* Edinburgh: T&T Clark, 1986.

———. *Following Jesus: Discipleship in the Gospel of Mark.* JSNTSup 4. Sheffield: JSOT Press, 1981.

———. "Mark's Preservation of the Tradition." Pages 21–34 in *L'Évangile selon Marc: Tradition et rédaction.* Edited by M. Sabbe. BETL 34. Leuven: Leuven University Press, 1988.

———. "Mark's Readers: A Profile." Pages 839–55 in *The Four Gospels 1992: Festschrift Frans Neirynck.* Vol. 2. Edited by Frans Van Segbroeck, Christopher M. Tuckett, Gilbert Van Belle, and Joseph Verheyden. BETL 100. Leuven: Leuven University Press, 1992.

———. Review of *The Disciples according to Mark: Markan Redaction in Current Debate*, by C. Clifton Black. *JTS* 41 (1990): 602–7.

———. *The Temptation and the Passion: The Markan Soteriology*. SNTSMS 2. Cambridge: Cambridge University Press, 1965.

———. *The Temptation and the Passion: The Markan Soteriology*. 2nd ed. SNTSMS 2. Cambridge: Cambridge University Press, 1990.

Bilezikian, Gilbert G. *The Liberated Gospel: A Comparison of the Gospel of Mark and Greek Tragedy*. Grand Rapids: Baker, 1977.

Bird, Michael F. "Mark: Interpreter of Peter and Disciple of Paul." Pages 39–61 in *Paul and the Gospels: Christologies, Conflicts and Convergences*. Edited by Michael F. Bird and Joel Willitts. LNTS 411. London: T&T Clark, 2011.

———. "Tearing the Heavens and Shaking the Heavenlies: Mark's Cosmology in Its Apocalyptic Context." Pages 45–59 in *Cosmology and New Testament Theology*. Edited by Jonathan T. Pennington and Sean M. McDonough. LNTS 355. London: T&T Clark, 2008.

Bitzer, Lloyd F. "The Rhetorical Situation." *PR* 1 (1968): 1–14.

Black, C. Clifton. *The Disciples according to Mark: Markan Redaction in Current Debate*. 2nd ed. Grand Rapids: Eerdmans, 2012.

———. "Kennedy and the Gospels: An Ambiguous Legacy, A Promising Bequest." Pages 63–80 in *Words Well Spoken: George Kennedy's Rhetoric of the New Testament*. Edited by Clifton Black and Duane F. Watson. SRR 8. Waco, TX: Baylor University Press, 2008.

———. "Lightfoot, Robert Henry (1883–1953)." *DBI* 2:77–78.

———. *The Lord's Prayer*. IRUSC. Louisville: Westminster John Knox, 2018.

———. *Mark*. ANTC. Nashville: Abingdon, 2011.

———. *Mark: Images of an Apostolic Interpreter*. SPNT. Minneapolis: Fortress; Edinburgh: T&T Clark, 2001.

———. "The Persistence of the Wounds." Pages 47–85 in *Lament: Reclaiming Practices in Pulpit, Pew, and Public Square*. Edited by Sally A. Brown and Patrick D. Miller. Louisville: Westminster John Knox, 2005.

———. *Reading Scripture with the Saints*. Eugene, OR: Wipf & Stock; Cambridge: Lutterworth, 2014, 2015.

———. "Redaction Criticism." Pages 491–95 in *Encyclopedia of the Historical Jesus*. Edited by Craig A. Evans. New York: Routledge; London: Taylor & Francis, 2008.

———. "Redaction Criticism, New Testament." *OEBI* 2:240–51.

———. Review of *Ancient Rhetoric and the Synoptic Problem: Clarifying Markan Priority*, by Alex Damm. *RBL* (2015). https://www.sblcentral.org/home.

———. Review of *A History of the Interpretation of the Gospel of Mark: Through the Nineteenth Century*, 3 vols., by Sean P. Kealy. *CBQ* 73 (2011): 391–92.

———. Review of *Jesus, a New Vision: Spirit, Culture, and the Life of Discipleship*, by Marcus J. Borg. *Int* 43 (1989): 422–24.

———. Review of *Mark: A Reader-Response Commentary*, by Bas M. F. van Iersel. *CBQ* 62 (2000): 570–72.

———. Review of *Sowing the Gospel: Mark's World in Literary-Historical Perspective*, by Mary Ann Tolbert. *CBQ* 54 (1992): 382–84.

———. *The Rhetoric of the Gospel: Theological Artistry in the Gospels and Acts*. 2nd ed. Louisville: Westminster John Knox, 2013.

Black, Matthew. *An Aramaic Approach to the Gospels and Acts*. 2nd ed. Oxford: Clarendon, 1954.

Blackman, E. Cyril. "Is History Irrelevant for the Christian Kerygma?" *Int* 21 (1967): 435–46.

Blatherwick, David. "The Markan Silhouette?" *NTS* 17 (1971): 184–92.

Bligh, Philip H. "A Note on *Huios Theou* in Mark 15:39." *ExpTim* 80 (1968): 51–53.

Blount, Brian K. *Go Preach! Mark's Kingdom Message and the Black Church Today*. Maryknoll, NY: Orbis, 1998.

———. "Preaching the Kingdom: Mark's Call for Prophetic Engagement." *PSB* 15 (1994): 33–56.

Bobertz, Charles A. *The Gospel of Mark: A Liturgical Reading*. Grand Rapids: Baker Academic, 2016.

Boismard, Marie-Émile. *L'Évangile de Marc: Sa Préhistoire*. EBib, n.s. 26. Paris: Gabalda, 1994.

Bolt, Peter G. *Jesus' Defeat of Death: Persuading Mark's Early Readers*. SNTSMS 125. Cambridge: Cambridge University Press, 2003.

Bond, Helen K. *The First Biography of Jesus: Genre and Meaning in Mark's Gospel*. Grand Rapids: Eerdmans, 2020.

———. "A Fitting End? Self-Denial and a Slave's Death in Mark's *Life of Jesus*." *NTS* 65 (2019): 425–42.

———. "Paragon of Discipleship? Simon of Cyrene in the Markan Passion Narrative." Pages 18–35 in *Matthew and Mark across Perspectives: Essays in Honour of Stephen C. Barton and William R. Telford*. Edited by Kristin A. Bendoraitis and Nijay K. Gupta. LNTS 538. London: Bloomsbury T&T Clark, 2016.

Boomershine, Thomas E. "Mark the Storyteller: A Rhetorical-Critical Investigation of Mark's Passion and Resurrection Narrative." PhD diss., Union Theological Seminary (New York City), 1974.

Booth, Wayne C. *The Rhetoric of Fiction*. 2nd ed. Chicago: University of Chicago Press, 1983.

Borg, Marcus J. *Jesus, a New Vision: Spirit, Culture, and the Life of Discipleship*. New York: Harper & Row, 1987.

———. "An Orthodoxy Reconsidered: The 'End-of-the-World Jesus.'" Pages 207–17 in *The Glory of Christ in the New Testament: Studies in Christology in Memory of George Bradford Caird*. Edited by L. D. Hurst and N. T. Wright. Oxford: Clarendon, 1987.

Boring, M. Eugene. "The Christology of Mark: Hermeneutical Issues for Systematic Theology." *Semeia* 30 (1984): 125–53.

———. *Mark: A Commentary*. NTL. Louisville: Westminster John Knox, 2006.

Bormann, Lukas. "Kulturwissenschaft und Exegesis: Gegenwärtige Geschichtsdiskurse und die biblische Geschichtskonzeption." *EvT* 69 (2009): 166–85.

Bornkamm, Günther, Gerhard Barth, and Heinz Joachim Held. *Tradition and Interpretation in Matthew*. Translated by Percy Scott. NTL. Philadelphia: Westminster, 1963.

Bosworth, A. B. "History and Artifice in Plutarch's *Eumenes*." Pages 56–89 in *Plutarch and the Historical Tradition*. Edited by Philip A. Stadter. London: Routledge, 1992.

Botner, Max. "Has Jesus Read What David Did? Probing Problems in Mark 2:25–26." *JTS* 69 (2018): 484–99.

Boulogne, J. "Les συγκρίσεις de Plutarque: Une rhétorique de la συγκρίσεις." Pages 32–44 in *Rhetorical Theory and Praxis in Plutarch*. Edited by L. van der Stockt. CEC 11. Leuven: Peeters, 2000.

Bowman, John. *The Gospel of Mark: The New Christian Jewish Passover Haggadah*. StPB 8. Leiden: Brill, 1965.

Brandenburger, Egon. *Markus 13 und die Apokalyptik*. FRLANT 134. Göttingen: Vandenhoeck & Ruprecht, 1984.

Brandon, S. G. F. *Jesus and the Zealots: A Study of the Political Factor in Primitive Christianity*. Manchester: Manchester University Press, 1967.

Breytenbach, Cilliers. "Alternation between Aorist, Historical Present and Imperfect: Aspects of Markan Narrative Style." *ETL* 95 (2019): 529–65. Repr., pages 179–219 in Cilliers Breytenbach, *The Gospel according to Mark as Episodic Narrative*. NovTSup 128. Leiden: Brill, 2021.

———. "Current Research on the Gospel according to Mark: A Report on Monographs Published from 2000–2009." Pages 13–32 in *Mark and Matthew I, Comparative Readings: Understanding the Earliest Gospels in Their*

First-Century Settings. Edited by Eve-Marie Becker and Anders Runesson. WUNT 271. Tübingen: Mohr Siebeck, 2011. Repr., pages 377–407 in Cilliers Breytenbach, *The Gospel according to Mark as Episodic Narrative*. NovTSup 128. Leiden: Brill, 2021.

———. "Das Evangelium nach Markus: Verschlüsselte Performanz?" Pages 87–114 in *Reading the Gospel of Mark in the Twenty-First Century: Method and Meaning*. Edited by Geert van Oyen. BETL 301. Leuven: Peeters, 2019. Repr., pages 468–97 in Cilliers Breytenbach, *The Gospel according to Mark as Episodic Narrative*. NovTSup 128. Leiden: Brill, 2021.

———. "Das Markusevangelium, Psalm 110,1 und 118,22f.: Folgetext und Prätext." Pages 197–222 in *The Scriptures in the Gospels*. Edited by Christopher M. Tuckett. BETL 131. Leuven: Peeters, 1997. Repr., pages 246–93 in Cilliers Breytenbach, *The Gospel according to Mark as Episodic Narrative*. NovTSup 128. Leiden: Brill, 2021.

———. "Die Vorschriften des Mose im Markusevangelium: Erwägungen zur Komposition von Mk 7,9–13; 10,2–9 und 12,18–27." *ZNW* 97 (2006): 23–43. Repr., pages 433–55 in Cilliers Breytenbach, *The Gospel according to Mark as Episodic Narrative*. NovTSup 128. Leiden: Brill, 2021.

———. "The Gospel according to Mark: The Yardstick for Comparing the Gospels with Ancient Texts." Pages 179–200 in *Modern and Ancient Literary Criticism of the Gospels: Continuing the Debate on Gospel Genre(s)*. Edited by Robert Matthew Calhoun, David P. Moessner, and Tobias Nicklas. WUNT 451. Tübingen: Mohr Siebeck, 2020. Repr., pages 41–65 in Cilliers Breytenbach, *The Gospel according to Mark as Episodic Narrative*. NovTSup 128. Leiden: Brill, 2021.

———. *The Gospel according to Mark as Episodic Narrative*. NovTSup 128. Leiden: Brill, 2021.

———. "The Minor Prophets in Mark's Gospel." Pages 27–37 in *The Minor Prophets in the New Testament*. Edited by M. J. J. Menken and S. Moyise. LNST 377. London: T&T Clark, 2009. Repr., pages 456–77 in Cilliers Breytenbach, *The Gospel according to Mark as Episodic Narrative*. NovTSup 128. Leiden: Brill, 2021.

———. *Nachfolge und Zukunftserwartung nach Markus: Eine methodenkritische Studie*. ATANT 71. Zürich: Theologischer Verlag, 1984.

Broadhead, Edwin K. *Prophet, Son, Messiah: Narrative Form and Function in Mark 14–16*. JSNTSup 97. Sheffield: Sheffield Academic, 1994.

———. Review of *The Disciples according to Mark: Markan Redaction in Current Debate*, by C. Clifton Black. *PRSt* 17 (1990): 83–84.

Brooks, James A. *Mark*. NAC 23. Nashville: Broadman, 1991.

Brown, Raymond E. *The Death of the Messiah: From Gethsemane to the Grave.* 2 vols. ABRL. New York: Doubleday, 1994.

——. *The Gospel according to John (xiii–xxi).* AB 29A. Garden City, NY: Doubleday, 1970.

——. "Jesus and Elisha." *Per* 12 (1971): 85–104.

——. "The Kerygma of the Gospel according to John: The Johannine View of Jesus in Modern Studies." *Int* 21 (1967): 387–400.

Brown, Raymond E., and John P. Meier. *Antioch and Rome: New Testament Cradles of Catholic Christianity.* New York: Paulist, 1983.

Buber, Martin. *Between Man and Man.* Translated by Ronald Gregor Smith. London: Kegan Paul, 1947.

Bultmann, Rudolf. *Das Evangelium des Johannes erklärt, mit Ergänzungsheft.* 2 vols. KEKNT 2. 11th ed. Göttingen: Vandenhoeck & Ruprecht, 1950.

——. "Der Glaube an Gott den Schöpfer." *EvT* 1 (1934–1935): 175–89. ET on pages 171–82 in *Existence and Faith: Shorter Writings of Rudolf Bultmann.* Edited by Schubert M. Ogden. Cleveland: World, 1960.

——. *The History of the Synoptic Tradition.* Translated by John Marsh. Rev. ed. New York: Harper & Row, 1963.

——. "Is Exegesis without Presuppositions Possible?" Pages 143–53 in *New Testament and Mythology and Other Basic Writings.* Edited and translated by Schubert M. Ogden. Philadelphia: Fortress, 1984.

——. "The Primitive Christian Kerygma and the Historical Jesus." Pages 15–42 in *The Historical Jesus and the Kerygmatic Christ: Essays on the New Quest of the Historical Jesus.* Edited by Carl E. Braaten and Roy A. Harrisville. Nashville: Abingdon, 1964.

——. *Theology of the New Testament.* 2 vols. Translated by Kendrick Grobel. New York: Scribner's Sons, 1951, 1955.

Burdon, Christopher. *Stumbling on God: Faith and Vision through Mark's Gospel.* London: SPCK; Grand Rapids: Eerdmans, 1990.

——. "Such a Fast God—True and False Disciples in Mark's Gospel." *Theology* 90 (1987): 89–97.

Burkett, Delbert. *The Case for Proto-Mark: A Study in the Synoptic Problem.* WUNT 399. Tübingen: Mohr Siebeck 2018.

——. *Rethinking the Gospel Sources: From Proto-Mark to Mark.* London: T&T Clark, 2004.

Burkill, T. Alec. *Mysterious Revelation: An Examination of the Philosophy of St. Mark's Gospel.* Ithaca, NY: Cornell University Press, 1963.

Burridge, Richard A. *What Are the Gospels? A Comparison with Graeco-Roman Biography.* 3rd ed. Waco, TX: Baylor University Press, 2018.

Busemann, Rolf. *Die Jüngergemeinde nach Markus 10: Eine redaktionsgeschicht-liche Untersuchung des 10. Kapitels im Markusevangelium.* BBB 57. Bonn: Hanstein, 1983.

Byrskog, Samuel. "The Early Church as a Narrative Fellowship: An Exploratory Study of the Performance of the *Chreia.*" *TTKi* 78 (2007): 207–26.

———. "The Eyewitnesses as Interpreters of the Past: Reflections on Richard Bauckham's *Jesus and the Eyewitnesses.*" *JSHJ* 6 (2008): 157–68.

———. *Jesus the Only Teacher: Didactic Authority and Transmission in Ancient Israel, Ancient Judaism and the Matthean Community.* CBNT 24. Stockholm: Almquist & Wiksell, 1994.

———. "Memory and Narrative—and Time." *JSHJ* 16 (2018): 108–35.

———. *Story as History—History as Story: The Gospel Tradition in the Context of Ancient Oral History.* WUNT 123. Tübingen: Mohr Siebeck, 2000.

———. "The Transmission of the Jesus Tradition: Old and New Insights." *EC* 1 (2010): 441–48.

———. "When Eyewitness Testimony and Oral Tradition Become Written Text." *SEÅ* 74 (2009): 41–53.

Cadbury, Henry Joel. *The Peril of Modernizing Jesus.* New York: Macmillan, 1937.

———. "Some Foibles of New Testament Scholarship." *JBR* 26 (1958): 213–16.

Cahill, Michael, ed. *The First Commentary on Mark: An Annotated Translation.* New York: Oxford University Press, 1998.

Caird, G. B. *New Testament Theology.* Edited and completed by L. D. Hurst. Oxford: Clarendon, 1994.

Camery-Hoggatt, Jerry. *Irony in Mark's Gospel: Text and Subtext.* SNTSMS 72. Cambridge: Cambridge University Press, 1992.

Campbell, Joseph. *The Hero with a Thousand Faces.* 2nd ed. Princeton: Princeton University Press, 1968.

Carrington, Philip. *The Primitive Christian Calendar: A Study in the Making of the Markan Gospel.* Cambridge: Cambridge University Press, 1952.

Catchpole, David. "On Proving Too Much: Critical Hesitations about Richard Bauckham's *Jesus and the Eyewitnesses.*" *JSHJ* 6 (2008): 169–81.

———. "The 'Triumphal' Entry." Pages 319–34 in *Jesus and the Politics of His Day.* Edited by Ernst Bammel and C. F. D. Moule. Cambridge: Cambridge University Press, 1984.

Chesterton, G. K. *Irish Impressions.* London: Collins Sons & Co., 1919.

Childs, Brevard S. *Biblical Theology in Crisis.* Philadelphia: Westminster, 1967.

———. *Introduction to the Old Testament as Scripture.* Philadelphia: Fortress, 1979.

———. *The New Testament as Canon: An Introduction.* Philadelphia: Fortress, 1985.

Chrysanthou, Chrysanthos S. *Plutarch's Parallel Lives: Narrative Technique and Moral Judgement.* TC 57. Berlin: de Gruyter, 2018.

Cobb, Laurel K. *Mark and Empire: Feminist Reflections.* Maryknoll, NY: Orbis, 2013.

Cohen, Shaye D. *The Significance of Yavneh and Other Essays in Jewish Hellenism.* TSAJ 136. Tübingen: Mohr Siebeck, 2010.

Colani, Timothy. *Jésus Christ et les Croyances messianiques de son Temps.* 2nd ed. Strasbourg: Treuttel et Wurtz, 1864.

Collingwood, R. G. *The Idea of History.* Rev. ed. Edited by Jan van der Dussen. Oxford: Oxford University Press, 1993.

Collins, John J. "Towards a Morphology of Genre." *Semeia* 14 (1979): 1–20.

Conzelmann, Hans. *The Theology of St. Luke.* Translated by Geoffrey Buswell. New York: Harper & Row, 1961.

Cook, John G. *The Structure and Persuasive Power of Mark: A Linguistic Approach.* SemeiaSt. Atlanta: Scholars Press, 1995.

Corbett, Edward P. J. *Classical Rhetoric for the Modern Student.* 2nd ed. New York: Oxford University Press, 1971.

Cotter, Wendy J. *The Christ of the Miracle Stories: Portrait through Encounter.* Grand Rapids: Baker Academic, 2010.

Cousar, Charles B. *A Theology of the Cross: The Death of Jesus in the Pauline Letters.* OBT. Minneapolis: Fortress, 1990.

Cox, Patricia L. *Biography in Late Antiquity: A Quest for the Holy Man.* Berkeley: University of California Press, 1983.

Cross, F. L., and E. A. Livingstone, eds. *The Oxford Dictionary of the Christian Church.* 2nd ed. New York: Oxford University Press, 1974.

Crossan, John Dominic. *The Historical Jesus: The Life of a Mediterranean Jewish Peasant.* San Francisco: HarperSanFrancisco, 1991.

Crossley, James G. "Mark, Paul and the Question of Influences." Pages 10–29 in *Paul and the Gospels: Christologies, Conflicts and Convergences.* Edited by Michael F. Bird and Joel Willitts. LNTS 411. London: T&T Clark, 2011.

Culpepper, R. Alan. *Anatomy of the Fourth Gospel: A Study in Literary Design.* Philadelphia: Fortress, 1983.

———. "The Christology of the Johannine Writings." Pages 66–87 in *Who Do You Say That I Am? Essays on Christology.* Edited by Mark Allan Powell and David R. Bauer. Louisville: Westminster John Knox, 1999.

———. "The Foundations of Matthean Ethics." Pages 359–79 in *Modern and Ancient Literary Criticism of the Gospels: Continuing the Debate on Gospel Genre(s).* Edited by Robert Matthew Calhoun, David P. Moessner, and Tobias Nicklas. WUNT 451. Tübingen: Mohr Siebeck, 2020.

———. *Mark.* SHBC. Macon, GA: Smyth & Helwys, 2007.

———. "Mark 10:50: Why Mention the Garment?" *JBL* 101 (1982): 131–32.

———. *Matthew: A Commentary.* NTL. Louisville: Westminster John Knox, 2021.

———. "The Prologue as Theological Prolegomenon to the Gospel of John." Pages

3–26 in *The Prologue of the Gospel of John: Literary, Theological, and Philosophical Contexts; Papers Read at the* Colloqueum Ioanneum *2013*. Edited by R. Alan Culpepper, Udo Schnelle, and Jan G. van der Watt. WUNT 359. Tübingen: Mohr Siebeck, 2016.

Cuvillier, Étienne. Review of *The Disciples according to Mark: Markan Redaction in Current Debate*, by C. Clifton Black. *ETR* 65 (1990): 272–73.

Dahl, Nils A. "The Crucified Messiah." Pages 27–47 in *Jesus the Messiah: The Historical Origin of Christological Doctrine*. Edited by Donald H. Juel. Minneapolis: Fortress, 1991.

———. *Jesus in the Memory of the Early Church*. Minneapolis: Augsburg, 1976.

———. "The Neglected Factor in New Testament Theology." Pages 153–63 in *Jesus the Messiah: The Historical Origin of Christological Doctrine*. Edited by Donald H. Juel. Minneapolis: Fortress, 1991.

———. "The Problem of the Historical Jesus." Pages 81–111 in Nils A. Dahl, *Jesus the Christ: The Historical Origins of Christological Doctrine*. Edited by Donald H. Juel. Minneapolis: Fortress, 1991.

Damm, Alex. *Ancient Rhetoric and the Synoptic Problem: Clarifying Markan Priority*. BETL 252. Leuven: Peeters, 2013.

Damon, Cynthia. "Death by Narrative in Suetonius' *Lives*." Pages 107–27 in *Ancient Biography: Identity through Lives*. Edited by Francis Cairns and Trevor Luke. ARCA Classical and Medieval Texts, Papers and Monographs 55. Prenton: Francis Cairns, 2018.

D'Angelo, Mary Rose. "*Abba* and 'Father': Imperial Theology and the Jesus Traditions." *JBL* 111 (1992): 611–30.

Danove, Paul. "The Characterization and Narrative Function of the Women at the Tomb (Mark 15,40–41.47; 16,1–8)." *Bib* 77 (1996): 375–97.

———. "The Narrative Rhetoric of Mark's Ambiguous Characterization of the Disciples." *JSNT* 20 (1998): 21–38. Repr., with elaboration, as "A Rhetorical Analysis of Mark's Construction of Discipleship." Pages 280–96 in *Rhetorical Criticism and the Bible*. Edited Stanley E. Porter and Dennis L. Stamps. JSNTSup 195. Sheffield: Sheffield Academic, 2002.

———. *The Rhetoric of the Characterization of God, Jesus, and Jesus' Disciples in the Gospel of Mark*. JSNTSup 290. New York: T&T Clark, 2005.

———. "The Rhetoric of the Characterization of Jesus as the Son of Man in Christ in Mark." *Bib* 84 (2003): 16–34.

Daube, David. *The New Testament and Rabbinic Judaism*. Salem, NH: Ayer, 1984.

Davies, Margaret. Review of *What Are the Gospels? A Comparison with Graeco-Roman Biography*, by Richard Burridge. *NBf* 74 (1993): 109–10.

Derrett, J. Duncan M. *The Making of Mark: The Scriptural Bases of the Earliest Gospel*. 2 vols. Shipston-on-Stour: Drinkwater, 1985.

Dewey, Joanna. "Mark as Interwoven Tapestry: Forecasts and Echoes for a Listening Audience." *CBQ* 53 (1991): 221–36.

———. *Markan Public Debate: Literary Technique, Concentric Structure, and Theology in Mark 2.1–3.6.* SBLDS 48. Chico, CA: Scholars Press, 1980.

Diagnostic and Statistical Manual of Mental Disorders. 5th ed. Washington, DC: American Psychiatric Publications, 2013.

Dibelius, Martin. "The First Christian Historian." Pages 123–37 in *Studies in the Acts of the Apostles.* Edited by Heinrich Greeven. Translated by Mary Ling. New York: Scribner's Sons, 1956. German original, 1951.

———. *From Tradition to Gospel.* Translated by Bertram Lee Woolf. New York: Scribner's Sons, 1965.

———. *Studies in the Acts of the Apostles.* Edited by Heinrich Greeven. Translated by Mary Ling. New York: Scribner's Sons, 1956. German original, 1951.

Diehl, Judith A. Review of *What Are the Gospels? A Comparison with Graeco-Roman Biography*, by Richard Burridge, 3rd ed. *CBQ* 82 (2020): 313–14.

Dippenaar, Michaelis Christoffel. "The Disciples in Mark: Narrative and Theology." *Taiwan Journal of Theology* 17 (1995): 139–209.

Dodd, C. H. *According to the Scriptures.* London: James Nisbet & Company, 1952.

———. *The Founder of Christianity.* London: Collins, 1971.

———. "The Framework of the Gospel Narrative." *ExpTim* 43 (1932): 396–400.

Donahue, John R. "Jesus as the Parable of God in the Gospel of Mark." *Int* 32 (1978): 369–86.

———. "A Neglected Factor in the Theology of Mark." *JBL* 101 (1982): 563–94.

———. "Redaction Criticism: Has the *Hauptstrasse* Become a *Sackgasse*?" Pages 27–57 in *The New Literary Criticism and the New Testament.* Edited by Elizabeth Struthers Malbon and Edgar V. McKnight. JSNTSup 109. Sheffield: Sheffield Academic, 1994.

———. Review of *The Disciples according to Mark: Markan Redaction in Current Debate*, by C. Clifton Black. *PSTJ* 42 (1989): 11–12.

Donahue, John R., and Daniel J. Harrington. *The Gospel of Mark.* SP 2. Collegeville, MN: Liturgical Press, 2002.

Donfried, Karl P., ed. *The Romans Debate.* Rev. ed. Peabody, MA: Hendrickson, 1991.

Dorian, Frederick. *The History of Music in Performance: The Art of Musical Interpretation from the Renaissance to Our Day.* New York: Norton, 1966.

Doudna, John Charles. *The Greek of the Gospel of Mark.* SBLMS 12. Philadelphia: Society of Biblical Literature and Exegesis, 1961.

Dowd, Sharyn Echols. *Prayer, Power, and the Problem of Suffering: Mark 11:22–25 in the Context of Markan Theology.* SBLDS 105. Atlanta: Scholars Press, 1988.

————. *Reading Mark: A Literary and Theological Commentary on the Second Gospel*. RNTS. Macon, GA: Smyth & Helwys, 2000.

Downey, Glanville. *A History of Antioch in Syria from Seleucus to the Arab Conquest*. Princeton: Princeton University Press, 1961.

Driediger-Murphy, Lindsay G. "'Do Not Examine, But Believe': A Classicist's Perspective on Teresa Morgan's Roman Faith and Christian Faith." *RelS* 54 (2018): 568–76.

Driggers, I. Brent. *Following God through Mark: Theological Tension in the Second Gospel*. Louisville: Westminster John Knox, 2007.

Droge, Arthur J., and James D. Tabor. *A Noble Death: Suicide and Martyrdom among Christians and Jews in Antiquity*. San Francisco: HarperCollins, 1992.

Duff, Timothy E. *Plutarch's* Lives: *Exploring Virtue and Vice*. Oxford: Clarendon, 1999.

Dunn, James D. G. "Altering the Default Setting: Re-envisaging the Early Transmission of the Jesus Tradition." *NTS* 49 (2003): 139–75. Repr., pages 41–79 in James D. G. Dunn, *The Oral Gospel Tradition*. Grand Rapids: Eerdmans, 2013.

————. *Jesus Remembered*. Christianity in the Making 1. Grand Rapids: Eerdmans, 2003.

————. "Jesus Tradition in Paul." Pages 155–78 in *Studying the Historical Jesus: Evaluations of the State of Current Research*. Edited by Bruce Chilton and Craig A. Evans. NTTS 19. Leiden: Brill, 1994.

————. *The Oral Gospel Tradition*. Grand Rapids: Eerdmans, 2013.

Dunn, James D. G., and James P. Mackey. *New Testament Theology in Dialogue: Christology and Ministry*. Philadelphia: Westminster, 1987.

Dwyer, Timothy. *The Motif of Wonder in the Gospel of Mark*. JSNTSup 128. Sheffield: Sheffield Academic, 1996.

Edwards, James R. *The Gospel according to Mark*. PNTC. Grand Rapids: Eerdmans; Leicester: Apollos, 2002.

————. "Markan Sandwiches: The Significance of Interpolations in Markan Narratives." *NovT* 31 (1989): 193–216.

Einstein, Albert. *Mein Weltbild*. 2nd ed. Amsterdam: Querido, 1934.

Elliott, John H. *A Home for the Homeless: A Sociological Exegesis of 1 Peter, Its Situation and Strategy*. Philadelphia: Fortress, 1981.

Erbse, Hartmut. "Die Bedeutung der Synkrisis in den Parellelobiographien Plutarchs." *Hermes* 84 (1956): 398–424.

Evans, C. Stephen. *The Historical Christ and the Jesus of Faith: The Incarnational Narrative as History*. Oxford: Clarendon, 1996.

Evans, Craig A. "How Mark Writes." Pages 135–48 in *The Written Gospel*. Edited by Markus Bockmuehl and Donald A. Hagner. Cambridge: Cambridge University Press, 2005.

———. *Mark 8:27–16:20*. WBC 34B. Nashville: Nelson, 2001.

———. Review of *L'Évangile de Marc: Sa Préhistoire*, by Marie-Émile Boismard. *CBQ* 58 (1996): 535–36.

———. "Source, Form and Redaction Criticism: The 'Traditional' Methods of Synoptic Interpretation." Pages 17–45 in *Approaches to New Testament Study*. Edited by S. E. Porter and D. Tombs. JSNTSup 120. Sheffield: Sheffield Academic, 1995.

Evans, Richard J. *In Defense of History*. New York: Norton, 2000.

Eyl, Jennifer. *Signs, Wonder, and Gifts: Divination in the Letters of Paul*. New York: Oxford University Press, 2019.

Fantin, Joseph D. Review of *The Purpose of Mark's Gospel: An Early Christian Response to Roman Imperial Propaganda*, by Adam Winn. *BSac* 169 (2012): 499–501.

Farmer, William R. *The Synoptic Problem: A Critical Analysis*. New York: Macmillan, 1964.

Farrer, Austin. *St Matthew and St Mark*. 2nd ed. Westminster: Dacre, 1966.

———. *A Study in St Mark*. London: Dacre, 1951.

Fenton, J. C. "Paul and Mark." Pages 89–112 in *Studies in the Gospels: Essays in Memory of R. H. Lightfoot*. Edited by D. E. Nineham. Oxford: Blackwell, 1955.

Feuerbach, Ludwig. *The Essence of Christianity*. Translated by George Eliot. New York: Harper & Row, 1957. German original, 1855.

Filannino, Francesco. *The Theological Programme of Mark*. WUNT 551. Tübingen: Mohr Siebeck, 2021.

Fischer, Cédric. *Les Disciples dans l'Évangile de Marc: Une grammaire théologique*. EBib n.s. 57. Paris: Gabalda, 2007.

Fishwick, Duncan. "A Critical Assessment: On the Imperial Cult in *Religions of Rome*." *RelStTh* 28 (2009): 129–74.

Fitzgerald, F. Scott. *The Crack-Up*. New York: Scribner's Sons, 1931.

Fitzmyer, Joseph A. Review of *Memory and Manuscript: Oral Traditions and Written Transmission in Rabbinic Judaism and Early Christianity*, by Birger Gerhardsson. *TS* 23 (1962): 442–57.

Fleddermann, Harry T. "The Flight of a Naked Young Man." *CBQ* 41 (1979): 412–18.

———. Review of *One Gospel from Two: Mark's Use of Matthew and Luke; A Demonstration by the Research Team of the International Institute for Renewal of Gospel Studies*, edited by David Peabody, Lamar Cope, and Allan J. McNicol. *CBQ* 66 (2004): 498–500.

Flesseman-van Leer, E. *Tradition and Scripture in the Early Church*. Assen: Van Gorcum, 1954.

Focant, Camille. *L'évangile selon Marc*. CBNT 2. Paris: Cerf, 2004.

Foote, Shelby. *The Civil War: A Narrative*. 3 vols. New York: Random House, 1958, 1963, 1974.

Fowl, Stephen. Review of *The Disciples according to Mark: Markan Redaction in Current Debate*, by C. Clifton Black. *JSNT* 13 (1990): 116.

Fowler, Robert. *Let the Reader Understand: Reader Response Criticism and the Gospel of Mark*. Minneapolis: Fortress, 1991.

France, R. T. *The Gospel of Mark: A Commentary on the Greek Text*. NIGTC. Grand Rapids: Eerdmans; Carlisle: Paternoster, 2002.

Francis, James A. "Truthful Fiction: New Questions to Old Answers on Philostratus' *Life of Apollonius*." *AJP* 119 (1998): 419–41.

Fredrickson, David. "What Difference Does Jesus Make for God?" *Di* 37 (1998): 104–10.

Fredriksen, Paula. "Arms and the Man: A Response to Dale Martin's 'Jesus in Jerusalem: Armed and Not Dangerous.'" *JSNT* 37 (2015): 312–25.

Frei, Hans W. *The Eclipse of Biblical Narrative: A Study in Eighteenth and Nineteenth Century Hermeneutics*. New Haven: Yale University Press, 1974.

Fretheim, Terence E. *God and World in the Old Testament: A Relational Theology of Creation*. Nashville: Abingdon, 2005.

———. *The Suffering of God: An Old Testament Perspective*. OBT. Philadelphia: Fortress, 1984.

Freyne, Sean. "The Geography of Restoration: Galilee-Jewish Relations in Early Jewish and Christian Experience." Pages 405–33 in *Restoration: Old Testament, Jewish, and Christian Perspectives*. Edited by J. M. Scott. JSJSup 72. Leiden: Brill, 2001.

Frickenschmidt, Dirk. *Evangelium als Biographie: Die vier Evangelien im Rahmen antiker Erzählkunst*. Tübingen: Francke, 1997.

Fried, Johannes. *Der Schleier der Erinnerung: Grundzüge einer historischen Memorik*. Munich: Beck, 2004.

Friedman, Richard Elliott. "Tabernacle." *ABD* 2:292–300.

Frye, Roland Mushat. "Literary Criticism and Gospel Criticism." *ThTo* 36 (1979): 207–19.

Fuller, Reginald H. *The Foundations of New Testament Christology*. London: Lutterworth, 1965.

Furnish, Victor Paul. *Jesus according to Paul*. UJT. Cambridge: Cambridge University Press, 1993.

———. "The Jesus-Paul Debate: From Baur to Bultmann." *BJRL* 47 (1964–1965):

342–81. Rev. repr., pages 17–50 in *Paul and Jesus: Collected Essays*. Edited by A. J. M. Wedderburn. JSNTSup 37. Sheffield: JSOT Press, 1989.

———. *The Moral Teaching of Paul: Selected Issues*. Rev. 2nd ed. Nashville: Abingdon, 1985.

———. "On Putting Paul in His Place." *JBL* 113 (1994): 3–17.

———. "Paul the Theologian." Pages 19–34 in *The Conversation Continues: Studies in Paul and John in Honor of J. Louis Martyn*. Edited by Robert T. Fortna and Beverly R. Gaventa. Nashville: Abingdon, 1990.

———. "Theology in 1 Corinthians." Pages 59–89 in *1 and 2 Corinthians*. Vol. 2 of *Pauline Theology*. Edited by David M. Hay. Minneapolis: Fortress, 1993.

———. "Theology in 1 Corinthians: Initial Soundings." Pages 246–64 in *Society of Biblical Literature 1989 Seminar Papers*. Edited by David J. Lull. Atlanta: Scholars Press, 1989.

Fusco, Vittorio. Review of *The Disciples according to Mark: Markan Redaction in Current Debate*, by C. Clifton Black. *Bib* 72 (1991): 123–27.

Gadamer, Hans-Georg. *Truth and Method*. Translated and edited by Garrett Barden and John Cumming. New York: Crossroad, 1975.

Gamble, Harry Y. *Books and Readers in the Early Church: A History of Early Christian Texts*. New Haven: Yale University Press, 1995.

Gamel, Brian K. *Mark 15:39 as a Markan Theology of Revelation: The Centurion's Confession as Apocalyptic Unveiling*. LNTS 574. London: Bloomsbury T&T Clark, 2017.

Garrett, Susan. *The Temptations of Jesus in Mark's Gospel*. Grand Rapids: Eerdmans, 1998.

Geddert, Timothy J. *Watchwords: Mark 13 in Markan Eschatology*. JSNTSup 26. Sheffield: JSOT Press, 1989.

Genette, Gérard. *Narrative Discourse: An Essay in Method*. Ithaca, NY: Cornell University Press, 1980.

Georgi, Dieter. *Die Gegner des Paulus im 2. Korintherbrief*. WMANT 11. Neukirchener-Vluyn: Neukirchener Verlag, 1964.

Georgia, Allan T. "Translating the Triumph: Reading Mark's Crucifixion Narrative against a Roman Ritual of Power." *JSNT* 36 (2013): 17–38.

Gerhardsson, Birger. *Memory and Manuscript: Oral Traditions and Written Transmission in Rabbinic Judaism and Early Christianity*. Translated by Eric J. Sharpe. ASNU 22. Uppsala: Gleerup; Copenhagen: Munksgaard, 1961.

———. *The Reliability of the Gospel Tradition*. Peabody, MA: Hendrickson, 2001.

———. "The Secret of the Transmission of the Unwritten Jesus Tradition." *NTS* 51 (2005): 1–18.

Geyer, Douglas W. *Fear, Anomaly, and Uncertainty in the Gospel of Mark.* ATLAMS 471. Lanham, MD: Scarecrow, 2002.

———. Review of *Rethinking the Gospel Sources: From Proto-Mark to Mark*, by Delbert Burkett. *RBL* (2005). https://www.sblcentral.org/home.

Gibson, Jeffrey B. "The Rebuke of the Disciples in Mark 8:14–21." *JSNT* 9 (1986): 31–47.

Gillespie, Thomas W. "A Case of 'Doctrinal Adhesion.'" *PSB* 24 (2003): 184–89.

Ginzberg, Louis. *The Legends of the Jews: Bible Times and Characters from Moses in the Wilderness to Esther.* 2 vols. Translated by Henrietta Szold and Paul Radin. Philadelphia: Jewish Publication Society, 2003.

Glasson, T. Francis. "Mark xv.39: The Son of God." *ExpTim* 80 (1969): 286.

Glasswell, M. E. "The Use of Miracles in the Markan Gospel." Pages 149–62 in *Miracles: Cambridge Studies in Their Philosophy and History.* Edited by C. F. D. Moule. London: Mowbray, 1965.

Gnilka, Joachim. *Das Evangelium nach Markus.* 2 vols. EKKNT 2/1–2. Neukirchen-Vluyn: Neukirchener Verlag, 1978, 1979.

Goodacre, Mark. "Scripturalization in Mark's Crucifixion Narrative." Pages 37–44 in *The Trial and Death of Jesus: Essays on the Passion Narrative in Mark.* Edited by Geert van Oyen and Tom Shepherd. CBET. Leuven: Peeters, 2006.

Goodwin, Doris Kearns. *Team of Rivals: The Political Genius of Abraham Lincoln.* New York: Simon & Schuster, 2006.

Goulder, Michael D. *The Evangelist's Calendar: A Lectionary Explanation of the Development of Scripture.* London: SPCK, 1978.

———. "The Pre-Marcan Gospel." *SJT* 47 (1994): 453–71.

Gray, John. *I and II Kings: A Commentary.* 2nd rev. ed. OTL. Philadelphia: Westminster, 1970.

Grayston, Kenneth. "The Study of Mark XIII." *BJRL* 56 (1974): 371–87.

Green, Joel B. Review of *The Disciples according to Mark: Markan Redaction in Current Debate*, by C. Clifton Black. *CBQ* 53 (1991): 314–15.

Greenberg, Moshe. "Exegesis." Pages 361–68 in *Studies in the Bible and Jewish Thought.* Philadelphia: Jewish Publication Society, 1995.

Guelich, Robert A. *Mark 1–8:26.* WBC 34A. Dallas: Word, 1989.

Gundry, Robert H. *Mark: A Commentary on His Apology for the Cross.* Grand Rapids: Eerdmans, 1993.

Gunkel, Hermann. *Schöpfung und Chaos in Urzeit und Endzeit: Eine religionsgeschichtliche Untersuchung über Gen 1 und Ap Joh 12.* Göttingen: Vandenhoeck & Ruprecht, 1895.

Hadas, Moses, and Morton Smith. *Heroes and Gods: Spiritual Biographies in Antiquity.* RP. New York: Harper & Row, 1965.

Haenchen, Ernst. *Der Weg Jesu: Eine Erklärung des Markus-Evangeliums und der kanonischen Parallelen.* Berlin: Alfred Töpelmann, 1966.

Hägg, Tomas. *The Art of Biography in Antiquity.* Cambridge: Cambridge University Press, 2012.

Halbwachs, Maurice. *Les cadres sociaux de la mémoire.* BEH 8. Paris: Michel, 2001. Original, 1925.

Hanson, James. "The Disciples in Mark's Gospel: Beyond the Pastoral/Polemical Debate." *HBT* 20 (1998): 128–55.

Hare, Douglas R. A. *The Son of Man Tradition.* Minneapolis: Fortress, 1990.

Harnack, Adolf von. *What Is Christianity?* Translated by Thomas Bailey Saunders. New York: Harper & Row, 1957. German original, 1899–1900.

Harner, Philip B. "Qualitative Anarthrous Predicate Nouns: Mark 15:39 and John 1:1." *JBL* 92 (1973): 75–87.

Harris, William V. *Ancient Literacy.* Cambridge: Harvard University Press, 1989.

Harrisville, Roy A. *The Miracle of Mark: A Study in the Gospel.* Minneapolis: Augsburg, 1967.

Hartman, Lars. *Prophecy Interpreted: The Formation of Some Jewish Apocalyptic Texts and of the Eschatological Discourse Mark 13 Par.* ConBNT. Lund: Gleerup, 1966.

Hatina, Thomas. *In Search of a Context: The Function of Scripture in Mark's Narrative.* LNTS 232. London: Sheffield Academic, 2002.

Hayes, John H., and Carl R. Holladay. *Biblical Exegesis: A Beginner's Handbook.* Atlanta: John Knox, 1982.

Hays, Richard B. *The Faith of Jesus Christ: An Investigation of the Narrative Substructure of Galatians 3:1–4:11.* 2nd ed. Grand Rapids: Eerdmans, 2002.

Henderson, John. "Was Suetonius' *Julius* a Caesar?" Pages 81–110 in *Suetonius the Biographer: Studies in Roman Lives.* Edited by Tristan Power and Roy K. Gibson. Oxford: Oxford University Press, 2014.

Henderson, Suzanne Watts. *Christology and Discipleship in the Gospel of Mark.* SNTSMS 135. Cambridge: Cambridge University Press, 2006.

———. "Was Mark a Supersessionist? Two Test Cases from the Earliest Gospel." Pages 145–68 in *The Ways That Often Parted: Essays in Honor of Joel Marcus.* Edited by Lori Barton, Jill Hicks-Keeton, and Matthew Thiessen. Atlanta: SBL Press, 2018.

Hengel, Martin. *Studies in the Gospel of Mark.* Translated by John Bowden. Philadelphia: Fortress 1985.

Henten, Jan Willem van. *The Maccabean Martyrs as Saviours of the Jewish People: A Study of 2 and 4 Maccabees.* JSJSup 57. Leiden: Brill, 1997.

Henten, Jan Willem van, and Friedrich Avemarie, eds. *Martyrdom and Noble*

Death: Selected Texts from Graeco-Roman, Jewish and Christian Antiquity. London: Routledge: 2002.

Hermogenes. "On Invention." Pages 107–13 in *Invention and Method: Two Rhetorical Treatises from the Hermogenic Corpus.* Translated by George A. Kennedy. WGRW 15. Atlanta: Society of Biblical Literature, 2005.

Herzog, William R., II. Review of *The Disciples according to Mark: Markan Redaction in Current Debate,* by C. Clifton Black. *TS* 51 (1990): 513–15.

Heschel, Abraham. *The Prophets.* New York: Harper & Row, 1982.

Hezser, Catherine. *Jewish Literacy in Roman Palestine.* TSAJ 81. Tübingen: Mohr Siebeck, 2001.

Hill, David. "Ernest Best: An Appreciation." *JSNT* 5 (1982): 3–6.

Hirsch, E. D., Jr. *Validity in Interpretation.* New Haven: Yale University Press, 1967.

Holland, Glenn S. *The Tradition That You Received from Us: 2 Thessalonians in the Pauline Tradition.* HUT 24. Tübingen: Mohr Siebeck, 1988.

Hooker, Morna D. *The Gospel according to Saint Mark.* BNTC. London: A & C Black, 1991.

———. *The Message of Mark.* London: Epworth, 1983.

———. Review of *The Disciples according to Mark: Markan Redaction in Current Debate,* by C. Clifton Black. *EpRev* 18 (1991): 86–87.

———. *The Son of Man in Mark.* Montreal: McGill University Press, 1967.

———. "Trial and Tribulation in Mark XIII." *BJRL* 65 (1982): 78–99.

———. "'What Doest Thou Here, Elijah?' A Look at St Mark's Account of the Transfiguration." Pages 59–70 in *The Glory of Christ in the New Testament: Studies in Christology in Memory of George Bradford Caird.* Edited by L. D. Hurst and N. T. Wright. Oxford: Clarendon, 1987.

Hope, Valerie M., ed. *Death in Ancient Rome: A Sourcebook.* London: Routledge, 2007.

Horsley, Richard A. *Jesus and the Spiral of Violence: Popular Jewish Resistance in Roman Palestine.* San Francisco: Harper & Row, 1987.

Hoskyns, Edwyn Clement, and Francis Noel Davey. *Crucifixion-Resurrection: The Pattern of the Theology and Ethics of the New Testament.* London: SPCK, 1981.

Howard-Snyder, Daniel. "Pistis, Fides, and Propositional Belief." *RelS* 54 (2018): 585–92.

Huebenthal, Sandra. *Das Markusevangelium als kollektives Gedächtnis.* FRLANT 253. Göttingen: Vandenhoeck & Ruprecht, 2014. English translation, *Reading Mark's Gospel as a Text from Collective Memory.* Grand Rapids: Eerdmans, 2020.

———. "Halbwachs, Maurice." Pages 247–49 in *Gedächtnis und Erinnerung: Ein interdisziplinäres Lexikon*. Edited by Nicholas Pethes and Jens Ruchatz. Hamburg: Rowohlt, 2001.

Hurtado, Larry. "Following Jesus in the Gospel of Mark—and Beyond." Pages 9–29 in *Patterns of Discipleship in the New Testament*. Edited by Richard N. Longenecker. Grand Rapids: Eerdmans, 1996.

———. "The Gospel of Mark: Evolutionary or Revolutionary Document?" *JSNT* 13 (1990): 15–32.

———. "Oral Fixation and New Testament Studies? 'Orality,' 'Performance,' and Reading Texts in Early Christianity." *NTS* 60 (2014): 321–41.

Hylen, Susan E. *Imperfect Believers: Ambiguous Characters in the Gospel of John*. Louisville: Westminster John Knox, 2009.

Iersel, Bas M. F. van. "The Gospel according to St Mark—Written for a Persecuted Community?" *NedTT* 34 (1980): 15–36.

———. *Mark: A Reader-Response Commentary*. Trans. W. H. Bisscheroux. JSNTSup 164. Sheffield: Sheffield Academic, 1998.

Incigneri, Brian J. *The Gospel to the Romans: The Setting and Rhetoric of Mark's Gospel*. BIS 65. Leiden: Brill, 2003.

Iverson, Kelly R. "Incongruity, Humor, and Mark: Performance and the Use of Laughter in the Second Gospel (Mark 8:14–21)." *NTS* 59 (2013): 2–19.

Jackson, Howard M. "The Death of Jesus in Mark and the Miracle from the Cross." *NTS* 33 (1987): 16–37.

Jackson, Shirley. "Memory and Delusion." *New Yorker*. 31 July 2015. https://www .newyorker.com/books/page-turner/memory-and-delusion.

Jackson, T. Ryan. *New Creation in Paul's Letters*. WUNT 272. Tübingen: Mohr Siebeck, 2010.

Jeffers, James S. *Conflict at Rome: Social Order and Hierarchy in Early Christianity*. Minneapolis: Fortress, 1991.

Jeremias, Joachim. *The Eucharistic Words of Jesus*. Translated by Norman Perrin. London: SCM, 1977.

———. *The Parables of Jesus*. 2nd rev. ed. Translated by S. H. Hooke. New York: Scribner's Sons, 1972.

———. *The Prayers of Jesus*. SBT, 2nd series 6. London: SCM, 1967.

Johnson, Andy. "The 'New Creation,' the Crucified and Risen Christ, and the Temple: A Pauline Audience for Mark." *JTI* 1 (2007): 171–91.

Johnson, Earl S., Jr. "Mark 15,39 and the So-Called Confession of the Roman Centurion." *Bib* 81 (2000): 406–13.

Johnson, Luke Timothy. *Living Jesus: Learning the Heart of the Gospel*. San Francisco: HarperCollins, 1999.

———. *Miracles: God's Presence and Power in Creation*. IRUSC. Louisville: Westminster John Knox, 2018.

Jones, J. Estill. Review of *The Disciples according to Mark: Markan Redaction in Current Debate*, by C. Clifton Black. *RevExp* 87 (1990): 129.

Jong, Irene J. F. de, René Nünlist, and Angus Bowie, eds. *Narrators, Narratees, and Narratives in Ancient Greek Literature: Studies in Ancient Greek Narrative*. MnemSup 257. Leiden: Brill, 2004.

Juel, Donald H. "Christian Hope and the Denial of Death: Encountering New Testament Eschatology." Pages 171–83 in *The End of the World and the Ends of God: Science and Theology on Eschatology*. Edited by John Polkinghorne and Michael Welker. Harrisburg, PA: Trinity Press International, 2000.

———. "Encountering the Sower: Mark 4:1–20." *Int* 56 (2002): 273–83.

———. "The Function of the Trial of Jesus in Mark's Gospel." Pages 83–104 in *Society of Biblical Literature 1975 Seminar Papers*. Edited by George MacRae. Missoula, MT: Scholars Press, 1975.

———. *The Gospel of Mark*. IBT. Nashville: Abingdon, 1999.

———. "The Image of the Servant-Christ in the New Testament." *SwJT* 21 (1979): 7–22.

———. *Mark*. ACNT. Minneapolis: Augsburg, 1990.

———. *A Master of Surprise: Mark Interpreted*. Minneapolis: Fortress, 1994.

———. *Messiah and Temple: The Trial of Jesus in the Gospel of Mark*. SBLDS 31. Missoula, MT: Scholars Press, 1977.

———. *Messianic Exegesis: Christological Interpretation of the Old Testament in Early Christianity*. Philadelphia: Fortress, 1988.

———. "The Origin of Mark's Christology." Pages 449–60 in *The Messiah: Developments in Judaism and Early Christianity*. Edited by James H. Charlesworth. Minneapolis: Fortress, 1992.

———. "The Parable of the Mustard Seed." Pages 355–67 in *Studies in Lutheran Hermeneutics*. Edited by John Reumann with Samuel H. Nafzger and Harold H. Ditmanson. Philadelphia: Fortress, 1979.

———. "Plundering Satan's House: Mark 5:1–20." *WW* 17 (1997): 278–81.

———. "The Strange Silence of the Bible." *Int* 51 (1997): 5–19.

Juel, Donald H., with James S. Ackerman and Thayer S. Wardshaw. *An Introduction to New Testament Literature*. Nashville: Abingdon, 1978.

Kähler, Martin. *The So-Called Historical Jesus and the Historic Biblical Christ*. Edited by Ernst Wolf. Translated by Carl E. Braaten. Philadelphia: Fortress, 1964.

Kant, Immanuel. *Religion within the Limits of Reason Alone*. Translated by Theodore M. Greene and Hoyt H. Hudson. New York: Harper & Row, 1960. Based on the 2nd German ed., 1794.

Käsemann, Ernst. "Blind Alleys in the 'Jesus of History' Controversy." Pages 23–65 in *New Testament Questions of Today*. Translated by W. J. Montague. Philadelphia: Fortress, 1969.

———. *Essays on New Testament Themes*. Translated by W. J. Montague. SBT 41. London: SCM, 1964.

———. *Jesus Means Freedom*. Translated by Frank Clarke. London: SCM, 1969. German original, 1968.

———. *The Testament of Jesus: A Study of the Gospel of John in the Light of Chapter 17*. London: SCM, 1968.

Kealy, Sean P. *A History of the Interpretation of the Gospel of Mark: Through the Nineteenth Century*. Vol. 1. Lewistown, NY: Mellen, 2007.

Keats, John. *The Complete Poetical Works and Letters of John Keats*. Cambridge Edition. Boston: Houghton, Mifflin and Company, 1899.

Kechagia, Eleni. "Dying Philosophers in Ancient Biography: Zeno the Stoic and Epicurus." Pages 181–99 in *Writing Biography in Greece and Rome*. Edited by Koen de Temmerman and Kristoffel Demoen. Cambridge: Cambridge University Press, 2016.

Keck, Leander E. *The Bible in the Pulpit: The Renewal of Biblical Preaching*. Nashville: Abingdon, 1978.

———. "Biblical Preaching as Divine Wisdom." Pages 137–56 in *A New Look at Preaching*. Edited by John Burke. GNS 7. Wilmington, DE: Glazier, 1983.

———. *Christ's First Theologian: The Shape of Paul's Thought*. Waco, TX: Baylor University Press, 2015.

———. "Derivation as Destiny: 'Of-ness' in Johannine Christology, Anthropology, and Soteriology." Pages 274–88 in *Exploring the Gospel of John in Honor of D. Moody Smith*. Edited by R. Alan Culpepper and C. Clifton Black. Louisville: Westminster John Knox, 1996.

———. "On the Ethos of Early Christians." *JAAR* 42 (1974): 435–42.

———. "Paul and Apocalyptic Theology." *Int* 38 (1984): 229–41.

———. "Toward the Renewal of New Testament Christology." *NTS* 32 (1986): 362–77.

———. *Who Is Jesus? History in Perfect Tense*. SPNT. Minneapolis: Fortress, 2001.

———. *Why Christ Matters: Toward a New Testament Christology*. Waco, TX: Baylor University Press, 2015.

Kee, Howard Clark. *Community of the New Age: Studies in Mark's Gospel*. Philadelphia: Westminster, 1977.

———. *Jesus in History: An Approach to the Study of the Gospels*. 2nd ed. New York: Harcourt Brace Jovanovich, 1977.

————. *Miracle in the Early Christian World: A Study in Sociohistorical Method.* New Haven: Yale University Press, 1983.

Keenan, John P. *The Gospel of Mark: A Mahayana Reading.* FMFS. Maryknoll, NY: Orbis, 1995.

Keener, Craig. *Christobiography: Memory, History, and the Reliability of the Gospels.* Grand Rapids: Eerdmans, 2019.

Keifert, Patrick. "Mind Reader and Maestro: Models for Understanding Biblical Interpreters." *WW* 1 (1981): 153–65.

Keillor, Garrison. *Lake Wobegon Days.* New York: Viking, 1985.

Kelber, Werner H. *The Oral and the Written Gospel: The Hermeneutics of Speaking and Writing in the Synoptic Tradition, Mark, Paul, and Q.* Philadelphia: Fortress, 1983. Rev. ed., VPT. Bloomington: Indiana University Press, 1997.

————, ed. *The Passion in Mark: Studies on Mark 14–16.* Philadelphia: Fortress, 1976.

————. "Redaction Criticism: On the Nature and Exposition of the Gospels." *PRSt* 6 (1979): 4–16.

Kelber, Werner, and Samuel Byrskog, eds. *Jesus in Memory: Traditions in Oral and Scribal Perspectives.* Waco, TX: Baylor University Press, 2009.

Kelley, Andrew J. "Miracles, Jesus, and Identity: A History of Research Regarding Jesus and Miracles with Special Attention to the Gospel of Mark." *CBR* 13 (2014): 82–106.

Kennedy, George A. *The Art of Persuasion in Greece.* Princeton: Princeton University Press, 1963.

————. *New Testament Interpretation through Rhetorical Criticism.* Chapel Hill: University of North Carolina Press, 1984.

Kermode, Frank. *The Genesis of Secrecy: On the Interpretation of Narrative.* Cambridge: Harvard University Press, 1979.

————. *The Sense of an Ending: Studies in the Theory of Fiction.* London: Oxford University Press, 1966.

Ketchum, Matthew James. "Haunting Empty Tombs: Specters of the Emperor and Jesus in the Gospel of Mark." *BibInt* 26 (2018): 219–43.

Keuth, Herbert. *The Philosophy of Karl Popper.* Cambridge: Cambridge University Press, 2005.

Kim, Tae Hun. "The Anarthrous *Huios Theou* in Mark 15,39 and the Roman Imperial Cult." *Bib* 79 (1998): 221–41.

Kingsbury, Jack Dean. *The Christology of Mark's Gospel.* Philadelphia: Fortress, 1983.

————. "The 'Divine Man' as the Key to Mark's Christology—The End of an Era?" *Int* 35 (1981): 243–57.

————. "The Gospel of Mark in Current Research." *RelSRev* 5 (1979): 101–7.

Kinneavy, James L. *Greek Rhetorical Origins of Christian Faith: An Inquiry*. New York: Oxford University Press, 1987.

Klauck, Hans-Josef. *Vorspiel im Himmel? Erzähltechnik und Theologie im Markus-prolog*. BTS 32. Neukirchener-Vluyn: Neukirchener Verlag, 1997.

Klostermann, Erich. *Das Markusevangelium*. 4th ed. HNT. Tübingen: Mohr Siebeck, 1950.

Klumbies, Paul-Gerhard. *Der Mythos bei Markus*. BZNW 108. Berlin: de Gruyter, 2001.

Knox, John. *Criticism and Faith*. Nashville: Abingdon-Cokesbury, 1952.

Koch, Dietrich-Alex. *Die Bedeutung der Wundererzählungen für die Christologie des Markusevangeliums*. BZNW 42. Berlin: de Gruyter, 1975.

Koester, Craig R. *The Word of Life: A Theology of John's Gospel*. Grand Rapids: Eerdmans, 2008.

Kok, Michael. "Does Mark Narrate the Pauline Kerygma of 'Christ Crucified'? Challenging an Emerging Consensus on Mark as a Pauline Gospel." *JSNT* 37 (2014): 139–60.

Konstan, David, and Robyn Walsh. "Civic and Subversive Biography in Antiquity." Pages 26–43 in *Writing Biography in Greece and Rome*. Edited by Koen de Temmerman and Kristoffel Demoen. Cambridge: Cambridge University Press, 2016.

Kugel, James L., and Rowan A. Greer. *Early Biblical Interpretation*. LEC 3. Philadelphia: Westminster 1986.

Kuhn, Thomas S. *The Structure of Scientific Revolutions*. Chicago: University of Chicago Press, 1962.

Kurzinger, Josef. "Die Aussage des Papias von Hierapolis zur literarischen Form des Markusevangelium." *BZ* 21 (1977): 245–64.

La Piana, George. "Foreign Groups in Rome during the First Centuries of the Empire." *HTR* 20 (1927): 183–403.

———. "The Roman Church at the End of the Second Century." *HTR* 18 (1925): 201–77.

Lambrecht, Jan. *Die Redaktion der Markus-Apokalypse: Literarische Analyse und Strukturuntersuchung*. AnBib 28. Rome: Pontifical Institute, 1967.

Lampe, G. W. H. "A.D. 70 in Christian Reflection." Pages 153–71 in *Jesus and the Politics of His Day*. Edited by Ernst Bammel and C. F. D. Moule. Cambridge: Cambridge University Press, 1984.

Lampe, Peter. *Die städtromischen Christen in den ersten beiden Jahrhunderten: Untersuchungen zur Sozialgeschichte*. 2nd ed. WUNT 2/18. Tübingen: Mohr Siebeck, 1987.

———. "Theological Wisdom and the 'Word about the Cross': The Rhetorical Scheme in 1 Corinthians 1–4." *Int* 44 (1990): 117–31.

Last, Richard. "Communities That Write: Christ-Groups, Associations, and Gospel Communities." *NTS* 58 (2012): 173–98.

Latzoo, Cyril. "The Story of the Twelve in the Gospel of Mark." *Hekima Review* [Nairobi] 13 (1995): 25–33.

Lausberg, Heinrich. *Handbook of Literary Rhetoric: A Foundation for Literary Study*. Translated by Matthew T. Bliss. Edited by David E. Orton and R. Dean Anderson. Leiden: Brill, 1998.

Leander, Hans. *Discourses of Empire: The Gospel of Mark from a Postcolonial Perspective*. Atlanta: Society of Biblical Literature, 2013.

LeDonne, Anthony, and Tom Thatcher, eds. *The Fourth Gospel in First-Century Media Culture*. LNTS 426. London: T&T Clark, 2011.

Lee-Pollard, Dorothy A. "Power as Powerlessness: A Key Emphasis in the Gospel of Mark." *SJT* 40 (1987): 173–88.

Levenson, Sam. *Everything but Money*. New York: Simon & Schuster, 1966.

Levin, Bernard. *Enthusiasms: Art, Literature, Music, Food, Walking*. New York: Crown, 1983.

Levine, Amy-Jill, with Marianne Blickenstaff, eds. *A Feminist Companion to Mark*. London: T&T Clark; Cleveland: Pilgrim, 2001.

Lewis, C. S. *The Lion, the Witch and the Wardrobe: A Children's Story*. New York: Collier, 1950.

Lewis, Jack P. "Jamnia after Forty Years." *HUCA* 71 (2000): 233–59.

Liew, Tat-siong Benny. *Politics of Parousia: Reading Mark Inter(con)textually*. BIS 42. Leiden: Brill, 1999.

Lightfoot, R. H. *The Gospel Message of St. Mark*. Oxford: Clarendon, 1950.

———. *History and Interpretation in the Gospels*. London: Hodder & Stoughton, 1935.

Lindars, Barnabas. *New Testament Apologetics*. London: SCM, 1961.

Lindemann, Andreas. "Literatur zu den Synoptischen Evangelien 1992–2000 (III): Das Markusevangelium." *TRu* 69 (2004): 369–423.

———. *Paulus im ältesten Christentum: Das Bild des Apostels und die Rezeption der paulinischen Theologie in der frühchristlichen Literatur bis Marcion*. BHT 58. Tübingen: Mohr Siebeck, 1979.

Loader, William. "Challenged at the Boundaries: A Conservative Jesus in Mark's Tradition." *JSNT* 19 (1997): 45–61.

Lounsbury, Richard C. *The Arts of Suetonius: An Introduction*. AUSS 3.3. New York: Lang, 1987.

Louth, Andrew. *Discerning the Mystery: An Essay on the Nature of Theology*. Oxford: Clarendon, 1983.

Lührmann, Dieter. *Das Markusevangelium*. HNT. Tübingen: Mohr Siebeck, 1987.

Luther, Martin. *Luther: Early Theological Works*. Edited by James Atkinson. Philadelphia: Westminster, 1962.

Luz, Ulrich. "Theologia crucis als Mitte der Theologie im Neuen Testament." *EvT* 34 (1974): 116–41.

Lyons, George. *Pauline Autobiography: Toward a New Understanding*. SBLDS 73. Atlanta: Scholars Press, 1985.

Lyons-Pardue, Kara J. *Gospel Women and the Long Ending of Mark*. LNTS 614. London: T&T Clark, 2020.

Mack, Burton L. *The Lost Gospel: The Book of Q and Christian Origins*. San Francisco: HarperSanFrancisco, 1993.

———. *A Myth of Innocence: Mark and Christian Origins*. Philadelphia: Fortress, 1988.

Mack, Burton L., and Vernon K. Robbins. *Patterns of Persuasion in the Gospels*. FF. Sonoma, CA: Polebridge, 1989.

Mackrell, Gerard. *The Healing Miracles in Mark's Gospel: The Passion and Compassion of Jesus*. Slough: St. Paul, 1987.

Macquarrie, John. *Principles of Christian Theology*. New York: Scribner's Sons, 1977.

Mainwaring, Simon. *Mark, Mutuality, and Mental Health: Encounters with Jesus*. SemeiaSt 79. Atlanta: Scholars Press, 2014.

Malbon, Elizabeth Struthers. "Echoes and Foreshadowings in Mark 4–8: Reading and Rereading." *JBL* 112 (1993): 211–30.

———. "Fallible Followers: Women and Men in the Gospel of Mark." *Semeia* 28 (1983): 29–48.

———. "Galilee and Jerusalem: History and Literature in Marcan Interpretation." *CBQ* 44 (1982): 242–55.

———. *In the Company of Jesus: Characters in Mark's Gospel*. Louisville: Westminster John Knox, 2000.

———. "The Jewish Leaders in the Gospel of Mark: A Literary Study of Markan Characterization." *JBL* 108 (1989): 259–81

———. *Mark's Jesus: Characterization as Narrative Christology*. Waco, TX: Baylor University Press, 2009.

———. *Narrative Space and Mythic Meaning in Mark*. San Francisco: Harper & Row, 1986.

———. Review of *The Disciples according to Mark: Markan Redaction in Current Debate*, by C. Clifton Black. *Int* 45 (1991): 82, 84.

———. "Texts and Contexts: Interpreting the Disciples in Mark." *Semeia* 62 (1993): 81–102.

Malcolm, Lois. "The Crucified Messiah and Divine Suffering in the Old Testament." Pages 136–44 in *"And God Saw That It Was Good": Essays on Creation and God in Honor of Terence E. Fretheim*. Edited by Frederick J. Gaiser and Mark A. Throntveit. WWSup 5. Saint Paul: Luther Seminary, 2006.

Maloney, Elliott C. *Semitic Interference in Marcan Syntax*. SBLDS 51. Chico, CA: Scholars Press, 1981.

Mann, C. S. *Mark: A New Translation with Introduction and Commentary*. AB 27. Garden City, NY: Doubleday, 1986.

Manson, T. W. *Studies in the Gospels and Epistles*. Edited by Matthew Black. Philadelphia: Westminster, 1962.

Marcus, Joel. "The Jewish War and the *Sitz im Leben* of Mark." *JBL* 111 (1992): 441–62.

———. "Mark—Interpreter of Paul." *NTS* 46 (2000): 473–87.

———. *Mark 1–8: A New Translation with Introduction and Commentary*. AB 27. New York: Doubleday, 2000.

———. "Mark 4:10–12 and Marcan Epistemology." *JBL* 103 (1984): 557–74.

———. *Mark 8–16: A New Translation with Introduction and Commentary*. AB 27A. New Haven: Yale University Press, 2009.

———. *The Mystery of the Kingdom of God*. SBLDS 90. Atlanta: Scholars Press, 1986.

———. "Scripture and Tradition in Mark 7." Pages 177–96 in *The Scriptures in the Gospels*. Edited by C. M. Tuckett. BETL 131. Leuven: Leuven University Press; Peeters, 1997.

———. *The Way of the Lord: Christological Exegesis of the Old Testament in the Gospel of Mark*. Louisville: Westminster John Knox, 1992.

Markowitsch, Hans. *Das Gedächtnis: Entwicklung, Funktionen, Störungen*. Munich: Beck, 2009.

Marshall, Christopher D. *Faith as a Theme in Mark's Narrative*. SNTSMS 64. Cambridge: Cambridge University Press, 1989.

Martin, Dale B. "Jesus in Jerusalem: Armed and Not Dangerous." *JSNT* 34 (2014): 3–24.

Martyn, J. Louis. "Epistemology at the Turn of the Ages: 2 Corinthians 5.16." Pages 269–87 in *Christian History and Interpretation: Studies Presented to John Knox*. Edited by W. R. Farmer, C. F. D. Moule, and R. R. Niebuhr. Cambridge: Cambridge University Press, 1967.

———. *Theological Issues in the Letters of Paul*. Nashville: Abingdon, 1997.

Marxsen, Willi. *Introduction to the New Testament: An Approach to Its Problems*. Translated by Geoffrey Buswell. Philadelphia: Fortress, 1968.

———. *Mark the Evangelist: Studies on the Redaction History of the Gospel*. Translated by James Boyce, Donald Juel, and William Poehlmann, with Roy A. Harrisville. Nashville: Abingdon, 1969. German original, *Der Evangelist Markus: Studien zur Redaktionsgeschichte des Evangeliums*. Göttingen: Vandenhoeck & Ruprecht, 1956.

Matera, Frank J. *The Kingship of Jesus: Composition and Theology in Mark 15*. SBLDS 66. Chico, CA: Scholars Press, 1982.

Matlock, R. Barry. *Unveiling the Apocalyptic Paul: Paul's Interpreters and the Rhetoric of Criticism*. JSNTSup 127. Sheffield: Sheffield Academic, 1996.

Mattingly, Garrett. *The Armada*. Boston: Houghton Mifflin, 1959.

Mauser, Ulrich. *Christ in the Wilderness: The Wilderness Theme in the Second Gospel and Its Basis in the Biblical Tradition*. SBT 39. London: SCM; Evanston, IL: Allenson, 1963.

McKane, Byron R. *Roll Back the Stone: Death and Burial in the World of Jesus*. Harrisburg, PA: Trinity Press International, 2003.

McKaughan, Daniel J. "Cognitive Opacity and the Analysis of Faith: Acts of Faith Interiorized through a Glass Only Darkly." *RelS* 54 (2018): 576–85.

McPherson, James. *Battle Cry of Freedom: The Civil War Era*. New York: Oxford University Press, 1988.

———. *For Cause and Comrades: Why Men Fought in the Civil War*. New York: Oxford University Press, 1997.

Meadors, Edward P. "Isaiah 40:3 and the Synoptic Gospels' Parody of the Roman Road System." *NTS* 66 (2020): 106–24.

Meagher, John C. *Clumsy Construction in Mark's Gospel: A Critique of Form- and Redaktionsgeschichte*. New York: Mellen, 1979.

———. "The Gospel of Mark: The Vulnerable Disciples." *Vid* 67 (2003): 779–803.

Meier, John P. *A Marginal Jew: Rethinking the Historical Jesus*. 5 vols. AYBRL. New York: Doubleday; New Haven: Yale University Press, 1991, 1994, 2001, 2009, 2016.

Menander Rhetor. *Menander Rhetor*. Edited with trans. and commentary by D. A. Russell and N. G. Wilson. Oxford: Clarendon, 1981.

Merkel, Helmut. "Peter's Curse." Pages 66–71 in *The Trial of Jesus: Cambridge Studies in Honour of C. F. D. Moule*. Edited by Ernst Bammel. SBT 2nd series 13. London: SCM, 1970.

Meye, Robert P. *Jesus and the Twelve: Discipleship and Revelation in Mark's Gospel*. Grand Rapids: Eerdmans, 1968.

Meyer, Ben F. *The Aims of Jesus*. London: SCM, 1979.

———. "Some Consequences of Birger Gerhardsson's Account of the Origins of the Gospel Tradition." Pages 424–40 in *Jesus and the Gospel Tradition*. Edited by Henry Wansbrough. JSNTSup 4. Sheffield: Sheffield Academic, 1991.

Meyer, Paul W. "Faith and History Revisited." *PSB* 10 (n.s. 1989): 75–83. Repr., pages 19–26 in Meyer, *The Word in This World: Essays in New Testament Exegesis and Theology*. Edited by John T. Carroll. NTL. Louisville: Westminster John Knox, 2004.

———. "'The Father': The Presentation of God in the Fourth Gospel." Pages 255–73 in

Exploring the Gospel of John in Honor of D. Moody Smith. Edited by R. Alan Culpepper and C. Clifton Black. Louisville: Westminster John Knox, 1996.

———. "The This-Worldliness of the New Testament." *PSB* 2 (1979): 219–31. Repr., pages 5–18 in Meyer, *The Word in This World: Essays in New Testament Exegesis and Theology.* Edited by John T. Carroll. NTL. Louisville: Westminster John Knox, 2004.

Millay, Edna St. Vincent. *The Letters of Edna St. Vincent Millay.* Edited by A. R. Macdougall. New York: Harper & Brothers, 1952.

Miller, David. "Conjectural Knowledge: Popper's Solution of the Problem of Induction." Pages 17–49 in *In Pursuit of Truth: Essays on the Philosophy of Karl Popper on the Occasion of His 80th Birthday.* Edited by Paul Levinson. Atlantic Highlands, NJ: Humanities; Sussex: Harvester, 1982.

———. *Critical Rationalism: A Restatement and Defence.* Chicago: Open Court, 1994.

Miller, Patrick D. "The Poetry of Creation: Psalm 104." Pages 87–103 in *God Who Creates: Essays in Honor of W. Sibley Towner.* Edited by William P. Brown and S. Dean McBride Jr. Grand Rapids: Eerdmans, 2000.

Miller, Richard Lawrence. *Lincoln and His World: The Early Years, Birth to Illinois Legislature.* Mechanicsburg, PA: Stackpole, 2006.

Miller, Susan. *Women in Mark's Gospel.* JSNTSup 259. London: T&T Clark, 2004.

Minear, Paul S. *The Bible and the Historian: Breaking the Silence about God in Biblical Studies.* Nashville: Abingdon, 2002.

Miscall, Peter. *The Workings of Old Testament Narrative.* Philadelphia: Fortress, 1983.

Mitchell, Margaret M. "Epiphanic Evolutions in Earliest Christianity." *ICS* 29 (2004): 183–204.

———. "Mark, the Long-Form Pauline εὐαγγέλιον." Pages 201–17 in *Modern and Ancient Literary Criticism of the Gospels: Continuing the Debate on Gospel Genre(s).* Edited by Robert Matthew Calhoun, David P. Moessner, and Tobias Nicklas. WUNT 451. Tübingen: Mohr Siebeck, 2020.

Moloney, Francis J. *The Gospel of Mark: A Commentary.* Peabody, MA: Hendrickson, 2002.

———. *The Johannine Son of Man.* BSR 14. 2nd ed. Rome: Libreria Ateneo Salesiano, 1978.

Momigliano, Arnaldo. *The Development of Greek Biography.* Exp. ed. Cambridge: Harvard University Press, 1993.

Moore, George Foot. *Judaism in the First Centuries of the Christian Era.* 2 vols. New York: Schocken, 1971.

Moore, W. Ernest. "'Outside' and 'Inside': Paul and Mark." *ExpTim* 103 (1992): 331–36.

Morgan, Robert. "The Historical Jesus and the Theology of the New Testament." Pages 187–206 in *The Glory of Christ in the New Testament: Studies in Christology in Memory of George Bradford Caird*. Edited by L. D. Hurst and N. T. Wright. Oxford: Clarendon, 1987.

———. Review of *The Disciples according to Mark: Markan Redaction in Current Debate*, by C. Clifton Black. *Theological Book Review* 1 (1989): 12.

Morgan, Teresa. "Faith in Dialogue." *JSNT* 40 (2018): 299–311.

———. "Introduction to *Roman Faith and Christian Faith*." *RelS* 54 (2018): 563–68.

———. "Response to My Commentators." *RelS* 54 (2018): 592–604.

———. Review of *The Son of God in the Roman World: Divine Sonship in Its Social and Political Context*, by Michael Peppard. *JTS* 64 (2013): 216–18.

———. "Roman Faith and Christian Faith." *NTS* 64 (2018): 255–61.

———. *Roman Faith and Christian Faith: Pistis and Fides in the Early Roman Empire and Early Churches*. Oxford: Oxford University Press, 2015.

Motyer, Stephen. "The Rending of the Veil: A Markan Pentecost?" *NTS* 33 (1987): 155–57.

Moule, C. F. D. *An Idiom Book of New Testament Greek*. 2nd ed. Cambridge: Cambridge University Press, 1959.

Moulton, James H. *Prolegomena*. Vol. 1 of *A Grammar of New Testament Greek*. 3rd ed. Edinburgh: T&T Clark, 1957.

Muddiman, John B. "The End of Markan Redaction Criticism?" Review of *The Disciples according to Mark: Markan Redaction in Current Debate*, by C. Clifton Black. *ExpTim* 101 (1990): 307–9.

Musurillo, Herbert, ed. *The Acts of the Christian Martyrs*. Oxford: Clarendon, 1972.

Myers, Ched. *Binding the Strong Man: A Political Reading of Mark's Story of Jesus*. Maryknoll, NY: Orbis, 1988.

Nadeau, Raymond. "Hermogenes' *On Stases*: A Translation with an Introduction and Notes." *SM* 31 (1964): 361–424.

Neffe, Jürgen. *Einstein: A Biography*. Translated by Shelley Frisch. New York: Farrar, Straus & Giroux, 2007.

Neirynck, Frans. *Duality in Mark: Contributions to the Study of the Markan Redaction*. BETL 31. Leuven: Leuven University Press, 1988.

———. "Paul and the Sayings of Jesus." Pages 265–321 in *L'Apôtre Paul: Personalité, style et conception du ministère*. Edited by A. Vanhoye. BETL 73. Leuven: Leuven University Press; Peeters, 1986.

———. "Urmarcus Révisé: La Théorie Synoptique de M.-É. Boismard, Nouvelle Manière." *ETL* 71 (1995): 166–75.

Neumann, James M. "The Gospel of the Son of God: Psalm 2 and Mark's Narrative Christology." PhD diss., Princeton Theological Seminary, 2020.

Nickelsburg, George W. E. "The Genre and Function of the Markan Passion Narrative." *HTR* 73 (1980): 153–84.

———. *Jewish Literature between the Bible and the Midrash: A Historical and Literary Introduction*. Philadelphia: Fortress, 1981.

Nineham, Dennis E. *The Gospel of St Mark*. PGC. Baltimore: Penguin Books, 1963.

O'Brien, Kelli S. "Innocence and Guilt: Apologetic, Martyr Stories, and Allusion in the Markan Trial Narratives." Pages 205–28 in *The Trial and Death of Jesus: Essays on the Passion Narrative in Mark*. Edited by Geert van Oyen and Tom Shepherd. CBET. Leuven: Peeters, 2006.

O'Connor, Flannery. *Mystery and Manners: Occasional Prose*. Edited by Sally and Robert Fitzgerald. New York: Farrar, Straus & Giroux, 1961.

O'Connor, Maurice John-Patrick. *The Moral Life according to the Gospel of Mark*. LNTS 667. London: Bloomsbury T&T Clark, 2022.

Oden, Thomas C., and Christopher A. Hall, eds. *Mark*. ACCSNT 2. Downers Grove, IL: InterVarsity Press, 1998.

Ollenburger, Ben C. "Israel's Creation Theology." *ExAud* 3 (1988): 54–71.

Outler, Albert C. "The 'Logic' of Canon-Making and the Tasks of Canon and the Tasks of Canon-Criticism." Pages 263–76 in *Texts and Testaments: Critical Essays on the Bible and Early Church Fathers*. Edited by W. Eugene March. San Antonio: Trinity University Press, 1980.

Overbeck, Franz. "Über die Anfänge der patrischen Literatur." *HZ* 48 (1882): 417–72.

Oyen, Geert van. *The Interpretation of the Feeding Miracles in the Gospel of Mark*. CBRA 4. Brussels: Koninkluke Vlaamse Academie van Belgie voor Wetenschappen en Kunsten, 1999.

———. "The Meaning of the Death of Jesus in the Gospel of Mark: A Real Reader Perspective." Pages 229–45 in *The Trial and Death of Jesus: Essays on the Passion Narrative in Mark*. Edited by Geert van Oyen and Tom Shepherd. CBET. Leuven: Peeters, 2006.

Painter, John. "When Is a House Not a Home? Disciples and Family in Mark 3:13–35." *NTS* 45 (1999): 498–513.

Pais, Abraham. *"Subtle Is the Lord . . .": The Science and Life of Albert Einstein*. Oxford: Clarendon; New York: Oxford University Press, 1982.

Parker, Dorothy. *The Algonquin Wits*. Edited by Robert E. Drennan. Kensington: Citadel, 1985.

Parsenios, George L. *Departure and Consolation: The Johannine Farewell Discourses in Light of Greco-Roman Literature*. NovTSup 117. Leiden: Brill, 2005.

———. *Rhetoric and Drama in the Johannine Lawsuit Motif.* WUNT 258. Tübingen: Mohr Siebeck, 2010.

Peabody, David B. *Mark as Composer.* NGS 1. Macon, GA: Mercer University Press, 1987.

Peabody, David, Lamar Cope, and Allan J. McNicol. *One Gospel from Two: Mark's Use of Matthew and Luke; A Demonstration by the Research Team of the International Institute for Renewal of Gospel Studies.* Harrisburg, PA: Trinity Press International, 2002.

Peppard, Michael. *The Son of God in the Roman World: Divine Sonship in Its Social and Political Context.* Oxford: Oxford University Press, 2011.

Perelman, Chaim, and Lucie Olbrechts-Tyteca. *The New Rhetoric: A Treatise on Argumentation.* Translated by John Wilkinson and Purcell Weaver. Notre Dame: University of Notre Dame Press, 1969.

Perrin, Norman. "The Evangelist as Author: Reflections on Method in the Study and Interpretation of the Synoptic Gospels and Acts." *BR* 17 (1972): 5–18.

———. "The Interpretation of the Gospel of Mark." *Int* 30 (1976): 115–24.

———. "Towards an Interpretation of the Gospel of Mark." Pages 1–78 in *Christology and a Modern Pilgrimage: A Discussion with Norman Perrin.* Edited by Hans Dieter Betz. Claremont: The New Testament Colloquium, 1971.

———. *What Is Redaction Criticism?* GBS. Philadelphia: Fortress, 1976.

Pesch, Rudolf. *Das Markusevangelium.* 2 vols. HTKNT 2. Freiburg: Herder, 1976, 1977.

———. *Das Markusevangelium.* 2nd ed. 2 vols. HTKNT 2. Freiburg: Herder, 1980.

———. *Naherwartungen: Tradition und Redaktion in Mk 13.* KBANT. Düsseldorf: Patmos, 1968.

Peterson, Dwight N. *The Origins of Mark: The Markan Community in Current Debate.* BibInt 48. Leiden: Brill, 2000.

Pethes, Nicolas. *Kulturwissenschaftliche Gedächtnistheorien: Zur Einführung.* Hamburg: Junius, 2008.

Pilch, John J. "Death with Honor: The Mediterranean Style Death of Jesus in Mark." *BTB* 2 (1995): 65–70.

Pilgaard, Aage. "Apokalyptik als bibeltheologisches Thema: Dargestellt an Dan 9 und Mark 13." Pages 180–200 in *New Directions in Biblical Theology: Papers of the Aarhus Conference, 16–19 September 1992.* Edited by Sigfried Pedersen. NovTSup 76. Leiden: Brill, 1994.

Pitre, Brent. *Jesus and the Last Supper.* Grand Rapids: Eerdmans, 2015.

Placher, William C. "How the Gospels Mean." Pages 27–42 in *Seeking the Identity of Jesus: A Pilgrimage.* Edited by Beverly Roberts Gaventa and Richard B. Hays. Grand Rapids: Eerdmans, 2008.

———. *Mark*. Belief. Louisville: Westminster John Knox, 2010.

———. "Narratives of a Vulnerable God." *PSB* 14 (1993): 134–51.

———. *Narratives of a Vulnerable God: Christ, Theology, and Scripture*. Louisville: Westminster John Knox, 1994.

Pluckrose, Helen, and James Lindsay. *Cynical Theories: How Activist Scholarship Made Everything about Race, Gender, and Identity—and Why This Harms Everybody*. Durham, NC: Pitchstone, 2020.

Polkinghorne, Donald E. "Narrative Psychology and Historical Consciousness." Pages 12–45 in *Erzählung, Identität, Historische Bewusstsein: Die psychologische Konstruktion von Zeit und Geschichte, Erinnerung, Geschichte Identität 1*. Edited by Jürgen Straub. Translated by Alexander Kochinka and Jürgen Straub. Frankfurt: Suhrkamp, 1998.

Polkinghorne, John. *Beyond Science: The Wider Human Context*. Cambridge: Cambridge University Press, 1996.

———. *The Quantum World*. London: Longman, 1985.

Popper, Karl R. *Conjectures and Refutations: The Growth of Scientific Knowledge*. 3rd ed. London: Routledge & Kegan Paul, 1969.

———. *The High Tide of Prophecy: Hegel, Marx, and the Aftermath*. Vol. 2 of *The Open Society and Its Enemies*. London: Routledge & Sons, 1945.

———. *Knowledge and the Mind-Body Problem: In Defence of Interaction*. Edited by M. A. Notturno. London: Routledge, 1994.

———. "Knowledge: Subjective versus Objective." Pages 58–77 in *A Pocket Popper*. Edited by David Miller. Oxford: Fontana, 1983.

———. *The Logic of Scientific Discovery*. New York: Basic Books, 1959.

———. *Objective Knowledge: An Evolutionary Approach*. Rev. ed. Oxford: Clarendon; New York: Oxford University Press, 1979.

———. *The Poverty of Historicism*. 2nd ed. London: Routledge & Kegan Paul, 1960.

———. *Realism and the Aim of Science*. London: Routledge, 1983.

Posner, Richard A. *How Judges Think*. Cambridge: Harvard University Press, 2008.

Pourcq, Maarten de, and Geert Roskam. "Mirroring Virtues in Plutarch's Agis, Cleomenes, and the Gracchi." Pages 163–80 in *Writing Biography in Greece and Rome: Narrative Technique and Fictionalization*. Edited by Koen de Temmerman and Kristoffel Demoen. Cambridge: Cambridge University Press, 2016.

Power, Tristan. "The Endings of Suetonius's *Caesars*." Pages 58–77 in *Suetonius the Biographer: Studies in Roman Lives*. Edited by Tristan Power and Roy K. Gibson. Oxford: Oxford University Press, 2014.

Praet, Danny. "The Divided Cloak as *Redemptio Militiae*: Biblical Stylization and Hagiographical Intertextuality in Sulpicius Severus' *Vita Martini*." Pages

133–59 in *Writing Biography in Greece and Rome: Narrative Technique and Fictionalization*. Edited by Koen de Temmerman and Kristoffel Demoen. Cambridge: Cambridge University Press, 2016.

Price, Reynolds. *Three Gospels: The Good News according to Mark; The Good News according to John; An Honest Account of a Memorable Life*. New York: Scribner, 1996.

Pritchard, James B., ed. *The Ancient Near East: An Anthology of Texts and Pictures*. Princeton: Princeton University Press, 1971.

Rad, Gerhard von. *Genesis: A Commentary*. Rev. ed. Translated by John H. Marks. OTL. Philadelphia: Westminster, 1972.

———. "The Theological Problem of the Old Testament Doctrine of Creation." Pages 177–86 in Gerhard von Rad, *From Genesis to Chronicles: Explorations in Old Testament Theology*. Edited by K. C. Hanson. Minneapolis: Fortress, 2005.

Räisänen, Heikki. Review of *The Disciples according to Mark: Markan Redaction in Current Debate*, by C. Clifton Black. *TeolT* 96 (1991): 80–81.

Rajak, Tessa. "Dying for the Law: The Martyr's Portrait in Jewish-Greek Literature." Pages 39–67 in *Portraits: Biographical Representation in Greek and Latin Literature of the Roman Empire*. Edited by M. J. Edwards and Simon Swain. Oxford: Clarendon, 1997.

Ranke, Leopold von. *The Secret of World History: Selected Writings on the Art and Science of History*. Edited by Roger Wines. New York: Fordham University Press, 1981.

Redman, Judith C. S. "How Accurate Are Eyewitnesses? Bauckham and the Eyewitnesses in the Light of Psychological Research." *JBL* 129 (2010): 177–97.

Reimarus, Hermann Samuel. *Fragments*. Edited by Charles H. Talbert. Translated by Ralph S. Fraser. LJS. Philadelphia: Fortress, 1972. German original, 1778.

Reiprich, Torsten. *Das Mariageheimnis: Maria von Nazareth und die Bedeutung familiärer Beziehungen im Markusevangelium*. FRLANT 223. Göttingen: Vandenhoeck & Ruprecht, 2008.

Renan, Ernst. *The Life of Jesus*. 23rd ed. Revised by John Henry Allen. New York: Random House, 1927. French original, 1863.

Renoir, Jean. Introduction to *La Règle du jeu*. New York: Criterion Collection, 2004.

Rhoads, David, and Joanna Dewey, and Donald Michie. *Mark as Story: An Introduction to the Narrative of a Gospel*. Minneapolis: Fortress, 2012.

Riches, John. *Conflicting Mythologies: Identity Formation in the Gospels of Mark and Matthew*. SNTW. Edinburgh: T&T Clark, 2000.

Riesner, Rainer. *Jesus als Lehrer: Eine Untersuchung zum Ursprung der Evangelien-Überlieferung*. WUNT 2/7. Tübingen: Mohr Siebeck, 1981.

Riley, Harold. *The Making of Mark: An Exploration*. Macon, GA: Mercer University Press, 1990.

Robbins, Vernon K. *Jesus the Teacher: A Socio-rhetorical Interpretation of Mark*. Philadelphia: Fortress, 1984.

Robinson, James M. *The Problem of History in Mark*. SBT 21. London: SCM, 1957.

Robinson, John A. T. *The Priority of John*. London: SCM, 1985.

Rohde, Joachim. *Rediscovering the Teaching of the Evangelists*. Translated by Dorothea M. Barton. NTL. Philadelphia: Westminster, 1968. German original, 1966.

Romaniuk, Kazimierz. "Le Problème des Paulinismes dans l'Évangile de Marc." *NTS* 23 (1977): 266–74.

Rosenblatt, Roger. *The Man in the Water: Essays and Stories*. New York: Random House, 1994.

Roskam, Hendrika Nicoline. *The Purpose of the Gospel of Mark in Its Social and Religious Context*. NovTSup 114. Leiden: Brill, 2004.

Rothschild, Clare K. "'Have I Not Seen Jesus Our Lord?!' (1 Cor 9:1c): Faithlessness of Eyewitnesses in the Gospels of Mark and Paul." *ASE* 31 (2014): 29–51.

Rousée, J.-M. Review of *The Disciples according to Mark: Markan Redaction in Current Debate*, by C. Clifton Black. *RB* 96 (1989): 474–75.

Rowland, Christopher. *The Open Heaven: A Study of Apocalyptic in Judaism and Early Christianity*. New York: Crossroad, 1982.

Rowlingson, Donald T. "The Moral Context of the Resurrection Faith." Pages 415–25 in *Christ and Spirit in the New Testament in Honour of Charles Francis Digby Moule*. Edited by Barnabas Lindars and Stephen S. Smalley. Cambridge: Cambridge University Press, 1973.

Rutherford, Ian. *Canons of Style in the Antonine Age: Idea-Theory in Its Literary Context*. Oxford: Clarendon, 1998.

Sabin, Marie Noonan. *Reopening the Word: Reading Mark as Theology in the Context of Early Judaism*. Oxford: Oxford University Press, 2002.

Sandburg, Carl. *Abraham Lincoln: The Prairie Years*. 2 vols. New York: Harcourt, Brace & Company, 1926.

———. *Abraham Lincoln: The War Years*. 4 vols. New York: Harcourt, Brace & Company, 1939.

Sanders, E. P. *Jesus and Judaism*. Philadelphia: Fortress, 1985.

———. *Paul and Palestinian Judaism: A Comparison of Patterns of Religion*. Philadelphia: Fortress, 1977.

Schacter, Daniel L. *Seven Sins of Memory: How the Mind Forgets and Remembers*. New York: Houghton Mifflin, 2002.

Schildgen, Brenda Deen. *Power and Prejudice: The Reception of the Gospel of Mark*. Detroit: Wayne State University Press, 1999.

Schleiermacher, Friedrich Daniel Ernst. *The Life of Jesus*. Edited by Jack D. Verhey-den. Translated by S. MacLean Gilmour. LJS. Philadelphia: Fortress, 1975. German original, 1864.

Schmidt, T. E. "Mark 15:16–32: The Crucifixion Narrative and the Roman Trium-phal Procession." *NTS* 41 (1995): 1–18.

Schmithals, Walter. *Das Evangelium nach Markus*. OTKNT 2/1–2. Gütersloh: Gerd Mohn; Würzburg: Echter, 1979.

Schröter, Jens. *Erinnerung an Jesu Worte: Studien zur Rezeption der Logienüber-lieferung in Markus, Q, und Thomas*. WMANT 76. Neukirchen-Vluyn: Neukirchener Verlag, 1997.

———. "The Gospels as Eyewitness Testimony? A Critical Examination of Richard Bauckham's *Jesus and the Eyewitnesses*." *JSNT* 31 (2008): 195–209.

Schüssler Fiorenza, Elisabeth. *Jesus: Miriam's Child, Sophia's Prophet: Critical Issues in Feminist Theology*. New York: Continuum: 1994.

———. "The Phenomenon of Early Christian Apocalyptic: Some Reflections on Method." Pages 295–316 in *Apocalypticism in the Mediterranean World and the Near East: Proceedings of the International Colloquium on Apocalypti-cism, Uppsala, August 12–17, 1979*. Edited by David Hellholm. 2nd ed. Tübin-gen: Mohr Siebeck, 1989.

Schweitzer, Albert. *The Quest of the Historical Jesus*. Translated by W. Montgomery, J. R. Coates, Susan Cupitt, and J. Bowden. London: SCM, 2000.

———. *The Quest of the Historical Jesus: First Complete Edition*. Edited by John Bowden. Minneapolis: Fortress, 2001.

Schweizer, Eduard. "Anmerkungen zur Theologie des Markus." Pages 35–46 in *Neo-testamentica et Patristica: Freundesgabe O. Cullmann*. NovTSup 6. Leiden: Brill, 1962.

———. "Die theologische Leistung des Markus." *EvT* 24 (1964): 337–55.

———. *The Good News according to Mark*. Translated by Donald H. Madvig. At-lanta: John Knox, 1970.

———. "Mark's Contribution to the Quest of the Historical Jesus." *NTS* 10 (1964): 421–32.

Schwöbel, Christoph. "Reconciliation: From Biblical Observations to Dogmatic Reconstruction." Pages 13–38 in *The Theology of Reconciliation*. Edited by Colin E. Gunton. London: T&T Clark, 2003.

Scott, James C. *Domination and the Arts of Resistance: Hidden Transcripts*. New Haven: Yale University Press, 1990.

Sehgal, Parul. "The Ghost Story Persists in American Literature. Why?" *New York Times*. 22 October 2018. https://www.nytimes.com/2018/10/22/books/re view/ghost-stories.html.

Selvidge, Marla J. "Mark 5:25–34 and Leviticus 15:19–20: A Reaction to Restrictive Purity Legislations." *JBL* 103 (1984): 619–23.

Senior, Donald. *The Passion of Jesus in the Gospel of Mark*. Wilmington, DE: Glazier, 1984.

Shenk, Joshua Wolf. *Lincoln's Melancholy: How Depression Challenged a President and Fueled His Greatness*. Boston: Houghton Mifflin, 2005.

Shepherd, Tom. "The Irony of Power in the Trial of Jesus and the Denial by Peter—Mark 14:53–72." Pages 229–45 in *The Trial and Death of Jesus: Essays on the Passion Narrative in Mark*. Edited by Geert van Oyen and Tom Shepherd. CBET. Leuven: Peeters, 2006.

Sheppard, Gerald T. "Canonical Criticism." *ABD* 1:861–66.

Shinal, Myrick C., Jr. *Miracles and the Kingdom of God: Christology and Social Identity in Mark and Q*. Minneapolis: Fortress, 2018.

Shiner, Whitney T. "The Ambiguous Pronouncement of the Centurion and the Shrouding of Meaning in Mark." *JSNT* 22 (2000): 3–22.

———. *Follow Me! Disciples in Markan Rhetoric*. SBLDS 145. Atlanta: Scholars Press, 1995.

———. *Proclaiming the Gospel: First-Century Performance of Mark*. Harrisburg, PA: Trinity Press International, 2003.

Shively, Elizabeth E. "A Critique of Richard Burridge's Genre Theory: From a One-Dimensional to a Multi-Dimensional Approach to Gospel Genre." Pages 97–112 in *Modern and Ancient Literary Criticism of the Gospels: Continuing the Debate on Gospel Genre(s)*. Edited by Robert Matthew Calhoun, David P. Moessner, and Tobias Nicklas. WUNT 451. Tübingen: Mohr Siebeck, 2020.

Shively, Elizabeth E., and Geert van Oyen, eds. *Communication, Pedagogy, and the Gospel of Mark*. RBS 83. Atlanta: SBL Press, 2016.

Sim, David C. "Matthew's Use of Mark: Did Matthew Intend to Supplement or to Replace His Primary Source?" *NTS* 57 (2011): 176–92.

Sittler, Joseph. *The Eloquence of Grace: Joseph Sittler and the Preaching Life*. Edited by James M. Childs Jr. and Richard Lischer. IPS. Eugene, OR: Wipf & Stock, 2012.

Smalley, Stephen S. "Redaction Criticism." Pages 181–98 in *New Testament Interpretation: Essays on Principles and Methods*. Edited by I. Howard Marshall. Exeter: Paternoster, 1977.

Smith, D. Moody. *The Composition and Order of the Fourth Gospel: Bultmann's Literary Theory*. YPR 10. New Haven: Yale University Press, 1965. Repr., with a foreword by R. Alan Culpepper. JMS. Eugene, OR: Wipf & Stock, 2015.

———. *Interpreting the Gospels for Preaching*. Philadelphia: Fortress, 1980.

————. *Johannine Christianity: Essays on Its Setting, Sources, and Theology*. Columbia: University of South Carolina Press, 1984.

————. *The Theology of the Gospel of John*. NTT. Cambridge: Cambridge University Press, 1995.

————. "Why Approaching the New Testament as Canon Matters." *Int* 40 (1986): 407–11.

Speiser, E. A. *Genesis*. AB 1. Garden City, NY: Doubleday, 1964.

Spivey, Robert A., D. Moody Smith, and C. Clifton Black. *Anatomy of the New Testament: A Guide to Its Structure and Meaning*. 8th ed. Minneapolis: Fortress, 2019.

Standaert, B. H. M. G. M. *L'Évangile selon Marc: Composition et genre littéraire*. Brugge: Sint Andreisabdij, 1978.

Stanton, Graham N. *Jesus and Gospel*. Cambridge: Cambridge University Press, 2004.

Stegemann, Ekkehard. "Zur Rolle von Petrus, Jakobus, und Johannes." *TZ* 42 (1986): 366–74.

Stein, Robert H. "Is the Transfiguration (Mark 9:2–8) a Misplaced Resurrection-Account?" *JBL* 95 (1976): 79–96.

————. "The Proper Methodology for Ascertaining a Markan Redaction History." *NovT* 13 (1971): 181–98.

————. "The 'Redaktionsgeschichtlich' Investigation of a Markan Seam (Mc 1.21f.)." *ZNW* 61 (1970): 70–94.

————. "What Is *Redaktionsgeschichte*?" *JBL* 88 (1969): 45–56.

Sternberg, Meir. *The Poetics of Biblical Narrative: Ideological Literature and the Drama of Reading*. Bloomington: Indiana University Press, 1985.

Stock, Augustine. *Call to Discipleship: A Literary Study of Mark's Gospel*. GNS 1. Wilmington, DE: Glazier, 1982.

Stockt, Luc van der. "Compositional Methods in the *Lives*." Pages 321–32 in *A Companion to Plutarch*. Edited by Martin Beck. Malden, MA: Wiley-Blackwell, 2014.

Strauss, David Friedrich. *The Life of Jesus Critically Examined*. Edited by Peter Hodgson. Translated by George Eliot. 4th ed. LJS. Philadelphia: Fortress, 1972. German original, 1835.

Strecker, Georg. "The Historical and Theological Problem of the Jesus Question." *TJT* 6 (1990): 201–23.

Streeter, B. H. *The Four Gospels: A Study of Origins*. New York: Macmillan, 1925.

Strelan, Richard E. "The Fallen Watchers and the Disciples in Mark." *JSP* 20 (1999): 73–92.

Stroup, George W. *The Promise of Narrative Theology: Recovering the Gospel in the Church*. Atlanta: John Knox, 1981.

Suhl, Alfred. *Die Funktion der alttestamentlichen Zitate und Anspielungen in Markusevangelium*. Gütersloh: Gütersloher Verlagshaus, 1965.

Sumney, Jerry L. *Identifying Paul's Opponents: The Question of Method in 2 Corinthians*. JSNTSup 40. Sheffield: JSOT Press, 1990.

Svartvik, Jesper. *Mark and Mission: Mark 7:1–23 in Its Narrative and Historical Contexts*. CBNT 32. Stockholm: Almqvist & Wiksell International, 2000.

———. "Matthew and Mark." Pages 27–49 in *Matthew and His Christian Contemporaries*. Edited by David C. Sim and Boris Repschinski. LNTS 333. London: T&T Clark, 2008.

Swanson, Reuben, ed. *New Testament Greek Manuscripts: Mark*. Sheffield: Sheffield Academic; Pasadena: William Carey International University Press, 1995.

Sweat, Laura C. *The Theological Role of Paradox in the Gospel of Mark*. LNTS 492. London: Bloomsbury T&T Clark, 2013.

Taeger, Jens-Wilhelm. Review of *The Disciples according to Mark: Markan Redaction in Current Debate*, by C. Clifton Black. *TLZ* 115 (1990): 590.

Tagawa, Kenzo. *Miracles et évangile: La pensée personnelle de l'évangéliste Marc*. EHPR 62. Paris: Universitaires de France, 1966.

Talbert, Charles H. *Learning through Suffering: The Educational Value of Suffering in the New Testament and in Its Milieu*. Collegeville, MN: Liturgical Press, 1991.

———. Review of *What Are the Gospels? A Comparison with Graeco-Roman Biography*, by Richard Burridge. *JBL* 112 (1993): 714–15.

———. *What Is a Gospel? The Genre of the Canonical Gospels*. Philadelphia: Fortress, 1977.

Tannehill, Robert C. "The Disciples in Mark: The Function of a Narrative Role." *JR* 57 (1977): 386–405. Repr., pages 134–57 in *The Interpretation of Mark*. Edited by William Telford. SNTI. Edinburgh: T&T Clark, 1995.

Tàrrech, Armand Puig i. "Holy Spirit and Evil Spirits in the Ministry of Jesus." Pages 365–93 in *The Holy Spirit and the Church according to the New Testament: Sixth International East-West Symposium of New Testament Scholars, Belgrade, August 25 to 31, 2013*. Edited by Predrag Dragutinovic, Karl-Wilhelm Niebuhr, and James Buchanan Wallace, in cooperation with Christos Karakolis. WUNT 354. Tübingen: Mohr Siebeck, 2016.

Taylor, Nicholas H. Review of *Rethinking the Gospel Sources: From Proto-Mark to Mark*, by Delbert Burkett. *JSNT* 28 (2006): 57–58.

Taylor, Vincent. *The Gospel according to St. Mark: The Greek Text with Introduction, Notes, and Indexes*. London: Macmillan, 1952.

———. *The Gospel according to St. Mark: The Greek Text with Introduction, Notes, and Indexes*. 2nd ed. London: Macmillan, 1966.

Teachout, Terry. *Duke: A Life of Duke Ellington*. New York: Gotham Books, 2013.

Telford, William R. *The Barren Temple and the Withered Tree: A Redaction-Critical Analysis of the Cursing of the Fig-Tree Pericope in Mark's Gospel and Its Relation to the Cleansing of the Temple Tradition*. JSNTSup 1. Sheffield: JSOT Press, 1980.

———. "The Pre-Markan Tradition in Recent Research (1980–1990)." Pages 693–723 in *The Four Gospels 1992: Festschrift Frans Neirynck*. Vol. 2. Edited by Frans Van Segbroeck, Christopher M. Tuckett, Gilbert Van Belle, and Joseph Verheyden. BETL 100. Leuven: Leuven University Press; Peeters, 1992.

———. Review of *The Gospel to the Romans: The Setting and Rhetoric of Mark's Gospel*, by Brian J. Incigneri. *JTS* 58 (2007): 206–14.

———. *The Theology of the Gospel of Mark*. NTT. Cambridge: Cambridge University Press, 1999.

Terrell, George. *Christianity at the Cross-Roads*. London: Longmans, Green, & Co., 1909.

Terrien, Samuel. *The Elusive Presence: Toward a New Biblical Theology*. RP 26. San Francisco: Harper & Row, 1978.

Thatcher, Tom. "The Gospel Genre: What Are We Looking For?" *ResQ* 39 (1994): 129–38.

Theissen, Gerd. *The Gospels in Context: Social and Political History in the Synoptic Tradition*. Minneapolis: Fortress, 1991.

———. "Lokalkoloritforschung in den Evangelien: Plädoyer für die Erneuerung einer alten Fragestellen." *EvT* 45 (1981): 481–99.

———. *Urchristliche Wundergeschichten: Ein Beitrag zur formgeschichtlichen Erforschung der synoptischen Evangelien*. Gütersloh: Mohn, 1974. English translation, *The Miracle Stories of the Early Christian Tradition*. Edited by John Riches. Translated by Francis McDonagh. Philadelphia: Fortress, 1983.

Theissen, Gerd, and Annette Merz. *The Historical Jesus: A Comprehensive Guide*. Translated by John Bowden. Minneapolis: Fortress, 1998.

Thiessen, Matthew. "The Many for One or One for the Many? Reading Mark 10:45 in the Roman Empire." *HTR* 109 (2016): 447–66.

Thompson, Marianne Meye. *The God of the Gospel of John*. Grand Rapids: Eerdmans, 2001.

———. *The Humanity of Jesus in the Fourth Gospel*. Philadelphia: Fortress, 1988.

———. *John: A Commentary*. NTL. Louisville: Westminster John Knox, 2015.

Thrall, Margaret E. "Elijah and Moses in Mark's Account of the Transfiguration." *NTS* 16 (1970): 305–17.

Thurber, James. *Fables for Our Time and Famous Poems Illustrated*. New York:

Harper & Row, 1940. Reprinted in *The Thurber Carnival*, New York: The Modern Library, 1957.

Tillich, Paul. *The Shaking of the Foundations*. New York: Scribner's Sons, 1948.

Timpte, Katherine Joy Kihlstrom. *The Transformational Role of Discipleship in Mark 10:13–16: Passage Towards Childhood*. LNTS 650. London: T&T Clark, 2021.

Tolbert, Mary Ann. *Sowing the Gospel: Mark's World in Literary-Historical Perspective*. Minneapolis: Fortress, 1989.

Treggiari, Susan. *Roman Marriage: Iusti Coniuges from the Time of Cicero to the Time of Ulpian*. Oxford: Clarendon, 1991.

Trevor-Roper, Hugh. "History and Imagination." *TLS*. 25 July 1980: 833–35.

Trillin, Calvin. "An Attempt to Compile a Short History of the Buffalo Chicken Wing." Pages 268–75 in *The Tummy Trilogy: American Fried; Alice, Let's Eat; Third Helpings*. New York: Farrar, Straus & Giroux, 1994.

Troeltsch, Ernst. "Historiography." Pages 716–23 in *Encyclopedia of Religion and Ethics*. Edited by James Hastings. New York: Scribner's Sons, 1922.

Tuchman, Barbara W. *The Guns of August*. New York: Ballantine, 1962.

———. *The March of Folly: From Troy to Vietnam*. New York: Knopf, 1984.

Turner, Cuthbert Hamilton. *The Language and Style of the Gospel of Mark: An Edition of C. H. Turner's "Notes on Marcan Usage" Together with Other Comparable Studies*. Edited by J. Keith Elliott. NovTSup 71. Leiden: Brill, 1993.

———. "Marcan Usage: Notes, Critical and Exegetical, on the Second Gospel." *JTS* old series 25 (1923): 377–86; 26 (1924): 12–20, 145–56, 225–40, 337–46; 27 (1925): 58–62; 28 (1926): 9–30, 349–62; 29 (1927): 257–89, 346–61.

Twain, Mark. *Mississippi Writings: The Adventures of Tom Sawyer, Life on the Mississippi, Adventures of Huckleberry Finn, Pudd'nhead Wilson*. Edited by Guy Cardwell. The Library of America. New York: Library Classics of the United States, 1982.

Twelftree, Graham H., ed. *The Cambridge Companion to Miracles*. Cambridge: Cambridge University Press, 2011.

———. *In the Name of Jesus: Exorcism among Early Christians*. Grand Rapids: Baker Academic, 2007.

Tyson, Joseph. "The Blindness of the Disciples in the Gospel of Mark." *JBL* 80 (1961): 261–68.

Ulansey, David. "The Heavenly Veil Torn: Mark's Cosmic *Inclusio*." *JBL* 110 (1991): 123–25.

Verheyden, Joseph. "Before Embarking on an Adventure: Some Preliminary Remarks on Writing the NTP Commentary on the Gospel of Mark." *StPatr* 44 (2010): 145–56.

———. "The Reception History of the Gospel of Mark in the Early Church:

Adventuring in Still Largely Unexplored Territory." Pages 395–428 in *Reading the Gospel of Mark in the Twenty-First Century: Method and Meaning*. Edited by Geert van Oyen. BETL 301. Leuven: Peeters, 2019.

Vermes, Géza. *Jesus the Jew: A Historian's Reading of the Gospels*. London: SCM, 1973.

Via, Dan O., Jr. *The Ethics of Mark's Gospel: In the Middle of Time*. Philadelphia: Fortress, 1985.

———. *Kerygma and Comedy in the New Testament: A Structuralist Approach to Hermeneutic*. Philadelphia: Fortress, 1975.

Vines, Michael. *The Problem of the Markan Genre: The Gospel of Mark and the Jewish Novel*. AcBib 3. Atlanta: Society of Biblical Literature, 2002.

———. "The 'Trial Scene' Chronotype in Mark and the Jewish Novel." Pages 189–203 in *The Trial and Death of Jesus: Essays on the Passion Narrative in Mark*. Edited by Geert van Oyen and Tom Shepherd. CBET. Leuven: Peeters, 2006.

Volkmar, Gustav. *Die Religion Jesu*. Leipzig: Brockhaus, 1857.

Vorster, W. S. "Literary Reflections on Mark 13:5–37: A Narrated Speech of Jesus." *Neot* 21 (1987): 203–24.

Votaw, Clyde Weber. *The Gospels and Contemporary Biographies in the Greco-Roman World*. FBBS. Philadelphia: Fortress, 1970.

Waetjen, Herman C. *A Reordering of Power: A Socio-political Reading of Mark's Gospel*. Minneapolis: Fortress, 1989.

Walker, William O., Jr. Review of *One Gospel from Two: Mark's Use of Matthew and Luke; A Demonstration by the Research Team of the International Institute for Renewal of Gospel Studies*. Edited by David Peabody, Lamar Cope, and Allan J. McNicol. *JBL* 110 (1991): 346–48.

Wall, Robert W. "Reading the New Testament in Canonical Context." Pages 370–93 in *Hearing the New Testament: Strategies for Interpretation*. 2nd ed. Edited by Joel B. Green. Grand Rapids: Eerdmans, 2010.

Walsh, Jerome T. "Elijah." *ABD* 2:463–66.

Wansbrough, Henry, ed. *Jesus and the Oral Gospel Tradition*. JSNTSup 64. Sheffield: Sheffield Academic, 1991. Repr., London: T&T Clark, 2004.

Watson, David F. *Honor among Christians: The Cultural Key to the Messianic Secret*. Minneapolis: Fortress, 2010.

Watson, Francis, and Mark Seifrid. "*Quaestiones disputatae*: Roman Faith and Christian Faith." *NTS* 64 (2018): 243–55.

Watts, Rikki. *Isaiah's New Exodus in Mark*. WUNT 88. Tübingen: Mohr Siebeck, 1997. Repr., Grand Rapids: Baker Academic, 2001.

Weeden, Theodore. *Mark: Traditions in Conflict*. Philadelphia: Fortress, 1971.

Weiss, Johannes. *Das älteste Evangelium: Ein Beitrag zum Verständnis des Markus-*

Evangeliums und der ältesten evangelischen Überlieferung. Göttingen: Vandenhoeck & Ruprecht, 1903.

———. *Jesus' Proclamation of the Kingdom of God.* Translated and edited by Richard Hyde Hiers and David Larimore Holland. LJS. Philadelphia: Fortress, 1971. German original, 1892.

Weiss, Meir. "Die Methode der 'Total-Interpretation.'" Pages 88–112 in *Congress Volume Uppsala 1971.* Edited by P. A. H. de Boer. VTSup 22. Leiden: Brill, 1972.

Weisse, C. H. *Die Evangelienfrage in ihrem gegenwärtigen Stadium.* Leipzig: Breitkopf & Härtel, 1856.

Wellhausen, Julius. *Einleitung in die drei ersten Evangelien.* Berlin: Georg Reimer, 1905.

Welzer, Harald. *Das kommunikative Gedächtnis: Eine Theorie der Erinnerung.* 2nd ed. Munich: Beck, 2008.

Wendt, Heidi. "Secrecy as Pauline Influence on the Gospel of Mark." *JBL* 140 (2021): 579–600.

Wenham, David. *Paul: Follower of Jesus or Founder of Christianity?* Grand Rapids: Eerdmans, 1995.

Werner, Martin. *Der Einfluss paulinischer Theologie im Markusevangelium: Eine Studie zur neutestamentlichen Theologie.* BZNW 1. Giessen; Töpelmann, 1923.

Wienér, Claude. "Voyant Qu'il Avait Ainsi Expiré (Marc 15,39)." Pages 551–81 in *Pense la Foi.* Edited by J. Doné and C. Theobald. Paris: Assas Éditions, 1993.

Wilder, Amos. *The Bible and the Literary Critic.* Minneapolis: Fortress, 1991.

Wiles, Maurice. *The Making of Christian Doctrine.* Cambridge: Cambridge University Press, 1967.

Wilke, C. G. *Der Urevangelist: Oder, Exegetische kritische Untersuchung über das Verwandtschaftsverhältnis der drei ersten Evangelien.* Dresden: G. Fleischer, 1838.

Willert, Niels. "Martyrology in the Passion Narratives of the Synoptic Gospels." Pages 15–43 in *Contextualizing Early Christian Martyrdom.* Edited by Jakob Engberg, Uffe Holmsgaard Eriksen, and Anders Klostergaard Petersen. ECCA 8. Frankfurt am Main: Lang, 2011.

Williams, Joel F. "Foreshadowing, Echoes, and the Blasphemy at the Cross (Mark 15:29)." *JBL* 132 (2013): 913–33.

Wills, Gary. *Lincoln at Gettysburg: The Words That Remade America.* New York: Simon & Schuster, 1992.

Wimsatt, William K., Jr., and Monroe C. Beardsley. "The Intentional Fallacy." *SR* 54 (1946): 468–88.

Winn, Adam. *Mark and the Elijah-Elisha Narrative: Considering the Practice of Greco-Roman Imitation in the Search for Markan Source Material.* Eugene, OR: Wipf & Stock, 2010.

———. *The Purpose of Mark's Gospel: An Early Christian Response to Roman Imperial Propaganda.* WUNT 2/245. Tübingen: Mohr Siebeck, 2008.

———. *Reading Mark's Christology under Caesar: Jesus the Messiah and Roman Imperial Ideology.* Downers Grove, IL: InterVarsity Press, 2018.

———. "Resisting Honor: The Markan Secrecy Motif and Roman Political Ideology." *JBL* 133 (2014): 583–601.

Wire, Antoinette Clark. *The Case for Mark Composed in Performance.* BPC 3. Eugene, OR: Cascade, 2011.

Wischmeyer, Ods, David C. Sim, and Ian J. Elmer, eds. *Paul and Mark: Comparative Essays Part I; Two Authors at the Beginnings of Christianity.* BZNW 198. Berlin: de Gruyter, 2014.

Wolff, Hans Walter. *Anthropology of the Old Testament.* Philadelphia: Fortress, 1974.

Wolterstorff, Nicholas. *Lament for a Son.* Grand Rapids: Eerdmans, 1987.

Worrall, John. "'Revolution in Permanence': Popper on Theory-Change in Science." Pages 75–102 in *Karl Popper: Philosophy and Problems.* Edited by Anthony O'Hear. RIPS 39. Cambridge: Cambridge University Press, 1995.

Wrede, William. *Das Messiasgeheimnis in den Evangelien: Zugleich ein Beitrag zum Verständnis des Markusevangeliums.* Göttingen: Vandenhoeck & Ruprecht, 1901.

———. *The Messianic Secret.* Translated by J. C. G. Greig. LTT. Cambridge: James Clarke, 1971. German original, 1901.

Wright, N. T. *The Climax of the Covenant: Christ and the Law in Pauline Theology.* Minneapolis: Fortress, 1992.

———. *Jesus and the Victory of God.* Minneapolis: Fortress, 1996.

———. *The New Testament and the People of God.* Minneapolis: Fortress, 1992.

Yarbro Collins, Adela. "The Apocalyptic Rhetoric of Mark 13 in Historical Context." *BR* 41 (1996): 5–36.

———. *The Beginning of the Gospel: Probings of Mark in Context.* Minneapolis: Fortress, 1992.

———. "Establishing the Text: Mark 1:1." Pages 111–27 in *Texts and Contexts: Biblical Texts in Their Textual and Situational Contexts; Essays in Honor of Lars Hartman.* Edited by T. Fornberg and D. Hellholm, assisted by C. D. Hellholm. Oslo: Scandinavia University Press, 1995.

———. "From Noble Death to Crucified Messiah." *NTS* 40 (1994): 481–503.

———. "Is Mark's Gospel a Life of Jesus? The Question of Genre." Pages 1–38 in *The Beginning of the Gospel: Probings of Mark in Context*. Minneapolis: Fortress, 1992.

———. *Mark: A Commentary*. Hermeneia. Minneapolis: Fortress, 2007.

———. "Mysteries in the Gospel of Mark." Pages 11–23 in *Mighty Minorities? Minorities in Early Christianity—Positions and Strategies: Essays in Honour of Jacob Jervell on His 70th Birthday, 21 May 1995*. Edited by David Hellholm, Halvor Moxnes, and Turid Karlsen Seim. Oslo: Scandinavian University Press, 1995.

———. Review of *The Disciples according to Mark: Markan Redaction in Current Debate*, by C. Clifton Black. *CRBR* 4 (1991): 169–71.

Zahn, Theodor. "Der Geschichtsschreiber und sein Stoff im Neuen Testament." *ZWKL* 9 (1888): 581–96.

Index of Modern Authors

Index of Subjects

Adam, 294–96
Akiba, Rabbi, 230, 244, 414
anointing of Jesus by the unnamed
  woman, 26, 185, 334–35, 412–13
Anselm of Canterbury, 121
apocalyptic eschatology, 110–11, 179,
  198n24, 286–87, 329, 425; book of
  Jubilees, 298–300; Elijah's return, 3,
  17, 31, 219–23, 275n46, 351–52; Jewish
  apocalypticism, 17, 46n9, 99, 102, 179,
  181, 298–300, 377, 405; Mark's creation
  theology, 286–87, 297, 298–300; millenarianism, 198n24, 200, 287, 298; Olivet
  Discourse, 23–25, 44, 249, 301–2, 329–30;
  Paul and Mark on the cross, 280; stories
  of suffering in Mark, 240–41; transfiguration of Jesus, 17, 122–23, 213–14, 218–22,
  223, 293, 396–99
Apollonius of Tyana, 185
Apostolic Constitutions, 38, 51n7
apostolocity: the early church's recognition of Mark's Gospel, 49–51, 56, 186–87;
  notion of, 49–51, 51n9
Aquinas, Thomas, 170
Armada, The (Mattingly), 194
authorship of Mark's Gospel, 1, 48–56,
  186–87; patristic authors on Mark the
  Evangelist, 37–38, 46–47, 48–56, 169–70;
  patristic authors on Peter-Mark-Rome
  connection, 37–38, 46–47, 50–51, 54;
  personification and the "personality" of
  Mark, 49–55; and portrayal of Mark as
  biographical subject, 54–55, 197

baptism: Jesus's, 2–3, 31, 122, 178, 213–18,
  223, 248n4, 292–93, 352, 376–77; ritual of,
  153, 408
Barabbas, 29, 251, 348–49
Bartimaeus, 19–20, 146, 147, 251, 259, 409
"biblical theology movement," 64, 67–68
βίος (genre of ancient biography): Burridge's
  thesis on correlation between the gospels
  and Greco-Roman βίος, 137–41; Mark's
  Gospel as, 54–55, 136–41, 173n156, 191, 197

Cayce, Edgar, 134
Christobiography (Keener), 139
Christology, Markan, 3, 10, 78, 99–101, 168,
  180–81, 214, 219, 293–94, 415, 423–24;
  and discipleship, 19–20, 182, 233–34; and
  John's Christology, 247, 248–49, 254;
  Mark's passion narrative, 278–79, 281–82;
  and Paul on the crucifixion, 278–79,
  281–82; "Son of God," 3, 177–78, 180–81,
  214, 253–55, 294–95, 398; "Son of Man," 6,
  17, 181, 213, 218–19, 253–55, 293–96
Claudius, 40
Composition and Order of the Fourth
  Gospel, The: Bultmann's Literary Theory
  (Smith), 80–81
composition criticism, 83, 109–10, 313. See
  also passion narrative (revenants in)
creation theology, 286–300; creation and
  creaturely dependence (Psalm 104), 289;
  creation and order (ordered restoration), 288–89, 293–96; creation as
  new creation, 290–91, 297; creation as
  origination, 289–90, 291–93; creation

of a people (Israel), 287–88, 297–98;
dimensions of creation in Mark, 291–98;
and Mark's apocalypticism, 286–87, 297,
298–300; Old Testament biblical beliefs
about creation, 287–98
Crusaders, The (1935 film), 379

*Das Markusevangelium als kollektives
Gedachtnis* (Huebenthal), 151–55
Davidic monarchy, 23, 96, 100–101, 217,
288–89, 293
Diagnostic and Statistical Manual of Mental Disorders, 5th ed., 381
Disciples according to Mark, The (Black).
See redaction criticism (reflections on
Black's *Disciples according to Mark*)
discipleship, 2, 16–20, 182–86, 258–60,
399–401; the anonymous disciples,
184–85, 335–36; Bauckham on the Twelve
as eyewitnesses, 145–51; commissioning
of the Twelve to extend Jesus's ministry,
12; ethics of, 18–19; and exegetical studies
for preachers (preaching from Mark's
Gospel), 375, 385–87, 392–95, 399–401,
407–9; filling out of the Twelve (names
and ordering), 7–8; in John's Gospel,
258–60; Juel on the disciples' problem,
126–27; and Markan Christology, 19–20,
182, 233–34; in Markan scholarship and
redaction criticism of the past thirty
years, 98–111; and moral responsibility,
183; Olivet Discourse and the disciples'
questions, 306–7, 309, 310, 311; and
reintegration into a new/surrogate
family, 43, 182, 298, 387; and self-denial/
self-sacrifice, 2, 182; the suffering of
Jesus and, 231–34, 242–43; the Twelve's
misunderstandings, lack of faith, and
refusals to understand Jesus, 33, 101–2,
183–84, 259–60, 392–95, 399–401, 407–9;
twinned tales of Jesus's ministry and
ministry of the Twelve (6:1–13), 385–87;
women disciples at the crucifixion and
empty tomb, 31–32, 34, 100, 276, 353–54,
355–56, 418–19. *See also* redaction criticism and the disciples in Mark

divorce, 18–19, 297
Domitian, 159, 365

Elijah, 3, 17, 31, 219–23, 237–38, 275n46,
351–52, 388, 417
Elisha, 11, 237–38
epideictic rhetoric, 156, 307–13
Evangelium als Biographie (Frickenschmidt), 138–39

family: discipleship and reintegration
into a surrogate family, 43, 182, 298, 387;
early Christian worship in houses as real
and surrogate families, 43, 387; Jesus's
redefinition of, 8
farewell address, Jesus's. *See* Olivet Discourse (rhetorical analysis of Mark 13)
Feast of Booths (Tabernacles), 221
feeding of the five thousand, 13, 337–39,
389
feeding of the four thousand, 15, 337–39
fig tree, withering of, 21, 25, 231, 315, 320,
410–11
First Commentary on Mark, The: An Annotated Translation (Cahill), 170
*Following Jesus: Discipleship in the Gospel
of Mark* (Best), 85–86
form criticism (*Formgeschichte*), 59–61, 65,
69, 213; and currents in recent Markan
scholarship, 138–39, 146, 154, 163–64; and
redaction-critical method, 59–61, 63–64,
69, 92–93

genre criticism, 138
Gerasene demoniac, exorcism of, 10–11,
249, 295, 380–82
Gethsemane, 27–28, 186, 233, 234–42, 252,
339–41, 347, 384, 414–15
Gnosticism, 53
God (θεός) in Mark's Gospel, 179–80, 211–
28; and Jesus's death, 213–14, 222–27, 293;
Juel's exegetical focus, 120–23, 127, 133,
212; presentation of God in the passion
narrative, 277–78; self-concealing revelation, 227–28; "Son of God," 3, 177–78,
180–81, 214, 253–55, 294–95, 398; triptych
of Jesus's baptism, transfiguration, and
death, 213–14, 293, 352–53

tinguishing features, 178–79; God (θεός), 179–80; the "good news" of the kingdom of God, 178; the Holy Spirit (Markan pneumatology), 178, 181–82; Jesus, 180–81; key metaphor of sonship, 180–81; the kingdom and scriptural prophecy of preparing the "way of the Lord," 178, 215; the kingdom of God, its agent and power, 177–82; the secrecy motif, 64–65, 168, 187–88, 228, 266–67; unresolved tension, 179, 188, 211–13, 227, 374

Mary Magdalene, 31–32, 33, 34, 148–49, 258, 276, 353–54

Mary the mother of James and Joses, 31–32, 34, 100, 276, 353–54

Memory and Manuscript (Gerhardsson), 143–45

memory and oral performance in the Jesus traditions, 141–57; Bauckham on the gospels as eyewitness testimony, 145–51; Byrskog on eyewitnesses and oral transmission in early Christian communities, 148–51; Dunn on the gospels and oral tradition, 142–43, 156–57; Gerhardsson on the evangelists' use of a pregospel tradition of memory material, 143–45, 151; Huebenthal on Mark and the community of memory ("social memory theory"), 151–55; Shiner on Mark's techniques of oral performance, 155–56

millenarianism, 198n24, 200, 287, 298

miracles, 166–67, 185–86, 208, 249, 257–58. *See also* healings, Jesus's

Miracles: God's Presence and Power in Creation (Johnson), 167

Monarchian gospel prologues, 37, 51n7, 52, 53, 55

Moses, 14, 17, 22, 219–21, 223, 397

Nero, 1, 40–41, 157–58, 422

"new criticism," 69, 70

Old Testament: creation theology and dimensions of creation in Mark, 287–98; and the Markan passion narrative, 357–58; and Mark's prologue introducing

Jesus, 3, 216–17, 292–93; studies of Mark's use of Jewish Scriptures and tradition, 95–96, 165–66

Olivet Discourse (rhetorical analysis of Mark 13), 301–30; alliteration, 322; antistrophe (ἐπιφορά), 321–22; antithesis, 323; aposiopesis, 324; apposition, 324; Aristotelian strategies, 314–16; arousal (ἀνάστασις), 324; arrangement (*taxis* or *dispositio*), 309–13; assonance, 323; asyndeton (*dissolutio*), 322; chiasmus, 323; clarity, 319; the conclusion (*proemium* or *exordium*), 309–10, 327; *controversia*, 324; correctness of style and Mark's Greek, 318–19; deliberative rhetoric, 307–8; "the desolating sacrilege" (τὸ βδέλυγμα τῆς ἐρημώσεως), 326–27; the disciples' questions and Jesus's replies, 306–7, 309, 310, 311; *ecphrasis*, 324; ellipsis, 324; epanalepsis, 322; epanaphora, 321; epideictic rhetoric, 156, 307–13; evaluating in accordance with Greco-Roman rhetorical norms, 302, 327–30; exigence or urgency, 305–6, 308, 316–17; figures of speech, 320–24; figures of thought, 324–27; homoeopropheron, 322; homoeoptoton (*exornatio*), 321; homoeoteleuton, 322; hyperbaton, 323; inartificial proofs and artificial proofs, 313–16; as Jesus's apocalyptic farewell address (*Abschiedsrede*), 23–25, 44, 249, 304–5; Jesus's authoritative pronouncements, 311; Jesus's commissions or prohibitions, 311; Jesus's exhortations, 310–11; Jesus's predictions of future occurrences, 310–11; *logos*, *pathos*, and *ēthos* of Jesus, 316–17, 327–28; Mark's apocalyptic perspective, 23–25, 44, 249, 301–2, 329–30; Mark's audience, 125n26, 302n9, 303–4, 310, 312, 327; the *narratio*, 310–12; ornamentation (diction and composition), 319–25; parallelism, 320–21; parenthesis (*interpositio*), 323–24; the *peroratio* (or *epilogos*), 312–13, 327; pleonasm, 325; polyptoton, 321; polysyndeton, 322; progressive escalation to an emotional climax, 311–12; propriety,

Peter: denial of Jesus, 183–84; interrogations at the high priest's court, 342–45,
347; Jesus's rebuttal of (Mark 8:31–38),
392–95; patristic authors on Peter-Mark-
Rome connection, 37–38, 46–47, 50–51,
54; proposal for three tents to be built for
Jesus, 221; and Simon the Cyrene, 349–50
philosophy of science, Popper's, 112–18
Pilate, 13, 29–32, 44, 191–92, 251, 345–48,
355, 374, 389
pistis/fides (trust/faith) in the early Roman
empire and early Christianity, 160–63
Popper, Sir Karl Raimund, 112–18
postcolonial readings of Mark, 159–60
postmodernism, 200
preaching from Mark's Gospel (exegetical
studies for preachers), 371–420; the death
of John the Baptist (6:14–29), 387–89;
discipleship, 375, 385–87, 392–95, 399–
401, 407–9; the eschatological nearness
of the kingdom of God (1:9–15), 376–78;
the exorcism of the Gerasene demoniac
(5:1–20), 380–82; healings of Jairus's
daughter and the chronically bleeding
woman (5:21–43), 382–85; healings of the
daughter of a gentile Syro-Phoenician
woman and the gentile deaf-mute
(7:24–37), 390–92; humor, 378–80,
409–11; Jesus's anointing by the nameless
woman (14:3–9), 412–13; Jesus's answer to
the question, "what must I do to inherit
eternal life?" (10:17–31), 404–6; Jesus's
entrance into Jerusalem (11:1–11), 409–12;
Jesus's first prediction and the disciples'
repudiation (8:31–38), 392–95; Jesus's
second prediction and the disciples'
incomprehension (9:30–37), 399–401;
Jesus's third prediction and the disciples'
misunderstanding (10:32–52), 407–9;
from the Last Supper to Gethsemane
(14:22–42), 413–15; original epilogue and
empty tomb (16:1–8), 418–20; parables
in Mark, 378–80; passion narrative and
Jesus's crucifixion (15:16–39), 415–17;
Peter's confession that Jesus is the Christ
and Jesus's rebuke (8:27–38), 394–96;

tales of Jesus's ministry and ministry of
the Twelve (6:1–13), 385–87; the transfiguration (9:2–9), 396–99; "whoever is
not against us is for us" (9:38–50), 401–4;
Year B in the Revised Common Lectionary, 371–76
pre-Markan tradition, 72–73, 90, 95–98,
357–58
Problem of History in Mark, The (Robinson), 111
Prokofiev, Sergei, 331–32
"Proper Method for Ascertaining a Marcan *Redaktionsgeschichte*, The" (Stein),
77–78

Quest of the Historical Jesus (Schweitzer),
78–80

redaction criticism (Markan *redaktionsgeschichtlich*), 57–75, 201–2; assumption of
Markan priority (the "Markan hypothesis"), 58, 64, 72, 84; Best on, 60, 78, 79,
84–94, 103, 108, 110; and the "biblical
theology movement," 64, 67–68; in context of twentieth-century theology and
scholarship, 62–68; continued quest for
Mark's sources and traditions, 72–73, 90,
95–98, 357–58; contributions, 68–71, 75;
emphasis on the evangelists as literary
authors, 59–62, 68–71, 266; emphasis on
the evangelists as theologians (religious
thinkers), 60–62, 69–71, 110–11, 188,
266–67; emphasis on the evangelists' historical and social contexts, 61–62, 71, 74;
emphasis on the gospel as literary entity
to be interpreted holistically, 61–62; Juel's
opposition, 128–29; liabilities, 71–74, 75;
new insights to problems raised by other
theological movements, 64–68, 92–93;
and old quest for the historical Jesus,
64–67, 92–93; perceived continuity with
previous exegetical methods, 63–64, 69,
92–93; and Popper's criteria for verifying
a scientific theory, 116–18; post–World
War II popularity, 63; profile of the
method, 58–62; relevant scholarly tendencies of the past thirty years, 94–111;

Index of Scripture

26:31–35	224	24:15–16	5	8:2–5	232
26:31–37	31	24:16	28	8:5	230
26:37	224	24:19–20	299	12:23	383
27:21	221	25:47–52	278n55, 409	13:1–3	314n39
29:43–44	221	26:11–12	221	13:7	314n39
31:12–17	290, 291			15:6–15	183
31:16	289n11	**Numbers**		15:7–11	412
33:18–23	14	1:4–16	7, 297	15:11	26
34:6–7	5	3:10	224	17:6	12
34:21	6	3:26	224	18:11	332n4
34:22	299	3:44–51	409	18:15	220, 293, 397
34:28	3, 292	3:45–51	278n55	19:15	12, 28, 385
34:29–35	220	5:2	380	19:21	299
38:18	224	6:6	380	21:3	20
		9:6	380	21:22–23	32
Leviticus		11:1–35	13	22:22	18
1:2	14	13:1–16	7, 297	24:1	18
2:13	300, 403	14:10	219	24:1–4	42
11:1–47	15, 42	14:10b	397	24:10–22	183
11:7–8	11, 380	14:11	15	24:14	19, 183, 260
12:1–8	11, 237	15:15	289n11	25:1–3	24
13:1–14:47	5	15:37–41	14	25:5–6	22, 96
14:5–6	292	18:19	289n11, 300, 403	30:3–4	314n39
14:30–32	292	19:1–22	237	31:1–33:29	304n19
14:48–57	5	19:2	20, 411	32:1–43	288
15:19–20	383	19:11–13	383	32:5	15
15:19–30	11, 237	19:13	292	32:6c–d	288
16:1–34	413	19:20–21	292	32:20	15
16:29	6	22:35	329n67	33:1–29	24
17–26	297	24:16	11		
18:13–16	388	27:15–17	13, 338	**Joshua**	
18:16	13	28:26	299	15:25	8
19:3	405			23:1–24:30	24, 304n19
19:18	23, 42, 180, 184, 249n6, 260	**Deuteronomy**		23:13	402
20:9	183	2:30	184	**1 Samuel**	
20:21	13, 388	4:35	23	4:17	140n22
21:23	224	4:36	397	6:6	6
22:1–16	42	5:12–15	6	6:7	20
22:4b–6a	380	5:13–21	183	10:1	26, 226n40
22:32	273	5:16	14, 96, 183, 260	10:1–8	20, 335, 411
23:15–20	299	5:16–20	19, 405	10:6	216
23:39–43	221	5:18	18	12:1–25	304n19
24:3	224	6:4	184, 260	15:22	23, 42, 184
24:5–9	6	6:4–5	23, 42, 180, 249n6, 297	17:43	15, 391
24:8	289n11	8:2	178	21:1–6	6, 42

10:17	318n53	23:1–39	185	28:19	33, 179, 391
10:17–18	24	23:9	406	28:19–20	32
10:19	318n53	23:11–12	400	28:20	33
10:19–20	24	24:3	304n15		
10:25	8	24:5	318n53	**Mark**	
10:40	401	24:14	318n53	1:1	3, 16, 17, 24, 26, 28, 31,
10:42	402	24:15	318n53		33, 34, 44, 70, 135n4,
11:5	3	24:22a	318n53		153, 177, 179, 180,
11:11	402	24:29	318n53		181, 190, 204, 205,
11:27	247	24:30	318n53		214, 215, 216, 235,
12:18	217	24:34	318n53		248, 274, 276, 282,
12:22–23	409	24:42	318n53		291, 293, 297, 345,
12:28	376	25:1–30	25		394, 423
12:32	246	25:13	85	1:1–3	2
13:13–15	379	26:3	28	1:1–11	218, 219, 220
13:18–23	180	26:47	341n23	1:1–13	153n80
13:32	379	26:51–52	395	1:1–15	2–3, 179, 389
13:43	34, 219, 397, 418	27:1	341–42n23	1:2	42, 179, 204, 333, 407
13:51–52	184	27:15	341n23	1:2–3	3, 42, 157n101, 178,
13:57b	387	27:18–25	29		215, 216, 224, 232,
14:26	332n4	27:19	282n61		248, 277, 291
14:28–33	184	27:20	341n23	1:2–8	221
15:23	390	27:24	341n23	1:2–15	154
15:24	391	27:25	341–42n23	1:2a	214
16:7–12	184	27:32	349	1:2b	215
16:17–23	234	27:38	350n37	1:2c	215
16:18–19	7	27:44	350n37, 359n61	1:3	3, 181, 215, 382, 407
17:12–13	179	27:46	351	1:3a	215
17:19–20	184	27:51	225	1:3b	215
17:23b	184	27:51–53	359n61	1:4	3, 215, 291, 300, 419
17:24–27	22	27:51–54	44n7, 278	1:4–8	2, 178, 215, 248,
18:6	402	27:51b–53	282n61		248n4, 291–92, 377
18:10	402	27:54	31, 224, 276n48, 417	1:4–11	147, 204
18:14	402	27:55–56	359n61	1:4a	291
18:16	385	27:59	355	1:4b	292
18:17	391	27:62–66	32	1:4c	292
19:9	18	27:64	341–42n23	1:5	3, 179, 217, 223, 297
19:28	7, 17, 297, 405	28:2	355, 359n61	1:6	3, 18, 31, 277n53,
20:1–16	180	28:2–4	418		293n19
20:16	400	28:5	355	1:6–7	223
21:1–11	20	28:8	32	1:6a	292
21:9	181, 252, 410, 412	28:8–20	186	1:8	3, 8, 182, 292
21:15	181	28:8b–20	211	1:8–11	178
21:32	21	28:9–10	33	1:9	34, 140n22, 215, 222,
22:1–4	27, 413	28:11–15	34		223, 248, 297
22:1–10	339	28:16–20	234		

Index of Other Ancient Sources